Law and Interdisciplinarity

Law and Interdisciplinarity

Edited by

Phillip Hellwege and Marta Soniewicka

Mohr Siebeck

Phillip Hellwege, holds the Chair of Private Law, Commercial Law, and Legal History at the University of Augsburg.
orcid.org/0000-0001-9012-2682

Marta Soniewicka, is associate professor at the Department of Philosophy of Law and Legal Ethics, Faculty of Law and Administration, Jagiellonian University.
orcid.org/0000-0003-3409-7819

The publication has been supported by a grant from the Faculty of Law and Administration under the Strategic Programme Excellence Initiative at Jagiellonian University.

ISBN 978-3-16-163881-7 / eISBN 978-3-16-163882-4
DOI 10.1628/978-3-16-163882-4

The Deutsche Nationalbibliothek lists this publication in the Deutsche Nationalbibliographie; detailed bibliographic data are available at *https://dnb.dnb.de.*

Published by Mohr Siebeck Tübingen, Germany, 2024. www.mohrsiebeck.com

The book was printed by Laupp & Göbel in Gomaringen on non-aging paper and bound by Buchbinderei Nädele in Nehren.

Printed in Germany.

Preface

On 15 and 16 October 2021, colleagues from the Faculty of Law and Administration of the Jagiellonian University in Kraków and from the Faculty of Law of the University of Augsburg came together in Kraków for the tenth Kraków-Augsburg Symposium. The tradition of the Kraków-Augsburg Symposia was established in 2002 by Prof. Dr. Dr. h.c. Dr. h.c. *Jerzy Stelmach* of Kraków and Prof. Dr. Dr. h.c. *Reiner Schmidt* of Augsburg, and these symposia are the core of the academic cooperation and friendship between both faculties. Each symposium has a different general theme. That of the tenth symposium has been "Interdisciplinary approaches to law", and the present volume, even though it has a slightly different title, collects the presentations of that symposium complemented by further contributions. The conceptual design of the symposium as well as of the present volume will be fully unfolded in the introductory chapter. And though a preface is not the place to unfold the conceptual design of a publication, it is a place to give thanks: We would like to thank our respective faculties and universities for funding the present publication. Then, our thanks go to Mohr Siebeck for including the present volume in its publishing programme. Finally, we would like to thank *Michael Friedman* for his critical comments on an earlier draft of this volume and for correcting the English. With respect to the English, we have asked him to strive for the internal consistency of each contribution, so that some contributions appear in British English, others in American English. The volume has been peer reviewed.

Augsburg and Kraków, November 2023

Phillip Hellwege
Marta Soniewicka

Foreword

No single person has been more important for the cooperation between the law faculties of the Jagiellonian University of Kraków and the University of Augsburg – a cooperation that now exists for more than a quarter of a century – than Prof. Dr. Dr. h.c. Dr. h.c. *Jurek* (or *Jerzy*) *Stelmach*. His 70th birthday in February 2024 is reason enough for reflection on his contribution to the Polish-German legal dialogue in particular and to legal academia in general.

It is only one out of many yields from the fruitful cooperation between both faculties that a series of edited volumes has been established. These volumes collect the presentations of the Kraków-Augsburg Symposia held every two years – alternately in Kraków and in Augsburg – and they are thus a chronicle of the ongoing Polish-German legal dialogue between both faculties. Originally, they were published under the series title "Kraków-Augsburg Studies in Law" ("Krakauer-Augsburger Rechtsstudien") with Wolters Kluwer.[1] The present volume is the second to appear with Mohr Siebeck.[2]

The opening contribution to the first volume is authored by Prof. *Stelmach*; it is entitled "Philosophy of Law in the Post-Modern Era", and the contribution is representative of his entire oeuvre.[3] He deliberately leaves unanswered the question whether legal philosophy belongs to the discipline of philosophy or law. Instead of focusing on such theoretical debates, he demands with practical rigour that we should "keep doing our job" ("weiter unser Ding machen") or otherwise change our profession. Ultimately, he explains, the philosophy of law is part of social philosophy or the general methodology of science, but he chooses to leave its classification in a state of uncertainty, observing that only the future will prove whether it will develop into a more technically understood theory of the doctrinal study of law. The essay is also for a second reason characteristic of Prof. *Stelmach*'s thinking and writing. In just under six pages, he

[1] *J. Stelmach/R. Schmidt* (eds.), Probleme der Angleichung des europäischen Rechts (2004); Information als Gegenstand des Rechts (2006); Rechtliche Steuerung von Wirtschaftsprozessen (2008); Wettbewerb der Staaten – Wettbewerb der Rechtsordnungen (2010); Grenzen der rechtsdogmatischen Interpretation (2011); *H. Bauer/D. Czybulka/W. Kahl/J. Stelmach/A. Voßkuhle* (eds.), Öffentliches Wirtschaftsrecht im Zeitalter der Globalisierung (2012); *J. Stelmach/R. Schmidt* (eds.), Die Rolle des Rechts in der Zeit der wirtschaftlichen Krise (2013); *idem/idem/P. Hellwege/M. Soniewicka*, Normschaffung (2017).

[2] *P. Hellwege/M. Soniewicka* (eds.), Die Einheit der Rechtsordnung. Annäherungen – Bestandsaufnahmen – Reflexionen (2020).

[3] *J. Stelmach*, Rechtsphilosophie in der Nach-Neuzeit, in: Probleme der Angleichung (n. 1), 9–18.

is, while meeting the highest academic standards, able to outline the development of post-war legal philosophy, including the philosophies of *Arthur Kaufmann*, *Gustav Radbruch*, *Jürgen Habermas*, *Ronald Dworkin*, *Robert Alexy*, *Richard Posner*, and *Theodor W. Adorno*; thereafter, he moves on to address the articulation of new theories, an idea he rejects with disarming clarity. Instead of developing such new theories, he argues, the invitation should be accepted to complete existing legal philosophy in its topicality, an invitation that is implicit in existing legal philosophy.

All articles that Prof. *Stelmach* contributed to the "Kraków-Augsburg Studies in Law" are characterised by such a combination of high theoretical awareness and pragmatism. For instance, he calls for putting an end to the interminable discussions on the ontological nature of law. Instead, he argues, we should turn to a much-needed analysis of the problems associated with the economic effectiveness of law.[4] Thereby, he proves to clearly grasp the limitations of theoretical discourse on law: Without knowing the preconditions for an effective law, without knowing why law works in some situations whereas it does not work in other situations, any legal discourse on a meta-theoretical level will remain stuck in a vacuum. Furthermore, he is critical of the creation of legal myths and of oversimplification. According to him, it is moreover possible to accept two mutually contradictory statements at the same time as long as they can be justified by similar or identical means.[5] In yet another contribution, he claims that all correctly formulated and applied methods of interpretation are equally legitimate. Theories of interpretation are incapable of capturing the specificities and particularities of all thinkable cases, and if they try, they become overly complicated and incapable of being applied. Even the idea of objectivity in legal interpretation proves to be "completely useless" for legal practice.[6] Finally, it is characteristic of Prof. *Stelmach*'s original thinking when, in an essay co-authored with his student *Bartosz Brożek*, he discusses the phenomenon of the dysfunctionality of law.[7] According to them, law is dysfunctional when it does not accomplish to a sufficient degree its fundamental purposes – justice, security, and economic efficiency. The provisional nature of "crisis economy" measures that are implemented as a reaction to the many destabilising factors which an economy witnesses during a period of instability is based on the simple fact that nobody knows anything about the true causes and consequences of anything. This makes, *Stelmach* and *Brożek* observe, the

[4] *J. Stelmach*, Acht Voraussetzungen für ein effektives Recht, in: Rechtliche Steuerung (n. 1), 9–21.

[5] *J. Stelmach*, Die Scheinbarkeit des Problems des Wettbewerbs von Rechtsordnungen, in: Wettbewerb der Staaten (n. 1), 9–15.

[6] *J. Stelmach*, Die unbegrenzte Interpretation, in: Grenzen der rechtsdogmatischen Interpretation (n. 1), 9–18.

[7] *J. Stelmach/B. Brożek*, Ökonomische Ursachen für Dysfunktionen des Rechts, in: Die Rolle des Rechts (n. 1), 203–213.

thesis of the dysfunctionality of law in times of economic turmoil seem almost trivial.

Next to the monographs, edited volumes, and other publications, his essays in the "Kraków-Augsburg Studies in Law", which I was able to cover here only by way of example, seem more like small add-ons. Mention should be made of "Methods of Legal Reasoning" (together with *Brożek*, 2006), "Philosophy in Science" (together with *Brożek*, *Janusz Maczka* and *Wojciech P. Grygiel*, 2011), the co-editorship of the monumental "The Many Faces of Normativity" in 2013, bringing together fourteen renowned authors and including an essay by Prof. *Stelmach* on "Naturalistic and Antinaturalistic Fallacies in Normative Discourse", the "The Art of Legal Negotiations" (together with *Brożek*, 2013), and the "Theorie der juristischen Verhandlungen" ("Theory of Legal Negotiations", together with *Brożek*, 2014). There are further important books, among others those co-authored with *Michael Heller*. These volumes are not listed here as they are not accessible to readers not familiar with the Polish language.

Prof. *Stelmach*'s impressive productivity, his ingenuity, his kindness, and his humour were and are formative for the development of the relationship between the two faculties in Kraków and Augsburg. The award of an honorary doctorate in 2011 by the Faculty of Law of the University of Augsburg – the University of Heidelberg had previously honoured him with the same distinction – was an expression of the high esteem in which Prof. *Stelmach* is held not only for his person and his academic work, but also for his contribution to mediating between Polish and German law.

In his work, Prof. *Stelmach* focuses especially on hermeneutics. According to him, law and the discovery of law do not end in relativism. The act of understanding is always a form of "being-in-the-world". This may be taken quite literally. Prof. *Stelmach* is a committed collector of art, especially of Polish contemporary art. His house is more a gallery than a residence. If one teasingly asked him whether he is rather a gallery owner or an academic, one would fall short as he is also a successful entrepreneur. As long-standing dean of the Faculty of Law and Administration, he was successful in acquiring the site for the University's new campus on the Vistula, and he was responsible for the restoration of the run-down Palais Larisch, now one of the architectural pearls of the Kraków Faculty of Law and Administration. Academic, gallery owner, or entrepreneur? Prof. *Stelmach* is all of these. Thus, his personal life mirrors his theoretical thinking: he impersonates several prima facie contradictory functions or standpoints simultaneously – and even with synergistic effects.

Prof. *Stelmach* is an exemplary and successful university teacher. He has supervised and promoted twenty PhD students. The success of his students, among others *Bartosz Brożek*, *Marta Soniewicka*, and *Wojciech Załuski,* prove his fruitful manner and stimulating aura. He and his wife *Ela* are generous, exemplary, and amiable hosts. Their open house is one of the intellectual centres of Kraków. Joint forays through the narrow streets and hidden corners of

Kraków are part of the invigorating and friendly exchange with Prof. *Stelmach*: In a small forgotten antique shop, an interesting graphic may be found in some dusty chest of drawers. The fact that life has secrets to offer is one of the lessons to learn from *Jurek Stelmach*.

Augsburg, November 2023 Reiner Schmidt

Table of Contents

Part 4
Law and Politics

Part 5
Law and Economics

Part 6
Law and Psychology

Part 1

Introduction

Law and Interdisciplinarity

Phillip Hellwege and *Marta Soniewicka*

I. Towards more interdisciplinarity in legal scholarship

A. The doctrinal study of law in continental European legal scholarship

The doctrinal study of law has a long tradition both in Poland and Germany, and the same is – with gradual differences – true for the entirety of continental Europe.[1] Continental European legal systems are largely codified, and the doc-

[1] On the situation in Poland, see *J. Wróblewski*, Pisma wybrane (2015); *idem*, Paradygmat dogmatyki prawa a prawoznawstwo, in: S. Wronkowska/M. Zieliński (eds.), Szkice z teorii prawa i szczegółowych nauk prawnych (1990), 38–42; *S. Wronkowska* (ed.), Z teorii i filozofii prawa Zygmunta Ziębińskiego (2007); *A. Peczenik*, Theory of Legal Science (1984); *idem*, Scientia Iuris. Legal Doctrine as Knowledge of Law and as a Source of Law (2005). In

trinal study of the respective codes is at the heart of continental European legal scholarship. Continental European scholars often contrast their approach to the study of law with that of their US colleagues, who traditionally have a stronger interest in interdisciplinary legal scholarship – at the expense of, as continental European legal academics often claim, the doctrinal study of law.[2]

B. Law and interdisciplinarity in US legal scholarship

The emphasis of US legal scholarship on interdisciplinarity is signalled by the combination of the word "law" with extra-legal concepts and disciplines in

addition, see *A. Aarnio*, On Paradigm of Legal Dogmatics – Problems of Scientific Progress in Legal Research, in: P. Trappe (ed.), Contemporary Conceptions of Law (1982), 135–136. For comparative reflections, see *H. Kötz*, Rechtsvergleichung und Rechtsdogmatik, in: idem, Undogmatisches. Rechtsvergleichende und rechtsökonomische Studien aus dreißig Jahren (2005), 64–79, 68; *P. Sahm*, Elemente der Dogmatik (2019), 24 ff.; *A. Stark*, Interdisziplinarität der Rechtsdogmatik (2020), 156 ff. In addition, see *C. Bumke*, Rechtsdogmatik. Eine Disziplin und ihre Arbeitsweise. Zugleich eine Studie über das rechtsdogmatische Arbeiten Friedrich Carl von Savignys (2017), 16. With a different view, *N. Jansen*, Rechtsdogmatik im Zivilrecht, in: T. Gutmann et al. (eds.), Enzyklopädie zur Rechtsphilosophie (2011), http://www.enzyklopaedie-rechtsphilosophie.net/inhaltsverzeichnis/19-beitraege/98-rechts-dogmatik-im-zivilrecht (last accessed 21 August 2023); *O. Lepsius*, Kritik der Dogmatik, in: G. Kirchhof et al. (eds.), Was weiß Dogmatik? Was leistet und wie steuert die Dogmatik des Öffentlichen Rechts? (2012), 39–62, 46 ff.; *M. Jestaedt*, Wissenschaftliches Recht. Rechtsdogmatik als gemeinsames Kommunikationsformat von Rechtswissenschaft and Rechtspraxis, in: Kirchof et al. (eds.), op.cit., 117–137, 117 f.; Jansen, Lepsius and Jestaedt claim that the doctrinal study of law is unique to Germany. More nuanced, *M. Flohr*, Rechtsdogmatik in England (2017), passim; *G. Kirchhof/S. Magen*, Dogmatik: Rechtliche Notwendigkeit und Grundlage fächerübergreifenden Dialogs – eine systematisierende Übersicht, in: Kirchhof et al. (eds.), op.cit., 151–172, 151 f., 158; *R. Stürner*, Das Zivilrecht der Moderne und die Bedeutung der Rechtsdogmatik, JuristenZeitung 2012, 10–24, 13; *P.-C. Müller-Graff*, Zur Integrationskraft zivilrechtlicher Dogmatik im Querschnitt von Referenzgebieten. Zugleich ein Blick in das Unionsrecht, in: T. Lobinger et al. (eds.), Zur Integrationskraft zivilrechtlicher Dogmatik (2014), 121–137, 122.

[2] On interdisciplinarity in US legal scholarship, especially on the exchange between law and the social sciences, see *O. Lepsius*, Sozialwissenschaften im Verfassungsrecht – Amerika als Vorbild?, JuristenZeitung 2005, 1–13, 4 ff.; *M. Reimann*, Die Propria der Rechtswissenschaft, in: *C. Engel/W. Schön* (eds.), Das Proprium der Rechtswissenschaft (2007), 87–99, 96 f.; *N. Petersen*, Braucht die Rechtswissenschaft eine empirische Wende?, Der Staat 49 (2010), 435–455, 435 f. However, Anglo-American scholarship, too, is familiar with something equivalent to the doctrinal study of law, see *Sahm* (n. 1), 26 ff. For an introduction to disputes in the US on interdisciplinarity in law, see *S. Kirste*, Voraussetzungen von Interdisziplinarität der Rechtswissenschaften, in: idem (ed.), Interdisziplinarität in den Rechtswissenschaften. Ein interdisziplinärer und internationaler Dialog (2016), 35–85, 35 f. Nevertheless, the doctrinal study of law is traditionally not as strong in the US as in Germany, see *M. Reimann*, Die Fremdheit des amerikanischen Rechts – Versuch einer historischen Erklärung, in: K. Krakau/F. Streng (eds.), Konflikt der Rechtskulturen? Die USA und Deutschland im Vergleich (2003), 23–36, 35.

order to define numerous interdisciplinary fields of study, the most prominent example up to now being law and economics.[3] Other examples include law and neurosciences (neurolaw), law and emotions, and law and literature. However, these fields of study do not simply combine two disciplines. Law and economics is, for example, dominated by *behavioural* law and economics, which stresses the limits of rationality and incorporates cognitive studies on biases and heuristics into both law and economics. Thus, behavioural law and economics combines law, economics, psychology, and cognitive sciences.

Neurolaw, to take another example, combines research from neuroscience and cognitive science with law.[4] Like behavioural law and economics, neurolaw is concerned with exploring the limits of rationality and the irrational dimensions of cognition. The study of the neural basis of cognitive processes, taking into account the important role of emotions, is used in the analysis of the conceptual and procedural assumptions of criminal law, including the question of assigning responsibility or determining insanity. Representatives of this field of study question the concept of free will, which can have a significant impact on the premises of criminal responsibility. They study the ability to consciously discern one's own actions in minors or mentally ill people, and they discuss issues surrounding the application of modern technologies, such as functional magnetic resonance imaging (fMRI), in evidentiary proceedings.

Law and emotions results from the affective turn in science in the 1990s. It partially overlaps with behavioural law and economics as well as with law and neurosciences. However, there are several important differences between these fields that are worth highlighting. Behavioural law and economics as well as law and neurosciences are primarily concerned with the study of cognition and decision-making, although they also emphasize the role of emotions in the context of cognition. Law and emotions, on the other hand, focuses primarily on the study of emotions and their relationship to law. All three question the narrow understanding of rationality and pay attention to the cognitive functions of emotions. However, behavioural law and economics and neurolaw remain

---

[3] *S. Henry*, Interdisciplinarity in the Fields of Law, Justice, and Criminology, in: R. Frodeman et al. (eds.) The Oxford Handbook of Interdisciplinarity (2017), 397–411, 397.

[4] *M. Pardo/D. Patterson*, Minds, Brains, and Law: The Conceptual Foundations of Law and Neuroscience (2013); *A. D'Aloia/M.C. Errigo* (eds.), Neuroscience and Law. Complicated Crossing and New Perspectives (2020); *S. Fuselli*, Neurocorrection. On the use of neuroevidence for criminals, Teoria e Critica della Regolazione Sociale 22/1 (2021), 209–229; *idem*, Mental integrity protection in the neuro-era. Legal challenges and philosophical background, BioLaw 2020, 413–429; *M. Ienca/R. Andorno*, Towards new human rights in the age of neuroscience and neurotechnology, Life Sciences, Society and Policy 13/5 (2017), 1–27; *J.K. Bublitz/R. Merkel*, Crimes Against Minds: On Mental Manipulations, Harms and a Human Right to Mental Self-Determination in Criminal Law, Philosophy 8 (2014), 51–77; *B. Brożek/J. Hage/N.A. Vincent* (eds.), Law and Mind. A Survey of Law and the Cognitive Science (2021); *J. Stelmach/B. Brożek/Ł. Kurek*, Philosophy in Neuroscience (2013).

within the paradigm of rationality as the privileged form of cognition, and their goal is to correct irrational aspects of the cognitive process or to correct the law in order to reconcile legal concepts and procedures with the results of scientific research. Both fields of study enjoy considerable recognition in scientific circles, as they are methodologically uniform, have clear and specific practical goals, are epistemologically conventional, and strive – simultaneously – for both the greatest possible scientificity and certainty of research. Law and emotions research is much more eclectic in terms of both methods and goals, less epistemologically conventional, and thus less recognized. Law and emotions questions the opposition between reason and emotion and rejects reducing emotions to deviations from rationality; it draws on a number of disciplines, including cognitive science or neuroscience, but primarily on the humanities and social sciences, without claiming to follow the paradigm of the natural sciences.

Overall, US scholars go so far as stressing that the study of law is only feasible with interdisciplinary input. *Alan M. Dershowitz*, for example, points out:[5]

> "Law, by its very nature, must be interdisciplinary. It is impossible to understand a legal system without recourse to history, psychology, economics, philosophy, and other academic disciplines. Law provides the structure for decision-making, but the structure is dependent on substantive rules that reflect the deeper concerns of a society. […] The law has varied over time in its emphasis on particular disciplines. There was a time when psychology was at the forefront, then sociology and now economics. To every discipline there is apparently a season, but there is no season for law shorn of other disciplines. Law without interdisciplinary input is like a beautiful wine decanter without the wine."

This statement is rooted in the legal realism that gained much more recognition in Anglo-American legal systems than in their continental European counterparts, which are rather dominated by the positivist formal approach and the idea of the independence of legal studies. The representatives of legal realism claimed that instead of dealing with abstract considerations about the nature of law, one should concentrate on the study of "real law" (living law), i.e. what judges do.[6] They referred to "real" law as "law in action", this contrasted with "law in books" – the latter being law understood as a system of rules, judgments, concepts, and legal categories. The representatives of legal realism argued for incorporating such disciplines as economics, psychology, sociology, and politics into legal theory and practice, as well as into legal education. This attitude resulted in the development of the law and economics movement as

[5] *A.M. Dershowitz*, The Interdisciplinary Study of Law: A Dedicatory Note on the Founding of the NILR, Northwestern Interdisciplinary Law Review 1 (2008), 3–6, 3–5.

[6] *O.W. Holmes Jr.*, The Path of the Law, Harvard Law Review 10(8) (1897), 457–478, 460 f.; *J. Frank*, What Courts Do in Fact – Part One, Illinois Law Review 26(6) (1931–1932), 645–666; *idem*, What Courts Do in Fact – Part Two, Illinois Law Review 26(7) (1931–1932), 761–784.

well as psychological and sociological jurisprudence. In the second half of the twentieth century, new trends emerged: critical legal studies (CLS) and feminist jurisprudence. Representatives of CLS claim that law is political in nature and is related to the socially created identity of legal entities. Accordingly, they argue that law cannot refer to abstract categories and entities, but should consider social and political conditions as well as real, rather than ideal, assumptions about human qualities, abilities, and behaviour. From this, further trends emerged, such as feminist legal theory or critical race theory. These trends question the mainstream legal concepts from the perspective of gender or race, claiming that such concepts are based on categories that do not consider the experience of different genders or ethnic minorities; law, therefore, is used as a tool of social oppression.

C. Towards more interdisciplinarity in continental European legal scholarship

In the past decades, legal academia has, however, seen dynamic developments on both sides of the Atlantic. On the one hand, the doctrinal study of law seems to have gained importance in US law schools. Most prominently, there is the project on the "foundations of private law", also labelled as "new private law". It has a stronger focus on the doctrinal study of law than traditional US legal scholarship.[7] On the other hand, interdisciplinary approaches to the study of law have (again) gained importance in continental European legal academia.[8]

---

[7] *E.G. Hosemann*, "The New Private Law": Die neue amerikanische Privatrechtswissenschaft in historischer und vergleichender Perspektive, Rabels Zeitschrift für ausländisches und internationales Privatrecht 78 (2014), 37–70. With respect to England, *Flohr* (n. 1), passim, speaks not of a convergence of English and German legal scholarship, but of a transformation in difference ("Transformation in Differenz"), in order to signal the many differences between the emerging doctrinal study of law in England and the traditional doctrinal study of law in Germany.

[8] In 2012, *Lepsius* (n. 1), 46 f., observed that German legal academia has more or less limited itself to the doctrinal study of law only in the past 30 years. However, it seems that since 2012 the pendulum has swung in another direction. Lepsius's observation goes hand in hand with *Stark* (n. 1), 10, who points to the fact that in the nineteenth and early twentieth centuries, German legal scholars did work interdisciplinarily. In the text following this footnote, however, it will become clear that Lepsius simplifies the developments in Germany, thus only describing a general trend. Furthermore, see *J. Croon-Gestefeld*, Interdisziplinäres Arbeiten der Zivilgerichte, in: G. Christandl et al. (eds.), Intra- und Interdisziplinarität im Zivilrecht (2018), 51–69, 53; *Kirste* (n. 2), 36. From a Dutch perspective, see *B. van Klink/S. Taekema*, in: Kirste (n. 2), 87–102, 88. By contrast, in Polish legal academia, there is a clear understanding that interdisciplinary approaches to law date back to the beginning of the twentieth century and that they have continued to thrive since that time: *L. Petrażycki*, Zarys filozofii prawa (1900); *idem*, Wstęp do nauki prawa i moralności (1905, 1959); *idem*, Teoria prawa i państwa w związku z nauką o moralności (1907, 1959–1960) – these works were originally published in Russian and translated into Polish many years later. These

In Germany, for example, it seems that law and economics first appeared in the 1980s.[9] Today it is especially the study of tort law which is influenced by economic insights and theories, but the importance of an economic analysis of law goes beyond the sphere of tort law. Nevertheless, there still are considerable differences in how far economic insights are made use of in different areas of law.[10] In an influential paper from 2012, the *Wissenschaftsrat* (Science and Humanities Council, an important advisory body in the fields of science and the humanities) demanded that German legal academia, among other things, intensify its interdisciplinary efforts and that it move away from a predominantly doctrinal approach to the study (and teaching) of law.[11] Yet, it would be an oversimplification to think that the *Wissenschaftsrat caused* legal scholars to intensify their interdisciplinary research. It seems rather that the *Wissenschaftsrat* picked up on an already existing trend towards more interdisciplinarity in legal academia and that its paper of 2012 functioned as a point of reference for a general debate on this trend,[12] thereby reinforcing it. And indeed, the assertion at the beginning of this paragraph that law and economics seems to have first appeared in the 1980s is itself an oversimplification: In his contribution to the present volume, *Wolfgang Wurmnest* points out that "Germany [has] a long tradition of applying economic insights to shape the body of competition law" that goes back to the nineteenth century.[13] It seems that the fruitful interactions between economics and competition law only again gained

---

approaches were revived in the 1960s, thanks to *Kazimierz Opałek*, Swoistość prawoznawstwa a problem integracji, Państwo i Prawo 4/5 (1966), 628–741; *idem*, Problemy "wewnętrznej" i "zewnętrznej" integracji nauk prawnych. Krakowskie, Studia Prawnicze 1/2 (1968), 7–30. The discussions have again gained attention in the 1990s, see *J. Łakomy*, Interdyscyplinarność i integracja zewnętrzna nauk prawnych w świetle postmodernistycznej krytyki, Archiwum Filozofii Prawa i Filozofii Społecznej 2011, 29–45.

[9] *G. Rühl*, Ökonomische Analyse des Rechts, in: J. Krüper (ed.), Grundlagen des Rechts (4th edn., 2021), 248–268, 248.

[10] *Rühl* (n. 9), 248 ff.; *Croon-Gestefeld* (n. 8), 57. See also the discussions by *Kasiske*, p. 209, below; *Derek*, p. 229, below.

[11] *Wissenschaftsrat*, Perspektiven der Rechtswissenschaft in Deutschland. Situation, Analysen, Empfehlungen (2012), 7 f., 29, 36 f., 43 f., 60.

[12] The debates initiated by the Wissenschaftsrat go beyond the claim for more interdisciplinarity in legal scholarship, see, e.g., *T. Gutmann*, Intra- und Interdisziplinarität: Chance oder Störfaktor?, in: E. Hilgendorf/H. Schulze-Fielitz (eds.), Selbstreflexion der Rechtswissenschaft (2nd edn., 2021), 93–118; *A. von Arnauld*, Öffnung der öffentlich-rechtlichen Methode durch Internationalität und Interdisziplinarität: Erscheinungsformen, Chancen, Grenzen, Veröffentlichungen der Vereinigung der Deutschen Staatsrechtlehrer 74 (2015), 39–81; *R. Stürner*, Die Zivilrechtswissenschaft und ihre Methodik – zu rechtsanwendungsbezogen und zu wenig grundlagenorientiert?, Archiv für die civilistische Praxis 214 (2014), 7–54; see also the contributions by *S. Grundmann*, *T. Gutmann*, *C. Hillgruber*, *S. Lorenz*, *S. Rixen*, and *M. Stolleis*, in: JuristenZeitung 2013, 693–714.

[13] *Wurmnest*, p. 242, below.

momentum in the second half of the twentieth century.[14] An analogous observation is made by *Phillip Hellwege* in his contribution on law and emotions.[15] These observations go hand-in-hand with analysis made by *Alexander Stark*, who rightly recalls that developments have always been multifaceted and overlapping, but never clear cut:[16]

> "In den letzten 150 Jahren wechselten sich Phasen der Offenheit und [...] Geschlossenheit mit anderen Wissenschaften kontinuierlich ab. [...] Es sind in aller Regel Phasen relativer Offenheit und relativer Geschlossenheit, die sich – teils überschneidend – abwechseln."

> "In the past 150 years, phases of openness and [...] closedness towards other disciplines have alternated continuously. [...] Generally, these were phases of relative openness and relative closedness that alternated and that at times overlapped."

By contrast, in Poland there is much greater awareness than in Germany that interdisciplinary approaches to the study of law have a long tradition and that these approaches have gone through various stages of development. In Poland, such approaches to the study of law first occurred in the beginning of the twentieth century and developed from debates on law as a scientific discipline.[17] These debates were both ontological (concerning the question of the nature of law) and epistemological (concerning the question of methods applied to law). The integration of other disciplines – mainly psychology and sociology – into legal scholarship was part of the process of the naturalization of law and ethics.[18] Naturalistic jurisprudence, as it emerged, aimed at the application of scientific knowledge to legal theory and practice. The most prominent representative of Polish psychological jurisprudence was *Leon Petrażycki*, who understood law as a psychological phenomenon.[19] The second stage appeared in the second half of the twentieth century, and it was *Kazimierz Opałek* and *Jerzy Wróblewski* who revived discussions on the integration of extra-legal discipli-

---

[14] *Wurmnest*, pp. 251 ff., below.

[15] *Hellwege*, p. 360 and p. 393, below.

[16] *Stark* (n. 1), 12. In addition, see *Croon-Gestefeld* (n. 8), 52 f.; *S. Kirste*, Einleitung, in: idem (n. 2), 9–17, 10; *idem* (n. 2), 36; *D. Grimm*, Notwendigkeit und Bedingungen interdisziplinärer Forschung in den Rechtswissenschaften, in: Kirste (n. 2), 21–34, 21.

[17] *J. Stelmach/B. Brożek*, Methods of Legal Reasoning (2006), passim.

[18] *H. Kelsen*, What is Justice? Justice, Law, and Politics in the Mirror of Science (1971), distinguished between analytical, normative, psychological, and sociological jurisprudence. Although he argued in favour of normative jurisprudence that was based on the strict separation of law from other disciplines, he claimed that psychological and sociological jurisprudence deal with the study of different aspects of law than analytical or normative jurisprudence, and thus they are not mutually exclusive, but rather complementary.

[19] *L. Petrażycki*, Teoria prawa (n. 8); *idem*, Über die Motive des Handelns und über das Wesen der Moral und des Rechts (1907); *idem*, Wstęp do nauki polityki prawa (1968); *idem*, O nauce, prawie i moralności. Pisma wybrane (1985); *idem*, Methodologie der Theorien des Rechts und der Moral. Zugleich eine neue logische Lehre von der Bildung der allgemeinen Begriffe und Theorien (1933).

nes into legal scholarship.[20] These discussions had mainly a methodological character. The two authors distinguished between external and internal integration, and they further distinguished three types of external integration: unification, coordination, and cooperation.[21] The third stage took place after the political transformation of Poland in 1989.[22] In the communist era, the official paradigm of social sciences was Marxist-Leninist doctrine. In response – to minimize ideological corruption of legal thought and to safeguard its autonomy – Polish legal scholars followed during the communist era a formal legal positivism known for its methodological conservatism, and special emphasis was put on conceptual and linguistic analysis as well as on logic. Poland's transformation into a liberal democracy resulted in emancipation from Marxist-Leninist doctrine and opened new perspectives – both methodological and theoretical – in law, and that is why, with respect to Poland, it is also possible to speak of a recent trend towards more interdisciplinary in legal scholarship. The most significant example of such new approaches to the study of law was inspired by the law and economics movement, which gained ground in connection with Poland's transformation into a free market economy.[23] The openness of legal scholarship to extra-legal disciplines resulted in a debate between modern and postmodern approaches to law.[24] In the last and current stage of interdisciplinary studies of law, the debate over the naturalization of law has regained special attention.[25] It was mainly caused by the rapid development of new technologies, chiefly in the fields of biotechnology[26] and computer

---

[20] *Opałek,* Problemy (n. 8); *idem,* Swoistość prawoznawstwa (n. 8). In addition, see *idem,* Interdyscyplinarne związki prawoznawstwa, Studia Filozoficzne 2/3 (1985), 17–29; *idem/J. Wróblewski,* Zagadnienia teorii prawa (1969); *idem/idem,* Prawo, metodologia, filozofia, teoria prawa (1991).

[21] *Opałek,* Problemy (n. 8), 7; *Łakomy* (n. 8).

[22] *Łakomy* (n. 8).

[23] *J. Stelmach/B. Brożek/W. Załuski,* Dziesięć wykładów o ekonomii prawa (2007); *J. Stelmach/M. Soniewicka* (eds.), Analiza ekonomiczna w zastosowaniach prawniczych (2007).

[24] See pp. 36 ff., below.

[25] *J. Stelmach/B. Brożek/M. Hohol,* The Many Faces of Normativity (2013); *J. Stelmach/B. Brożek/Ł. Kurek/K. Eliasz* (eds.), Naturalizm prawniczy: stanowiska (2015); *J. Stelmach/B. Brożek/Ł. Kurek/K. Eliasz* (eds.), Naturalizm prawniczy: interpretacje (2015); *J. Stelmach/B. Brożek/Ł. Kurek* (eds.), Naturalizm prawniczy: granice (2017).

[26] *J. Stelmach/B. Brożek/M. Soniewicka* (eds.), Studies in the Philosophy of Law, vol. 5: Law and Biology (2010); *J. Stelmach/M. Soniewicka/W. Załuski* (eds.), Studies in the Philosophy of Law, vol. 4: Legal Philosophy and the Challenges of Biosciences (2010).

science[27] but also in the area of cognitive science;[28] it was progress in the latter discipline that led to the emergence of a new field of study called neurolaw.[29]

D. The reasons for the trend towards more interdisciplinarity in legal scholarship

This brings us to the reasons for the trend towards more interdisciplinarity in legal scholarship. In Western Europe, the 1960s were a phase of societal transformation, and as a consequence legal scholarship opened up to the social sciences.[30] In Poland, it was in the aftermath of the 1989 political and economic transformation that Polish legal scholarship opened up to new perspectives. And today, we simultaneously experience a number of fundamental – societal, technical, and environmental – challenges, transformations, and crises: globalization, climate change, digitalization, decolonization, and demographic changes, to name just five examples. These challenges, transformations, and crises also challenge traditional law along with the lawyers who have to understand these challenges, transformations, and crises in order to develop legal answers to them. This requires an openness to other disciplines. Furthermore, we are experiencing an ongoing and accelerated advance in extra-legal disciplines, and these advances pose the question whether the law is still based on accurate extra-legal assumptions. At the same time, legal scholarship is experiencing an ongoing process of internationalization – again as a response to the many challenges, transformations, and crises which cannot be solved on a purely national level. In a process of legal internationalization, it is difficult to have purely doctrinal discussions in law, as law is mostly national and for that reason inapt for the framing of international discussions.[31] Finally, the many challenges, transformations, and crises lead to increased legislative activity. With respect to this last point, *Christoph Engel* and *Wolfgang Schön* observe:[32]

"Dass die Rechtswissenschaft diese Grundlagenfächer in den vergangenen einhundert Jahren dennoch aus dem Kernbereich ihrer Arbeit weitgehend verdrängen konnte, scheint seinen wesentlichen Grund in der relativen Stabilität des Forschungsgegenstandes zu besitzen. Wenn Kerngebiete des Rechts – etwa der Grundrechtsabschnitt der Verfassung oder die allgemeinen Grundlagen des Bürgerlichen Rechts und des Strafrechts – in ihrer positivrechtli-

---

[27] See *B. Fischer/A. Pązik/M. Świerczyński* (eds.), Prawo sztucznej inteligencji i nowych technologii (2021).

[28] *M. Jakubiec,* Interdisciplinary jurisprudence: between law, cognitive science and new technologies, in: B. Brożek et al. (eds.), Perspectives on Interdisciplinarity (2021), 79–98.

[29] *B. Brożek/J. Hage/N. Vincent* (eds.), Law and Mind: A Survey of Law and Cognitive Sciences (2021); *B. Brożek,* The Legal Mind: A New Introduction to Legal Epistemology (2020).

[30] *Grimm* (n. 16), 21 f. On the following account, see in addition, *Stark* (n. 1), 202 ff.

[31] *T. Duve*, Internationalisierung und Transnationalisierung der Rechtswissenschaft, in: D. Grimm et al. (eds.), Rechtswege. Kontextsensible Rechtswissenschaft vor der transnationalen Herausforderung (2015), 167–195, 180 ff. In addition, see *Kirste* (n. 2), 59.

[32] *C. Engel/W. Schön*, Vorwort, in: idem (n. 2), IX–XIV, XI.

chen Fassung über Jahrzehnte unverändert bleiben, treten die außerrechtlichen Konstituanten dieser Normsysteme zunehmend in den Hintergrund. In Rechtsprechung und Literatur entwickelt sich ein selbsttragendes Kontinuum von Präzedenzfällen und 'Meinungen', die die Fähigkeit zu[r] […] organischen Fortentwicklung in sich trägt […]."

"The ability of legal scholarship to push aside scholarship on the foundations of law in the past one hundred years seems to be explained by the relative stability of its research object. If the core areas of law – such as the constitution's section on basic rights or the foundational provisions of private and criminal law – remain for decades unaltered, the extra-legal foundations of these normative systems continuously recede. Case law and literature develop a self-sustaining continuum of precedents and doctrines, which itself is capable of organic development."

The current trend towards more interdisciplinarity in legal academia has different – positive and negative – (side) effects. German universities come, for example, under increasing pressure to generate third-party research funding, especially from funding bodies such as the *Deutsche Forschungsgemeinschaft* (German Research Foundation) or the European Research Council. It seems that legal research proposals following a purely doctrinal research agenda are less likely to attract third-party funding than those going beyond such an approach.[33] The same tendency can be seen in Poland, where research funding agencies emphasize interdisciplinarity. Consequently, scholars may for purely monetary reasons move towards a more interdisciplinary approach. However, interdisciplinary research driven by the motivation of attracting funding and not by an intrinsic motivation may be problematic for the reasons which *Jerzy Stelmach* explores in his contribution to the present volume: researchers may simply follow "cognitive fashions".[34] In all, this seems to be a negative side effect of the trend towards more interdisciplinarity in legal research. A positive effect is the general openness and breadth of interdisciplinary approaches that we find in Polish and German legal scholarship – an openness and breadth that is not visible at first sight as in both countries interdisciplinary discussions in law are usually embedded in specialized fields such as medical law or relate to specific problems such as digitalization.[35]

---

[33] *N. Jansen*, Rechtsdogmatik, Rechtswissenschaft und juristische Praxis. Zum gesellschaftlichen Ort und wissenschaftlichen Selbstverständnis universitärer Rechtsdogmatik, Archiv des öffentlichen Rechts 143 (2018), 623–658, 629; *H. Rottleuthner*, Methodologie und Organisation der Rechtswissenschaft, in: E. Hilgendorf/H. Schulze-Fielitz (eds.), Selbstreflexion der Rechtswissenschaft (2nd edn., 2021), 241–257, 256. On the interest of research funding bodies in interdisciplinary research, see *Kirste* (n. 2), 62. With respect to Poland, see *B. Brożek*, What is interdisciplinarity?, in: Brożek (n. 28), 11–32, 11.

[34] See *Stelmach*, pp. 49 f., below. *Dershowitz* (n. 5), 3–5, speaks of "season", see p. 6, above.

[35] See, e.g., the contributions by *U.M. Gassner* and *J. Kersten*, in: J. Soentgen et al. (eds.), Umwelt und Gesundheit (2020), and the contribution by *U.M. Gassner* and *F. Steger*, in: U.M. Gassner et al. (eds.), Geschlecht und Gesundheit (2018).

E. Reflecting on interdisciplinary research in law

The trend towards more interdisciplinarity raises numerous questions: What do legal scholars mean when referring to the concept of interdisciplinarity? Is it possible to distinguish different types or grades of interdisciplinarity? What are the functions of interdisciplinary arguments in legal debates? Are there common problems which legal scholars face when engaging in interdisciplinary research regardless of which area of law they are working in and regardless of which discipline they are cooperating with? And is there an interdependence between a given national legal system and interdisciplinary research? Are, for example, interdisciplinary research questions which legal scholars ask dependent on the national legal system they come from? And are the functions of interdisciplinary findings in legal debates dependent on the specific national legal system in the context of which such debates are conducted?

Despite the trend towards more interdisciplinarity in legal scholarship, it seems that these and related questions have hitherto not attracted much attention: Continental European legal scholars increasingly engage in interdisciplinary research without much reflection on the specificities of interdisciplinary research in law.[36] Against this background, the present volume wishes to explore these questions. Nota bene, it wishes only to *explore* these questions. It does not envisage the development of final answers and at most wishes to develop tentative answers. And the last three questions posed in the preceding paragraph already suggest that it wishes to explore these questions also from comparative perspectives, specifically by engaging in a Polish-German dialogue. Furthermore, the questions already hint at what the present volume wishes to achieve and what it is not meant to accomplish: It is, except for one contribution, not engaging in an interdisciplinary exchange with scholars from non-legal disciplines.[37] Rather, the present volume offers reflections by legal scholars on interdisciplinary legal research in their fields of specialization.

The remainder of this introductory chapter serves two purposes. First, we wish to expand on the above questions in detail in order to unfold the present volume's specific focus. However, the present volume does not adopt a top-down approach. Beyond the first three introductory chapters, the contributions to the present volume do not engage in general debates and do not make general observations on interdisciplinary research in law, nor do they engage in any sort of meta-discourse. We thereby want to avoid what *Stelmach* calls in his contribution "sterile academic disputes about interdisciplinarity itself".[38] Rather, the present volume adopts a bottom-up approach. We have invited

---

[36] See *Stark* (n. 1), passim. For international reflections on interdisciplinarity in legal scholarship, see the contributions in *S. Kirste* (ed.), Interdisziplinarität in den Rechtswissenschaften. Ein interdisziplinärer und internationaler Dialog (2016).

[37] The exception is the contribution authored by *Marschler*, pp. 95 ff., below.

[38] *Stelmach*, p. 49, below.

numerous scholars from Poland and Germany to reflect on interdisciplinary research or to discuss examples of interdisciplinary debates in their fields of legal specialization. We have not imposed any further restrictions on these scholars, and as a consequence their contributions reflect how legal scholars understand the concept of interdisciplinarity as well as the diversity of interdisciplinary research in law. For each Polish contribution, we have then invited a German colleague to comment on the main Polish contribution from the perspective of German legal scholarship and *vice versa*. We find these comments essential in implementing the aforementioned comparative approach and in reflecting on the interdependence between a given positive national legal system and interdisciplinary research. The commentators were asked to focus on the interdisciplinary aspects of the contribution they commented on, and they were in particular invited to address the following aspects and questions:

"How would you define the relationship between law and the extra-legal discipline in the paper you comment on? Is it an interdisciplinary reflection *on* law? Or are interdisciplinary/extra-legal insights/findings applied *in* the legal discourse? Are the different disciplines separated from each other? Or is it even a further relationship?

Polish commentators are asked to comment on papers authored by German colleagues and *vice versa*. We are particularly interested in reflections on whether in your own legal system the interdisciplinary approach as presented in the paper you comment upon runs very differently or whether it runs in parallel.

Finally, we are interested in reflections on the reasons for the differences or commonalities which you identify: Is the legal framework simply a different one so that there is no room for interdisciplinary arguments in your own legal system? Should/could the discourse in your country run parallel and is there, thus, no justification for the observed differences? Is interdisciplinarity therefore perhaps a vehicle for different legal systems to converge? Or is the state of the art in the extra-legal discipline different?"

When formulating these questions, we were aware that the main contributions will be so diverse that not all commentators would be able to answer all questions alike and that some commentators would even be unable to address any of these questions. In all, the function of these questions was simply to give the commentators guidance without binding them to these questions.

When developing this specific design of the present volume, we hoped that the entirety of the contributions would allow us to identify common themes and problems of interdisciplinary legal scholarship and that the entirety of contributions would allow us to explore, and to develop tentative answers to, the aforementioned questions – tentative answers which may in turn be the starting point for further debates on law and interdisciplinarity or which other scholars may wish to challenge. And this brings us to the second purpose which this introductory chapter serves. When devising the present volume's specific design and when formulating the questions which we wished to explore, we naturally started with top-down thinking. However, by signalling to the authors that these questions were only meant to give them guidance (in order to enhance the volume's overall coherence), we secured the present volume's bottom-up approach, and we hope that, as a consequence, our analysis is not a sterile academic dispute on interdisciplinarity itself as warned against by *Stelmach*. Thus, in this introductory chapter we would like to link our top-down ideas which we had developed when first planning the present volume with the tentative answers which we have distilled from the different contributions, thereby presenting an overall analysis on law and interdisciplinarity.

II. Defining interdisciplinarity: a fruitless endeavour?

Readers of a volume titled "Law and Interdisciplinarity" will expect the authors to implement a clear and uniform definition of the very concept of interdisciplinarity. Interdisciplinary research is usually understood as integrating methods and/or concepts from different disciplines into one.[39] Interdisciplinarity is often distinguished from multi- and transdisciplinarity. Multidisciplinarity aims at studying the same problem from the perspective of different disciplines, without integrating the methods and concepts of these disciplines into one. Instead, the various disciplines stand side by side. Accordingly, in multidisciplinary conferences and publications, specialists from different disciplines present different views on a shared problem. Transdisciplinarity is "defined as a common system of axioms that transcends the scope of disciplinary worldviews through an overarching synthesis, such as anthropology conceived as the science of humans."[40] In a nutshell, interdisciplinarity is described as integrating, blending, combining, and linking different disciplines as well as allowing for interaction between different disciplines within a principally designated discipline; multidisciplinarity as coordinating, sequencing, and juxtaposing various disciplines in a dialogue, with the danger of producing a series of monologues instead of a dialogue; and transdisciplinarity as transcending, transgressing, and transforming different disciplines. With respect to the concept of interdisciplinarity, *Stanley Fish* accurately points out that the "dream of a unified field of knowledge" is utopian by definition and results in "the religion of interdisciplinarity", by which he means

[39] *J.T. Klein*, Typologies of Interdisciplinarity: The Boundary Work of Definition, in: Frodeman (n. 3), 21–34. In addition, see *Henry* (n. 3); *B. Brożek* (n. 33), 12 f.; *W. Załuski*, The pitfalls of interdisciplinarity, in: Brożek (n. 28), 175–192, 175.

[40] *Klein* (n. 39), 29.

"the hope that we can put all the jobs of work – all the so-called disciplines – together and form one large and unified field of knowledge (call it cultural studies) to replace the fractured and fragmented knowledges now given us by separate departments and schools."[41]

In fact, such synthesis will turn out to be "a grab-bag of disparate elements held together by the conceptual equivalent of chicken-wire, or by shifting political and economic alliances, or by a desire to control the production and dissemination of knowledge."[42] Other authors add further concepts to the discussion, such as cross- and pluridisciplinarity. Within, the concept of interdisciplinarity, some authors further distinguish between indiscriminate, pseudo, auxiliary, composite, supplementary, and unifying interdisciplinarity. And other authors speak of methodological, conceptual, and temporary interdisciplinary.[43] *Bartosz Brożek*, for example, differentiates between two main types of interdisciplinarity – methodological and theoretical interdisciplinarity. The former aims at bringing together the methods from various disciplines into a new field of study, the latter at integrating methods from other disciplines into a leading discipline.[44]

However, it seems that there are no generally accepted definitions of the aforementioned concepts. Furthermore, some scholars claim that these definitions are unhelpful for reflections on the current state of interdisciplinary legal research because such research is so multifaceted that any enumeration of concepts describing it has to be non-exhaustive.[45] Finally, it seems that there is no example of interdisciplinary research in law that can be labelled exclusively with one of these concepts. Most research, rather, represents a mix of them. In order to avoid what *Stelmach* calls "sterile academic disputes about interdisciplinarity itself",[46] we wish not to further reflect on the different definitions and distinctions of interdisciplinarity. We will adopt a different starting point that is more in line with the bottom-up approach which we wish to follow.

---

41 *S. Fish*, Professional Correctness: Literary Studies and Political Change (1999), 73.

42 *Fish* (n. 41), 74.

43 On these different concepts and classifications, see *Klein* (n. 39), 29; *Stark* (n. 1), 173; *Kirste* (n. 2), 55 ff., 63 ff.; *van Klink/Taekema* (n. 8), 87 ff.; *M. Jungert*, Was zwischen wem und warum eigentlich? Grundsätzliche Fragen der Interdisziplinarität, in: idem et al. (eds.), Interdisziplinarität. Theorie, Praxis, Probleme (2010), 1–12, 1 ff.

44 *B. Brożek* (n. 33), 12 f.

45 Similarly, *M. Jakubiec/P. Urbańczyk/B. Brożek*, Introduction, in: Brożek et al. (n. 28), 7–10, 7, reject the helpfulness of these concepts and classifications.

46 *Stelmach*, p. 49, below. Such approach follows from the bottom-up approach adhered to in the present volume, see pp. 13 f., above.

III. A different starting point: the doctrinal study of law

Above, interdisciplinary research in law has been contrasted with the doctrinal study of law, which is still at the heart of continental European legal scholarship. Reflections on the latter concept may allow us to develop an answer to the question of what legal scholars – or one should rather say: continental European scholars engaged in the doctrinal study of law – mean when speaking of interdisciplinarity.[47]

In Poland, the doctrinal study of law is called *dogmatyka*, in Germany *Dogmatik* (dogmatics) or, in order to distinguish it from dogmatic theology, *dogmatyka prawa* or *Rechtsdogmatik* (legal dogmatics). In English, the term dogmatics is primarily linked to dogmatic theology.[48] It is only rarely found with reference to legal scholarship, and the phrase "doctrinal study of law" or "doctrinal legal scholarship" seems to be more widely spread.[49] In fact, there is a methodological link between dogmatic theology and the doctrinal study of law. This link is at the heart of the contributions of *Franciszek Longchamps de Bérier* and *Thomas Marschler*.[50] Both authors thereby pick up on a dialogue between legal scholars and theologians that has recently been initiated by *Georg Essen* and *Nils Jansen*.[51] And it is because of the methodological link between the doctrinal study of law and dogmatic theology that *Marschler* and *Longchamps de Bérier* also make reference in their contributions to the doctrinal study of law as dogmatics, a term which other authors to the present volume have by and large tried to avoid.

Marschler observes that "it is repeatedly emphasized that there is no consensus in the definition of legal dogmatics",[52] citing, among others, *Bernd*

---

[47] A similar approach is adopted by *Gutmann* (n. 12), 93 ff.

[48] *A.C. Outler*, Doctrines and Dogmas, Religious, in: The New Encyclopaedia Britannica, vol. 17 (15th edn., 2007), 394; Dogmatic, in: J.A. Simpson/E.S.C. Weiner (eds.), The Oxford English Dictionary, vol. 4 (2nd edn., 1989), 929.

[49] See the examples cited by *Sahm* (n. 1), 26 ff.

[50] *Longchamps de Bérier*, pp. 75 ff., below *Marschler*, pp. 95 ff., below.

[51] *G. Essen/N. Jansen* (eds.), Dogmatisierungsprozesse in Recht und Religion (2011). In addition, see *Sahm* (n. 1), passim. Sceptically, *Jestaedt* (n. 1), 118: "[A]llenfalls die Theologie [kann] noch mit einem – wohl stärker dem Namen denn der Sache nach – analogen disziplinären Format aufwarten, […]." ("It is, at best, theology that can come up with an analogous disciplinary concept – yet probably more in name than in substance […].").

[52] *Marschler*, p. 97, below.

Rüthers:[53] "The concept [of legal dogmatics] is presumed to be known, but it is rarely and mostly only scarcely defined." *Oliver Lepsius* adds:[54]

"Eine klare Aufgabenbeschreibung, Funktionsvorstellung oder gar Begriffsbildung gibt es nicht. Man gewinnt eher den Eindruck, bei Dogmatik handele es sich um einen Evidenzbegriff, der allseitige Wertschätzung und Zustimmung genießt, individuell aber durchaus unterschiedlich verstanden wird."

"There is no clear understanding of what legal dogmatics is supposed to achieve, no clear understanding of its functions and no clear definition. It rather seems that legal dogmatics is a concept that goes without saying and that enjoys universal esteem and approval, but one that is understood differently individually."

Nevertheless, legal academia is currently witnessing (again) an increasing interest in, and ongoing debates on, the characteristics of what in Germany is called *Rechtsdogmatik*, with different scholars stressing different aspects.[55] This increased interest in defining the concept of *Rechtsdogmatik* is, here again, most probably a result of the many challenges which law faces today and which produces today's trend towards more interdisciplinarity in legal scholarship: When scholars of one discipline open up to other disciplines, they

---

[53] *B. Rüthers*, Rechtsdogmatik als Schranke des Richterrechts?, Jahrbuch des öffentlichen Rechts der Gegenwart 64 (2016), 309–343, 313: "Der Begriff [der Dogmatik] wird als bekannt vorausgesetzt, aber selten und meistens spärlich definiert." The translation is taken from *Marschler*, p. 97, below. Similarly, *B. Rüthers/C. Fischer/A. Birk*, Rechtstheorie mit Juristischer Methodenlehre (12th edn., 2022), para. 309; *C. Waldhoff*, Kritik und Lob der Dogmatik. Rechtsdogmatik im Spannungsfeld von Gesetzesbindung und Funktionsorientierung, in: Kirchhof et al. (n. 1), 17–37, 21; *B. Grzeszick*, Steuert Dogmatik? Inwiefern steuert die Dogmatik des Öffentlichen Rechts? Gibt es eine rechtliche Steuerungsfunktion jenseits der Rechtsdogmatik?, in: Kirchhof et al. (n. 1), 97–109, 98; *A. Voßkuhle*, Was leistet Rechtsdogmatik? Zusammenführung und Ausblick in 12 Thesen, in: Kirchhof et al. (n. 1), 111–114, 111.

[54] *Lepsius* (n. 1), 40.

[55] See, e.g., most recently and all with references to older literature, *Rüthers/Fischer/Birk* (n. 53), para. 309 ff.; *Jansen* (n. 33), 623 ff.; *idem* (n. 1); *Bumke*, (n. 1), passim; *idem*, Erzeugung und Gebrauch von Wissen in der Rechtsdogmatik, in: I. Augsberg/G.F. Schuppert (eds.), Wissen und Recht (2022), 443–486; *idem*, Rechtsdogmatik. Überlegungen zur Entwicklung und zu den Formen einer Denk- und Arbeitsweise der deutschen Rechtswissenschaft, JuristenZeitung 2014, 641–650; *Sahm* (n. 1), passim; *J. Lennartz*, Dogmatik als Methode (2017), passim; *Stark* (n. 1), 21 ff., 77 ff.; *T. Lobinger*, Perspektiven der Privatrechtsdogmatik am Beispiel des allgemeinen Gleichbehandlungsrechts, Archiv für die civilistische Praxis 216 (2016), 28–106, 34 ff.; *Stürner* (n. 12), 10 ff.; *idem* (n. 1), 10 ff.; *Gutmann* (n. 12), 94 ff.; *M. Goldmann*, Dogmatik als rationale Rekonstruktion: Versuch einer Metatheorie am Beispiel völkerrechtlicher Prinzipien, Der Staat 53 (2014), 373–399; see also the contributions in *G. Kirchhof/S. Magen/K. Schneider* (eds.), Was weiß Dogmatik. Was leistet und wie steuert die Dogmatik des öffentlichen Rechts? (2012), and see especially the overview by *Waldhoff* (n. 53), 22 ff. From the older literature and from a historical perspective, see especially *M. Herberger*, Dogmatik. Zur Geschichte von Begriff und Methode in Medizin und Jurisprudenz (1981).

need an understanding of the specificities of their own discipline. Despite the observation that different scholars stress different aspects when it comes to defining the concept of *Rechtsdogmatik*, it seems safe to summarize the essence of the doctrinal study of law in the words of *Rüthers*, *Christian Fischer*, and *Axel Birk* as

> "die Erläuterung der für das geltende Recht maßgeblichen Begründungen und Lösungsmuster. Damit sind alle Lehrsätze, Grundregeln und Prinzipien erfaßt, sowohl diejenigen, die im Gesetz zu finden sind, als auch diejenigen, die Rechtswissenschaft und Rechtspraxis dem Gesetz hinzugefügt haben. Die Dogmatik soll das geltende Recht mit rationaler Überzeugungskraft erklären."[56]

> "the description of the rationales and approaches [*Lösungsmuster*, literally: solution patterns] of the law as it is in force. This includes all theorems, fundamental rules, and principles regardless of whether they are made explicit in the law itself or whether legal academia and legal practice have added them to the law [or better: have found them to be inherent in the law]. The doctrinal study of law is intended to explain the law as it is in force with rational persuasiveness."

And *Arthur Kaufmann* explains:[57]

> "Der Rechtsdogmatiker fragt nicht, was Recht überhaupt ist und ob, unter welchen Umständen, in welchem Umfang und auf welche Weise es Rechtserkenntnis gibt. Das heißt nicht notwendig, daß die Rechtsdogmatik unkritisch verführe; aber auch wo sie kritisch vorgeht, etwa eine Norm des Gesetzes kritisch überprüft, argumentiert sie stets systemimmanent, das geltende System bleibt unangetastet."

> "A doctrinal law scholar does not ask what law is and whether – and under what circumstances, to what extent, and in what way – there is cognition of law. This does not necessarily imply that the doctrinal study of law is uncritical; but even where it critically reflects upon the law, where, for example, it critically analyses a legal rule, it always uses arguments that are internal to the system. The system as it is in force remains untouched."

On the basis of these two explanations, it is possible to identify a number of elements that are characteristic of the doctrinal study of law and that distinguish it from other disciplines. The first element, however, does not appear in these two explanations but is taken for granted in a codified legal system: Doctrinal scholars of law wish to "explain the law as it is in force with rational persuasiveness", and in a codified legal system the law in force is a code or at least a statute. Doctrinal scholars of law thus focus on legal norms as contained in codes and statutes as authoritative texts. The aim of the doctrinal study of law is to understand and explain each legal norm of a given legal system. To this end, scholars of the doctrinal study of law use arguments that are internal to the system. In the process of understanding and explaining a legal norm,

---

[56] *Rüthers/Fischer/Birk* (n. 53), para. 311.

[57] *A. Kaufmann*, Rechtsphilosophie, Rechtstheorie, Rechtsdogmatik, in: W. Hassemer et al. (eds.), Einführung in die Rechtsphilosophie und Rechtstheorie der Gegenwart (9th edn., 2016), 1–22, 1.

they start with the legal norm's wording, analyse its *telos*, place it in its systematic legal context, and take into account its legislative history. They work on the assumption that a legal system is a coherent and self-contained whole. When analysing the legal norm's wording, when analysing its telos, and when putting it in its systematic legal context, doctrinal scholars of law, thus, identify other norms as argumentative points of reference. Thereby, they assume that in the process of analysing the law they reconstruct the legal system as a coherent whole as it is hypothesised to have been enacted by the legislature. Finally, as *Rüthers*, *Fischer*, and *Birk* point out, doctrinal scholars of law do not restrict themselves to the norm itself. They identify theorems, fundamental rules, and principles seen to be inherent in the law, which they in turn apply to interpret single legal norms. And the identification and critical discussion of such theorems, fundamental rules, and principles has indeed seen a renaissance in the doctrinal study of law.[58] The overall aim of the exercise is, as *Rüthers*, *Fischer*, and *Birk* point out, to explain each single norm "with rational persuasiveness", or, in the words of *Martin Eifert*, with a focus primarily on the application of the law:[59]

> "Dogmatik ist danach vor allem eine kohärenzsichernde, operationalisierende Zwischenschicht zwischen den Rechtsnormen und der Rechtsanwendung im Einzelfall."

> "Accordingly, [legal] dogmatics is foremost an intermediate layer that operates between legal rules as in force and as applied in individual cases and that serves to ensure overall coherence."

The aim to explain each single norm "with rational persuasiveness" points to another characteristic element of the doctrinal study of law: It is an argumentative or discursive discipline. Unlike the natural sciences, there is no right or wrong. Depending on the weight that one attaches to a specific argument, depending on the systematic legal context into which one sets a specific legal norm, depending on the fundamental rules and principles which one accepts to be inherent in the law, and depending on the weight that one attaches to these fundamental rules and principles, the interpretation of a legal norm may differ. Thus, German scholars of the doctrinal study of law do not label a legal interpretation as right or wrong.[60] Rather, they use the concepts of tenable (*vertretbar*) and untenable (*unvertretbar*).[61] Whether a legal interpretation is tenable

[58] See the discussion of *M. Grünberger/N. Jansen*, Perspektiven deutscher Privatrechtstheorie, in: idem (eds.), Privatrechtstheorie heute. Perspektiven deutscher Privatrechtstheorie (2017), 1–44, 1 ff.

[59] *M. Eifert*, Zum Verhältnis von Dogmatik und pluralisierter Rechtswissenschaft, in: Kirchhof et al. (n. 1), 79–96, 81.

[60] *Rüthers/Fischer/Birk* (n. 53), para. 316; *Rüthers* (n. 53), 323; *Jansen* (n. 33), 630.

[61] *Rüthers/Fischer/Birk* (n. 53), para. 320.

will foremost be decided by reference to the standards of legal methodology.[62] And the doctrinal discourse between legal academia and legal practice (especially in the courts) will identify that legal interpretation amongst all tenable interpretations which has the most persuasive power. If such an interpretation is identifiable, German lawyers speak of a *herrschende Meinung* (predominant opinion) where that interpretation is predominant both in the case law and in academic writing; of a *herrschende Lehre* (predominant teaching) where that interpretation is predominant in academic writing but not in case law; or of *ständige Rechtsprechung* (established case law) where that interpretation is predominant in the case law but not necessarily in academic writing.

What are the functions of the doctrinal study of law? *Rüthers*, *Fischer*, and *Birk* work out different functions:[63] (1) It is clear that the doctrinal study of law serves the function of systematizing the law as it is in force. (2) The doctrinal study of law has a stabilizing function; it is a function that is of utmost importance in a legal system that is not based on binding precedents, but in which a judge is bound only to the legal norm as enacted by the legislature: Of the multitude of possible legal interpretations, one interpretation will be accepted as the most persuasive, and legal actors as well as citizens will rely on courts following such interpretations. Thus, the doctrinal study of law will lead to legal certainty. (3) It also leads to the rationalization and legitimization of law by explaining the law with rationale persuasiveness. (4) Furthermore, it serves the function of reducing the argumentative workload which legal actors have to assume in order to support a given legal solution. If legal actors adopt an interpretation that has been accepted as the most persuasive, their argument may be brief. (5) By contrast, if legal actors wish to depart from an interpretation that has been accepted as the most persuasive, then they have to invest more time to argue their case. They have to present their specific interpretation with “rationale persuasiveness”, knowing that this specific interpretation departs from the interpretation that is accepted by other legal actors as the most convincing. (6) The doctrinal study of law is at the heart of teaching, a point that is stressed by *Longchamps de Bérier*;[64] *Marschler* simply speaks of its “didactic purposes”.[65] This didactic function of the doctrinal study of law is based directly on its systematizing function. (7) Just above we have written that scholars of the doctrinal study of law “assume that in the process of analysing the law they reconstruct the legal system as a coherent whole as it is hypothesised to have been enacted by the legislature.” Yet it has been observed that the

---

[62] On the contested relationship between the doctrinal study of law and legal methodology, see *Kirchhof/Magen* (n. 1), 155 f.; *Bumke*, (n. 1), 113 ff.

[63] *Rüthers/Fischer/Birk* (n. 53), para. 321 ff. In addition, see *Rüthers* (n. 53), 333 ff.; *Bumke* (n. 1), 45 ff.; *Voßkuhle* (n. 53), 112; *Stark* (n. 1), 115 ff. (speaking not of the functions of the doctrinal study of law, but of the reasons for engaging in such study).

[64] *Longchamps de Bérier*, pp. 81 f., below.

[65] *Marschler*, p. 98, below.

doctrinal study of law is not limited to reconstructing the authoritative text as it was enacted. Indeed, it is an illusion that the doctrinal study of law is limited to reconstructing the law. It has an innovative function. By interpreting, for example, an old statute in the light of a new statute, by applying an old statute to new factual situations, by finding certain theorems, fundamental rules, and principles to be inherent in the law, or by simply arguing in favour of one out of many possible interpretations as being the most persuasive, doctrinal scholars of law may in fact construct the law.[66]

To fulfil these functions, it is of importance that one of the many tenable interpretations emerges as the most persuasive. This brings us to a further characteristic element of the doctrinal study of law that distinguishes it from other academic disciplines. It is, as has already been pointed out, a discursive discipline. *Rüthers*, *Fischer*, and *Birk* speak of "legitimation through explanatory reasoning".[67] In other academic disciplines, it is of the utmost importance who was the first to make a specific finding. In the doctrinal study of law, numerous scholars will, together with legal practice, work out that interpretation that is accepted as the most persuasive. To that end, it is at the heart of the doctrinal study of law that this interpretation will be reformulated again and again. And it may not be the scholar who has formulated an interpretation for the first time, but – often – the scholar who has formulated such interpretation with the most "rationale persuasiveness" who is cited most.

There is yet a further difference between the doctrinal study of law and other disciplines: The interpretation that is accepted as the most persuasive may change over time, an observation that relates to the innovative function of the doctrinal study of law. There is by definition no finality in the findings of the doctrinal study of law. The reasons why the predominant opinion as to which interpretation is the most convincing may change over time are diverse. (1) It may, for example, be that only over time does it become clear that a certain interpretation is not workable or that it has undesired implications. (2) It may be that the legislature reforms one part of the legal system and that this reform has distant effects on the interpretation of a specific legal norm in other parts of the legal system. (3) Or it may be that it takes some time before somebody thinks of a novel interpretation and that it takes then again more time before that interpretation is accepted as being the most rationally persuasive interpretation, first in legal literature and then by the case law. An example of this phenomenon is discussed by *Thilo Rensmann*:[68] Up until the early 2000s, the concepts of human dignity and inalienable human rights in Art. 1 of the

---

[66] *Sahm* (n. 1), 195; *F. Schorkopf*, Dogmatik und Kohärenz, in: Kirchhof et al. (n. 1), 139–149, 146; *Lobinger* (n. 55), 47 f.

[67] *Rüthers/Fischer/Birk* (n. 53), para. 320, citing the book title of *F. Eckhold-Schmidt*, Legitimation durch Begründung (1974).

[68] See *Rensmann*, pp. 118 f., below.

German Constitution, the so-called Basic Law (*Grundgesetz* – GG), were interpreted as referring to meta-positive law. It was only at that time that *Matthias Herdegen* first formulated the idea of understanding both concepts as notions of positive law. More often than not, however, the interpretation that is accepted as the most persuasive does not change over time. In that case, scholars engaged in the doctrinal study of law simply perpetuate in their writings the existing patterns of argumentation, thereby openly acknowledging continuity: the doctrinal study of law holds available "for legal practice a reservoir of legal knowledge".[69]

There is a final difference between the doctrinal study of law and other disciplines which becomes important when reflecting on interdisciplinary legal research. In general, one speaks of interdisciplinary research when two or more academic disciplines come together to address a single research question.[70] However, what kind of *research* questions are addressed by scholars who undertake the doctrinal study of law? And is it that only *scholars* engage in the doctrinal study of law? Scholars from non-legal disciplines may be tempted to answer the first question in the negative: Scholars undertaking the doctrinal study of law do not address any research questions at all. They simply engage in the same work as judges and all other practising lawyers: "The doctrinal study of law is an application-oriented discipline."[71] Scholars undertaking the doctrinal study of law engage, together with judges and all other practising lawyers, in the ongoing work of interpreting and applying legal norms. Or, as *Rüthers*, *Fischer*, and *Birk* put it:[72]

> "Dogmatik entsteht aus dem Zusammenwirken von Rechtswissenschaft und Justiz. Dabei hat allerdings die Justiz wegen der Rechtskraft ihrer letztinstanzlichen Entscheidungen regelmäßig das 'letzte Wort'."

> "The doctrinal study of law is based on a cooperation between legal academia and the judiciary. The judiciary has, however, the 'last word' due to the force of its last instance decisions."

Whereas courts and practising lawyers immediately apply their interpretation to a single case, scholars engaged in the doctrinal study of law will critically analyse the interpretation of legal norms by courts and by practising lawyers, they will critically reflect on the application of such interpretation to individual cases, they will try to foresee the implication of such interpretations for future

---

[69] *Bumke* (n. 1), 2: "ein Wissensreservoir für die Praxis".

[70] *M. Martinek*, Die Autonomie oder die gescheiterte Interdisziplinarität der Rechtswissenschaft, juris – Die Monatszeitschrift 2018, 447–454, 447; Interdisziplinär, in: Duden. Deutsches Universalwörterbuch (7th edn., 2011), 925.

[71] *Stark* (n. 1), 166: "Rechtsdogmatik ist eine gebrauchsorientierte Disziplin."

[72] *Rüthers/Fischer/Birk* (n. 53), para. 314. In addition, see *Bumke* (n. 1), 15; *idem* (n. 55), 477; *Lepsius* (n. 1), 42; *Jestaedt* (n. 1), 117, 127; *Stark* (n. 1), 81 ff. Finally, see the discussions by *Jansen* (n. 33), 638 ff.; *Rottleuthner* (n. 33), 257 ff.

cases, and they will try to test these interpretations by applying them to hypothetical cases. However, there is no fundamental difference between the work of judges and all other practising lawyers, on the one hand, and the described scholars on the other hand. Rather, there seems to be only a gradual difference. Judges and other practising lawyers try to resolve the case in front of them, and to that end they interpret the legal norm which they wish to apply. Legal academics try to foresee the implications of a given possible interpretation for all future cases, and they try to analyse the implications of a given possible interpretation for the entire legal system.

The preceding summary of the characteristic elements of the doctrinal study of law raises numerous further questions. Is it, for example, possible to call the doctrinal study of law a *scientific* discipline as German legal scholars traditionally do ("Rechts*wissenschaft*")?[73] International readers may find some of the aforementioned elements questionable, for example, the claim that the doctrinal study of law has an innovative function and that academics participate in fulfilling this function. Does it not fall solely on the legislature and the judiciary to further develop the law? Finally, the preceding summary allows one to dive into comparative reflections on the doctrinal study of law:[74] Is the doctrinal study of law unique to Germany, as Germany legal scholars often claim? In fact, there seems to be little difference between Polish and German doctrinal legal scholarship, and the claim by German legal academics that the doctrinal study of law is unique to Germany may simply reflect their ignorance of Polish legal scholarship. Is it then perhaps unique to continental Europe? Or does Anglo-American legal scholarship know something equivalent to the doctrinal study of law? The answers to these last three questions very much depend on which of the aforementioned elements are regarded as constitutive for the doctrinal study of law.[75] Yet this introduction is not the place to further reflect on these and other questions.

IV. Going beyond the doctrinal study of law

The preceding reflections on the doctrinal study of law have simply served to pave the ground for developing an answer to the question of what continental European scholars (undertaking doctrinal study) of law mean when speaking

[73] See, e.g., *Jansen* (n. 33), 638 ff.; *Rüthers/Fischer/Birk* (n. 53), para. 280 ff.; *U. Neumann*, Wissenschaftstheorie der Rechtswissenschaft, in: Hassemer et al. (n. 57), 351–364; *T. Kuntz*, Auf der Suche nach einem Proprium der Rechtswissenschaft. Sinn und Unsinn des Bemühens um disziplinäre Identität, Archiv für die civilistische Praxis 219 (2019), 254–299. See *Stelmach/Brożek* (n. 17).

[74] See the references in n. 1, n. 2, and n. 7, above.

[75] *Stark* (n. 1), 156 ff.; *Kirchhof/Magen* (n. 1), 158.

of interdisciplinarity, and in the present section we wish to carve out the meaning of interdisciplinarity in legal scholarship by contrasting interdisciplinarity with the doctrinal study of law. In interdisciplinary research, two or more academic disciplines come together to address a single research question. But when is it feasible to say that two disciplines come together? The answer to this question depends on a further question: What are the constitutive elements of an academic discipline? Most scholars will agree that an academic discipline is constituted by the use of distinct methods. However, some scholars claim that an academic discipline is also defined by its distinct concepts, its distinct research objectives, its distinct problem awareness, and its distinct research goals.[76] Again, we wish to avoid the "sterile academic disputes about interdisciplinarity itself" described by *Stelmach*.[77] After having defined what legal academics mean when speaking of the doctrinal study of law, we rather want to begin our reflections with the hypothesis that legal scholars work interdisciplinarily whenever they go beyond the limits of the doctrinal study of law. *Kaufmann* explains that the "doctrinal study of law [...] always uses arguments that are internal to the [legal] system".[78] Scholars engaged in the doctrinal study of law could thus speak of interdisciplinarity whenever they transcend a specific legal system. In the abstract, this statement seems conclusive; however, further reflection is demanded in regard to three points: (1) research on the foundations of law, (2) the use of extra-legal concepts in law, and (3) law and politics.

A. Research on the foundations of law

First, there are *Grundlagenfächer*.[79] The word *Grundlagen* translates as foundations, and *Grundlagenfächer* are those (legal) (sub-)disciplines that relate to the foundations of law: comparative law, legal philosophy, legal theory, legal history, legal sociology, legal anthropology, and, arguably, law and economics. Are *Grundlagenfächer* examples of interdisciplinary research?

With reference to comparative law, the answer is in the negative. In order to study a foreign legal system, comparative lawyers need to apply (foreign) legal methods and (foreign) legal concepts; their research object is the law, and they have a legal research goal as well as legal problem awareness. Yet it may be necessary to transcend legal methods and to use non-legal concepts in order to

---

[76] *Van Klink/Taekema* (n. 8), 89.

[77] *Stelmach*, p. 49, below.

[78] *Kaufmann* (n. 57), 1.

[79] On the concept of legal Grundlagenfächer as distinguished from the doctrinal study of law, see, e.g., *O. Muthorst*, Grundlagen der Rechtswissenschaft. Methode – Begriff – System (2nd edn., 2019), § 2 para. 24; *J. Krüper*, Für wen dieses Buch geschrieben ist, wie und warum, in: idem (n. 9), 17–21, 19; *A. Funke*, Rechtswissenschaftliches Grundlagencurriculum – Funktionen und Formen, in: J. Krüper (ed.), Rechtswissenschaft lehren. Handbuch der juristischen Fachdidaktik (2023), 383–408, 384 ff.

contextualize foreign law and to properly understand it. Even then, the research object and the ultimate research goal are still defined by the discipline of law, and comparative scholars rarely engage in proper interdisciplinary research. They usually simply rely on the findings of other disciplines when they are faced with the task of contextualizing a foreign legal system in order to properly understand it. When comparative lawyers not only wish to study a foreign law but also wish to compare two or more legal systems, they need to apply the same methods that are shared by all comparative disciplines such as comparative literature and comparative sociology.[80] Even though comparative legal scholars are aware of the links between these different comparative disciplines, they usually do not engage in interdisciplinary research when comparing two or more legal systems. They simply apply comparative legal methods as they are taught in law schools. In all, comparative law in itself is not an example of interdisciplinary research. Nevertheless, comparative legal research questions may invite scholars of comparative law to engage in interdisciplinary research.

With reference to legal philosophy, *Kaufmann* notes that it "is a branch of philosophy, not of legal science".[81] Yet it would be wrong to conclude that legal philosophy is not an example of interdisciplinary scholarship. *Kaufmann* himself adds:[82]

> "In der Rechtsphilosophie fragt der Jurist, die Antwort gibt der Philosoph. Deshalb muss ein zünftiger Rechtsphilosoph auch in beiden Disziplinen zu Hause sein, in der Rechtswissenschaft und in der Philosophie […]."

> "Within the philosophy of law, questions are asked by the lawyer, and answers are given by the philosopher. Therefore, a legal philosopher must be at home in both disciplines, in law and in philosophy […]."

Accordingly, legal philosophy is an interdisciplinary endeavour par excellence. The example of legal philosophy already points to a general problem of inter-

---

[80] See *R. Michaels*, The Functional Method of Comparative Law, in: M. Reimann/R. Zimmermann (eds.), The Oxford Handbook of Comparative Law (2006), 339–382, and the contributions in *M. Adams/M. Van Hoecke* (eds.), Comparative Methods in Law, Humanities and Social Sciences (2021). *M. Adams/M. Van Hoecke*, Conclusion: challenges of comparison, in: ibid., 246–263, 263, however, want to speak of a shared "research design rather than a research method". Finally, see *M. Cottier*, Interdisziplinäre Rechtsvergleichung. Elemente einer rechtssoziologisch fundierten Rechtsvergleichung am Beispiel des Familien- und Erbrechts, in: C. Boulanger et al. (eds.), Interdisziplinäre Rechtsforschung. Eine Einführung in die geistes- und sozialwissenschaftliche Befassung mit dem Recht und seiner Praxis (2019), 109–123. Of course, there is no clear-cut distinction between studying a foreign legal system and comparing it with other legal systems. The endeavour to describe a foreign legal system in own's one language requires comparative methods.

[81] *Kaufmann* (n. 57), 1: "Die Rechtsphilosophie ist ein Zweig der Philosophie, nicht ein Zweig der Rechtswissenschaft."

[82] *Kaufmann* (n. 57), 1.

disciplinary research: In matters of philosophy, as *Karl Jaspers* has noted, everyone considers himself an expert and competent to make judgments.[83] Thus, citing *Gustav Radbruch*, *Kaufmann* accurately points out that

> "[g]enauso ist es bei den Juristen. Fast jeder hält sich in den Dingen der Rechtsphilosophie für sachkompetent, mag er sich auch niemals ernstlich mit der Philosophie beschäftigt haben. Am ausgeprägtesten zeigte sich dieser juristische Scientismus um die Jahrhundertwende bei der sog. Allgemeinen Rechtslehre, dieser 'Euthanasie der Rechtsphilosophie',[84] wo der juristische 'Spezialist' das Geschäft des Philosophierens in die Hand nehmen, die Rechtsphilosophie also in eine 'Juristenphilosophie' ummünzen wollte. Das Ergebnis einer solchen juristischen Inzucht ist bestenfalls eine Vulgär-Philsophie [...]; in der Regel ist es platter Dilettantismus."

> "[t]he same is true of lawyers. Almost everyone considers himself competent in legal philosophy, even if he has never seriously engaged in philosophy. This legal scientism was most clearly visible at the turn of the twentieth century in the so-called General Theory of Law, that peculiar 'euthanasia of legal philosophy' where the specialist lawyer wanted to take philosophy into his own hands and remodel it into a 'philosophy of lawyers.' The result of this type of 'legal inbreeding' is, at best, a vulgarized philosophy [...]; usually, it is a banal dilettantism."[85]

Kaufmann warns against philosophical dilettantism performed by lawyers and legal dilettantism performed by philosophers, stressing that knowledge of both disciplines is necessary for the fruitful marriage of philosophy and law. In our volume, *Stelmach*, *Marta Soniewicka*, *Wojciech Załuski*, and *Łukasz Kurek* provide philosophical analyses of legal or meta-legal problems,[86] and each has a background in both disciplines.

Legal history, too, is an interdisciplinary endeavour: Legal historians have to apply legal methods and historical methods. When they compare different legal systems of the past or when they compare a legal system of the past with today's law, they need, furthermore, to apply comparative methods. Moreover, if legal historians wish to contextualize their findings, they need to apply further methods. Finally, if they engage in research in, for example, economic or social legal history, they cannot restrict their research object, their concepts, their problem awareness, their research goal, or their objectives to the legal world; instead they must first fully understand the economic or social dimension of their research question. To do so, legal historians often cooperate with historians, social historians, or economic historians, each of them working with his or her distinct method, concepts, problem awareness, research goals, and objectives.

---

[83] *K. Jaspers*, Einführung in die Philosophie (25th edn., 2005), 21 ff.

[84] Kaufmann cites *G. Radbruch*, Rechtsphilosophie (9th edn., 1983), 114. We were not able to verify the quote in the edition to which we had access.

[85] *Kaufmann* (n. 57), 6.

[86] *Stelmach*, pp. 49 ff., below; *Soniewicka/Wesołowska*, pp. 319 ff., below; *Załuski*, pp. 397 ff., below; *Kurek*, pp. 425 ff., below.

Thus, *Grundlagenfächer* such as legal philosophy and legal history are examples of interdisciplinary research. Nevertheless, we do not immediately think of *Grundlagenfächer* as possible examples of interdisciplinary research, and the reasons may be simple:[87] *Grundlagenfächer* are an integral part of the curriculum of every law school, they could be described as legal sub-disciplines, and it is usually lawyers who engage in research in – and teach – *Grundlagenfächer*. Indeed, German legal academics stress that legal scholarship cannot be reduced to the doctrinal study of law, and some say that one should rather speak of legal scholarships in the plural (*Rechtswissenschaften*) instead of legal scholarship in the singular (*Rechtswissenschaft*) in order to signal that there is more to legal scholarship than the doctrinal study of law.[88] *Matthias Jestaedt* speaks of "legal scholarship(s) as disciplinary cluster of normative disciplines".[89]

The fact that *Grundlagenfächer* may count as examples of interdisciplinary research is, finally, confirmed with reference to law and economics. Most lawyers will probably first think of law and economics when being asked for an example of interdisciplinary research. This is also reflected in the present volume, which features six contributions in the field of law and economics.[90] However, law and economics is today so well established that it is looked upon as a *Grundlagenfach*. This is at least the case in Germany,[91] but one may of course disagree with this classification.

B. Extra-legal concepts and value systems

Secondly, legal norms regularly use concepts that may be understood to refer to something outside the legal system: good morals, fairness, reasonableness, good faith and fair dealing, or human dignity. Of course, it is possible to define these concepts as legal concepts. Then they are part of the legal system, and when analysing them it is consequently possible to use "arguments that are

---

[87] Compare *Grimm* (n. 16), 23.

[88] See *Eifert* (n. 59), 87; *M. Jestaedt*, Rechtswissenschaft als normative Disziplin. Banalität, Komplexität und Brisanz der Klassifikationsfrage, in: *Kirste* (n. 2), 103–114, 110; *Gutmann* (n. 12), 108 f.

[89] *Jestaedt* (n. 88), 110: "Rechtswissenschaft(en) als disziplinäres Cluster normativer Disziplinen". This raises the question as to the relationship between the doctrinal study of law and research on the foundations of law. This relationship should not be described as antagonistic. There is indeed abundant literature stressing the importance of overcoming any form of antagonism with respect to legal history and the doctrinal study of law, see e.g. *E. Picker*, Rechtsdogmatik und Rechtsgeschichte, Archiv für die civilistische Praxis 201 (2001), 763–859. For an interesting holistic approach, see *M. Auer*, Zum Erkenntnisziel der Rechtstheorie. Philosophische Grundlagen multidisziplinärer Rechtswissenschaften (2018).

[90] *Kasiske*, pp. 209 ff., below; *Derek*, pp. 229 ff., below; *Wurmnest*, pp. 241, below; *Długosz*, pp. 271 ff., below; *Blicharz*, pp. 283 ff., below; *Willems*, pp. 309 ff., below.

[91] *Rühl* (n. 9), 248 ff.

internal to the system".[92] For example, § 138(1) of the German Civil Code (*Bürgerliches Gesetzbuch* – BGB) reads:

"Ein Rechtsgeschäft, das gegen die guten Sitten verstößt, ist nichtig."

"A legal transaction which is contrary to good morals is void."

Good morals in the sense of § 138(1) BGB may be understood as a legal concept, and they are, indeed, understood to reflect fundamental constitutional values, foremost the basic rights as codified in the German constitution.[93] Even though, private law scholars transcend the German Civil Code when interpreting § 138(1) BGB in such a vein, they still use "arguments that are internal to the [entire legal] system".[94] Yet it is also feasible to interpret § 138(1) BGB as referring to an extra-legal value system.[95] Such an understanding immediately raises the question of how to ascertain such extra-legal values. Legal methods will not be of any help. An interdisciplinary approach is necessary.

Thilo Rensmann and *Monika Florczak-Wątor* discuss in their contributions another example of the phenomenon that legal norms use concepts that may be understood as referring to something outside the legal system: human dignity and inalienable human rights.[96] Both concepts are mentioned in Art. 1 GG:

"(1) Die Würde des Menschen ist unantastbar. Sie zu achten und zu schützen ist Verpflichtung aller staatlichen Gewalt.
(2) Das Deutsche Volk bekennt sich darum zu unverletzlichen und unveräußerlichen Menschenrechten als Grundlage jeder menschlichen Gemeinschaft, des Friedens und der Gerechtigkeit in der Welt.
(3) Die nachfolgenden Grundrechte binden Gesetzgebung, vollziehende Gewalt und Rechtsprechung als unmittelbar geltendes Recht."

"(1) Human dignity shall be inviolable. To respect and protect it shall be the duty of all state authority.
(2) The German people therefore acknowledge inviolable and inalienable human rights as the basis of every community, of peace and of justice in the world.
(3) The following basic rights shall bind the legislature, the executive and the judiciary as directly applicable law."[97]

Are human dignity and inalienable human rights legal or extra-legal (meta-positive) concepts? And what does it mean for the process of analysing both concepts if they are such extra-legal concepts? Is research into the meaning of human dignity and inalienable human rights as extra-legal concepts an example of interdisciplinary scholarship in law? Readers may be tempted to answer the

---

[92] *Kaufmann* (n. 57), 1.
[93] *J. Neuner*, Allgemeiner Teil des Bürgerlichen Rechts (13th edn., 2023), § 46 para. 13.
[94] *Kaufmann* (n. 57), 1.
[95] *Neuner* (n. 93), § 46 para. 12.
[96] See *Rensmann*, pp. 113 ff., below, and *Florczak-Wątor*, pp. 151 ff., below.
[97] https://www.gesetze-im-internet.de/englisch_gg/ (last accessed 19 July 2023).

last question in the negative. If they are, for example, philosophical concepts, then it would be sufficient, one could argue, to consult philosophers and ask them for the meaning of these concepts. What would be needed is a division of labour between two disciplines rather than interdisciplinarity. However, even as extra-legal concepts human dignity and inalienable human rights serve specific normative functions that cannot be disregarded when analysing them. And how constitutional law uses these concepts defines these normative functions. That is the essence of the contributions of *Rensmann* and *Florczak-Wątor*, and that is the reason why their contributions rightly belong in this volume.

However, readers may still disagree, and they may disagree for good reason: It seems that in the example discussed by *Rensmann* and *Florczak-Wątor* interdisciplinarity is an unfulfilled promise. According to both authors, human dignity and inalienable human rights may be understood to stand "outside or above positive law"[98] or as something "primary to the law",[99] as notions that "transcend positive law"[100] or as "meta-positive values".[101] And both authors refer to the philosophical, theological, political, cultural, and social foundations of human dignity and inalienable human rights.[102] Yet constitutional law scholars who follow such an understanding seem to rarely engage in any interdisciplinary collaboration with scholars from the respective disciplines so as to give content to these notions.[103] Quite to the contrary, it seems that German constitutional lawyers have simply adapted legal methods to cope with human dignity as a meta-positive concept, and the question may be asked whether German constitutional law scholars have thereby tried to find an argumentative construct allowing them to refrain from conducting interdisciplinary research. *Rensmann* himself points to the "pluralistic conception of human dignity" and cites *Theodor Heuss* in stating that it "could be understood theologically by some, philosophically by others and ethically by yet others."[104] And *Florczak-Wątor* notes that human dignity "is a semantically open concept that evolves over time and space. Any legal definition of dignity would be imperfect, as it would further limit the very concept and rapidly become outdated."[105] Indeed, it seems that collaboration with a single extra-legal discipline for the purpose of giving content to the notion of human dignity would be at odds with its pluralistic conception.

---

[98] *Florczak-Wątor*, p. 155, below.

[99] *Florczak-Wątor*, p. 151, below.

[100] *Rensmann*, p. 114, below.

[101] *Rensmann*, p. 116, below.

[102] See, e.g., *Rensmann*, p. 116, below, and *Florczak-Wątor*, p. 154, below.

[103] For an example of interdisciplinary (or rather multidisciplinary) discussions, see the contributions in *D. Grimm/A. Kemmerer/C. Möllers* (eds.), Human Dignity in Context. Explorations of a Contested Concept (2018).

[104] *Rensmann*, p. 123, below.

[105] *Florczak-Wątor*, p. 154, below.

C. Law and politics

Finally, the contributions authored by *Aqilah Sandhu* and *Monika Kawczyńska* raise the question whether it is possible to speak of interdisciplinarity whenever legal actors transcend the sphere of law.[106] Both authors discuss the current and highly problematic relationship between the European Court of Justice (ECJ), the European Court of Human Rights (ECtHR), and national constitutional courts. The two authors claim that these courts have left the sphere of law and entered the sphere of politics. However, this alone does not allow invocation of the notion of interdisciplinarity. Even if these courts leave the sphere of legal methods, they do not seem to apply methods of political science. Instead, they simply substitute political debates. Yet it follows from this observation that legal academics cannot restrict themselves to legal methodology when analysing the judgments of these courts. They have to apply methods of extra-legal disciplines, too. In all, the contributions of *Sandhu* and *Kawczyńska* are invitations to engage in interdisciplinary research.

V. Integrating extra-legal findings into law

It is possible to reflect on the specificities of interdisciplinary research in law also from a different angle. In order to develop this perspective, let us start by pondering two questions: When do lawyers work interdisciplinarily? And when is it necessary for them to work interdisciplinarily? With respect to continental European legal scholarship, the tentative answer to the former question is: far too rarely! For a long period of time, continental European legal scholars have predominantly adopted a doctrinal approach to the study of law.[107] However, the obvious answer to the latter question is: always! After all, law regulates all aspects of life. As *Stephan Kirste* writes:[108]

> "Disziplinübergreifende Diskurse verbessern die Fähigkeit zur Problemlösung. Rechtswissenschaften als praktische Wissenschaften sollen helfen, soziale Konflikte zu lösen und Prinzipien bereithalten, um diese zukünftig gar nicht erst aufkommen zu lassen. Partizipieren die Rechtswissenschaften nicht in interdisziplinären Diskursen mit solchen Wissenschaften, die den Realbereich des Rechts erforschen, verliert die Jurisprudenz die Fähigkeit, ihren genuinen Zielen zu genügen."

---

[106] *Sandhu*, pp. 169 ff., below, and *Kawczyńska*, pp. 187 ff., below.

[107] See p. 3, above.

[108] *Kirste* (n. 2), 63. In addition, see *Gutmann* (n. 12), 101; *S. Grundmann/H.-W. Micklitz/M. Renner*, Privatrechtstheorie – eine Einführung, in: idem, Privatrechtstheorie, vol. 1 (2015), 1–38, 1; *K. Langenbucher*, Interdisziplinäre Forschung im Unternehmensrecht – auf dem Weg zu einer cognitive corporate governance?, Zeitschrift für Unternehmens- und Gesellschaftsrecht 2019, 717–759, 718.

"Discourse across disciplines improves the ability to solve problems. Legal scholarship as a practical discipline aims at solving social conflicts, and it should have available strategies to prevent such conflicts from arising in the future. If legal scholarship does not engage in interdisciplinary discourse with those disciplines that study the factual context of law, legal scholarship will lose the ability to serve this very purpose."

Do legal scholars consequently need to always engage in interdisciplinary work for the simple reason that the law regulates extra-legal phenomena such that it is simply impossible for legal scholars to, as *Kaufmann* claims, exclusively use "arguments that are internal to the [legal] system".[109] In his contribution to the present volume, *Wurmnest* observes that "[m]ost commentators agree that legal rules applying to the economy should make economic sense".[110] Do legal scholars thus have to engage in interdisciplinary economic research whenever they interpret legal rules applying to the economy? *Peter Kasiske* would probably agree with the observation that his paper[111] still follows the observations made by *Franz von Liszt*'s (1851–1919) in 1892:[112]

"Wer aber das Verbrechen bekämpfen will, muß das Verbrechen kennen, er muß es studieren nicht als begriffliche Abstraktion, sondern als Erscheinung, als Ereignis des gesellschaftlichen sowohl, wie des individuellen Lebens."

"He who wants to fight crime has to understand crime; he must study it, not as conceptual abstraction, but as a phenomenon, as incident of societal as well as individual life."

In essence, *Kasiske* argues that behavioural economics is an analytical tool to understand crime as "incident [...] of individual life". If we further understand criminal law as a measure to fight crime, we need to integrate the findings of behavioural economics in criminal law. Should criminal law scholars consequently engage in interdisciplinary research in behavioural economics in order to ensure that they fully understand crime? *Hellwege*, in his contribution,[113] cites *Eric A. Posner*:[114] "The role of the emotions is much neglected in legal theory. This should be puzzling, because emotions play an important role in many areas of the law." Does it follow that legal scholars regularly need to engage in interdisciplinary research on emotions? The representatives of law and emotion indeed argue, as *Soniewicka* and *Julia Wesołowska* point out in

[109] *Kaufmann* (n. 57), 1.

[110] *Wurmnest*, p. 241, below.

[111] *Kasiske*, pp. 209 ff., below.

[112] *F. von Liszt*, Die Zukunft des Strafrechts. Vortrag, gehalten in der Budapester juristischen Gesellschaft, den 4. April 1892, in: idem, Strafrechtliche Aufsätze und Vorträge, vol. 2 (1905), 1–24, 3.

[113] *Hellwege*, p. 362, below.

[114] *E.A. Posner*, Law and the Emotions, Georgetown Law Journal 89 (2001), 1977–2012, 1977.

their contribution,[115] that interdisciplinary research on emotions would significantly increase our understanding of law.

Thus, the aforementioned questions link to the reasons for today's trend towards more interdisciplinarity in legal scholarship, as have been discussed above:[116] In the past, legal scholars have worked on the assumption that the law reflected state-of-the-art extra-legal insights. There was no need for them to engage in interdisciplinary research. However, the accelerated advance in extra-legal disciplines poses the question whether the law is still based on accurate extra-legal assumptions. However, we do not wish to once again articulate reflections on the reasons for the trend towards more interdisciplinarity in legal scholarship. Rather, in the present section of our introduction we would like to pose a different question: Is it feasible to speak of interdisciplinarity whenever lawyers integrate such extra-legal findings in law?

In the preceding section of this introductory chapter, we have reflected on when it is possible to say that legal scholars transcend the limits of the doctrinal study of law and whether it is possible to speak of interdisciplinarity whenever they do transcend such limits. In the present section we focus on the opposite situation, where lawyers integrate extra-legal findings into the law. This difference may be expressed as follows: In the case of *Grundlagenfächer*, one may speak of interdisciplinary approaches *to* law. When lawyers integrate extra-legal findings into the law, it is perhaps more apt to speak of interdisciplinary approaches *in* law. And when it comes to interdisciplinary approaches *in* law, we have a problem with the general definition of interdisciplinarity as being two or more academic disciplines coming together and cooperating to address a single research question. In the text above we have already discussed two questions:[117] What kind of research questions are addressed by scholars undertaking the doctrinal study of law? And is it only scholars who engage in the doctrinal study of law? We have already claimed that scholars from non-legal disciplines will be tempted to answer the first question in the negative: Scholars who undertake the doctrinal study of law do not address any research questions at all. They simply engage in the same practical work as judges and all other practising lawyers. They engage, together with judges and all other practising lawyers, in the ongoing work of interpreting and applying legal norms. However, is it then at all possible to speak of interdisciplinary research when we want to describe interdisciplinary approaches *in* law? In order to develop an answer to these questions, it is advisable to differentiate between three situations in which legal scholars may want to integrate extra-legal findings into law: (1) When lawyers engage in legislative debates, (2) when lawyers

---

[115] *Soniewicka/Wesołowska*, pp. 319 ff., above.

[116] See p. 11, above.

[117] See, p. 23, above.

develop arguments *de lege ferenda*, and (3) when lawyers interpret and analyse positive law.

A. Lawyers engaging in legislative debates

Lawyers who engage in legislative debates and in research that is supposed to pave the ground towards legislation cannot limit themselves to use arguments that are internal to the legal system. Legislatures always address extra-legal problems, and lawyers engaging in legislative debates should have an understanding of these problems. Legal rules that, for example, aim at regulating the economy should make economic sense. This requires interdisciplinary expertise on the side of lawyers engaging in such debates, and it requires interdisciplinary research or even interdisciplinary cooperation. Indeed, legislation should always be preceded by interdisciplinary research, and the observation that modern legislation is often of poor quality may be explainable by reference to the fact that legislatures work too hastily, that they do not wait for the findings of extra-legal research addressing the specific problem which the legislation in the making aims to solve or that they ignore such findings for political reasons. In such cases the legitimization of law is in danger. However, lawyers engaging in legislative debates and in research that paves the ground for legislation cannot limit themselves to understanding the extra-legal problem which the legislature wishes to address. In addition, they have to ensure that the norm they are proposing will not cause inconsistencies in the legal system and that it does not conflict with the legal system's "theorems, fundamental rules, and principles regardless of whether they are made explicit in the law itself or whether legal academia and legal practice" have found them to be inherent in the law.[118] Furthermore, they have to ensure that the norm they are proposing will be interpreted and applied in a way which the legislature envisages. This is the task of scholars engaged in the doctrinal study of law.[119] The interdisciplinary challenges which lawyers face in legislative debates and the institutional framework for addressing these challenges are fully discussed by *Matthias Rossi*.[120]

B. Lawyers developing arguments de lege ferenda

What has been said about lawyers who engage in legislative debates and who conduct research that paves the ground for legislation is also true for those scholars developing arguments *de lege ferenda*, that is to say, for those scholars who criticise positive law as deficient and who, in a next step, propose

[118] *Rüthers/Fischer/Birk*, (n. 53), para. 311.

[119] *O. Behrends*, Das Bündnis zwischen Gesetz und Dogmatik und die Frage der dogmatischen Rangstufen, in: idem/W. Henkel (eds.), Gesetzgebung und Dogmatik (1989), 9–36, 9.

[120] *Rossi*, pp. 55 ff., below.

legislative reform. They may apply methods of doctrinal study of law when, for example, they argue that a given legal norm creates inconsistencies with other legal norms. They then exclusively use "arguments that are internal to the [legal] system".[121] However, they may go beyond the doctrinal study of law when, for example, they argue that a legal norm did not resolve the extra-legal problem which it was supposed to address, they argue that the extra-legal problem has changed, they argue that new extra-legal insights change our understanding of the extra-legal problem which the legislature had addressed, or when they argue that the legal norm had unwanted extra-legal side effects. They are only able to develop such arguments properly if they engage in interdisciplinary research. Thus, when lawyers develop arguments *de lege ferenda* – when they criticise positive law and propose legislative reform – they actually have to integrate interdisciplinary research on two distinct levels of analysis: first, on the level of criticising the *lex lata* and, secondly, on the level of developing proposals for legislative reform.

C. Lawyers interpreting and analysing positive law

Finally, lawyers interpreting and applying the law may primarily follow a doctrinal approach to the study of law. However, we have already seen situations in which even lawyers interpreting and applying the law have to go beyond using "arguments that are internal to the [legal] system":[122] Certain legal provisions may refer to extra-legal value systems or other extra-legal phenomena, the understanding of which require interdisciplinary expertise. Furthermore, some argue that open-textured norms invite the incorporation of interdisciplinary insights into the law.[123] At times, legislatures may even intentionally use open-textured concepts when drafting a legal provision in order to leave interpretative room for new extra-legal scientific insights or for societal change. Moreover, if legal academia accepts a specific private law theory as being reflected and inherent in a specific private law codification, legal scholars may in turn apply this private law theory to analyse and interpret that codification, thereby again incorporating interdisciplinary insights into the law.[124] Finally, each legal norm has a rationale, a specific purpose which it serves, and this rationale is of utmost importance for the interpretation of that legal norm.

---

[121] *Kaufmann* (n. 57), 1.

[122] *Kaufmann* (n. 57), 1. On the following points, see *Stark* (n. 1), 233 ff.; *Croon-Gestefeld* (n. 8), 61; *H. Hamann*, Marken- und Wettbewerbsrecht als Vorbilder für die Vertragsauslegung? Demoskopische Befragungsmethoden und ihre ungewisse Zukunft, in: Christandl et al. (n. 4), 135–153, 147 ff. In addition, see *C. Gusy*, "Wirklichkeit" in der Rechtsdogmatik, JuristenZeitung 1991, 213–222.

[123] With reference to empathy, see *A. Beckers*, Empathie im Wettbewerbsrecht: Gesellschaftliche Rationalitätskonflikte statt Emotionen des Verbrauchers, in: *M.C. Gruber/S. Häußler*, Normen der Empathie (2012), 93–114, 95.

[124] See, e.g., *H. Unberath*, Die Vertragsverletzung (2007), passim.

More often than not it is an extra-legal rationale allowing the incorporation of extra-legal insights into the legal discourse. A prime example is the systematization of consumers' withdrawal rights in light of an economic analysis of law.[125] In each of these example, positive law contains what *Stark* calls "interdisciplinary docking points".[126] The direct link between interdisciplinarity and the doctrinal study of law is at the heart of *Stark*'s monograph. He speaks of an "Interdisciplinarity of Legal Dogmatics",[127] thereby suggesting that interdisciplinary approaches may be inherent to the doctrinal study of law and contrasting his understanding of what he believes to be the orthodox view that interdisciplinarity and the doctrinal study of law are mutually exclusive or at least opposing concepts.

VI. Different types and grades of interdisciplinarity in law

As mentioned before, literature differentiates between numerous concepts describing situations in which two or more disciplines come together, and it further distinguishes different forms of interdisciplinarity. Instead of engaging in what *Stelmach* calls "sterile academic disputes about interdisciplinarity itself",[128] we wish to simply identify and describe different types and grades of interdisciplinarity in legal research by drawing on the contributions to the present volume.

A. Disciplinary boundaries

Against the background that the doctrinal study of law is characterized by a number of distinct elements,[129] it does not come as a surprise that the disciplinary boundaries between it and non-legal disciplines have thus far not broken down. On the contrary, most authors to the present volume stress or at least work from the assumption that the doctrinal study of law is an academic discipline in its own right.[130] Such a starting point or assumption directly affects how interdisciplinary research is perceived. However, it has already become clear that law cannot be reduced to the doctrinal study of law. There is also research on the foundations of law (*Grundlagenfächer*). The disciplinary boundaries between the *Grundlagenfächer* and their neighbouring disciplines

---

[125] *E. Eidenmüller*, Die Rechtfertigung von Widerrufsrechten, Archiv für die civilistische Praxis 210 (2010), 67–104.

[126] *Stark* (n. 1), 233: "interdisziplinäre Andockstellen".

[127] *A. Stark*, Interdisziplinarität der Rechtsdogmatik (2020).

[128] *Stelmach*, p. 49, below. Such an approach follows from the bottom-up approach adhered to in the present volume, see pp. 13 f., above.

[129] See pp. 17 ff., above.

[130] In addition, see *Kirste* (n. 16), 9; *Stark* (n. 1), 13; *Bumke* (n. 55), 469 f.

have at times disappeared.[131] Furthermore, it seems that there are numerous examples of an ongoing and stable cooperation between law and non-legal disciplines. Here again, the *Grundlagenfächer* and their neighbouring disciplines may be cited as examples,[132] and the example of law and economics suggests that a permanent and stable cooperation between law and a non-legal discipline will lead, at least in German legal scholarship, to the formation of a new legal *Grundlagenfach*.[133]

It is possible to link these observations with theoretical debates. *Brożek* distinguishes four options for defining the relationship between extra-legal findings and law: separation, supervenience, reduction, and coherence.[134] Separation is firmly based on *Hans Kelsen*'s "pure theory of law", which is free from any external elements.[135] According to the second option, legal facts supervene natural facts as some representatives of the naturalization of law claim,[136] in particular proponents of the evolutionary approach to law.[137] The third option aims at the translation of legal norms into descriptive statements, a typical approach followed by representatives of legal realism.[138] The fourth option aims at coherence between legal and scientific findings. According to *Brożek*, naturalized law must be interdisciplinary: it has to be consistent with scientific knowledge.[139] Yet the naturalization of law that is rooted in the philosophy of the Enlightenment has been frequently objected to as corrupting the humanities and the social sciences with its expansion of natural sciences into fields where they do not belong. Furthermore, it is claimed that the naturalization of law results in unjustified reductionism, confusion, and an oversimplification of legal problems.[140] Finally, *Załuski* mentions the deceptive similarity of concepts which may result in equivocation, the problem of incorrect reductionism, or the pars pro toto error. It is worth mentioning that there are, of course, also non-naturalistic interdisciplinary approaches to law, such as law and litera-

---

131 See pp. 25 ff., above.

132 See pp. 25 ff., above.

133 See p. 28, above.

134 *B. Brożek*, O naturalizacji prawa, in: J. Stelmach et. al. (eds.), Naturalizm prawniczy. Interpretacje (2015), 26; see also *Jakubiec* (n. 28), 80 f.

135 *H. Kelsen*, Die Reine Rechtslehre (1934).

136 See *B. Brożek/A. Rotolo/J. Stelmach* (eds.), Supervenience and Normativity (2017).

137 *W. Załuski*, Evolutionary Theory and Legal Philosophy (2009); *idem*, Law and Evil. The Evolutionary Perspective (2018).

138 *Stelmach/Brożek* (n. 13).

139 On the resulting pitfalls, see *J. Stelmach*, Kirchmanns Fluch, in: F. Saliger et. al. (eds.), Rechtsstaatliches Strafrecht. Festschrift für Ulfrid Neumann zum 70. Geburtstag (2017), 445–452; *Załuski* (n. 39), 175–192.

140 See, e.g., *I. Domurath*, The politics of interdisciplinarity in law, in: M. Bartl/J.C. Lawrence (eds.), The Politics of European Legal Research (2022), 140–158. Furthermore, see *Soniewicka/Wesołowska* pp. 319 ff.

ture.[141] This last observation reminds us that the boundaries between law and extra-legal findings cannot be described only in terms of separation, supervenience, reduction, and coherence and that coherence is not only a result of the naturalization of law. If we focus on disciplinary boundaries, it is obvious that it is postmodern approaches to law that undermine not only the positivistic idea of law but also the division between different extra-legal disciplines and legal scholarship. Postmodern approaches to law advocate integration of law with other disciplines, plurality of methods, deconstruction of concepts, and a fragmentation of legal studies.[142]

B. Inbound and outbound interdisciplinarity

Where interdisciplinary research is based on the assumption that law is still a discipline in its own rights, lawyers engage more often than not in what one could call "inbound interdisciplinarity". Legal scholars apply extra-legal insights or concepts in order to advance the law or their understanding of the law. Most contributions to the present volume are examples of this type of interdisciplinarity. However, there is also research which one could call "outbound interdisciplinarity". Legal scholars introduce legal insights or concepts into extra-legal disciplines. There are four contributions to the present volume that engage in such type of interdisciplinary research, one of which is a comment from the perspective of the respective extra-legal discipline.[143]

C. Different grades of inbound interdisciplinarity

Restricting oneself to inbound interdisciplinarity, it is possible to distinguish different grades of interdisciplinary research. (1) Above, interdisciplinary research has been defined as two or more academic disciplines cooperating to address a single research question.[144] The definition sounds as if the involved disciplines identify their research object and define their research question together on equal terms and then explore that research object in a wholistic

---

[141] *J.B. Baron*, Law, Literature, and the Problems of Interdisciplinarity, Yale Law Journal 108 (1999), 1059–1085. In addition, see *J.M. Balkin/S.V. Levinson*, Law and the Humanities: An Uneasy Relationship, Yale Journal of Law and the Humanities 18 (2006), 155–187.

[142] *G. Minda*, Postmodern Legal Movements. Law and Jurisprudence at Century's End (1995); *L. Morawski*, Co może dać nauce prawa postmodernizm? (2001); *J. Stelmach*, Ponowoczesna filozofia prawa, in: idem (ed.), Studia z filozofii prawa (2003), 15–21; *A. Sulikowski*, O ponowoczesnej teorii prawa, in: idem (ed.), Z zagadnień teorii i filozofii prawa. W poszukiwaniu podstaw prawa (2006), 241–257; *M. Zirk-Sadowski*, Postmodernistyczna jurysprudencja?, in: M. Błachut (ed.), Z zagadnień teorii i filozofii prawa. Ponowoczesność (2007), 24–41; *T. Biernat/M. Zirk-Sadowski*, Politics of law and legal policy between modern and postmodern jurisprudence (2008).

[143] *Longchamps de Bérier*, pp. 75 ff., below; *Marschler*, pp. 95 ff., below; *Blicharz*, pp. 283 ff., below; *Willems*, pp. 309 ff., below.

[144] See pp. 24 f, above.

fashion with each discipline adding its own specific disciplinary perspective, using its own research concepts and methods. There are examples of interdisciplinary research of this kind, especially in *Grundlagenfächer*.[145] Such research may be called cooperative interdisciplinarity. We have labelled it above as integrative because this form of research integrates the methods of different disciplines.[146] However, there are also other forms of interdisciplinary research. (2) Most contributions to the present volume are examples of interdisciplinary research that one could label as the import model. Above, we have also used the terms "integrative interdisciplinarity" and "interdisciplinary approaches *in* law":[147] Scholars engaged in the doctrinal study of law integrate extra-legal findings into the law; the research objective and the research goal are defined by doctrinal scholars of law alone, and they then turn to extra-legal disciplines for support. The support given by the extra-legal disciplines may differ: Doctrinal scholars of law may simply import findings of extra-legal disciplines or use respective concepts. (3) By contrast, *Grundlagenfächer* are examples of "interdisciplinary approaches *to* law".[148] Legal scholars go beyond the doctrinal study of law and take an outward perspective on the law.[149] However, there is no exact dividing line between interdisciplinary research *in* law and interdisciplinary approaches *to* law, as the contributions to the present volume prove: In a first step, extra-legal disciplines may be used to test the law (interdisciplinary approaches *to* law), and in a second step the question may be raised whether it is possible to integrate extra-legal insights into the law (interdisciplinary approaches *in* law). (4) Finally, it is possible to identify research which may be labelled as "approaches *to* law", but where it is actually doubtful whether it is correct to speak of interdisciplinarity. Some of the contributions to the present volume refer to research on the importance of anchoring effects in judicial decision making.[150] The respective research has legal actors and their decision making as the research object. However, the methods, concepts, objectives, and goals of the respective research seem to be exclusively those of extra-legal disciplines. Consequently, it is questionable to speak of interdisciplinary research.

---

[145] In addition to Grundlagenfächer as examples of such cooperating interdisciplinarity, see, e.g., *U.M. Gassner/F. Steger*, Geschlechtergerechte Medizin – juristische und ethische Aspekte, in: U.M. Gassner et al. (eds.), Geschlecht und Gesundheit (2018), 209–251.

[146] See, p. 15, above.

[147] See, p. 33, above.

[148] See, p. 33, above.

[149] See, pp. 24 ff., above.

[150] *Kasiske*, p. 219, below; *Derek*, p. 232, below; *Soniewicka/Wesołowska*, p. 321, below.

D. Different grades of integrative interdisciplinarity

In the last paragraph the term integrative interdisciplinarity has been used to describe what scholars undertaking the doctrinal study of law regularly do when engaging in interdisciplinary work: They integrate extra-legal findings into the law. The research objective and research goal are defined by doctrinal scholars of law alone, and they then turn to extra-legal disciplines for support. The definition of interdisciplinary research as two or more academic disciplines coming together to address a single research question again sounds as if representatives of different disciplines work together or as if a representative of one discipline adopts the concepts and methodologies of other disciplines. However, with integrative interdisciplinarity, there are foremost two different grades of interdisciplinarity: (1) doctrinal scholars of law integrating research findings of other disciplines in their own research; (2) different levels of division of labour. Legal scholars generally accept that integrating the findings of other disciplines into legal discourse is a form of interdisciplinarity. As *Stark* observes:[151]

"Es ist [...] nicht überraschend, dass nicht alles, was 'interdisziplinär' heißt, interdisziplinär ist. Als interdisziplinär ausgewiesene Forschung ist oftmals nicht mehr als 'halbherzige Multidisziplinarität' – [...] nebeneinander stehende Disziplinarität. Interdisziplinarität grenzt sich von dem allein auf das bloße Zusammentreffen beschränkten Format der Multidisziplinarität dadurch ab, dass Begriffe, Theorien, Wissensbestände, Erklärungsansätze, Modelle, Konzepte oder Ideen einer anderen Disziplin in die eigendisziplinäre Arbeit einbezogen werden. Anders als bei Multidisziplinarität findet hier eine Einbeziehung bzw. Integration von Erkenntnissen einer Nachbardisziplin statt."

"It is [...] not surprising that not everything that is called 'interdisciplinary' may actually count as interdisciplinary. Research labelled as interdisciplinary is often nothing more than 'half-hearted multi-disciplinarity' – different disciplines standing side by side [...]. Interdisciplinarity is distinguished from multi-disciplinarity, which is a simple meeting of different disciplines by the fact that concepts, theories, findings, explanations, models, concepts, or ideas of another discipline are included in own's one disciplinary work. Unlike multi-disciplinarity, interdisciplinarity involves the inclusion or integration of findings from a neighbouring discipline."

Stark speaks of an integrational model of interdisciplinarity based on the independence of each discipline. According to this model, the doctrinal study of law is an academic discipline in its own right and interdisciplinarity simply means integrating the findings of an extra-legal discipline in law ("interdisciplinarity approaches *in* law"):[152]

"Wenn eine Disziplin ihren Status nicht aufgeben will, muss sie Interdisziplinarität von ihrem disziplinären Boden aus betreiben. Interdisziplinarität wird disziplinäre vollzogen. Eine interdisziplinär orientierte Rechtsdogmatik zielt darauf, Erkenntnisse anderer Disziplinen,

[151] *Stark* (n. 1), 193.

[152] *Stark* (n. 1), 193. See also ibid., 181.

'zu sammeln, zu koordinieren und zu bewerten' und für die Beantwortung der eigenen Fragestellung zu verwenden. Disziplinen ändern durch Interdisziplinarität zwar ihren Wissensbestand, nicht aber ihre Identität."

"If a discipline does not want to give up its status [as an independent discipline], it has to carry out interdisciplinary research on its own disciplinary ground. Interdisciplinarity is pursued on a disciplinary basis. A doctrinal study of law that is open to interdisciplinarity aims at 'collecting, coordinating and assessing' the findings of other disciplines and using them to answer its own questions. When pursuing interdisciplinary research, disciplines expand their knowledge base, but they do not change their identity."

Similarly, *Hans Christian Röhl* writes:[153]

"'Öffnung der Methode' meint [...] die Bereitschaft, Methoden zu verwenden, die nicht zum klassischen Methodenrepertoire der Rechtswissenschaft gehören oder Ergebnisse zu rezipieren, die andere Wissenschaften mit derartigen Methoden erzielt haben."

"'Opening up methodologies' is [...] the willingness to use methods that do not belong to the classical methodological repertoire of legal scholarship or to receive results that other sciences have achieved with such methods."

According to *Röhl*, legal scholars engage in interdisciplinary research whenever they integrate the research results of other disciplines into their own research. However, *Thomas Gutmann* disagrees:[154]

"Die aufklärende Funktion insbesondere der sozialwissenschaftlichen und der ökonomischen Beobachtung des Rechts [...] hat Bedeutung [...] für die [...] Rechtsdogmatik, die [...] versuchen sollte, ihr jeweiliges Rechtsgebiet auf eine Weise zu systematisieren, die nicht schon in empirischer Hinsicht dysfunktional ist. Das alles setzt jedoch noch keine Interdisziplinarität im eigentlichen Sinn voraus, sondern nur die Bereitschaft, die einschlägigen Debatten und Ergebnisse der anderen Einzelwissenschaften [...] zur Kenntnis zu nehmen."

"The explanatory value of research on law, especially that conducted by the social sciences and economics, [...] is of importance [...] for the [...] doctrinal study of law, which [...] should attempt to systematize the respective area of law in a way that is not already dysfunctional in empirical terms. However, this does not require true interdisciplinarity, but simply the willingness to take note of the relevant debates and the research results of other disciplines."

Yet it seems that *Gutmann*'s view is not generally shared. It seems to be generally accepted by legal scholars that integrating the findings and insights of extra-legal disciplines is true interdisciplinarity. Indeed, the contributions to the present volume all follow such an approach. And it is for this reason why

---

153 *H.C. Röhl*, Öffnung der öffentlich-rechtlichen Methode durch Internationalität und Interdisziplinarität: Erscheinungsformen, Chancen, Grenzen, Veröffentlichungen der Vereinigung der Deutschen Staatsrechtlehrer 74 (2015), 7–37, 27 ff. Röhl, however, qualifies his assertion on p. 28 by saying that this is rather an example of legal scholarship, and that one *may* speak of interdisciplinary scholarship.

154 *Gutmann* (n. 12), 101 f.

Wojciech Dajczak and *Herbert Zech* remind us that it is essential to teach the basics of digitalization to students of law in order to furnish them with the necessary expertise to integrate extra-legal findings into legal debates on digitalization,[155] and one may add that the same holds true for other extra-legal disciplines. This brings us back to *Kaufmann*'s warning against dilettantism:[156] He observed that "legal scientism" may lead to the decline of legal sub-disciplines such as legal philosophy or legal history. Legal academics researching these sub-disciplines need to have an understanding of philosophy and history. And representatives of legal realism suggested already at the end of the nineteenth and the beginning of the twentieth centuries that legal education would benefit from incorporating courses in economics, philosophy, psychology, or sociology into the curriculum.[157] Today, *Dershowitz* makes the following demand:[158]

> "Today's law student must be familiar with developments not only in the social sciences, but in the hard sciences as well. Criminal lawyers must understand genetics, DNA, basic scientific methodology, false positives and false negatives as well as the limitations on memory, eyewitness identification, and other such issues. Fortunately, these subjects have become far more accessible through excellent books and websites. It is not enough for a practicing lawyer today to be adept at legal research. She must also know how to do research in a wide range of other disciplines."

However, what about division of labour? *Lepsius* claims that a division of labour between representatives of different disciplines, too, amounts to interdisciplinarity.[159] Indeed, there should be no difference between the situations in which a doctrinal scholar of law simply integrates existing findings into law and in which a doctrinal scholar asks an extra-legal scholar to formulate extra-legal insights which the legal scholar then wishes to integrate in law. However, one has to be cautious: Often lawyers will ask individuals working in extra-legal disciplines to assist them with the clarification of the facts of a given case. The representative of the extra-legal discipline will then prepare an expert opinion. This is not an example of interdisciplinary research, and it is not even research.[160]

---

155 *Dajczak*, pp. 499 ff., below; *Zech*, pp. 517 ff., below.
156 See p. 27, above.
157 See the references in n. 6, above.
158 *Dershowitz* (n. 5), 5.
159 *Lepsius* (n. 2), 3 ff.
160 *Hellwege*, p. 371, below.

VII. The design and structure of the present volume

Against the background of what has been said so far, it is possible to reflect on the title and the structure of the present volume. It assembles the papers presented at a symposium held in October 2021 in Kraków, complemented by further contributions. The symposium's title was "Interdisciplinary approaches *to* law". However, it has become clear that this title is too narrow to cover the diverse presentations collected in the present volume. The title "Law and Interdisciplinarity" seems best at capturing just how multifaceted interdisciplinary research in law may be. Structuring the present volume has been a challenge. We have decided to start with three introductory chapters that are not complemented by a comparative comment;[161] these are followed by two contributions on "Law and Theology" for the simple reason that they discuss the starting point of our reflections on law and interdisciplinarity: the concept of dogmatics. Both contributions adopt what we have called above an "outbound perspective".[162] Some readers may disagree whether the four contributions which then follow belong in a volume on "law and interdisciplinarity".[163] However, for exactly this reason we have decided to continue with these contributions as they challenge our thinking as to what legal scholars mean when referring to the concept of interdisciplinarity. In order to give structure to the volume, we have decided to group all contributions under headings signalling the extra-legal discipline which is discussed or touched upon in these contributions. However, for two reasons readers should be warned that these headings are, as is often the case, simplifications: (1) Interdisciplinary research in law rarely relates to one extra-legal discipline alone. Economics, for example, is today strongly influenced by psychology.[164] (2) *Soniewicka* and *Wesołowska* as well as *Załuski* appear under the heading "Law and Psychology", but their papers adopt rather a philosophical approach to psychological problems or phenomena.[165]

VIII. Common themes and problems

In this last part of our introductory chapter, we wish to present common themes and problems encountered in interdisciplinary research in law. We would like

---

[161] *Stelmach*, pp. 49 ff., below; *Rossi*, pp. 55 ff., below.

[162] *Longchamps de Bérier*, pp. 75 ff., below *Marschler*, pp. 95 ff., below.

[163] *Rensmann*, pp. 113 ff., below; *Florczak-Wątor*, pp. 151 ff., below; *Sandhu*, pp. 169 ff., below, and *Kawczyńska*, pp. 187 ff., below.

[164] See, e.g., *Wurmnest*, p. 253, below; *Soniewicka/Wesołowska*, p. 324, below.

[165] *Soniewicka/Wesołowska*, pp. 324 ff., below; *Załuski*, pp. 397 ff., below. In addition, see *Kaspar*, p. 415, below.

to focus on what has been called above the inbound perspective of interdisciplinary legal research, and more specifically on what has above been labelled integrative interdisciplinary research: doctrinal scholars of law integrating extra-legal insights into the law when interpreting and applying positive law. It has been pointed out that doctrinal scholars of law need docking points in positive law to be able to integrate extra-legal insights into the law.[166] *Grimm* provides an example: When legal scholars in the course of interpreting and analysing positive law wish to consider extra-legal findings on social change, a possible docking point may be the rationale of a legal norm:[167]

"Sozialer Wandel ist juristisch nur normvermittelt von Interesse. Ihm kommt nicht als solchem juristische Relevanz zu, sondern nur dann, wenn er die Verwirklichung des Normzwecks bei unveränderter Interpretation gefährden würde."

"In law, social change is of interest only if it is linked to legal norms. Social change is not in itself legally relevant; rather, it assumes relevance only when an unaltered interpretation of a norm would endanger realization of the norm's rationale."

And *Stark* observes in a more generalized fashion:[168]

"Ausschlaggebend für die Relevanz nachbardisziplinärer Erkenntnisse ist das rechtsdogmatische Erkenntnisinteresse. […] Interdisziplinarität ist deshalb als Transformationsprozess zu verstehen. Die nachbardisziplinären Erkenntnisse sollen nicht eins-zu-eins von der Rechtsdogmatik verwendet werden. Sie sind im Lichte des rechtsdogmatischen Erkenntnisinteresses und des jeweiligen rechtlichen bzw. rechtsdogmatischen Kontexts zu deuten und zu bewerten."

"The specific research interest in the doctrinal study of law is decisive for the relevance of extra-legal findings. […] For that reason, interdisciplinarity is to be understood as a transformation process. Extra-legal findings cannot be copied and pasted by scholars engaged in the doctrinal study of law. Such findings are to be interpreted and evaluated in the light of the specific research interests of the doctrinal study of law and the legal and doctrinal contexts."

This process of transformation – one could also speak of a process of translation[169] – is central to integrative interdisciplinary work. In the past, we have above all seen heated debates on how to integrate economic insights into law,[170] but the underlying problem is universal. Moreover, it is not only scholars interpreting and applying positive law who engage in integrative interdiscipli-

[166] See p. 36, above.

[167] *Grimm* (n. 16), 27.

[168] *Stark* (n. 1), 230. In addition, see *Bumke* (n. 55), 469 f.

[169] See *Dajczak*, p. 510, below.

[170] See, e.g., *S. Grundmann*, Methodenpluralismus als Aufgabe. Zur Legalität von ökonomischen und rechtsethischen Argumenten in Auslegung und Rechtsanwendung, Rabels Zeitschrift für ausländisches und internationales Privatrecht 61 (1997), 423–453.

nary work. Lawyers engaging in legislative debates and lawyers developing arguments *de lege ferenda* may do so, too.[171]

In the beginning of our introductory chapter, we asked the question whether there is an interdependence between a given national legal system and interdisciplinary research, and it does not come as a surprise that there is such interdependence. This is, for example, shown in the contribution authored by *Florczak-Wątor*.[172] *Florczak-Wątor* analyses how differently the Polish and German constitutions frame the concepts of human dignity and inalienable human rights and how this affects doctrinal legal scholars' interdisciplinary thinking on both concepts.

However, it surprised us that the integration of extra-legal findings into law is not so much affected by black-letter law but rather by theorems, fundamental rules, and principles which are found to be inherent in the law. A perfect example is offered by the contributions authored by *Kasiske* and *Michał Derek*.[173] Both authors are doctrinal law scholars. However, it seems that they put different emphasis on the theorems, fundamental rules, and principles that are found to be inherent in the law and which limit, as *Derek* argues, the application of extra-legal findings in the doctrinal discourse on law. However, these theorems, fundamental rules, and principles seem to be identical in Polish and German criminal law. The dividing line between both authors needs to be drawn somewhere else. *Kasiske* stresses in his paper that he is arguing from "a strictly social science perspective",[174] and it seems that *Derek* would not disagree with such a perspective. However, *Kasiske* takes this perspective as a starting point to reflect on positive criminal law, and it seems that *Derek* disagrees with this part of *Kasiske*'s contribution. The dialogue between *Załuski* and *Johannes Kaspar* shows that those principles derived from the respective constitutions – and that are again similar in both legal systems – are of the same importance as factors that limit the application of extra-legal findings in law.[175] Moreover, *Wurmnest* and *Długosz* remind us that theorems, fundamental rules, and principles which are found to be inherent in the law, as well as constitutional principles, may not only limit the integration of extra-legal insights when interpreting and applying positive law, but that they may equally hinder the integration of extra-legal insights by legislatures.[176] After all, legislatures do not work in a legal vacuum. *Wurmnest* and *Długosz* again refer to principles that are similar in Germany and Poland.

---

[171] See pp. 31 ff., above; *Rossi*, pp. 55 ff. below.

[172] *Florczak-Wątor*, pp. 151 ff., below. For further examples, see *Rensmann*, pp. 113 ff., below; *Hellwege*, p. 378, below.

[173] *Kasiske*, pp. 209 ff., below; *Derek*, pp. 229 ff., below. In addition, see the contributions by *Laskowska-Litak*, pp. 463 ff., below; *Kim*, pp. 487 ff., below.

[174] *Kasiske*, p. 210, below.

[175] *Załuski*, pp. 397 ff., below; *Kaspar*, pp. 411 ff., below.

[176] *Wurmnest*, pp. 241 ff., below; *Długosz*, p. 276, below.

The reasons why we nevertheless see disagreement between *Kasiske* and *Derek*, between *Załuski* and *Kaspar*, and between *Ewa Laskowska-Litak* and *Daria Kim* is explainable by reference to the doctrinal study of law as a discursive discipline that aims at explaining positive law with rational persuasiveness.[177] When it comes to assessing the factual basis of a case, extra-legal disciplines take the lead, and they simply have to persuade legal actors of the correctness of their findings. However, when it comes to integrating extra-legal findings into the interpretation of law, it is not enough that legal actors are persuaded by the correctness of extra-legal findings. A lawyer will have to convince other lawyers that the legal interpretation which integrates extra-legal findings is the one that has the most persuasive power. Extra-legal scholars may think that extra-legal findings will make the task of the lawyer easier, as extra-legal scholars may think that the lawyer should simply follow the interpretation that is in accordance with the extra-legal findings. Yet the opposite is the case. For the lawyer the task of integrating extra-legal findings into the law adds a further variant to the complex process of legal interpretation and legal argumentation. This observation follows directly from *Stark*'s assertion that the doctrinal study of law pursues interdisciplinarity on its own disciplinary grounds:[178] extra-legal factors lose their compelling persuasive power and become one out of many points of refence in a complex doctrinal analysis. The picture is further complicated by the fact that the social sciences and humanities rarely present universally accepted insights and that the insights of different extra-legal disciplines may even conflict with each other.[179] Then it is on legal actors to decide which insights they wish to follow.

The conclusion that the doctrinal study of law pursues interdisciplinarity on its own disciplinary grounds, a determination which includes the characterization of the doctrinal study of law as a discursive discipline, explains why *Rossi*, *Wurmnest*, and *Długosz* all agree that it is not the way forward to formalize or institutionalize the ways in which extra-legal insights are integrated into the law.[180]

These observations also allow us to develop an answer to the question whether interdisciplinarity is a vehicle allowing different legal systems to converge. New extra-legal research may in all legal systems alike raise the question of whether the law is still based on accurate extra-legal assumptions. However, it has become clear by now that lawyers may develop different answers as to how to integrate these extra-legal findings into the law.[181]

---

[177] See pp. 20, above.

[178] See p. 40, above.

[179] *Florczak-Wątor*, p. 154, above; *Wurmnest*, p. 256, below; *Willems*, p. 309, below; *Soniewicka/Wesołowska*, pp. 324 ff., below.

[180] *Rossi*, pp. 55 ff., below; *Wurmnest*, p. 247 f., below; *Długosz*, p. 273, below.

[181] *Florczak-Wątor*, pp. 164 f., below.

That leaves us with a further point. In her paper, *Kim* speaks of interdisciplinarity as "an excursion", pointing out that there is no "universal step-by-step methodology for conducting interdisciplinary research" in law.[182] Further, *Stelmach* observes that recourse to interdisciplinarity often follows cognitive fashions.[183] We doubt that it is possible to overcome these problems. First, interdisciplinary research in law is too multifaceted. A single step-by-step methodology for conducting interdisciplinary research is simply unthinkable. It would, by contrast, seem sufficient to simply adhere to the different methodologies of the involved discipline. Secondly, recourse to interdisciplinarity indeed follows cognitive fashions, personal taste, personal expertise, or, as *Dershowitz* puts it, seasons.[184] However, such interdisciplinary research will, in the worst case, simply lack the "rationale persuasiveness" that is always of primary importance in legal discourse.

There are two final observations worth making: (1) The way legal scholars understand the concept of interdisciplinarity ultimately depends on the philosophical foundations of a legal system. Unlike US legal scholarship, continental European legal scholarship is positivist. And that is why the present chapter started with the doctrinal study of law in approaching the topic "law and interdisciplinarity".[185] It follows that the great divide in the way we perceive interdisciplinarity in law is one existing not between different continental European legal systems, but between continental European legal systems on the one hand and the US on the other hand. (2) Nevertheless, we first presented a generally accepted definition of interdisciplinarity.[186] Still, we have not followed that line and have instead called any efforts to define interdisciplinarity "a fruitless endeavour". The reason is simple: Most contributions to the present volume do not meet that generally accepted definition of interdisciplinarity! Should we as editors subsequently have rejected these contributions as being based on erroneous understandings of interdisciplinarity? No! These contributions rather represent how scholars engaged in the doctrinal study of law understand the concept of interdisciplinarity against the background of the specificities of their own discipline. And we as editors have understood it to be our task to pinpoint the elements of this specific understanding in the preceding introduction.

---

[182] *Kim*, p. 487, below.

[183] *Stelmach*, pp. 49 ff., below.

[184] *Dershowitz* (n. 5), 3–5. See, p. 6, above.

[185] See pp. 17 ff., above.

[186] See pp. 15 f., above.

Interdisciplinarity and the Dimensions of Legal Discourse

Jerzy Stelmach

I. The debate on "interdisciplinarity"

A. "Interdisciplinarity" means the "opening up" of one discipline of knowledge to the language, methods strategies, or insights developed in another academic discipline. In every case, however, interdisciplinarity means "opening up" to scientific knowledge as distinct from common knowledge or other non-scientific knowledge. This distinction is particularly crucial for any further considerations devoted to the cognitive status of legal discourse. Appealing to various concepts, views, and beliefs that do not even meet the "soft" requirements of science should not be equated with "interdisciplinary openness." Here I am highlighting the first of the problems that are usually overlooked in any discussion on interdisciplinarity. "Interdisciplinarity" is a concept that is ascribed an unequivocally positive meaning. "Interdisciplinary openness" has the objective of helping to "improve" and "develop" a given field of knowledge and should not lead to its regression or chaos. Of course, such a narrow sense of the term may also raise doubts. The development of many branches of science, not only the social sciences, but also logic and mathematics, have been inspired by speculative (metaphysical) philosophies, which certainly did not meet the standard requirements of science. The second problem concerns the postulate of intersubjectivity itself or, more precisely, two situations, the first being where interdisciplinarity acts as a normative postulate and the other being where it is a descriptive thesis. It is hard not to notice the difference between the statements: "Contemporary jurisprudence should be interdisciplinary" and "contemporary physics is an interdisciplinary science." The confusion of cognitive expectations with the actual state of development of certain fields of knowledge is, in my opinion, the cause of numerous misunderstandings and, as a result, sterile academic disputes about interdisciplinarity itself.

B. The three most important "sins" which are associated with the legal understanding of interdisciplinarity are "selectivity", "lack of competence", and "a lack of a distinction between theoretical and practical discourse." Referring to certain scientific views is sometimes done selectively, and reference to others occurs even "at random". "Recourse to interdisciplinarity" is often not intended to improve the specific legal discipline in which it is made, but rather to compensate for the "cognitive fashions" which prevail in legal scholarship at any given time. Over the course of my academic activity, I have observed a number of such interdisciplinary trends, ranging from philosophical positivism, logical empiricism, and analytical philosophy – both in the soft form (soft-shoe analysis) and in the harder, mathematical, and logical variety (horse-shoe analysis) – to economics and, more specifically, the economic analysis of law, psychology, and the neuroscience and cognitivism of the present. Of course, I am also aware of successful "interdisciplinary receptions", but the vast majority have actually been selective and very superficial in legal scholarship. Certainly, logical empiricism had a significant impact on the school of Scandinavian Legal Realism, where the reception of analytical philosophy was widespread and left its mark on both the philosophy and theory of law of the time, as well as on its legal dogmatics. In turn, the law and economics movement has enjoyed a stunning career in the US, while research in the field of neuroscience and cognitive science in law is also gaining in importance, although the latter now tends to be conducted in smaller "groups of believers". "Selectivity" most often results from the second of the aforementioned sins, namely the "lack of competence" in the fields of scientific knowledge which these lawyers refer to. In this case, they tend to appeal to the discipline because it is the current fashion, because others are already talking about it, because it is simply there. Although this sin is not inherently "deadly", it becomes so when lawyers continue to persistently discuss topics which they have no idea about. It is hard to blame lawyers for not being philosophers, linguists, logicians, economists, or specialists in psychology or neuroscience. Yet they can certainly be found guilty of "trespassing" in a field in which they fundamentally lack the requisite competence. On the other hand, the source of the "third sin" is caused by not distinguishing between areas of legal discourse having different cognitive status, namely theoretical and practical discourse. In my opinion, this is not only a "deadly sin" but perhaps also simultaneously the "original sin" because most debates on the interdisciplinarity of jurisprudence and other disputes closely related to it are burdened with this sin, in particular those concerning the "scientific nature of jurisprudence", and "the cognitive status of normative statements".

II. Two branches of discourse

A. Both of these branches of legal discourse exist independently of one another. Of course, the findings gleaned from theoretical discourse may have an impact on the decisions made in practical discourse, but demonstrating a closer relationship between them is a somewhat impossible undertaking.[1] This distinction, which is of key importance to most considerations in the field of legal epistemology, has somehow not been adopted very well in the fields of the philosophy and theory of law, or legal dogmatics. Much ink has been spilled on practical legal discourse, while little has been said on theoretical discourse, and almost nothing has been written on the mutual relations between these areas of discourse.[2] There are several reasons for this lack of interest. Supporters of the cognitive position in the dispute over the meaning of normativity, in both the supra-naturalistic and naturalistic senses, do not see the need to distinguish between the two areas of discourse, as they assume that the cognitive status of practical discourse is, or at least may be, the same as that of theoretical discourse. Meanwhile, the prescriptivists, in turn, focus their attention on the cognitive differences in practical discourse. Finally, for the majority of "ordinary lawyers" who do not have to deal with the philosophy and theory of law, considerations on the cognitive status of both branches of legal discourse turn out to not only be too difficult but also extremely inconvenient, because they violate the cognitive status quo that is fundamental to them, especially the principle regarding the homogeneity and integrity of legal knowledge. In any event, the entire discussion on the cognitive status of jurisprudence, and in particular on the scientific value of the methods used by lawyers which was initiated by *Julius Hermann von Kirchmann* with his "accusation" in the first half of the nineteenth century, concerned only practical discourse.[3] It seems as if theoretical discourse in the study of law and legal practice either does not exist at all or is without any significant importance. And yet it most certainly does exist, and its significance is as fundamental as that of practical discourse.

B. Theoretical legal discourse is open to any type of scientific knowledge, because the arrangements made within it are verified on the basis of strictly scientific criteria. Being scientific discourse, it can use any methods considered to be scientific, and their use will depend only on specific cognitive needs. These methods will find an application in both the "legal context of the discovery" and its "justification". In the "discovery" phase, empirical methods which are primarily in the repertoire of sciences such as psychology, biology, and medicine are most frequently employed. However, in the "justification" phase,

---

[1] The confirmation of this thesis is the ongoing is/ought debate, present in philosophy since Antiquity and in the philosophy of law since the nineteenth century. See *J. Stelmach*, A jeśli powinność nie istnieje, in: A. Brożek et al. (eds.), Fenomen normatywności (2013), 205.

[2] "Almost does not mean nothing, however", as I have written in an article devoted to the topic: *J. Stelmach*, Die Grenzen der juristischen Erkenntnis, in: B. Dauner-Lieb et al. (eds.), Festschrift für Horst Konzen zum siebzigsten Geburtstag (2006), 893–902, 893.

[3] *J.H. von Kirchmann*, Die Werthlosigkeit der Jurisprudenz als Wissenchaft (1848). See also *J. Stelmach*, Kirchmanns Fluch, in: F. Saliger et al. (eds.), Rechtsstaatliches Straftrecht. Festschrift für Ulfrid Neumann zum 70. Geburtstag (2017), 445–450, 445.

when theorems are formulated and models are built, the methods of more formal sciences, such as logic, mathematics, and economics are used. The context of the discovery precedes the proper interpretation, that is, practical discourse. At this stage of legal thought, empirical determinations are made, and evidence is collected. The justification, on the other hand, is carried out after the interpretation process is completed and is aimed at finding theoretical arguments to justify the previously made decision. Theoretical legal discourse is essentially interdisciplinary discourse. In none of its contexts – in neither the discovery nor its justification – is it specifically legal, because all of the cognitive methods and strategies employed are simply universal and meet the requirements of a strict understanding of what is scientific.

C. However, the issue of the interdisciplinary openness of practical legal discourse is somewhat different. The cognitive variety of this area of discourse, just like with any other practical discourse, cannot raise any doubts even for the adherents of the cognitive position. This is because in the world of obligations, different criteria are used for the recognition of judgments and normative statements. Truth in practical discourse is replaced by less stringent criteria, such as equity, fairness, reliability, validity, effectiveness, or efficiency. Admittedly, successive "cognitive revolutions" which have heralded "corrective programs" or "scientificization" through an interdisciplinary opening up of jurisprudence have had a significant impact on the development of legal thought and practice. Yet this has primarily been in their theoretical dimensions, while not necessarily being the case in terms of the practical discourse.[4] The potential for the direct use of scientific methods in practical legal discourse has turned out to be significantly limited, precisely because of the special cognitive status of the inquiry. We have learnt that the world of duty is governed by its own laws, laws which have little in common with the principles of science and scientific methods. Therefore, in the case of practical legal discourse, we can at best speak of "limited or indirect interdisciplinarity." Why? The answer to this question requires a slightly more extensive commentary on the possibility of directly using scientific methods in practical legal discourse.

Let us first consider the case of mathematics. I am unaware of any modern attempts to apply mathematical models in practical legal discourse.[5] However, mathematics is employed in theoretical legal discourse, for example probability calculus or statistical analysis. Of course, this may have some influence on the development and results of the cognitive activities carried out as part of practical discourse, but it is certainly not a direct impact.

---

[4] *J. Stelmach*, The Cognitive Approach in Legal Science and Practice: A History of Four Revolutions, in: B. Brożek et al. (eds.), Law and Mind. A Survey of Law and Cognitive Sciences (2021), 507–520, 507.

[5] For a possible historical attempt, see *Dajczak*, pp. 506 ff., below.

An even knottier case is that of the "reception of logic" in practical discourse. Regardless of the countless debates, disputes, and overbearing claims that have been made about the potential to use logic in practical legal discourse, the entire problem essentially boils down to the question of just what logic are we talking about here? After all, formal logic, by which I mean both classical propositional calculus and more specialized logics such as deontic and modal logic, cannot be applied to normative reasoning. A logic of norms has not yet been created, while "legal logic" or, more broadly, "practical logic" (with logic understood more narrowly, i.e. formally) unfortunately does not have many common points. Of course, such a view will not be shared by the declared adherents of legal logic. They most frequently formulate two arguments in favour of recognising the autonomy of legal logic. The first concerns the very concept of logic, which, in their opinion, can be understood more broadly and thus less formally. The second, on the other hand, is related to the possibility of considering certain principles of legal logic, such as *a fortiori* argumentation, to be fully logical. I do not share the view of the "optimists" for at least two different reasons. First of all, legal logic is a set of different rules and principles which, whilst entirely common sense, do not create any coherent system, let alone an axiomatic one. Second, all the rules and principles of legal logic, without exception, are questionable. While we can freely use various types of formal logics in theoretical legal discourse, we only have "legal logic" in practical legal discourse, and this, as I have tried to show, is simply not logic. Thus, it would in this case be difficult to talk about a genuine "interdisciplinary openness" because what would be the point? In terms of its cognitive status, "practical logic" is, to put it delicately, questionable.

The "opening up" of legal discourse to psychology took place in the first half of the twentieth century, and there is no doubt that the psychological "trend" has been a constant presence in theoretical legal discourse. The key question is the extent to which scientific psychology can be used in practical legal discourse, and in my opinion its scope of application is very limited. The theories and models built on the basis of scientific psychology are used to describe the real world, i.e. phenomena from the realm of being, the world of "is". That is why the direct application of these theories and models to the interpretation of the world of ought – without first adopting "strong" naturalistic assumptions about the possibility of reducing an "ought" to an "is" – is simply impossible. In practical legal discourse, scientific psychology is replaced by common or folk psychology. While this type of psychology uses a number of methods, including pre-comprehension and understanding, instinct, intuition, hunch, and insight, they do not meet the standard scientific requirements.[6] On the other hand, these methods allow for the construction of numerous extremely useful heuristics that allow the interpreter to find a "shortcut". This

[6] *J. Stelmach/Ł. Kurek*, Psychologia potoczna w myśleniu prawniczym (2022), 23 ff.

psychology, based on common sense, is in fact the "first psychology" that precedes a secondary scientific psychology, and it is considered by some, including myself, to be the only legitimate version. Although both psychologies seem to use different areas of our cognition, there are still many common points. For example, there is talk in hermeneutics of "putting oneself into the mental position of another person" as a cognitive (interpretative) strategy, while in psychology and cognitive science this is referred to as a "thought experiment". Perhaps the key concept of hermeneutics is "understanding", which again in psychology and cognitive science is known as the ability to "carry out mental simulations". In fact, it is the same thing all the time. I have no doubts that practical legal discourse is open to psychological reflection, but first and foremost to the everyday variety. It would, by contrast, be difficult to find examples of the direct application of theories and models from the field of scientific psychology in practical discourse.

Economic analysis is also reduced to the common normative variant in practical legal discourse. It is in this simplified, common-sense way that lawyers who are dealing with legal practice understand the key concepts of the economic analysis of law, in particular the concepts of efficiency and *homo economicus*. More in-depth research, taking into account the different variants of the economic analysis of law, appears in theoretical legal discourse, if at all. In any case, I have never met a practising lawyer who, when referring to economic "facts" or "concepts", would use more sophisticated tools developed on the basis of economic analysis of law, for example consciously choosing the concept of efficiency or game theory.

Legislation as an Interdisciplinary Challenge

On the Relationship between Democracy and Expertise

Matthias Rossi

I. Introduction

The relationship between law and extra-legal scholarship and extra-legal findings and, thus, the relationship between law and interdisciplinarity has been discussed a great many times. In the present volume, which collects papers given at the Kraków-Augsburg Symposium in 2021, a scholar from the Jagiellonian University in Kraków may be quoted in order to provisionally frame the topic:[1]

> "The interdisciplinarity of law is of a specific nature and this is implied by certain features of the law. First, it is not the aim of law to describe reality, nor does law explain human behaviour. Rather, it states the norms which are ruling the behaviour of people [...]. But if we accept a more inclusive way of defining interdisciplinarity, namely as an intellectual activity which concerns more than one discipline or harnessing results gained by different sciences, it transpires that law may be treated as interdisciplinary in many aspects."

The term "interdisciplinarity" itself is woolly. It is used in a variety of contexts and with varying content, indeed with varying precision.[2] The contributions in the present volume will also be based on different understandings of the term. From the perspective of a precise science, this is to be regretted. Yet a general definition could narrow the view from the outset and thereby hinder open-ended discussions of the concept. For this reason, the present contribution also refrains from giving a definition or even a paraphrasing of what is understood by interdisciplinarity. A brief discussion of the overall theme is nevertheless in order: It is possible to distinguish interdisciplinary approaches *to* law from interdisciplinary approaches *of* law. This small but subtle distinction is noteworthy because with the former approach the question is how other disciplines look at law, whereas with the latter the question is to what extent law takes other disciplines into account. The present contribution will be concerned only with the latter approach. Indeed, legal scholarship is open to the considerations of other disciplines. In particular, the empirical social sciences (above all political science) as well as economics are increasingly being included in legal treatises. Admittedly, an esteemed colleague has recently expressed skepticism about this form of "including refined morsels of bourgeois erudition" in legal scholarship, speaking of "Suhrkamp scholarship".[3] But it cannot be denied that legal scholarship is at any rate receptive and curious towards other disciplines, whereas the willingness of other disciplines to engage with legal scholars is rather low.[4]

In the following text, however, the focus is not on a perspective internal to legal scholarship that deals with the interdisciplinarity of the doctrinal study of

---

[1] *M. Jakubiec*, Interdisciplinary jurisprudence, in: B. Brożek et al. (eds.), Perspectives on Interdisciplinarity (2021), 79–98.

[2] See the inventory in *C. Boulanger/J. Rosenstock/T. Singelnstein* (eds.), Interdisziplinäre Rechtsforschung (2019), 3 ff. In addition, see *P. Richli*, Interdisziplinäre Daumenregeln für eine faire Rechtsetzung (2000), 8.

[3] *K. F. Gärditz*, JuristenZeitung 2021, 461–463, 462, alluding to a renowned publishing house whose books are perceived as setting the standard especially in the field of humanities, at least by the respective authors.

[4] Criticizing, inter alia, what the author finds to be an insufficient consideration of constitutional jurisprudence in historical scholarship, *D. Grimm*, Die Historiker und die Verfassung (2022), passim.

law. Rather, the focus will be on the role that interdisciplinarity plays, or should play, in the creation of statutory law: Political decision-making is always dependent on specialist expertise, and the interplay between democratically legitimized lawmaking and factually based knowledge often reveals that legislation is an interdisciplinary challenge. Insofar as doctrinal scholars of law primarily focus on the application of law, they do not face the same challenges as those lawyers who are engaged in the drafting of legislation. The question of how existing law is to be interpreted and applied is, with its deductive method, fundamentally different from the inductive method which is to be applied in legislation. Legal scholarship is therefore not only a discipline of interpretation; it is also normative and conceptual in nature.[5]

II. The need for interdisciplinarity in legislation

It should be beyond question that interdisciplinarity is necessary in lawmaking: "Law cannot be developed as a pure normative system, separated from the knowledge about the world."[6] Therefore "the interdisciplinarity of law is not only an option – it is a necessity,"[7] "an imperative" ("ein Gebot").[8] Assuming that law wants to shape a given (social) reality in a certain way, both the grasping of reality and an appreciation of how reality is shaped by law require interdisciplinary expertise. It follows that only an interdisciplinary approach to lawmaking can improve the quality of laws.[9]

A. Grasping reality

The power of law to shape and steer reality requires that lawmakers have a sufficiently good grasp of the reality the law seeks to influence. Coping with climate change is not possible without knowledge of the respective scientific contexts, curbing crime is hopeless without knowledge of its causes, and regulating the housing market through private civil law requires information about supply and demand. Without a reliable database, "good laws" cannot be made.

B. Shaping reality

The understanding of how reality is shaped by law also requires interdisciplinary insights. This applies above all to the (probable) future effects of law. Predictions about causal processes and probable behavioral patterns as well as

---

[5] *Richli* (n. 2), 114.
[6] *Jakubiec* (n. 1), 81.
[7] *Jakubiec* (n. 1), 82.
[8] For *Richli* (n. 2), 11 and 91, it is even a constitutional requirement.
[9] *Richli* (n. 2), 4.

the anticipation of undesirable side effects require knowledge that goes beyond the expertise of a single unit of a ministry that is usually tasked with formulating a law. This applies, for example, to technical developments in general and to their impact on financial instruments in particular, to give another example: It is impossible to introduce standards for the operation of fintech enterprises without understanding their technical functioning.[10]

C. The climate and COVID-19 crises as current examples

The question of whether legislative processes are, or should be, interdisciplinary tasks has often been raised, although under other headings.[11] In particular, when it comes to the inclusion of expert knowledge, the question regularly arises as to whether and how extra-legal expertise can be incorporated into the process of legislation. This is an enduring and fundamental question, one which is not to be answered primarily in legal terms or from the perspective of legal scholarship but is to be addressed first and foremost by politics itself. And it follows that this question also calls to the scene the social and political sciences.

The functions potentially served by the involvement of extra-legal experts in legislative processes overlap in part with those that the involvement of stakeholders is intended to fulfil. First, such involvement has a neutral information function, and it serves to safeguard the quality of legislation. It can also improve the acceptance of decisions made by the legislature. However, this improvement in acceptance is based less on the participatory involvement of potential addressees of legislation, and it thus cannot be explained in terms of a democratic coloring of the legislative process. Instead, it is their know-how that provides the experts with a purely rationally mediated legitimacy. Extralegal experts do not solely perform content-related tasks. They are often involved in decision-making for symbolic and tactical reasons. It has long been observed that highly complex and difficult political questions will be converted into seemingly soluble technical problems which can be presented in a dichotomous, right-wrong framework, thereby quickly establishing the desired solution and precluding alternate approaches.[12]

If extra-legal expertise is understood as scientific knowledge, the aforementioned question concerns nothing less than the relationship between science and politics. Both terms need to be defined in more detail, but in the present

[10] *Jakubiec* (n. 1), 88.

[11] See, above all *U. Smeddinck*, Intgegrierte Gesetzesproduktion (2006), passim, with numerous further references; *M. Rossi*, Betroffenenbeteiligung im Gesetzgebungsverfahren, Jahrbuch des öffentlichen Rechts der Gegenwart 62 (2014), 159–178; *S. Ledermann*, Evidenz und Expertise im vorparlamentarischen Gesetzgebungsprozess: Die Rolle von Verwaltung und externen Experten, Swiss Political Science Review 20/3 (2014), 453–485.

[12] In detail, *D.B. Bobrow/J. Dryzek*, Policy Analysis by Design (1987).

context it is sufficient to understand science (in a clearly oversimplified fashion) as a synonym for (high-quality) extra-legal knowledge and politics (in a similarly oversimplified vein) as a representative of the system of state or sovereign rule-making. It is possible to illustrate the reciprocal relationship between the "systems" of science and politics in almost all fields that have recently been the object of legislation: In technology and environmental law, for example, it is primarily scientific knowledge that influences the political will. In general economic policy, it is economic insights – to put it in perspective, one should rather speak of economic convictions – that influence politics. In the field of criminal law, the policies to be followed by the legislature are not only based on political convictions but also on empirically and psychologically based knowledge. The same applies to almost all areas of law.

In the last two or three years, the difficult relationship between science and politics has come to the attention of the general public, mainly due to two crises: the climate crisis and the COVID-19 crisis. The COVID-19 crisis has brought two aspects to light as if under a magnifying glass: On the one hand, it has shown how much politics is dependent on extra-legal knowledge that promises security, certainty, and clarity. These promises are of special importance in times of crisis because such times are characterized not only by time pressure but also by the complete lack of security, certainty, and clarity. On the other hand, the COVID-19 crisis has made it clear how much politicians rely on the power of scientific insights in times of crisis, i.e., how much they tend to implement expert assessments and recommendations directly instead of making their own decisions – yet decision-making always means weighing up and prioritizing. In retrospect, it is fair to say, with all due differentiation, that at times policymakers simply reacted to a certain situation by referring to "science" and did not even make an effort to "get ahead of the situation," i.e., to take the rudder into their own hands or to set the course. In this respect, the COVID-19 crisis – at least at the beginning – presented itself as an epistemic problem,[13] i.e. as being almost exclusively a question of knowledge, expertise, and competence.

For adherents of a strictly "follow-the-science" approach in politics, the first governmental reactions to the COVID-19 crisis were thus a further wake-up call supporting their approach, which they want to make fruitful for climate policy in particular. In the area of climate policy, the epistemic character of political controversies is particularly evident and has been so for some time, but because the consequences – unlike in the case of the COVID-19 crisis – are not immediately noticeable and because, moreover, causal relationships are incomparably more complex, expert knowledge has not been reflected in political measures to the extent that some would have liked. *Wolfgang Schäuble*, the

---

[13] In detail, *L. Münkler*, Expertokratie (2020), passim. In addition, see *A. Bogner*, Die Epistemisierung des Politischen (2021), passim.

former President of the German *Bundestag*, addressed these concerns in his speech as *Alterspräsident* (Chairman by Seniority) at the constituent session of the twentieth *Bundestag* on 26 October 2021:

"Das mitunter zähe Ringen um gesellschaftliche Mehrheiten sollten wir gerade auch denjenigen nahebringen, die mit Blick auf den Klimawandel von der Trägheit demokratischer Prozesse enttäuscht sind und sofortiges Handeln fordern. Ihre Motive sind nachvollziehbar, aber wissenschaftliche Erkenntnis allein ist noch keine Politik und schon gar nicht demokratische Mehrheit. Wer Ziele und Mittel absolut setzt, bringt sie gegen das demokratische Prinzip in Stellung. Übrigens kann die Wissenschaft genauso wenig letzte Gewissheit liefern, und in der Demokratie gibt es sowieso nicht die eine richtige Entscheidung. Genau damit müssen wir umgehen."[14]

"The at times difficult struggle to gain democratic majorities in society should be brought to the attention of those who, with regard to climate change, are disappointed by the sluggishness of democratic processes and demand immediate action. Their motives are understandable, but scientific knowledge is not in itself politics, and it certainly does not represent a democratic majority. Those who make ends and means absolute set them against democratic principles. Moreover, science is incapable of providing final certainty, and in democracy there is in any event never a single correct decision. This is precisely what we have to deal with."

D. The relationship between science and politics

For the relationship between science and politics, two statements are noteworthy. First, the statement: "scientific knowledge is not in itself politics, and it certainly does not represent a democratic majority," is significant. It implies two things. It differentiates between knowledge on the one hand and decision-making on the other. And in view of the principle of democracy, it empowers the majority to make decisions that are inconsistent with scientific knowledge. This statement touches on the age-old and large question of whether and under what conditions a democracy can produce "best" decisions and whether, in the final analysis, procedurally legitimized majority decisions are better than factually legitimized expert opinions. No less relevant, on the other hand, is the proposition that "[t]hose who make ends and means absolute set them against democratic principles." This proposition is not surprising, as it was also *Schäuble* who, at the beginning of the heated discussions about COVID-19 measures, reminded us that no constitutional value, not even the protection of health, was entitled to claim absolute priority over other values,[15] and only following this reminder did the political as well as the scientific discussion take on a more objective dimension. Above all, *Schäuble* is proposing that no expert know-

[14] Available at https://www.bundestag.de/parlament/praesidium/reden/2021/20211026-866254 (last accessed on 31 August 2023).

[15] https://www.tagesspiegel.de/politik/schauble-will-dem-schutz-des-lebens-nicht-alles-unterordnen-7507174.html (last accessed on 31 August 2023).

ledge, no matter how correct, should be implemented without further political debate, and he rejects the ideas of absolute expert knowledge and of decisions being without alternatives. Or formulated differently: Existing complexity must not be ignored, and it must not be reduced to such an extent that other aspects and interests, which should be considered in political debates too, are completely disregarded.

III. Instruments for ensuring interdisciplinary lawmaking

The extra-legal knowledge required in the legislative process is only partly available to the legislature. Consequently, individual experts or entire expert committees are involved in lawmaking. Yet this involvement is institutionalized only to a relatively small extent.[16] A look at legislative practice shows that there are no detailed procedures and only a few official institutions that ensure interdisciplinary lawmaking.

A. Preliminary phase

Looking at legislative processes in Germany, we find many ways in which extra-legal insights are introduced. These different ways may be categorized with reference to the involved actors, the degree of their independence, the reputation of their expertise, or the binding effect of their decisions. Moreover, it is possible to distinguish institutionalized instruments from informal ones. Without claiming to be exhaustive, the following account will mention some of the possible measures and institutions by first focusing on the different phases of lawmaking, starting with a preliminary phase. This phase is not regulated by constitutional law and only partly by the Rules of Procedure of the Federal Government (*Geschäftsordnung der Bundesregierung*). The fact that constitutional law entirely ignores and the Rules of Procedure mostly ignore the preliminary phase is noteworthy given its importance. It is this preliminary phase in which legislative ideas are born and formulated. At times, civil society is involved in this process: business associations, NGOs dedicated to certain aspects of the common good, and political parties. The importance of such informal and unofficial initiatives by such diverse actors from civil society should not be underestimated. These actors are much more than gateways for primarily politically motivated lobbying. Rather, from the perspective of those potentially affected by a law, they not only express wishes as to the paths to be taken but also contribute information that the legislature does not have at its immediate disposal – or that can be acquired only after extensive research – but which is nevertheless needed as part of the legislative process. In this respect,

---

16 Critical of this fact and demanding further institutionalization, *Richli* (n. 2), 91, 409.

stakeholder participation is an important point of entry for interdisciplinarity in the process of lawmaking.

B. Internal governmental drafting phase

In the internal governmental drafting phase, which precedes the introduction of a draft bill in the legislative process, interdisciplinarity is achieved not only by consulting those affected, but above all by consulting other specialized ministries. Of course, these consultations are also – and in coalition governments perhaps primarily – used to gain political influence. But ideally, such consultations make available the expertise of other ministries and, where appropriate, subordinated governmental agencies. This applies, for example, to consultations between the Ministry for Economic Affairs and the Ministry for the Environment on classic disputes between economics and ecology. The exchange of information between these ministries relates not only to the political goals to be implemented but also to an understanding of the reality to be shaped.

C. Parliamentary consultation phase

The same applies to the involvement of committees during the parliamentary consultation phase. Various specialized parliamentary committees are involved, and they will often hold expert hearings. The importance of such hearings should not be overestimated. After all, the experts are proposed by the individual parliamentary groups, and they are not always soberly detached from the political goals of the party which has advanced their names. Nevertheless, their involvement should also not be underestimated. The hearings of experts take place in public and are observed and digested, accordingly, by the public – at least by the media. This often gives them special weight.

D. Federal consultation phase

Today, the *Bundesrat* refrains from having regular expert hearings of its own. However, this should not obscure the fact that the *Bundesrat*'s involvement in the legislative process is a further gateway to interdisciplinary insights since the individual members of the *Bundesrat* are briefed accordingly by their own specialist ministries.

E. Informal and institutionalized expertise

In a final step, I want to move beyond the different phases of the legislative process and focus on a different aspect: the distinction between informal and institutionalized external expertise. The COVID-19 crisis may again be used for the purpose of illustration. Even though COVID-19 measures were from a legal perspective largely decided by the German states, they were in fact in a first step regularly prepared at the federal level. The state governments, as well as the federal government, drew in particular on the expertise of institutional actors, most importantly the Robert Koch Institute (an independent federal agency under the supervision of the Federal Ministry of Health), the Standing Commission on Vaccination (*Ständige Impfkommission*, a federal expert group appointed by the Federal Minister of Health), and the National Academy of Sciences (*Leopoldina – Nationale Akademie der Wissenschaften*). They competed with informal actors, associations, and other persons, such as individual scientists, in interpreting the current risk situation and recommending future policy. Regardless of the question of what role these actors should and may play in sovereign decision-making, the example illustrates that a state is well advised to maintain institutions that generate knowledge and to make it available when needed. This is another way of meeting the interdisciplinary challenges of lawmaking.

IV. Excursus: expert groups in EU lawmaking

Within the EU, a large part of national lawmaking is simply implementing European directives. The question of how expertise is held in reserve for, made available in, and incorporated into the European legislative process is thus of particular importance. Here the role of expert groups is central. This role has been excellently analyzed in a recent dissertation and may be summarized as follows.[17]

The focus needs to be on the European Commission: It has a monopoly-like right of legislative initiative and derived legislative powers. In practice, its power to shape legislation is countered by a particular need for information and networking with the regulatory environment due to a lack of personnel resources and political involvement. It has met this structural challenge primarily through a system of approximately 1,000 expert groups. These groups are not integrated into the institutional structure of the EU. Nevertheless, they have factually become an integral and essential part of the Commission's structures, and it is hard to imagine the process of European lawmaking without them.

Expert groups are involved in the stage of preparing legislation, specifically in the phases of legislative planning and drafting. They are part of the Commission's "internal" procedure, which is hardly regulated and which precedes actual decisions, with the formal decision-making power remaining exclusively with the Commission. The core of the regulatory regime, last reformed in 2016, establishes so-called horizontal provisions for the establishment and operation of expert groups. With this regulatory structure, regulation has left the realm of soft law. In the legal form of a resolution, it is now generally

---

[17] *A. Dankowski*, Expertengruppen in der europäischen Rechtsetzung (2019), 428.

binding but can be classified as an internal measure of self-organization, which in principle has no external effect.

Expert groups are characterized by great diversity and heterogeneity in composition, organization, tasks, and working methods. In general, they are composed of scientists, stakeholders, and officials from Member State authorities. Information on the individual groups and relevant documents are available via a publicly accessible register on the Commission's website. Moreover, it is at the Commission's discretion whether to use an expert group and whether and to what extent to take the recommendations and opinions of an expert group into account. In the area of risk regulation, there are, however, special features at issue and the European courts have: (1) indicated that the discretion to employ expert groups can be reduced to zero in individual cases; (2) granted the scientific opinions of expert groups a kind of binding force in the sense of a rule; and (3) formulated requirements for the opinions of the groups.

The task of the expert groups is to provide the Commission with the necessary expertise that the Commission requires to fulfil its duties. It is noteworthy, that the Commission's understanding of expertise is broad and encompasses not only scientific but also practical and interest-driven expertise. It follows that the Commission pursues a "democratization of expertise" and instrumentalizes expert groups as part of its governance strategy. The practical functions and modes of action of expert groups are complex and extend well beyond knowledge-generating advice. For example, expert groups also serve as a control mechanism of the Member States and the European Parliament vis-à-vis the Commission and assume a depoliticizing function in implementing legislation. There are no empirically verified findings on the actual influence of expert group advice on the Commission's activities. However, it can be assumed that it has a strong influence and also a de facto binding effect.

From a functional perspective, the involvement of expert groups is significant for European lawmaking in three respects: (1) It gives the Commission the expertise it needs in its legislative activities; (2) the Union's decision-making system gains in overall effectiveness and efficiency; and (3) the quality of legal acts is increased by improving the basis for decision-making.

Phenomenologically, expert group consultations can be classified as cooperative decision-making in the form of increasingly legalized participation in sovereign processes. In practice, expert groups are the most important direct consultation and participation mechanism of European institutions. As such, they also allow for lobbying at the European level with direct, permanent, and partially formalized access to sovereign decision-making. First and foremost, expert groups are functional bodies of the Commission. They form part of the European committee system, they network with European administrations, and they can thus be seen as an element of European governance.

V. Fundamental problems of interdisciplinary lawmaking

What has proved successful at the European level is at the same time evidence of the numerous fundamental problems associated with the inclusion of external knowledge in legislation. Three such problems are to be named here.

A. Reception and evaluation of external knowledge

The first problem concerns the problem of how external knowledge is translated into the legal sphere. So far, we have only sketched out the possibilities for bringing external knowledge into the political decision-making process. The quintessence of this brief description is that knowledge input is characterized by plurality. But this knowledge must also be comprehended and evaluated. This raises the question of whether the state decision-making organs have a sufficient and appropriate receptor system as interdisciplinary work naturally requires interdisciplinary competence.[18] However, the plurality of informants and information inevitably entails the danger of being overwhelmed. This is because the information provided to government institutions must be evaluated not only as it impacts their own areas of expertise but also in respect of their interactions with other disciplines and fields of knowledge. This is precisely the interdisciplinary challenge.

B. Relationship between knowledge and decision-making

The second problem is more concrete and can ultimately be solved in terms of procedural or organizational law. It lies in the ambivalence between knowledge and decision-making in a democracy: When there exists a need for expert advice, politicians and, above all, the general public will rate the reliability of an expert opinion higher, the more independent an expert is. Ideally, their involvement will be legitimized solely by their expertise. Yet, in order to strengthen their democratic legitimacy, they must be linked to the state's legislative bodies. This in turn often raises the suspicion of manipulative knowledge processing.

This tension cannot be completely eliminated, but it can certainly be reduced.[19] From the perspective of constitutional law, and thus also from the perspective of legitimacy, it is ultimately decisive that the democratically legitimized sovereign authority is both enabled to make decisions based on external expertise but at the same time retains the final right of decision. Contrary to the call to "follow the science" often heard in connection with climate change, it must not be overlooked – especially in a democracy – that every decision is only a prioritization and as such falls within the realm of politics. As true as it

---

[18] *Richli* (n. 2), 11.

[19] *Münkler* (n. 13), 648.

is that expertise is a basic requirement of politics, this expertise must be limited to the provision of provable facts. However, the evaluation of the facts is no longer the sole responsibility of science; it shares this task with politics. What consequences are ultimately to be drawn from the facts and their evaluation is the sole task of politics, and insofar as this policy is to be cast in legally binding forms, this task falls to parliaments.

It is only where one believes that political action should be determined in every respect and without exception by figures, data, and facts that one can argue for orienting politics exclusively on the question of who has the "better" data. However, even this basic assumption is wrong,[20] at least for liberal democracies. Rather, as argued by *Joseph Alois Schumpeter*, it must always be remembered that liberal democracy does not follow an explicit normative goal but only provides a method for establishing social order.[21] This method is dependent on knowledge but must always act on its own and with ultimate responsibility, both in cases of certain knowledge and in cases of ignorance.

Incidentally, but this should only be hinted at here, the problem can also be defused by ensuring, as far as possible, an expert consensus: Expert consensus indicates that the knowledge conveyed is not based on politically driven evaluations. If the expert consensus is also ensured on an interdisciplinary basis, there is a very high probability that it is correct.

C. Epistemization of politics

The third problem is of a more abstract nature. It consists in the danger of an increasing epistemization of politics, in other words, in the fact that a primarily political dispute is waged as a knowledge conflict. If, for example, theoretically grounded knowledge (expertise) and empirically acquired knowledge (experience) are irreconcilably opposed to each other, the concept of knowledge is understood as rational as well as emotional. This makes political debate difficult. As an example, one can refer to the discussion on penal policy. Today's crime statistics testify to increasing security (expertise), while the subjective perception of a majority of people indicates decreasing security (experience). Refugee policy and climate change are also examples of areas in which different types of "knowledge" are at odds with each other. Such an epistemocracy threatens to destroy democracy. For knowledge alone does not make decisions, nor does it eliminate the need for decisions. Rather, specialized knowledge from different disciplines must be transparently available to all participants in democratic discourse. *Alexander Bogner* provides a good summary of this idea's development:[22]

---

[20] *Bogner* (n. 13), 39.
[21] *A. Schumpeter*, Kapitalismus, Sozialismus und Demokratie (8th edn., 2005), 427.
[22] *Bogner* (n. 13), 13 ff.

For a long time, the belief in the rationality of the social order seemed so dominant that the limits of such a rational order were virtually ignored. And the limits lie primarily in the particular complexity of the actual foundations and their interrelationships of effects. The world is precisely not a closed, logical causal connection, and therefore the "belief that one could, if one only wanted to, master all things – in principle – by calculation," as *Max Weber* put it in his 1919 paper "Science as a Vocation," cannot suffice from the outset. In more recent times, emotionality seems to have replaced rationality as the decisive criterion for social and governmental order, and even, presumptuously, for a world order. Corresponding movements refer to philosophical guarantors who early on criticized and questioned the faith in knowledge of modernity. *Werner Heisenberg*'s uncertainty principle, according to which the very attempt to understand something changes the object of understanding, and *Erwin Schrödinger*'s thought experiment on a cat that is simultaneously alive and dead are only two striking examples of the questioning of secure knowledge.

VI. The imperative to obtain external expertise

Despite these basic problems, interdisciplinarity appears not only as a challenge. It is imperative to obtain external expertise if the aim is good legislation. Yet what constitutes good legislation? When is it better than good? What constitutes optimal legislation? Is the quality of legislation measured by compliance with its constitutional limits? By its comprehensibility? By its effectiveness? By the modalities of its enactment? And if there are several yardsticks that make up good legislation, which is the most relevant?

A. Countless criteria and systematizations

These questions cannot be answered conclusively here, if only because there are countless criteria and almost as many systematizations for quality standards, depending on the horizon of expectations and the specialist discipline. The much-cited *Mandelkern* Report from 2001,[23] for example, names necessity, proportionality, subsidiarity, transparency, accountability, accessibility, and simplicity as "general principles" on the way to better laws. In 2002, *Gunnar Folke Schuppert* was commissioned by the German Federal Ministry of Justice to draw up an expert report on "Good Legislation", which identified further – and different – standards.[24] The same applies to the results of the *Deutsche Juristentag* (Association of German Jurists), which dealt with "Ways

[23] The expert group, chaired by D. Mandelkern, had been convened by the European Ministers of Public Administration to prepare recommendations on the implementation of the Lisbon process.

[24] *G.F. Schuppert*, Gute Gesetzgebung, Zeitschrift für Gesetzgebung Vierteljahresschrift für staatliche und kommunale Rechtsetzung (special issue, 2003).

to Better Legislation" in September 2004.[25] In contrast, a study by *McKinsey*, commissioned by the German *Nationaler Normenkontrollrat* (an independent advisory body to the federal government) in 2019, highlighted only effectiveness, addressee-friendliness, and enforceability as key characteristics of good legislation, in addition to the required constitutional conformity.[26] From a normative perspective, it should be emphasized that – against the background of the large number and the sometimes seemingly arbitrary selection of different criteria – there is no legally binding standard that conclusively and bindingly defines criteria for good legislation. This applies to both the national and the European level.[27]

B. Constitutional requirements and standards of legislative prudence

Of course, there are several binding requirements that can be derived from constitutional law or primary Union law. It is thus possible to divide the manifold criteria according to their degree of bindingness into "hard" constitutional requirements and "soft" standards of legislative prudence.

1. Binding constitutional requirements

"Hard" constitutional requirements are quality requirements that not only have a binding effect but that ultimately decide on the constitutionality of laws. Nevertheless, they are not prerequisites for the validity of laws because all legal acts promulgated in conformity with the constitution are initially valid. They do, however, provide constitutional courts with standards on the basis of which legal norms can be declared invalid. They include (1) requirements relating in particular to the legislative procedure and (2) substantive limits that arise from fundamental rights, which, moreover, are based on the rule of law: The requirement of certainty, the principle of the protection of legitimate expectations, and the principle of proportionality formulate minimum requirements for the quality of laws, even though their enforcement still depends on how the court responsible in each case interprets them.

2. Non-binding standards of legislative wisdom

Beyond these "hard" minimum requirements, there are "soft" criteria flowing from non-binding standards of legislative wisdom. Non-compliance with these ultimately remains without (legal) consequences. Necessity, practicability,

---

[25] See especially, *P. Blum*, Wege zu besserer Gesetzgebung – sachverständige Beratung, Begründung, Folgeabschätzung und Wirkungskontrolle, in: Gutachten I zum 65. Deutschen Juristentag (2004), I 121.

[26] *Nationaler Normenkontrollrat* (ed.), Erst der Inhalt, dann die Paragrafen. Gesetze wirksam und praxistauglich gestalten (2019), 14.

[27] See the comparative comments by *Richli* (n. 2), 92.

acceptance, flexibility, learning ability, coherence, and efficiency are examples of such quality criteria on whose usefulness there is broad agreement, but whose assessment is nevertheless mostly in the eye of the beholder and whose disregard cannot, therefore, be established without further ado. This is particularly true with regard to the standard prescribing that only "just" laws can be good laws.

3. State policy objectives and maxims

Finally, these hard requirements and soft quality standards are interspersed with state policy objectives and maxims that the legislator is obliged to take into account but which regularly leave it such a broad scope for assessment that they are ultimately not legally binding. These requirements include, for example, state objectives relating to environmental protection and animal welfare (Art. 20a of the German Basic Law [*Grundgesetz* – GG]), as well as compliance with the overall economic balance (Art. 109(2) GG), the principle of economic efficiency (Art. 114(2) GG), or, on European level, the various cross-cutting clauses aimed, for example, at a high level of environmental protection (Art. 11 TFEU) or a high level of data protection (Art. 16 TFEU).

C. Requirements in terms of content and in terms of the legislative process

As has already been mentioned, a distinction can be made between requirements in terms of content and in terms of the legislative process. The procedural aspect can certainly be understood in an instrumental sense, as is also known from the administrative procedure. However, it serves more than mere functionality. The corresponding prerequisites create their own added value with regard to a wide range of quality requirements. Examples include the creation of transparency through hearings and the effect of acceptance through deliberative procedures. But is the inclusion of external expertise a prerequisite for good legislation? Good legislation is indeed characterized by the fact that it takes, in addition to the knowledge available internally, external expertise into account. Ideally, external expertise will only confirm internal knowledge, in which case its additional inclusion will do no harm. Yet at times external expertise will present itself as additional and diverging knowledge, in which case the relevant policy decisions may need to be reconsidered. And if internal assumptions and external expertise conflict, it must be transparently disclosed why a certain assumption is being followed.

From a legal and even constitutional perspective, there is much to be said for a principle according to which the legislature has to make use of external expertise. Ultimately, it is the requirements of the constitutional principle of proportionality – in particular the first, often neglected component of suitability – that demand from the legislature a reliable grasp of reality, which can often only be achieved with external expertise. And the constitutional necessity principle, with its prioritization of the mildest means, requires a comprehensive impact assessment, which is nowadays firmly anchored in the legislative process, at least for laws drafted at the national as well as at the European level. Such impact assessment again requires external expertise. Following a proven instrument in environmental law, legislators can be required to obtain the relevant information for legislation using the "best available technique", and such an optimization requirement would be violated if legislators failed to make use of existing external expertise.

The German *Bundesverfassungsgericht* (Federal Constitutional Court) has referred to such obligations of the legislature in various decisions, always placing greater emphasis on the procedural dimension when clear substantive standards were not tangible. The Court assumed a duty to ascertain the facts, which was not limited to general findings but also had to cover complex interrelationships regarding the overall economic situation.[28] In another decision, the Court obliged the legislature to deal with, and compare, the "state of the methodological discussion" of empirical social research and official statistics.[29] In quite general terms, it will be possible to assume that the legislature has a constitutional duty to forecast and observe the effects of legislation. This does not say anything about whether and to what extent the legislature must draw on external knowledge. But in general terms, the constitution certainly contains a prohibition against denying reality, and from this, conversely, follows the imperative to take notice of scientific knowledge.

However, in view of the basic problems regarding the relationship between science and politics in constitutional democracies, the imperative to obtain external expertise should not be understood as a constitutional requirement, the violation of which can result in the nullity of laws or call the constitutional courts into action. Rather, it is a standard of prudence that should be applied in a differentiated manner according to various criteria: the intensity of the intervention, its scope, and above all the revisability of the standards to be enacted. Particularly with regard to revisability, we should be warned against turning the imperative to obtain external expertise into a "hard" constitutional requirement: It is easier to correct a statutory provision than the case law of constitutional courts.

Incidentally, we would like to warn once again against the absolutization of expertise, both internal and external. The plural and liberal society lives from the parallelism of standards and discourse in multiple fields (medical, psychological, scientific, ethical, legal, and political), and it lives from the competition between such discourse. Freedom of opinion and freedom of science are both protected by fundamental rights, but while freedom of opinion has no qualitative minimum requirements, freedom of science imposes qualified

[28] BVerfG, judgment of 1 March 1979, BVerfGE 50, 290, 333.
[29] BVerfG, judgment of 15 December 1983, BVerfGE 65, 1 55.

rationality and thus quality requirements. This is what makes scientific knowledge so credible – at least for the vast majority of people. This credibility presupposes trust, and in this respect, Germany's *Bundespräsident* (Federal President) *Frank-Walter Steinmeier* may be quoted with a statement he made at the opening of a conference on the "Future of Democracy" on 15 November 2021:[30]

> "Wo Politik sich hinter Wissenschaft versteckt, oder umgekehrt, wo Politik sich an die Stelle der Wissenschaft setzt, ich könnte auch umgekehrt sagen, wo Politiker und Wissenschaftler sich gegenseitig benutzen, um Ziele durchzusetzen, da schwächen wir das Vertrauen sowohl in Wissenschaft wie in Demokratie."

> "When politics hides behind science or, alternatively, when politics takes the place of science – and, by further contrast, when politicians and scientists use each other to push through goals – that is when we weaken trust in both science and democracy."

VII. Conclusion

Legislation is an interdisciplinary challenge. The German legislature meets this challenge sometimes better, sometimes worse, but this observation does not in itself call for any immediate response. Rather, the legislative process as defined by the constitution already offers numerous possibilities for meeting interdisciplinary demands placed on legislation. It is pluralistic to a degree that there are sufficient opportunities for interdisciplinary findings to be taken into consideration. Thus, there is no need for introducing any formalized or institutional safeguard, for example in the form of a commission of experts that serves the function of implementing interdisciplinary insights in legislation. On the contrary, the fact that the many means of taking interdisciplinary insights into account are neither formalized nor institutionalized proves to be an advantage from both practical and theoretical perspectives: Any formal or institutional safeguard to integrate interdisciplinary insights into the legislative process could be in conflict with the principles of democracy and democratic legitimacy. Nevertheless, there is an overall need for greater sensitivity to the interdisciplinary challenges in legislation. Appropriately trained actors for the collection, reception, evaluation, processing, and implementation of interdisciplinary insights are needed, especially in the ministries which continue to play a key role in lawmaking. Above all, however, a broad public discussion appears necessary, a discourse that has to go beyond the discussions led by political parties and that is free from any ideological framing. Moreover, irrespective of

[30] *F.-W. Steinmeier*, Opening of the 12th Forum Bellevue "Was kann der Staat? Lektionen aus der Pandemie", 15 November 2021, 7, https://www.bundespraesident.de/SharedDocs/Downloads/DE/Reden/2021/11/211115-Forum-Bellevue-XII.pdf?__blob=publicationFile (last accessed 7 September 2023).

the question of how interdisciplinary insights can be introduced into legislation, time plays a central role in this respect: The legislative process must be decelerated so that it is possible to collect, receive, evaluate, process, and implement the relevant extra-legal knowledge. Finally, it needs to be remembered that legislation in democracies is, and has to be, open to making "wrong" decisions contrary to better knowledge. If such incorrect decisions are made, legislation can nevertheless, with the passage of time, successfully overcome its interdisciplinary challenges, namely by correcting laws. The fact that the legislature in a democracy always has the right to reform the law proves to be the most effective instrument for meeting the interdisciplinary challenges of lawmaking.

Part 2

Law and Theology

The Use of Law and Legal Studies for the Methodological Renewal of Dogmatic Theology

Franciszek Longchamps de Bérier

I. Dogma in law and theology

Law and legal studies have a remarkable amount in common with dogmatic theology. This observation may surprise, even astonish, some (especially lawyers), because the comparison refers to two separate worlds that are different in almost every respect. Yet to a person learned in both fields it should be apparent that they have developed in parallel ways. Theology has been using the word "dogma" in today's meaning since the eighteenth century,[1] and the term "deposit", as it appears in the key expression, "the deposit of faith", for even longer. "Deposit" is, in fact, a strictly legal term. In both form and meaning, it is derived from Roman law and continues to be used within the European legal tradition.[2] The law is aware of its dogmatic structures and, indeed, proud of its dogmatic analyses and interpretations. Therefore, it should not seem strange to consider how law may be able to contribute to dogmatic theology or, at least, whether it can helpfully encourage dogmatic theologians to focus attention on certain issues. Considering the above-mentioned parallelism of these two worlds, it seems legitimate to ask how legal disciplines may be able to support the work of dogmatic theologians, what problems the latter may helpfully be alerted to, i.e. what experience legal scholars may be able to helpfully offer specialists in dogmatic theology. Comparisons and analogies carry a high

---

[1] *K. Rahner/H. Vorgrimler*, Kleines Theologisches Wörterbuch (2nd edn., 1962), 73.

[2] See e.g. *W. Dajczak/T. Giaro/F. Longchamps de Bérier*, Prawo rzymskie. U podstaw prawa prywatnego (3rd edn., 2018), 554.

cognitive and "scientific" potential. Better reciprocal understanding between legal scholars and dogmatic theologians could become the basis for a mutual enrichment, i.e. new opportunities and advances resulting from looking at one's own field with a different kind of research and academic sensibility. These two fields of study do not come into contact very often: all the more, then, we should try – when the occasion arises – to find answers to questions about the message and possible contribution of dogmatic theology for law and legal studies.

Using dogma is typical of both the theological and legal disciplines. A nineteenth-century division, which is so characteristic of legal positivism, strongly distinguishes legal dogmatics from the so-called legal *Grundlagenfächer*, including legal history, legal philosophy, and theory of law. Dogmatics is practised by those legal scholars who deal with the law in force. They analyse its content, drawing conclusions about the content of binding norms from legal provisions. Their domain is the *lex lata*, i.e. "the existing law." This does not prevent them from considering which direction changes of law and statutes in force can or should take, and they, thus, also make propositions *de lege ferenda*, i.e. "under the pretence of what is to be proposed as law."

As regards theology, for a legal historian it is quite obvious that law originates from religion.[3] This was clearly reflected in Jewish, Roman, and Islamic law. The same was the case with law in ancient Greece and in almost all ancient societies, the legal heritage of which, however, did not bring any significant achievement to modern legal studies or legal culture. While, in today's globalising world, Islamic law does not seem to affect the laws of other legal traditions – as, at the most, it displaces them locally when it spreads along with followers of Islam – we see that Christian and Jewish, but above all Roman law forms the basis of modern legal systems and the contemporary way of thinking about the law. These legal traditions led to the creation of the European legal tradition that influenced the legal systems even of common law countries (of which England was the first). Of course, the European legal tradition is most clearly visible and strongly present in jurisdictions called – from the perspective of the common law – "continental" or simply "civil" law.

The real world of law is not divided in accordance with the structure of university law schools, which still today – at least in the civil law world – often reflect the tripartition into legal dogmatics, legal history, and legal philosophy. In both common law and civil law countries, a lawyer's work boils down to one thing, that is, *interpreting* the law. And this is, perhaps, the strongest basis for the parallelism that arouses our academic curiosity as to how enlightening the experiences of the legal world could be for dogmatic theology: *interpretatio*

[3] *P. Noailles*, Du Droit sacré au Droit civil. Cours de Droit Romain Approfondi 1941–1942 (1949), 16–20; *W. Uruszczak*, Historii państwa i prawa polskiego 966–1795 (4th edn., 2021), 92 f.

iuris and the interpretation of a dogma, which is also the everyday work of the theologian.

II. Dogma, law, and interpretation

The object is sometimes confused with, or even mistaken for, the subject. This is something that legal studies and dogmatic theology have in common. Lawyers discuss interpretation, providing a grounded reply to a question which law regulates with respect to an actual social situation. Experience proves that while maintaining even the highest restraint against being creative (i.e. so as not to convey one's own conclusions, solutions, or convictions to others while claiming or implying that this is what the applicable law actually states), the interpreting lawyer nevertheless gives a *specific* shape to what results from the general norms established for a particular situation. Sometimes the lawyer draws conclusions or poses theses that, after being transferred to academic research in law, can in turn influence the doctrine of the law or inspire changes in the law. If these changes match the direction desired by the lawgiver, a practising lawyer, or sometimes a law professor, or, more usually, a professional governmental legislator, can then transform the established arrangements into bills. More promptly, those arrangements can affect court rulings which have to embrace the whole legal argumentation, i.e. constantly interpret the law. As regards continental Europe,[4] the decisions of courts are not formally considered a source of law (it is quite different in common law), but it is rather case law along with all the interpretation encapsulated in courts' opinions that becomes the most important material for legal dogmatics and the object of legal studies. Many lawyers start their research by consulting the decisions of courts, i.e. by analysing the courts' reasoning, and at the same time searching for the regulations which are adequate to the particular problem the lawyer faces. Does not a dogmatic theologian similarly carry out interpretations that may later be introduced, as explanations, into the dogmatic tradition or inspire new formulations of dogma?

Obviously, in both cases, that of the lawyer and that of the theologian, at some point a subject has to step in, one who must authoritatively determine that a given interpretation is to be adopted as proper, decisive, or valid. In the world of law, such decisions, if in the hands of a single person, are taken by the sovereign. This is rarely the case today, so most often a collective sovereign expresses its opinion in a referendum or through representatives in the parliament. Supreme courts or constitutional tribunals are authorized to take final decisions. Thus, a lawyer does not herself take decisions! It is important that

---

[4] On the prohibition of law-making by interpretation, *L. Morawski*, Zasady wykładni prawa (2nd edn., 2010), 21 f.

she remembers that. She is but to interpret the law and suggest solutions. She is to serve others. In this, we must go back to what the law's role is. Though the aforementioned courts, which constitute the highest body in any given state or jurisdiction, are normally filled by lawyers, this is not necessarily a rule. It is not necessary for judges to be trained lawyers. Judges need only be reasonable people of sound mind and common life experience. Neither is the presence of lawyers in parliaments a rule, although it might be thought desirable for lawyers to be well-represented there for the efficiency and smoothness of the legislative process. Lawyers' participation in matters is similar to that of theologians. Referendums, statutes, and court rulings are binding for lawyers, just as papal or conciliar decrees and official pronouncements of the ordinary *magisterium* are for theologians. Courts have the last word, deciding upon the final interpretation that ends a given process. The legal situation appears, then, to be clear, at least momentarily. Will it remain so? What will it be in a year or in the next generation? The experience of legal history makes us very cautious about giving any positive reply to such a speculation.

An organised analysis of the *lex lata*, which is (as distinguished from legal philosophy and legal history) the domain of legal dogmatics, comes up against basic doubts about how to define it as a discipline within the arts or sciences. This is because, for their part, the history and philosophy of law have their own clear objects of study, as well as their own established methods, whereas, in legal dogmatics, the following, quite typical questions are being asked with the utmost anxiety:

> "What is legal science? What is its subject matter and its purpose? What are the ways in which to conduct academic research in law? How can one evaluate the results of this research? What is the value of the notions used in legal life (notions that are being studied), the notions used by legal disciplines (research notions), and how do they relate to each other? And, finally, what is law?"[5]

Roman law – the pillar of modern civilisation standing next to Christianity and Greek philosophy – left us only one actual definition of law.[6] We know it from the Digest, i.e. a collection of fragments of the works of ancient lawyers compiled in AD 533 by a commission appointed by the Byzantine Emperor *Justinian*. At the very beginning of the collection is a fragment of a handbook by the third century jurist *Ulpian*, who quotes the definition of law by the jurist *Celsus*: "ius est ars boni et aequi"[7] ("law is the art of what is good and just"). *Ulpian* believed that this definition was both original and well-expressed, and he refers to *Celsus* as *eleganter* to emphasize *Celsus*' subtle creativity and

---

[5] *F. Longchamps*, Z problemów poznania prawa (1968), 7 (author's translation).

[6] *H. Kupiszewski*, Prawo rzymskie a współczesność (2nd edn., 2013), 31.

[7] *Ulpian* D. 1.1.1: "ut eleganter Celsus definit, ius est ars boni et aequi".

innovativeness[8] (*Celsus* was much older than *Ulpian*, having written in the first half of the second century). *Celsus*' definition is, indeed, perfectly succinct. Each word is there to make us think, and each word forces us to interpret the entire definition. Most intriguing is the accuracy of the word *ars*. Translation into Greek – "techne" – would only seem to flatten the perspective, because we expect mastery rather than mere craft from good lawyers, and we would certainly all prefer to avail ourselves of the services of masters. Furthermore, the quotation from *Celsus*

> "invariably reminds us what determines the specific features of law. Law is *ars*, the art of arranging relations and finding solutions. Thus, in practice, it is not static legal or code regulations that count the most, but the efficient use of legal skills. Those skills, apart from the pure specific nature of law as art, have to take into account certain anthropological constants, many of which found verbal expression in Latin legal maxims. These constants are apparently the *causae* of the acceptability of particular norms and their consequences for man. This is because anthropological constants subjectively reflect the way people perceive themselves and the external world."[9]

The word *ars* indicates the nature of legal studies and facilitates its classification as a discipline, e.g. together with medicine, which is *ars par excellence*. First of all, however, *Celsus*' use of the word *ars* reminds us that law is a tool. And only a tool. It serves the objectives the determination of which is the domain of what we call legal policy. Law, then, is an instrument for the fulfilment of values. The Roman jurist *Celsus* expressed this idea in the above-mentioned words *bonum* and *aequum*. Law expresses values and makes it possible to discover them in man, in his traditions, and in his culture. This is why the above-mentioned remark on anthropological constants was made. It is because we can justly expect from legal studies that they shall analyse these constants. Law is not to create values. The idea of presenting it with such a task should be considered unrealistic or even dangerous. And if we reject *Nietzsche*'s thought and language, which insist on the multitude or variety of values, then we should expect that law would support and develop (i.e. multiply) *good*, as well as justice, equity, rightfulness, fairness. *Bonum et aequum*! *Celsus* defined law using the verb *est*: "is"; in legal language, this is a typical way of expressing *duty*. Thus, we can translate *Celsus*' definition as: "law is to be the art of what is good and just." A separate issue, of course, is just how "good" and "justice" are to be understood in a particular given place and time.

---

[8] *A. Carcaterra*, Concezioni epistemiche dei giuristi romani, Studia et Documenta Historiae et Iuris 54 (1988), 37–65, 60–63.

[9] *F. Longchamps de Bérier*, Common law a dekodyfikacja i globalizacja prawa, in: idem (ed.), Dekodyfikacja prawa prywatnego w europejskiej tradycji prawnej (2019), 19–51, 29 (author's translation).

III. Dogma, law, and classifications

A lawyer must be humble with regard to the matter on which she works and while using the tools necessary to practise her craft or art. Her task is to serve for the multiplication of good. And a dogmatic theologian needs to be even humbler, as his "systematic and methodical discovering of the reality of God's Revelation learnt through faith"[10] refers to Good with a capital "G". Moreover, scientific, i.e. organized, inquiry deals with the reflection of that reality "in the life of the society of the Church."[11] Neither a lawyer nor a theologian should mistake the object for the subject. In the case of the practice of dogmatic theology, this obligation is expressed, first of all, in a constant care to distinguish mere theological hypotheses and studies from the established teaching of faith, and not to present one's own theses or research results as the opinion of the Church itself before they officially, i.e. legally, become such an opinion.

In answer to the call to adhere firmly to the study-teaching distinction, and taking a broader perspective, one might propose a more general postulate: dogmatic theology requires one to fully develop the ability to make distinctions and follow them in a consistent and logical manner. As regards the lawyer, his job, to a large extent, boils down to classifying and suggesting distinctions. Theologians have been well aware of the need for distinctions for a long time, as they have been using the description of the relationship between essence and person that was provided by the ancient lawyer *Tertullian* in the debate on the Holy Trinity.[12] In any event, the best, i.e. victorious, "turns of events" in legal argumentation usually result from distinctions that are skilfully, intelligently, and unexpectedly implemented into a given discourse or analysis.

In considerations of the issue as to what extent law remains an ordinary tool, and whether the nature of law results in norms and typical regulatory phenomena, what is often indicated in the first place is the *autonomy* of law. Sometimes one might like to present such autonomy historically as law breaking away from religion, and later also from morality, and in the present day at least, as an independence from politics. Morality, politics, and law are different levels of evaluation or analysis, and even of discovering or establishing duty. In the reality which is regulated, i.e. put continuously in order, by law, these levels are not independent of one another. What is more, in the pragmatics of social life the mutual influences of these levels must be taken for granted. Thus, it is impossible to make these different levels abstract from one another, as a legal

---

[10] *W. Beinert*, Teologiczna teoria poznania (trans. J. Fenrychowa, 1998), 279 (author's translation).

[11] *Beinert* (n. 10), 279.

[12] Cf. e.g. *R. Zyzik*, Pojęcie osoby – jedno czy wiele?, Racjonalia. Z punktu widzenia humanistyki 2 (2012), 5–31, 10–12; *B. Huculak*, Początek i zarys dogmatu o Trójcy, Roczniki Teologiczne 63 (2016), 187–216, 206–209.

measure distinguishing them is aimed at describing and understanding their mutual influences only in order to subsequently show the relationships, first of all, between law and morality in the modern world. In contrast, legal positivism[13] attempted to deny those relationships, as it claimed that only or mainly the will of the legislator would count.

The postulate or thesis of the autonomy of law is no less a legal trick than that of distinguishing the levels of separating morality, politics, and law.[14] It is worth adopting this thesis on a working basis, but we should remember that the autonomy of law is not and never shall be complete. All that is needed is a *relative* autonomy of law, and such autonomy has already been expressed in treating law as a tool in the service of good, not as something used for itself or for the pure beauty of legal thought structures. Anyway, thinking about the autonomy of law is the result of the distinction made in canon law through specifying the difference between the external forum and the internal forum.[15] As a consequence, we treat the same situation in a completely different manner when it is described to the confessor as a sin and when the ecclesiastical court determines whether it is a crime or not. The actual dualism between canon law and civil law contributed to the adoption of the concept of the autonomous nature of the rules of law as compared to any other normative system governing a given society.[16] Such a dualism was clearly obvious in teaching, studies, doctrine, and practice from the time when universities were established up to the eighteenth century, i.e. in the era in which only those two areas were actually taught at all the law faculties of the world.

IV. Dogma, law, and the meaning of words

Today, dogmas have negative associations. Dogmatic theologians are particularly aware of this.[17] The picture is different with regard to legal studies, where, at least in civil law jurisdictions, the word "dogmatic" is perceived and treated in a completely neutral manner. First year law students, indeed, sometimes instinctively smile at the legal jargon they hear from a specialist such as a law professor, but after hearing the proper explanation of "dogmatic" in the legal

---

[13] Cf. *J. Finnis*, The Truth in Legal Positivism, in: R.P. George (ed.), The Autonomy of Law: Essays on Legal Positivism (1999), 195–214, 203–205.

[14] *G. Postema*, Law's Autonomy and Public Practical Reason, in: George (n. 13), 79–118, 80–88.

[15] *P. Erdö*, Foro interno e foro esterno nel diritto canonico, in: A. Skorupa (ed.), Forum externum i forum internum w prawie kanonicznym. Między prawem a sumieniem (2006), 37–60, 38 f.

[16] *M. Safjan*, Prawo, wartości i demokracja, Chrześcijaństwo, świat, polityka. Zeszyty społecznej myśli Kościoła 5/1 (2008), 5–23, 5.

[17] *J. Majewski*, Wprowadzenie do teologii dogmatycznej (2005), 16.

context, they start to use the same expressions themselves in a technical and dispassionate manner, proceeding to the pertinent agenda by means of the professionally used wording. After being introduced to what "dogmas" or the "dogmatics" mean in the legal context, first year law students seem to exhibit no peculiar reaction at all, as, from the beginning, they are aware of the technical nature of the expression. And, despite the acceptance of the tripartite distinction of law into dogmatics, philosophy, and history, every lawyer knows very well that law, by nature, is dogmatic and works with dogmas. Lawyers help to ensure the law's stability or even constancy. They serve the socially required permanence of law which, basically, promotes the postulate of the certainty of law (which was appreciated not only in the nineteenth century).[18]

Law is full of dogmas, i.e. statements of an obligatory nature, which express the truth of what law is in force or which solution is good, and which regulation should be adopted as just within the art of settling social relations in a particular situation that requires regulation. At various levels, law includes numerous inviolable basic theses on which argumentations are based. These are dogmatic argumentations. As a side note, it is worth noting that some techniques in law may make us think that constructions based on them are autonomous. Sometimes, the dogmatics of law is treated in a completely ahistorical manner, and, during reforms of higher education, a view can emerge that only such dogmatics should be the subject of legal studies. Thus, the history, philosophy, and especially theory of law are judged to play a purely ancillary role, as little more than didactic additions. Researchers and academic staff who limit their focus to legal dogmatics often behave as if they are the ones who hold all the cards in the legal world, although, in fact, in legal studies they do not necessarily lead the way. However, leaving aside the disputes of law professors on the curricula of legal studies, it is now time to postulate that – since dogmatic analyses are treated with such pride in law – theologians should also rid themselves of any complexes related to the word "dogma" and its usage.

V. Dogma and the methods of legal interpretation

Both theologians and lawyers know that the use of dogmas is the basic issue with regard to their discipline's methodology. In addition, many lawyers search for other methods that make it possible to describe and evaluate stability and changes in law. As regards modern civil law jurisdictions it is, unfortunately, not everyone who perceives (immediately, at least) the need to reach beyond dogmatics in order to interpret the law from the perspective of legal history. In

[18] Cf. two opinions: *J. Stelmach*, Czy interpretacja prawnicza może być gwarantem pewności prawa?, Forum Prawnicze 6 (2011), 17–22; *B. Brożek*, Pewność prawa jako stabilność strukturalna, Forum Prawnicze 6 (2011), 23–29.

common law countries, by contrast, the need for the historical perspective is obvious and accepted as being on the agenda, although (especially in case law jurisdictions) presenting historical development serves mainly argumentative purposes and the setting of precedents. This search for historical perspectives and the setting of precedents should serve, however, not to enable lawyers and judges to create the law, i.e. not to let them become lawgivers, but just to keep them within the realm of their own proper craft: to find and interpret the law in force.[19] Legal tradition consists of the precious deposit of law, i.e. useful regulations of historically-proven effectiveness that have the potential of being socially approved. Such approval leads to the internalization of norms by users of law. In consequence, it turns out that the deposit of legal experience passed on in legal tradition, and not the sheer will of the legislator, is what determines what is binding and why it is binding. It is true that Anglo-American legal systems have long been struggling with the unsolved (perhaps unsolvable) dispute on the role of a judge. This problem, which refers to the interpretation and application of law, has become universal within the last decades as European judges have become jealous about the power of common law judges.[20] The simplest approach to this issue is that of counteracting the judges' activism (law-making from the bench) by insisting on the requirement of judicial restraint. The fine line of using both attitudes and keeping a balance between them is in order to ensure that judges determine what the law *is* and not what it *should be*.

As experts in the history of dogma, theologians are aware of its development. It might be useful for them to be also aware that the methodology of legal studies, for pragmatic reasons, tells us to reach beyond dogmatics towards historical and comparative arguments:

> "This is because legal history should give to modern lawyers history as a practical tool. This is why we extend the area of legal experience by skilful combination of arguments typical not only of dogmatics, but also of comparative studies, according to various analyses. It is worth practising law in a historical manner because, in gaining such experience, we should not be limited to synchronic juxtapositions, i.e. to collations that disregard the differences of the ages. The synchronic juxtapositions serve only the dogmatic demonstration of comparison. The diachronic approach, on the other hand, is adequate to the practical history of law, as it shows the changes of structure and constructions in various jurisdictions at different stages of development and history."[21]

Researchers and academics who are concerned almost exclusively with legal dogmatics may start to unexpectedly move towards legal-comparative analyses when the development of law, to their surprise, tells them to go in a direction

---

[19] Cf. *H.L.A. Hart*, American Jurisprudence through English Eyes: The Nightmare and the Noble Dream, in: idem, Essays in Jurisprudence and Philosophy (1983), 123–144, 126.

[20] *A. Scalia*, Mullahs of the West: Judges as Moral Arbiters (2009).

[21] *F. Longchamps de Bérier*, Stałość a zmienność szczegółowych regulacji prawa spadkowego Niepodległej, Forum Prawnicze 2 (2018), 3–24, 4 (author's translation).

different from what they had expected on the basis of the applicable regulations, i.e. the law in force. In such cases, the easiest thing is for them to use synchronic comparative studies, i.e. studies that disregard the differences of the ages but juxtapose and analyse dogmatic solutions from different contexts of the present time. Usually, this only requires a glance at norms in other jurisdictions, and thus the law of various states. This can indeed be useful and instructive, but diachronic comparative studies are much more effective. These perceive things in a manner parallel to that of synchronic juxtapositions, but they also note the history of changes and directions of development, and are able, as a result of this, to juxtapose the regulations of various epochs. Thus, from a scientific point of view, it is more complex

> "to show changes in regulations and the resulting experience simultaneously in various jurisdictions and at different stages of their history. Similar tasks seem to be even more time-consuming in diachronic than in synchronic analyses and require a higher level of versatility."[22]

However, the implementation of the various methods together gives results that are useful for scholars with vision who are not afraid of diachronic comparisons.

We might think, for example, about the liturgical and legal consequences of the loss of the unity of the Church for systemic thinking about Revelation, comparing the situation under unity with the subsequent diversity of theological traditions. What happens if marriage loses the status of a sacrament and has to submit to state regulations whose tone conflicts with even the broadest interpretation of the Bible? We might mention the changes in the ecclesiology of the Church of England, and, for example, "annihilation" as a theological idea. We might consider whether the celibacy of priests and bishops is just a matter of discipline and what its ecclesial consequences are. How does it locate the relations between priesthood and monastic life? What should people think about the postulate for the deaconate of women? These are just observations noted casually by "a man on the outside" who dares to suggest that dogmatic theology should use dogmatic, historical, and comparative arguments all together, i.e. in both a synchronic and a diachronic way, despite the fear of coming across difficulties similar to those occurring in legal studies and despite the very high substantive and methodological requirements of such an approach.

[22] *F. Longchamps de Bérier*, Z uwag do metodologii nauki prawa prywatnego: argumenty historyczny, dogmatyczny i prawnoporównawczy na przykładzie darowizny na wypadek śmierci oraz zapisu windykacyjnego, in: A. Wudarski (ed.), Polska komparatystyka prawa. Prawo obce w doktrynie prawa polskiego (2016), 285–329, 322 (author's translation).

VI. Legal experience and meditation upon the Word

Interpretation is the lawyer's task and craft. Theology is not law, although it has sometimes attempted "pretend law", e.g. moral theology before the Second Vatican Council which was focused on case studies.[23] Liturgics cannot boil down to rubrics, as this is the lowest level of norms, rightly compared to stage directions. Among theologians, it is the liturgists who mainly need preparation and experience similar to that of lawyers, so that they can provide mature instructions and teachings, faithful to the whole system, which for its part is adequate to a given rite in the history of the church's prayer tradition. This is a huge responsibility, as the content and form of praying expresses the faith of God's people: *lex orandi – lex credendi*.[24] There are, unfortunately, numerous negative examples of incompetence or immaturity in the interpretations suggested by liturgists. It should be noted that this often results from the lack of proper legal skills and experience. Dogmatic theologians also sometimes face the question of methods of interpreting texts that actually regulate reality, as is the case with numerous decrees of councils or synods. Also, it is important for theology to consider individual decisions or sentences of Church bodies or courts. Thus, dogmatic theologians need to be able to respond to formulations that are expressed in legal language or that include norms and sanctions expressed in a way typical of legal regulations.[25] While the rubrics of liturgists are the lowest level and the most detailed form of regulation, it is necessary for dogmatic theologians to confront "great words" – such as the strongly penal *anathema sit*, which has often been used in the history of the Church.

Interpreting norms and regulations is, however, not just a matter of technique. A legal provision as a linguistic formulation or, more frequently, a whole series of such provisions are the basis for interpreting the disposition of a norm being a directive for the proper proceedings in a situation which the norm specified in its hypothesis. Any norm consists of a hypothesis that describes a situation in which a disposition provides the proper way of behaviour. Noncompliance with the disposition may be punished, as a legislator may attach in a norm the sanction that facilitates the fulfilment of the disposition. The sanction would be the third part of the norm. However, the existence of a

[23] *F. Greniuk*, Katolicka teologia moralna w poszukiwaniu własnej tożsamości (1993), 172.

[24] *A. Żądło*, Lex orandi – lex credendi w modlitwach nad darami Adwentu w Mszale Pawła VI. Studium hermeneutyczno-liturgiczne (2013), 19–65.

[25] *L. Jones Hall*, Roman Berytus. Beirut in Late Antiquity (2004), 201: "Religion found a voice which was legalistic. In other words, legal training gave religious leaders the tools of a lawyer – the framing of an indictment, the presentation of evidence, the plea for mercy or conviction, the stipulation of punishment. Such tools were used relentlessly and lawyer-like in the anathemas and counter-anathemas of the church controversies. Even reading the council minutes is reminiscent of reading the proceedings of a court case."

sanction does not seem necessary, as was already confirmed by Roman law.[26] Most of the statutes of Roman law had the nature of *leges imperfectae*, i.e. not only without the sanction of invalidity like *leges perfectae*, but even without predicting any consequences for non-observance of law, like *leges minus quam perfectae*.[27] If law is to order social situations, then the people who are aware of the need or necessity for such ordering should be satisfied with the directive of a proceeding – a guideline on how they should behave. In order to comply with that norm, they do not need any other motivation apart from the rational one. In the case of any inconvenience, they should recite: *dura lex sed lex* ("the law is harsh, but it is the law"),[28] since the observance of valid law constitutes a social value in itself. This is visible in the very nature of law, which is created to save people from chaos. However, this should only be done after carrying out the interpretation which reveals the content of the norm, i.e. specifies its hypothesis and disposition. Such interpretation makes it possible to determine which law applies. At this point, many people would probably like to quote the statement: *clara non sunt intepretanda* or, in other words, *interpretatio cessat in claris*.[29] It sounds reasonable that what is clear does not have to be interpreted. And the truth expressed in the language of the ancient Romans seems to explain the whole issue: interpretation is needed only when we are dealing with obscurity. First of all, however, we should note that the statement that an issue belongs to the category of *clara*, i.e. is clear and understandable, is already the result of an interpretation.[30] Thus, another statement is often used to oppose the above quotation. The statement is also formulated in Latin, but its contents are closer to the views of ancient Romans:[31] *omnia sunt intepretanda* ("everything is subject to interpretation").[32] Secondly, in a conflict situation,

[26] *Dajczak/Giaro/Longchamps de Bérier* (n. 2), 143 f.

[27] Cf. e.g. *T. Stawecki/P. Winczorek*, Wstęp do prawoznawstwa (4th edn., 2003), 86–90.

[28] Cf. *Ulpian* D. 40.9.12.1; *D. Liebs*, Lateinische Rechtsregeln und Rechtssprichwörter (6th edn., 1998), 69; *R. Domingo/J. Ortega/B. Rodríguez-Antolín*, Principios de derecho global. Aforismos jurídicos comentados (2003), 84 f.

[29] *S. Masuelli*, "In claris non sit interpretation". Alle origini del brocardo, Rivista di Diritto Romano 2 (2002), 401–424; *C. Drand*, Le caractère législatif de l'adage Interpretatio cessat in claris en droit français des contrats, Scientia Juris 2 (2013), 1–23/Revue générale du droit on line (2013): www.revuegeneraledudroit.eu/?p=7496 (accessed 27 November 2023).

[30] Cf. e.g. *P. Kroczek*, Zasada "clara non sunt interpretanda" w prawie kanonicznym (2nd edn., 2005).

[31] *W. Rozwadowski*, Etiam clarum ius exigit interpretationem, in: A. Choduń/S. Czepita (eds.), W poszukiwaniu dobra wspólnego. Księga jubileuszowa Profesora Macieja Zielińskiego (2010), 37–48, 46.

[32] *J. Leszczyński*, O pewnych aporiach normatywnej teorii wykładni prawa, Principia 61–62 (2015), 43–46; *A. Grabowski*, Clara non sunt interpretanda vs. omnia sunt interpretanda. A Never-Ending Controversy in Polish Legal Theory?, Revus. Journal for Constitutional Theory and Philosophy of Law 27 (2015), 67–97.

different opinions and ways of understanding may arise, consequently, what had at first seemed to be clear may not be clear anymore. And what I mean is not just perversity in interpretation aimed at the pursuit of personal interests, but the diversity resulting from different kinds of sensibility, habits, or ways of thinking. Dogmatic theology has the universal perspective of the whole Church, while law usually has a local perspective: it works and is interpreted within a given country or, even more locally, in one of the jurisdictions existing within the country. Moreover, we must remember that law is art, which is why its interpretation has to deal with the divergence of interpretative opportunities. However, it is incumbent upon law to find solutions, so, rather than asking questions, it always has to provide answers. And each reply must refer to a particular case, i.e. to a given social situation. Extending this reply to other, analogous replies is possible, but not essential. Sometimes a solution can be extended, and sometimes it has to be left on its own as a single case. The complexity of this issue can be illustrated with an example from common law, in which court decisions are openly treated as precedents and a source of law. Here, we see the clash of two approaches, expressed in two contradictory statements: *hard cases make bad law*[33] and *hard cases make good law*.[34] According to the latter, the adequacy of regulation is verified in difficult cases. Both rationality and consistency are, then, desirable, and we should keep following the law that makes it possible for us to solve even the most unusual of cases. According to the *hard cases make bad law* view, law is created for the normal course of human affairs and not for rare and absolutely unique situations, although the latter might constitute a legally interesting challenge. And it should be appreciated that, if law is indeed able to solve an untypical or borderline case, which raises numerous doubts or disputes, this does not therefore mean that a single result should be extended to other situations and treated as a precedent, i.e. as a breach in the current understanding of a given regulation or as a model for new rulings.

In society it is always possible to come across legal conflicts based on interpretation. A method that is commonly adopted is to start with linguistic interpretation and then to support this with logical interpretation. After all, legal conclusions should be based on the principles of logic. If these fail to give an unambiguous result, we can proceed to combine these with systemic or functional interpretations.[35] A functional interpretation would appear to include a teleological interpretation; this is because it analyses not only the objective to be fulfilled by the regulation but also its function in general. The systemic

[33] *Northern Securities Co. v. United States*, 24 S.Ct. 436, 468 (1904) (Holmes, J., dissenting): Great cases, like hard cases, make bad law. Cf. recently *L.H. Bloom*, Do Great Cases Make Bad Law? (2014).

[34] *A. Corbin*, Hard Cases Make Good Law, Yale Law Journal 33 (1923–1924), 78–82.

[35] For more, cf. *Morawski* (n. 4), 97–174.

interpretation, for its part, places the regulation within the context of the entire legal system in which and with which the provision applies.

The previously mentioned historical and comparative arguments do not allow us to be satisfied with the existing doctrine related to the method of interpretation. This method stems from the Enlightenment, which replaced tradition with reason. Up until that time, interpretation had begun with the question of how a given provision or regulation should be understood. Standard methods of interpretation had been set up by the Roman jurist *Paul* of the third century:

"[S]i de interpretatione legis quaeratur, in primis inspiciendum est, quo iure civitas retro in eiusmodi casibus usa fuisset: optima enim est legum interpres consuetudo."

"[I]f a question should arise about the interpretation of a statute, what ought to be looked into first is the law that the civitas had previously applied in cases of the same kind; for custom is the best interpreter of statutes."[36]

The idea can be explained as follows:

"Directives for the interpretation of a legal text in the Middle Ages referred to the experience of Roman law, from the legendary Laws of the Kings (*leges regiae*) and the Laws of the Twelve Tables from the mid-fifth century BC, up to Justinian's compilation from the sixth century AD. Lawyers first had to consider the customary understanding of a regulation, and, if that was fruitless, they were instructed to reach for *communis opinio doctorum*. The lawyers were searching for a convincing interpretation among the experts in a given field, hoping that there was some intellectual agreement of opinion among them. It was particularly important that scholars of different ages should think the same. It was only when consent was missing that lawyers studied a text for the purpose of carrying out a linguistic, functional, or systemic (as we would call it today) interpretation. These types of interpretation are always present in the dogmatic argument."[37]

Meditation upon the Word is the theologian's task and craft. Just as a lawyer must be constantly aware that he should begin with a text understood within the context of the tradition in which it is rooted, so a theologian must deal with exegesis and learn hermeneutics. The interpretation of the Bible is the basis for the theologian's ruminations because the results of dogmatic theology's investigations have to be made consonant with such interpretation. However, biblical interpretation is not the only basis of the theologian's work. He sees this as just one of the sources carried by the Tradition. From the point of view of a lawyer, however, the Tradition of the Church would be seen as a combination of norm and interpretation, where text is mixed with commentary. That is a reason for a lawyer to encourage a theologian to become acquainted with legal instruments and make use of them. Interpretative tools are used in law in an entirely natural manner, almost without being analysed; they are, after all, very familiar to lawyers and, indeed, used on a daily basis. Without such tools, a

[36] *Paulus* D. 1.3.37 (trans. D.N. MacCormick, in: A. Watson [ed.], The Digest of Justinian, vol. 1 [2nd ed., 1998]).

[37] *Longchamps de Bérier* (n. 22), 289 (author's translation).

lawyer would simply have no lawyerly equipment to use, and so, fundamentally, there would be no such thing as a "lawyer". There is no reason for a dogmatic theologian to be wary of those tools or sceptical of their specific features: they have already proven their use in legal exegesis. It would be profitable for a theologian to learn to use these tools himself, or at least to venture to discuss the results of his research with a lawyer. He should not do this in order to take over the juristic point of view or the legal sensibility or mentality, but as a verification of his own viewpoint. Law and learning about law can offer a mirror for dogmatic theology in which to see itself – for instance when research projects are undertaken, such as this very project on the methodological renewal of dogmatic theology. But it is not only on special occasions that this should occur. If we look at the methodologies of the arts and sciences, then it would appear that the heritage of legal studies is linked with theology in terms of basic questions concerning credibility and the scientific quality of the basis of research. Law is art, and it is also possible for dogmatic theology to develop as the art of interpretation. It would be worthwhile for theologians to trace the history of the critique of law, as it could have much to say as regards the critique of dogmatic theology. Neither a lawyer, nor a theologian makes decisions, although everyone expects them both to be able to give a clear reply to questions that arise in the practice of everyday life. While maintaining necessary restraint, they have to be able to formulate conclusions and postulates in a way that is convincing and reliably explained.

VII. Dogma and new challenges

As always in the history of the Catholic Church, new insights concerning Catholic dogmatics are being shaped right in front of our eyes. These insights appear as, fundamentally, dogmatic theses which are a response to particular ideas, questions, or utterances; even the *magisterium* of the Church takes part in formulating them. Of course, they should always be subject to historical and comparative reflection, but it seems a reasonable surmise that it would be worth submitting them to the evaluation of legal dogmatic analysis. As a beginning, we can have a look at the following four examples.

The first example concerns the question of the *actual faith* of a man and a woman when they contract marriage. The theological definition of marriage is given in the Code of Canon Law of 1983, where can. 1055 § 1 states that the marriage covenant "has, between the baptised, been raised by Christ the Lord to the dignity of a sacrament." Thus, the sacramental effect results from the situation itself of getting married and does not depend on the faith of the individuals who choose to do so. In the modern world, it is clear that many people fail to perceive that marriage should be a partnership for the whole of life, one which of its very nature is ordered to the well-being of the spouses and to the procreation and upbringing of children. Disturbances in the expression of individual will, including a large number of cases of immaturity of men and women when declaring their matrimonial consent, are nowadays subject to assessment by Church courts on a massive scale. It is no wonder, therefore, that pastoral concern encourages us to ask whether the marriage contracted by one who no longer believes, or perhaps has never believed, is actually a sacrament due only to the fact that he or she was baptised. If a person does not believe, how can he or she receive sacramental grace? Does such a person receive grace without having faith? How does this contribute to the good of the spouses or to the community of the Church as the people of God? The questions sound telling because they include a rhetorical *reductio ad absurdum*. "The point is that the condition for the meaningfulness of using the argument of coherence is having a consistent system of reference."[38] Canon law must remain such a system. As regards the legal viewpoint, a lawyer would encourage us to give up absolutely any idea of connecting the validity of the sacrament of marriage to the faith of the baptised who contract marriage. This is due to the fact that it is impossible to deal with the possible consequences of having to assess the faith, or rather the degree of lack of faith, of the individual man or woman. The criterion of the lack of faith is unclear and the degree of faith or the lack of it is absolutely immeasurable by a law that would not only have to assign the results as regards the declaration of will made by the marrying parties in the proper form and without impediments,[39] but also make the results depend on the subjective disposition of faith that, in the case of each contracting party, has a different intensity and quality. Just how can this be put into the language of dogmatics and then examined in the courts? From the legal point of view, the task seems to be completely impossible to perform.

Our second example is the postulate of an *ecological* sin. In the era of globalization, people perceive that particular decisions influence the state of the natural environment in the broader context. We live in this environment, and we try to analyse the influence – and seriously think about the consequences – of human behaviour and choices on a larger scale. If the warning against ecological sin[40] is not just a pastoral action but also, by holding up the possibility of committing actual sin in this regard, a means to powerfully draw the attention of the faithful to their own attitude towards the act of creation, and thus to the gifts received from God by the people living in a particular place and by all the people who inhabit the blue planet, then, together with the lawyers, we

[38] *G. Strzelczyk*, Niespójności katolickiej doktryny o sakramencie małżeństwa, Studia Teologii Dogmatycznej 2 (2016), 106–119, 118 (author's translation).

[39] Cf. *A. Bartczak*, Przygotowanie do zawarcia małżeństwa w świetle przemówienia Benedykta XVI do Roty Rzymskiej z 2011 r., Łódzkie Studia Teologiczne 20 (2011), 25–31, 26.

[40] *J. Babiński*, "Kwestia ekologiczna" w nauczaniu Jana Pawła II, Studia Gdańskie 30 (2012), 249–264, 252–255.

should analyse the actual normativity of the guidelines of the moral teaching on ecological sin. Who should be blamed and what for? How serious is that guilt? While replying to such questions from the faithful, we have to explain how responsibility is assigned as well as the moral and legal sanctions on the internal forum, and possibly the external forum, of the canon law. An adequate precision of teaching that seeks to formulate specific norms of behaviour in this area would appear to be no easy feat from a legal point of view.

The third example relates to the theses of *social* sin (if these turn out to be anything more than rhetoric). In this case, a lawyer is able to ask a very specific

> "question regarding the credibility and integrity of the proposals made in the public sphere, as well as the actions that are actually carried out there by the people performing functions in governmental bodies, with the cultural patterns and values promoted by them."[41]

Such questioning might coordinate analyses from the two fields, which is possible due to the plain parallelism between theology and law with regard to dogmatic thinking about man's actions. Law, in considering the evaluation of the act of a person which contravenes that person's duty in relation to the common good, can derive from or be inspired by theology. The reply to the lawyer's question falls within the field of the Church's social teaching. However, the issue raised by the lawyer's question concerns the dogmatic structure of the relationship between professed and proclaimed faith vis-à-vis responsibility for the practice of social life. It is obvious that every sin has social consequences. In distinguishing social sin as a special category, the lawgiver draws our attention to the harm we may do by directly threatening another person through certain behaviour. Due to the precision in the listing of such behaviour, which can be found in the exhortation by *John Paul II* "Reconciliatio et paenitentia",[42]

---

[41] *M. Zubik*, O "grzechach społecznych" przeciwko ustawie zasadniczej, Państwo i Prawo 1 (2018), 3–23, 4 (author's translation).

[42] *John Paul II*, Post-synodal Apostolic Exhortation 'Reconciliation and penance', 2 December 1984, point 16: "a direct attack on one's neighbor and more exactly, in the language of the Gospel, against one's brother or sister. They are an offense against God because they are offenses against one's neighbor. [...] Likewise, the term *social* applies to every sin against justice in interpersonal relationships, committed either by the individual against the community or by the community against the individual. Also social is every sin against the rights of the human person, beginning with the right to and including the life of the unborn or against a person's physical integrity. Likewise social is every sin against others' freedom, especially against the supreme freedom to believe in God and adore him; social is every sin against the dignity and honor of one's neighbor. Also social is every sin against the common good and its exigencies in relation to the whole broad spectrum of the rights and duties of citizens. The term social can be applied to sins of commission or omission – on the part of political, economic or trade union leaders, who though in a position to do so, do not work diligently and wisely for the improvement and transformation of society according to the requirements and potential of the given historic moment; as also on the part of workers who through absenteeism or non-cooperation fail to ensure that their industries can continue to

a lawyer is given the means to analyse the degree of blameworthiness in the situation and, for instance, to consider prohibiting a particular act or targeting it with a sanction. Due to the parallelism of the structure of dogmatic thinking, which is characteristic of both the methodology of dogmatic theology and the lawyer's workshop, condemnation can be translated into incrimination.

Considering social sin, we note that it is much more difficult to clarify what a *structural* sin is and what its consequences are for an acting subject. This is our fourth and last example and is based on the observation of the structures of evil existing in today's world. What I am referring to are negative human behaviour that forms complex dependencies determining bad social relations in the sphere of the economy, politics, or culture. We call such sins "structural" because, although they are always embedded in particular people, they attain the power of supra-individual structures due to socialization and the institutionalization of personal life.[43] The result of the structures of evil is their determining the life of the perpetrators of sin and its victims – which is why a lawyer is naturally motivated to bring a series of specific questions to the issue. For example, when can we say that law itself participates in creating the structure of evil? Can we hope to design and introduce regulations that enable us to remove, or at least reduce, the blameworthiness of the people who happen to participate in evil? To what extent can law counteract the creation or continued existence of the structures of sin as such? How can individual people influence law within those structures? To what extent and up to what point do we owe obedience to the law involved in the structures of evil?[44]

Each of the four examples we have looked at has referred to a thesis that is so new in the Church that it requires further refinement by dogmatic theology. In modern theology, "new methods are practised without their prior theorising,"[45] which is why we tried to look at each of these theses from the perspective of the legal sensibility and legal studies in order to suggest the proper verification of both the methods and the structure. It is clear that this was, indeed, achieved, although the results and the satisfaction of the lawyer were every time different. Naturally, satisfaction is to be assessed according to perspectives that comport with the legal instruments applied in each case, and to the potential of describing and ordering the social reality. Each thesis would, separately, be subject to the historical or comparative reflection that is undertaken

---

advance the well-being of the workers themselves, of their families and of the whole of society."

[43] *P. Bortkiewicz*, Grzech strukturalny. Próba definicji, Czterdzieści i Cztery 44/5 (2012), 8–19, 13 f.

[44] *F. Longchamps de Bérier*, Prawo wobec grzechu strukturalnego, in: A. Dębiński et al. (eds.), Abiit, non obiit. Księga poświęcona pamięci ks. prof. Antoniego Kościa SVD (2013), 767–777, 767.

[45] *R. Winling*, Teologia współczesna 1945–1980 (trans. K. Kisielewska-Sławińska, 1990), 473 (author's translation).

within legal studies. So far, we have only attempted to suggest legal *dogmatic* analyses, as these seem to be closest to the work of dogmatic theologians. In each case, the result probably says a lot about the degree of, and potential for, the refinement of each of the theses.

VIII. The mirror of dogmatic theology

Law and legal studies convince us that we do not have to be ashamed of dogma. They encourage us to develop dogmatic theology as the art of interpretation. And since the life of law and the craft of lawyers is essentially interpretation, it would probably be worthwhile for dogmatic theologians to become knowledgeable about legal methods. How can they accomplish this? First, they must become acquainted with the basic methods of legal interpretation: linguistic, systemic, and functional. This will facilitate understanding and increase the self-confidence of those who, within dogmatic theology, come across expressions of a legal nature or significance. Second, they should look at a given regulation not only according to its dogmatic structure, but also taking into account the interpretative conclusions resulting from arguments of a historical or comparative nature. This will make it possible to place the discussed normative issues or solutions in their broader context. And this will in turn facilitate the evaluation of their efficiency and, at times, enable theologians to predict a dogma's development and prepare for possible changes or mutations in it.

There is no harm in dogmatic theologians tracing the critique of law, as this might give them more to say as regards the critique of dogmatic theology. This might also help them reinforce the credibility and scientific and cognitive nature of their own research. Thus, dogmatic theologians should not be afraid to consider their theses or research results from the perspective given by legal studies. Comparisons between the two fields are methodologically justified, as both fields develop in a parallel manner. It is appropriate for them to use each other's instruments, and the relationship between dogmatic theology and law, including legal studies, can be mutually beneficial. Law and legal studies can be treated as the useful mirror of dogmatic theology. Looking at law and legal studies from the perspective of dogmatic theology is a different task, but it could result in interesting descriptions, comparisons, and juxtapositions, and, in consequence, suggestions or reinforcement for legal arrangements. For this, however, a separate study is needed.

Legal and Theological Dogmatics

Thomas Marschler

I. Introduction

Even though jurisprudence did not derive its understanding of dogmatics from theology, but from its encounter with medicine,[1] the identical naming of a core discipline is noted with interest in both theological and legal literature. In this respect, it may come as a surprise that detailed comparisons between legal and theological dogmatics, which elaborate differences as well as similarities, are rarely found. Discussions in legal handbooks are scarce, and even recent monographic contributions to the theory of legal dogmatics often avoid bridging to theology. Nevertheless, there are exceptions. In interdisciplinary research projects featuring the participation of Catholic theologians, the legal scholar *Nils Jansen* has dealt with "Processes of Dogmatization in Law and Religion" ("Dogmatisierungsprozesse in Recht und Religion"), and in this context he has reflected on the specific nature of legal dogmatics.[2] In his dissertation on the "Interdisciplinarity of Legal Dogmatics" ("Interdisziplinarität der Rechtsdogmatik"), *Alexander Stark* discusses parallels and differences with theological

[1] See *M. Herberger*, Dogmatik. Zur Geschichte von Begriff und Methode in Medizin und Jurisprudenz (1981); for a brief summary see: *idem*, Rechtsdogmatik, in: J. Ritter et al. (eds.), Historisches Wörterbuch der Philosophie, vol. 8 (1992), 266–272.

[2] See *G. Essen/N. Jansen* (eds.), Dogmatisierungsprozesse in Recht und Religion (2011); see also *N. Jansen*, Kanonisierungs- und Dogmatisierungsprozesse in Recht und Religion. Historisch-vergleichende Beobachtungen, in: I. Augsberg/G.F. Schuppert (eds.), Wissen und Recht (2022), 487–506.

dogmatics.[3] *Philipp Sahm* sees in "dogmatic thinking" ("dogmatische Denkform") (*Erich Rothacker*) a principle that connects both disciplines, making the structural comparison the central thread of his study on legal dogmatics.[4] He observes an absence of similar efforts on the theological side:

"Theologen [...] erwähnen die Rechtsdogmatik wenn überhaupt nur selten. Und falls doch, dann erfolgt der Verweis auf die Rechtsdogmatik in apologetischer Absicht, wonach auch irdisch orientierte Juristen, die anders als Theologen gewöhnlich nicht unter dem Verdacht frommer Naivität stehen, ganz selbstverständlich Dogmatik betreiben."[5]

"Theologians [...] mention legal dogmatics, if ever, only rarely. And if they do, then reference to legal dogmatics is made with an apologetic intention: also worldly orientated jurists, who – unlike theologians – are not under the suspicion of pious naivety, pursue, perfectly naturally, dogmatics."

A look at current introductory literature of both Catholic and Protestant provenance could easily confirm this judgment. The only theological contribution I know of dedicated to a direct comparison of the dogmatics of both disciplines is a paper authored by the Protestant theologian *Michael Welker*, intended as an outsider's perspective on recent legal debates.[6] It is therefore to be wel-

---

[3] *A. Stark*, Interdisziplinarität der Rechtsdogmatik (2020), 56–60.

[4] *P. Sahm*, Elemente der Dogmatik (2019); he writes in his summary on 195: "Die Gegenüberstellung der Rechtsdogmatik mit der theologischen Dogmatik zeigt die charakteristischen Merkmale der dogmatischen Denkform. Diese zeichnet sich zunächst dadurch aus, dass sich das dogmatische Denken auf einer spezifisch mittleren Abstraktionshöhe abspielt. Sodann wird deutlich, dass sich die Dogmatiken jeweils einem Primärtext unterwerfen, der Gegenstand und Ziel ihrer hermeneutischen Bemühungen ist. Gleichzeitig wird diese Bindung an den Primärtext unterlaufen, indem die Dogmatiker um ihres Primärtextes willen dessen Interpretationsbedürftigkeit einräumen müssen und sich so Freiräume schaffen. So wird der Primärtext für den unvermeidlichen Beitrag des Interpreten geöffnet und seine alleinige Stellung als autoritative Quelle unterlaufen. Der Primärtext wird folglich nicht nur rekonstruiert, sondern auch konstruiert. Die dogmatische Argumentation ist ferner von einem spezifischen Geltungsanspruch gekennzeichnet, der den Dogmatikern argumentative Spielregeln in Form einer Pflicht zu loyaler Textauslegung auferlegt." ("A comparison of legal dogmatics with theological dogmatics reveals the characteristics of dogmatic thinking. Dogmatic thinking is characterized firstly by a specifically middle level of abstraction. Secondly, the comparison makes clear that both legal and theological dogmatics submit to a primary text that is the object and objective of their hermeneutical efforts. At the same time, the binding force of the primary text is undermined by the dogmatists – for the sake of the primary text – having to concede the need for interpretation and thus creating freedom for themselves. Thereby, the text is opened to the inevitable input of the interpreter and its sole role as an authoritative text is undermined. Consequently, the primary text is not only reconstructed, but it is also constructed. Moreover, dogmatic argumentation is characterised by a specific claim to validity, which imposes argumentative rules on the dogmatist in the form of a duty to interpret the primary text loyally.").

[5] *Sahm* (n. 4), 34.

[6] See *M. Welker*, Juristische und theologische Dogmatik, Evangelische Theologie 75 (2015), 325–341.

comed that *Franciszek Longchamps de Bérier* is now continuing the interdisciplinary dialogue by explaining several dimensions of the dogmatic method in legal sciences that could be instructive for dogmatic theology. In response to his contribution, I will look at common definitions and descriptions of legal and theological dogmatics in order to take up some of his observations and add further aspects of comparison. Like *Longchamps de Bérier*, I will judge primarily from a Roman Catholic professional perspective.

II. Definitions of legal dogmatics

Longchamps de Bérier offers a definition of legal dogmatics[7] that emphasizes three aspects in particular: (1) The primary subject of dogmatics is the *lex lata*. Its valid principles can be understood as "dogmas", of which therefore the law is "full".[8] (2) The analysis of the law, connected with classifications and proposals for distinctions,[9] has a practical goal: dogmatic conclusions should serve the application of the law. (3) Dogmatics can help prepare future legislation through critical, innovative proposals. Even if it is repeatedly emphasized that there is no consensus in the definition of legal dogmatics,[10] these basic elements are (with different emphasis) regularly found,[11] sometimes enriched by further aspects. An example is the proposal that *Christian Bumke* places at the beginning of his monograph on the subject:

---

[7] "Dogmatics is practised by those legal scholars who deal with the law in force. They analyse its content, drawing conclusions about the content of binding norms from legal provisions. Their domain is the lex lata, i.e. 'the existing law.' This does not prevent them from considering which direction changes of law and statutes in force can or should take, and they, thus, also make propositions de lege ferenda, i.e. 'under the pretence of what is to be proposed as law.'" *Longchamps de Bérier*, p. 76, above.

[8] "Law is full of dogmas, i.e. statements of an obligatory nature, which express the truth of what law is in force or which solution is good, and which regulation should be adopted as just within the art of settling social relations in a particular situation that requires regulation." *Longchamps de Bérier*, 82, above.

[9] See *Longchamps de Bérier*, p. 80, above: "classifying and suggesting distinctions".

[10] See *B. Rüthers*, Rechtsdogmatik als Schranke des Richterrechts?, Jahrbuch des öffentlichen Rechts der Gegenwart 64 (2016), 309–343, 313: "Der Begriff wird als bekannt vorausgesetzt, aber selten und meistens spärlich definiert" ("The concept is presumed to be known, but it is rarely and mostly only scarcely defined"); *C. Waldhoff*, Lob und Kritik der Dogmatik, in: G. Kirchhof et al. (eds.), Was weiß Dogmatik? (2012), 17–37, 21: "Was juristische Dogmatik oder Rechtsdogmatik ist, ist allerdings bis heute unklar." ("However, it remains unclear just what juridical or legal dogmatics is.").

[11] According to *Sahm* (n. 4), 17, there has been a "stable core of meaning in the definitions of dogmatics over the past hundred years" ("in den vergangenen hundert Jahren einen zeitlich stabilen Bedeutungskern der Dogmatikdefinitionen"); they all sounded "very similar" ("sehr ähnlich") (ibid., 39).

"Die Rechtsdogmatik lässt sich als eine Disziplin beschreiben, die das positive Recht durchdringen und ordnen will, um die rechtliche Arbeit anzuleiten, und jene Fragen zu beantworten sucht, die die Rechtspraxis aufwirft. Sie bemüht sich darum, die Vorstellungen und Einsichten über das Recht zu sichten und zu sichern, indem sie Begriffe formt, Unterscheidungen einführt, Figuren oder Prinzipien erarbeitet und den Stoff ordnet. Sie hinterfragt die bestehenden Vorstellungen oder Entscheidungen der Praxis, greift Neuerungen auf und prüft den daraus resultierenden Veränderungsbedarf, zeichnet nach und vor. Auf diese Weise hält sie ein Wissensreservoir für die Praxis vor, trägt zur Erlernbarkeit der praktischen Rechtsarbeit bei und leistet einen Beitrag zur Rationalisierung und damit auch zur Legitimierung des Rechts."[12]

"Legal dogmatics may be described as a discipline that wishes to permeate and map out positive law. It thereby aims to guide any engagement with law and to answer questions raised by legal practice. It seeks to screen and collect perceptions on, and insights into, the law by shaping concepts, introducing distinctions, elaborating ideas and principles, and sorting the legal material. It questions existing legal views and decisions of legal practice, takes up new developments and analyses any resulting need for change – it looks both back and ahead. In so doing, legal dogmatics holds available for legal practice a reservoir of legal knowledge, it contributes to the learnability of practical legal work as well as to the rationalization and, thus, also the legitimization, of law."

In addition to a more precise description of the systematizing task of legal dogmatics and its interaction with practice, *Bumke* mentions the function of legal dogmatics for didactic purposes and for the legitimization of law.

III. Definition and subject of theological dogmatics

In theology, as in jurisprudence, dogmatics as a disciplinary name has been established in the course of modern times. Since the middle of the seventeenth century, the term has appeared in textbook titles, and at the beginning of the nineteenth century it came to prevail as a name for the primarily theoretical reflection on Christian doctrine.[13] While academic theology in the Middle Ages was regarded as a unity, clearly distinguished only from canon law, in the post-Reformation period a gradual specialization and division took place, the result of which are the sub-disciplines currently represented in theological faculties. Among them, dogmatics is found in the area of systematic theology. For centuries, contributions to theological dogmatics, with few exceptions, came almost exclusively from scholars specialized in this area, who had close ties to academic teaching.[14] By contrast, the field of participants in legal dogmatics

---

[12] *C. Bumke*, Rechtsdogmatik (2017), 1 f.

[13] See *H. Filser*, Dogma, Dogmen, Dogmatik. Eine Untersuchung zur Begründung und zur Entstehungsgeschichte einer theologischen Disziplin von der Reformation bis zur Spätaufklärung (2000), 628–661.

[14] *W. Hassemer*, Dogmatik zwischen Wissenschaft und richterlicher Pragmatik: Einführende Bemerkungen, in: Kirchhof et al. (n. 10), 3–15, 11, gives a negative answer to the

has been much broader, insofar as "judges, academic staff at the federal courts and in the large law firms, administrative officials or lawyers" ("Richter, wissenschaftliche Mitarbeiterinnen an den Bundesgerichten und in den großen Anwaltsfirmen, Verwaltungsbeamte oder Rechtsanwälte")[15] are involved together with legal scholars.

The fact that the term "dogmatics" – the science "of dogmas" – was established for reflection on the doctrine of faith in its narrower sense documents a turning away from older scholastic theology, which was accused by humanists and reformers as embodying an excess of useless speculation not serving the faith. Since then, the "positive" method gained in importance in Catholic theology, with the method aiming at a precise presentation of the doctrine of faith from Scripture and Tradition, thereby being withdrawn from scholastic discussions and largely renouncing speculative questions.[16] While the "theologia positiva" initially supplemented the scholastic mode of presentation in the seventeenth century,[17] it became dominant after the latter's collapse from the mid-eighteenth century. At the beginning of the nineteenth century, and in the wake of German Idealism and Romanticism, under the title of "Dogmatics" a new synthesis was sought between positive and speculative elements, a synthesis which remained authoritative in the subsequent Neo-Scholastic movement. Theological dogmatics continues to follow this basic model to this day. However, significant changes and differentiations have taken place both in exegetical and speculative method as well as in the understanding of their inner connection.[18]

The subject of dogmatics is the entire content of the revealed faith as normatively attested in the teaching of the Church (in its "dogmas").[19] Especially the second criterion designates a Catholic proprium; Protestants do not recognize a living ecclesiastical *magisterium* "of those who have received through Episcopal succession the sure gift of truth" (*Dei Verbum* 8). They therefore determine the content of faith in a different way (recurring to the self-

---

question "whether everything that jurisprudence produces may be considered legal dogmatics" ("ob all das, was Rechtswissenschaft produziert, als Rechtsdogmatik gelten darf"). This certainly also applies to the contributions of dogmatic theologians.

[15] *Bumke* (n. 12), 15.

[16] See *M.-J. Congar*, Théologie, in: Dictionnaire de théologie catholique, vol. 15 (1946), 341–502, 432.

[17] In the seventeenth century, one finds theological treatises which are structured within the framework of scholastic tradition but draw their arguments in large part (Ruiz de Montoya) or almost completely (Petavius, Thomassin) from Patristic sources. From the end of the seventeenth century, book titles like "dissertatio scholastico-dogmatica" became common.

[18] See the programmatic guidelines of Vatican II in Optatam totius (1965), 16.

[19] See *T. Marschler*, Dogmatik, II. Theologisch, in: Staatslexikon online (8th edn., 2022), https://www.staatslexikon-online.de/Lexikon/Dogmatik (last accessed on 27 September 2022); *idem*, Dogmatik als Wissenschaft, in: B.P. Göcke/L.V. Ohler (eds.), Die Wissenschaftlichkeit der Theologie, vol. 2 (2019), 101–138.

interpreting Bible, creeds of the ancient Church or personal inner testimony of the Holy Spirit). In Catholic understanding, dogmatics has to do with descriptive, indicative propositions, whose content has to fulfill two criteria: on the one hand, to be part of God's self-disclosure to mankind, represented in Scripture and Tradition, and on the other hand, to be officially attested by the Church (in various ways) as content of revelation.[20] The testimony of the Church establishes neither the affiliation of a truth to revelation nor man's obligation to believe, but only makes both clearly recognizable. Thus, the ecclesiastical judgment of faith differs from legislation in its proper sense.[21] The distinction between sources of revelation and testifying instances, between constitutive and interpretive theological *loci*, already developed in the influential treatise on the theological sources of knowledge by *Melchor Cano* ("De locis theologicis", 1563), is of central importance. The work of theologians has traditionally been viewed as an interpretive source of second rank because it lacks the certainty of testimony that belongs to the official doctrinal statements of the Church and to its faith as a whole.

IV. Main steps of theological dogmatics

On this basis, three central and interpenetrating steps of theological dogmatics can be distinguished. There are fundamental parallels to the description of legal dogmatics,[22] but at the same time we encounter important differences.

---

[20] See *First Vatican Council*, Dei Filius (1870), c. 3 (DH 3011): "Porro fide divina et catholica ea omnia credenda sunt, quae in verbo Dei scripto vel tradito continentur et ab Ecclesia sive solemni iudicio sive ordinario et universali magisterio tamquam divinitus revelata credenda proponuntur."

[21] *M.J. Scheeben*, Glaubensregel, in: J. Hergenröther/F.P. Kaulen (eds.), Wetzer und Welte's Kirchenlexikon, vol. 5 (2nd edn., 1888), 685–693, 688: "Allerdings sind die auctoritativen Bestimmungen der kirchlichen Lehrgewalt insofern keine eigentlichen Gesetze, als sie nur ein von Gott gegebenes Gesetz declariren; ja meistens auch insofern, als sie ein bereits geltendes Gesetz nur nachdrücklicher einschärfen." ("However, the authoritative rules of ecclesiastical doctrine are insofar not themselves actual laws as they only reproduce a law given by God; indeed, they are not actual laws also insofar as they only strongly inculcate a law that already is in force."). *Waldhoff* (n. 10), 27, points out: "Dogmatik ist nicht Rechts-, sondern Rechtserkenntnisquelle." ("Dogmatics is not a source of law but only a source of finding the law."). In the context of dogmatic theology, this applies not only to scholarly contributions but also to the official teachings of the Church – the "legislator" in a strict sense is God alone.

[22] See R. Dreier's three-prong description of legal dogmatics as referenced in *O. Lepsius*, Kritik der Dogmatik, in: Kirchhof et al. (n. 10), 39–62, 42: "Dogmatik besitze drei Dimensionen: eine empirische Dimension, die auf die Sammlung und Sichtung des positiven Rechtsstoffs gerichtet ist, eine analytische, die auf die begrifflich-systematische Durchdringung des positiven Rechts gerichtet ist, sowie eine normative, rechtsethische Dimension, die

A. Identification and explication of the contents of revelation from Scripture and Tradition under the guidelines of ecclesiastical testimony

The first task of dogmatics is to precisely identify the contents of revelation from the aforementioned sources and, in doing so, to distinguish them from facts that do not meet the relevant criteria. Since God's revelation is addressed to all people of all times, dogmas apply to the whole church, while laws are, with the exception of public international law, regional. In this respect, theological dogmatics has a broader perspective than legal dogmatics.[23] On the other hand, the material theological dogmatics has to deal with is not ready-made in the same way as the norms in a code of laws. This is especially true in light of more recent theories of revelation, which understand revelation as the event of God's communication with mankind, in which his personal self-disclosure and not the transmission of propositional truths is the central point (although propositional truths are indispensable for human understanding of God and his intentions). The source text of theological dogmatics is not simply "the Bible";[24] this is because Scripture is not identical with revelation, which takes place in different ways in human history, but is instead a medium (albeit an excellent one) of faith and ecclesiastical testimony. Furthermore, the Bible contains much that is not relevant to the understanding of revelation. What is "to be believed" has been raised within the community of the Church in a process of scriptural tradition and interpretation over centuries and, in many cases, has been defined in normative statements. Tracing these historical processes of dogmatization is inseparable from an accurate understanding of dogmatic content. Thus, the famous core formula of the First Ecumenical Council of Nicaea (325), according to which Christ the Son is "of one substance with the Father", can be understood correctly only if one reads it against the background of the (philosophical) prehistory of the term *homousios* and as a response to Arius's subordinationist Christology, anathematized (without mentioning his name) in the appendix of the Nicene symbolum. For the first time, a non-biblical term was used here to determine as precisely as possible the orthodox understanding of a central article of faith and to reject an opposing interpretation (the Son as the first creature of the Father). By making a distinction between "explicit" and

den Bezug zur praktischen Vernunft herstellt." ("Dogmatics has three dimensions: an empirical dimension that is directed at collecting and looking through the positive law; an analytical dimension that is directed at the conceptual-systematic reviewing of the positive law; and a normative, legal-ethical dimension that establishes a link to practical reason.").

[23] See *Longchamps de Bérier*, p. 87, above.

[24] The tendency to parallelize "the Bible" and "current law" as the primary texts of theological and legal dogmatics is characteristic for *Sahm* (n. 4), 53 f. It fits well with a Protestant understanding of dogmatics (see *Welker* (n. 6), 333). The decisive question a theologian, unlike a lawyer, has to ask is not whether a book belongs to the canon of Scriptures or whether the biblical text is reliable (see *Sahm* (n. 4), 80 f.), but rather which statements derived from the Bible can be regarded as God's revelation (and why).

"implicit" content of revelation, theologians acknowledge the possibility of genuine dogmatic development that takes place in the progressive reflection on God's word expressed in human words. There is a broad consensus across all major Christian denominations and theologies regarding the conviction that revelation itself is definitively completed because God's self-communication in Christ cannot be surpassed.[25] Because, unlike the sources of legal dogmatics, all constitutive sources of theological dogmatics are withdrawn from future change or increase,[26] progress can only take place in the interpretation of these sources.

A further challenge for dogmatic theology consists in the fact that the Church's affirmation of the contents of revelation is neither uniform nor always unambiguous. Dogmas in the narrower sense are the precisely formulated decisions of doctrinal questions by Councils or (in more recent times, after the clarification of papal infallibility) by the pope alone, usually linked to canonical sanctions.[27] One can speak of "dogmata declarata" here. However, such definitions remain comparatively rare and do not follow a certain plan. They are often reactions to contemporary discussions; therefore, they do not provide a complete systematic treatment of the respective topics. The Second Vatican Council, unlike previous councils, presented overall theological drafts, especially in its major dogmatic constitutions on revelation (*Dei Verbum*) and on the Church (*Lumen gentium*). At the same time, however, it established a new form of conciliar teaching emphasizing pastoral goals and dispensing with the juridical precision of earlier dogmatic definitions or condemnations, though not with doctrinal claims in general. Controversies about the correct hermeneutics in dealing with the texts of Vatican II still preoccupy dogmatic theologians more than half a century after the end of the Council.

---

[25] Problems connected with the strict distinction between the event of revelation and its interpretation cannot be discussed here. Only few Christian denominations, such as the Mormon Church, acknowledge the principle of continuing revelation through living prophets.

[26] See *Rüthers* (n. 10), 320 f.; *Sahm* (n. 4), 106 f. *N. Jansen*, Dogmatisierungsprozesse in Recht und Religion: Einführung, in: Essen/Jansen (n. 2), 1–22, 8, considers this a fundamental difference between legal and theological processes of dogmatization: "Ein Diskurs von Normsetzern (Gesetzgebern, aber auch Gerichten) und Rechtsanwendern, wie er das Recht kennzeichnet, konnte sich in der christlichen Religion deshalb nie herausbilden. Eine Externalisierung von Problemen, die sich innerhalb des theologischen Diskurses argumentativ nicht lösen lassen, auf politische oder juristische Entscheidungsinstanzen war damit ausgeschlossen." ("For that reason, a discourse between lawmakers (the legislature as well as the courts) and those applying the law, as is characteristic for law, was never able to develop in Christianity. An externalization of problems that could not be solved argumentatively within the theological discourse onto political or legal decision makers was thereby excluded.").

[27] *Longchamps de Bérier*, p. 85, above, correctly points out that dogmatic theologians will often encounter texts of juridical character, which require them to have a certain skill of interpretation.

The Church's doctrine of faith is not constituted solely by the formal definitions of councils and popes. There is content which has been consistently and unchallengedly attested by the Church, whereas there was no need to protect it through official dogmatization. Since the nineteenth century, theologians speak of an attestation in "living doctrinal tradition" by the "ordinary and universal magisterium" as distinguished from the acts of the "extraordinary magisterium" (definitions of the councils and papal *ex cathedra* decisions). If one wants to use juridical terms, the solemnly defined dogmas can be compared as suggested by *Matthias Joseph Scheeben* to the "statutory law" or "written law", while the "dogmata non declarata", truths of faith attested by the ordinary *magisterium*, are given "in the form of a kind of customary law".[28] It is obvious that the latter is actually the more original way in which the rule of faith has been transmitted in the Church, even if the tendency towards formal definitions and thus towards a juridification of the Church's doctrine of faith has become more and more evident over time.

The treatment of the so-called secondary objects of dogmatics is more difficult.[29] These doctrines, although not considered formally revealed, are "required for the holy keeping and faithful exposition of the deposit of faith". In 1989, Pope *John Paul II* added a paragraph to Canon Law (CIC 1983, can. 750, § 2), requiring that these teachings "must be firmly accepted and held".[30] This is obviously less than faith in the sense of the divine virtue required for dogmas, but it is more than the mere acceptance in "religious reverence" that Catholics are generally supposed to have towards the statements of the *magisterium*, even if they are not definitive. Some theologians have criticized the expansion of the claim to infallibility, which has been carried out here, as an encroaching innovation.[31] A hotly disputed question in the contemporary Catholic Church, the

---

[28] *Scheeben* (n. 21), 687 f.

[29] See *D. Hercsik*, Die Grundlagen unseres Glaubens. Eine theologische Prinzipienlehre (2005), 176–180, 184.

[30] *John Paul II*, Motu Proprio Ad tuendam fidem (1998), https://www.vatican.va/content/john-paul-ii/de/motu_proprio/documents/hf_jp-ii_motu-proprio_30061998_ad-tuendam-fidem.html (last accessed on 25 October 2022): "Furthermore, each and everything set forth definitively by the Magisterium of the Church regarding teaching on faith and morals must be firmly accepted and held; namely, those things required for the holy keeping and faithful exposition of the deposit of faith; therefore, anyone who rejects propositions which are to be held definitively sets himself against the teaching of the Catholic Church." Theological criticism of the increased demands of the ecclesiastical magisterium can be likened to lawyers' complaints that supreme courts are expanding their authority to interpret the constitution without an explicit mandate; see *Lepsius* (n. 22), 43 f.

[31] See *M. Rehak*, Wie weit reicht die Unfehlbarkeit des kirchlichen Lehramts? Can. 750 § 2 CIC und die Lehre von den "Katholischen Wahrheiten", in: F.X. Bischof/G. Essen (eds.), Theologie, kirchliches Lehramt und öffentliche Meinung. Die Münchener Gelehrtenversammlung von 1863 und ihre Folgen (2015), 153–192.

exclusion of women from sacramental ordinations, belongs to the realm of these secondary objects.

Once one has identified a "revealed truth" (or a doctrine to be distinguished from it) according to the dogmatic criteria, its exact content remains to be determined. This, too, is one of the central tasks of dogmatic theology. From a Catholic point of view, the dogmatic formulations of the Church, which are often the result of long collective reflection, represent a binding framework of orientation. Therefore, they were called *norma proxima fidei* in older theology and were placed before Scripture and Tradition in the theological order of knowledge. This entails the danger of "dogmatism" that reads historical sources exclusively in the light of dogmatic interpretations (analogous dangers are discussed in legal dogmatics). After the crisis of modernism in the early twentieth century, Catholic theology has learned to understand more deeply the historicity of revelation itself. Now it has been recognized that scriptural exegesis and the historiography of dogma must in principle be methodologically independent of dogmatic prescriptions. *Longchamps de Bérier* rightly points out that exegetical and hermeneutical skills are just as indispensable for the dogmatic theologian as for the lawyer.[32] Since the inclusion of historical and comparative perspectives has become a matter of course since the end of Neo-Scholasticism, at least in German-speaking countries, theology will not have to learn too much from legal dogmatics on this point.[33] Perhaps the reverse learning path can be taken here – within legal scholarship, the complaint is expressed that dogmatic interpretation shows a tendency to de-temporalize or de-contextualize its sources and to tune out comparative perspectives.[34]

Just as the work of dogmatic theology does not begin simply with the examination of ecclesiastical formulas, it does not end with it either. Even the earliest councils show that practically all ecclesiastical decisions raise numerous follow-up questions. For example, when the Council of Chalcedon (451) confessed Christ as "one person in two natures," it did not provide a definition of what exactly was to be understood by these terms. It was left to the theologians to ponder such problems. They were encouraged to submit proposals for further

[32] See *Longchamps de Bérier*, p. 88, above.

[33] This refers to the advice given by *Longchamps de Bérier*, p. 83, above: "As experts in the history of dogma, theologians are aware of its development. It might be useful for them to be also aware that the methodology of legal studies, for pragmatic reasons, tells us to reach beyond dogmatics towards historical and comparative arguments". Currently, the accusation of unhistorical thinking is only occasionally raised against representatives of analytical theology.

[34] See *Lepsius* (n. 22), 40: "Die dogmatischen Abhandlungen unserer Tage scheuen den historischen Rückblick, den philosophischen Tiefblick, den sozialwissenschaftlichen Rundblick oder gar den politischen Ausblick." ("Today's dogmatic treatises eschew the historical view back, the in-depth view into philosophical insights, the panoramic view of the social science as well as the political outlook.").

dogmatic development; this has a parallel in the critical-innovative dimension of legal dogmatics.[35] The acceptance or rejection of these proposals falls within the competence of ecclesiastical authorities (as in the field of law, legislature and courts are responsible for the reception of dogmatic proposals). However, even popes and bishops are dependent on the expertise of dogmatic theology, as can be illustrated by the history of every doctrinal decision.

Statements of theological dogmatics, we said at the beginning, are descriptive, indicative propositions. Two important comments must be made here. "Dogmatics" as a theological discipline came into existence from a point in time when scholarly reflection on the doctrine of faith had been separated from reflection on the precepts and virtues ordering Christian life (in moral theology). This separation was unknown in pre-Reformation theology, as can be easily verified in medieval *Summae* and Commentaries on the Sentences. In a broader sense, the principles of theological ethics officially taught by the Church could be called "dogmata practica",[36] considered in moral theology as "ethical practical dogmatics". One may ask whether moral theology understood in this way would not correspond more directly to legal dogmatics than the systematic interpretation of faith. In addition, the Catholic Church has its universal canon law, which formulates norms based on dogmatic and moral principles and which can develop its own legal dogmatics. It is noticeable that the case studies *Longchamps de Bérier* discusses in the last part of his contribution could also be assigned to these two disciplines: The concepts of ecological or structural/social sin are to be treated by moral theology as well as by dogmatics; the question of whether active faith must be a prerequisite for the validity of sacramental marriage is inextricably linked to the canonical understanding of marriage consensus.

A second remark: In formulating indicative propositions, dogmatics as "science of the dogmas (of faith)" always pursues a practical goal. Already since *Tertullian* (†220), long before the Church made its first dogmatic decisions, the doctrine of faith was understood as the "norm of faith" (*regula fidei*). This normative claim is affirmed in the authoritative presentation of the *credenda* by ecclesiastical creeds. Symbols of faith are necessary to protect the identity of the ecclesiastical community, to reject threats from false teachings and to enable the transmission of faith in catechesis. In this respect, dogmatics can be described as both an expression and a stabilization of a social practice. At the same time, it illustrates the conviction that the confession of the articles of faith (at least to a certain extent) is indispensable for each individual person's relationship with God and for receiving the grace of salvation. Therefore, the "doctrine of salvation" as reflected in dogmatics undoubtedly has practical relevance for the faithful. In the Middle Ages, theology sometimes defined itself

---

[35] See *Longchamps de Bérier*, p. 77 and p. 93, above.

[36] See *J. Brinktrine*, Einleitung in die Dogmatik (1951), 26.

as "practical science" because it wanted to be an introduction to the path of salvation opened by God, providing deeper understanding. In contrast to legal dogmatics, however, theological dogmatics is not focused on the solution of practical problems. It is not concerned with bridging the gap between general, abstract norms and the case-by-case decisions[37] that a court cannot avoid.[38] In the Catholic Church there is no ecclesiastical jurisdiction dealing with questions of faith in distinction from the *magisterium*. At best, theological dogmatics succeeds in improving and deepening the understanding of revealed faith in the Church as a whole, or at least for individual believers.

B. Systematic connection and further development of dogmatic statements

The identification and precise determination of the content of faith from its constitutive sources described so far is followed by systematic reflection. Its goal is to show inner connections between the individual doctrinal statements and their integration into an overall view that is as coherent as possible and determined by consistent principles. When theology as science emerged with the scholasticism of the twelfth and thirteenth centuries, closely connected to the establishment of the universities, its epistemological model was taken from the Second Analytics of *Aristotle*. According to the philosopher, scientific knowledge is mainly generated by logically correct conclusions drawn from basic propositions. *Thomas Aquinas*[39] applied this model to theology by qualifying the revealed articles of faith as participation in the *scientia Dei et beatorum*, i.e., a higher science, to which theology relates as *scientia subalternata*, the same way, for example, engineering science relates to physics. Although medieval scholasticism never carried out this method consistently, it has remained dominant in Catholic dogmatics into the modern era. Theologians were now willing to include purely philosophical premises in order to derive conclusions from revealed principles. This conclusive procedure has close counterparts in modern theories of science. Nevertheless, it has come under criti-

---

[37] See *Waldhoff* (n. 10), 26. The definition of legal dogmatics as an "operationalizing intermediate layer between legal norms and the application of law in individual cases" ("operationalisierende Zwischenschicht zwischen den Rechtsnormen und der Rechtsanwendung im Einzelfall") (*M. Eifert*, Zum Verhältnis von Dogmatik und pluralisierter Rechtswissenschaft, in: Kirchhof et al. (n. 10), 79–96, 81) cannot be transferred to theological dogmatics. See *Sahm* (n. 4), 72.

[38] "Der Unterschied zwischen theologischen und juristischen Dogmatikern besteht darin, dass die theologischen Dogmatiker keinem Entscheidungszwang ausgesetzt sind" ("The difference between theological and legal dogmatists is that theological dogmatists are under no obligation to decide."): *Sahm* (n. 4), 173.

[39] See *Congar* (n. 16), 378–392; *M. Grabmann*, Die theologische Erkenntnis- und Einleitungslehre des hl. Thomas von Aquin auf Grund seiner Schrift In Boethium de trinitate im Zusammenhang der Scholastik des 13. und beginnenden 14. Jahrhunderts dargestellt (1948); *J.-P. Torrell*, Le savoir théologique chez saint Thomas, Revue thomiste 96 (1996) 355–396.

cism in recent theology because of its tendency towards unhistorical argumentation (especially in the Neo-Scholasticism that prevailed between around 1850 and 1950). Since then, hermeneutic methods of interpretation as developed in modern humanities have been adopted to a large extent. Nevertheless, important systematic contributions are still characterized by a logically coherent unfolding of fundamental principles, which, of course, must be historically reflected. The "hierarchy of truths" (Vatican II, *Unitatis Redintegratio* 11) given in revelation itself, i.e., the insight into the theological priority of certain truths of faith over others, serves as a fundamental ordering principle. Insofar as consistency, rational accessibility and communicability of Christian doctrine are clarified by systematic presentation, the dogmatic *intellectus fidei* has implicit relevance for the justification of faith in the face of critical inquiries on the part of philosophical reason. Every dogmatic system implies the decision in favour of certain philosophical premises. While in Christian antiquity and in the Middle Ages the dominant paradigms were first Platonism and then Aristotelianism, the situation has changed considerably in modern times. Since the middle of the nineteenth century, the aforementioned Neo-Scholastic movement, with the support of the ecclesiastical *magisterium*, pursued the goal of bringing the premises of Thomistic Aristotelianism once again to general acceptance within Catholic philosophy and theology. After Vatican II, Neo-Scholasticism came to a rapid end. Since then, a diversification has taken place in Catholic dogmatics that goes far beyond the variety of theological schools existing in earlier centuries.

C. Explanation of Christian doctrine in contemporary contexts

A third task of theological dogmatics has received greater attention only in the last few decades: the effort to make the ecclesiastical doctrine of faith plausible in changing forms of thought as well as in changing cultural and linguistic situations, in dialogue with contemporary sciences, worldviews and religions. In fact, dogmatic judgments of the Church and their interpretation by theologians have always been made under the auspices of changing philosophical, but also political and social conditions. The concept of transubstantiation could not have been established at the beginning of the thirteenth century without the reception of Aristotelian metaphysics. The definition of the doctrinal and jurisdictional primacy of the pope by the First Vatican Council (1870) is to be understood against the background of political developments after 1789. Dogmas must therefore be interpreted not only with respect to their conditions of origin; under changing circumstances, they may need to be supplemented and to be placed into new contexts of meaning. For example, the Second Vatican Council explained the previous Council's definition of papal infallibility in its larger ecclesiological context and introduced a counterweight to papal absolutism with the doctrine of episcopal collegiality. Dogmatics can and should formulate constructive suggestions for such updates.[40] However, it must continue to be recognized that "translating" dogma does not mean an exchange of its meaning. The Catholic Church does not recognize a formal abandonment of dogmatic statements of the past on the argument that its judgments are no longer understandable or that they are based on erroneous premises. This would be difficult to reconcile with the statements about the stability of dogmatic teaching in Vatican I (see Dogmat. Konstitution *Dei Filius*, can. 4, *Denzinger-Hünermann* 3043) and the chapters on "sacred tradition" in Vatican II (cf. *Dei Verbum* 7–10). In fact, some demands for a "transformation of the form of thought" within dogmatic theology no longer touch solely on previous interpretations of Christian dogmas, but on the dogmas as such. Theologians, who, for example, follow *Immanuel Kant* in refuting the pre-modern understanding of metaphysics will find it difficult to make sense of the dogmas of the "one divine nature in three persons", of the "one person of Christ in two natures" or of the "transubstantiation" of bread and wine in the Eucharist. This fundamental criticism is often accompanied by an appeal to historical-critical exegesis. In recent times, demands for changes in previous church teachings, as evidenced for example by the hermeneutical basic text of the "Synodal Path" (*Synodaler Weg*) in Germany,[41] are often raised with reference to two further criteria. One is the "sense of faith of the faithful", now understood as the current majority opinion of church members or as their refusal to adopt certain official positions of the *magisterium*. In addition, reference is made to "signs of the times" (cf. Vatican II, *Gaudium et Spes* 4), phenomena and developments of the present age which are conceived as "effects of the Spirit in society and in history"[42] and as manifestations of divine revelation for a certain time. Gender equality, democratic standards regarding participation and separation of powers, or the evaluation of sexuality in the humanities can be used as benchmarks for changes in ecclesiastical doctrine. The shifts in theological epistemology associated with these criteria are currently giving rise to serious controversy.[43] It remains to be seen whether, on this basis, certain parts of the doctrine of the Church will in the future be more closely aligned with profane legal systems, which are subject to constant change in the process of social transformation.

[40] See the remarks in *L. Scheffczyk*, Grundlagen des Dogmas. Einleitung in die Dogmatik (1997), 180–189.

[41] *Büro des Synodalen Weges* (ed.), Orientierungstext. Auf dem Weg der Umkehr und der Erneuerung. Theologische Grundlagen des Synodalen Weges der katholischen Kirche in Deutschland (2022).

[42] *P. Hünermann*, Dogmatische Prinzipienlehre. Glaube – Überlieferung – Theologie als Sprach- und Wahrheitsgeschehen (2003), 223.

[43] See *T. Marschler*, Zeichen der Zeit als neuer locus theologicus?, in: J.-H. Tück/ M. Striet (eds.), Jesus Christus – Alpha und Omega. Festschrift H. Hoping (2021), 38–56. English version: https://churchlifejournal.nd.edu/articles/signs-of-the-times-as-a-new-locus-theologicus/ (last accessed on 18 October 2022).

V. Conclusion

Our incomplete comments on the relationship between theological and legal dogmatics based on the definitions of the terms have shown that considerable parallels can indeed be discovered if the respective methods are described from a certain abstracting distance. One could easily extend the comparison to the storage and relief function of dogmatics and its didactic dimension, or reflect on specific problems associated with dogmatic thinking.[44] On the other hand, it cannot be overlooked that the different character of legal and theological principles and the diverging perspective of dogmatic statements in the two disciplines set limits on the comparison. Therefore, direct interdisciplinary contact between legal and theological dogmatics will probably remain rare in the future.

[44] *M. Jestaedt*, Wissenschaftliches Recht. Rechtsdogmatik als gemeinsames Kommunikationsformat von Rechtswissenschaft und Rechtspraxis, in: Kirchhof et al. (n. 10), 117–137, identifies four threats to legal dogmatics (131–136): dogmatism (the danger of "excessive disciplinary auto-reference"); exclusive or inclusive universalism (perceiving the dogmatic method as the only true method within the entire discipline or as the synthesis of all other methods); systematism (a compulsive fitting of all facts into the scheme of dogmatics); integralism (a blurring of the boundaries between knowledge and generation of law). All four points are relevant (mutatis mutandis) for theological dogmatics as well.

Part 3

Law and Extra-Legal Value Systems

Inalienable Human Rights

An Interdisciplinary Challenge to the Discipline of Law

Thilo Rensmann

I. Introduction

In the first article of Germany's federal constitution (the *Grundgesetz* – Basic Law), the German people profess their faith in inviolable human dignity and inalienable human rights.[1] This solemn pledge is explicitly protected against

[1] Art. 1(1) and (2) Basic Law. English translation available at https://www.gesetze-im-internet.de/englisch_gg/englisch_gg.html#p0019 (last accessed on 28 September 2022).

constitutional amendment[2] and therefore belongs – as the Federal Constitutional Court (*Bundesverfassungsgericht*) puts it – to the "eternal" principles which define the "constitutional identity" of the Federal Republic of Germany.[3]

Whilst human dignity has been fully embraced in German constitutional practice and is indeed today considered the hallmark of Germany's constitutional identity,[4] inalienable human rights, despite their equally prominent position in the Constitution, have long lain dormant in constitutional jurisprudence and scholarship. The Federal Constitutional Court only rediscovered the constitutional dimension of inalienable human rights in the early 2000s.[5] Since then, the Court has increasingly referred to inalienable human rights, in particular to rationalise the interaction between constitutionally entrenched fundamental rights on the one hand and European and international human rights on the other.[6]

The renaissance of inalienable human rights reached its preliminary peak in an order handed down by the Federal Constitutional Court in April 2021.[7] In this decision the Court emphasised that from a German constitutional perspective the commitment to inalienable human rights provides the common reference point for the determination of the proper relationship between the German bill of rights, the EU Charter of Fundamental Rights[8] and the European Convention on Human Rights.[9]

It is against this backdrop that the present chapter will attempt to establish why inalienable human rights have long been neglected and what accounts for their sudden renaissance. A special emphasis will be placed on the methodological dimension of this process. It will be demonstrated that the difficulty of capturing the legal meaning of a notion specifically intended to transcend positive law has from the outset posed a tremendous interdisciplinary challenge to the discipline of law and that this challenge has still not yet been fully mastered.

---

[2] Art. 1(3) Basic Law.

[3] Federal Constitutional Court, judgment of 30 June 2009, BVerfGE 123, 267, para. 218.

[4] See *M. Baldus*, Kämpfe um Menschenwürde: Die Debatten seit 1949 (2016).

[5] See pp. 138 ff., below.

[6] See pp. 144 ff., below.

[7] Federal Constitutional Court, order of 27 April 2021, BVerfGE 158, 1; for a detailed analysis see pp. 145 ff., below.

[8] Charter of Fundamental Rights of the European Union, as amended on 12 December 2007, Official Journal of the European Union 2012 C 236/391 (hereinafter: EU Charter).

[9] Convention for the Protection of Human Rights and Fundamental Freedoms, 4 November 1950, ETS 5 (hereinafter: ECHR).

II. Inalienable human rights as an interdisciplinary challenge

The Basic Law acknowledges inviolable human dignity and inalienable human rights as the "basis of every community, of peace and of justice in the world."[10] Human dignity and human rights must thus be respected and protected by "all state authority",[11] regardless of when and where it is exercised. Given their timeless and universal quality, human dignity and human rights are accordingly not established by constitutional fiat but simply reaffirmed by constitutional creed: the German people as the *pouvoir constituant* humbly "profess their faith"[12] in human dignity and human rights and thereby recognise that their otherwise unbridled power is reined in by the constant duty to respect and protect these meta-positive values.

In discharging this duty, the framers of the Basic Law "transformed"[13] human dignity and inalienable human rights into a bill of "fundamental" rights.[14] According to the wording and systematic structure of Art. 1 Basic Law, it is only via the medium of such positive fundamental rights that human dignity and inalienable human rights partake in the supremacy of the constitution and thus bind all three branches of government "as directly applicable law".[15]

However, given the stated object and purpose of fundamental rights as a means of respecting and protecting human dignity and inalienable human rights, these meta-positive values continue to play a significant role in interpreting the constitutionally entrenched bill of rights.[16] Moreover, human dignity and inalienable human rights belong to the "eternal" principles protected against constitutional amendment.[17] When interpreting fundamental rights and reflecting on the immutable "identity"[18] of the constitution, constitutional lawyers are thus confronted with the difficult task of establishing the specifically *legal* meaning of foundational values to which the constitution itself ascribes a meta-positive quality. This poses a considerable challenge to the discipline of law. Without overstretching the concepts of "law" and the "discipline of law",[19]

---

[10] Art. 1(1) and (2) Basic Law.

[11] Art. 1(1)(2) Basic Law.

[12] Art. 1(2) Basic Law.

[13] As to the notion of "transformation" in the deliberations of the Parliamentary Council on the draft text of the Grundgesetz, see *M. Hong*, Der Menschenwürdegehalt der Grundrechte (2019), 208 with further references.

[14] Art. 1(3) Basic Law refers to constitutionally entrenched "fundamental rights" as opposed to the meta-positive "human rights" acknowledged in Art. 1(2) Basic Law.

[15] Art. 1(3) in conjunction with Art. 20(3) Basic Law.

[16] On this interpretative function, see pp. 141 ff., below.

[17] Art. 79(3) Basic Law.

[18] See n. 3, above.

[19] As to the problem of determining the "identity" of the discipline of law in an interdisciplinary context, see *S. Kirste*, Voraussetzungen von Interdisziplinarität der Rechtswis-

legal scholarship is inevitably reliant on transdisciplinary assistance and interdisciplinary exchange in its effort to unearth the deeper philosophical, theological, political, cultural, and social roots which inform the proper understanding of human dignity and inalienable human rights.[20]

III. Inalienable human rights, human dignity and the discipline of law

It is therefore not surprising that ever since the Basic Law entered into force in 1949, constitutional jurisprudence and scholarship have been battling to make sense of the invocation of human dignity and inalienable human rights. In the judicial and academic responses to this methodological conundrum, three main approaches can be distinguished: Firstly, the acknowledgement that meta-positive values are beyond the reach of the discipline of law; secondly, the adaptation of legal methodology to the meta-positive object of interpretation; and thirdly, *vice versa*, the adaptation of the object of interpretation to legal methodology.

A. Beyond the discipline of law: marginalisation of inalienable human rights

Following the first approach, constitutional scholars have long marginalised the significance of the human rights clause in Art. 1(2) Basic Law. The invocation of inalienable human rights continues to be considered a "misplaced preambular paragraph"[21] or a mere reference to the "abstract idea"[22] of human rights and thus largely devoid of tangible substance.

Some early commentators did in fact recognise the intended link[23] between Art. 1(2) Basic Law and the emerging body of international human rights.[24] However, since the 1948 Universal Declaration of Human Rights[25] was a non-binding political resolution and it was to take until the mid-1970s for a treaty-based "International Bill of Rights" to enter into force,[26] Art. 1(2) Basic Law

---

senschaften, in: idem (ed.), Interdisziplinarität in den Rechtswissenschaften (2016), 35–85, 38–45.

[20] As to human dignity, see, e.g. *D. Grimm* et al. (eds.), Human Dignity in Context (2018); as to human rights see the contributions in *Kirste* (n. 19), 343–430.

[21] *H. Dreier*, Art. 1 Abs. 2, para. 11, in: idem (ed.), Grundgesetz-Kommentar (3rd edn., 2018).

[22] *C. Walter*, Art. 1 Abs. 2, paras. 35, 37, 42, in: W. Kahl et al. (eds.), Bonner Kommentar zum Grundgesetz (Looseleaf, 214th instalment, 2021).

[23] See pp. 121, below.

[24] *G. Dürig*, Art. 1, para. 55, in: idem/T. Maunz (eds.), Grundgesetz: Kommentar (1958).

[25] Universal Declaration of Human Rights, G.A. Res. 217A (III), U.N. Doc A/810, 71 (1948) (hereinafter: UDHR).

[26] See pp. 138 ff., below.

remained – at least for the time being – beyond the cognition of the discipline of law.[27]

B. Eclectic interdisciplinarity: elevation of human dignity to a constitutional supernorm

In stark contrast, the invocation of human dignity in Art. 1(1) Basic Law has, from the very beginning, been fully espoused by constitutional scholarship.[28] Despite being of an even more abstract nature than inalienable human rights, human dignity quickly developed into a constitutional "supernorm"[29] radiating into every corner of the legal system.[30]

Initially, the problem of the meta-positive origin of human dignity was predominantly viewed through the lens of the second approach, the adaptation of constitutional methodology to the object of interpretation. This approach is based on the assumption that the constitutional reference to human dignity is either declaratory of, or a *renvoi* to, a meta-positive principle. According to *Günter Dürig*, the most famous and influential early representative of this approach,

> "the moral value of human dignity, by having been incorporated into the positive constitution, has, from the perspective of positive law, simultaneously become a legal value so that positive law itself now mandates its still unfamiliar and therefore admittedly difficult legal interpretation."[31]

In *Dürig*'s view, the affirmation of human dignity in the positive constitution did not, however, change its meta-positive nature.[32] The meaning of human dignity as a "legal value" therefore continued to be informed by its meta-positive origin. *Dürig*, like many other pioneering legal scholars of the 1950s assumed that the pre-constitutional roots of human dignity, and hence the key to its understanding as a parallel "legal value", lay primarily in the Christian *imago dei*-doctrine and its "personalist" application in Catholic and Protestant social thought.[33] Although this Christian natural law approach did not find any

---

[27] *Dürig* (n. 24), paras. 55 f.

[28] See *Baldus* (n. 4), 60–88, 104–184, 246–250 with further references. For one of the very few authors who, in keeping with the first approach, considers the human dignity clause beyond the cognition of the discipline of law and hence largely devoid of legal meaning, see *E. Forsthoff*, Die Umbildung des Verfassungsgesetzes, in: E. Barion et al. (eds.), Festschrift für Carl Schmitt (1959), 35–62, 53.

[29] *Baldus* (n. 4), 14, 28, 253.

[30] *Baldus* (n. 4), 246 f.

[31] *Dürig* (n. 24), para. 1 (translation by the author).

[32] *Dürig* (n. 24), paras. 2, 73.

[33] *Dürig* (n. 24), para. 15. As to other authors following this Christian natural law approach, see *Baldus* (n. 4), 78–81, 241–243.

convincing support in the *travaux préparatoires*,[34] it remained the prevailing understanding of the human dignity clause during the first two decades after the Basic Law entered into force.[35]

Later, *Dürig* openly admitted that his more or less direct recourse to natural law and Christian social thought – interspersed with elements of Kantian philosophy – found little support in traditional legal hermeneutics.[36] His methodological approach was, as he put it, a "pilot project" largely conducted as a "blind flight" with the aid of a "compass" he had "cobbled together" himself.[37]

Dürig's eclectic approach has nevertheless remained influential to this day.[38] In an increasingly secularised and pluralistic society, it is, however, not so much his Christian reading of the dignity clause but rather his methodological point of departure which lives on in today's constitutional discourse. *Dürig*'s assumption that human dignity provides a gateway to the meta-positive world of ideas has subsequently encouraged many others to interpret the dignity clause in the light of their own preferred theological, philosophical or social theory.[39]

Consequently, we are faced today with a bewildering multitude of understandings of human dignity as a legal concept. Given the diversity and at times contradictory nature of the meta-positive ideas projected onto the dignity clause, all attempts at creating a workable synthesis by finding an "interdisciplinary consensus"[40] have been doomed to failure.[41]

It has thus become increasingly clear that only a legal approach severed from any particular meta-positive school of thought is capable of providing a generally accepted understanding of human dignity as the highest constitutional value.

C. The turn to positive law: re-emergence of inalienable human rights

Dürig's pioneering interpretation of Art. 1 formed part of the leading commentary on the Basic Law, at the time jointly edited by himself and the now disgraced[42] *Theodor Maunz*. Since its first edition in 1958, the commentary has been published as a looseleaf binder with a view to keeping it constantly up to

---

[34] See pp. 121 ff., below.

[35] *Baldus* (n. 4), 98.

[36] *G. Dürig*, Dankrede am 65. Geburtstag, Jahrbuch des öffentlichen Rechts der Gegenwart NF 36 (1987), 91–103, 95.

[37] *Dürig* (n. 36), 95 (translation by the author).

[38] See *Baldus* (n. 4), 237.

[39] See *Baldus* (n. 4), 98–103 with further references.

[40] As to such attempts, see *Baldus* (n. 4), 241 f.

[41] *Baldus* (n. 4), 260, 429.

[42] See *M. Stolleis*, Theodor Maunz: Ein Staatsrechtslehrerleben, Kritische Justiz 26 (1993), 393–396.

date.[43] Against this backdrop it is telling that *Dürig*'s commentary on Art. 1(1) and (2) Basic Law remained unchanged until 2003/2004, when it was completely reworked by *Matthias Herdegen*.[44]

In his new commentary, *Herdegen* advocates a distinctly "legal reading" (*staatsrechtliche Betrachtung*)[45] of the pledge to human dignity and inalienable human rights that is strictly limited to established methods of constitutional interpretation.[46] Human dignity and human rights are, accordingly, largely severed from their meta-positive origins and treated as – or at least equated to – notions of positive law.[47] The object of interpretation is thus adapted to legal methodology.

In search of reliable guideposts for the interpretation of human dignity and human rights within the realm of positive law, *Herdegen* places a particular emphasis on Art. 1(2) Basic Law as a gateway to the fundamental values of the international community.[48] Based on the observation that the drafters had modelled the first two paragraphs of Art. 1 Basic Law on the Universal Declaration of Human Rights,[49] he posits that the pledge to inalienable human rights "as the basis of every community, of peace and of justice in the world"[50] forms a bridge to the body of universal human rights recognised today as an integral part of positive international law.[51] These international human rights standards, in turn, are considered to provide essential guidance in the interpretation of both the dignity clause and the subsequent bill of fundamental rights.[52]

When *Herdegen*'s new commentary on Art. 1(1) and (2) Basic Law was first published, his "positivist" reinterpretation of *Dürig*'s – by then canonical – text was met with stinging criticism from other constitutional scholars. Initially, the focus of the debate was on the dignity clause. *Ernst Wolfgang Böckenförde*, a prominent constitutional lawyer and legal philosopher who had served on the Federal Constitutional Court from 1983 to 1996, accused *Herdegen* of having wilfully broken with the post-war constitutional consensus of human dignity

---

[43] *G. Dürig/T. Maunz*, Vorwort zur 1. Auflage, in: idem (eds.), Grundgesetz: Kommentar (1958).

[44] *M. Herdegen*, Art. 1 Abs. 1, in: G. Dürig et al. (eds.), Grundgesetz: Kommentar (2003); *idem*, Art. 1 Abs. 2, in: G. Dürig et al. (eds.), Grundgesetz: Kommentar (2004). The following citations refer to the newest edition (Looseleaf, 100th instalment, 2023).

[45] *Herdegen* (n. 44), Art. 1 Abs. 1, para. 20 ("staatsrechtliche Betrachtung").

[46] *Herdegen* (n. 44), Art. 1 Abs. 1, para. 20.

[47] *Herdegen* (n. 44), Art. 1 Abs. 1, para. 20.

[48] *Herdegen* (n. 44), Art. 1 Abs. 1, paras. 3, 42, 44.

[49] See also pp. 121 ff., below.

[50] Art. 1(2) Basic Law.

[51] *Herdegen* (n. 44), Art. 1 Abs. 1, paras. 3, 42, 44; *idem.*, Art. 1 Abs. 2, paras. 1 f., 22–35, 39–51.

[52] *Herdegen* (n. 44), Art. 1 Abs. 1, para. 42, 44; *idem.*, Art. 1 Abs. 2, paras. 47–51.

being firmly anchored in Christian natural law.[53] *Böckenförde* spoke of an "historic turning point" and a "watershed moment".[54]

The "Herdegen-Böckenförde debate" even made it to the frontpage of the *Frankfurter Allgemeine Zeitung*, Germany's leading conservative broadsheet.[55] The remarkable fact that a scholarly dispute about constitutional methodology became headline news highlights the pivotal role human dignity played and still plays in Germany's political culture. Human dignity not only defines the "identity" of the German constitution[56] but has at the same time, in a much broader sociological sense, become a crucial "integrative factor"[57] in the forging of Germany's distinctive identity as a nation.[58]

This may also explain why the pledge to inalienable human rights has until recently been largely neglected in German constitutional jurisprudence and scholoarship. Given that Germany was unable to boast an unbroken human rights tradition of its own, the fledgling (West) German democracy, in fleshing out its new identity, gravitated first towards the novel[59] and therefore more open constitutional concept of human dignity. Given that the overwhelming majority of the population were still practising Catholics and Protestants at this time, the concepts of Christian personalism and German idealism conjured up by the notion of human dignity seemed far better suited as a rallying point for Germany's new constitutional identity[60] than the more generic human rights tradition commonly associated with inalienable rights.[61]

It should have come as no surprise, therefore, that *Herdegen*'s interpretation of inalienable human rights as a normative bridge to international human rights law was considered just as "revolutionary"[62] as his "positivist" reinterpretation of the dignity clause. His critics insisted that the natural law notion of inalienable human rights cannot be magically transformed into a gateway to positive

---

[53] *E.-W. Böckenförde*, Die Würde des Menschen war unantastbar, Frankfurter Allgemeine Zeitung, 3 September 2003, 33.

[54] *Böckenförde* (n. 53), 33.

[55] Streit über Menschenwürde im Grundgesetz, Frankfurter Allgemeine Zeitung, 3 September 2003, 1.

[56] See n. 3, above.

[57] As to "integrative factors" and their origin in Rudolf Smend's "integration theory", see pp. 125 ff., below.

[58] As to the legal notion of national identity, see Art. 4(2) Treaty on European Union, 2012 Official Journal of the European Union C 326/13 (hereinafter: TEU).

[59] As to the novelty of human dignity as a legal concept, see pp. 121 ff., below.

[60] See *Baldus* (n. 4), 60–103.

[61] As to the link between inalienable rights and the human rights tradition, see pp. 121 ff. and pp. 145 ff., below.

[62] *C. Hillgruber*, Der internationale Menschenrechtsstandard – geltendes Verfassungsrecht?, in: G. Gornig et al. (eds.), Iustitia et Pax: Gedächtnisschrift für Dieter Blumenwitz (2008), 123–142, 128.

human rights law.[63] They argued that the drafters of the Basic Law purposefully ranked international treaties and general international law below the constitution.[64] This original intent would therefore be turned on its head if, via the pledge to inalienable human rights, international human rights law were suddenly elevated to the pinnacle of the constitution.[65] The constitutional floodgates would then be opened to the unfiltered influx of international human rights law, and the idiosyncrasies of Germany's celebrated post-war fundamental rights jurisprudence would gradually be washed away.[66] The novel "positivist" reading of the pledge to inalienable human rights would thereby lead inexorably to the erosion of Germany's constitutional identity.

IV. Inalienable human rights in the jurisprudence of the Federal Constitutional Court

The evolution of the jurisprudence of the Federal Constitutional Court points, however, in a different direction. Rather than eroding Germany's constitutional identity, the link established between the pledge to human dignity and inalienable human rights on the one hand and international human rights law on the other is in fact deeply embedded in Germany's constitutional DNA.

A closer look at the Federal Constitutional Court's case law demonstrates that the Court has in fact always been conscious of this essential connection between human dignity, inalienable human rights, positive constitutional law and the emergence of the international human rights system.

A. Context: the role of the Universal Declaration of Human Rights in the travaux préparatoires of the Basic Law

The genetic link between inalienable and international human rights finds its most conspicuous expression in the fact that the first two paragraphs of Art. 1 Basic Law echo – practically in *haec verba* – the preamble of the Universal Declaration of Human Rights.[67] This textual match is no coincidence. The *travaux préparatoires* document extensively that the drafters of the Basic Law

---

[63] *Hillgruber* (n. 62), 139. In a similar vein, *M. Jestaedt*, Selbstand und Offenheit der Verfassung gegenüber nationalem, supranationalem und internationalem Recht, in: J. Isensee/P. Kirchhof (eds.), Handbuch des Staatsrechts der Bundesrepublik, vol. 12 (3rd edn., 2014), § 264 para. 84.

[64] *Hillgruber* (n. 62), 139–142.

[65] *Hillgruber* (n. 62), 128 f.

[66] *Hillgruber* (n. 62), 129.

[67] UDHR, Preamble, para. 1: "Whereas recognition of the inherent dignity and of the equal and inalienable rights of all members of the human family is the foundation of freedom, justice and peace in the world, […]."

attached great importance to the Universal Declaration because it embodied a "common understanding"[68] of human rights, which, in 1948, had almost miraculously bridged the deepening ideological divide between East and West.[69] Taking the Declaration as a reference point for drafting the bill of fundamental rights was thus informed by the hope that a constitution anchored in this universal consensus could serve as a basis for Germany's swift reunification and reinstatement as an "equal partner"[70] within the international community.[71]

Accordingly, the pledge to human dignity and inalienable human rights in Art. 1(1) and (2) Basic Law refers to the common, universal understanding of these foundational values as laid down in the Universal Declaration. Whereas the reference to inalienable rights conjures up associations with the human rights tradition of the enlightenment, the simultaneous invocation of human dignity marks, however, a new departure in the evolution of human rights.

During the 1940s human dignity was a novel concept in the human rights domain.[72] Its emergence as the highest value underpinning the fledgling international human rights system therefore signalled a break with the previous human rights tradition in two important respects.

Firstly, human dignity was intended to provide human rights with a pluralistic foundation.[73] The aim of making human rights truly universal was irreconcilable with grounding them in any particular theory of natural law. In the Universal Declaration all references to nature and the Creator were accordingly erased from the classical templates and substituted by the notion of human dignity.[74] Human dignity was, however, not intended to be a full substitute for the omitted answers to the question of the ultimate foundation of human rights. The value of dignity operates rather as a "halt to reflection" (*Reflexionsstop*);[75] it marks the thin "overlapping consensus"[76] on which the modern edifice of international human rights law is built. In a similar vein, *René Cassin*, one of the "fathers" of the Declaration, described the function of human dignity as allowing the drafters

---

[68] UDHR, Preamble, para. 7.

[69] See *Hong* (n. 13), 241–244, 613 f. and *T. Rensmann*, Wertordnung und Verfassung (2007), 25–42, each with further references.

[70] See the Preamble of the Basic Law: "[...] Inspired by the determination to promote world peace as an equal partner in a united Europe [...]."

[71] *Rensmann* (n. 69), 25 f.

[72] *T. Rensmann*, Menschenwürde als universaler Rechtsbegriff, in: C. Thies (ed.), Der Wert der Menschenwürde (2009), 75–92.

[73] *Rensmann* (n. 72), 77–79, 85–89.

[74] *Rensmann* (n. 69), 15 f. with further references.

[75] *N. Luhmann*, Gibt es in unserer Gesellschaft noch unverzichtbare Normen? (1993), 19.

[76] *J. Rawls*, A Theory of Justice (revised edn., 1999), 340.

> "to take no position on the nature of man and of society and to avoid metaphysical controversies, notably the conflicting doctrines of spiritualists, traditionalist, and materialists regarding the origin of the rights of man."[77]

The French Catholic philosopher *Jacques Maritain* who in 1947 had been commissioned by UNESCO to preside over an interdisciplinary and intercultural "Committee on the Philosophic Bases of Human Rights" put it similarly:

> "The philosophies of our times, notwithstanding their divergencies, have deepened faith in the dignity of man."[78]

Given the variety of faiths and beliefs amongst the drafters of the Basic Law, this pluralistic conception of human dignity provided a welcome compromise position in the intense and divisive debates on the meta-positive origin of human rights during the drafting process.[79] The invocation of human dignity in Art. 1(1) Basic Law was thus also conceived as an "uninterpreted hypothesis" (*nicht interpretierte These*) which "could be understood theologically by some, philosophically by others and ethically by yet others."[80]

Secondly, human dignity also marked a substantive break with the prevailing liberal human rights tradition. The Universal Declaration is built on a "value system" in which human dignity as the highest value overarches the trinity of freedom, equality and brotherhood (or "solidarity" in modern parlance).[81] The ultimate goal of human rights is hence no longer limited to ensuring "freedom" in the sense of a "right to be let alone"[82] but extends to those societal conditions that are "indispensable for […] [a person's] dignity and the free and full development of his [or her] personality".[83]

This communitarian vision of freedom in dignity substantially changes the ambit and structure of human rights. The Universal Declaration not only guarantees classical negative rights but also social rights which typically require positive action by the State.[84] All human rights – liberal and social rights – are

---

[77] *R. Cassin*, La pensée et l'action (1972), 108; English translation by *J. Morsink*, The Universal Declaration of Human Rights (1999), 287.

[78] UNESCO (ed.), Human Rights: Comments and Interpretations (1949), 260.

[79] *Rensmann* (n. 69), 29–32.

[80] *T. Heuss*, Fourth Session of the Policy Committee (Grundsatzausschuss) of the Parliamentary Council, 23 September 1948, in: Deutscher Bundestag/Bundesarchiv (eds.), Der Parlamentarische Rat 1948–1949 – Akten und Protokolle, vol. 5/1 (1993), 67, 72 (translation by the author).

[81] Art. 1 UDHR and Preamble, para. 1. As to the conceptualisation of the UDHR as a value system, see *Rensmann* (n. 69), 29–32; *idem*, Normative Values in Modern Constitutionalism, in: C. Hugo/T.M.J. Möllers (eds.), Legality and Limitation of Powers (2019), 19–34, 24–26.

[82] *S. Warren/L. Brandeis*, The Right to Privacy, Harvard Law Review 4 (1890), 193–216, 193.

[83] Art. 22 UDHR.

[84] Art. 22–27 UHDR.

thus considered "inalienable"; they are – as it was later put – "indivisible, interdependent and interrelated".[85]

By tearing down the wall of separation established by the liberal human rights tradition between the governmental and societal spheres, human rights are, in addition, endowed with a constitutive and "transformative"[86] dimension. This finds its clearest expression in Art. 28 UDHR, according to which "everyone is entitled to a social and international order in which the rights and freedoms set forth in […] [the] Declaration can be fully realised". Human rights are thus understood not only as individual rights but also as normative "values" or "principles" which underpin and structure the social order at the domestic and international levels. As essential constitutional building blocks, they provide the "basis of every community […] in the world"[87].

The framers of the Basic Law recognised that their programmatic commitment to human dignity and the value system of the Universal Declaration inevitably encompassed these social and constitutive dimensions of human rights.[88] Yet, at the same time they were determined not to repeat the mistakes that had led to the downfall of the Weimar Republic. The Achilles' heel of the Weimar Constitution of 1919[89] was considered to have been its procedural, relativistic approach to democracy and, in particular, the weak normative power of fundamental rights.[90] As a response, Art. 1(3) Basic Law, which immediately follows the pledge to human dignity and inalienable human rights, declares the bill of fundamental rights binding on "the legislature, the executive and the judiciary as directly applicable law".

The goal of endowing fundamental rights with strict normativity and justiciability, however, seemed to militate against the incorporation of such positive human rights dimensions, which under the Weimar Constitution had been widely considered mere "programmatic" provisions devoid of any normative force.[91] In the process of drafting the Basic Law the issue of reconciling the programmatic commitment to human dignity and inalienable human rights, on the one hand, with the strict normativity of the new constitution, on the other, remained largely unresolved.[92] The social and constitutive dimensions of

---

[85] Vienna Declaration and Programme of Action, 25 June 1993, International Legal Materials 32 (1993), 1661, chapter I, para. 5.

[86] *K.E. Klare*, Legal Culture and Transformative Constitutionalism, South African Journal on Human Rights 14 (1998), 146–188.

[87] See Art. 1(2) Basic Law.

[88] See *Rensmann* (n. 69), 33–36.

[89] Constitution of the German Empire, 11 August 1919, Reichsgesetzblatt 1919, 1383.

[90] *Rensmann* (n. 69), 33; *idem* (n. 81), 26 f.

[91] *Rensmann* (n. 81), 27. See also *idem*, Domestic Courts as International Human Rights Courts: A German Perspective, in: S. Kadelbach et al. (eds.), Judging International Human Rights (2018), 471–496, 473 f.

[92] *Rensmann* (n. 69), 33–36, 40–42.

human dignity and inalienable human rights therefore did not find clear textual expression in the bill of fundamental rights. The tasks of completing the "human rights revolution"[93] proclaimed in the Universal Declaration and the first two paragraphs of Art. 1 Basic Law was therefore left primarily to the judiciary and in particular to the Federal Constitutional Court.[94]

B. History, philosophy and sociology: inalienable human rights as meta-positive values

1. Radbruch, Smend and the United Nations

The main battleground for the early jurisprudence of the Federal Constitutional Court on the relationship between inalienable human rights, human dignity and positive constitutional law was the equality of men and women, in particular in matrimonial and family matters.[95] Although gender equality had already featured amongst the fundamental rights of the Weimar Constitution,[96] it had not been considered a human right and consequently its personal ambit only extended to German nationals.[97] Equality of men and women was restricted to "civil rights" and, moreover, only guaranteed "in principle", thus leaving its interpretation open to unspecified limitations.[98] Whilst the Weimar Constitution explicitly stated that marriage "shall rest upon the equality of both sexes", this provision was placed in the programmatic and hence legally non-binding section on community life.[99]

Against this backdrop and the social reality in post-war West Germany, the elevation of the equality of men and women to a fundamental right of "all human beings"[100] binding on all three branches of government "as directly applicable law"[101] was nothing short of a revolution. This constitutional revolution was foreshadowed by the emergence of international human rights law. The Charter of the United Nations,[102] the new "constitution" of the international community, had prepared the ground by putting special emphasis on the close connection between human dignity, human rights and equal rights for men and

93 See *L.B. Sohn*, The New International Law: Protection of the Rights of the Individuals Rather Than States, American University Law Review 32 (1982–1983), 1–64, 1.

94 *Rensmann* (n. 91), 474.

95 As to the issue of equal pay for men and women, see *Rensmann* (n. 69), 76–81.

96 See n. 89, above.

97 Art. 109(1) and (2) Weimar Constitution.

98 Art. 109(2) Weimar Constitution.

99 Art. 119(1) Weimar Constitution. As to the programmatic nature, see Federal Constitutional Court, judgment of 18 December 1953, BVerfGE 3, 225, 242.

100 Art. 3(2) in conjunction with (1) Basic Law.

101 Art. 1(3) Basic Law.

102 Charter of the United Nations, 26 June 1945, 1 UNTS 15 (hereinafter UN Charter).

women.[103] Three years later the Universal Declaration of Human Rights resoundingly reaffirmed that "all human beings are born free and equal in rights"[104] and hence "entitled to all […] [human] rights […] without distinction of […] sex".[105] The Declaration explicitly stresses that gender equality also applies "to marriage, during marriage and at its dissolution".[106]

When the framers of the Basic Law took up the baton from the United Nations by recognising the equality of men and women as a human and fundamental right in Art. 3(2) Basic Law,[107] they were well aware of the revolutionary consequences of this move and therefore took the unusual step of suspending the revolution for almost four years. In order to allow sufficient time for Parliament to eliminate all patriarchal privileges from existing legislation, Art. 117(1) Basic Law set forth that all law inconsistent with Art. 3(2) Basic Law was to "remain in force until adapted to that provision, but not beyond 31 March 1953."[108]

The deadline passed without Parliament having been able to agree on the reforms necessary to bring all pre-constitutional statutes in line with the principle of gender equality.[109] The government and the parliamentary majority saw in particular no need to amend matrimonial and family law. They argued that the subservience of women within the family was anchored in Christian natural law and that the equality clause of Art. 3(2) Basic Law in its interplay with the constitutional protection of marriage and the family (Art. 6(1) Basic Law) ought to be interpreted accordingly.[110] This view was seconded by *Dürig*[111] and other constitutional scholars who championed a Christian natural law interpretation of human dignity and inalienable human rights.[112]

---

[103] UN Charter, Preamble, Art. 1(3), 13(1)(b), 55(3), 76.

[104] Art. 1 UDHR.

[105] Art. 2(1) UDHR.

[106] Art. 16(1) UDHR.

[107] See Art. 1(3) Basic Law.

[108] On the continuing validity of pre-constitutional law according to Art. 123(1) Basic Law see *T. Rensmann*, Die Einheit der Rechtsordnung auf Grundlage der Grund- und Menschenrechte, in: P. Hellwege/M. Soniewicka (eds.), Die Einheit der Rechtsordnung (2020), 83–105, 91.

[109] See Federal Constitutional Court, judgment of 18 December 1953, BVerfGE 3, 225, 226; *T. Darnstädt*, Verschlusssache Karlsruhe (2018), 98–100.

[110] See Federal Constitutional Court, judgment of 29 July 1959, BVerfGE 10, 59, 63–65; *Darnstädt* (n. 109), 98–100.

[111] *G. Dürig*, Art. 3 II GG – vom verfassungsrechtlichen Standpunkt gesehen, Zeitschrift für das gesamte Familienrecht 1 (1954), 2–5, 4. As to Dürig's Christian interpretation of human dignity, see pp. 117 ff., above.

[112] See Federal Constitutional Court, judgment of 29 July 1959, BVerfGE 10, 59, 72 with further references.

As soon as the deadline set in Art. 117(1) Basic Law had passed, the matter was brought before the Federal Constitutional Court.[113] In a curious procedural twist, the Court was confronted with the issue in the context of a reference by a higher regional court challenging the "constitutionality" of Art. 117(1) Basic Law.[114] The case thus raised the intriguing question of "unconstitutional constitutional law"[115] and thereby elevated the issue of gender equality to a meta-positive level.

The referring court argued that Art. 117(1) Basic Law had created "legal chaos" by having rendered large parts of matrimonial and family law void after the constitutional deadline lapsed.[116] Given that no amending legislation had been passed, the judiciary was now left without any statutory guidance as to how to fill the ensuing gaps; this, in turn, was considered by the referring court as violating the principle of legal certainty, which, as a core tenet of the rule of law, was argued to be binding not only on all constituted State power but also on the *pouvoir constituant* itself. For this reason, the referring court asked the Federal Constitutional Court to rule that the statutory provisions affected by the principle of gender equality were to remain in force until the legislature had addressed the situation.

Had the reference been successful, the gender equality revolution would have been delayed even further. As chance would have it, however, the revolution had already reached the Federal Constitutional Court. The judge rapporteur in this case was *Erna Scheffler*, the first and for many years only female justice on the Federal Constitutional Court.[117] Prior to her appointment she had earned herself a reputation as a women's rights activist. In a high-profile presentation at the annual conference of the German Lawyer's Association (*Deutscher Juristentag*) in 1950 she had argued forcefully that Art. 3(2) Basic Law required the unconditional removal of all male privileges from the statute book.[118]

---

[113] Federal Constitutional Court, judgment of 18 December 1953, BVerfGE 3, 225.

[114] Federal Constitutional Court, judgment of 18 December 1953, BVerfGE 3, 225, 226 f.

[115] Federal Constitutional Court, judgment of 18 December 1953, BVerfGE 3, 225, 231–234.

[116] See Federal Constitutional Court, judgment of 18 December 1953, BVerfGE 3, 225, 226 f., 239.

[117] See *M. Hansen*, Erna Scheffler (1893–1983): Erste Richterin am Bundesverfassungsgericht und Wegbereiterin einer geschlechtergerechten Gesellschaft (2019); on her role in this particular case, *Darnstädt* (n. 109), 91–127; *T. Rensmann*, Abschied von Lüth? Zur Kontextualisierung und Historisierung von verfassungsgerichtlichen Leitentscheidungen, in: T. Groh et al. (eds.), Verfassungsrecht, Völkerrecht, Menschenrechte – Vom Recht im Zentrum der Internationalen Beziehungen. Festschrift für Ulrich Fastenrath (2019), 55–77, 67–71.

[118] *E. Scheffler*, Gleichberechtigung der Frau: In welcher Weise empfiehlt es sich, gemäß Art. 117 des Grundgesetzes das geltende Recht an Art. 3 Abs. 2 des Grundgesetzes anzupassen?, Verhandlungen des Deutsches Juristentages 38 (1950), B 3–B 30.

In her new role as justice at the Federal Constitutional Court, *Scheffler* managed to convince her male colleagues on the bench to grasp the opportunity presented by these proceedings and spell out clearly the proper understanding of Art. 3(2) Basic Law in matrimonial and family law.[119] The case pitted the natural law reading embraced by the parliamentary majority against the pluralistic understanding of human dignity and human rights espoused by the United Nations, the drafters of the Basic Law and *Scheffler*.

The Court acknowledged the, albeit highly unlikely, possibility of "unconstitutional constitutional law" and considered its power of judicial review, in such exceptional instances, to extend to original constitutional law.[120] The Federal Constitutional Court based this extraordinary power on the close link between the Federal Republic of Germany's constitutional identity and the historical context in which the Basic Law was drafted. In the eyes of the Federal Constitutional Court, the experience of the Nazi dictatorship had discredited a strictly positivist approach to the law since some of the worst injustice perpetrated during the "Third Reich" had been committed under the cloak of properly enacted statutes.[121] Consequently, the drafters of the Basic Law had opted for a value-oriented conception of the rule of law and had entrenched basic tenets of justice in Art. 1 and 20 Basic Law.

The Court stressed that by having been incorporated into positive constitutional law, human dignity, inalienable human rights and other principles of "substantive justice" had not lost their meta-positive quality.[122] Accordingly, the Federal Constitutional Court considered the *pouvoir constituant* itself to have been bound by such principles of justice. In order to delineate more precisely the limits of the otherwise unfettered power of constitution-making, the Court relied on *Gustav Radbruch*'s famous formula:[123]

"The conflict between justice and legal certainty may well be resolved in this way: The positive law, secured by legislation and power, takes precedence even when its content is unjust and fails to benefit the people, unless the conflict between statute and justice reaches such an intolerable degree that the statute, as 'flawed law', must yield to justice."[124]

In the case at issue, the reliance of the Court on the *Radbruch* formula was significant because it underscored the paramount importance attached by the Federal Constitutional Court to the rule of law, legal certainty and the supremacy of the positive constitution. The strong emphasis on legal certainty as the

---

[119] *Darnstädt* (n. 109), 108–120.

[120] Federal Constitutional Court, judgment of 18 December 1953, BVerfGE 3, 225, 231–236.

[121] Federal Constitutional Court, judgment of 18 December 1953, BVerfGE 3, 225, 232.

[122] Federal Constitutional Court, judgment of 18 December 1953, BVerfGE 3, 225, 233.

[123] Federal Constitutional Court, judgment of 18 December 1953, BVerfGE 3, 225, 232 f.

[124] *G. Radbruch*, Statutory Lawlessness and Supra-Statutory Law (1946), Oxford Journal of Legal Studies 26 (2006), 1–11, 7 (translated by B. Litschewski/S.L. Paulson).

default position in the *Radbruch* formula reflected the Federal Constitutional Court's consciousness of a second historical lesson to be gleaned from Germany's recent dictatorial past. Since the Nazi regime in its constitutional theory and practice had in fact relied heavily on its own – Darwinist – version of natural law,[125] the dangers of value-free positivism needed to be carefully balanced against the hazards of an unqualified reliance on natural law.

The Federal Constitutional Court thus unequivocally rejected any direct recourse to natural law. Due to the multitude of approaches and theories associated with this indeterminate notion, natural law as such was considered unsuitable as a basis for judicial review.[126]

In the case at hand, the Federal Constitutional Court assumed that the *pouvoir constituant*, by incorporating the pledge to human dignity and inalienable human rights into the constitution, had bound itself to meta-positive standards of justice.[127] However, bearing in mind that human dignity conjured up associations with Christian natural law theory,[128] this argument begged the question as to whether the pledge in Art. 1(1) and (2) Basic Law referred to a Christian understanding of justice after all. Notwithstanding, the Federal Constitutional Court insisted that in view of the pluralistic composition of the Parliamentary Council (the *Parlamentarischer Rat* – the body which had drafted the Basic Law), the interpretation of human dignity and human rights in the light of any particular faith or belief would be incompatible with the original intent.[129]

Given that the Federal Constitutional Court therefore assumed that recourse to any *specific* strand of natural law was impermissible, the question arose as to how else to determine the substance of human dignity, inalienable human rights and other principles of justice. In the context of his formula, *Radbruch* provided the following answer:

> "There are principles of law […] that are weightier than any legal enactment, so that a law in conflict with them is devoid of validity. These principles are known as natural law or the law of reason. To be sure, their details remain open to question, but the work of centuries has in fact established a solid core of them, and they have come to enjoy such far-reaching consensus in the so-called declarations of human and civil rights that only the dogmatic sceptic could entertain doubts about […] them."[130]

Radbruch's formula is thus based on a universal, pluralistic and dynamic notion of justice which leaves the "details" of its ultimate origin (such as nature or reason) open and instead relies on a global consensus evolving over time

---

[125] See *Rensmann* (n. 69), 29 f.; *idem* (n. 108), 87–90, 104.

[126] See Federal Constitutional Court, judgment of 29 July 1959, BVerfGE 10, 59, 81.

[127] Federal Constitutional Court, judgment of 18 December 1953, BVerfGE 3, 225, 233.

[128] See pp. 117, above.

[129] Federal Constitutional Court, judgment of 18 December 1953, BVerfGE 3, 225, 233 f.

[130] *G. Radbruch*, Five Minutes of Legal Philosophy (1945), Oxford Journal of Legal Studies 26 (2006), 13–15, 14 f. (translated by B. Litschewski/S.L. Paulson).

("the work of centuries") and finding its authoritative expression in successive human rights declarations.[131] Several references to the Universal Declaration of Human Rights,[132] to the French Declaration of the Rights of Man and of the Citizen[133] and to the American human rights tradition[134] in the Federal Constitutional Court's early jurisprudence bear witness to the influence of *Radbruch*'s thinking in this regard.

The Federal Constitutional Court found additional support for such a pluralistic and dynamic approach in *Rudolf Smend*'s "theory of integration", which was very influential in constitutional scholarship and judicial practice during the formative years of the Federal Republic of Germany.[135] In his pioneering interdisciplinary study *Verfassung und Verfassungsrecht* (The Constitution and Constitutional Law), first published in 1928 during the Weimar Republic, *Smend* combined legal theory and doctrine with sociological methodology.[136] He conceptualised the social phenomenon (the "reality") of the State as a constant process of "integration".[137] In this process the constitution is considered a decisive "integrative factor".[138] In particular, fundamental rights are accordingly not perceived primarily as "technical legal norms" but rather as the proclamation of a "cultural" or "value system" in the name of which a people aspire to be constitutionally united.[139] In *Smend*'s view fundamental rights are hence the source of the legitimacy of a given legal order and the embodiment of its object and purpose. As a matter of legal doctrine, he posited that fundamental rights therefore assume an important "directive function" in the sense that the "value system" established by them provides essential guidance for the interpretation of the entire legal order.[140]

Applied to the Basic Law, *Smend*'s theory, however, assumed a new, universal dimension: In Art. 1 Basic Law the German people profess their faith in human dignity and inalienable human rights "as the basis of every community, of peace and of justice in the world". Since 1949 it is thus the "value system"

---

[131] See also *G. Lohmann*, Menschenrechte und Recht. Zu Gustav Radbruchs "Fünfter Minute", in: Kirste (n. 18), 361–368.

[132] Federal Constitutional Court, order of 17 January 1957, BVerfGE 6, 55, 73; Federal Constitutional Court, order of 30 June 1964, BVerfGE 18, 112, 118; Federal Constitutional Court, order of 4 May 1971, BVerfGE 31, 58, 68.

[133] Federal Constitutional Court, judgment of 15 January 1958, BVerfGE 7, 198, 208.

[134] Federal Constitutional Court, judgment of 15 January 1958, BVerfGE 7, 198, 208 (with reference to *Palko v. Connecticut*, 302 US 319 [1937]).

[135] See *Rensmann* (n. 69), 107–113.

[136] *R. Smend*, Verfassung und Verfassungsrecht (1928), reprinted in: idem, Staatsrechtliche Abhandlungen (2nd edn., 1968), 119–276.

[137] *Smend* (n. 136), 136–142.

[138] *Smend* (n. 136), 189–198.

[139] *Smend* (n. 136), 264 f.

[140] *Smend* (n. 136), 265.

of the international community in the name of which the German people have vowed to be constitutionally united.

In relation to the debate about gender equality, *Smend*'s integration theory thus offered two important arguments against an instrumentalisation of Christian natural law in order to preserve male privileges in matrimonial and family law.[141] Firstly, in the dynamic process of integration the German people had chosen the core humanitarian values of the UN Charter and Universal Declaration of Human Rights as their constitutional rallying point, namely human dignity, inalienable human rights and equal rights for men and women. Secondly, in the light of this fundamental constitutional decision, the interpretation of marriage and family as legal notions had thus to be based on the "directive dimension" of this "value system" rather than on static notions of natural law or traditional values.

In the case at hand, the Federal Constitutional Court, however, still needed to overcome the argument made by the referring court that, due to its general and "ideological" nature, the principle of gender equality was not amenable to judicial application without a prior concretisation by the legislature.[142] In the eyes of the referring court, the *pouvoir constituant* had therefore in effect relinquished large swathes of matrimonial and family law to the subjective preferences of the judiciary and had accordingly acted with intolerable disregard for the principles of legal certainty and the rule of law.[143]

The Federal Constitutional Court conceded that legal certainty itself belonged to the indispensable conditions for a just constitutional order and that, in extreme cases, its violation could thus render a constitutional provision void.[144] At the same time, however, the Court insisted that the enactment of Art. 117(1) Basic Law had not transgressed these outer boundaries.

In support of this assessment the Court pointed out that the process of constitution-making itself frequently requires that legal certainty be balanced against substantive principles of justice and that the *pouvoir constituant* enjoyed a large margin of appreciation in this regard.[145] The Federal Constitutional Court highlighted that the equality of men and women must also be considered a fundamental tenet of justice and that the goal of its effective implementation would accordingly justify a certain interference with the principle of legal certainty.[146]

---

[141] In a closely related case (Federal Constitutional Court, judgment of 29 July 1959, BVerfGE 10, 59), in which Erna Scheffler also acted as judge rapporteur, she explicitly relied on Smend in her draft judgment to counter the argument that Art. 3(2) Basic Law ought to be interpreted in the light of Christian natural law, see *Darnstädt* (n. 109), 122 f.

[142] See Federal Constitutional Court, judgment of 18 December 1953, BVerfGE 3, 225, 239.

[143] See Federal Constitutional Court, judgment of 18 December 1953, BVerfGE 3, 225, 239.

[144] Federal Constitutional Court, judgment of 18 December 1953, BVerfGE 3, 225, 237.

[145] Federal Constitutional Court, judgment of 18 December 1953, BVerfGE 3, 225, 237 f.

[146] Federal Constitutional Court, judgment of 18 December 1953, BVerfGE 3, 225, 238.

In the opinion of the Court, any legal uncertainty caused by Art. 117(1) Basic Law would at any rate not have reached the "intolerable" degree required by the *Radbruch* formula. The Court drew attention to the fact that Art. 3(2) Basic Law supplied the judiciary with a sufficiently objective standard to fill any gaps created by Parliament having failed to introduce amending legislation within the constitutional deadline. Importantly, this implied the recognition of a constitutive or transformative dimension of fundamental rights since the Court considered Art. 3(2) Basic Law to provide guidance in the adjudication of the relationship between private individuals in matrimonial and family matters.[147]

At this juncture the Court used the opportunity to make some important general observations on the methodological challenges presented by the Basic Law having endowed the universal values of human dignity and inalienable human rights, and hence also the principle of gender equality, with the status of "directly applicable" constitutional law.[148] The key contentions can be summed up as follows:[149]

(a) Due to their general and "programmatic" nature, fundamental rights cannot be interpreted in the positivist tradition in which the judicial branch is perceived to be completely controlled by statutory provisions and in this sense "*en quelque façon nulle*".[150]

(b) The open-textured nature of human and fundamental rights requires, rather, that these rights be fleshed out by the judiciary. Under the Basic Law the judiciary is therefore assigned a new role which is more akin to the judicial function in common law systems.

(c) In this new role judges remain subject to the rule of law. The rationality and objectivity of their judgments is primarily secured by the time-honoured methods of the common law tradition.

(d) Human and fundamental rights jurisprudence, hence, gradually develops from the abstract "first principles" laid down in the bill of rights into an increasingly differentiated body of case law. By virtue of the rule-of-law principle, this case law exerts a certain *stare decisis* effect. This in turn contributes to the gradual emergence of a "common law" of human and fundamental rights.

(e) Given the universal nature of the underlying values of human dignity and inalienable human rights, jurisprudence from other jurisdictions following the

---

[147] *Rensmann* (n. 117), 71.

[148] Federal Constitutional Court, judgment of 18 December 1953, BVerfGE 3, 225, 239–247.

[149] See also *Rensmann* (n. 117) 64–67.

[150] See *C. de Montesquieu*, De l'Esprit des Lois (1748), Livre XI, Chapitre VI.

same "value system" needs to be accorded "decent respect".[151] Comparative law hence becomes a key element of fundamental rights adjudication.[152]

(f) A central function of the judiciary is to translate the abstract principles of human and fundamental rights into individual justice.[153] This can be achieved only if "all relevant circumstances of the individual case are taken into account".[154] Since the judicial function therefore increasingly turns on the proper assessment of the factual context of a given case, fundamental rights jurisprudence is increasingly dependent on trans- and interdisciplinary assistance. In this context, *Martin Drath*, at the time one of *Scheffler*'s fellow justices on the bench, urgently called on constitutional scholars and practitioners "to venture beyond the traditional limits of their discipline and methodology and seek intensive cooperation with other humanities, in particular the social sciences."[155]

When *Scheffler* read out the Court's judgment confirming the constitutionality of Art. 117(1) Basic Law on 18 December 1953, she and her fellow justices had not only taken gender equality but indeed the overall "human rights revolution" a decisive step forward. It was the first time the Court unequivocally recognised the two innovations introduced by the Universal Declaration into the human rights tradition: firstly, the universal and pluralistic understanding of human dignity and inalienable human rights, and secondly, the constitutive and transformative dimension of human and fundamental rights which provide "guidelines and impulses"[156] for all areas of law, including matrimonial and family law.

At the same time the Court supplied the judiciary with a toolbox for transporting the "guidelines and impulses" of the "value system" of international human rights into the entire legal system and thereby into the fabric of German society. Both for gender equality and the "human rights revolution" at large, this was to be, however, only the first episode in the ongoing and probably never-ending journey towards "the full realization of [the] pledge"[157] to human dignity and inalienable human rights.

---

[151] The link between "inalienable" or "unalienable" human rights and the duty to pay "decent respect to the opinions of mankind" was first established in the United States Declaration of Independence, 4 July 1776, paras. 1 f.; see *M. Risse*, On American Values, Unalienable Rights, and Human Rights: Some Reflections on the Pompeo Commission, Ethics & International Affairs 34 (2020), 13–31, 15–19.

[152] Federal Constitutional Court, judgment of 18 December 1953, BVerfGE 3, 225, 244.

[153] Federal Constitutional Court, judgment of 18 December 1953, BVerfGE 3, 225, 243.

[154] See Federal Constitutional Court, judgment of 15 January 1958, BVerfGE 7, 198, 212 (translation by the author).

[155] *M. Drath*, Die Grenzen der Verfassungsgerichtsbarkeit, in: Veröffentlichungen der Vereinigung der Deutschen Staatsrechtslehrer 9 (1950), 17–116, 111 (translation by the author).

[156] See Federal Constitutional Court, judgment of 15 January 1958, BVerfGE 7, 198, 205.

[157] UDHR, Preamble, para. 7.

2. Evolving standards of decency and the Universal Declaration of Human Rights

The first decision containing an explicit reference to the human rights clause in Art. 1(2) Basic Law concerned an extradition request by France in relation to a Yugoslav member of the French Foreign Legion who had fled to Germany.[158] The legionnaire was accused of having killed at least eleven civilians in a targeted attack carried out jointly with other comrades during their service in Algeria. Under French law he faced the death penalty.[159] A German court granted the extradition request in accordance with the terms of a bilateral extradition treaty. The legionnaire filed a constitutional complaint against the authorisation of his extradition. He argued that Art. 102 Basic Law had abolished capital punishment[160] and that exposing him to the risk of the death penalty thus violated his right to life under Art. 2(2) Basic Law.[161]

In the proceedings before the Federal Constitutional Court the German government submitted that the abolition of capital punishment did not belong to the "meta-constitutional values" recognised by Art. 1(1) and (2) Basic Law and was therefore simply based on a "positive decision" of the German *pouvoir constituant*.[162] Art. 102 Basic Law could thus not be considered to stand in the way of the complainant's extradition since both the prosecution and the execution of the sentence lay exclusively within the responsibility of France.

In its decision of 30 June 1964, the Federal Constitutional Court dismissed the constitutional complaint as unfounded. The Court agreed with the German government that, interpreted in its constitutional context and in the light of its object and purpose, Art. 102 Basic Law could not be considered to impede extradition to countries which had not yet abolished the death penalty.[163] This restrictive approach was based primarily on the "openness" of the constitution to international law and on the fact that at the time the death penalty was considered lawful under both international law and the majority of domestic legal orders.

The Court argued that the Basic Law, being underpinned by a pronounced "openness to international law" in principle, requires respect for the laws and legal views of foreign States even if they are not fully consistent with the "value order" of the German constitution.[164] In this context the Federal Constitutional

[158] Federal Constitutional Court, order of 30 June 1964, BVerfGE 18, 112.

[159] As to the facts, see Federal Constitutional Court, order of 30 June 1964, BVerfGE 18, 112, 112 f.

[160] Art. 102 Basic Law reads: "Capital punishment is abolished".

[161] Federal Constitutional Court, order of 30 June 1964, BVerfGE 18, 112, 114.

[162] Federal Constitutional Court, order of 30 June 1964, BVerfGE 18, 112, 114 f. (translations by the author).

[163] Federal Constitutional Court, order of 30 June 1964, BVerfGE 18, 112, 116–121.

[164] Federal Constitutional Court, order of 30 June 1964, BVerfGE 18, 112, 121. This is by now established case law, see, e.g. Federal Constitutional Court, order of 6 July 2005,

Court put special emphasis on the role of human rights as both the foundation and the limit of international cooperation in criminal matters.[165]

On the one hand the Court stressed that mutual legal assistance contributes to ensuring the prosecution and punishment of human rights violations "which are of common concern to all States".[166] In the present case a war crime was at issue: the complainant was accused of extrajudicial killings committed as a member of the armed forces during an armed conflict. On the other hand, given that the "openness" of the constitution to international law is itself premised on an international legal order rooted in "inalienable human rights",[167] the inviolability of these meta-constitutional values also defines the limits of the duty to respect the idiosyncrasies of other legal systems.[168]

At the heart of the case therefore lay the question as to whether the constitutional decision to abolish capital punishment in Art. 102 Basic Law was an emanation of inalienable human rights or not. In making this assessment, the Federal Constitutional Court could not rely on binding international law as such since the European Convention on Human Rights had not yet been ratified by France and the International Human Rights Covenants[169] were still under negotiation. The Court was therefore once again faced with the methodological problem of identifying those timeless and universal human rights which according to Art. 1(2) Basic Law are "the basis of every community, of peace and of justice in the world".

In order to establish the compatibility of the death penalty with such universal standards of justice, the Court proceeded to analyse the "legislation" and

BVerfGE 113, 154, para. 24: "[…] [T]he Basic Law proceeds on the basis that the state constituted by it is integrated into the system of international law of the community of States […] [and] it [therefore] requires that, in particular in matters of judicial assistance, the structures and contents of foreign legal systems and views of the law must in principle be respected […], even if in detail they do not comply with German views." English translation available at http://www.bverfg.de/e/rs20050706_2bvr225904en.html (last accessed on 28 September 2022).

[165] See also Federal Constitutional Court, order of 4 May 1971, BVerfGE 31, 58, a private international law case in which the Federal Constitutional Court enlarges upon the principles established in the *Death Penalty* case. At 75 f. the Federal Constitutional Court explicitly cites Art. 1(2) Basic Law both in support of the principle of "openness to international law" and with a view to defining its limits.

[166] Federal Constitutional Court, order of 30 June 1964, BVerfGE 18, 112, 121.

[167] See, with explicit reference to Art. 1(2) Basic Law, Federal Constitutional Court, order of 4 May 1971, BVerfGE 31, 58, 76.

[168] See the explicit reference to Art. 1(2) Basic Law in the arguments submitted by the Federal Government, Federal Constitutional Court, order of 30 June 1964, BVerfGE 18, 112, 114.

[169] International Covenant on Economic, Social and Cultural Rights, 16 December 1966, UNTS 993, 3; International Covenant on Civil and Political Rights, 16 December 1966, UNTS 999, 171.

"public opinion" of the "civilized world".[170] Importantly, the Federal Constitutional Court referred to the "standard of civilisation *reached today*"[171] and thereby echoed the dynamic approach of the US Supreme Court which – only a few years before in a comparable factual setting – had similarly interpreted the constitutional bill of rights in the light of "evolving standards of decency that mark the progress of a maturing society".[172]

At this juncture the Federal Constitutional Court for the first time explicitly recognised the pivotal role of the Universal Declaration of Human Rights as an authoritative restatement of inalienable human rights. Whilst the Court also referred to the European Convention on Human Rights, this was not motivated by its status as treaty law or as a reflection of a specifically European standard but rather by the fact that the Convention perceives itself merely as a means of reiterating and enforcing "rights stated in the Universal Declaration".[173]

In keeping with its previous jurisprudence,[174] the Federal Constitutional Court in addition undertook a comparative analysis of the attitude of foreign legal orders to the death penalty.[175] The particular attention paid by the Court to the "leading democracies of the Western world" is primarily attributable to the backdrop of the Cold War and to (West) Germany's special political status at the time.[176] However, the implied emphasis on democratic governance and the values of the "free world" also points to the fact that the *tertium comparationis* of any meaningful comparison must be the shared and effective commitment to the "common standard of achievement"[177] formulated in the Universal Declaration.

The result of this comparative analysis was crystal clear: The Universal Declaration had not outlawed the death penalty, its lawfulness was explicitly reaffirmed in the European Convention on Human Rights and the majority of States, including France and other "leading democracies", had retained capital punishment. Hence there was no doubt that at the time the imposition of the

---

[170] Federal Constitutional Court, order of 30 June 1964, BVerfGE 18, 112, 117.

[171] Federal Constitutional Court, order of 30 June 1964, BVerfGE 18, 112, 117 (emphasis added).

[172] *Trop v. Dulles* 356 US 86, 101 (1958). On the influence of the Universal Declaration of Human Rights on this case, see *T. Rensmann*, The Constitution as a Normative Order of Values, in: P.-M. Dupuy et al. (eds.), Völkerrecht als Wertordnung. Festschrift für Christian Tomuschat (2006), 259–278, 269 f.

[173] ECHR, Preamble, para. 5. See also Federal Constitutional Court, order of 4 May 1971, BVerfGE 31, 58, 68, with explicit reference to the Preamble.

[174] See Federal Constitutional Court, judgment of 18 December 1953, BVerfGE 3, 225, 244 and pp. 125 ff., above.

[175] Federal Constitutional Court, order of 30 June 1964, BVerfGE 18, 112, 118.

[176] Federal Constitutional Court, order of 30 June 1964, BVerfGE 18, 112, 118 (translation by the author).

[177] UDHR, Preamble, para. 8.

death penalty was compatible with the pledge to human dignity and inalienable human rights in Art. 1(1) and (2) Basic Law.

The Court seemed to suggest, however, that this assessment was not carved in stone and pointed to the continuing "general discourse" on the legitimacy and utility of the death penalty.[178] In the eyes of the Federal Constitutional Court, domestic public opinion and the "decent opinions of mankind"[179] thus deserve particular attention when monitoring "evolving standards of decency". This, in turn, involves, as the Court explicitly pointed out, the need to interact with other disciplines, since public opinion is shaped by a multitude of social, historical, philosophical and theological factors.[180]

Last but not least, the Federal Constitutional Court made some significant observations on the relationship between inalienable human rights and national constitutional identity. Whilst otherwise in agreement with the submissions of the Federal Government, the Court emphasised that the importance of Art. 102 Basic Law reached far beyond its status as positive constitutional law:

> "[Article 102 Basic Law] [...] is a decision of great significance in terms of state policy and legal policy. It contains a commitment to the fundamental value of human life and to a conception of the state which stands in marked contrast to the views of a political regime to which individual life meant little and which therefore blatantly abused the arrogated right over the life and death of the citizen. This decision must be understood against the backdrop of the particular historical situation in which it was made. It cannot therefore imply a value judgement on other legal orders which have not had this experience with a system of injustice and which – due to a different historical development, other political circumstances and a different political philosophy – have not made such a decision for themselves."[181]

Inalienable human rights thus allow for constitutional pluralism to accommodate different historical experiences, cultural traditions and philosophical outlooks. Within the limits set by inalienable human rights such pluralism requires mutual tolerance[182] and thus respect for the "constitutional identity" of other States. This also holds true for the human right to life which is at the heart of some of the most divisive issues in modern societies, such as the death penalty, abortion or the "right to die". As illustrated by the example of the death penalty, each domestic "constitutional decision" on these matters at the same time contributes to the universal discourse on "evolving standards of decency". Also in this sense, Art. 102 Basic Law was indeed a "decision of great significance". It stood at the beginning of a growing European and international consensus that "the abolition of the death penalty is essential for the protection of th[e]

---

[178] Federal Constitutional Court, order of 30 June 1964, BVerfGE 18, 112, 118.

[179] See n. 151, above.

[180] Federal Constitutional Court, order of 30 June 1964, BVerfGE 18, 112, 118.

[181] Federal Constitutional Court, order of 30 June 1964, BVerfGE 18, 112, 117 (translation by the author).

[182] See also Federal Constitutional Court, order of 4 May 1971, BVerfGE 31, 58, 75.

right [to life] and for the full recognition of the inherent dignity of all human beings".[183]

C. The turn to positive law: inalienable human rights as international human rights

Up until the early 2000s, inalienable human rights only received scant attention in the Federal Constitutional Court's jurisprudence.[184] This is primarily attributable to the fact that the Basic Law internalised the essential pillars of the "value system" of the Universal Declaration of Human Rights[185] and that constitutionally entrenched fundamental rights therefore provided the Federal Constitutional Court with a sufficient basis to uphold "substantive justice" within the German legal order.[186] The Court's rapidly expanding fundamental rights jurisprudence quickly coalesced into established case law and any remaining need for "meta-positive" reassurance was exclusively projected onto the dignity clause. At the same time, the international pedigree of human dignity and its inextricable connection with inalienable human rights faded into oblivion.

1. Consolidation of international human rights law, European integration and the end of the cold war

The renewed interest in inalienable human rights by the beginning of the new millennium can be attributed to several factors:

First, human rights gained a firm foothold in positive international law. By virtue of the two International Covenants[187] and a number of other "Core International Human Rights Instruments",[188] the rights laid down in the Universal

---

[183] ECtHR, *Al Nashiri v. Romania*, App. No. 33234/12, 31 May 2018, § 727.

[184] Subsequent to Federal Constitutional Court, order of 30 June 1964, BVerfGE 18, 112, explicit references to Art. 1(2) Basic Law can be found in Federal Constitutional Court, order of 4 May 1971, BVerfGE 31, 58, 75 f.; Federal Constitutional Court, order of 18 July 1973, BVerfGE 35, 382, 407; Federal Constitutional Court, judgment of 23 April 1991, BVerfGE 84, 90, 121; Federal Constitutional Court, judgment of 14 May 1996, BVerfGE 94, 49, 102 f.; Federal Constitutional Court, judgment of 3 March 2004, BVerfGE 109, 279, 310.

[185] See pp. 121, above.

[186] It was probably only a Freudian slip but nevertheless telling that, in one of the few instances in which the Federal Constitutional Court referred to Art. 1(2) Basic Law, the Court in Federal Constitutional Court, order of 18 July 1973, BVerfGE 35, 382, 407, referred to "fundamental rights" rather than "human rights" as "the basis of every community in the world."

[187] See n. 169, above.

[188] For a list of these treaties, see *United Nations, Office of the High Commission for Human Rights*, The Core International Human Rights Instruments and their Monitoring Bodies, available at https://www.ohchr.org/en/core-international-human-rights-instruments-and-their-monitoring-bodies (last accessed on 28 September 2022).

Declaration of Human Rights have been transformed into binding treaty law and become subject to the supervisory jurisdiction of the respective treaty bodies. It is also recognised today that certain fundamental human rights have become "constitutional" principles of the international legal order and therefore belong to the indispensable core of peremptory norms of general international law (*jus cogens*).[189]

At the regional level, following the accession of the Middle and Eastern European States in the 1990s and early 2000s, the European Convention of Human Rights has developed into a pan-European human rights standard. Since the entry into force of Protocol XI in 1998, individuals are granted direct access to the European Court of Human Rights.[190]

Second, the collapse of the Soviet Union gave rise to the hope that the "end of history"[191] had been reached and that the international legal order was "gradually developing [into an] international community of democratic states under the rule of law".[192] Against this backdrop the Federal Constitutional Court posited with increasing confidence that general rules of international law recognise a "minimum standard of human rights"[193] and that certain "fundamental human rights" have attained the status of *jus cogens*.[194]

Third, in the aftermath of German reunification the Federal Constitutional Court was compelled to revisit the problem of transitional justice and the concomitant tension between positive law and substantive justice. The Court perceived this as an opportunity to move inalienable human rights from the lofty heights of meta-positive ideas to the supposedly firmer ground of positive law. In the *Border Guard* cases, the Federal Constitutional Court endorsed the approach of the criminal courts[195] which, when applying the *Radbruch* formula, had relied heavily on the International Covenant on Civil and Political Rights to determine the intolerable degree of injustice required to override the

---

[189] Art. 53 Vienna Convention on the Law of Treaties, 23 May 1969, UNTS 1155, 331; *International Law Commission*, Articles 40 and 41 of the Articles on the Responsibility of States for Internationally Wrongful Acts 2001, General Assembly resolution 56/83, Annex, 12 December 2001, UN Doc. A/56/49(Vol. I)/Corr.4.

[190] Protocol No. 11 to the Convention for the Protection of Human Rights and Fundamental Freedoms, Restructuring the Control Machinery Established Thereby, ETS No. 155.

[191] See *F. Fukuyama*, The End of History and the Last Man (1992).

[192] Federal Constitutional Court, order of 14 October 2004, BVerfGE 111, 307, para. 36. English translation available at http://www.bverfg.de/e/rs20041014_2bvr148104en.html (last accessed on 28 September 2022).

[193] Federal Constitutional Court, order of 25 March 1981, BVerfGE 57, 9, 25. For further references see *D. Wolff*, Der Einzelne in der offenen Staatlichkeit (2020), 199–227.

[194] Federal Constitutional Court, order of 26 October 2004, BVerfGE 112, 1, para. 98.

[195] See in particular Federal Court of Justice, judgment of 3 November 1992, BGHSt 39, 1.

principle of *nulla poena sine lege*.[196] In a decision on expropriation in the former Soviet occupation zone, the Federal Constitutional Court perceived Art. 1(2) Basic Law as a gateway to *jus cogens*. Addressing the substantive limits imposed on the *pouvoir constituant* and the legislature when amending the constitution,[197] the Court thus equated "fundamental tenets of justice" (*grundlegende Gerechtigkeitspostulate*) with peremptory norms of general international law.[198]

Fourth, with the accelerating activity and growing institutional strength of the European Court of Human Rights, the Federal Constitutional Court became increasingly conscious of the fact that it had lost its exclusive position as the "ultimate guardian" of human dignity and inalienable human rights in Germany.[199] More and more individuals availed themselves of the possibility of challenging Federal Constitutional Court decisions before the Strasbourg court. This led to some high-profile cases in which the European Court of Human Rights questioned key aspects of fundamental rights doctrine in Germany. The political discontent caused by this development prompted the Federal Constitutional Court to reconsider the relationship between the German constitution and the European Convention on Human Rights. Art. 1(2) Basic Law offered the constitutional anchor necessary for the desired realignment of the judicial dialogue between the Karlsruhe and Strasbourg courts.

Finally, the move towards an "ever closer union"[200] within the process of European integration has led to a significant shift of power with regard to fundamental rights protection. In its seminal *Solange II* decision, the Federal Constitutional Court finally acknowledged that (secondary) EU law, in view of its primacy over domestic law, may not be reviewed against the yardstick of German fundamental rights.[201] The Court added, however, the important caveat that Germany will only honour the primacy of EU law "as long as" (*solange*)

---

[196] Federal Constitutional Court, order of 24 October 1996, BVerfGE 95, 96. For further details, see *T. Rensmann*, Systemunrecht und die Relativität des absoluten Rückwirkungsverbots, in: J. Menzel et al. (eds.), Verfassungsrechtsprechung (3rd edn., 2017), 606–613.

[197] See Art. 79(3) Basic Law.

[198] Federal Constitutional Court, order of 26 October 2004, BVerfGE 112, 1, para. 97: "In Article 1.2 and Article 25 sentence 1 of the Basic Law, the Basic Law also adopts the gradual recognition of the existence of mandatory provisions, that is, provisions that are in the individual case not open to disposition by the states (*ius cogens*)." English translation available at http://www.bverfg.de/e/rs20041026_2bvr095500en.html (last accessed on 28 September 2022).

[199] See, e.g. *H. Steinberger*, Entwicklungslinien in der neueren Rechtsprechung des Bundesverfassungsgerichts zu völkerrechtlichen Fragen, Zeitschrift für ausländisches öffentliches Recht und Völkerrecht 48 (1988), 1–17, 8.

[200] See Art. 1 TEU.

[201] Federal Constitutional Court, order of 22 October 1986, BVerfGE 73, 339, 387.

the Union "guarantees a level of [fundamental rights] protection […] essentially comparable to that afforded by the Basic Law."[202]

Since the proclamation of the Charter of Fundamental Rights and its elevation to the status of binding primary law,[203] the *Solange*-caveat has become virtually moot. This has shifted attention beyond positive fundamental rights to the protection of Germany's "constitutional identity" and thus to the commitment to human dignity and inalienable human rights.[204] With reference to the fact that the Basic Law has "not giv[en] up the final responsibility" for protecting these values,[205] the Federal Constitutional Court insists on the right to "identity review" of EU law.[206] In this particular context, however, the Court has up to this point exclusively referred to the dignity clause of Art. 1(1) Basic Law, presumably because human dignity is more evocative of Germany's idiosyncratic constitutional tradition than inalienable human rights.[207] Yet, as the recent *Ökotox* decision demonstrates, the pledge to inalienable human rights has nevertheless become a key concept in recalibrating the balance of power between the Federal Constitutional Court and the ECJ in the domain of fundamental rights protection.[208]

2. Inalienable human rights as a gateway to international human rights

The backdrop for the spectacular comeback of inalienable human rights was provided by the *Görgülü* case, which concerned the status of judgments of the European Court of Human Rights within the German legal order.[209] At issue was a constitutional complaint by *Kazim Görgülü*, the father of *Christopher*,

---

[202] See Art. 23 (1) Basic Law in which the Solange-caveat was codified.

[203] See Art. 6(1) TEU.

[204] See Art. 23(1)(3) in conjunction with Articles 79(3) and 1(1) and (2) Basic Law.

[205] As to this formulation see Federal Constitutional Court, order of 26 October 2004, BVerfGE 112, 1, 26: "[…] without giving up the final responsibility for respect for human dignity and for the observance of fundamental rights by German state authority"; with particular reference to EU law, see Federal Constitutional Court, judgment of 30 June 2009, BVerfGE 123, 267, 400 f.: "The Basic Law strives to integrate Germany into the legal community of peaceful and free states, but does not waive the sovereignty contained in the last word of the German constitution as a right of the people to take constitutive decisions concerning fundamental questions as to its own identity." English translation available at http://www.bverfg.de/e/es20090630_2bve000208en.html (last accessed on 28 September 2022).

[206] See Federal Constitutional Court, judgment of 30 June 2009, BVerfGE 123, 267, 353 f.; Federal Constitutional Court, order of 15 December 2015, BVerfGE 140, 317, paras. 42 f.; Federal Constitutional Court, order of 6 November 2019, BVerfGE 152, 216, para. 49.

[207] See also pp. 118 ff., above.

[208] See pp. 145 ff., below.

[209] Federal Constitutional Court, order of 14 October 2004, BVerfGE 111, 307. For a more detailed analysis, see *Rensmann* (n. 91), 485–492.

who was born out of wedlock and whose mother had given him up for adoption.[210] *Görgülü* had unsuccessfully sought custody of his son before German courts. He took the matter to the European Court of Human Rights, which found a violation of Art. 8 ECHR.[211] A regional court nevertheless continued to deny *Görgülü* access to his son, arguing that the European Court of Human Rights judgment had no binding effect within the German legal order. *Görgülü* filed a constitutional complaint arguing that the regional court had failed to implement the Strasbourg judgment properly.

In its decision of 14 October 2004, the Federal Constitutional Court thoroughly reassessed the relationship between the Convention system and the German constitutional order. The central issue to be resolved was the question as to whether the disregard of a European Court of Human Rights judgment by a domestic court could as such be challenged before the Federal Constitutional Court by means of a constitutional complaint.

The extent to which European Court of Human Rights judgments must be followed by German courts primarily depends on the pertinent provisions of the Convention and their status within the German legal order. In *Görgülü* the Court reaffirmed the generally accepted view that the Convention is endowed with the domestic status of the statute giving parliamentary assent[212] to the ratification of the Convention.[213] Given that the European Convention on Human Rights does thus not possess constitutional status, a constitutional complaint cannot be based directly on a violation of the Convention or the disregard of a European Court of Human Rights judgment. However, in a decisive strategic move the Federal Constitutional Court nevertheless endowed the Convention with "constitutional significance" and hence proceeded to assume control over the proper interpretation and application of Convention rights within the German legal order.[214]

The main lever for this partial "constitutionalisation" of the Convention is the commitment to inalienable human rights in Art. 1(2) Basic Law which – as the Federal Constitutional Court put it – "accords special protection to the core

---

[210] As to the facts, see Federal Constitutional Court, order of 14 October 2004, BVerfGE 111, 307, 308–313.

[211] ECtHR, *Görgülü v. Germany*, App No 74969/01, 26 February 2004.

[212] See Art. 59(2) Basic Law.

[213] Federal Constitutional Court, order of 14 October 2004, BVerfGE 111, 307, 317.

[214] Federal Constitutional Court, order of 14 October 2004, BVerfGE 111, 307, 317. This move was prepared by Federal Constitutional Court, order of 26 March 1987, BVerfGE 74, 358, 370, and Federal Constitutional Court, order of 29 May 1990, BVerfGE 82, 106, 114, which, however, rely on the "openness to international law" rather than Art. 1(2) Basic Law. On these decisions, see *Steinberger* (n. 199), 7–9.

of international human rights."[215] The Federal Constitutional Court was, however, careful not to attach "direct constitutional status" to the Convention via the "gateway" of Art. 1(2) Basic Law[216] since this would not only have elevated the Convention guarantees to the constitutional level but also incorporated them as such into the core of the "eternal" principles exempt from constitutional amendment.[217] Instead, the Federal Constitutional Court posited "a constitutional duty" to interpret the "content and scope" of German fundamental rights in the light of the Convention.[218] It derived this duty from Art. 1(2) Basic Law in conjunction with the more general principle of the "openness" of the Constitution to international law.[219]

Accordingly, whenever German courts fail to pay due regard to the Convention or judgments of the European Court of Human Rights, they not only violate the rule-of-law principle, which requires them to respect the binding force of the Convention as a federal statute (Art. 20(3) Basic Law), but also – in view of the Convention's "radiating effect"[220] on the German bill of rights – infringe the fundamental right corresponding to the Convention guarantee.[221] The Federal Constitutional Court thereby opened up the possibility for individuals to challenge court decisions on the basis of the Convention not having been properly applied. Via this partial "constitutionalisation" of the Convention, the Federal Constitutional Court thus established itself as the ultimate (domestic) guardian of the Convention within the German legal order. Whilst from the external perspective of international law the European Court of Human Rights retains the "last word"[222] on the proper interpretation of Convention guarantees, the Court can at least since *Görgülü* lay claim to having the first say in matters pertaining to the German legal order.

---

[215] Federal Constitutional Court, order of 14 October 2004, BVerfGE 111, 307, 329. English translation available at http://www.bverfg.de/e/rs20041014_2bvr148104en.html (last accessed on 28 September 2022).

[216] Thus the formulation in Federal Constitutional Court, judgment of 4 May 2011, BVerfGE 128, 326, 369. English translation available at http://www.bverfg.de/e/rs20110504_2bvr236509en.html (last accessed on 28 September 2022). See also Federal Constitutional Court, order of 14 October 2004, BVerfGE 111, 307, 317.

[217] See Art. 79(3) Basic Law.

[218] Federal Constitutional Court, order of 14 October 2004, BVerfGE 111, 307, 329.

[219] Federal Constitutional Court, order of 14 October 2004, BVerfGE 111, 307, 329.

[220] As to this notion, see Federal Constitutional Court, judgment of 15 January 1958, BVerfGE 7, 198, 207.

[221] Federal Constitutional Court, order of 14 October 2004, BVerfGE 111, 307, 330.

[222] Federal Constitutional Court, order of 14 October 2004, BVerfGE 111, 307, 319. On the problem of both the Federal Constitutional Court and the ECtHR laying claim to having the "last word" see *Rensmann* (n. 91), 487–489.

D. Return to values and traditions: inalienable human rights as common law

1. From international to general human rights

In *Görgülü* it remains somewhat obscure how the Federal Constitutional Court conceptualises the link between inalienable and international human rights. The term "*international* human rights"[223] and the simultaneous reliance on the "openness to international law" suggest that the Court equates "inalienable human rights" with positive "international human rights law". Equally ambiguous is the limitation of the relevant spectrum of international human rights to their "core".[224] Whilst the reasoning in *Görgülü* appears to be based on the assumption that all Convention rights are reflective of this core, later decisions suggest that the "international human rights core" refers exclusively to peremptory norms of international law.[225]

In its subsequent jurisprudence on the status of the European Convention on Human Rights within the German legal order, the Federal Constitutional Court has apparently tried to dispel the impression of simply equating inalienable rights with international human rights. This seems to be the reason why the Court, in more recent cases, has dropped the reference to "*international* human rights". The constitutional pledge to inalienable human rights is now simply interpreted as a substantive orientation towards "human rights".[226] The latest judgment in this line of jurisprudence describes Art. 1(2) Basic Law as a "manifestation of *general* human rights".[227]

According to the Federal Constitutional Court's established jurisprudence, other human rights treaties must also be taken into account when interpreting the German bill of fundamental rights. This applies in particular to the two International Human Rights Covenants[228] and other "Core International Human Rights Instruments",[229] such as the United Nations Convention on the Rights

---

[223] Federal Constitutional Court, order of 14 October 2004, BVerfGE 111, 307, 329.

[224] Federal Constitutional Court, order of 14 October 2004, BVerfGE 111, 307, 329.

[225] Federal Constitutional Court, order of 15 December 2015, BVerfGE 141, 1, para. 76: "[T]he Basic Law distinguishes not only between international treaty law and the general rules of international law, but also between peremptory provisions that may not be modified even by the constitutional legislature (*Verfassungsgeber*) – particularly inviolable and inalienable human rights (Art. 1(2) GG) – and other international law […]." English translation available at http://www.bverfg.de/e/ls20151215_2bvl000112en.html (last accessed at 28 September 2022).

[226] Federal Constitutional Court, judgment of 4 May 2011, BVerfGE 128, 326, 369.

[227] Federal Constitutional Court, judgment of 12 June 2018, BVerfGE 148, 296, para. 130 (emphasis added). See, however, Federal Constitutional Court, judgment of 19 May 2020, BVerfGE 154, 152, para. 94–96, which still refers to "international human rights".

[228] Federal Constitutional Court, order of 16 December 2021, 1 BvR 1541/20, para. 107. English translation available at http://www.bverfg.de/e/rs20211216_1bvr154120en.html (last accessed on 28 September 2022).

[229] See n. 188, above.

of Persons with Disabilities.[230] Whilst one would intuitively agree that these treaties are also emanations of "general human rights", other treaties designated as human rights instruments[231] would require closer scrutiny, in particular if they relate to contentious issues and are only supported by a limited number of Contracting States.

2. Common constitutional traditions and the Universal Declaration of Human Rights

Until recently, the Court had never convincingly explained how the reference to inalienable human rights as a meta-positive concept could serve as a gateway to positive international human rights law. With its *Ökotox* decision the Federal Constitutional Court has now provided this missing link.[232]

At issue was a constitutional complaint in which a pharmaceutical company claimed that a marketing authorisation granted to a competitor for a veterinary medicinal product was based on the impermissible use of the complainant's business secrets and therefore in violation of its fundamental rights.[233] The authorisation was granted by a German agency under the provisions of the German Medicinal Products Act (*Arzneimittelgesetz*), which implements a corresponding EU directive.[234]

Since the Federal Constitutional Court's ground-breaking *Right to be Forgotten* decisions, the yardstick against which the Court measures the domestic application of EU law depends on whether the matter is fully determined by EU law or not.[235] If this is not the case, the fundamental rights of the Basic Law apply;[236] if the matter is, however, fully harmonised by EU law, the EU Charter provides the relevant standard of review.[237]

---

[230] Federal Constitutional Court, order of 16 December 2021, 1 BvR 1541/20, para. 102.

[231] As to the reverse problem of individual rights which are not explicitly designated as human rights, see *Rensmann* (n. 91), 487–489.

[232] Federal Constitutional Court, order of 27 April 2021, BVerfGE 158, 1. English translation available at http://www.bverfg.de/e/rs20210427_2bvr020614.html (last accessed on 28 September 2022).

[233] As to the protection of business secrets both under Art. 12(1) in conjunction with 19(3) Basic Law and under Art. 16 EU Charter, see Federal Constitutional Court, order of 27 April 2021, BVerfGE 158, 1, paras. 47–52, 75 f.

[234] Directive 2001/82/EC of 6 November 2001 on the Community code relating to veterinary medicinal products, Official Journal of the European Union 2001 L 311/1.

[235] Federal Constitutional Court, order of 6 November 2019, BVerfGE 152, 152; Federal Constitutional Court, order of 6 November 2019, BVerfGE 152, 216.

[236] Federal Constitutional Court, order of 6 November 2019, BVerfGE 152, 216; Federal Constitutional Court, order of 27 April 2021, BVerfGE 158, 1, paras. 35, 45.

[237] Federal Constitutional Court, order of 6 November 2019, BVerfGE 152, 152; Federal Constitutional Court, order of 27 April 2021, BVerfGE 158, 1, paras. 35, 56.

Rather than deciding the threshold issue as to whether the applicable EU directive left any latitude to German authorities, the Court in the *Ökotox* case immediately proceeded to review the constitutional complaint against the yardstick of *both* the German bill of rights and the EU Charter.[238] The Federal Constitutional Court based this cumulative or hybrid approach on the general assertion that German and EU fundamental rights are typically congruent, with the consequence that the applicable standard of review could in most future cases be left undecided.[239]

The Federal Constitutional Court's contention that fundamental rights standards under German and EU law are in most instances identical, is based on two initial observations: The starting point of the Court's reasoning is the important unifying role played by the European Convention on Human Rights, on which the interpretation of both German fundamental rights[240] and the EU Charter[241] heavily rely.[242] The Court then proceeds to emphasise that all three instruments – the German bill of fundamental rights, the EU Charter and the European Convention – are "rooted in common constitutional traditions and are thus a manifestation of common European and universal values".[243]

The Court argues that these common values and traditions are based on the "shared commitment to human dignity"[244] which in turn finds its "reference point" in the Universal Declaration of Human Rights".[245] Whilst the European Convention on Human Rights explicitly establishes this link to the Universal Declaration in its preamble,[246] the fundamental rights of the Basic Law are embedded in this modern human rights tradition by virtue of the pledge to human dignity and inalienable human rights in Art. 1(1) and (2) Basic Law.[247] The Court stresses that the EU Charter similarly recognises human dignity as the "real basis of human rights"[248] and in its preamble "invokes […] the inviolable and inalienable human rights enshrined in international conventions and in the European Convention on Human Rights".[249] In addition, both the EU Charter and the Treaty on European Union highlight the importance of "constitutional

---

[238] Federal Constitutional Court, order of 27 April 2021, BVerfGE 158, 1, paras. 45–55, 56–81.

[239] Federal Constitutional Court, order of 27 April 2021, BVerfGE 158, 1, paras. 45–81.

[240] See pp. 134 ff. and pp. 144 f., above.

[241] See Art. 52 (3) and 53 EU Charter.

[242] Federal Constitutional Court, order of 27 April 2021, BVerfGE 158, 1, para. 57.

[243] Federal Constitutional Court, order of 27 April 2021, BVerfGE 158, 1, para. 57.

[244] Federal Constitutional Court, order of 27 April 2021, BVerfGE 158, 1, para. 72.

[245] Federal Constitutional Court, order of 27 April 2021, BVerfGE 158, 1, para. 63.

[246] See n. 173, above; Federal Constitutional Court, order of 27 April 2021, BVerfGE 158, 1, para. 61.

[247] Federal Constitutional Court, order of 27 April 2021, BVerfGE 158, 1, paras. 59 f.

[248] Explanations relating to the Charter, Official Journal of the European Union 2007 C 303/17; Federal Constitutional Court, order of 27 April 2021, BVerfGE 158, 1, para. 62.

[249] Federal Constitutional Court, order of 27 April 2021, BVerfGE 158, 1, para. 68.

traditions common to the Member States" as a "source"[250] of fundamental rights.[251]

The Federal Constitutional Court therefore perceives the fundamental rights of the Basic Law, the European Convention and the EU Charter as "manifestations" of the "common values" laid down in the Universal Declaration of Human Rights.[252] Echoing the methodological approach in its early jurisprudence,[253] the Court conceptualises the development of human and fundamental rights at the domestic, regional and international levels as a constant process of further "fleshing out" (*Konkretisierung*) the "value system" of the Universal Declaration. The Court considers the codification of bills of rights in constitutions and treaties to be the first step in this process.[254] The task of "further refining"[255] human rights standards then passes to the domestic constitutional and apex courts as well as to the European Court of Human Rights and the European Court of Justice.[256]

According to the Federal Constitutional Court, this process unfolds in a common "legal sphere" (*Rechtsraum*)[257] which is defined by the shared commitment to human dignity and the value system of the Universal Declaration. The Court primarily refers to the "European legal sphere", which is composed of the Council of Europe, the European Union and their respective member States.[258] In applying the common values to individual cases, their courts thus contribute to the development of "common European standards of fundamental rights" which gradually evolve into regional common law (*ius publicum europaeum*).[259]

However, given that non-European States and other regional human rights systems also follow the lodestar of the Universal Declaration of Human Rights, a larger "legal sphere", that of "constitutional democracies" and their constitutional or apex courts, also comes into play.[260] In this context the Court points

---

[250] See Federal Constitutional Court, order of 27 April 2021, BVerfGE 158, 1, para. 71.

[251] Art. 52(4) EU Charter; Art. 6(3) TEU.

[252] See Federal Constitutional Court, order of 27 April 2021, BVerfGE 158, 1, para. 57.

[253] See pp. 125 ff., above.

[254] Federal Constitutional Court, order of 27 April 2021, BVerfGE 158, 1, paras. 41, 56, 63, 68. For an early expression of this idea, see Federal Constitutional Court, judgment of 23 October 1952, BVerfGE 2, 1, 13 and Federal Constitutional Court, judgment of 17 August 1956, BVerfGE 5, 85, 140.

[255] Federal Constitutional Court, order of 27 April 2021, BVerfGE 158, 1, para. 68.

[256] Federal Constitutional Court, order of 27 April 2021, BVerfGE 158, 1, paras. 57, 65, 69, 70, 72.

[257] Federal Constitutional Court, order of 27 April 2021, BVerfGE 158, 1, para. 71. See also Federal Constitutional Court, order of 18 November 2020, 2 BvR 477/17, para. 26.

[258] Federal Constitutional Court, order of 27 April 2021, BVerfGE 158, 1, para. 71.

[259] Federal Constitutional Court, order of 27 April 2021, BVerfGE 158, 1, para. 71.

[260] Federal Constitutional Court, order of 27 April 2021, BVerfGE 158, 1, para. 70. As to the Court's earlier references to (leading) democracies, see pp. 134 ff., above.

in particular to the significance of the fundamental rights jurisprudence of the US and Canadian Supreme Courts.[261] At the same time, however, the Federal Constitutional Court emphasises that due to Germany's integration into Europe and the "openness" of the constitution to European law,[262] particular weight must be attached to the European tradition and to the development of human rights.[263]

The Federal Constitutional Court argues that within these "legal spheres" the courts are joint trustees[264] of the common value system of the Universal Declaration. With regard to the "European legal sphere", the Federal Constitutional Court describes this fiduciary duty as a responsibility to "promote [...] the reinforcement of common European standards of fundamental rights" and to further their effectiveness and legal certainty by "prevent[ing] friction and conflicting value decisions in the protection of fundamental rights."[265]

In Art. 1(2) Basic Law this fiduciary duty is accorded a "constitutional dimension". By virtue of this constitutional duty, not only the European Convention but also the EU Charter and the constitutional traditions common to the Member States and other constitutional democracies must be taken into account when interpreting German fundamental rights.[266] This duty is mirrored in the EU Charter, which explicitly sets forth that its rights and principles must be interpreted in harmony with the European Convention and the common constitutional traditions of the Member States.[267]

The Federal Constitutional Court places particular emphasis on the fact that the constitutional traditions of the Member States are primarily reflected in the jurisprudence of their constitutional and apex courts.[268] It stands to reason that the Federal Constitutional Court, when interpreting the EU Charter, thereby attributes particular weight to its own case law. This is not only due to the sheer volume of fundamental rights jurisprudence that has been produced by the Court since it took up its work more than 70 years ago; more importantly, the fact that the Federal Constitutional Court itself now has a long-standing practice of interpreting German fundamental rights in the light of the European

[261] See Federal Constitutional Court, order of 27 April 2021, BVerfGE 158, 1, para. 70, in conjunction with the reference to Federal Constitutional Court, judgment of 22 February 2011 BVerfGE 128, 226, 253, 267.

[262] Federal Constitutional Court, order of 27 April 2021, BVerfGE 158, 1, para. 71.

[263] Federal Constitutional Court, order of 27 April 2021, BVerfGE 158, 1, para. 60.

[264] As to the role of domestic courts as trustees of the observance of international human rights, see *H. Lauterpacht*, An International Bill of the Rights of Man (1945), 185.

[265] Federal Constitutional Court, order of 27 April 2021, BVerfGE 158, 1, para. 71.

[266] Federal Constitutional Court, order of 27 April 2021, BVerfGE 158, 1, paras. 69, 70.

[267] Art. 52(3) and 52(4) EU Charter.

[268] Federal Constitutional Court, order of 27 April 2021, BVerfGE 158, 1, paras. 57, 69, 70, 72.

Convention[269] – and the case law of constitutional and apex courts of the Member States[270] – means that its jurisprudence incorporates and consolidates "common European standards of fundamental rights".[271] The Federal Constitutional Court thus seems to suggest that German fundamental rights jurisprudence offers – to use a term popularised by a former British prime minister – "oven-ready" interpretative solutions for the EU Charter on Fundamental Rights.

V. Conclusion

Inalienable human rights transcend positive law and are therefore difficult to grasp for the discipline of law. In its quest for the essence of inalienable human rights, the Federal Constitutional Court has thus ventured beyond the realm of positive law, ultimately finding firm ground in traditions, values and a non-binding political resolution, the Universal Declaration of Human Rights. From a legal perspective this raises many vexing issues that can be adequately resolved only on the basis of transdisciplinary assistance and interdisciplinary exchange.

The Federal Constitutional Court's approach touches upon some of the key challenges currently facing international human rights. How, for example, does the discipline of law approach the interpretation of the Universal Declaration as a non-binding political instrument? Is the Declaration interpreted in the same way as a binding human rights treaty? The Federal Constitutional Court advocates a dynamic approach which echoes the "living instrument" doctrine of the European Court of Human Rights.[272] In contrast, the final report of the Commission on Unalienable Rights,[273] an interdisciplinary panel of experts established in 2017 by then US Secretary of State *Michael Pompeo*, insists on a strict "originalist" reading of the Declaration and thus delegitimises many subsequent developments in international human rights law.[274]

---

[269] See pp. 144 f., above.

[270] See the references in Federal Constitutional Court, order of 27 April 2021, BVerfGE 158, 1, para. 70.

[271] Federal Constitutional Court, order of 27 April 2021, BVerfGE 158, 1, para. 71.

[272] See the Federal Constitutional Court's repeated emphasis on the fact that the human rights tradition is open to further development, Federal Constitutional Court, order of 27 April 2021, BVerfGE 158, 1, paras. 46, 56, 60, 65, 71.

[273] *Commission on Unalienable Rights*, Report of the Commission on Unalienable Rights, 26 August 2020, available at https://2017-2021.state.gov/report-of-the-commission-on-unalienable-rights/ (last accessed on 28 September 2022).

[274] See *K. Young*, Human Rights Originalism, Georgetown Law Journal 110 (2022), 1–91; from a philosophical perspective, *Risse* (n. 151), 13–31.

The Federal Constitutional Court's invocation of traditions and values must also be considered carefully in the light of more recent attempts, most prominently by Russia, to utilise "traditional values" as a means of undermining international human rights protection.[275] It is therefore important to unpack the fundamentally different meanings and functions ascribed by the Federal Constitutional Court to traditions[276] and values[277] in its most recent jurisprudence.

Last but not least, the question as to how to accommodate the universality of inalienable human rights and the political and cultural idiosyncrasies of individual States[278] raises one of the perennial problems of international human rights protection. The latest example is provided by the claim of the People's Republic of China to "human rights with Chinese characteristics".[279] This renewed reliance on the theory of cultural relativism highlights the enduring need to rest the universality of human rights on solid conceptual foundations.[280]

The future of domestic and international human rights protection will thus depend not least on the ability of the law to successfully master the interdisciplinary challenge posed by the inalienability of human rights.

---

[275] See, e.g. *A. Faiola*, How Putin is weaponizing "traditional values" to defend Russian aggression in Ukraine, Washington Post, 23 March 2022, available at https://www.washingtonpost.com/world/2022/03/23/putin-russia-ukraine-orthodox/ (last accessed on 28 September 2022); *C. McCrudden*, Human Rights and Traditional Values, in: U. Braxi et al. (eds.), Law's Ethical, Global and Theoretical Contexts – Essays in Honour of William Twining (2018), 38–72.

[276] See *S. Cassese*, Ruling from Below: Common Constitutional Traditions and Their Role, NYU Environmental Law Journal 29 (2021), 591–618; *M. Krygier*, Law as Tradition, Law and Philosophy 5/2 (1986), 237–262.

[277] For a legal perspective on values and "orders of values", see *Rensmann* (n. 69); from a sociological perspective, see *H. Joas*, Die Sakralität der Person (2nd edn., 2019), 251–281; *idem*, Value Generalization, Limitations and Possibilities of a Communication about Values, Zeitschrift für Wirtschafts- und Unternehmensethik 9 (2008), 88–96.

[278] See pp. 134 ff., above with regard to Federal Constitutional Court, order of 30 June 1964, BVerfGE 18, 112. This issue is also raised in the Ökotox decision, see Federal Constitutional Court, order of 27 April 2021, BVerfGE 158, 1, para. 73.

[279] *State Council Information Office of the People's Republic of China* (PRC), Progress in Human Rights over the 40 Years of Reform and Opening Up in China (2018), available at http://english.www.gov.cn/archive/white_paper/2018/12/13/content_281476431737638.htm (last accessed on 28 September 2022).

[280] *Yu-Jie Chen*, China's Challenge to the International Human Rights Regime, NYU Journal of International Law and Politics 51 (2019), 1179–1222.

Human Dignity, Inalienable Human Rights, and Interdisciplinarity[*]

Monika Florczak-Wątor

I. Inalienable human rights as a problem requiring interdisciplinary analysis

Human dignity and human rights can be discussed on different levels, these including the philosophical, theological, normative, political and sociological levels.[1] However, a discussion limited to only one level does not capture the complexity of these phenomena. Consequently, the adoption of an interdisciplinary approach is required. This is due to the fact that human dignity and human rights are philosophical and theological categories that – as fundamental values for the functioning of the individual, society and the state – constitute the axiological foundation of national and international legal orders.[2] They are concepts that are primary to the law[3] and are thus legally undefinable. However, the law requires the clarification of their essence, which, as is generally accepted, cannot be done solely on the basis of one particular philosophical or theological theory. The common contemporary expectation that human dignity and human rights will have a pluralistic and universal nature, and that reflection

---

[*] The research has been supported by a grant from the Heritage Priority Research Area under the Strategic Programme Excellence Initiative at Jagiellonian University.

[1] *M. Cohn/D. Grimm*, "Human dignity" as a constitutional doctrine, in: M. Tushnet et al. (eds.), Routledge Handbook of Constitutional Law (2012), 193–203, 193.

[2] See *D. Feldman*, Human Dignity as a Legal Value, Public Law (1999), 682–702.

[3] See *M. Piechowiak*, What are Human Rights? The Concept of Human Rights and Their Extra-Legal Justification, in: R. Hanski/M. Suksi (eds.), An Introduction to the International Protection of Human Rights. A Textbook (1999), 3–14, 5 f.

on them will shape community-building thinking, creates a need to seek out their broader legitimacy and justification.[4] This is precisely the possibility offered by an interdisciplinary approach, which allows legal analysis to take the findings of other scientific disciplines into account.

Thilo Rensmann's paper entitled "Inalienable Human Rights: An Interdisciplinary Challenge to the Discipline of Law" perfectly demonstrates this need to include an interdisciplinary perspective in the consideration of concepts fundamental to contemporary human rights doctrine. The author takes Art. 1 of the German Basic Law (*Grundgesetz* – GG) as a starting point, which proclaims that human dignity and inalienable human rights must be respected and protected and that the basic rights bind the legislative, executive and judicial authorities. He explains the relationship between inalienable human rights and human dignity, showing the different ways in which German legal scholarship and the Federal Constitutional Court (*Bundesverfassungsgericht*) have sought to clarify these concepts and tried to justify them.

Rensmann's findings are worth holding up against Polish legal scholarship's and the Polish Constitutional Court's understanding of human dignity and human rights, as well as the extent to which this understanding is determined by the aforementioned interdisciplinary approach. However, it must be clarified at the outset that the constitutional regulations on human dignity and human rights in the two states are not identical, although they are undoubtedly similar, especially as the 1997 Constitution of the Republic of Poland[5] was inspired, *inter alia*, by the German Basic Law and the jurisprudence of the Federal Constitutional Court. Hence, before going on to analyse the relevant constitutional provisions of both countries, it is worth pointing out the basic differences in their actual wording.

II. Comparison of the wording of the constitutional regulations

Article 30 of the Polish Constitution (hereinafter: PC), which is key to the issues under analysis, proclaims the inherent and inalienable dignity of the human being as the source of his or her rights and freedoms and states that dignity is inviolable and its respect and protection are the duty of public authorities. Article 1(1) GG similarly states that human dignity is inviolable and its respect and protection are the duty of all state authorities, but it further declares in Art. 1(2) that the German people recognise inviolable and inalienable human

[4] See *M. Piechowiak*, Problem aksjologicznej legitymizacji uniwersalnego systemu ochrony praw człowieka, in: E. Karska (ed.), Globalne problemy ochrony praw człowieka (2015), 86–100.

[5] The Constitution of the Republic of Poland as adopted on 2 April 1997 (Journal of Laws No. 78, item 483 with amendments).

rights as the basis of every human community and of peace and justice in the world. In addition, Art. 1(3) GG stipulates that, as directly applicable law, the fundamental rights regulated in the German Constitution bind the legislature, the executive and the judiciary.

Three differences in the wording of the Polish and German constitutional regulations therefore need to be highlighted at this point. Firstly, Art. 1(2) GG attributes inalienability to human rights, whereas Art. 30 PC relates inalienability to dignity. Secondly, Art. 30 PC uses the concept of inherence to characterise dignity, which is not the case in Art. 1 GG. Thirdly, these two provisions describe the relationship between dignity and human rights somewhat differently. Article 30 PC identifies dignity as the source of human rights, making it a primary concept not only in relation to law, but also in relation to human rights. Article 1(2) GG, on the other hand, exposes the community-based approach to human rights, stating that human rights are the basis of human society, peace and justice. Hence, in the German discussion on human rights in the context of their inalienability and their relationship to dignity, the link between constitutional and international reflection is strong, which is not the case in the Polish discussion on this matter.

It should be added that the Polish Constitution – apart from the aforementioned Art. 30 – refers to the concept of dignity in two other places. The Preamble calls upon all those who will apply this Constitution to do so by "taking care to preserve the inherent dignity of the human being". Article 233(1) PC, in turn, prohibits the restriction of dignity during states of emergency, thus classifying dignity as a non-derogable right. In addition, in the most recent literature, one may encounter a statement that the principle of the protection of human dignity is expressed by all provisions of the Polish Constitution concerning the rights and freedoms of an individual. Such a position is presented, for example, by *Leszek Garlicki*, a former judge of the Polish Constitutional Court and an editor of one of the most widely read commentaries on the Polish Constitution, who, commenting on the aforementioned Art. 30, stated: "constitutionally established rights and freedoms constitute, in their totality, a system for respecting human dignity".[6] The Polish Constitutional Court, which, in general, shares this standpoint, emphasises, however, that although manifestations of the protection of human dignity may in fact be discerned in many provisions of the Constitution, the identification of the infringement of every right and freedom with the infringement of human dignity "would in fact oversimplify the meaning and normative content of Article 30 of the Polish Constitution. This is because it encompasses the most important values, which do not benefit from other, independent guarantees on constitutional grounds, and which touch

---

[6] *L. Garlicki*, Art. 30, in: idem/M. Zubik (eds.), Konstytucja Rzeczypospolitej Polskiej. Komentarz, vol. 2 (2016), 41.

upon the essence of the position of the individual in society, his or her relation to other persons and to public authority".[7]

III. Dignity as a key concept for understanding the concept of inalienable human rights

In his contribution, *Rensmann* strongly emphasises dignity as a concept that determines the manner in which we understand the concept of inalienable human rights. While sharing this view, it should be added that human dignity is first and foremost a philosophical and theological category; hence, religious concepts, including Catholic social teaching and Christian personalism, as well as philosophical concepts, including Stoicism, Judaism and, later, the natural law school, have had a significant impact on shaping the contemporary understanding of this concept. For German and Polish constitutional traditions, two sources of inspiration were of particular importance – Christian thought, linking the concept of dignity to the creation of a human being in the image of God, and Kantian thought, perceiving dignity through the prism of the prohibition of instrumental treatment of human beings.[8] In the latter understanding, the essence of human dignity is the subjectivity (autonomy) and freedom of self-determination of individuals, which is a consequence of their possession of reason and free will. Such an understanding of dignity excludes the acceptance of any manifestation of a depersonalisation of a human being – of treating him or her as a means to achieve certain ends.[9]

Rensmann rightly points out that not only is it impossible, but that there is also no need to seek a legal definition of human dignity. This is because it is a semantically open concept that evolves over time and space.[10] Any legal definition of dignity would be imperfect, as it would further limit the very concept and rapidly become outdated. However, the absence of a universally accepted legal definition of dignity does not mean that the concept has no normative content. This is given by the characteristics attributed to dignity, namely inherence, universality, inalienability and inviolability. It follows from these char-

[7] Polish Constitutional Court, judgment of 5 March 2003, K 7/01.

[8] *M. Soniewicka/J. Holocher*, Human Dignity in Poland, in: P. Becchi/K. Mathis (eds.), Handbook of Human Dignity in Europe (2019), 697–718.

[9] See Polish Constitutional Court, judgments of 9 July 2009, SK 48/05; 30 September 2008, K 44/07; 24 February 2010, K 6/09.

[10] Similarly, see *M. Krzemiński/A. Grabowski/J. Holocher/M. Latacz*, Zasada godności człowieka jako źródła wolności i praw, in: M. Florczak-Wątor/A. Grabowski (eds.), Argumenty i rozumowania prawnicze w konstytucyjnym państwie prawa. Komentarz (2021), 967. On the multiple meanings of human dignity across the constitutional jurisprudence of different systems, see: *P.G. Carozza*, Human dignity in constitutional adjudication, in: T. Ginsburg/R. Dixon (eds.), Comparative Constitutional Law (2011), 459–472, 460–465.

acteristics that dignity is a permanent (vested in a human being by virtue of the very fact of being a human being), absolute (it is not subject to limitations[11]) and primary (it stands outside or above positive law) category.[12] This way of clarifying the idea of dignity is sufficient for the law to capture its essence. It is supplemented by the negative aspect of dignity, which is the prohibition of instrumental treatment of human beings.

Polish legal scholarship and the jurisprudence of the Polish Constitutional Court strongly emphasise that the protection of dignity is not subject to gradation, that the weighing of human dignity against other constitutional values is excluded and that any violation of dignity is *ex definition* illegal.[13] It is also impermissible to restrict dignity in the name of the "common good of all citizens", although the latter is more prominent in the systematics of the Constitution than dignity, since the common good is mentioned as the fundamental value in Art. 1, which opens the Polish Constitution. As stated by the Constitutional Court, "the protection of the common good, even the most obvious one, cannot take the form of a violation of inalienable human dignity".[14]

The understanding of dignity in German legal scholarship and the jurisprudence of the Federal Constitutional Court as presented by *Rensmann* is very close to that existing in the Polish constitutional order. This fact may not come as a surprise as this is the understanding of dignity accepted in democratic states. However, the differences concern the manner in which the concept of dignity is justified, its sources, its genesis and the translation of the understanding of dignity into the understanding of inalienable human rights.

In his paper, *Rensmann* shows how the reading of Art. 1(1) and (2) GG by German legal doctrine has evolved. This is symbolised by the updating of a leading commentary on the German Constitution as occurred 20 years ago. For the first few decades after its adoption, the interpretation of Art. 1(1) GG was determined by *Günter Dürig*'s view that dignity has a meta-positive character and is firmly rooted in Christian natural law.[15] The turn towards positivism made by *Matthias Herdegen* in his new version of the commentary on Art. 1(1) GG consisted of detaching dignity from its meta-positive genesis and considering it as a concept within the scope of positive law.[16] This change allowed for the rediscovery of the constitutional dimension of inalienable human rights in Art. 1(2) GG, which thus became – as *Rensmann* notes in his paper – "a

---

[11] *Soniewicka/Holocher* (n. 8).

[12] *Garlicki* (n. 6), 30.

[13] Polish Constitutional Court, judgment of 28 June 2016, K 31/15; *Krzemiński/Grabowski/Holocher/Latacz* (n. 10), 978.

[14] Polish Constitutional Court, judgment of 20 March 2006, K 17/05.

[15] *G. Dürig*, in: idem/T. Maunz (eds.), Grundgesetz. Kommentar (1958), Art. 1 para. 55.

[16] *M. Herdegen*, in: G. Dürig et al. (eds.), Grundgesetz. Kommentar (2003), Art. 1 Abs. 1; *idem*, in: G. Dürig et al. (eds.), Grundgesetz. Kommentar (2004), Art. 1 Abs. 2.

bridge to the body of universal human rights recognised today as an integral part of positive international law".[17]

In Polish legal doctrine, such a strong turn towards a positivist reading of dignity – and consequently this rediscovery of the constitutional dimension of inalienable human rights – has never taken place. Dignity as a source of rights and freedoms within the meaning of Art. 30 PC has a strong axiological tinge, constituting "a bridge between the world of values and the world of norms".[18] As the Polish Constitutional Court stated, "the legislator has given human dignity a constitutional significance, making it the plane of reference for the system of values around which the Constitution is built, and at the same time the foundation of the entire legal order in the State".[19] The Constitutional Court defines dignity as "the fundamental value of the legal order"[20] and as "a constitutional value of central importance for the construction of the axiology of the current constitutional solutions",[21] through the prism of which all other provisions on the rights, freedoms and duties of the individual should be interpreted and applied.

However, Art. 30 PC is not only axiological but also normative in nature.[22] The dignity expressed therein is both a principle-postulate (*zasada-postulat*) and a principle-norm (*zasada-norma*).[23] In the former sense, the inherent dignity of a human being constitutes an objective that the state should aim to realise. It implies an obligation to interpret *in dubio pro dignitate* the particular norms of the system for the protection of individual rights. In this second sense, dignity is a real category that the normative system is intended to protect. It is a legal principle of a normative nature, from which there arise specific

---

[17] *Rensmann*, p. 119, above.

[18] *J. Zajadło*, Godność i prawa człowieka (Ideowe i normatywne źródła przepisu art. 30 Konstytucji), Gdańskie Studia Prawnicze 3 (1998), 53–62, 58. See also *M. Granat*, Godność człowieka z art. 30 Konstytucji RP jako wartość i jako norma prawna, Państwo i Prawo 8 (2014), 3–22.

[19] Polish Constitutional Court, judgment of 4 April 2001, K 11/00: "Ustrojodawca nadał godności człowieka znaczenie konstytucyjne czyniąc z niej płaszczyznę odniesienia dla systemu wartości, wokół którego zbudowano Konstytucję a zarazem fundament całego porządku prawnego w Państwie."

[20] Polish Constitutional Court, judgment of 30 October 2006, P 10/06: "fundamentalna wartość porządku prawnego".

[21] Polish Constitutional Court, judgment of 30 September 2008, K 44/07; see also Polish Constitutional Court, judgment of 22 January 2013, P 46/09: "pojęciu godności ludzkiej należy przypisać charakter wartości konstytucyjnej o centralnym znaczeniu dla zbudowania aksjologii obecnych rozwiązań konstytucyjnych".

[22] *P. Polak/J. Trzciński*, Konstytucyjna zasada godności człowieka w świetle orzecznictwa Trybunału Konstytucyjnego, Gdańskie Studia Prawnicze 40 (2018), 258–274, 264.

[23] *J. Zajadło*, Godność jednostki w aktach międzynarodowej ochrony praw człowieka, Ruch Prawniczy, Ekonomiczny i Socjologiczny 2 (1989), 103–117, 115.

obligations – as indicated in the second sentence of Art. 30 PC – that are incumbent on public authorities.

IV. Dignity as a community-building concept under international law

The Universal Declaration of Human Rights (UDHR),[24] which, as *Rensmann* points out, has strongly determined the understanding of Art. 1(2) GG, has never been of as much importance for the Polish Constitutional Court's interpretation of Art. 30 PC. The latter provision, unlike its German counterpart, does not explicitly refer to the idea expressed in the UDHR of making human dignity and human rights the basis for freedom, justice and peace in the world. Nor does the Polish Constitutional Court draw on international human rights law to construct the pluralistic concept of dignity or the communitarian vision of freedom that *Rensmann* writes about.

This different distribution of emphases in the German and Polish constitutional regulations is certainly a consequence of the fact that the constitutionalisation of the idea of dignity in both countries took place at different historical moments. Indeed, the German Constitution was adopted just after the Second World War, when the concept of dignity appeared in international law as a reaction to the atrocities of Nazism and fascism, the enslavement of human beings and their objectification. The Preamble to the Charter of the United Nation,[25] adopted at the time, emphasised the need "to reaffirm faith in fundamental human rights, in the dignity and worth of the human person". In turn, the Universal Declaration of Human Rights stated that "the peoples of the United Nations have in the Charter reaffirmed their faith in fundamental human rights, in the dignity and worth of the human person" and that "recognition of the inherent dignity and of the equal and inalienable rights of all members of the human family is the foundation of freedom, justice and peace in the world". In this way, human dignity was closely linked to inalienable human rights, and both values were recognised as the basis of freedom, justice and peace in the world. Similarly, the problem was subsequently expressed in international human rights covenants.[26] These included, on the one hand, a reminder that "in accordance with the principles proclaimed in the Charter of the United Nations, recognition of the inherent dignity and of the equal and inalienable rights of all

---

[24] Universal Declaration of Human Rights, G.A. Res. 217A (III), U.N. Doc A/810, 71 (1948) (hereinafter: UDHR).

[25] Charter of the United Nations, 26 June 1945, 1 UNTS 15 (hereinafter UN Charter).

[26] See International Covenant on Economic, Social and Cultural Rights, 16 December 1966, UNTS 993, 3; International Covenant on Civil and Political Rights, 16 December 1966, UNTS 999, 171.

members of the human family is the foundation of freedom, justice and peace in the world" and, on the other hand, a statement that "these rights derive from the inherent dignity of the human person". The covenants, like the Declaration before it, thus highlighted the particular characteristic of dignity, which is its inherent nature, but at the same time, they emphasised that dignity was not only linked to individual rights as their source but also had the status of a legal principle.

In acts of constitutional rank, the idea of protecting human dignity was first proclaimed in the inter-war period. The Weimar Constitution (*Weimarer Reichsverfassung*) of 1919 mentioned dignity in the context of social rights,[27] and the Irish Constitution of 1937 pointed to the need to ensure the individual's "dignity and freedom".[28] The constitutionalisation of the imperative to respect and protect dignity, however, did not fully occur until after the Second World War in response to massive human rights violations. The German Constitution adopted in 1949 was strongly influenced both by this particular post-war historical moment and by the Universal Declaration of Human Rights. However, Poland, which, like other countries in Central and Eastern Europe, remained enslaved by the communist regime at the time, did not participate in these discussions on the need to protect dignity and human rights that took place immediately after the Second World War. References to dignity in the constitutions of the countries of Central and Eastern Europe appeared only after the fall of communism in 1989. The differences in the wording of Art. 1 GG and Art. 30 PC must therefore be seen through the prism of these two different historical moments, which were separated by more than 40 years of different experiences.

Two sources of ideological and normative inspiration can be discerned in the content of Art. 30 PC. The first is the aforementioned preambles of the international human rights covenants, and the second is Art. 1 GG.[29] The first works on Art. 30 PC, which appeared shortly after the entry into force of this provision, emphasised its similarity to Art. 1 GG and the need to draw on the achievements of German scholarship and jurisprudence in reconstructing its meaning. Shortly after the entry into force of the Polish Constitution and referring to the concept of dignity appearing in its Art. 30, eminent Polish philosopher and legal theorist *Jerzy Zajadło* wrote:

> "The Constitutional Court, interpreting the Constitution, will thus have to specify both the content of the concept in question and its normative (meta-normative?) functions. […] It is therefore likely to draw on the very rich jurisprudence of the Federal Constitutional Court of Germany, on the one hand, and to draw on the German scholarship of constitutional law,

[27] Constitution of the German Empire, 11 August 1919, Reichsgesetzblatt 1919, 1383.

[28] Constitution of Ireland, 1 July 1937.

[29] *L. Bosek*, Gwarancje godności ludzkiej i ich wpływ na polskie prawo cywilne (2012); *Soniewicka/Holocher* (n. 8).

on the other. These references, however, will only be of a subsidiary nature, as they concern the legal system of another state and are difficult to transfer directly to the ground of Polish constitutional practice."[30]

The meta-positivist understanding of dignity is therefore strongly rooted in the tradition of Polish constitutionalism. At the same time, however, the principle of respecting and protecting human dignity has had a positivised character since the beginning of the political transformation in Poland. Initially, it was derived from the principle of a democratic state ruled by law as introduced into Art. 1 of the 1952 Constitution[31] by the December Amendment of 1989.[32] The Constitutional Court, by reference to the aforementioned principle of a democratic state ruled by law, also deduced, from dignity, the fundamental rights of the individual that were not protected by the 1952 Constitution then in force, such as the right to the protection of life, the right to privacy or the right to a fair trial. This technique of deriving rights and freedoms from dignity by referring to the principle of the democratic state ruled by law is clearly illustrated by the resolution of 17 March 1993, W 16/92, in which the Polish Constitutional Court stated:

"Permitting a research experiment without the consent of the person on whom the experiment is performed violates the principle of a democratic state ruled by law by violating the dignity of the human being reduced in such a case to the role of an experimental object."[33]

It is worth noting that the principle of the democratic state ruled by law was of fundamental importance in the process of discovering the rights and freedoms subject to constitutional protection during this period immediately preceding the adoption of the current Constitution.[34] The leading character of this principle undoubtedly resulted in the marginalisation of the principle of protecting human dignity as a basis from which one could derive such rights and freedoms. This situation changed only to a limited extent after the entry into force of the 1997 Constitution. Although it proclaims the protection of dignity, its Art. 30 is, in practice, much less frequently invoked in the jurisprudence of the Polish Constitutional Court than its Art. 2 expressing the principle of a democratic state ruled by law.

---

[30] *Zajadło* (n. 18), 53 f.

[31] The Constitution of the People's Republic of Poland as adopted on 22 July 1952 (Journal of Laws of 1976, No. 7, item 36 with amendments).

[32] The Amendment Act to the Constitution of the People's Republic of Poland as adopted on 29 December 1989 (Journal of Laws of 1989, No. 75, item 444).

[33] "Dopuszczenie bowiem eksperymentu badawczego bez zgody osoby, na której eksperyment jest dokonywany, narusza zasadę demokratycznego państwa prawa poprzez pogwałcenie godności człowieka sprowadzonego w takim przypadku do roli obiektu doświadczalnego."

[34] *Garlicki* (n. 6), 32.

V. Absolutisation of dignity and the inalienability of human rights

There is a very strong conviction in Polish legal scholarship and jurisprudence that dignity is subject to absolute protection, while the rights and freedoms derived from it may, and even should, be subject to limitations. The Constitutional Court emphasises in its case law that

"human dignity appears as a transcendent value […] [and therefore] cannot be lost by a human being. In this sense, a human being always retains his dignity and no behaviour, including the actions of the legislator, can deprive him of this dignity".[35]

The rights and freedoms rooted in dignity inherit, in a sense, its characteristics, that is, inviolability, inalienability and its inherent nature. However, most of these rights and freedoms are not absolute and may – or even must – be subject to limitations under the conditions set out in the Constitution, though it is impermissible to violate their essence. The prohibition against infringing the essence of rights and freedoms is a consequence of the anchoring of freedoms and rights in dignity, which is absolute in nature and thus cannot be subject to limitations. The relationship between a right or freedom and dignity also determines the extent of its protection. The stronger this link is, the higher the level of protection required.[36]

The relationship between rights and freedoms, on the one hand, and human dignity, on the other hand, determines, in light of the jurisprudence of the Polish Constitutional Court, the existence of two categories of rights and freedoms: those which are of a fundamental nature and cannot be limited, and those which may be subject to limitations. The difference between these two categories of rights and freedoms was explained by the Constitutional Court in its judgment of 15 November 2000, P 12/99, as follows:

"Among the rights for which Art. 30 of the Constitution is the source, of primary importance are those which, by referring directly to the essence of human dignity and expressing its quintessence, have the character of fundamental rights. As a rule, the legislator is not only entitled to question these rights but also to restrict them. Their content is not dependent on the will of the legislator, still less on the bodies applying the law, be they public administration bodies or courts. Hence, they are referred to as inherent rights. The constitutional proclamation of the inviolability of human dignity is undoubtedly connected with this category of rights of an inherent nature. […] From fundamental [inherent] rights, one should distinguish those which are not a simple emanation of human dignity and aim at securing other

[35] Polish Constitutional Court, judgment of 9 July 2009, SK 48/05: "godność człowieka jawi się jako wartość transcendentna […] [i dlatego] nie może zostać przez człowieka utracona. W tym znaczeniu człowiek zawsze zachowuje godność i żadne zachowania, w tym również działania prawodawcy, nie mogą go tej godności pozbawić". See also *Polak/ Trzciński* (n. 22), 258.

[36] See Polish Constitutional Court, judgment of 30 October 2006, P 10/06.

human rights and freedoms. They are rights enabling the realisation of other rights and freedoms. The constitutional legislator, as well as the ordinary legislator, may shape these rights, searching for an optimum model which will, on the one hand, create the possibility of their protection and, on the other hand, create instruments which guarantee the possibility of the realisation of other constitutional values. Obviously, the legal norms established in this respect must take into account the axiology of a democratic state ruled by law."[37]

In the case that gave rise to this ruling, the Constitutional Court recognised the right of access to court as a right belonging to the latter category, stressing that it was not an absolute right. However, the category of rights of a procedural nature, which are not a simple emanation of dignity, could also include, for example, the right to petition, the right to asylum and freedom from extradition.

The inviolable and inalienable rights immanent to dignity may thus not be restricted, but in practice they are not considered to be absolutely protected, as the legislator may restrict the exercise of these rights under the conditions set out in the Constitution. Such conditions are determined primarily by Art. 31(3) PC, which stipulates that limitations on the enjoyment of constitutional freedoms and rights may be established only by statute and only when they are necessary in a democratic state for its security or public order, or for the protection of the environment, health and public morals, or the freedoms and rights of others. At the same time, the provision stipulates that these limitations must not affect the essence of the freedoms and rights. However, this difference between a "limitation of a right" and a "limitation of the possibility to exercise a right" is not always discernible in the jurisprudence of the Constitutional Court, which, in this respect, has not formulated any specific criteria for distinguishing between these two types of limitations. Moreover, the Court does not seem to attach much importance to this distinction, and the conditions listed in Art. 31(3) PC are most often referred to as conditions attached to the restriction of a right, rather than conditions attached to restrictions on the possibility of exercising that right. A good example in this respect is the right to the protec-

[37] "Pośród praw, dla których źródłem jest art. 30 konstytucji podstawowe znaczenie mają te, które przez to, że nawiązują wprost do istoty godności ludzkiej i wyrażają jej kwintesencję, mają charakter praw fundamentalnych. Ustawodawca z reguły nie może ich nie tylko kwestionować, ale i ograniczać. Nie są one w zasadniczej swojej treści uzależnione od woli prawodawcy, a tym bardziej od organów stosujących prawo, bez względu na to czy będą to organy administracji publicznej czy sądy. Stąd określa się je mianem praw przyrodzonych. Z nimi wiąże się niewątpliwie konstytucyjna teza o nienaruszalności godności człowieka. [...]. Od praw fundamentalnych (przyrodzonych) należałoby odróżnić te, które nie są prostą emanacją godności ludzkiej a stanowią jedynie formę lub jedną z form zabezpieczenia praw człowieka. Mają więc charakter praw umożliwiających realizację innych praw i wolności. Te ustrojodawca, a także zwykły ustawodawca, może kształtować, poszukując optymalnego modelu, który z jednej strony będzie stwarzać możliwość ich ochrony, z drugiej zaś – kreować instrumenty gwarantujące możliwość realizowania innych konstytucyjnych wartości. Oczywiście, że stanowione w tym zakresie normy prawne muszą uwzględniać aksjologię demokratycznego państwa prawnego."

tion of life, which, according to the Court, is not absolute and is subject to limitations, although it is undoubtedly closely related to dignity and, in this sense, undoubtedly meets the abovementioned criteria of a fundamental (inherent) right. In a 2008 judgment concerning a provision allowing public authorities to shoot down a passenger aircraft used as a means of terrorist attack, the Constitutional Court stated that it

> "unequivocally gives priority to the values of human life and dignity. These values are the foundation of European civilisation and determine the semantic content of the concept of humanism, which is central in our culture (including our legal culture). They are inalienable in the sense that they do not allow for 'suspension' or 'abolition' in a specific situational context. Humanism is not an attitude that, as a kind of decorum, is cultivated only in times of peace and prosperity, but a value whose particular test is precisely in crisis situations, sometimes extremely difficult ones. From the point of view of the most rudimentary assumptions of our legal system, a different conception would be unacceptable."[38]

At the same time, however, in an abortion ruling issued 11 years earlier, the Constitutional Court recognised that the legal protection of life is progressive and may be subject to limitations, albeit only in justified cases. At that time, the Court did not consider an abortion performed on account of a woman's difficult financial situation to be such a justified case.[39]

VI. Community versus national thinking on dignity and inalienable human rights

Rensmann concludes his remarks on inalienable human rights by pointing out that in recent case law, of which the *Ökotox* decision[40] is a representative example, the Federal Constitutional Court views the fundamental rights contained in the German Basic Law, the European Convention on Human Rights[41] and

---

[38] See Polish Constitutional Court, judgment of 30 October 2008, K 44/07: "Trybunał Konstytucyjny jednoznacznie przyznaje priorytet wartościom, którymi są życie i godność człowieka. Wartości te stanowią fundament europejskiej cywilizacji i wyznaczają treść znaczeniową centralnego w naszej kulturze (także prawnej) pojęcia humanizmu. Są one niezbywalne w tym sensie, że nie dopuszczają 'zawieszenia' lub 'zniesienia' w konkretnym kontekście sytuacyjnym. Humanizm nie jest postawą, którą w charakterze swoistego decorum kultywuje się wyłącznie w czasach pokoju i dobrobytu, ale wartością, której szczególnym probierzem są właśnie sytuacje kryzysowe, niekiedy skrajnie trudne. Z punktu widzenia najbardziej rudymentarnych założeń naszego systemu prawnego koncepcja odmienna byłaby nie do przyjęcia."

[39] See Polish Constitutional Court, judgment of 28 May 1997, K 26/96.

[40] Federal Constitutional Court, order of 27 April 2021, BVerfGE 158, 1.

[41] Convention for the Protection of Human Rights and Fundamental Freedoms, 4 November 1950, ETS 5.

the EU Charter of Fundamental Rights[42] as "manifestations" of the "common values" laid down in the Universal Declaration of Human Rights. The Court argues that all three of the abovementioned legal instruments are rooted in common constitutional traditions and are thus a manifestation of common European and universal values, and that these common values and traditions are based on a common commitment to respect for human dignity, which in turn finds its point of reference in the Universal Declaration of Human Rights.

However, in its recent jurisprudence, the Polish Constitutional Court has clearly departed from such communitarian thinking. A good example in this regard is its judgment of 7 October 2021, K 3/21, in which the Court declared, *inter alia*, the partial unconstitutionality of Art. 2 of the Treaty on European Union (TEU), according to which the European Union is founded on the values of respect for human dignity, freedom, democracy, equality, the rule of law and human rights. The Polish Constitutional Court held that

> "[t]he content of Art. 2 TEU, while deriving from the constitutional traditions of nation states, draws heavily on the content and interpretation of Art. 2 of the Constitution of the Republic of Poland as one of the largest EU member states with a centuries-old legal culture."[43]

Thus, the Court came to the conclusion that the Polish understanding of the principle of a democratic state ruled by law as expressed in Art. 2 PC should determine the direction of interpretation of Art. 2 TEU by the Court of Justice of the European Union (CJEU). In its further arguments, the Court questioned the possibility of a uniform understanding of the values on which the EU is based. Indeed, as was stated:

> "Article 2 TEU lists the values of the EU by means of vague and indefinite phrases, as the content of these phrases does not encompass a complete set of constitutive characteristics [...]. Each of these terms has a rich and varied content in the legal culture of the EU Member States. And since Art. 2 TEU (read in conjunction with the TEU Preamble) mentions reconstructed rather than created values, it should also take into account the understanding of these terms in various European democracies, especially ones such as the Polish democracy, which has a centuries-old tradition. It follows from the phrase 'are common' in Art. 2 TEU that the values listed therein are part of common traditions, not that they are to be 'communalised' through the law-making interpretation of EU bodies. The values constituting national identity cannot be imposed on any nation at all as a result of the CJEU's interpretation of treaty law."[44]

---

[42] Charter of Fundamental Rights of the European Union, as amended on 12 December 2007, Official Journal of the European Union 2012 C 236/391.

[43] "Treść art. 2 TUE, wywodząc się z tradycji konstytucji państw narodowych, czerpie w znacznym stopniu z treści i wykładni art. 2 Konstytucji RP jako jednego z największych państw członkowskich UE, mającego wielowiekową kulturę prawną."

[44] "Art. 2 TUE wymienia wartości UE przy pomocy zwrotów nieostrych i niedookreślonych, gdyż treść tych zwrotów nie obejmuje kompletnego zespołu cech konstytutywnych [...]. Każdy z tych terminów ma w kulturze państw członkowskich UE bogatą i różnorodną

It should be added that this ruling concerned the right of access to court, which is undoubtedly a fundamental right under Polish case law and an inalienable human right under German case law. The Polish Court held that there is no possibility of a "communitarisation" of this right, as it is a value constituting the Polish national identity, and the understanding of this right cannot "be imposed on any nation as a result of the CJEU's interpretation of treaty law". This is therefore a completely different approach to the problem of inalienable human rights from that of the Federal Constitutional Court in its jurisprudence and from that presented in *Rensmann*'s paper.

VII. Conclusions

It is generally accepted that the basic concepts defining a European legal culture, such as dignity or human rights, should be uniformly understood in countries belonging to this culture. The analysis of the concept of dignity in German and Polish constitutional jurisprudence and its translation into the concept of inalienable human rights, however, leads to the conclusion that there are significant differences in the perception, description and justification of human dignity and inalienable human rights. While the German Constitutional Court tries to give these concepts a universal meaning by referring to the Universal Declaration of Human Rights and the common constitutional traditions of the EU Member States, the Polish Constitutional Court defines these concepts exclusively through the prism of the Polish Constitution and Polish constitutional identity. These differences arise not so much from the wording of the constitutional regulation on human dignity – although, as mentioned, some differences can also be seen in this respect – but rather from the two constitutional courts referencing differently understood constitutional traditions, social expectations, historical experiences and even well-known theories and philosophies. The jurisprudence of the German Constitutional Court also shows consistency in developing both concepts in a certain direction, as described by *Rensmann*, whereas in the jurisprudence of the Polish Constitutional Court, we observe a new approach to these issues, which is the result of a collision course with EU law and EU integration that started in 2017. While earlier, for many years, the Polish Constitutional Court referred to German jurisprudence when defining

treść. Skoro zaś art. 2 TUE (rozumiany wespół z preambułą TUE) wymienia wartości odtworzone, a nie stworzone, to powinien również uwzględniać rozumienie tych pojęć w różnych europejskich demokracjach, zwłaszcza takich jak posiadająca wielowiekowe tradycje demokracja polska. Z zawartego w art. 2 TUE sformułowania 'są wspólne' wynika, że wartości tam wymienione należą do wspólnych tradycji, a nie to, że mają podlegać 'uwspólnotowieniu' w drodze prawotwórczej wykładni organów UE. Wartości składające się na tożsamość narodową w ogóle nie mogą być narzucane jakiemukolwiek narodowi w efekcie wykładni prawa traktatowego przez TSUE."

concepts such as dignity or democracy, which were introduced into the Polish Constitution after taking inspiration from the German Constitution, in its most recent jurisprudence the Court has strongly distanced itself from the universal (European) understanding of these concepts, emphasising the specificity of the domestic context that should be taken into account. This makes it possible to conclude that adopting an interdisciplinary approach for the analysis of basic legal concepts does not always lead to the universalisation of these concepts and their commonality.

Part 4

Law and Politics

The Judicial Dialogue in the EU between Law and Politics*

Aqilah Sandhu

I. Introduction

In his laudatory address to the academic community of the Jagiellonian University at the honorary degree ceremony, *Reiner Schmidt* called the relationship between European law and the constitutional laws of the Member States "one of the most interesting questions"[1] of our times. He concluded that whereas the Federal Constitutional Court's (*Bundesverfassungsgericht*) normative programme was the enforcement of the law (i.e. of the German Constitution – the *Grundgesetz*), the European Court of Justice's (ECJ) programme was the subordination of law to the political programme of the European Union. He called into question whether the courts were overburdened with crucial political questions, especially with regard to the "teleology of the European project", which is left open in the primary law of the EU.

The question as to which Court has the last word and whether primary law is politicised has been accompanying the process of integration for a long time

* The author is grateful for financial support of the Young Researchers Travel Scholarship Program of the University of Augsburg. The last substantive update of this paper dates back to May 2022.

[1] *R. Schmidt*, Should monetary policy be taken to court? ("Gehört die Geldpolitik vor die Richter?"), address to the JU academic community at the conferral of the doctorate honoris causa, 15 October 2021, Krakow.

and keeps recurring. There is a tradition of accusing the ECJ of overstepping its limits as defined in the Treaties.[2] This has also been repeatedly voiced by judges of the Federal Constitutional Court. *Dieter Grimm*, former judge of the Federal Constitutional Court, for example, famously called the ECJ a "court with an agenda".[3] According to him, the ECJ is neither a guardian of the interests of the Member States nor a neutral arbiter, but rather a political institution with a one-sided bias in favour of European integration. From a methodological perspective, the scope of Union law is defined by means of teleological interpretation based on the objectives set out in the Treaties. Thereby, however, the ECJ has been overstretching the *effet utile* leading to the broadening of the scope of Union law far beyond the Union's original competence.[4]

In the European court system, national constitutional courts and the ECJ engage in a vivid judicial dialogue. This dialogue is not a purely legal one, but also a platform to fathom the respective powers – which is however, a highly political question. It is, of course, true that there is no sharp line between the interpretation of the law and judicial law-making, and that especially constitutional courts are inherently political actors. Yet the judicial dialogue in the EU adds another dimension to this old debate, which is mainly led with regard to the horizontal separation of powers in nation-states. In the EU, important legal issues are negotiated in an overarching judicial dialogue, replacing democratic debate in the competent parliamentary system, Treaty revision procedures or Treaty amending conventions. The pinnacle was reached in the dispute concerning the Public Sector Purchase Programme (PSPP), which almost led to direct conflict between the courts (see below II). Recapitulating the famous *Schmitt-Kelsen* debate on the legitimacy of the jurisprudence of constitutional courts (III), this contribution analyses the relevance of the judicial dialogue in the European court system (IV). It then questions the legitimacy of a predomi-

[2] See *M. Dougan*, The Bubble that Burst: Exploring the Legitimacy of the Case Law on the Free Movement of Union Citizens, in: M. Adams et al. (eds.), Judging Europe's Judges. The Legitimacy of the Case Law of the European Court of Justice (2013), 127–154, 128 (for further references); for an early critique, see *H. Rasmussen*, On Law and Policy in the European Court of Justice. A Comparative Study in Judicial Policy-Making (1986); *P. Neill*, The European Court of Justice: A Case Study in Judicial Activism (1995).

[3] *D. Grimm*, Europa ja – aber welches? Zur Verfassung der europäischen Demokratie (2016), 16. This criticism was repeated by the former President of the German Constitutional Court and member of its second senate responsible for the PSPP judgment, Andreas Voßkuhle, as cited by *A. Kaufmann*, "Befangener kann man nicht sein", Legal Tribune Online, 22 June 2021, https://www.lto.de/recht/justiz/j/ex-bverfg-praesident-andreas-vokuhle-zu-europischer-rechtsgemeinschaft-rechtsstaatlichkeit-ezb-entscheidung-eugh-polen-ungarn/ (accessed on 25 February 2022). The statement was originally made by *R. Wahl*, Das Recht der Integrationsgemeinschaft Europäische Union, in: C. Franzius et al. (eds.), Beharren. Bewegen. Festschrift für Michael Kloepfer zum 70. Geburtstag (2013), 233–259, 248.

[4] In the field of data protection, see e.g. *A. Sandhu*, Grundrechtsunitarisierung durch Sekundärrecht (2021), 56–61.

nantly indirect dialogue between the ECJ and national constitutional courts (V), which in recent times has taken the form of actual policy-shaping (VI). The traditional indirect dialogue has led not only to the migration of legal concepts to substantive law, but also to their adaptation in methodological terms. Teleological judicial interpretation is replacing political debate. The loss of democratic transformation is multiplied in the EU as a multi-level system. As will be shown in this contribution, the extension of the German Constitutional Court's competence by reference to its responsibility with regard to European integration under Article 23(1) of the Constitutio (*Integrationsverantwortung*) closely resembles the much criticised and strained use of *effet utile* by the ECJ.

II. Primacy of EU law and political promises

With the Federal Constitutional Court's *PSPP* judgment of May 2020,[5] the dispute between national constitutional courts and the ECJ on the last word in the supranational order of the European Union had reached yet another peak. The Federal Constitutional Court for the first time applied its *ultra vires* doctrine and declared a judgment of the ECJ concerning the Public Sector Purchase Programme of the European Central Bank to be "simply not comprehensible and arbitrary from an objective perspective so that, to this extent, the judgment was rendered *ultra vires*".[6] On the occasion of this ruling, what had traditionally been seen as a "cooperative relationship"[7] between both courts was now denounced as a euphemism, a "sham cooperation" or a "confrontational relationship"[8]. Although the Federal Constitutional Court was one of the first

[5] BVerfG, judgment of 5 May 2020, 2 BvR 859/15. One year later, the Court dismissed applications for an order of execution of its judgment as they went "beyond the factual and legal circumstances of the matter decided [in the PSPP judgment] and thus exceeded the permissible scope of an order of execution", BVerfG, order of 29 April 2021, 2 BvR 1651/15, para. 82.

[6] BVerfG, judgment of 5 May 2020, 2 BvR 859/15, para. 116. The official translation is somewhat unfortunate and perhaps misleading, as the ECJ's judgment of 11 December 2018, Case C-493/17 – Weiss and Others, which was declared inapplicable by the BVerfG, was very well studied and indeed "comprehensible". However, the legal reasoning of the ECJ was considered inacceptable and intransparent, especially from a methodological perspective (in the German original: "schlechterdings nicht mehr nachvollziehbar"). Regarding this translation, see *F. Schorkopf*, Antwort auf eine entgrenzte Politik, Frankfurter Allgemeine Zeitung, Einspruch Exklusiv, 5 May 2020.

[7] This phrase goes back to the Maastricht judgment of the BVerfG, judgment of 12 October 1993, 2 BvR 2134/92, 2 BvR 2159/92, BVerfGE 89, 155, 175.

[8] *W. Kahl*, Optimierungspotenzial im "Kooperationsverhältnis" zwischen EuGH und BVerfG, Neue Zeitschrift für Verwaltungsrecht 39 (2020), 824–828, 827.

courts in the European Community to acknowledge the primacy of EU law,[9] it actually arrogated for itself the right to declare EU law inapplicable if it was necessary to safeguard state sovereignty and the national identity along with the principle of conferral, and thus the power to exercise judicial oversight over the ECJ. For some, these red lines seemed more like "a dictate" than an offer of dialogue with the EU Court.[10] In reaction to the *PSPP* judgment, the European Commission initiated infringement proceedings against Germany under Art. 258 TFEU. It found that with the Constitutional Court's ruling, Germany had violated "the general principles of autonomy, primacy, effectiveness and uniform application of Union law" and had failed to comply with Art. 267 TFEU as interpreted in light of the principle of sincere cooperation expressed in Art. 4(3) TEU.[11] The subsequent statement of Germany of August 2021 led to the closure of the infringement proceedings. In its statement, Germany formally reaffirmed the principles of autonomy, primacy, and effectiveness of Union law. It expressly recognised the authority of the ECJ in the EU, and it declared its intention to use all means at its disposal to actively avoid a repetition of an *ultra vires* finding in the future.[12] This last concession must be considered as an empty promise if it is not to be understood as being in conflict with the fundamental principle of judicial independence, guaranteed by Art. 97 of the German *Grundgesetz* and a basic element of the rule of law, a common value[13] on which the EU is founded. The German government cannot coerce the Federal Constitutional Court to abandon its *ultra vires* review without violating judicial independence.[14] Furthermore, the reserved oversight powers are an

[9] Albeit with a reasoning different than that of the ECJ, see BVerfG, order of 22 October 1986, 2 BvR 197/83, BVerfGE 73, 330, 374 (Solange II); *D. Grimm*, Der Dialog zwischen EuGH und BVerfG und das PSPP-Urteil, AnwBl Online (2021), 150–151, 151.

[10] *Kahl* (n. 8), 827.

[11] European Commission, Letter of Formal Notice, 9 June 2021, https://ruleoflaw.pl/wp-content/uploads/2022/02/doc-1-LFN-to-DE-EN.pdf (last accessed on 25 February 2022).

[12] European Commission, Press Release, 2 December 2021, https://ec.europa.eu/commission/presscorner/detail/de/inf_21_6201; for a summary of the proceedings, see Deutscher Bundestag, Aktueller Begriff Europa, Nr. 09/21, 23 December 2021, https://www.bundestag.de/resource/blob/873842/4b6dd11dc21afcfcb1ffa49cc665fe5b/Vertragsverletzungsverfahren-geg-BRD-data.pdf; Germany's full statement is available at https://ruleoflaw.pl/wp-content/uploads/2022/02/doc-2-DE-reply-to-LFN-de.pdf (each last accessed on 25 February 2022).

[13] On the rule of law as a common and fundamental EU value, see the settled case law of the CJEU, judgment of 16 February 2022, C-156/21 and C-157/21 – Hungary and Poland/Parliament and Council; judgment of 24 June 2019, C-619/18 – Commission/Poland.

[14] See also the critique of *M. Ruffert*, Verfahren eingestellt, Problem gelöst?, VerfBlog 2021/12/07, DOI: 10.17176/20211208-022437-0. Moreover, the Federal Constitutional Court is not integrated into the regular court system but is a distinctive constitutional organ as stipulated in § 1 of the Act on the Federal Constitutional Court (BVerfGG): "The Federal Constitutional Court shall be a federal court of justice which is autonomous and independent of all other constitutional organs." With a view to the interest of the Commission in lowering the standard

expression of the Member States' sovereignty as explicitly recognised in Art. 4(2) TEU, and as such they are not contrary to the primacy of EU law but merely mark the limits of EU competence. They are also grounded in Art. 23(1)(3) of the *Grundgesetz*, declaring the establishment of the European Union as well as Treaty amendments to be subject to Art. 79(2) and (3) of the *Grundgesetz*. In particular, Art. 79(2) and (3) *Grundgesetz* protect constitutional identity, the principles of the rule of law and democracy and the inviolability of human dignity. This provision is the legal basis for the reserved powers of the Federal Constitutional Court.[15] Thus, it is the German *Grundgesetz* itself that places the outermost limits on the otherwise unquestioned precedence of EU law over national law.

Germany also expressed its commitment to formalise and institutionalise the so far merely informal dialogue ongoing between the ECJ and national supreme courts in order to foster a common understanding within the European network of courts (*Gerichtsverbund*). It suggested the instalment of a "platform of European Judges" to act as consultative body.[16] This entity could complement the already existing Conference of the Heads of the Supreme Courts of the EU Member States.[17]

III. The inherent political character of constitutional courts

The question as to which court has the final say in the vertically integrated judicial system of the EU leads to the problem of politicisation of the jurisdiction of the courts. As the president of the ECJ has put it: "By drawing the borderline between law and politics, courts in fact are drawing the contours of

of review of the ECJ, see the critique of *K.F. Gärditz,* Ein Staatsstreich von oben?, Frankfurter Allgemeine Zeitung, Einspruch Exklusiv, 12 July 2021, https://www.faz.net/aktuell/politik/einspruch-exklusiv-ein-staatsstreich-von-oben-17434747.html (last accessed on 25 February 2022).

[15] See e.g. BVerfG, judgment of 30 June 2009, 2 BvE 2/08, para. 208; BVerfG, order of 1 December 2020, 2 BvR 1845/18, para. 40.

[16] Statement of Germany (n. 12), 4. There are already informal horizontal meetings between the supreme courts of the Member States: Since 2004, they have exchanged their ideas in the Network of the Presidents of the Supreme Judicial Courts of the EU, https://www.network-presidents.eu. However, this does not include the constitutional courts; Germany, for instance, is represented by the Bundesgerichtshof (BGH). The Conference of European Constitutional Courts established in 1972 brings together 46 European constitutional courts and is not limited to the EU Member States, https://www.confeuconstco.org/en/common/home.html.

[17] The heads of the supreme courts of the EU Member States (i.e. the constitutional courts) meet in conferences to discuss the role of the ECJ, see e.g. BVerfG, Press Release No. 13/2022 of 22 February 2022.

their own legitimacy."[18] The principle of separation of powers aims at drawing the line between law and politics. This is also true for the EU, where "legitimacy requires power to be allocated in accordance with the Treaties. An EU court will be deprived of its legitimacy [...] if it intrudes into the political sphere, at either EU or national level [...]".[19] It is thus of vital importance for a court's legitimacy not to intrude into the political process.

A. The role of constitutional courts in Kelsen's theory

Yet, when it comes to EU politics, the Federal Constitutional Court is no less a relevant political player than the ECJ, although the first usually raises its admonishing finger towards the latter for overstepping its powers. Instead, albeit without advocating a rigid distinction between law and politics in the sense of *Carl Schmitt*, who for his part functionally separated the legislature from the judiciary,[20] the political ambitions of both courts have to be seen critically. To *Schmitt*, constitutional jurisdiction was incompatible with the constitution being a mere political compromise between the dominant social forces. Establishing a constitutional jurisdiction which encompassed the power to annul laws enacted by the legislature would inevitably turn courts into political actors.[21] However, *Hans Kelsen* contended that

> "[t]he view that only legislation and not the 'actual' judiciary is political is just as wrong as the view that only legislation is a productive creation of law whereas judicial activity is only a reproductive application of law."[22]

The Federal Constitutional Court, in particular, is a political institution and certainly has an active, policy-shaping function, as, in the sense of *Kelsen*, constitutional questions are always political questions.

Nevertheless, *Kelsen*'s pure theory of law was not an illusionary vision of law created in a social and moral vacuum. Instead, he recognised that constitutional law was inextricably intertwined with politics, that law was the product

---

[18] *K. Lenaerts*, The Court's Outer and Inner Selves: Exploring the External and Internal Legitimacy of the European Court of Justice, in: M. Adams et al. (n. 2), 13–60, 13; on the importance of contextualisation of judicial rulings due to the inherent interest of the courts to expand their judicial powers, *O. Lepsius*, Kontextualisierung als Aufgabe der Rechtswissenschaft, Juristenzeitung 74 (2019), 793–802, 799.

[19] *Lenaerts* (n. 18), 14.

[20] *C. Schmitt*, Der Hüter der Verfassung (1931), 595.

[21] See the analysis of *R.C. van Ooyen*, Die Funktion der Verfassungsgerichtsbarkeit in der pluralistischen Demokratie und die Kontroverse um den "Hüter der Verfassung", in: idem (ed.), Hans Kelsen. Wer soll der Hüter der Verfassung sein? (2nd edn., 2019), VII–XXIII, XVI.

[22] *H. Kelsen*, Wer soll der Hüter der Verfassungs sein?, Die Justiz 6 (1931), 576–628, 586: "Die Meinung, daß nur die Gesetzgebung, nicht aber die 'echte' Justiz politisch sei, ist ebenso falsch wie die, daß nur die Gesetzgebung produktive Rechtserzeugung, die Gerichtsbarkeit aber nur reproduktive Rechtsanwendung sei." (Author's translation).

of social influences and a compromise between different interest groups, and that judgments of constitutional courts are political in nature.[23] Law is thus "politics in a congealed form."[24] However, the process of judicial interpretation and the application of the law should abstain from practising politics.[25] *Kelsen* warned that constitutional jurisdiction can be a means of safeguarding democracy if that constitution abstains from "phraseology".[26] In order to prevent a power shift away from the democratically elected legislature, i.e. the parliament, towards the judiciary, both the standard of review of the court and its legal requirements and principles had to be precisely defined in the constitution.[27] The next section discusses the political nature of the judicial dialogue and *Kelsen*'s theory in the European context.[28]

B. Phraseology in the EU Treaties

The ECJ has historically had a "gap-filling function"[29] due to the vagueness of the Treaties in the early phase of the integration process. Primary law leaves unresolved the question of what is the ultimate goal of the European project – which is fundamental to the process of European integration. According to Art. 1(2) TEU, "[t]his Treaty marks a new stage in the process of creating an ever closer union among the peoples of Europe", but what is the ultimate goal

[23] *H. Kelsen*, Was ist Reine Rechtslehre? (1953), in: H. Klecatsky et al. (eds.), Die Wiener Rechtstheoretische Schule. Ausgewählte Schriften von Hans Kelsen, Adolf Julius Merkl und Alfred Verdross, vol. 1 (1968), 611–629, 620; *idem* (n. 22), 587. See also *H. Dreier*, Hans Kelsen's Wissenschaftsprogramm, in: M. Jestaedt/S.L. Paulson (eds.), Kelsen im Kontext. Beiträge zum Werk Hans Kelsens und geistesverwandter Autoren (2019), 29–66, 30.

[24] *Dreier* (n. 23), 30.

[25] *Kelsen* (n. 23), 620.

[26] *H. Kelsen*, Wesen und Entwicklung der Staatsgerichtsbarkeit, VVDStRL 5 (1929), 30–88, 70. See also *H. Dreier*, Hans Kelsen (1881–1973), in: Jestaedt/Paulson (n. 23), 1–26, 14.

[27] *Dreier* (n. 26), 14: "präzise Kontrollmaßstäbe".

[28] More in-depth studies examine the state-centred logic of pure legal theory specifically in relation to the European Community, see e.g. *I. Weyland*, The Application of Kelsen's Theory of the Legal System to European Community Law – The Supremacy Puzzle resolved, Law and Philosophy 21 (2002) 1–37; *T. Ehs* (ed.), Hans Kelsen und die Europäische Union (2008); *J. Busch/T. Ehs*, The EU as Rechtsgemeinschaft. A Kelsenian Approach to European Legal Philosophy, Rivista Internazionale di Filosofia del Diritto 2 (2008), 195–223; *S.-P. Hwang*, Demokratie im Mehrebenensystem: Integrationsfest oder integrationsoffen? Überlegungen zum Demokratiebegriff beim Lissabon-Urteil des BVerfG im Lichte des Schmitt-Kelsen-Gegensatzes, Rechtswissenschaft 2 (2013), 166–192. These studies tackle the question of parliamentary sovereignty of the Member States, the principle of supremacy of EU law and the applicability of Kelsen's theory to the EU as a political Union, which is special in that it has "a constitution without a state" (*H. Brunkhorst*, A Polity without a State? European Constitutionalism between Evolution and Revolution, ARENA Working Paper 14 (2003), 1–30, 19). They do not deal with the role of the ECJ as a "constitutional court" or as a political actor in the EU, where the counter-majoritarian problem is even more pressing.

[29] *Lenaerts* (n. 18), 15.

of this ever closer union? A federal state or only the smoothest possible internal market for persons, services, goods and capital? The final goal of the integration of Europe remains undefined in the Treaties.

For decades, however, the political integration of Europe has not been decided solely at the conferences in Rome, Maastricht, Amsterdam, Nice or Lisbon. It was very much negotiated between Luxembourg and Karlsruhe. It was the ECJ that established the principle of absolute primacy of Union law,[30] which was codified only in 2009 in Declaration no. 17 annexed to the Treaty of Lisbon.[31] The problem of the elusiveness of the Treaty provisions creating excess space for the "interpretative autonomy of the Court" had been identified in academic literature before, especially with regard to the internal market rules, which "leave open a host of vital questions".[32] And, as *Kelsen* prominently warned, it is especially true for the ECJ that "the less precise the mandate on the basis of which a court is asked to operate, the more power is delegated to that court to select among plausible alternatives."[33] The judiciary is given a power equivalent to that of the lawmaker if the constitution refers to formulistic principles like "fairness", "justice", "freedom", "equity" or "morality", without further specifying their content.[34] Delegating the definition of such values to the constitutional judiciary may turn out to be "highly dangerous"[35] if these principles are the standard of review for determining the validity of a legal norm. It is even more dangerous considering the power of the ECJ to set aside laws enacted by the parliaments of the Member States. Whereas the EU Treaty provisions are often criticised for being too detailed and thus creating an inflexible framework,[36] the recent rule of law controversy has shown that despite the vagueness of the values of the EU, their breach by the Member States may be sanctioned. The ECJ upheld the general regime of conditionality for the protection of the EU budget (Regulation 2020/2092).[37] It aims at protecting the financial interests of the EU and ensuring that financing is in line with the values set out in Art. 2 TEU. Art. 2 TEU could be regarded as a

---

[30] ECJ, judgment of 15 July 1964, Case 6/64 – Costa/E.N.E.L. See also *K.J. Alter*, Establishing the Supremacy of European Law (2003).

[31] See also BVerfG, judgment of 30 June 2009, 2 BvE 2/08, para. 331 – Lisbon, stating that the Declaration merely "confirms the legal situation as interpreted by the Federal Constitutional Court."

[32] *S. Weatherill*, The Court's Case Law on the Internal Market: "A Circumloquacious Statement of the Result, Rather than a Reason for Arriving at It"?, in: Adams et al. (n. 2), 87–108, 108.

[33] *Weatherill* (n. 32), 90.

[34] *Kelsen* (n. 26), 69; especially in the internal market context, "definitional precision remains elusive", as pointed out by *Weatherill* (n. 32), 95.

[35] *Kelsen* (n. 26), 69.

[36] *Grimm* (n. 3), 104.

[37] Judgment of 16 February 2022, Case C-156/21 and 157/21 – Hungary and Poland/Parliament and Council.

phraseological constitutional provision *par excellence*, referring, as it does, to principles such as "freedom, democracy, equality, [and] the rule of law", yet without contour and precision, thus granting the quasi-constitutional court of Europe a power that must be perceived as "absolutely intolerable" in the spirit of *Kelsen*.[38] With regard to its aims and values, the integration programme of the EU is not sufficiently precise.

IV. Necessity of the judicial dialogue

As the EU is not a superstate, being described instead as a "non-hierarchical and polycentric polity",[39] an omnipotent ECJ is met with distrust by the democratically legitimised constitutional courts of the Member States.[40] At the same time, however, judicial dialogue in the EU is intrinsic to its "multi-layered human rights architecture".[41] This encompasses not only the dialogue between the highest constitutional courts and the ECJ within the Union, but also that between Strasbourg and Luxemburg, a dialogue which is explicitly enshrined in the Declaration on Art. 6(2) of the EU Treaty, annexed to the Final Act of the Intergovernmental Conference which adopted the Treaty of Lisbon.[42]

---

[38] He warned that such formulas serving as "political decoration of the Constitution" ("dem politischen Schmuck der Verfassung dienenden Formeln") may easily be confused with material provisions on fundamental rights and freedoms. A constitutional court may thus annul a law referring to undefined principles such as "justice". In so doing, it would acquire an unacceptably unlimited political power ("eine Machtvollkommenheit [...], die schlechthin als unerträglich empfunden werden muss"), *Kelsen* (n. 26), 69–70. The rule of law has been substantiated by the ECJ in its case law and defined in Recital 3 of EU Regulation 2020/2092. Art. 2 TEU was also addressed in the Lisbon judgment; however, the Federal Constitutional Court left open its legal character and made clear that the value-clause does not provide the EU with a "Kompetenz-Kompetenz", thus respecting the principle of conferral, judgment of 30 June 2009, 2 BvE 2/08, para. 332.

[39] *F. Snyder*, General Course on Constitutional Law of the European Union (1995), 55.

[40] *F.W. Scharpf*, Legitimationskonzepte jenseits des Nationalstaats, in: G.F. Schuppert et al. (eds.), Europawissenschaft (2005), 705–742, 728, also points to the possibility of the legislature to react to a decision of the Federal Constitutional Court by amending the constitution, whereas the ECJ's decisions are almost engraved in stone with regard to the complex Treaty ratification process.

[41] *F. Fabbrini*, The EU Charter of Fundamental Rights and the Rights to Data Privacy: The EU Court of Justice as a Human Rights Court, in: S. de Vries et al. (eds.), The EU Charter of Fundamental Rights as a binding instrument. Five years old and growing (2015), 261–286, 281.

[42] According to the Declaration "the Conference notes the existence of a regular dialogue between the [Court of Justice] and the [ECtHR]; such dialogue could be reinforced when the Union accedes to that Convention."

Union law is very much a product of transnational comparative reasoning, marked by the migration of methodological instruments.[43] Consequently, the ECJ has learned from the national constitutional courts. The principle of proportionality is, for example, widely considered as having successfully migrated from German law into Union law.[44] And when reading the reasoning of the ECJ in its case law on fundamental rights, one can certainly not deny the obvious impact of the Federal Constitutional Court's jurisprudence.[45]

A. Direct dialogue

Apart from the dialogue between the ECtHR and the ECJ, there is also the institutionalised dialogue between the ECJ and national courts – including constitutional courts – according to Art. 267 TFEU. The term "dialogue between courts" has its origin in the context of preliminary proceedings. As a Union of law, the EU is founded on the very fundamental premise that the Member States' judicial systems are governed by the rule of law. The direct dialogue only functions if it is practised by independent courts. The preliminary procedure is considered to be the "keystone" in the judicial system of the EU. It sets up "a dialogue between one court and another, specifically between the Court of Justice and the courts and tribunals of the Member States".[46] The object of this dialogue is to secure the uniform interpretation of EU law and thereby to ensure the consistency, full effect and autonomy of EU law in the Member States.[47] Yet this dialogue has until recently rarely been relied on by the constitutional courts of the Member States, especially the Federal Constitutional Court. It is only in the past 15 years that references for a preliminary ruling have been submitted to the ECJ by the Italian (2008), Spanish (2011), French

---

[43] *E. Stein*, Lawyers, Judges and the Making of a Transnational Constitution, American Journal of International Law 75 (1981), 1–27; *F. Mancini*, The Making of a Constitution for Europe, Common Market Law Review 26 (1989), 595–614; *A. Stone Sweet*, The Judicial Construction of Europe (2004).

[44] On this, see *S. Choudhry* (ed.), The Migration of Constitutional Ideas (2008).

[45] ECJ, Joined Cases C-293/12 and C-594/12, para. 37: In the context of the storage of all telecommunications traffic data for several months, the Federal Constitutional Court considered the provision at issue to be disproportionate by, inter alia, referring to the "diffuse sense of threat" and "a sense of being permanently monitored" as a result of data storage.[45] One is very much reminded of this wording when reading the Digital Rights judgment only four years later, where the ECJ declared the underlying Data Retention Directive null and void, arguing that data retention without the users' knowledge "is likely to generate in the minds of the persons concerned the feeling that their private lives are the subject of constant surveillance."

[46] ECJ, Opinion 2/13, 18 December 2014, para. 176 – Accession to the ECHR.

[47] ECJ, Opinion 2/13, 18 December 2014, para. 176 – Accession to the ECHR.

(2013), and German (2014) constitutional courts.[48] And for the most part, the questions referred did not concern fundamental rights. One may wonder why such a direct dialogue has taken so long to develop.

Rulings of the ECJ under Art. 267 TFEU bind the referring court.[49] They are not directly binding upon the parties involved. Only the final decision of the referring court (applying the ECJ's interpretation) binds the parties of the proceedings (*inter partes*). The preliminary decision of the ECJ is binding only insofar as it answers the specific questions referred to it. "Dialogue" thus seeks to describe the binding effect of a preliminary ruling which is neither *erga omnes* nor *inter partes* in a strict sense. In a broader sense, and according to the *acte clair* or *acte eclairé* doctrine, these rulings factually bind all other national courts as well once they are confronted with a similar case.[50]

B. Indirect dialogue

Whereas direct dialogue between the ECJ and national constitutional courts has a relatively short history, the informal, non-institutionalised dialogue has a long tradition. One may distinguish this from the horizontal dialogue between the national courts, which is very intense. The latter takes place in informal meetings and conferences, but also in academic literature. In the landmark decision on the *Right to be Forgotten II*, the Federal Constitutional Court referred to the Austrian Constitutional Court, the Constitutional Court of Belgium, the French *Conseil constitutionnel* and the Italian *Corte costituzionale* in order to justify the review of the domestic application of EU law by German authorities on the basis of the EU Charter. Also, the famous *Solange II* decision of the Federal Constitutional Court was preceded by the *Frontini* case of the Italian *Corte costituzionale*, in which the *Corte* reserved to itself the right to adjudicate on the compatibility of Community legislation with fundamental rights under the Italian Constitution.[51] Particularly in *Solange II*, the Federal Constitutional Court aimed at pressuring the ECJ to improve fundamental rights protection to a standard equivalent to that of the national level, with the objective of increasing convergence between the two legal orders.

---

[48] *A. Lang*, How Constitutional Courts talk to each other: The Potential of the Preliminary Reference Procedure for Europe's pluralist Verfassungsverbund, VerfBlog 2014/11/28, DOI: 10.17176/20170601-145708.

[49] *AG Warner*, Opinion Case 112/76, ECR 1977, 1658, 1662 – Manzoni.

[50] In more detail on this aspect, see *Sandhu* (n. 4), 219–225.

[51] *P. Mengozzi*, A European Partnership of Courts. Judicial Dialogue between the EU Court of Justice and National Constitutional Courts, Il Diritto Dell'Unione Europea 3 (2015), 701–720. He also reports that the famous Solange II decision of the Federal Constitutional Court was preceded by the ground-breaking Granital decision of the Italian Corte Costituzionale. Wolfgang Zeidler, then President of the Federal Constitutional Court, and Antonio La Pergola, the reporting judge of the Granital case in 1984, had exchanged views previously at a meeting at the University of Bologna.

More dominant in public discourse is the indirect dialogue between the ECJ and the Member States' constitutional courts as a "non-hierarchical and polycentric polity".[52] This judicial dialogue is even more powerful than the Treaties. Major steps in the development of fundamental rights in the EU have resulted from the dialogue between the judges of, on the one hand, the ECJ and, on the other hand, the national constitutional courts. Emphasising the importance of the non-institutionalised judicial dialogue between the ECJ and national constitutional courts is more than subscribing to "a cliché" in EU constitutional law.[53] Rather, the indirect dialogue is perhaps its cornerstone.

V. Legitimacy of the dialogue

This raises the question of the legitimacy of such a dialogue that determines the scope of the ECJ's jurisdiction, especially in the field of fundamental rights protection. Article 51 of the Charter, from the outset, seems to set clear and precise boundaries on the jurisdiction of the ECJ. Its para. 1 limits the binding-force of the Charter *vis-à-vis* the Member States to situations where "they are implementing Union law". Paragraph 2 ensures that the Charter "does not extend the field of application of Union law beyond the powers of the Union or establish any new power or task for the Union, or modify powers and tasks as defined in the Treaties." Yet the jurisprudence of the ECJ has vastly expanded the scope of application of fundamental rights over the last few years.[54] Article 51 of the Charter is a compromise, consolidating the ECJ jurisprudence on the one hand and leaving enough room for interpretation with dynamic reference to EU law on the other. The jurisprudence on the applicability of the Charter to measures of the Member States is therefore often of a political or even constituent nature.[55] The extensive interpretation of the scope of application of the Charter has been countered by the national constitutional courts – especially the German, Italian and French courts – in order to protect their national identity and the principle of conferral.[56] When the ECJ expands its jurisdiction by adopting a broad definition of the "scope of Union law", the national constitutional courts threaten to activate their review mechanisms in turn.

In the field of fundamental rights protection, the ECJ has increasingly adjudicated cases that fall within the exclusive competence of the Member States,

---

[52] *Snyder* (n. 39), 55.

[53] *Fabbrini* (n. 41), 280 f.

[54] See especially the judgment of 29 February 2013, Case C-617/10 – Fransson.

[55] *D. Grimm*, Recht oder Politik? (2017), 19.

[56] In the ruling on the counter-terrorism database, the Federal Constitutional Court of Germany directly replied to the Fransson judgment, demanding a restrictive interpretation of the ECJ's ruling, see BVerfG, judgment of 24 April 2013, 1 BvR 1215/07, para. 91.

e.g. cases touching on criminal law, private law, citizenship law or the relationship between state and church. The case law of the ECJ on the church's right to self-determination in individual labour law matters and the prohibition of discrimination on grounds of religion was criticised by legal commentators as "massive encroachments on core elements of national identity such as the basic relationship between state and church".[57] The ECJ has ruled on a case concerning discrimination by the church on grounds of religion, leaving aside Art. 17 TFEU, which in turn is relevant with view to the question of competence.[58] It could do so, because Directive 2000/78/EC on equal treatment in employment and occupation, concretising the general prohibition of discrimination, has a broad scope of application. According to Art. 17 TFEU, the Union respects and does not prejudice the status under national law of churches and religious associations or communities in the Member States. In this case however, the Court put aside the Member State's concern regarding its national identity by assuming that the EU legislature had taken this provision into account when adopting the directive.[59] Granting effective judicial review even in cases where the relation of Member States with churches and religious associations is concerned is in principle necessary and in line with secondary law. However, the Member States' reservations and the EU's duty of neutrality as expressed in Art. 17 TFEU must be given at least some consideration in the reasoning on this issue.

Instead of merely defending their constitutional orders, many national constitutional courts have adopted the practice of including the Charter into their respective standard of review. The Federal Constitutional Court for the first time applied the EU Charter of Fundamental Rights in the *Right to be Forgotten II* decision,[60] which some view as a sign of appeasement politics.[61] Others however, have rightly warned that applying the Charter straightforwardly could result in an interpretive hegemony in Europe.[62] The Federal Constitutional Court has thereby secured its position as the "ultimate guardian" of fundamental rights.

---

[57] *Kahl* (n. 8), 826.

[58] ECJ, judgment of 17 April 2018, Case C-414/16 – Egenberger, now subject to a constitutional complaint currently pending before the BVerfG, 2 BvR 934/19.

[59] ECJ, judgment of 17 April 2018, Case C-414/16, para. 57 – Egenberger.

[60] BVerfG, order of the First Senate of 6 November 2019, 1 BvR 276/17.

[61] The BVerfG itself stresses that it should conduct its review "in close cooperation with the Court of Justice of the European Union", ibid., para. 68, and acknowledges the ECJ's "final authority for interpreting EU law", para. 69 (official translation).

[62] See *Rensmann*, pp. 113 ff., 148 ff., above, on the Federal Constitutional Court's tendency to interpret the EU Charter in the light of its own case law.

VI. From dialogue to policy-making

It is not the application of the Charter by the Federal Constitutional Court that gives rise to criticism, but rather the underlying reasoning. It seems to be more politically motivated than normatively guided. Thereby, the Federal Constitutional Court seems to succumb to the same methodological fallacies as the often rightly criticised ECJ: The law is subordinated to a political aim – instead of being the normative programme of the court itself. Whereas the ECJ centres its arguments around the *effet utile*, which mostly trumps legitimate national interests, the Federal Constitutional Court refers to "its responsibility with regard to European integration (*Integrationsverantwortung*)" under Art. 23(1) of the *Grundgesetz*[63] in order to justify the application of the Charter. This *Integrationsverantwortung* can be viewed as the argumentative counterpart to *effet utile*. It is only seemingly a more integrationist, EU friendly approach. In fact, the Court thereby claims an inherently political responsibility in order to define its own jurisdiction. *Integrationsverantwortung* was initially ascribed to the political constitutional organs, especially the federal government and the federal German parliament, the *Bundestag*. In its *Lisbon* decision, the Federal Constitutional Court initially referred to this "responsibility for integration" as a "special responsibility" that is incumbent on the legislative bodies and the federal government within the context of integration, thereby ensuring democratic participation in the ratification process and preserving the principle of conferral.[64] This responsibility is an expression of the limits on European integration as framed in the *Grundgesetz*. German state organs are not authorised to transfer sovereign power to the EU and are thus prohibited from conferring upon the EU the competence to decide on its own powers.[65] While ensuring that adherence to the European integration agenda is incumbent on all constitutional organs – albeit only within their respective constitutional powers – it does not allow the government to encroach upon the judiciary or vice versa. So, for example, referring to the *PSPP* judgment, the German federal government cannot prevent the Federal Constitutional Court from exercising its reserved oversight powers when asserting its *Integrationsverantwortung*. Conversely, the Federal Constitutional Court cannot expand its own jurisdiction beyond the limits set out in the *Grundgesetz* by asserting the exercise of its *Integrationsverantwortung*. And yet, this is what occurred in the *Right to be Forgotten II* decision, where the Federal Constitutional Court derived the standard of review from Art. 23(1) of the *Grundgesetz* in conjunction with the

[63] BVerfG, order of 6 November 2019, 1 BvR 276/17, para. 53.

[64] BVerfG, judgment of 30 June 2009, 2 BvE 2/08, para. 236.

[65] BVerfG, judgment of 12 October 1993, 2 BvR 2134, 2159/92, BVerfGE 89, 155, 187; BVerfG, judgment of 5 May 2020, 2 BvR 859/15, para. 102, 116; for an extensive analysis, see *Sandhu* (n. 4), 216–218.

provisions on its role with regard to fundamental rights protection.[66] Only by applying the Charter in cases within the scope of application of fully harmonised EU law is the court able to fulfil its role of providing comprehensive fundamental rights protection *vis-à-vis* German state authorities. The Federal Constitutional Court as a state organ possesses a genuine *Integrationsverantwortung* with regard to the participation of the Federal Republic of Germany in the EU, just like the parliaments at the federal or state level or like the federal or state governments.

However, the ruling of the Federal Constitutional Court in the Right to be Forgotten II case gives rise to two issues. Firstly, it conflicts with the explicit wording of Art. 93(1) no. 4a of the *Grundgesetz*, defining the relevant standard of review for constitutional complaints before the Federal Constitutional Court. The provision only refers to the infringement of basic rights and certain similar rights under the *Grundgesetz*. It does not include the EU Charter or the European Convention on Human Rights. The Federal Constitutional Court's ruling thus amounts to an amendment of the *Grundgesetz*.[67]

Secondly, fully harmonised EU law is not "state authority" in the sense of Art. 1(1) of the *Grundgesetz* and attributable to the German state alone. While stressing that EU law partially takes precedence over constitutional law, the Federal Constitutional Court at the same time tacitly centralises Art. 267 TFEU-proceedings at the federal level in fundamental rights questions. Ordinary courts may still initiate preliminary proceedings under Art. 267 TFEU to review the compatibility of a national provision within the scope of EU law in terms of fundamental rights.[68] More likely, however, they will refer to the Constitutional Court as the instance of final resort in fundamental rights protection (Art. 267[3] TFEU) and thus refrain from referrals to the ECJ. The minute differentiation between binding standards set by EU law and a Member State's discretion[69] then becomes irrelevant. In any case, the Federal Constitutional Court is competent to adjudicate, albeit with a differing standard of review (*Grundgesetz* rights or Charter rights). The Federal Constitutional Court has thereby secured comprehensive fundamental rights protection *vis-à-vis* the entire German state authority in all its manifestations. In doing so it provides a purely teleological reasoning for the expanded standard of review. This comes

---

[66] BVerfG, order of 6 November 2019, 1 BvR 276/17, para. 53.

[67] *D. Preßlein*, Grundgesetz vs. Grundrechtecharta? Zur "europäisierten Grundrechtsprüfung" des BVerfG nach den Beschlüssen zum "Recht auf Vergessen" und "Europäischer Haftbefehl III", Europarecht 56 (2021), 247–274, 247.

[68] BVerfG, order of 6 November 2019, 1 BvR 276/17, para. 66: "As the organ guaranteeing comprehensive fundamental rights protection at the domestic level, the Federal Constitutional Court must review the decisions of the ordinary courts in this respect." ("Als Garant eines umfassenden innerstaatlichen Grundrechtsschutzes hat das Bundesverfassungsgericht die Fachgerichte diesbezüglich zu kontrollieren.") (Official translation).

[69] See e.g. BVerfG, order of 21 March 2018, 1 BvF 1/13, paras. 20–22.

very close to the one-sided methodology practised by the ECJ. *Wolfgang Kahl* brings it sharply to the point:

> "Both sides are concerned with staking their 'claims' or 'territory' in order not to be marginalized as a 'player' in the European constitutional court network, whereby power considerations, the urge for cross-border glamour, external impact and perception (by the media and the public) as well as personal sensitivities and vanities are also at play […]."[70]

But while the amendments made by the Federal Constitutional Court to the *Grundgesetz* can be either adopted or rejected with a two-thirds majority in the German *Bundestag*, implicit treaty amendments made by the ECJ can effectively not be revoked as such action would require an unanimous decision by all Member States and a subsequent ratification process.

Just as the ECJ seeks to fill the gaps in the Treaties by means of judicial activism, the Federal Constitutional Court seeks to fix perceived deficiencies in the fundamental rights protection in the European legal order. Accepting the fact that according to the far-reaching jurisprudence of the ECJ much of the national legal order is within the scope of the Charter, rendering inapplicable the German *Grundgesetz*, the Federal Constitutional Court argues that it cannot "withdraw from fundamental rights protection in such constellations" because it would no longer be able to fulfil its role.[71] Is this an implicit hint that the ECJ does not fulfil this role sufficiently or that it is not intended to be a European Constitutional Court? For clearly, if the Federal Constitutional Court retreated on fundamental rights questions, the ECJ would inevitably take its place. This is rightly detected as an architectural deficit in the European legal order, above all for an individual citizen who is deprived of the constitutional right to complain in all cases fully harmonised by EU law and is forced to assert that German ordinary courts violated one's right to a lawful judge by refusing to initiate a long-winded preliminary procedure before the ECJ. The Federal Constitutional Court refers to exactly this

> "gap in protection arising from the application of EU fundamental rights by the ordinary courts […] because individuals have no direct recourse to the Court of Justice of the European Union for asserting a violation of EU fundamental rights in such cases."[72]

However, in claiming to improve the doubtlessly insufficient legal recourse for individuals under EU law, the Federal Constitutional Court has adopted a political function far beyond its jurisdictional powers under the *Grundgesetz*. It is not the duty of the courts to correct deficiencies in the EU legal system. Judicial review by the national constitutional courts seeks to compensate for the narrow admissibility requirements for individual actions under Art. 263 TFEU. Case law can be seen as a form of counterweight to the dysfunctional

---

[70] *Kahl* (n. 8), 825 f. (author's translation).

[71] BVerfG, order of 6 November 2019, 1 BvR 276/17, para. 60.

[72] BVerfG, order of 6 November 2019, 1 BvR 276/17, para. 61 (official translation).

system of checks and balances in the EU. The lack of individual protection is a problem of primary law – selective relief by individual Member States only adds a horizontal dimension of inequality to the unsatisfactory fundamental rights protection in the EU. In order to change this – admittedly unsatisfactory – situation, the Treaties need to be amended. The situation is widely seen to be unsatisfactory, but changes to it should come from amendments to the Treaties by the responsible legislative bodies.

The diminishing relevance of the Federal Constitutional Court should not be countered with equally teleological reasoning, but with a more precise definition of the jurisdiction of the ECJ in the Treaties. Both courts should refrain from referring to a political object in order to justify either preserving or extending their powers.

VII. Concluding remarks: cooperation or confrontation?

The First Senate's expansion of fundamental rights review with reference to its *Integrationsverantwortung* proves to be a positive gesture of cooperation only at the surface. In fact, it enables an independent application of the EU Charter and secures the Member State's sovereignty of interpretation in fundamental rights issues even in cases determined by Union law.

Over the course of time, the "dialogue between courts" has been torn from its original context and turned into a judicial technique that goes well beyond what the law had in mind. It is rooted neither in a democratically legitimised process nor an accepted legal method provided or backed by primary law or by the constitution. Judicial dialogue has become a self-employed term, a projection of the respective expectations of each legal system. The Courts no longer interpret the law within their respective jurisdictions – they have seized the law in their own interests. The "dialogical logic"[73] has become an unquestioned and unchallenged axiom in legal literature. Primary law is reduced to a document that merely reproduces and codifies ECJ jurisprudence instead of canalising or limiting its power. According to the principle of conferral, the EU cannot determine its own powers. Yet, if the Court interprets EU law extensively, it acquires *Kompetenz-Kompetenz* – disregarding the fact that the ECJ is also subject to conferral.

Only a decentralised application of EU law as well as respect for the principles of subsidiarity and proportionality and the principle of conferral can lead to a proper functioning of the EU judicial system. The law is the main force of the EU as a community of law.

Perhaps the ECJ will, in reaction to the decentralised application of the Charter, learn once again from the national constitutional courts and define a

[73] *G. Buchholtz*, DÖV 2017, 837–845, 845.

core of the Charter that is not at the disposal of the Member States. And perhaps national identity will be found to be equivalent with a European identity in some regards – just as fundamental rights protection is made equivalent on both levels.[74]

[74] The recent arrest warrant case merges Art. 4 of the EU Charter and Art. 79(3) of the Grundgesetz in a ruling involving the protection of the constitutional identity, BVerfG, order of 1 December 2020, 2 BvR 1845/18.

The Relation between "the Courts of the Last Word": Judicial Dialogue or Diverging Monologues?

Monika Kawczyńska

I. The judicial dialogue in the EU: the influence of politics on law

The article by *Aqilah Sandhu*, "The Judicial Dialogue in the EU between Law and Politics", illustrates the influence of politics on law by outlining the relationship between the German Constitutional Court and the European Court of Justice (ECJ). The author convincingly argues that both courts "engage in a vivid judicial dialogue" on "highly political question[s]".[1] In fact, the relationship between the constitutional courts of the Member States and the ECJ is a part of broader and highly complex political and legal dynamics and processes. Constitutional courts interact with the respective national Member State's legislative and executive branches, while the ECJ interacts with EU institutions and Member States acting through their governments, as well as with the parties to the proceedings brought before it.[2] Both courts – the national constitutional court and the ECJ – tend to uphold their position as "the court of the last word" or "an ultimate arbiter" in their respective legal orders. Since accession to the European Union, the national constitutional courts perform a dual role. They are judicial bodies that, on the one hand, ensure compliance with the respective constitution at the national level and, on the other hand, operate within the structure of the European Union ensuring compliance with EU law.

---

[1] *Sandhu*, p. 170, above.

[2] *M. Claes*, Luxembourg, Here We Come? Constitutional Courts and the Preliminary Reference Procedure, German Law Journal 16 (2015), 1331–1342, 1335.

According to the theory of role splitting (*dédoublement fonctionnel*), bodies or institutions can split their role by fulfilling tasks at two levels of decision-making in the legal orders to which they belong.[3]

Sandhu rightly indicates that due to the "vagueness of the Treaties" the ECJ historically acquired "a gap-filling function".[4] Since the 1960s the ECJ has been playing a key role as "a motor" of European integration.[5] Exercising its competence, it has been presenting dynamic methods of treaty interpretation and has established the foundations of the Union's constitutional order. The ECJ frequently refers to "meta-teleological" arguments, invoking the telos of the whole legal order and the function and consequences of a particular interpretation adopted. In its judgments the ECJ invokes effectiveness (*effet utile*), uniformity, legal certainty and the protection of individual rights as meta-purposes of the EU legal order.[6] Consequently, it is broadly accepted among scholars that the ECJ employs teleological or purposive reasoning, where law is interpreted in the service of an objective that advances European integration.[7] Judicial activism of the ECJ is often perceived by the Member States as being *ultra vires*. EU action that exceeds the limits of its competence consists not only in the adoption of legal acts that are *ultra vires* in relation to the Treaty articles on which they are based, but may also take the form of *ultra vires* interpretation of Treaty provisions or rules made thereunder by the EU courts.[8]

The thesis supported by the ECJ since the 1970s that Union law enjoys "absolute" or "unconditional" primacy over national constitutional provisions is generally not accepted by national constitutional courts. The constitution remains at the top of the hierarchy of legal norms, and EU law can be applied to national law only under the limits and conditions set by the constitution.[9] In national legal orders the constitutional courts retain their mandate to uphold the constitution and formulate their own conceptualization of the relationship between national and EU law. This has resulted in various doctrines imposing limits on the effects of EU law in three main areas: fundamental rights,

[3] *J. Temple Lang*, The Duties of National Courts under Community Constitutional Law, European Law Review 22 (1997), 3–18, 3.

[4] *Sandhu*, p. 175, above.

[5] *T. Horsley*, Reflections on the role of the Court of Justice as the "motor" of European integration: Legal limits to judicial lawmaking, Common Market Law Review 50 (2013), 931–964, 934.

[6] *J. Komarek*, Legal Reasoning in EU law, in: A. Arnull/D. Chalmers (eds.), The Oxford Handbook of European Union Law (2015), 28–51, 46.

[7] *G. Conway*, The Limits of Legal Reasoning and the European Court of Justice (2012), 22; *A. Albors-Llorens*, The European Court of Justice. More than a Teleological Court, Cambridge Yearbook of European Legal Studies 2 (1999), 373–398, 382.

[8] *P. Craig*, The ECJ and the ultra vires action: A conceptual analysis, Common Market Law Review 48 (2011), 395–437, 395.

[9] *B. de Witte*, Direct Effect, Primacy, and the Nature of the Legal Order, in: P. Craig/G. de Búrca (eds.), The Evolution of EU Law (2021), 187–227, 217.

conferral of competence (*ultra vires* review) and, more recently, national constitutional identity.[10]

Sandhu discusses the politically influenced interaction between the German Constitutional Court and the ECJ, which has developed in the aftermath of the seminal case *Internationale Handelsgesellschaft* concerning the primacy of EU secondary legislation over the German Basic Law (*Grundgesetz*).[11] Admittedly, the jurisprudence of the German Constitutional Court has played an important role for the constitutional basis of German participation in the ongoing European integration process, but it also has been significant for the development of jurisprudence in other EU Member States.[12] On one hand, the primacy of EU law is generally accepted as part of the acquis and as a consequence of the Basic Law's openness towards integration and European law.[13] On the other hand, the German Constitutional Court has repeatedly challenged the ECJ's viewpoint on the "unconditional primacy of EU law" by formulating judicial reservations in three contexts so as to have account of exceptional circumstances:[14] first, the protection of fundamental rights on the EU level at a degree substantially similar to that required unconditionally by the German Constitution,[15] while progressively accepting the presumption of equal standards;[16] second, *ultra vires* review as to whether EU legal acts remain within the competence of the EU, declaring acts that transgress these borders to be *ultra vires*;[17] third, the identity review as to whether an act of EU law infringes national constitutional identity and is thus inapplicable in Germany.[18]

Sandhu states that the dispute between national constitutional courts and the ECJ "had reached yet another peak" in the case concerning the Public Sector

---

[10] *Claes* (n. 2), 1335.

[11] ECJ, judgment of 17 December 1970, Case 11/70 – Internationale Handelsgesellschaft.

[12] *A. von Bogdandy/M. Kottmann/C. Antpöhler/J. Dickschen/S. Hentrei/M. Smrkolj*, Reverse Solange – Protecting the Essence of Fundamental Rights against EU Member States, Common Market Law Review 49 (2012), 489–519, 489.

[13] *A. Voßkuhle*, European Integration Through Law: The Contribution of the Federal Constitutional Court, European Journal of Sociology 58 (2017), 145–168, 148.

[14] *D. Grimm/M. Wendel/T. Reinbacher*, European Constitutionalism and the German Basic Law, in: A. Albi/S. Bardutzky (eds.) National Constitutions in European and Global Governance: Democracy, Rights, the Rule of Law (2019), 407–492, 423–426.

[15] BVerfG, order of 29 May 1974, 2 BvL 52/71 – Solange I.

[16] BVerfG, order of 22 October 1986, 2 BvR 197/83 – Solange II; BVerfG, order of 7 June 2000, 2 BvL 1/97 – Banana Market.

[17] BVerfG, judgment of 12 October 1993, 2 BvR 2134, 2159/92 – Treaty of Maastricht; BVerfG, judgment of 30 June 2009, 2 BvE 2/08 et al. – Treaty of Lisbon; BVerfG, order of 6 July 2010, 2 BvR 2661/06 – Honeywell; BVerfG, order of 14 January 2014, 2 BvR 2728/13 et al. – OMT.

[18] BVerfG, judgment of 30 June 2009, 2 BvE 2/08 et al. – Treaty of Lisbon; BVerfG, order of 14 January 2014, 2 BvR 2728/13 et al. – OMT; BVerfG, judgment of 18 July 2005, 2 BvR 2236/04 – European Arrest Warrant I.

Purchase Programme (PSPP).[19] Indeed, since the *Maastricht* judgment the German Constitutional Court has taken a careful approach to the *ultra vires* doctrine, applying it for the first time in the *PSPP* judgment of May 2020.[20] It held that the review undertaken by the ECJ with regard to whether the ECB's decisions on the PSPP satisfy the principle of proportionality was not comprehensible. The judgment in the *Weiss* case[21] was thus rendered *ultra vires*, exceeding the judicial mandate conferred upon the ECJ in Art. 19(1)(2) TEU and inapplicable in Germany. When the Commission instituted infringement proceedings under Art. 258 TFEU,[22] the German Constitutional Court partially retreated from its position, rejecting two requests seeking an order of execution for the *PSPP* judgment.[23] Moreover – as reported by the Commission – in its reply to the letter of formal notice, the German government provided very strong commitments. In particular, it has committed itself to use "all the means at its disposal to avoid, in the future, a repetition of an *ultra vires* finding, and take an active role in that regard".[24] However, it has been argued that the Commission closed the infringement proceedings due to some misunderstanding or rather a very optimistic reading since the German federal government cannot take any "active role" that would compromise the independence of constitutional judges.[25]

In her contribution, *Sandhu* shows that it "is the indirect dialogue between the ECJ and the constitutional courts in the EU" that is "[m]ore dominant in public discourse".[26] In fact, the example of Germany opposing the judicial activism of EU judges is not an isolated one. Also in other European countries the highest national courts are challenging the ECJ's case law. Recent examples include the Italian Constitutional Court with its counter-limits doctrine (*Taricco*),[27] the Czech Constitutional Court (*Holubec*),[28] the Danish Supreme Court (*Ajos*)[29] or the Spanish Supreme Court (*Junqueras*).[30] Though, it should be noted that in the *Taricco II* case, the ECJ partially reversed its previous ruling that had raised allegations of a violation of national constitutional

[19] *Sandhu*, p. 171, above.

[20] BVerfG, judgment of 5 May 2020, 2 BvR 859/15 – PSPP.

[21] ECJ, judgment of 11 December 2018, C-493/17 – Heinrich Weiss and Others.

[22] https://ec.europa.eu/commission/presscorner/detail/EN/INF_21_2743.

[23] BVerfG, order of 29 April 2021, 2 BvR 1651/15.

[24] https://ec.europa.eu/commission/presscorner/detail/en/inf_21_6201.

[25] *M. Wendel*, Constructive Misunderstandings – How the PSPP Conflict was Eventually Settled and How it Reflects Constitutional Pluralism, in: M. Avbelj (ed.), The Future of EU Constitutionalism (2023), 53–70, 65.

[26] *Sandhu*, p. 180, above.

[27] Italian Constitutional Court, order of 23 November 2016, case 24/2017.

[28] Czech Constitutional Court, judgment of 31 January 2012, case ÚS 5/12.

[29] Danish Supreme Court, judgment of 6 December 2016, case 15/2014.

[30] Spanish Supreme Court, order of 9 January 2020, case 20907/2017.

identity.[31] The judicial dialogue was conducted in a reasonable manner at the final stage of the case, thereby preventing an open conflict between EU law and Italian constitutional law.[32]

Unlike in Germany, in Poland there is a different nature of political involvement by the Constitutional Court. The Polish Constitutional Court is currently considered to be effectively assisting the executive and legislative powers by legitimizing their political authority. Before the constitutional crisis in Poland, the most common problem of politicization concerned the ideological involvement of judges or their support for political parties, combined with encroachment on the powers of the legislature, which also involved the issue of judicial activism.[33] As soon as the political party "Law and Justice" (PiS) won the parliamentary elections in November 2015, the myth of the apolitical nature of the Polish Constitutional Court collapsed.[34] It became a tool of political struggle, in which opposing parties sought to secure the largest possible number of judges. Admittedly, there are guarantees in the Polish Constitution that ensure the apolitical nature of judges in general, who, during their term of office, are not permitted to belong to a political party or a trade union or to perform public activities incompatible with the principles of the independence of the courts and judges. Nevertheless, the judges are chosen individually by the *Sejm*, the lower house of the Polish Parliament, whose connection to political parties is self-evident.

According to the European Commission, Poland currently lacks a legitimate means of constitutional review since such review can no longer be guaranteed by an independent constitutional court.[35] In its resolution the European Parliament condemned the use of the judicial system for political purposes and described the Polish Constitutional Court as "illegitimate".[36] Also as regards the domestic legal order, the view is expressed that due to numerous violations concerning the election of judges to seats already occupied and due to abuses of the procedure for issuing rulings, Poland currently lacks an institution that

---

[31] ECJ, judgment of 8 September 2015, Case C-105/14 – Taricco and Others; ECJ, judgment of 5 December 2017, Case C-42/17 – M.A.S. and M.B. (Taricco II).

[32] *A. Marciano*, The Dialogue between Courts in the so-called Taricco Saga, in: K. Lenaerts et al. (eds.), Building the European Union: The Jurist's View of the Union's Evolution (2021), 237–244, 244.

[33] *K. Otręba*, Rozważania o władzy Trybunału Konstytucyjnego jako problem polityczny, Przegląd Prawa Konstytucyjnego 12 (2018), 58–67, 60.

[34] *A. Sulikowski*, Trybunał Konstytucyjny a polityczność. O konsekwencji upadku pewnego mitu, Państwo i Prawo 4 (2016), 3–14, 3.

[35] European Commission, Reasoned proposal in accordance with Article 7(1) TEU regarding the rule of law in Poland for a Council Decision on the determination of a clear risk of a serious breach by the Republic of Poland of the rule of law, Brussels, 20 December 2017 COM (2017) 835 final.

[36] European Parliament, Resolution of 21 October 2021 on the rule of law crisis in Poland and the primacy of EU law (2021/2935(RSP)).

meets the criteria for a constitutional court.[37] A former judge of the Polish Constitutional Court accurately described that the Court's current function is understood to be "à rebours" and that it is no longer consistent with the model of a constitutional body appointed to review legislation adopted by a political majority in defence of a democratic minority.[38]

II. Affirming the supremacy of the Polish Constitution: cooperation and favourable predisposition towards EU law

In assessing the position towards EU law, two phases can be distinguished in the jurisprudence of the Polish Constitutional Court. The turning point was the change in its composition in December 2016 after the end of President *Andrzej Rzepliński*'s term of office. The first phase can be described as "cooperation", where the Polish Constitutional Court firmly upheld the primacy of the Polish Constitution over EU law, but it did so with a favourable predisposition towards the process of European integration. The second phase, which can be kindly described as "confrontation", involves issuing judgments beneficial to the current political actors in order to legitimize systemic changes to the constitutional order, responding to critical rulings of international tribunals and justifying the rejection of unfavourable judgments. It might be argued that the state of constitutional jurisprudence reflects to a large extent the status of the political relations between the Republic of Poland and the European Union as a supranational organization.

In the first phase, the Polish Constitutional Court examined – within its competence to review the conformity of international agreements to the Constitution (Art. 188(1)) – the Accession Treaty and certain provisions of the Treaties establishing and amending the Communities and the European Union that were inherent in the application of the Accession Treaty.[39] In its judgment K 18/04, the Court firmly stated that "the Constitution – due to its exceptional power – remains the supreme law of the Republic of Poland" in relation to all binding international agreements. This also applies to ratified international agreements delegating to an international organization "the competence of organs of state authority in relation to certain matters". Thus "given its supreme legal force (Art. 8(1)), the Constitution enjoys precedence of binding force and application within the territory of the Republic of Poland".

---

[37] *W. Wróbel*, Skutki rozstrzygnięcia w sprawie K 3/21 w perspektywie Sądu Najwyższego i sądów powszechnych, Europejski Przegląd Sądowy 12 (2021), 19–25, 20.

[38] *M. Pyziak-Szafnicka*, Trybunał Konstytucyjny á rebours, Państwo i Prawo 5 (2020), 25–45, 43 f.

[39] Polish Constitutional Court, judgment of 11 May 2005, K 18/04, para. 4.2.

The cited ruling has determined the line of jurisprudence of the Polish Constitutional Court in its subsequent case law concerning the relationship of Polish law with EU law. In the judgment relating to the Lisbon Treaty,[40] the Court defined the limit on the transfer of powers "in relation to certain matters". Accordingly, it is prohibited to confer all powers vested in a given organ of state authority or to confer all powers within a given scope. The powers covered by the prohibition of conferral are determined by the constitutional identity of the state and cover matters belonging to the core that are cardinal to the foundations of the political system. The catalogue of non-transferable powers includes the provisions defining the fundamental principles of the Constitution and provisions relating to the rights of individuals such as: human dignity, democracy, the rule of law, social justice, subsidiarity and the competence to create powers. In that regard, the Member States remain the subjects of the integration process and maintain *Kompetenz-Kompetenz*.[41] Thus, the Polish Constitutional Court used the counter-limits doctrine in order to set the boundaries of European integration and to protect national constitutional identity.

In a seminal case concerning Council Regulation (EC) No. 44/2001 (Brussels I), the Polish Constitutional Court positioned itself as "a court of the last word" and as an "ultimate arbiter" in relation to constitutional issues.[42] It directly reviewed the conformity of an act of EU secondary legislation with the Polish Constitution in the course of proceedings which were commenced by constitutional complaint. The admissibility of such review was closely related to the type of proceedings submitted for the protection of constitutional rights and freedoms of the individual. The Court assumed that "a normative act" within the meaning of Art. 79(1) of the Constitution may not only be a normative act issued by one of the organs of the state, but also a legal act issued by an organ of an international organization. It held that due to the content of Art. 8(1) of the Constitution, the Court is obliged to perceive its position in such a way that in fundamental matters concerning systemic issues it is "the Court which will have the last word" with regard to the Polish Constitution. In attributing to itself the ability to review acts of secondary EU law, the Polish Constitutional Court softened its position, indicating that "the non-conformity of EU law to the Constitution should have the character of *ultima ratio*, and ought to appear only when all other ways of resolving a conflict between Polish norms and the norms of the EU legal order have failed". In the case at hand, the Constitutional Court had no doubts as to the compatibility of the provisions of the contested Council Regulation with the constitutionally guaranteed right

---

[40] Polish Constitutional Court, judgment of 24 November 2010, K 32/09, para. 2.1.

[41] The Court upheld its position in a case concerning the ratification of the European Council Decision 2011/199/EU amending Art. 136 of the TFEU, judgment of 26 June 2013, K 33/12, para 6.3.

[42] Polish Constitutional Court, judgment of 16 November 2011, SK 45/09, para. 2.4.

to a fair trial, and thus there was no need to submit a question for a preliminary ruling.[43]

Despite its firm stance on the principle of the absolute primacy of the Constitution and despite claiming the ultimate authority in this respect, the Court developed the approach of an "EU-friendly" interpretation of national law. The principle of "favourable predisposition towards the process of European integration and the cooperation between states" was derived from the Preamble and Art. 9 of the Polish Constitution, according to which the Republic of Poland shall respect international law binding upon it. Already in its ruling on the Treaty of Accession, the Court stated that Art. 8(1) of the Constitution, which states that the Constitution is the "supreme law of the Republic of Poland", is accompanied by the requirement to respect and to be favourably inclined towards appropriately drafted and binding regulations of international law.[44]

Within this phase of jurisprudence, three examples of such an approach can be mentioned. Firstly, in the judgment concerning the European Arrest Warrant,[45] despite finding the provision of the statute implementing EU law incompatible with the Polish Constitution, the Court recommended the necessary amendment to the Constitution enabling a full implementation of the Council Framework Decision 2002/584. To this end, an important adjustment was introduced to Art. 55 of the Polish Constitution, the adjustment being directly related to Polish membership in the European Union. The new provision envisages an exception to the prohibition against extraditing Polish citizens, allowing the surrender the requested person to other EU Member States on the basis of the European Arrest Warrant[46]. Secondly, in the judgment concerning the compatibility of the excise duty with Art. 90 TEC (now Art. 110 TFEU), the Court decided to discontinue the proceedings in order to prevent a possible divergence in the jurisprudence following a preliminary ruling by the ECJ in a pending case concerning the same legal provisions.[47] The Court retreated, giving precedence in interpretation of the Treaties to ECJ, so as to eliminate not only "the overlapping of the jurisdiction of the two courts or concurrent rulings on the same legal issues", but also "any dysfunctionality in relations". Thirdly, in the case already referred to on the constitutionality of Council Regulation (EC) No 44/2001, the Polish Constitutional Court significantly limited the possibility of reviewing EU secondary legislation and adopted an approach similar to that of the German Constitutional Court in *Solange II* or of the ECtHR in *Bosphorus*.[48] Accordingly, when filing a constitutional complaint challenging

[43] ECJ, judgment of 22 October 1987, Case C-314/85 – Foto-Frost.

[44] Polish Constitutional Court, judgment of 11 May 2005, K 18/04, para. 2.2.

[45] Polish Constitutional Court, judgment of 27 April 2005, P 1/05.

[46] Act amending the Constitution of the Republic of Poland of 8 September 2006, Journal of Laws No. 200, item 1471.

[47] Polish Constitutional Court, order of 19 December 2006, P 37/05.

[48] ECtHR, judgment of 30 June 2005, applications no. 45036/98 – Bosphorus/Ireland

EU secondary legislation, an applicant has to demonstrate as "probable that the challenged act of EU secondary legislation causes a considerable decline in the standard of protection of rights and freedoms, in comparison with the standard of protection guaranteed by the Constitution".[49] It follows, that the Polish Constitutional Court firmly established a presumption of an adequate level of protection for the rights and freedoms of individuals in the EU legal system, such as that guaranteed at constitutional level.

III. Declaring the incompatibility of EU norms with the Polish Constitution: confrontation or an open conflict?

The second and current phase of the judicial relationship between the "courts of the last word" is characterized by the Polish Constitutional Court's rendering of "retaliatory" judgments in response to specific rulings of the ECJ. The motions for such rulings have been formed upon political request of the prime minister or the prosecutor general and the legal questions have been submitted by judges of the Disciplinary Chamber of the Supreme Court who are directly interested in a given outcome. Identifying the ECJ rulings as being issued *ultra vires*, the Polish Constitutional Court has clearly departed from the view expressed in the case concerning the Accession Treaty that "the assessment of the case law of any jurisdictional body of the European Communities is clearly outside the cognition of the Constitutional Court, strictly defined in Art. 188 of the Constitution".[50]

The responses of the European Union to illiberal democracies demonstrate that there has been a shift from a political to a judicial enforcement of values. In view of the ineffectiveness of political mechanisms for protecting the rule of law, the role of "guardian" was assumed by the ECJ in the framework of proceedings provided for in the Treaties, which are not designed for systemic protection of the rule of law. Firstly, this assumed role explains the infringement actions brought by the Commission against Poland under Art. 258 TFEU concerning the retirement age of Supreme Court judges[51] and judges of common courts and prosecutors;[52] concerning the Disciplinary Chamber of the Supreme Court;[53] and concerning the "muzzle law" threatening judges with disciplinary proceedings for applying EU law.[54] Secondly, this assumed role underlies the preliminary ruling procedure instituted by judges whose indepen-

[49] Polish Constitutional Court, judgment of 16 November 2011, SK 45/09, para. 8.5.

[50] Polish Constitutional Court, judgment of 11 May 2005, K 18/04, para 9.1.

[51] ECJ, judgment of 24 June 2019, case C-619/18 – Commission/Poland.

[52] ECJ, judgment of 5 November 2019, case C-192/18 – Commission/Poland.

[53] ECJ, judgment of 15 July 2021, case C-791/19 – Commission/Poland.

[54] AG Collins, opinion of 15 December 2022, case C-204/21 – Commission/Poland.

dence was threatened by the actions of the legislative and executive branches of government[55] or by courts from other EU Member States concerned about mutual trust in judicial cooperation in criminal matters.[56] Thirdly, this assumed role emerges in interim measures applied in infringement cases instituted by the European Commission related to the functioning and organization of the Polish Supreme Court.[57] It must not be ignored that in two cases Art. 279 TFEU was the legal basis for imposing a financial penalty for Poland's failure to comply with the orders on interim measures. The ECJ awarded the European Commission a fine of half a million Euros per day in the *Turów Mine* case and one million Euros per day in the *Disciplinary Chamber of the Supreme Court* case.[58]

The reason for the Polish Constitutional Court's first ruling on a challenge to the constitutionality of the EU Treaties was the ECJ's order on interim measures to suspend the application of the provisions underlying the functioning of the Disciplinary Chamber of the Supreme Court.[59] In response, on the very same day in July 2021 the Constitutional Court delivered its judgment in case P 7/20 replying to the legal question submitted by the Disciplinary Chamber on the review of Art. 4(3)(2) TEU in conjunction with Art. 279 TFEU.[60] The question was brought the day after the first interim measure was issued, in which the ECJ ordered the suspension of the provisions of the Act on the Supreme Court underlying the jurisdiction of the Disciplinary Chamber in disciplinary cases concerning judges.[61] The problem formulated by the Disciplinary Chamber concerned the constitutionality of the legal norm derived from the provisions of the TEU and the TFEU, according to which a Member State is obliged to implement provisional measures relating to the structure and functioning of its constitutional organs, including those of the judiciary. In assessing the *ultra vires* review of ECJ judgments, the Polish Constitutional Court pointed out that the constitutional courts of the Member States are "com-

[55] ECJ, judgment of 19 November 2019, cases C-585/18, C-624/18, and C-625/18 – A.K. and others; judgment of 26 March 2020, cases C-558/18 and C-563/18 – Miasto Łowicz and others; judgment of 6 October 2021, case C-487/19 – W.Ż.; judgment of 2 March 2021, case C-824/18 – A.B. and others; judgment of 16 November 2021, cases C-748/19 to C-754/19 – W.B. and others; judgment of 22 March 2022, case C-508/19 – M.F.

[56] ECJ, judgment of 25 July 2018, case C-216/18 PPU – LM; judgment of 22 February 2022, cases C-562/21 PPU and C-563/21 PPU – X and Y.

[57] ECJ, order of 17 December 2018, case C-619/18 R – Commission/Poland; order of 8 April 2020, case C-791/19 R – Commission/Poland; order of 14 July 2021, case C-204/21 R – Commission/Poland.

[58] ECJ, order of 20 September 2021, case C-121/21 R – Czech Republic/Poland; order of 27 October 2021, case C-204/21 R – Commission/Poland.

[59] ECJ, order of 14 July 2021, case C-204/21 R – Commission/Poland.

[60] ECJ, order of 8 April 2020, case C-791/19 R – Commission/Poland.

[61] Disciplinary Chamber of the Supreme Court, order of 9 April 2020 referring a question of law in case P 7/20.

petent to protect their own constitutional identity in the process of European integration", as had been stated in Germany, the Czech Republic, Denmark, France, Spain, Romania and Italy. It discussed in more detail the application of *ultra vires* review of EU acts by the German Constitutional Court, in particular in the case of *Honeywell and Outright Monetary Transactions*.[62] The Court declared that if the ECJ exceeds the limits of its conferred powers and the principles of subsidiarity and proportionality, or enters arbitrarily into the area of constitutional identity, the *ultra vires* review of such law-making activity is not excluded in terms of the Polish Constitution. It is significant that the Polish authorities very often refer to the practice of other Member States, thereby implicitly arguing that there is nothing exceptional about their opposition to EU institutions as they are safeguarding the rule of law. In conducting an *ultra vires* review, the Polish Constitutional Court, as it indicated, assessed not the merits of the interim order, but only the constitutionality of its consequences. It ruled that Art. 4(3) TEU in conjunction with Art. 279 TFEU violates the Polish Constitution to the extent that the ECJ imposes *ultra vires* obligations on Poland in ordering interim measures relating to the organization and jurisdiction of Polish courts as well as the procedure to be followed before those courts. The Court concluded that the principles of primacy and of direct effect of EU law do not apply to those measures.

In the referred case, the constitutional problem was artificially created by the Disciplinary Chamber so as to serve the current political objectives. The verdict issued with the participation of a "double" judge[63] was intended to justify the failure of the Polish authorities to enforce the interim order concerning the suspension of the operation of the Disciplinary Chamber. The judgment of the Constitutional Court has consequences only in the internal legal order and does not derogate from a norm of EU law deemed incompatible with the Polish Constitution, but – as was clearly indicated – it excludes its applicability before national authorities. It must be emphasized that the judgment does not have any effect in the sphere of EU law; in particular, it does not deprive the interim measures issued on the basis of Art. 279 TFEU of their effectiveness, nor does it relieve Poland of the obligation to enforce them.

The Polish authorities attempted to take advantage of the above judgment in August 2021 by filing an application for the cancellation of the interim order. The government claimed that the provisional measures were contrary to the national constitutional order, in which the Constitutional Court "must be regarded as the court having the last word". In this context it was submitted that the ECJ ruled *ultra vires* and exceeded the limits of its competence since the Treaties do not confer on the EU any competence in the area of the organization

---

[62] Polish Constitutional Court, judgment of 14 July 2021, P 7/20.

[63] Polish Constitutional Court, order of 15 June 2021, case P 7/20, on the exclusion of Judge J. Piskorski.

of the national judiciary. It remains the exclusive sovereign competence of the Member States. Poland's application was dismissed because, according to the principle of primacy, a Member State's reliance on rules of national law, even of a constitutional nature, cannot be allowed to undermine the unity and effectiveness of EU law. The judgment of the Polish Constitutional Court could therefore not be regarded as a "change of circumstances", within the meaning of Art. 163 of the Rules of Procedure, that was capable of calling into question the assessments set out in the interim order.[64]

What caused even more controversy in the relationship between "the courts of the last word" was the judgment of the Polish Constitutional Court issued in October 2021, concerning the constitutional review of EU primary law that establishes the basis of European integration.[65] The motion was initiated by the prime minister in order to neutralize the significance of the ECJ rulings and interim orders concerning the independence of judges and to create a guise of legality for the Polish authorities refusing to enforce the referenced verdicts. The prime minister, formally seeking to subject the constitutionality of treaty norms to scrutiny, in fact expected a review of the ECJ's jurisprudence on the independence of judges. In case K 3/21, the Polish Constitutional Court declared unconstitutional Art. 1(1) and (2) TEU in conjunction with Art. 4(3) TEU to the extent that EU institutions act beyond the limits of the competences conferred in the Treaties, with the result that the Constitution is not recognized as the supreme law in the national legal order and Poland cannot function as a sovereign and democratic state. In addition, the Court ruled that the second subparagraph of Art. 19(1) TEU is unconstitutional to the extent that it grants national courts the power to disapply provisions of the Constitution and review the legality of the procedure for appointing judges. The Court stated that the ECJ's jurisprudence on the independence of Polish judges is "a clear manifestation of the creation of new powers without due authorization (*ultra vires*) and that it is contrary to the principles of proportionality and subsidiarity, involving obvious interference in the area of Polish constitutional identity".

The ruling was controversial not only because of its merits, but also for the reason that the written reasons were published as late as November 2022, more than a year after the verdict was issued. Additionally, the judge-rapporteur published an *ad vocem* letter in which he referred to the dissenting opinions of the five judges, revealing how the deliberations proceeded in reaching the verdict.[66] He expressed his personal opinion on the judgment, indicating that "it is a precedent in the legal dialogue on EU federalization. Until now, the overwhelming part of the Polish and European jurisprudence has remained

[64] ECJ, order of 6 October 2021, case C-204/21 R-RAP – Commission/Poland.

[65] Polish Constitutional Court, judgment of 7 October 2021, case K 3/21.

[66] Ad vocem of 16 November 2022 of Judge Bartłomiej Sochański to the dissenting opinions to the judgment K 3/21.

uncritical and even approving towards the law-making interpretation of the ECJ". It must be underlined that in accordance with the international obligations imposed on Poland and Art. 9 of the Polish Constitution, concerning the observance of binding international law, this judgment did not have any effect on the validity of EU law and its application. The decisions of national constitutional courts may not be the basis for evading obligations under EU law. The Polish courts are at the same time bound and entitled to disapply a provision of law, court ruling or practice that would prevent them from fulfilling these obligations.

In December 2021 the European Commission decided to open an infringement procedure against Poland because of serious concerns with respect to the Constitutional Court and its recent case law challenging the primacy of EU law.[67] Similar to the *PSPP* case in Germany, the judgments were considered to be in breach of the general principles of autonomy, primacy and effectiveness as well as of the uniform application of Union law and the binding effect of ECJ rulings. Moreover, the Commission stated that Poland has failed to fulfil its obligations under Art. 19(1) TEU since "the Constitutional Tribunal no longer meets the requirement of an independent and impartial tribunal previously established by law". The Polish government's reply to the letter of formal notice and the reasoned opinion did not address the given concerns. Thus, in February 2023 the Commission decided to refer the case to the ECJ for violations of EU law by the Constitutional Court.[68] The featured case will be an ultimate test in the relationship between "the courts of the last word", because the ECJ will be confronted in the adjudication process with the infringement of fundamental principles of EU law resulting from jurisprudence of the national constitutional court.

IV. Direct dialogue through preliminary ruling procedure: is it still feasible?

Sandhu points to Art. 267 TFEU as an important basis for a "direct dialogue between the courts". However, the constitutional courts of the Member States were for a considerable time hesitant to refer questions to a preliminary ruling. This was primarily because they conceptualized their special role in the legal system as the ultimate arbiters of constitutionality review and did not regard themselves as ordinary courts of European law.[69] The literature made reference to the "doctrine of displacement" that the ECJ had applied and that

[67] https://ec.europa.eu/commission/presscorner/detail/en/ip_21_7070, INFR(2021)2261.

[68] https://ec.europa.eu/commission/presscorner/detail/EN/IP_23_842; case C-147/23 – Commission/Poland.

[69] *Claes* (n. 2), 1331 f.

marginalises constitutional courts with respect to their place in constitutional law and policy. This approach underlined the diminution of their role in cooperation with the ECJ, allowing constitutional courts to be replaced by the common courts.[70]

The only and historic preliminary question submitted by the German Constitutional Court occurred in 2014 and concerned the validity of the Outright Monetary Transactions (OMT) Programme.[71] The referral can hardly be perceived as a conciliatory gesture since the Court announced its willingness to declare the OMT Programme an *ultra vires* act violating German constitutional identity.[72] Also the Polish Constitutional Court decided in 2015 to submit a preliminary question to the ECJ under Art. 267 TFEU on the validity of the directive on the common system of value added tax.[73] The request was made after the Polish Commissioner for Civic Rights had requested a ruling that national provisions precluding the application of a reduced rate of VAT to the supply of electronic books and other electronic publications did not comply with the Polish Constitution.[74] The case was brought due to complaints from citizens about differences in the tax rate for publications made available on a physical medium as compared to those transmitted electronically. This distinction raised questions in view of the principle of equal treatment and the constitutional guarantee of equality in bearing public burdens. Consequently, the Polish Constitutional Court decided to stay proceedings and to refer the preliminary questions alleging a violation of essential formal consultation requirements with the European Parliament and infringement of the principle of fiscal neutrality. The ECJ ruled that an analysis of the claims had not revealed any circumstances that would affect the validity of the directive. Two months following the judgment, the Polish Commissioner for Civic Rights withdrew the application and requested that the proceedings at the Polish Constitutional Court be discontinued. The amendment to the VAT directive enabling Member States to apply the same VAT rates to electronically supplied publications as to publications on any physical medium was finally adopted as part of the VAT digital single market package.[75]

---

[70] *J. Komárek*, The Place of Constitutional Courts in the EU, European Constitutional Law Review 9 (2013), 420–450, 449.

[71] ECJ, judgment of 16 June 2015, case C-62/14 – Peter Gauweiler and Others.

[72] *M. Payandeh*, The OMT Judgment of the German Federal Constitutional Court: Repositioning the Court within the European Constitutional Architecture, European Constitutional Law Review 13(2017), 400–416, 404.

[73] ECJ, judgment of 7 March 2017, case C-390/15 – Rzecznik Praw Obywatelskich (RPO).

[74] Polish Constitutional Court, order of 7 July 2015, case K 61/13.

[75] Council Directive (EU) 2018/1713 of 6 November 2018 amending Directive 2006/112/EC as regards rates of value added tax applied to books, newspapers and periodicals, Official Journal of the European Union L 286/20–21.

Recently, considerable steps have been taken by the Polish Constitutional Court to exclude the possibility of submitting preliminary questions. Firstly, these steps related to the ECtHR judgment in the *Xero Flor* case, stating that the Polish Constitutional Court could not be considered a "tribunal established by law" within the meaning of Art. 6(1) of the European Convention on Human Rights (ECHR) due to the unlawful appointment of its judges.[76] In its "retaliatory" judgment in the case K 6/21, the Polish Constitutional Court held that the first sentence of Art. 6(1) ECHR is incompatible with the Constitution to the extent that the concept of a court used in that provision includes the Constitutional Court.[77] It held that "the very guarantees of that provision do not apply to the Constitutional Court". Consequently, it should be considered that it also does not meet the requirements of a "national court" specified in Art. 267 TFEU. Secondly, the inability to submit preliminary questions emerged from the statements of the Court's new vice-president, whose election procedure was directly criticized by the *Xero Flor* judgment. He published an article regarding preliminary questions in which he surprisingly stated that the Polish Constitutional Court is not a court "within the meaning of Art. 267 TFEU, as it is not a court within the meaning of Art. 45(1) of the [Polish] Constitution, nor within the meaning of Art. 6(1)" ECHR. Therefore, the Court "should be released from the obligation to submit a preliminary question when confronted with a problem related to EU law".[78] Thirdly, there is a case pending before the Polish Constitutional Court based on a request submitted by the Polish prosecutor general,[79] who, in response to a preliminary question from the Supreme Court regarding the retirement age of judges,[80] questioned the constitutionality of Art. 267 TFEU. The prosecutor general has challenged the provision establishing the foundation for Polish courts to refer questions for a preliminary ruling on the ground that it contradicts the principles of legalism and legal certainty as well as the principle of supremacy of the Constitution. The request concerns a review of the constitutionality of Art. 267 TFEU, allowing – in the view of the prosecutor general – the national courts to refer preliminary questions having no bearing on the subject matter of the main case. It is likely that the Constitutional Court will rule in accordance with the prosecutor general's request as it has already in the past repeatedly contested the primacy of EU law as well as the ECJ's exclusive authority to provide a binding interpretation of the

---

[76] ECtHR, judgment of 7 May 2021, application no. 4907/18 – Xero Flor/Poland.

[77] Polish Constitutional Court, judgment of 24 November 2021, K 6/21.

[78] *M. Muszyński*, Pytanie prejudycjalne jako instrument wykładni prawa UE: istota, granice i możliwości kontroli, Prokuratura i Prawo 7–8 (2020), 84–112, 92–94.

[79] Request of the Prosecutor General of 23 August 2018 in case K 7/18.

[80] Polish Supreme Court, order of 2 August 2018 for the preliminary ruling in case C-522/18 – Zakład Ubezpieczeń Społecznych.

Treaties. According to the established jurisprudence of the ECJ,[81] this would not be an obstacle to referring new cases to the ECJ, but judgments issued in response to preliminary references would raise constitutional concerns in the Polish legal order.

V. Fundamental rights and the Polish Constitutional Court's "right to resistance"

Sandhu argues that the German Constitutional Court "secured its position as the 'ultimate guardian' of fundamental rights".[82] The Polish Constitutional Court appears to perform the same role. It presumes that the standard of protection guaranteed by the Polish Constitution is equal to or higher than that guaranteed in EU law or by the European Convention on Human Rights. As an example of this approach, mention can be made of one of the many recent and disputed rulings in which the Polish Constitutional Court attributed to itself the right to review a resolution of the Polish Supreme Court.[83] The resolution at issue secured in the Polish legal order the effects of the ECJ's judgment in the case *A.K.*, holding that a court can be considered to be unlawfully composed when the ruling is delivered with the participation of judges selected by the non-independent National Council of Judiciary.[84] The Court found Art. 6(1) ECHR to be an adequate standard for review, since it shows close links – and in fact "normative identity" – with the constitutional right to a court provided for in Art. 45(1) of the Polish Constitution. On the other hand, the Court explicitly declined a review in light of the EU Charter of Fundamental Rights, since it does not "constitute a separately ratified international agreement or part of a treaty subject to the ratification procedure". In addition, contrary to the case law of the ECJ,[85] the Court indicated that the Charter may not be regarded as a source of universally binding law in Poland because Poland signed the so-called Polish-British Protocol. This is in line with the position of the Polish authorities, who refer very conservatively to the Charter, seeing it as an indefinite instrument that can serve as a basis for redefining the rights and freedoms set forth in the Constitution. Consequently, unlike the German Constitutional Court, its Polish counterpart expressly refused to include the Charter in its standard of review.

---

[81] ECJ, judgment of 22 June 2010, cases C-188/10 and C-189/10 – Aziz Melki and Sélim Abdeli; judgment of 11 November 2014, case C-112/13 – A./B.; judgment of 15 January 2013, case C-416/10 – Jozef Križan; judgment of 23 November 2021, case C-564/19 – IS.

[82] *Sandhu*, p. 181, above.

[83] Polish Constitutional Court, judgment of 20 April 2020, U 2/20.

[84] Polish Supreme Court, resolution of 23 January 2020, BSA I-4110-1/20.

[85] ECJ, judgment of 21 December 2011, cases C-411/10 and C-493/10 – N.S. and others.

Differently from Germany, in the case of Poland the problematic relationship with the ECtHR cannot be overlooked. Beginning in 2021, the ECtHR has issued a number of rulings concerning changes relating to the Polish judiciary and the independence of judges, declaring these changes incompatible with Art. 6(1) ECHR as regards the right to a fair hearing and the right to a tribunal established by law. In response to these rulings, the national authorities questioned their validity and binding force. To reinforce his claims, the Polish prosecutor general, who is a major supporter of the changes in Poland's judiciary, has filed motions with the Polish Constitutional Court with the express purpose of declaring any unfavourable ECtHR rulings as legally non-existent.

In May 2021, the ECtHR issued a landmark judgment in the *Xero Flor* case, in which it stated that participation of an unlawfully elected judge in a panel of the Polish Constitutional Court which discontinued the proceedings initiated by a constitutional complaint resulted in a violation of Art. 6(1) ECHR.[86] In reaching its verdict, the ECtHR applied the three-step test set out in the *Guðmundur Andri Ástráðsson* case,[87] consequently finding that the grave irregularities encountered in the judicial election procedure deprived the applicant of the right to a "tribunal established by law". As a direct response, the Polish Constitutional Court delivered a ruling in case K 6/21 in which it held that the first sentence of Art. 6(1) ECHR is incompatible with the Constitution to the extent that the concept of a tribunal used in that provision includes the Constitutional Court.[88] The Court stated that no national or international authority has the competence to undermine the status of the Court's judges, and any attempt to do so amounts to a violation of Poland's constitutional principles. In the referenced judgment, the Court openly stated that it does not have to meet international standards. In other words, it does not have to be independent and impartial; it does not have to hear a case within a reasonable time; nor does it have to be properly established by law. If one did not know the situational context and the reasons why the prosecutor general submitted the motion, it would seem that the conclusion reached by the Polish Constitutional Court was preposterous.

In a series of consecutive rulings, the ECtHR has evaluated the procedures for appointing judges of both the Polish Supreme Court as well as the common courts under the participation of the reformed National Council of the Judiciary, pronouncing them incompatible with the standards guaranteed by the Convention.[89] In turn, the Polish prosecutor general filed a motion alleging that the

---

[86] ECtHR, judgment of 7 May 2021, application no. 4907/18 – Xero Flor/Poland.

[87] ECtHR, judgment of 1 December 2020, application no. 26374/18 – Guðmundur Andri Ástráðsson/Iceland.

[88] Polish Constitutional Court, judgment of 24 November 2021, ref. no. K 6/21, OTK ZU A/2022, poz. 9.

[89] ECtHR, judgment of 29 June 2021, applications no. 26691/18 and no. 27367/18 – Broda and Bojara/Poland; judgment of 22 July 2021, application no. 43447/19 –

ECtHR shaped a completely new standard under the Convention in disregard of the will of the contracting states to the Convention. In his view, the actions of the ECtHR authorize the Constitutional Court to assess the compatibility of the normative content identified in these rulings with the Constitution. Also, the lower house of the Polish Parliament, in its submission to the Constitutional Court, asserted that deriving norms from the Convention that were not subject to the ratification procedure amounts to a violation of the Constitution and can be considered *ultra vires*. In a precedent-setting ruling in case K 7/21, the Court ruled that Art. 6(1) ECHR is incompatible with the Polish Constitution insofar as it allows national courts or the ECtHR to review the statutes concerning the organization of the judiciary, the jurisdiction of the courts and the law concerning the National Council of the Judiciary.[90] The Court expressed a surprising thesis justifying its position as to the incompatibility of one of the basic provisions of the Convention with the Polish Constitution. It held that the previous activity of constitutional courts in the field of international law has been restrained, but the new situation has created a helpful concept allowing national courts to challenge the supremacy of international law. In effect, it defended the possibility of rejecting international obligations, including judgments of the ECtHR. Academic literature has labelled this concept the "constitutional right to resistance".[91] Unfortunately, the Constitutional Court completely distorted the meaning of this idea, as the right to resistance was in fact designed to enhance the protection of human rights and democracy. The authors of the referenced concept pointed out that only international norms which disregard fundamental rights and suffer from democratic deficiencies should be unenforceable in the domestic legal order. In the case in question, precisely the opposite situation occurred, as it is the norms of international law that protect human rights and democratic principles in a state where the norms of national law are in breach of the rule of law. In the section on the effects of the judgment, the Constitutional Court pointed out that the four explicitly mentioned judgments of ECtHR issued on the basis of Art. 6(1) ECHR "do not have in Poland the attribute provided for in Art. 46 of the Convention (obligation of enforceability), as being rendered on a basis that lies outside the scope of the State's legal obligations." The decision can be seen as circumventing the limitations placed on the Court's jurisdiction as defined by the Constitution, which includes a review only of legal norms and excludes a review of judicial decisions of international courts. Such a practice is also inconsistent with Art. 9 of the Polish Constitution, which demands the observance of binding international law.

Reczkowicz/Poland; judgment of 8 November 2021, application no. 49868/19 and no. 57511/19 – Dolińska-Ficek and Ozimek/Poland; judgment of 3 February 2022, application no. 1469/20 – Advance Pharma/Poland.

[90] Polish Constitutional Court, judgment of 10 March 2022, K 7/21.

[91] *A. Peters*, Supremacy Lost: International Law Meets Domestic Constitutional Law, Vienna Online Journal on International Constitutional Law 3 (2009), 170–198, 195.

VI. Conclusions

As far as the German Constitutional Court is concerned, it is still possible to speak, as *Sandhu* does, of a judicial dialogue with the ECJ, even if both courts are "inherently political". The relationship between the "courts of the last word" in Karlsruhe and Luxembourg was never easy, but it has always been based on dialogue and mutual respect. It seemed that with the *PSPP* decision, the dialogue had ended, while with the order of April 2021 the German Constitutional Court seemed to return to a more conciliatory tone.[92] Nevertheless, the example of the Italian Constitutional Court and the *Taricco* saga indicates that it is also the ECJ that may retreat from its position, positively contributing to an ongoing conversation between European courts.[93]

The case of Poland is rather different. The state that was presented as a successful example of constitutional transition and economic transformation has substantially deviated from principles that the country had accepted as part of the Copenhagen criteria. Since the change of political power in October 2015, one can observe an "anti-constitutional populist backsliding"[94] that is gradually heading towards an authoritarian regime. One of the features of the Polish leadership's political program is to take a "tough" stance toward the EU. This is reflected in the functioning of the Constitutional Court, whose "capture" began as soon as the political party "Law and Justice" (PiS) won the parliamentary elections. This happened initially by introducing three unlawfully elected judges to already occupied seats, then by changing the rules of procedure, and finally by power in the Court being taken over by people close to political actors, who arbitrarily select the composition of judicial panels and determine the order of cases to be heard.

The Polish Constitutional Court has become a political "tool" in the battle against the international tribunals that are safeguarding the rule of law and the protection of human rights. Apart from the ECJ, it is impossible to ignore the relationship of the Polish Constitutional Court with the ECtHR, which until the *Xero Flor* judgment was based on mutual respect. In proceedings before the Constitutional Court, the ECtHR's human rights jurisprudence had been cited repeatedly to strengthen arguments for the protection of constitutional rights, and the provisions of the Convention were invoked by parties as a standard for constitutionality review. The opposition against international tribunals mani-

---

[92] *P. Hilpold*, So Long Solange? The PSPP Judgment of the German Constitutional Court and the Conflict between the German and the European "Popular Spirit", Cambridge Yearbook of European Legal Studies 23 (2021), 159–192, 159.

[93] *M. Bonelli*, The Taricco Saga and the consolidation of judicial dialogue in the European Union, Maastricht Journal of European and Comparative Law 25 (2018), 357–373, 372.

[94] *W. Sadurski*, How Democracy Dies (in Poland): A Case Study of Anti-Constitutional Populist Backsliding, Sydney Law School Research Paper 18/01 (2018), 1–72, 9.

fests itself through artificially created constitutional issues and the filing of motions by the executive branch, especially by the prime minister and the prosecutor general. In March 2023, even the President of the Republic submitted a motion regarding the constitutionality of amendments that had been made to the Act on the Supreme Court so as to comply with milestones that had been agreed with the European Commission in order to unlock payments from the National Recovery and Resilience Plan. In addition, the verdicts of international tribunals are challenged through legal questions formulated by the Disciplinary Chamber of the Supreme Court as a reaction to the ECJ's[95] and the ECtHR's[96] questioning of the Court's independence.

Therefore, with respect to Poland, one can speak of diverging monologues instead of a judicial dialogue with the ECJ or even a trialogue with the ECtHR. Each of the tribunals is perceiving its role as "the court of last word" in their respective legal orders and delivers its position in the form of an assertive monologue. The rendered verdicts exist side by side, often leading to contradictory results that threaten the principle of legal certainty. In times of political turmoil, every reaction gives rise to a corresponding reaction. Laws enacted by Polish political authorities that violate constitutional and conventional standards are challenged either before the ECJ in the form of infringement actions filed by the European Commission or in the form of preliminary questions submitted by Polish courts. Or these laws are challenged before the ECtHR in the form of complaints brought by Polish citizens or persecuted judges. In response, the Polish Constitutional Court reviews cases, at the request of those directly concerned, so as to justify the refusal to enforce the judgments of international tribunals or to legitimize controversial legislative changes, in effect aiming to change the constitutional order. In such a political system, national and patriotic values play an integral role, so that the Constitutional Court appears as the designated guardian of sovereignty, ideological values and constitutional identity. Thus, the Polish Constitutional Court falls in line with the practice of other courts, which tend to abuse the concept of constitutional identity or constitutional pluralism to justify violations of EU values and the principle of sincere cooperation, thereby effectively assisting the governing political authorities.[97]

---

[95] ECJ, judgment of 19 November 2019, cases C-585/18, C-624/18 and C-625/18 – A.K. and others, followed by the judgment of the Polish Supreme Court of 5 December 2019 in case III PO 7/18.

[96] ECtHR, judgment of 22 July 2021, application no. 43447/19 – Reczkowicz / Poland.

[97] *R. Kelemen/L. Pech,* The Uses and Abuses of Constitutional Pluralism: Undermining the Rule of Law in the Name of Constitutional Identity in Hungary and Poland, Cambridge Yearbook of European Legal Studies 21 (2019), 59–74, 69.

Part 5

Law and Economics

Criminal Law and Behavioral Law and Economics

Peter Kasiske

I. Introduction

Since its first emergence in the seventies of the past century, behavioral economics has grown to become a significant branch in the field of economic sciences. By examining how people make judgments and come to a decision, it has replenished important economic models by adding valuable new insights, thus revising the concept of the so-called *homo economicus*. Furthermore, these insights also have proven to be of great value for jurisprudence. In Europe and Germany, capital market law and consumer protection law in particular have already received valuable stimuli from behavioral economics.[1] Criminal law in

[1] *L. Klöhn*, Kapitalmarkt, Spekulation und Behavioral Finance (2006); *D. Enste/M. Ewers/C. Heldmann/R. Schneider*, Verbraucherschutz und Verhaltensökonomik (2016); *L. Oehler/A. Reisch*, Behavioral Economics – Eine neue Grundlage für die Verbraucherpolitik, Vierteljahreshefte zur Wirtschaftsforschung 78 (2009), 30–43; *A. Sibony/G. Helleringer*, EU Consumer protection and Behavioural Sciences: Revolution or Reform?, in: A. Alemanno/A. Sibony (eds.), Nudge and the Law. A European Perspective (2015), 209–234.

Germany, however, has yet to adopt behavioral economic insights,[2] while other nations such as the United States or Israel have shown themselves considerably more open minded towards ideas from behavioral economics even in the field of criminal law.[3] This may be due to the fact that the economic approach to criminal law has hitherto been met with rather substantial skepticism by German criminal law scholars.[4] Discussing a behavioral economics approach to the crime of fraud, the following article tries to show that behavioral economics can offer valuable insights for criminal law and is therefore worthy of an unbiased reception.

II. The importance of behavioral models for the law

From a strictly social sciences perspective, criminal law is just a means to shape and control human behavior. The rules of the criminal code are supposed to provide that certain forms of behavior, such as murder or theft, are not accepted by the collective. This purpose is meant to be achieved by threatening the citizen with sanctions in the event he fails to refrain from said behavior. *Georg Wilhelm Friedrich Hegel* stated the opinion that such an understanding of criminal law treats the citizen unduly like a dog that is being trained by its owner.[5] Such a view may indeed be inappropriate if one questions the criminal law regarding its legitimacy and its purpose. The same view may prove helpful, however, if one asks how criminal law can achieve this purpose. Just as training a dog demands knowledge regarding the behavior of dogs, criminal law, as far as it aims to control the behavior of humans, requires an idea on how humans actually behave. Just as an economist who studies the consequences of human decisions in the field of economics, a researcher in the field of criminal law requires a behavioral model in order to predict how the rules of criminal law affect the conduct of the people.

---

[2] *M. Englerth*, Der beschränkt rationale Verbrecher – Behavioral Economics in der Kriminologie (2010).

[3] *R. McAdams/T. Ulen*, Behavioral Criminal Law and Economics, in: N. Garoupa (ed.), Encyclopedia of Law and Economics, vol. 3 (2nd edn., 2009), ch. 16; *A. Harel*, Behavioral Analysis of Criminal Law, in: E. Zamir/D. Teichmann (eds.), The Oxford Handbook of Behavioral Economics and the Law (2014), 568–598.

[4] *P. Wittig*, Der rationale Verbrecher (1993), 126–129; *S. Harrendorf/B. Geng*, Der rational kalkulierende Verbrecher? Zu Entwicklung, Stand und Zukunftsperspektiven ökonomischer Kriminalitätstheorien, in: J. Körner et al. (eds.), Recht trifft Wirtschaft (2019), 181–212.

[5] *G.W.F. Hegel*, Grundlinien der Philosophie des Rechts (1821), § 99.

A. Homo economicus as a behavioral model

The dominant behavioral model in economics is that of *homo economicus*, as it forms the bases of rational choice theory. It explains human behavior as the result of decisions made by a rational agent. His behavior is therefore predictable if his preferences are known. *Homo economicus* tends to display three certain characteristics: First, he is motivated only by self-interest, which means that he aims exclusively to maximize his utility function. Secondly, he continually acts rationally in the sense that he always choses whichever option facilitates his self-interest best when offered various alternatives of decision. And finally, he is always capable of acting upon those decisions. Therefore, he does not let himself get irritated by his emotions or his urges.[6]

It is obvious, that *homo economicus* is not a truly realistic depiction of human individuals, who – of course – are influenced in their behavior by their feelings and who by no means always strive for the maximization of their utility function but who can also act in an altruistic manner. But contrary to popular belief, the concept of *homo economicus* does not claim to project a realistic depiction of human nature. It rather illustrates a conscious simplification, which reduces complex human motives and behaviors to a few characteristic traits. Only through this simplification is *homo economicus* able to fulfill its function as a parameter within the framework of mathematical formalizations, which economists utilize in order to predict human decision-making behavior. Hence it is not necessary for the concept of *homo economicus* to be based on a framework that accurately captures human nature and human behavior in its entirety. What matters is whether the concept can help make verifiable predictions regarding reality.[7] For a long time, economists were convinced that the concept of *homo economicus* could provide just that. Even if it does not project correctly how concrete individuals will make their decisions, it is capable of predicting what decisions can be expected from a multitude of human beings.

B. Behavioral economics

Through behavioral economics this assumption has been challenged. Behavioral economics combines elements of economics and psychology to understand how people make decisions and how they act upon those decisions. Unlike rational choice theory, behavioral economics does not try to construct a simplified model of behavior based on more or less plausible assumptions of human conduct. Instead behavioral economists use laboratory and field experiments and analysis of archival data to find out how people make decisions in

---

[6] *G. Kirchgässner*, Homo oeconomicus – The Economic Model of Behavior and its Applications in Economics and other Social Sciences (2008), 12–17.

[7] *Englerth* (n. 2), 43–45 referring to *M. Friedman*, The Methodology of Positive Economics, in: idem (ed.), Essays in Positive Economics (1953), 3–43, 9–15.

the real word. Behavioral economists have examined the actual decision-making behavior of humans in a multitude of experiments. By confronting countless groups of test subjects with various fictional decision-making scenarios, asking, for example, whether the subjects would pocket the winnings of a lottery jackpot or if they would rather invest said winnings in hopes of winning an even higher jackpot. The results of these experiments have shown that people often act contrary to what the rational-choice-approach would lead one to believe. It appears, that irrational behavior in many cases is not a neglectable exception but the rule. Human beings regularly make predictable and pervasive mistakes in their judgment and decision-making. Behavioral economists have identified biases that distort our reception of reality and therefore our judgments. And they have shown that under cognitive or information constraints humans fall back on certain heuristics. Those shortcuts and rules of thumb are often useful, but under certain circumstances they lead to errors. They may obstruct the ability to properly estimate probabilities and risks.[8] While rational choice theory is based on the behavior of a rational and self-interested *homo economicus*, according to behavioral economics the conduct of real people regularly displays bounded rationality, bounded willpower and bounded self-interest. As a consequence behavioral economists assume that the *homo economicus* model of rational choice theory in many cases will fail to correctly predict the typical behavior of people.[9] This does not mean, however, that behavioral economics seeks to completely dismiss the concept of *homo economicus* as a behavioral model. The insights of behavioral economics do not force the conclusion that human behavior is irrational to an extent that makes is impossible to design a behavioral model that allows reliable predictions. A valuable finding of behavioral economics is that the mistakes people are making in their judgments and decisions can also be predicted.[10] So the structural flaws in human decision-making that behavioral economics has identified can themselves be modelled. Thus it should be possible to adjust the shortcomings of the *homo economicus*-model by integrating some of the insights of behavioral economics.[11]

C. Behavioral models in law: What role do behavior models play in law and criminal law in particular?

Jurisprudence first became aware of *homo economicus* through the economic analysis of law. Since the discipline first emerged in the United States in the

---

[8] For an overview, see *H. Beck*, Behavioral Economics – Eine Einführung (2014), 25–94; *D. Kahnemann*, Thinking, Fast and Slow (2011).

[9] *C. Jolls/C. Sunstein/R. Thaler*, A Behavioral Approach to Law and Economics, Stanford Law Review 50 (1998), 1471–1550, 1476.

[10] *T. Ulen*, The Importance of Behavioral Law, in: Zamir/Teichmann (n. 3), 94–124, 94.

[11] *Beck* (n. 8), 9; *Jolls/Sunstein/Thaler* (n. 9), 1487.

second half of the preceding century, this school of thought has also gained traction in continental Europe and has therefore been incorporated in more and more legal systems. The economic analysis of law examines which economic effects originate from legal norms or decisions. For this purpose it makes use of the tools of rational choice theory and asks how a rational and self-serving individual would most likely react towards those norms and decisions.[12] Thus the economic analysis of law takes resort to the behavior model of the *homo economicus*.

Criminal law as well has been made the subject of economic analysis. Especially the research of *Gary Becker* and *Isaac Ehrlich* proved influential on criminology and public policy on crime and law enforcement.[13] *Becker* and *Ehrlich* postulated that, in general, criminals are rational actors who reflect upon the cost-to-benefit-ratio before committing any crimes. While the benefits would be the expected monetary and nonmonetary returns of the criminal activity, discounted by their probabilities of realization, the costs of the crime would include formal and informal sanctions (like social stigma or the loss of lawful employment) discounted by the probabilities of detection and punishment. *Becker* offers an account of *homo economicus* when he states that "human behavior can be viewed as involving participants who (1) maximize their utility (2) from a stable set of preferences and (3) accumulate an optimal amount of information and other inputs in a variety of markets".[14]

Despite some reservations, the economic analysis of law has gained considerable influence in German civil law.[15] At the same time it has not met with equal success in criminal law theory. The approach of *Becker* and *Ehrlich* has been countered by German scholars with the argument that the *homo economicus* model is an undue simplification which does not live up to the complexity of the social and psychological reality of criminal behavior.[16] However, the fact that the behavioral model of *homo economicus* has been dismissed by German criminal law theory does not mean that it has no place in German criminal law practice. Criminal law is always dependent on assumptions made in regard of human behavior. And if one examines the assumptions on human behavior that lie beneath most concepts and rules of German criminal law, one will inevitably encounter *homo economicus*. I want to illustrate this point by reference to the German criminal law provision on the crime of fraud.

---

[12] *T. Micelli*, The Economic Approach to Law (2004), 1 f.

[13] *G. Becker*, Crime and Punishment: An Economic Approach, The Journal of Political Economy 76 (1968), 169–217; *I. Ehrlich*, The Deterrent Effect of Capital Punishment: A Question of Life and Death, American Economic Review 65 (1975), 397–417.

[14] *G. Becker*, The Economic Approach to Human Behaviour (1976), 14.

[15] *H.-D. Assmann/C. Kirchner/E. Schanze*, Ökonomische Analyse des Rechts (1993); *H. Eidenmüller*, Effizienz als Rechtsprinzip (4th edn., 2015).

[16] *Wittig* (n. 4), 126–128; *T. Singelnstein/M. Kunz*, Kriminologie (8th edn., 2021), 176–178; *Harrendorf/Geng* (n. 4), 191–193.

III. A behavioral economics approach to the crime of fraud

The crime of fraud is defined in § 263(1) of the German *Strafgesetzbuch* (Criminal Code):

> "Wer in der Absicht, sich oder einem Dritten einen rechtswidrigen Vermögensvorteil zu verschaffen, das Vermögen eines anderen dadurch beschädigt, daß er durch Vorspiegelung falscher oder durch Entstellung oder Unterdrückung wahrer Tatsachen einen Irrtum erregt oder unterhält, wird mit Freiheitsstrafe bis zu fünf Jahren oder mit Geldstrafe bestraft."

> "Whoever, with the intention of obtaining an unlawful pecuniary benefit for themselves or a third party, damages the assets of another by causing or maintaining an error under false pretences or distorting or suppressing true facts incurs a penalty of imprisonment for a term not exceeding five years or a fine."[17]

This rule contains assumptions regarding the behavior of three different persons: the victim, the potential offender and the judge who must pass judgment on the convicted delinquent.

A. Assumptions on the behavior of the offender

According to § 263(1) *Strafgesetzbuch*, a person who has committed fraud can be sentenced with imprisonment of up to five years. It is thus assumed that the imposition of a penalty or its threat has an effect on the behavior of (potential) offenders. In what follows, I want to concentrate on the behavioral effects of the threat of punishment.

1. The concept of general deterrence and the rational criminal

It is widely accepted that one purpose of threatening punishment is general deterrence. According to this concept, a reasonable number of possible offenders will refrain from committing a crime because they want to avoid punishment. Yet such a discouragement can only come into effect if the offender in fact considers the risk of punishment and weighs it against the possible benefits before committing a crime. It is obvious that the theory of deterrence necessitates a rationally acting offender, who, driven by his self-interest, wants to avoid the negative consequences of punishment.[18] In other words, § 263(1) *Strafgesetzbuch* (like, on the basis of the deterrence theory of punishment, all other crimes in the criminal code) treats the potential offender as a *homo economicus*.

---

[17] English trans. by M. Bohlander/U. Reusch: www.gesetze-im-internet.de/englisch_stgb/index.html (last accessed 10 July 2022).

[18] *S. Laudien*, Der homo oeconomicus und das Strafrecht, in: A. Dieckmann/C. Sorge (eds.), Der homo oeconomicus in der Rechtsanwendung (2016), 233–253, 237; *S. Shavell*, Criminal Law and the Optimal Use of Nonmonetary Sanctions as a Deterrent, Columbia Law Review 85 (1985), 1232–1262, 1235.

There has already been a multitude of objections against general deterrence as an aim of punishment. One common objection, for example, is that the severity of the punishment is not the sole factor in the benefit-risk-assessment of the possible offender. In most cases, the risk of getting caught at all would be a much more dominant factor in his assessment.[19] If a potential offender assumes he will not even be detected or cannot be identified as the offender, the severity of the potential punishment will play next to no role in his calculations. Correspondingly, the effect of a potential punishment-threat will be very small. The economic analysis of criminal law has always taken this aspect into consideration and has therefore incorporated the risk of detection in its decision-making model.[20] It also added the concept of moral cost to take account of the fact that criminal behavior is influenced not only by deterrence but also by social norms and values.[21]

Another criticism cannot, however, be remedied by adjusting the decision-making-model: It is safe to assume that there are cases where the offender does no benefit-risk-assessment at all before committing the crime. A majority of crimes are committed spontaneously without any prior considerations. Moreover, there are also offenders who are in an emotional state of emergency during which they are incapable of judging the consequences of their behavior in a rational manner. Also, there are crimes which are committed under the influence of alcohol and/or drugs, a state which compromises immensely the capacity for making rational decisions. Especially with violent crimes or sex crimes, a rationally acting offender, who assesses all benefits and risks, can be considered an exception.[22]

Yet there are several areas of crime where the behavioral model of a rational criminal is appropriate. This applies especially for fraud or other types of so-called white collar crimes. Offenders committing this kind of crime mostly act prudentially and are driven by an egoistic self-interest.[23] It therefore seems at least reasonable to assume that a serious risk of a severe punishment could discourage potential offenders from committing a crime.[24]

---

[19] *A. Bottoms/A. von Hirsch*, The Crime-Preventive Impact of Penal Sanctions, in: P. Kane/H. Kritzer (eds.), The Oxford Handbook of Empirical Legal Research (2010), 96–124, 101–103.

[20] *Becker* (n. 13), 180.

[21] *E. Posner*, Law and Social Norms (2000), 88–111.

[22] *D.A. Anderson*, The Deterrence Hypothesis and Picking Pockets at the Pickpocket's Hanging, American Law and Economics Review 4 (2002), 295–313, 308; *P. Robinson*, The Role of Deterrence in the Formulation of Criminal Law Rules: At Its Worst When Doing Its Best, Georgetown Law Journal 91 (2003) 949–1002, 956 f.

[23] See *R. Paternoster/S. Tibbets*, White-Collar-Crime and Perceptual Deterrence, in: S. van Slyke et al. (eds.), The Oxford Handbook of White-Collar-Crime, 622–641 (2016), who attribute a larger deterrence effect to informal sanctions than to formal punishment.

[24] *T. Hörnle*, Straftheorien (2nd edn., 2017), 27.

2. General deterrence and behavioral economics

However, such an assessment requires the correct perception and processing of information regarding the probability and severity of punishment. The behavioral model of *homo economicus* considers these abilities as a given, although experimental studies suggest that humans are exposed to various distorting effects when in the process of risk assessment. This could first be of consequence on the level of perceiving the information that is necessary for such an assessment. A potential offender may have access to data regarding the objective risk of detection and punishment, perhaps because there are well-known incidents, where someone already has been arrested and put on trial for committing such a crime. Yet this does not automatically support the conclusion that he will process the information at hand in a rational manner. According to insights of behavioral economics regarding what is known as the *availability heuristic*, the ability to form a subjective prognosis of probability depends crucially on how well the person has the relevant information available in their memory. For example, regarding the probability assessment for getting involved in a traffic accident, it makes a big difference whether someone has obtained the available information from immediate personal experience, from the personal account of a close acquaintance or from media coverage. If someone has experienced a traffic accident either personally or has heard the account from a close acquaintance, this information will become engrained much deeper in their memory in contrast to their obtaining the same information from media coverage. Concordantly, this information is either more or less available for their risk assessment. Humans that have experienced an incident either themselves or in their immediate circle estimate the likelihood of that event occurring again higher than humans that have received their information solely from the media.[25] Therefore, it might very well make a difference for a potential offender whether he has knowledge of other offenders in his immediate circle who were caught or if he merely has once taken note of abstract data regarding the police clearance rate for that offence. Similarly, it can also be relevant that the availability of such data can be overshadowed by better availability of contrary information, e.g. where a potential offender has knowledge of cases in his immediate circle that have neither been detected nor caught and the offenders secured valuable monetary or nonmonetary returns through their criminal activity.[26]

Additional cognitive distortion effects are also to be expected in the processing of information within a risk assessment. Behavioral economists have grappled intensely with the question of how humans assess risk. They found that people often tend to assess their situation significantly more optimistically than objectively appropriate. For example, the probability of being affected by

[25] *Beck* (n. 8), 43.

[26] *Englerth* (n. 2), 218.

an adverse event is oftentimes underestimated. In the area of criminal behavior, such an *overconfidence bias* could lead criminals to underassess their risk of being detected and convicted by law enforcement authorities.[27]

One of the most influential concepts of behavioral economics is *prospect theory*, which deals particularly with decisions as to risks.[28] While rational choice theory assumes that a rational agent chooses between risky prospects by comparing expected utility values (i.e. the weighted sum of adding the respective utility values of payoffs multiplied by their probabilities), prospect theory states that people evaluate outcomes based on the change they represent from an initial reference point rather than based on the nature of the outcome itself.[29] Applied to the concept of general deterrence, this leads to the conclusion that the deterrence effect of punishment is nonlinear. Thus it can be assumed that beyond a certain threshold, a further aggravation of punishment does not carry any more weight for a potential offender. For instance, while the risk assessment outcome could be significantly affected depending on whether the threatened punishment for a crime is either a fine of zero or 2,000 Euros, there is next to no effect on the assessment if the fine alternates between 10,000 or 12,000 Euros.[30] Ultimately, behavioral economics does not question the logic of deterrence in general. But its insights allow for a more differentiated approach, which in return introduces chances for more efficient crime control.

3. Prospect theory applied to the abandonment of an attempt

Prospect theory not only sheds a new light on general deterrence. Its findings on risk-averse and risk-seeking patterns are also of interest for the assessment of other legal provisions that deal with situations where an offender has to make a decision under conditions of uncertainty. Consider, for example, the abandonment of an attempted crime. Statutory provisions could provide that an offender may secure impunity if he gives up the plan to commit a crime that has already begun. The reasoning behind such a rule is that the possibility of impunity should motivate the offender not to carry on with an already commenced crime.[31] Especially in cases of attempted murder, he will be provided with an incentive to spare his victim. One flaw in this argument is its precondition of the offender knowing about the legal consequences of abandonment.

---

[27] *McAdams/Ulen* (n. 3), ch. 16; *N. Garoupa*, Behavioral Economic Analysis of Crime: A Critical Review, European Journal of Law and Economics 15 (2003), 5–15, 9.

[28] *D. Kahnemann/A. Tversky*, Prospect Theory: An Analysis of Decision under Risks, Econometrica 47 (1979), 263–291.

[29] *Kahnemann/Tversky* (n. 28), 273.

[30] *C. Jolls*, On Law Enforcement with Boundedly Rational Actors, in: F. Parisi/V. Smith (eds.), The Law and Economics of Irrational Behavior (2004), 268–286, 282.

[31] *W. LaFave*, Criminal Law (6th edn., 2017), 807; *American Law Institute*, Model Penal Code Part I, Commentaries, vol. 2 (1985), 359.

It seems reasonable to expect this rarely to be the case. But from the perspective of prospect theory, this reasoning has another weakness, especially when the offender does not have a chance to secure complete impunity but only a less harsh punishment.

To exemplify: A shoots B in an attempt to kill B, but the first shot only injures B slightly. A still has a bullet remaining, and he knows that B could identify him. A now has the choice to either complete his offence or to abandon his attempt. If he abandons his attempt, he could definitely avoid a severe punishment for attempted murder, yet he would have to expect a definite, albeit less severe, punishment for a completed battery. By completing the murder, he could significantly minimize his risk of getting caught at all. However, should he get caught, the punishment would be much more severe.

Is it realistic to assume that A would choose to abandon his attempt at murder in this situation? According to prospect theory, individuals making a decision under risk tend to value gains and losses differently, placing more weight on perceived gains than on perceived losses. This means that the risk assessment depends primarily on whether the actual decision-making situation is about limiting losses already incurred or about preserving or expanding chances of winning. In the former case, people typically tend to act more risk-seeking, which means they are willing to accept further losses in order to compensate for already incurred losses, whereas in the latter case they tend to act more risk-averse if already realized profits are at stake.[32] In our example, from A's point of view his choice is about how to limit already incurred losses in the form of punishment risks in an already disadvantageous situation. According to the claims of prospect theory, he would now be inclined to accept further losses if in return he stands the chance of avoiding a certain loss. The option of abandonment, which means a lower but more certain loss, would therefore be less attractive than the option of simply completing the offence, by which he could avoid punishment entirely.

B. Assumptions on the behavior of the sentencing judge

Most legal systems grant the judge substantial discretion in determining the sentence, thus enabling him to take into account all circumstances of the concrete case and the individual character of the offender. This assumes that the decision of the judge is guided by the relevant facts alone, while disregarding any other influences. Again, from a behavioral economics perspective this premise seems doubtful. Experimental studies suggest that people, even when consciously disregarding irrelevant considerations, are still subject to unconscious distortionary influences when exercising their discretionary power.

---

[32] *D. Kahnemann/A. Tversky*, The Framing of Decisions and the Psychology of Choice, Science 211 (1981), 453–458, 454.

One example for such a distorting influence is the anchoring effect. According to this phenomenon people, who must decide upon a certain value on a scale, are generally oriented towards a reference point that is currently available in their consciousness.[33] This anchoring effect influences not only our decisions when making estimates, but also comes into play when we must decide upon a certain value within a given scope of discretion. The efficacy of the anchoring effect in sentencing has been proven by an empirical study in which experienced judges have been asked to impose a sentence on an offender based on a described rape case. Beforehand, they have been told what level of punishment a legal layman has deemed appropriate. It became apparent that the sentences given by the judges was significantly higher when the lay prosecutor also favored a high sentence, whereas the sentencing of the judges was much more lenient when the layman favored a lower sentencing. Evidently the assessment of the layman set an anchor that influenced the professional judges decisions in a certain direction.[34] Another study on the decision making of juries in litigation cases reached similar results.[35]

In addition to information visibly connected to the subject matter of the decision, judgments can also be distorted by influences whose connection to the decision is not even consciously perceived. Studies have shown that anchors can be set by any arbitrary information even where it is obviously irrelevant to the decision. These studies have shown that, when assessing damages, judges are influenced by any random numeric value that was currently available in their consciousness. Behavioral economics call this noise effects.[36] It is long been known that judges in different places often decide dissimilarly upon identical cases. Research traces this back to the fact that different places tend to generate different decision-making habits and manners of exercising discretion.[37] The findings of behavioral economics on noise indicate that in addition to this cultural effect, other distorting factors that are deeply rooted in human behavior come into play as well.

In the face of these results, the assumption of the law that a judge would base his sentencing judgment solely on objective criteria proves to be an illusion. But behavioral economics also give a hint on how such distorting effects in decision-making behavior can be counteracted. If one cannot avoid

---

[33] *D. Teichmann/E. Zamir*, Judicial Decision-Making, in: Zamir/Teichmann (n. 3), 664–702, 678; *M. Englerth*, Behavioral Law and Economics – eine kritische Einführung, in: C. Engel et al. (eds.), Recht und Verhalten (2007), 60–132, 82 and 94.

[34] *B. Englich/T. Mussweiler*, Anchoring Effects in the Courtroom, Journal of Applied Social Psychology 31 (2001), 1535–1551, 1546.

[35] *G.B. Chapman/B. Bornstein*, The More You Ask for the More You Get: Anchoring in Personal Injury Verdicts, Applied Cognitive Psychology 10 (1996), 519–540.

[36] *D. Kahnemann/O. Sibony/C. Sunstein*, Noise (2021), 9.

[37] *C. Pfeiffer*, Glasnost in der Strafjustiz – Empirische Forschung auf der Suche nach Strafzumessungsgerechtigkeit, Deutsche Richterzeitung (1990), 441–445, 444.

anchoring effects, then the anchors should represent information that does not distort the judgment. For example, it would make sense to collect sentencing decisions in a database. If judges were obliged to consult such data base before each decision, they would be influenced by the sentencing in comparable constellations and not by arbitrary anchor values. So from a behavior-economics position, there is a lot that argues for the use of sentencing guidelines.[38] Of course this would lead to a standardization of sentencing that might restrict the scope of judicial discretion. But in individual cases justice could still be done by allowing a deviation from the guidelines if this can be explicitly justified by the circumstances of the individual case.

C. Assumptions regarding the behavior of the victim

From a behavioral economics view, the offense of fraud is particularly interesting because this crime is designed not only on assumptions relating to the behavior of offenders and judges but also on suppositions regarding the behavior of potential victims. The crime of fraud is supposed to penalize manipulations by means of communication that cause victims to harm their own assets. The idea of penalizing fraud is to protect the autonomy of individual decisions and behavior, as far as that behavior has an effect on someone's assets. The concept behind this design is that in a market economy all agents should carry out their transaction with other parties according to their individual preferences.[39] Autonomous action requires not only freedom from constraint but also freedom from errors and misconceptions. Only one who is fully aware of the circumstances and consequences of a decision can make a truly autonomous and self-determined decision. That is why protection against willfully caused asset-relevant misconceptions is essential for every market-based economic system. Criminal law contributes to this protection by penalizing willful deceit.

1. The concept of deceit and the information model

The most obvious case of deceit is an explicit lie, in which the offender states false facts to provide the victim with inaccurate information to compromise the latter's decision-making basis. The untrue statement of a seller that an offered carpet stems from Persia will lead the victim to the incorrect conclusion that the requested price is appropriate, thus leading to the sale of an inferior product for an excessive price. Incorrect information does not necessarily need to be conveyed by spoken or written word but can also be encompassed in certain behavior. If someone dresses up as a police officer to confiscate allegedly counterfeit money, he does not need to explicitly mention that he is a police officer. The appearance in uniform in itself already conveys that statement. The

---

[38] *Kahnemann/Sibony/Sunstein* (n. 36), 24.

[39] *M. Mansdörfer*, Zur Theorie des Wirtschaftsstrafrechts (2011), 218.

outlined cases have in common that the offender deceitfully interferes with the perception of the victim by providing them with inaccurate information. Thereby he provokes a misconception which in turn leads to an economically disadvantageous decision.

The underlying assumption of penalizing deceit is that decisions like those described above always result from either insufficient or incorrect information. According to this information model of decision-making, a person with comprehensive and accurate information at their disposal will always make a rational and economically prudent decision. So once more we encounter *homo economicus* as a behavioral model. In accordance with that understanding of human behavior, criminal law only has to ensure that no incorrect information is transmitted, whereas responsibility for the completeness of the information on which a decision is made falls entirely on the potential victim. If relevant information is not known to an actor, he is expected to ask his transactional partner, who in return is now obliged to truthfully disclose this information. Only very seldom does there exist an obligation to correct a misperception about certain circumstances without being asked. A violation of these obligations can then be punishable as fraud by omission. But in general, in a market economy it is everyone's own responsibility to base his decisions on sufficient information.[40] If we assume with the information model that rational decisions are only a are only a matter of the participants possessing the right amount of truthful information, then criminal law must only prevent intentional misinformation against which a victim cannot defend himself. This defenselessness results from the fact that in economic transactions we typically have to trust in the truthfulness of the information we receive, as we cannot verify it without further effort.

2. Flaws in the information model

From the perspective of behavioral economics, such an information model of fraud seems incomplete. Misconceptions and unfavorable decisions often result not from inaccurate information but from flawed information processing. According to the information model of fraud, the processing of information is solely the potential victim's responsibility. But what if the potential victim's information processing can also be compromised by manipulations against which he is defenseless?

Restrictions and errors in information processing are a central field of research in behavioral economics. Behavioral experiments have shown that human beings have only a limited ability to absorb and then correctly process information. A well-studied effect in that context is what is termed information

[40] *Mansdörfer* (n. 39), 221.

overload.[41] If a person is exposed to more information than he can absorb, he will fall back on unconscious mechanisms (heuristics) to make the amount of information manageable. However, this can lead to inaccurate conclusions, even if the information the conclusion is based on is correct. How is this possible? In the case of information overload, the information that has been perceived first regularly is remembered best and therefore forms the basis of the decision. Although later information is initially consciously perceived, it does not remain in the memory to the same extent and thus will probably not be taken into account in the decision-making process. An example: When dealing with capital investment, private investors are often provided with a large amount of complex information when talking to their investment advisors. This can cause information overload. If during those talks the chances of profit have been discussed first, while the risks have been discussed at the end, it is to be expected that the information regarding the potential benefits has been better absorbed by the investor than the information regarding the risks.[42] So, although all relevant information has been conveyed accurately, the investor might assess the risk-reward-ratio incorrectly and will, concordantly, make a non-rational choice.

Another important phenomenon in the context of information processing is the "framing effect". It describes how our information processing is strongly affected by the way the information is presented. When people have to make risky economic decisions, those decisions often depend on the way the relevant information is conveyed to them. In a behavioral economics study the test subjects were presented with two questions:

1. Would you participate in a lottery where there is a 10% chance of winning 95 Euros and a 90% chance of losing 5 Euros?

2. Would you pay 5 Euros to participate in a lottery where there is a 10% chance of winning 100 Euros and a 90% chance of winning nothing?

The chance of turning a profit or the risk of suffering a loss, respectively, are statistically identical in both scenarios. Under the premise that individuals make rational choices when given accurate information, one would expect that in both scenarios the proportion of subjects that would participate in the lottery would be approximately the same. But this is not the case. In fact, question 1 induced far more participants to turn down the opportunity of participation than question 2 did.[43] Apparently it makes a substantial difference whether a decision-making problem is presented as a choice between a win and a likely loss or a win and just a cost.

---

[41] *K. Keller/R. Staelin*, Effects of Quality and Quantity of Information on Decision Effectiveness, Journal of Consumer Research 14 (1987), 200–213, 212.

[42] *R. Eberius*, Regulierung der Anlageberatung und Behavioral Finance (2013), 105.

[43] *Kahnemann/Tversky* (n. 32), 453; *Kahnemann* (n. 8), 448.

It is obvious that mechanisms like framing or information overload can be used to manipulate other people and entice them to a certain behavior. Sales techniques, as they are taught in seminars to sales representatives, often just comprise instructions on how to specifically frame an offer to make it appear more attractive to potential buyers. The insights of behavioral economics can be used to protect consumers from the abusive application of such practices. Consumer protection law, for example, has been inspired by behavioral economics to apply new solutions in certain areas. Not long ago, consumer protection law solely followed the approach of the "information model" to protect consumers from poor decisions. Thus it obliged sellers and manufacturers to provide more and more extensive information.[44] Meanwhile, based on the insights of behavioral economics, there has been growing recognition that not only does more information not necessarily lead to more rational decisions, but that it can also lead to an information overload which may result in an even more disadvantageous decision-making behavior.[45] Therefore investor protection today regulates not only the amount of information but also how this information has to be presented to potential customers. For example, providers of financial services are obliged to summarize the most crucial information and then illustrate it in an intuitive graphic.[46]

D. Consequences for the concept of fraud

The insights of behavioral economics regarding the structural deficits of human information processing are also of interest when analyzing the offense of fraud. Perhaps criminal law should draw the same conclusions as consumer protection law and stop relying exclusively on the information model. If the manipulation of information processing can be as effective as the conveying of false information, then it could be prudent to have the crime of fraud apply to such cases as where an offender purposely causes his victim to erroneously process information. I would like to illustrate this point by giving an example:

Mister X is sending letters offering "Investment Certificates" to people who are interested in safe low-risk investments for retirement income. In fact, the "Investment Certificates" have a very high risk of default and are therefore not suited for purposes of retirement income. Mister X knows that his prospective customers are seeking exclusively low-risk investments.

If Mister X advertises the "Investment Certificates" explicitly as suitable for retirement income or if he provides incorrect details regarding the certificates'

---

[44] *D. Zimmer*, Vom Informationsmodell zu Behavioral Finance: Brauchen wir Ampeln oder Produktverbote für Finanzanlagen?, Juristenzeitung 2014, 714–721, 715.

[45] *G. Spindler*, Behavioural Finance and Investor Protection Regulations, Journal of Consumer Policy 34 (2011), 315–336, 321.

[46] *T.M.J. Möllers/E. Kernchen*, Information Overload am Kapitalmarkt, Zeitschrift für Gesellschaftsrecht (2011), 1–26, 17.

risks, this would be chargeable fraud, because the misrepresentation of facts would qualify as deception within the meaning of § 263(1) *Strafgesetzbuch*. But if Mister X is familiar with behavioral economics, it might not even be necessary for him to explicitly deceive his victims. Instead, he could achieve his goal in a more subtle fashion. For example, he could make use of framing effects in presenting the information on his product. He could thus lead the readers to incorrectly conclude that the product is suitable for generating retirement income despite all the provided information being technically correct. This result could be achieved by emphasizing the earnings potential over the risk of loss and therefore manipulating information processing in a way that gives the reader a false overall impression. Mister X could also make use of information overload effect by providing an overabundance of detailed information in a way that a significant number of potential purchasers will be too overwhelmed to take these risks into consideration when making their decision.

Does this conduct constitute deception in terms of the crime of fraud? After all, the offender is providing only correct information and no inaccurate facts. On the other hand, he is ensuring that the provided information will most likely be processed incorrectly.

German criminal law recognizes fraud by "deception with true facts". The idea is that several pieces of information, each true in itself, can be presented in an overall fashion that deceives the victim. In this line of thought, the German *Bundesgerichtshof* (Federal Court of Justice) identified deception in a case where the offender had offered a fee-based route planner online.[47] However, only in a very hidden part of the website did he point out that use of the route planner was subject to a charge. Anyone who did not discover this notice on the extensive page could, by the design of the page, get the impression that the route planner was being offered free of charge. Decisive for the Court's conclusion was the offender's very aim to create such a false impression.

Yet the Court's reasoning is not very convincing. After all, deception is an objective element of the offense. Consequently, it cannot be inferred from the offender's subjective intention alone.

From the perspective of behavioral economics, however, the result could very well be justified based on objective criteria: By the website's design, the offender caused information overload among his victims. Affected by this overload, they were unable to perceive the decisive piece of information among the multitude of items presented: the service being subject to a charge. As a result, their lack of information led them to falsely conclude the offer was free of charge.

Could the concept of "deception with true facts" also cover cases of framing where, even though all the information is perceived correctly, its particular presentation leads to incorrect information processing and thus to an error?

---

[47] BGH, judgment of 5 March 2014, 2 StR 616/12.

Such an interpretation would, however, be irreconcilable with the explicit wording of § 263(1) *Strafgesetzbuch*, since the provision requires an action under false pretenses or either a distortion or suppression of true facts, which means that criminal liability is constituted by conveying incorrect information and not by manipulation of information processing.[48] To subsume a behavior like manipulative framing under § 263(1) *Strafgesetzbuch* would therefore be an impermissible analogy.

E. Fraud without deceit?

As we have seen, in German criminal law fraud requires a deceptive manipulation of the bases of information. A similar approach is found in the criminal law of the United Kingdom and the United States, where the offense of fraud requires a false representation of facts.[49] However, it is not imperative to define fraud so narrowly. Other legal systems define fraud in a broader sense and do not require deceit by false representation of facts. For instance, in Art. 286 § 1 of the Polish Penal Code, fraud is defined as follows:

"Kto, w celu osiągnięcia korzyści majątkowej, doprowadza inną osobę do niekorzystnego rozporządzenia własnym lub cudzym mieniem za pomocą wprowadzenia jej w błąd albo wyzyskania błędu lub niezdolności do należytego pojmowania przedsiębranego działania, podlega karze pozbawienia wolności od 6 miesięcy do lat 8."

"Whoever, with the purpose of gaining a material benefit, causes another person to disadvantageously dispose of his own or someone else's property by misleading him, or by taking advantage of a mistake or inability to adequately understand the action undertaken shall be subject to the penalty of deprivation of liberty for a term of between six months and eight years."[50]

Accordingly, Polish criminal law does not require deceit in the sense that the offender must create a misconception in the victim. Instead, it is sufficient if the offender merely exploits a misconception no matter how this misconception came into existence. Therefore, an offender could be held responsible for provoking a misconception of the victim by manipulatively framing information and thus causing the victim to dispose of his assets in a disadvantageous fashion.

Now, which solution is more sensible from a criminal policy perspective? The German model follows the information model and presumes that victims only need protection from deceptions, because there is almost no way to protect oneself against false information when dealing with strangers in business. On

[48] *R. Hefendehl*, in: Münchener Kommentar zum Strafgesetzbuch, vol. 5 (4th edn., 2022), § 263 para 36.

[49] See UK Fraud Act of 2006; *LaFave* (n. 31), 1261.

[50] English translation by International Money Laundering Information Network: www.imolin.org/imolin/amlid/data/pol/document/act_6_of_june_1997_the_penal_code.html (last accessed 10th July 2022).

the other hand, how received information is processed lies within the personal responsibility of each individual.[51]

From the perspective of behavioral economics, the information model seems dubious, and thus the Polish conception of fraud has its merits, since it takes into account that a misconception can be caused not only by deceit but also by more subtle forms of manipulation. On the other hand, a behavioral-economic understanding of fraud would not necessarily presuppose that the mere exploitation of a misconception is to be declared a punishable offense. One could object that only causing a misconception constitutes an injustice that must be punishable by law, while simply exploiting such a misconception is merely morally reprehensible. This is apparently how the legislatures in Germany, the United Kingdom and the Unites States see the matter. But one could think of extending the crime of fraud to all cases in which the perpetrator provokes a misconception in the victim, regardless of whether this is done by transmitting incorrect information or by deliberately manipulating information processing.

If fraud were to be extended to an intentional manipulation of information processing as well, this would significantly expand the range of punishable behavior. Would this not pose a risk of criminalizing sales tactics and marketing strategies that are common and accepted in our market economy? It would not. This is because the offense of fraud not only requires an intended causation of a misconception but also requires the victim to dispose of his assets in a harmful fashion as a direct result of this misconception. This is not the case where, as a result of the misconception, the victim merely makes a transaction that he otherwise would not have made. If the victim receives goods or services in return which are objectively worth their price, then there is no damage to the assets of the victim. A buyer that has been enticed to purchase an unwanted product is not a victim of fraud just because the seller elicited a misconception.[52] Here, the buyer is already adequately protected by civil law.

If, on the other hand, targeted manipulations are used to entice the victim to dispose of his assets in an economically damaging way, then it seems reasonable to punish the offender for committing fraud. In essence, the wrongfulness associated with fraud stems not from the way an error was induced by the offender but rather from the offender's attempt to damage the victim's assets so as to enrich himself. What needs to be taken into account as well is the fact that criminal law is supposed to serve especially the protection of the weak.[53] Fraudsters do not search for their victims among their attentive and critical

---

[51] *R. Kölbel*, in: H. Achenbach et al. (eds.), Handbuch Wirtschaftsstrafrecht (5th edn., 2019), 706: "in principle the recipient is responsible for misunderstandings" (author's translation).

[52] *Hefendehl* (n. 48), § 263 para 817.

[53] *R. Vergho*, Das Leitbild eines verständigen Durchschnittsverbrauchers und das Strafrecht – ein inkongruentes Verhältnis, Zeitschrift für Wirtschafts- und Steuerstrafrecht (2010), 86–93, 92.

contemporaries but among the gullible and naive. These groups of persons need protection not only from explicit deceptions but also from other forms of manipulation.

That is why it is not appropriate to resort to the standards of consumer protection law when determining the standard of protection of criminal law in respect of fraud. Consumer protection law in Germany is defined by the law of the European Union. According to that body of law, the applied standard is that of an consumer who is reasonably well informed and reasonably observant and circumspect.[54] This standard regulates what can be expected from a consumer when doing business with honest enterprises. Therefore, it is applicable, for instance, when dealing with the question of whether an advertisement is of a misleading character.

Conversely, fraud is about protection from behavior that is designed to willfully damage the assets of the victim. In that case, the point of reference cannot be a standardized average consumer. The level of protection needs to be determined in accordance with what degree of observance and circumspection can actually be expected of people who are typically the victims of fraudsters. Here, the insights of behavioral economics can be helpful in ensuring that assessment of the degree to which people need protection from a manipulation of their decision-making behavior is based on a realistic foundation.

IV. Conclusion

Behavioral economics is of interest not only for criminology but also for the doctrinal study of criminal law. The preceding remarks have shown that the normative evaluations of criminal law are in many respects dependent on models that contain assumptions about the expected behavior of the norm's addressees. In this context, criminal law usually falls back on the behavioral model of *homo economicus*, which assumes a rationally acting utility maximizer. However, this model has its deficiencies, not only in the description of criminal behavior but also concerning the behavior of judges or potential victims. Behavioral economics does not aim to completely replace *homo economicus*. However, it can add important insights to this model and thus improve its informative value as a behavioral model for criminal law.

---

[54] See Directive 2005/29/EC (2005) concerning unfair business-to-consumer commercial practices, recital no. 5.

The Limits of the Application of Behavioral Economics to Criminal Law*

Michał Derek

I. Introduction

Peter Kasiske's paper "Criminal Law and Behavioral Law and Economics" is inspiring. He argues that the findings of behavioral economics are of importance not only for capital market law and consumer protection law, but also for criminal law. This is, he claims, especially true for its insights on the bounded rationality, the bounded willpower, and the bounded self-interest of "real people". *Kasiske* does not, however, explicitly work out the boundaries of the application of behavioral economics to criminal law. Furthermore, a complete picture also demands emphasizing the potential dangers of using behavioral economics in criminal law. The aim of the present comment is therefore to point out the limits of a potential utilization of behavioral economics in criminal law, to explicitly draw the readers' attention to the potential dangers of such an application, and thereby to express doubts concerning the use of behavioral economics in criminal law. Foremost, criminal law is based on and requires precise and axiologically founded criteria. Yet these criteria may conflict with those on which behavioral economics is founded. Consequently, behavioral economics needs to be applied to criminal law with the greatest care. Moreover, it is impossible to interpret criminal law provisions exclusively in the light of the *homo economicus* model or the limited rationality model

* The publication was funded by the Faculty of Law and Administration of the Jagiellonian University within the Priority Research Area FutureSoc under the program "Excellence Initiative – Research University" at the Jagiellonian University in Krakow.

because criminal law legislation cannot be reduced to these models. Criminal law legislation is shaped by a range of value judgments and policy considerations that go beyond these models. At the same time, it needs to be stressed that the purpose of the present paper is not to question the findings of behavioral economics itself.

II. Functions of criminal law and criminal justice and the axiological neutrality of behavioral economics

Kasiske addresses an interdisciplinary dilemma concerning the complex issue of the vision of human nature to be adopted in law as well as in economics, ethics, and political philosophy. In the context of criminal law, the dilemma is at the heart of the problems of defining the functions of criminal law and criminal justice. At the beginning of his paper *Kasiske* states – and he repeats this assertion throughout his contribution – that criminal law is a means to shape and control human behavior. This is the reason why, according to *Kasiske*, we need to understand how humans actually behave, with behavioral economics being key to such an understanding. It is already this starting point underlying *Kasiske*'s entire paper that I would like to question: The functions of criminal law and criminal justice can simply not be reduced to "training" people. Such instrumentalization of criminal law and criminal justice to control society would raise the question of the limits of state powers. The protection of human dignity requires that we do not treat people as objects in order to achieve good results by shaping their behavior in a desired way.[1] It is thus unsurprising that literature describes behavioral economics as evoking the risk of manipulation when used in legislation,[2] and this holds equally true when criminal law and criminal justice are instrumentalized to interfere with the freedom of individuals.

A discussion of the utilization of behavioral economics in criminal law thus needs to be preceded by a general analysis of the functions of criminal law and criminal justice,[3] which for certain are not limited to "controlling society". For example, the retrospective or retributive theory considers criminal justice as a way to answer a wrongful act that has already been committed.[4] Furthermore, an oft mooted point is that punishment is mainly to confirm the responsibility

---

[1] *W. Wróbel/A. Zoll*, Polskie prawo karne. Część ogólna (2014), 25; *M. Królikowski/R. Zawłocki*, Introduction, in: M. Królikowski/R. Zawłocki (eds.), Kodeks karny. Część ogólna. Komentarz do artykułów 1–116 (2021), § 24.

[2] *R. Zyzik*, Behawioralna analiza prawa (2021), 113.

[3] *Zyzik* (n. 2), 116.

[4] *D. Lyons*, Ethics and the Rule of Law (1984), 145–167.

of persons for their acts.[5] *Antony Duff* expressed the idea that the crucial role of criminal law is to define public wrongs.[6] It "defines certain kinds of wrong and provides for the perpetrators to be called to account, condemned and punished",[7] and it is the responsibility of society to "try to bring [the perpetrator] to recognise, and to see the need to make moral reparation for, what he has done".[8] Furthermore, it is claimed that society needs criminal law and that it needs to enforce criminal sanctions to preserve its existence.[9] Finally, criminal justice is a way for society to express its disapproval of the perpetrator's behavior. According to *Joel Feinberg*:

> "Punishment is a conventional device for the expression of attitudes of resentment and indignation, and of judgements of disapproval and reprobation, either on the part of the punishing authority himself or of those 'in whose name' the punishment is inflicted. Punishment, in short, has a *symbolic significance* largely missing from other kinds of penalties."[10]

It should be noted that one must consider all these concepts when discussing the shape of criminal law. Whenever we wish to consider potential criminal law instruments, we cannot limit ourselves to their influence on possible offenders. After all, criminal law may also be described as: (1) a way to unify a society which shares certain values; (2) a method for making somebody responsible for his actions; (3) a means to answer a wrong which has already been committed; and (4) a symbolic model illustrating wrong behavior and its public consequences, this being a model independent of the "real" moral and legal condition of the members of society. Whilst not denying that behavioral economics is a relevant factor, there are significant others which cannot be omitted. In other words, the functions of criminal justice and criminal law are multidimensional.[11] By contrast, *Kasiske* focuses solely on the preventive function of criminal law and criminal justice, and he does not mention the possible incompatibility of behavioral economics with its other functions.

The limited influence of behavioral economics on criminal law is also a result of the claim that the former is treated as axiologically neutral: It is not

---

[5] *Wróbel/Zoll* (n. 1), 415.

[6] *R.A. Duff*, Answering for the Crime. Responsibility and Liability in the Criminal Law (2007), 89.

[7] *R.A. Duff/S. Marshall*, Public and Private Wrongs, in: J. Chalmers et al. (eds.), Essays in Criminal Law in Honour of Sir Gerald Gordon (2010), 70–85, 71.

[8] *Duff/Marshall* (n. 7), 75.

[9] *P. Devlin*, The Enforcement of Morals (1965), 10–18. But see also the reply by *R. Dworkin*, Lord Devlin and the Enforcement of Morals, Yale Law Journal 6 (1966), 986–1005.

[10] *J. Feinberg*, The Expressive Function of Punishment, The Monist 49 (1965), 397–423, 400 (emphasis in the original).

[11] *Wróbel/Zoll* (n. 1), 39.

attached to a given moral concept or set of values.[12] *Avishalom Tor* noted that behavioral economics

"is not committed to any specific legal goal or value system. In this sense, the behavioral approach is fundamentally different from normatively committed legal methodologies, such as the economic analysis of law or rights-based theories. At most, the behavioral analysis of law may be committed to the instrumental value of integrating empirical evidence on human behavior into legal analysis, where relevant."[13]

On the other hand, the dilemmas encountered in criminal law are of a moral and philosophical nature *par excellence*.[14] From this perspective, the potential impact of behavioral economics on criminal law seems to be much more modest. The admissibility of the use of behavioral economics in criminal law depends on the compliance of the former with the axiological assumptions of the latter. In conclusion, criminal law has only a limited need to predict the typical behavior of people. The norms created by society may demand more than average individuals comply with, especially if one takes seriously the first and fourth functions mentioned above. In other words, it is far from clear that criminal law needs to correspond (or should correspond) with the "real" behavior of citizens in order to perform its proper role.

III. The judge, the offender, and the victim

In his exemplary discussion of § 263(1) of the German Criminal Code (*Strafgesetzbuch* – StGB), *Kasiske* claims criminal law provisions contain "assumptions regarding the behavior of three different persons: the victim, the potential offender and the judge who must pass judgment on the convicted delinquent".[15] I, too, will discuss these three different actors and will begin with the sentencing judge.

A. The sentencing judge

The most promising object of research in behavioral economics in criminal law is the sentencing judge. This corresponds with the view expressed by *Tor* that behavioral economics may be used to improve legal procedures.[16] Accordingly, it is legislation on criminal procedure which may profit most from the findings of behavioral economics. *Kasiske* discusses, for example, anchoring effects.[17]

---

[12] *Zyzik* (n. 2), 67. See also *A. Tor*, The Methodology of the Behavioral Analysis of Law (2008), 314.

[13] *Tor* (n. 12), 314.

[14] *J. Zajadło*, Po co prawnikom filozofia prawa? (2008), 10.

[15] *Kasiske*, p. 214, above.

[16] *Tor* (n. 12), 315.

[17] *Kasiske*, pp. 219 f., above.

Another example is the finding that the more tired judges are, the less likely they are to release the accused on parole.[18] It seems that behavioral sciences allow us to better understand how sentencing judges reach their decisions, and this may in turn help to create better conditions for those judging or conducting a criminal trial and help to improve the legal framework defined by legislation on criminal procedure. Principles and procedures such as judicial independence, the taking of evidence, and the free appraisal of evidence – not to mention the overall efficiency of proceedings – could certainly be more fully attained if we were to use the knowledge available concerning the nature of human decisions.

B. The potential offender

According to *Kasiske* the findings of behavioral economics may allow us to better understand general deterrence – more specifically the impact that information on the severity of punishment and on potential impunity may have on potential offenders.[19] This aspect of his paper seems more problematic. As I mentioned above, whilst it is true that one of the aims of punishment is deterrence, it is not the only aim. For example, when defining the potential punishment for a prohibited act, the legislature has to assess the abstract wrongfulness of the prohibited act. Above all, the upper limit of the punishment cannot exceed the importance of the protected legal good (e.g. life, health, liberty) and the harmfulness of the action. What is more, focusing on the deterrent effect of the punishment for the members of society bears the risk that the punishment might *a priori* exceed the degree of culpability of the individual perpetrator. This is, however, excluded by Art. 53 of the Polish Criminal Code, and it is also excluded in German law. In other words, the frame of punishment as defined by a criminal provision reflects more than possible findings on the punishment's deterrent effect on the potential offender.

It should be noted that behavioral economics applied directly to criminal law creates the danger of shaping the latter into a technocratic system which enables a given group to shape society. The overemphasis of deterrence carries with it the risk that the society or the government will take aim at political goals by simply *using* a potential offender. Criminal law as an instrument to influence human behavior is dangerous because such instrumentalization makes criminal law omnipresent and results in excessive interference with rights of the individual. To apply behavioral economics to criminal law may lead to

[18] *R. Zyzik*, Dlaczego zmęczenie decyzyjne może być zagrożeniem dla niezawisłości sędziego?, Forum Prawnicze 3 (2014), 17–24, 22.

[19] *Kasiske*, pp. 214 ff., above.

inconsistencies with the *ultima ratio* principle, which may be derived from the principle of proportionality.[20]

In all, one can hardly argue, as *Kasiske* does, that Art. 286 § 1 of the Polish Criminal Code or § 263(1) *Strafgesetzbuch* implicitly reveals a *homo economicus* attitude when, for example, the former provision states that one guilty of fraud is liable to "imprisonment for a term between six months and eight years". Since the scope of possible punishment results from the wrongfulness of the prohibited behavior, it depends on many factors, such as the type and nature of the infringed legal good, the scale of damage caused, the importance of the duties breached by the offender, the intent and motivation of the offender, or the type of standard of care breached.[21] Again, having account of the offender's reasons for committing the crime is but one of many crucial elements in settling upon the appropriate punishment. In other words, the scope of possible punishment established in the criminal provision does not depend solely on influencing the potential offender as the basic aim of the punishment is not to shape his behavior.

Let us consider a further example discussed by *Kasiske*: His justification for the impunity offered to a perpetrator who voluntarily abandons the further commitment of an attempt makes reference to the potential offender's reasoning.[22] He argues that "the possibility of impunity should motivate the offender not to carry on with an already commenced crime".[23] However, it is not entirely clear that the potential offender's reasoning is the only correct point of reference. Rather, one could argue that the perpetrator who abandons the further commission of an attempt simply *deserves* not to be punished.[24] Both from the retributive and the utilitarian position, it is possible to argue that anything praiseworthy done after the offender has taken direct and immediate steps towards the realization of the offence needs to be taken into consideration in his favor.[25] Accordingly, it is simply *fair* to treat such an offender – regardless of the effect that his initial decision had on society (including other potential

---

[20] *K. Wojtyczek*, Zasada proporcjonalności jako granica prawa karania, Czasopismo Prawa Karnego i Nauk Penalnych 2 (1999), 33–51.

[21] See Art. 115 § 2 of the Polish Criminal Code – addressed to the court assessing the social harmfulness of an act in concreto.

[22] According to Art. 15 § 1 of the Polish Criminal Code: "Anyone who has voluntarily abandoned the commission of a prohibited act or has prevented the result that constitutes an element of the prohibited act shall not be liable to a penalty for the attempt". See translation of the provisions of the Polish Criminal Code on the website: sip.legalis.pl (last accessed 8 February 2023).

[23] *Kasiske*, p. 217, above.

[24] *S. Tarapata/P. Zakrzewski*, Dobrowolność jako warunek czynnego żalu, in: J. Majewski (ed.) Czynny żal jako okoliczność wpływająca na odpowiedzialność karną. Pokłosie XIV Bielańskiego Kolokwium Karnistycznego (2018), 25–46, 37.

[25] *M. Derek*, Karnoprawne znaczenie woli dzierżyciela dobra prawnego (2021), 313–315.

offenders) – better than the one who completed the attempt and fully carried out the offence.

The above remarks should not be taken to mean that there is never the need to seek out measures which might motivate an individual to avoid committing a crime. However, one has to bear in mind the limits which insights of behavioral economics may have in criminal law. For example, it is a valuable insight of behavioral economics that there is a need to react differently depending on the character of the crime: One may consider defining different punishments for "white-collar crimes" and other crimes.[26]

C. The victim

The most interesting part of *Kasiske*'s paper concerns the position of the victim in the crime of fraud. *Kasiske* claims, *inter alia*, that the point of reference in fraud "cannot be a standardized average consumer" but "needs to be determined in accordance with what degree of observance and circumspection can actually be expected of people who are typically the victims of fraudsters".[27] This point touches upon a fundamental question about the level of protection on the side of the victim as well as the level of care and the level of resilience we require from the victim and – correspondingly – about the standard of care and conduct on the side of the offender. Therefore, *Kasiske*'s assertion may raise doubts.

Firstly, it is not immediately apparent that criminal law should be based on a mirror image of what a "real human" is like. *Kasiske* states that "behavioral economists assume that the *homo economicus* model of rational choice theory in many cases will fail to correctly predict the typical behavior of people".[28] Yet perhaps we do not need to use the typical behavior of individuals to establish what we understand as a "model victim" in criminal law. There is a clear distinction in the theory of law between the "model pattern" and the "descriptive model". The former establishes a binding rule ("how it should be like"), while the latter is a projection of a phenomenon ("how it is").[29] The descriptive model is expected to explain the real functioning of the phenomenon in question while the model pattern shows the features, these including the axiological or economic goals which the phenomenon *should* meet. As a result, the latter is independent from the actual state of affairs.[30] In criminal law, lawgivers are not obliged to follow the descriptive model, but they may define the subject or phenomenon on axiological grounds, something which is not infrequently more

---

[26] *Zyzik* (n. 2), 69.

[27] *Kasiske*, p. 227, above.

[28] *Kasiske*, p. 212, above.

[29] *I. Dąbska*, Dwa studia z teorii naukowego poznania (1962), 21–31; *M. Rodzynkiewicz*, Modelowanie pojęć w prawie karnym (1998), 12.

[30] *K. Lipiński*, Wzorce osobowe w prawie karnym (2020), 44 f.

demanding than a pure description of "how it is". The desires expressed in criminal legislation may stem variously from economics, ethics, political philosophy, and the surrounding culture.[31] Even if the majority of people do not behave in a certain way, legal norms may oblige them to do so.[32] Theoretically criminal law may demand from the victim a resilience which the average individual is incapable of showing. In all, behavioral economics and criminal law are two separate areas. Whilst behavioral economics describes and predicts behaviors in practice, criminal law labels some behaviors punishable and is of a strictly normative nature rather than a descriptive one.[33]

However, this leaves us with the question of how to define the standard of protection on the side of the victim as well as the level of care and resilience which we require from the victim. Should we require from the victim a maximum standard, a standard exceeding the average, the statistical average, or should the standard be aligned to a person who does not act as reasonably as the average victim? A maximum standard is to be rejected on the ground of *impossibilium nulla obligatio est*.[34] To align the standard to a person who is not as reasonable as the average seems problematic, too: The criminal liability of potential offenders is overly extended by essentially abstaining from requiring any level of care from the victim.[35] Polish legal scholarship and the judiciary opt for a level that exceeds the average standard, but that is still lower than the maximum standard. It is referred to as the concept of the reasonable or honest man.[36] This means that the concept of the bounded rationality of the individual does not define what we expect from the victim, and, in turn, it therefore also does not define the victim's standard of protection.

The consequences of the adoption of such a standard are important, and they go beyond the crime of fraud. A threat, for example, is only punishable if there is a *justifiable* fear on the part of the victim that the threat will be carried out,[37] and the case law evaluates this fear objectively.[38] A persistent harassment of another person requires that this person feel *justifiably* endangered,[39] i.e. that a

[31] *Rodzynkiewicz* (n. 29), 79.

[32] *Lipiński* (n. 30), 45.

[33] *Rodzynkiewicz* (n. 29), 11 f.

[34] *Wróbel/Zoll* (n. 1), 324 f.

[35] *Lipiński* (n. 30), 166–172. See also *Rodzynkiewicz* (n. 29), 126.

[36] *Lipiński* (n. 30), 174–178.

[37] Art. 190 § 1 of the Polish Criminal Code: "Anyone who threatens to commit an offence to the detriment of another person or his or her family or household member, where there is a justifiable fear that the threat will be carried out, shall be liable to a fine, community sentence or imprisonment for a maximum term of two years."

[38] See Court of Appeal in Poznań, judgment of 5 May 2022, II Aka 22/22.

[39] Art. 190a § 1 of the Polish Criminal Code: "Anyone who, through persistent harassment of another person or another person's family or household member, creates a justified sense of danger, humiliation or anguish or significantly violates the person's privacy, shall be liable to imprisonment going for a term between six months and eight years."

reasonable man would feel endangered.[40] Similarly, the crime of physical or mental maltreatment requires an objective assessment of whether the conduct at issue would cause one to "seriously suffer" and not merely an assessment of the victim's subjective feeling of having seriously suffered.[41]

How then should we tackle the crime of fraud? *Kasiske* rightly notes that fraud is committed even when the victim is naïve. In Polish case law it is well established that even careless victims are protected.[42] The Supreme Court has stated that someone is misled regardless of whether he should have been more careful when making the transaction.[43] As a result, the crime of fraud is committed even if the victim could have prevented the fraud by being attentive and professional.[44] Is this, as *Kasiske* might argue, the result of applying the insights of behavioral economics? I do not think so. The crime of fraud may be just an exception to the rule that the insufficient behavior of the victim reduces the blameworthiness of the act committed by the offender. Regardless of the issue of the "average consumer", criminal law may protect even a careless victim because of the presumed imbalance or disparity between the parties.

The standard of protection on the side of the victim and, correspondingly, the level of care and resilience we require from the victim may, thus, depend on the specific crime, and one may argue that such standard should not simply reflect the average individual's behavior and abilities, but that the specificities of the crime need to be taken into consideration. For example, in the case of fraud or offences against sexual freedom, criminal law needs to protect also naïve or weak victims, thereby extending the offender's criminal liability. On the other hand, in traffic offences, the insufficient behavior of a victim should limit the accused criminal liability.

As stated above, my intent is not to question behavioral economics. However, it has become clear that introducing behavioral economics to criminal law requires limitations. One could argue that criminal law would still have good reasons to recognize the contribution made by a careless victim of a traffic accident even if behavioral economics recognized the bounded rationality of drivers. For a number of reasons which are mostly axiological, criminal law may "raise the bar" and demand a higher standard of care or a higher level of resilience from a victim, even if the average person usually finds it difficult to

---

[40] District Court in Gliwice, judgment of 11 May 2018, VI Ka 333/18.

[41] Supreme Court, judgment of 11 February 2003, IV KKN 312/99. Art. 207 § 1 of the Polish Criminal Code: "Anyone who mentally or physically maltreats his or her family or household member or another person being in a permanent or temporary relationship of dependence to the offender, shall be liable to imprisonment for a term going between three months and five years."

[42] See e.g. Supreme Court, judgments of 11 August 2021, IV KK 502/20, and of 26 August 2021, V KK 297/21.

[43] Supreme Court, judgment of 19 February 2021, III KK 35/19.

[44] Supreme Court, judgment of 13 January 2010, II KK 150/09.

meet such expectations. Knowledge about "framing" or "information overload" may obviously help to properly interpret criminal provisions. Yet the answer may be found not only in behavioral economics but also in the axiological foundations of criminal law.

Finally, let us return to the position of the offender. *Kasiske* notes that "according to behavioral economics the conduct of real people regularly displays bounded rationality, bounded willpower and bounded self-interest".[45] Should the standard of protection in relation to the victim, which goes hand in hand with the level of care and the standard of resilience we require from the victim, be mirrored to the perpetrator? It is indeed worth considering whether bounded rationality or willpower should result in lowering the standard of conduct we require from the offender in every case. This would demand that we rethink the classic concept according to which criminal liability correlates to the ability of the perpetrator to act freely. The assumption that the offender has limited rationality and willpower inevitably changes the interpretation of provisions on a mistake of fact or of law as a defense, as well as on the imputation of culpability. It is criminal law, however, which should answer the question whether such use of behavioral economics is desired.

IV. Conclusion

Behavioral economics certainly presents challenges for criminal law. It demands that we rethink and reexamine the concept of a human who is responsible for his or her actions. However, it is also far from surprising that criminal law may be skeptically predisposed towards behavioral economics. Whilst the research of the latter "can offer valuable insights for criminal law", it is equally important to show that there are limits on the application of behavioral economics to criminal law. The idea of bounded willpower or bounded rationality may certainly be treated as relevant factors, but there are many more elements which are strictly connected with the principles of law which the lawgiver or the judge should bear in mind when, respectively, adopting provisions which describe prohibited acts and formulating judgments. There is also a serious danger when using behavioral economics in criminal law, specifically a "direct use of behavioral economics" that does not observe that behavioral economics and criminal law have different functions and different theoretical foundations (the former being descriptive and the latter being normative). The sphere of description and predictions cannot simply be transferred to the area of normativity. The aims of criminal law, the protection of the dignity of the person, the principle of proportionality, the standard of protection on the side of the victim, or the standard of care on the side of the offender – these are some of the

[45] *Kasiske*, p. 212, above.

axiologically grounded elements which limit the influence of behavioral economics on criminal law and which should not be considered as being less important than behavioral economics itself.

The Interplay of Law and Economics in Competition Law

From the Humble Beginnings to the More Economic Approach*

Wolfgang Wurmnest

I. Introduction

It is a simple truth that the two disciplines of law and economics can have a particularly fruitful relationship in the area of economic regulation. Most commentators agree that legal rules applying to the economy should make economic sense. Otherwise unwarranted welfare losses will occur. Having said

---

* The text draws to a very large extent from *W. Wurmnest*, Marktmacht und Verdrängungsmissbrauch (2nd edn., 2012). I warmly thank *Martin Fischer* for his linguistic review of the manuscript and *Svenja Langenhagen*, *Justin Röper* and *Luca Wölk* for their work on the footnotes.

that, the legal system also has certain needs and peculiarities that must be respected in order to create an optimal regulatory framework.

One of the key areas of economic regulation is competition (antitrust) law,[1] the rules of which seek to maintain unfettered competition on the market. In Germany, there is a long tradition of applying economic insights to shape the body of competition law. This joint venture is certainly one of the earliest "law & economics" movements, one that started in the nineteenth century. With the benefit of hindsight, one can see that not all of the effects of this collaboration have been favourable for competition, even though things have generally improved significantly over the course of time. This chapter will examine two major developments that took place in Germany and consider the lessons which can be learned about the sound interplay between law and economics in the area of competition law.

The first part adopts a historical perspective, analysing the interplay between law and economics over the course of the development of the modern German legal system. It will therefore start in 1871, when Germany became a unified state. In the decades that followed, more and more markets came to be controlled by various types of collusion amongst competitors to the detriment of free and unfettered competition. Unlike in the US, where the Sherman Act was passed in 1890,[2] it took much longer to develop a modern competition law in European states. In Germany the first modern competition act was adopted only in 1957 after an intense debate, and even this act was far from perfect. However, in the same year the European Economic Community was established, which has over the years developed a powerful competition law system. Today, the interpretation and application of the European competition rules strongly shapes the national competition rules of the EU Member States. National competition laws are also to a large extent harmonised with the EU rules.

Against this background, the second part of this chapter will take a closer look at the "more economic approach" to the interpretation and application of competition law. This approach has been introduced incrementally by the EU Commission over the last two decades and bases the application of competition law to a greater extent on robust economic insights. The debate on the "more economic approach" was strongly influenced by US developments, which will also be briefly explained.

The final part will explain three lessons that can be learned from the long history of competition law and economics in Europe.

[1] The notions of "competition" and "antitrust" law are used synonymously in this chapter.

[2] 26 Stat. 209 (1890). On the passing of this Act, see *H.B. Thorelli*, The Federal Antitrust Policy (1955), 164 ff.; *R.J.R. Peritz*, Competition Policy in America, 1888–1992: History, Rhetoric, Law (1996), 9 ff.

II. The difficult beginnings: no competition law, please!

A. The German cartelisation movement and its backing by economic thought

After the German unification in 1871, the increased industrialisation led to various waves of economic booms, but also to oversupply and price crashes. As a result, German industries looked for a means to consolidate supply and demand. More than in other European States,[3] it was typical for competitors to restrict competition through agreements on, for example, output restriction, price fixing or market allocation, although these arrangements were in the beginning often local in reach and fluid.[4] The first German-wide institutionalised cartels were formed in 1876 in the steel industry and in the potash mining sector – the latter cartel was actually an initiative of state-owned companies in Prussia and Saxony-Anhalt.[5] Towards the end of the nineteenth century, cartels spread not only to more and more industries but also became significantly more stable and organised,[6] and individual members were sometimes forced to join the cartel, occasionally even by the state.[7]

This approach was backed by prevailing German economic theory. The *Historische Schule* led by the economist *Gustav (von) Schmoller* saw the formation of large business associations and monopolies as a natural consequence of the ongoing process of industrialisation in a modern economy. Cartels, they believed, aimed at "saving production costs and furthering technical improvements in production".[8] In line with historic precursors they regarded these eco-

---

[3] See *U. Wengenroth,* Die Entwicklung der Kartellbewegung bis 1914, in: H. Pohl (ed.), Kartelle und Kartellgesetzgebung in Praxis und Rechtsprechung vom 19. Jahrhundert bis zur Gegenwart (1985), 15–27, 16: "Allenfalls in Österreich, Belgien und – mit Abstrichen Frankreich – können wir tendenziell ähnliche Entwicklungen beobachten, ohne daß die Kartelle dort vor dem ersten Weltkrieg eine ebenso beherrschende Stellung wie in Deutschland erreichten."

[4] *H. Roth*, Die Kartellverordnung vom November 1923 und ihre Bonner Variante, Jahrbuch für Wirtschaftsgeschichte 3/4 (1962), 11–56, 11, points out that cartels in the various German states were formed as early as the first third of the nineteenth century but that these structures saw a particular boom after the foundation of the German Reich; see also *F. Kleinwächter*, Die Kartelle: ein Beitrag zur Frage der Organisation der Volkswirtschaft (1883), 138, pointing out that many cartels were formed after the economic crash of 1873.

[5] *H.G. Schröter*, Kartellierung und Dekartellierung 1890–1990, Vierteljahrschrift für Sozial- und Wirtschaftsgeschichte 81 (1994), 457–493, 459.

[6] *Schröter* (n. 5), 459. On the economic factors that supported the establishment of such structures, see *Wengenroth* (n. 3), 17 ff.

[7] On the legitimisation of the Potash Mining Syndicate in 1910 by the German legislature, see *K.W. Nörr*, Die Leiden des Privatrechts (1994), 17 f.

[8] *G. von Schmoller*, Verhandlungen der am 28. und 29. September 1894 in Wien abgehaltenen Generalversammlung des Vereins für Socialpolitik über die Kartelle und über das ländliche Erbrecht (1895), in: Verein für Socialpolitik (ed.), 234: "[Kartelle sind] gleichsam

nomic power structures as a form of self-governance which helped realise economies of scale and organise the market to avoid ruinous competition. Far-reaching agreements amongst competitors were seen to have saved markets from "falling prices, bankruptcy, capital devaluation, dismissal of workers and breadlessness".[9] The Austrian economist *Friedrich Kleinwächter* characterised cartels as "modern guilds"[10] and emphasised that cartels were "children born out of necessity" to overcome economically difficult times of oversupply.[11]

Given that cartels and monopolies were regarded as an essential component of industry, the German legislature at first refrained from enacting modern competition legislation. The coming of the twentieth century did not bring much change, and the war economy in World War I even fostered cooperation amongst competitors.[12] During the debate on possible legislative action against the cartels, the Sherman Act was noted but a reception of US law was generally rejected. The view prevailed that unlike in the US, where trusts had – in the words of *Schmoller* – established "a system of robbery and fraud" making far-reaching prohibitions necessary, the German cartels worked for the benefit of the general public, and thus such legislation to restrict the establishment of such structures was thought unnecessary.[13] What followed was that Germany turned into a country of cartels ("Land der Kartelle").[14]

B. The embracing of economic teachings by the Reichsgericht

That cartels could spread across industry and trade was possible only because German courts did not develop rules for the protection of the competitive process based on the general provisions of private law. When the establishment of cartels increased significantly, those who were affected by such structures tried to seek redress before the ordinary courts under the general rules of law.[15] The discussion largely hinged on the question of whether outsiders or those cartel members that were sanctioned by the cartel for not complying with its rules

eine naturgesetzliche, […] nicht zu hindernde, auf Ersparung an Produktionskosten und technische Verbesserungen der Produktion gerichtete Entwicklung [der modernen Wirtschaft]".

[9] *L. Brentano*, Über die Ursachen der heutigen socialen Noth (1889), 23: "Preissturz, Bankrott, Kapitalentwerthung, Arbeiterentlassung und Brodlosigkeit".

[10] *Kleinwächter* (n. 4), 179: "moderne Zünfte".

[11] *Kleinwächter* (n. 4), 143: "Kinder der Not".

[12] See *O. Lehnich*, Der Gegenwärtige Stand der Kartellfrage, Zeitschrift für die gesamte Staatswissenschaft 87 (1929), 501–544, 502.

[13] *Von Schmoller*, as cited by *J. von Hein*, Die Rezeption US-amerikanischen Gesellschaftsrechts in Deutschland (2008), 117 f.

[14] *Schröter* (n. 5), 457; *J. Basedow*, Kartellrecht im Land der Kartelle: zur Entstehung und Entwicklung des Gesetzes gegen Wettbewerbsbeschränkungen, Wirtschaft und Wettbewerb 2008, 270–273, 270.

[15] On the early case law, see *R. Schröder*, Die Entwicklung des Kartellrechts und des kollektiven Arbeitsrechts durch die Rechtsprechung des Reichsgerichts vor 1914 (1988), 9 ff.

could claim damages or injunctions. Ordering such legal consequences required that the conspirators had engaged in unlawful behaviour. Against this background, it was argued that price-fixing agreements and similar arrangements were void for infringing freedom of trade (*Gewerbefreiheit*) as enshrined in § 1 *Gewerbeordnung* and thus should be unenforceable against those who infringed the agreement. Alternatively, the general clauses of tort law could have served as a basis for redress against cartels. After the adoption of the *Bürgerliches Gesetzbuch* (BGB), businesses tried to rely on, *inter alia*, § 823(1) BGB to stop the anti-competitive conduct of their competitors and contractual partners. To the detriment of competition, both approaches were rejected by the *Reichsgericht* (Imperial Supreme Court) in a series of judgments handed down between 1890 and 1902.[16]

From the perspective of the interplay between law and economics, the 1897 judgment on the Saxon wood pulp cartel is of particular relevance here. The case concerned an agreement in which the producers of wood pulp in Saxony agreed to market their products only via a central sales point to ensure reasonable prices above the competitive level. It was alleged that one of the cartel members sold its products directly to customers, thereby bypassing the cartel's centralised sales system. The association in charge of the organisation of the cartel therefore claimed a contractual penalty from the member for violation of the agreement. To avoid payment, the cartel member claimed that the contract setting up the cartel was void. This argument was rejected by the *Reichsgericht*. The court cited *Kleinwächter*'s work and referred to the works of other economists to explain why cartels are necessary to avoid ruinous competition.[17] Against this background the court argued that agreements concluded "in good faith" to ensure reasonable prices in the industry were valid, and as a result contractual penalties for violations of such an agreement were enforceable. That courts in other jurisdictions, namely in the US, had declared such contracts to be null and void, was noted by the court (which even cited comparative sources),[18] without however much attention being paid to the reasons motivating those judgments.

C. Weimar Republic: controlling abuses of economic power

During the Weimar Republic (1919–1933), the German economic mainstream believed that an economic order based on cartels and other collective actors was a natural consequence of capitalism. The teachings of economists like *Werner Sombart*, who argued that economic concentration is typical for an

[16] RG, judgment of 25 June 1890, RGZ 28, 238 – Rabattkartell Buchhandel; RG, judgment of 4 Feburary 1897, RGZ 38, 155 – Sächsisches Holzstoffkartell; RG, judgment of 14 December 1902, RGZ 56, 271 – Börsenverein des deutschen Buchhandels.

[17] RG, judgment of 4 Feburary 1897, RGZ 38, 155, 157 – Sächsisches Holzstoffkartell.

[18] RG, judgment of 4 Feburary 1897, RGZ 38, 155, 159 – Sächsisches Holzstoffkartell.

advanced capitalistic economy,[19] and *Eugen Schmalenbach*, who posited that the increased amount of fixed costs in industrial mass production leads to massive overproduction and thus forced businesses to cooperate,[20] were readily received by lawyers and used to justify cartels and other forms of economic concentration.[21]

Germany was, however, tormented by a galloping inflation and an economic crisis in the post-war period, and the legislature came under pressure to take at least some steps to restrict price increases stemming from cartel formations. What arose from this was that in 1923, a time when around 1,500 cartels were operating in Germany,[22] the *Verordnung gegen Missbrauch wirtschaftlicher Machtstellungen* (KartellVO)[23] (Ordinance against the Abuse of Economic Positions of Power) was enacted.

This instrument, which was drafted in less than four weeks, was born of out necessity "to do something" to counter the economic crisis.[24] Given that cartels were seen by many as a useful means of structuring the economy, the KartellVO did not declare price-fixing conspiracies and other form of anticompetitive agreements as illegal and void. The German legislature merely allowed for a little more control over the cartel's conduct.[25] Accordingly, the power to terminate cartel agreements by cartel members for good cause was strengthened (§ 8 KartellVO), and a mild form of oversight for potential abuses was established via a special cartel court (§ 9 KartellVO). In addition, the Ministry of Economic Affairs was empowered to have prices and terms reviewed by the courts on the basis of public policy standards (§ 10 KartellVO). Despite its modest scope, the KartellVO was subject to fierce criticism by lawyers, and the *Deutsche Juristentag* of 1928 demanded a long list of changes to strengthen the powers of cartels.[26]

Given the paucity of remedies under the KartellVO, persons affected by the cartels also had to rely on the general provisions of private law to seek justice.

---

[19] On Sombart's teachings, see *Nörr* (n. 7), 70.

[20] *E. Schmalenbach*, Die Betriebswirtschaftslehre an der Schwelle der neuen Wirtschaftsverfassung, Zeitschrift für Handelswissenschaftliche Forschung 22 (1928), 241–251, 241 ff.

[21] *Nörr* (n. 7), 70 f.

[22] *Roth* (n. 4), 16, referring to an estimation of *Metzner*, Industrie- und Handelszeitung, Karlsruhe 27 November 1925. See also *R. Liefmann*, Kartelle und Trusts und die Weiterbildung der volkswirtschaftlichen Organisation (6th edn., 1924), 18 (estimating that thousands of cartels had existed or existed in Germany at the time).

[23] Verordnung gegen Missbrauch wirtschaftlicher Machtstellungen, Reichsgesetzblatt 1923 I, 1067 ff., corrected in Reichsgesetzblatt 1923 I, 1071.

[24] See *Nörr* (n. 7), 54 ff.

[25] See *J. Jickeli*, Das Kartellrecht in der Weimarer Republik – Lehren für das europäische Kartellverbot, in: A. Hoyer et al. (eds.), Gedächtnisschrift für Jörn Eckert (2008), 405–424, 415 ff.

[26] Verhandlungen des Fünfunddreißigsten Deutschen Juristentages 1928 (Salzburg), vol. 2 (1929), 851 f.

Even though the *Reichsgericht* in 1897 had not stopped the cartelisation process by declaring anticompetitive agreements void, it did accept that certain abusive practices of cartels could be prohibited under the general rules of tort and unfair competition law. The leading case was decided in 1931 and concerned exclusionary conduct that today would be scrutinised under predatory pricing standards. Specifically, several large producers of petrol had cooperated to divide Germany into various geographic zones with uniform prices. An independent petrol station that purchased petrol from a foreign competitor had refused to adjust its petrol prices to the level set forth by cartel, so the cartelists ensured that all the petrol stations in the surrounding area undercut the prices of the independent seller. The independent petrol station sued the producers to obtain an injunction. As the predatory pricing strategy could not be stopped on the basis of the KartellVO, given that the cartel merely coordinated their behaviour via an information exchange that was not covered by the cartel concept under the Ordinance (which demanded a legally binding agreement),[27] the *Reichsgericht* had to take recourse to the general clause of unfair competition law as well as to § 826 BGB to find that such anticompetitive conduct was *contra bonos mores*.[28] The court was well aware that price cutting, as such, is the essence of competition and should not be prohibited by the law.[29] But given that particular circumstances of the case, the systematic undercutting was regarded as an unlawful manoeuvre to drive the independent petrol station out of business rather than an instance of lawful price competition. Otherwise, reasoned the German court, an economically healthy outsider confronted by a powerful group of competitors with deep pockets would have no choice but to exit the market or raise its prices to the level of those of the cartel, even if the cartelists because of their higher cost of production could not compete on the merits with the outsider. In declaring the coordinated price cutting as unlawful, the *Reichsgericht* discarded expert opinions by *Rudolf Callmann*,[30] *Rudolf Isay*[31] and *Hans Carl Nipperdey*,[32] three renowned competition law experts who had argued that the price-cutting conduct was lawful.

---

[27] See *Nörr* (n. 7), 96. In addition, undercutting the prices of outsiders was not actionable under Sec. 9 KartVO, see RG, judgment of 9 January 1928, RGZ 119, 366, 369 – Linoleum-Konvention.

[28] RG, judgment of 18 December 1931, RGZ 134, 342, 350 ff. – Benrather Tankstelle.

[29] RG, judgment of 18 December 1931, RGZ 134, 342, 355 – Benrather Tankstelle.

[30] *R. Callmann*, Außenseiter und Kampfpreise, Juristische Wochenschrift 1930, 1647–1650.

[31] *R. Isay*, Der Vernichtungszweck im Wettbewerbsrecht, Gewerblicher Rechtsschutz und Urheberrecht 1929, 1368–1380, 1370 ff.

[32] *H.C. Nipperdey*, Wettbewerb und Existenzvernichtung, Kartell-Rundschau 1930, 127–152.

D. The road towards a modern competition law: changes in economic and legal thinking

After the Nazis came to power, the concentration of power in the economy gained further ground. This collaboration helped the government to control and direct private economic activities. During the course of World War II, the Ministry of Economics even tightened the grip on cartels to ensure a strong platform for war production.[33]

The excesses of economic concentration that were already visible during the Weimar Republic and which reached their peak during the Third Reich led, however, to a shift in economic and legal thinking. At the beginning of the 1930s, a group of scholars centred around the economist *Walter Eucken* and the lawyers *Franz Böhm* and *Hans Großmann-Doerth* established a school of thought which elaborated an economic and legal framework to protect competition and to push back the teachings articulated by the Historic School and related approaches.[34] This circle was referred to as the Freiburg School, as *Eucken* held a chair at the University of Freiburg and *Böhm* started his academic career there before he was later removed from university service for criticising the Nazis' oppression of Jews.[35]

Unlike *Schmoller* and *Kleinwächter*, *Eucken* and *Böhm* were very sceptical about the positive effects of widespread collaboration amongst competitors. They had seen how cartels and monopolies could effectively control competition and eliminate economic freedom of other market players. Therefore, the idea of a limitation of private power through law became one of the key ideas of this line of thought, and later the term "Ordoliberalism" was established as a general term for conceptions of a legal and economic order based on this belief.

The ordoliberal economists rejected the economic justification of cartels and monopolies that had dominated until then. *Eucken* emphasised that the process of competition will be inhibited if private businesses obtain too much economic power over their competitors. Authorities should intervene to ensure free

---

[33] On the competition policy of the Third Reich, see *Nörr* (n. 7), 131 ff.; *A. Pöting*, Die Kartellgesetzgebung als Instrument staatlicher Wirtschaftslenkung im Zeitalter des Nationalsozialismus (2006), 83 ff.

[34] See *F. Böhm/W. Eucken/H. Großmann-Doerth*, Unsere Aufgabe, printed as the preface to: *F. Böhm*, Die Ordnung der Wirtschaft als geschichtliche Aufgabe und rechtsschöpferische Leistung (1937), VII–XXI, IX ff.

[35] On the foundation of the Freiburg School, see *A. Heinemann*, Die Freiburger Schule und ihre geistigen Wurzeln (1989), 8 ff.; *D.J. Gerber,* Constitutionalizing the Economy: German Neo-liberalism, Competition Law and the "New" Europe, The American Journal of Comparative Law 42 (1994), 25–84, 28 ff.

competition and ban economic concentrations as far as possible.[36] One Freiburg economist, *Leonhard Miksch*, even went so far as demanding far reaching public intervention, namely to control *all* dominant firms so that they act "as if" they were controlled by competition,[37] but that view was not shared by other scholars.

To overcome the lack of comprehensive private law regulations directed at stopping anti-competitive conduct, *Böhm*, who had already spoken out sharply against abuses of market power in his habilitation thesis,[38] started to work on a private law doctrine to prevent restrictions of competition. One of his key ideas was that cartels and dominant firms should not be allowed to rely on the principle of freedom of contract, guaranteed under private law, to restrict the freedom of action of other market participants to the detriment of the competitive process.[39]

The sceptical views of the Freiburg scholars regarding cartels and monopolies were matched, to a large extent, by the interests of the Western Allies, above all those of the Americans. In the immediate aftermath of the war there was a strong interest in dissolving German cartels and monopolies, which had greatly promoted the German war economy and the Nazi-regime.[40] Even though the beginning of the Cold War led to a more forgiving view of the Western-German economic structures, the Americans were very firm in their belief that without proper competition law, Western Germany should not be allowed to become a sovereign state.[41] At the same time, some ordoliberal thinkers gained important positions in post-war Germany and tried to

---

[36] *W. Eucken*, Die Wettbewerbsordnung und ihre Verwirklichung, ORDO: Jahrbuch für die Ordnung von Wirtschaft und Gesellschaft 2 (1949), 1–99, 64 ff.; *W. Eucken*, Grundsätze der Wirtschaftspolitik (1952), 334 ff.

[37] *L. Miksch*, Wettbewerb als Aufgabe: Grundsätze einer Wettbewerbsordnung (1947), 98 ff.

[38] See *F. Böhm*, Wettbewerb und Monopolkampf: Eine Untersuchung zur Frage des wirtschaftlichen Kampfrechts und zur Frage der rechtlichen Struktur der geltenden Wirtschaftsordnung (1933).

[39] Over the course of his career, *Böhm* developed different justifications for this general theme, see *K.W. Nörr*, An der Wiege deutscher Identität nach 1945: Franz Böhm zwischen Ordo und Liberalismus (1992), 1 ff.; *E.-J. Mestmäcker*, Das Privatrecht vor den Herausforderungen der wirtschaftlichen Macht, Rabels Zeitschrift für ausländisches und internationales Privatrecht 60 (1996), 58–71, 58 ff.

[40] The agreement reached at the Potsdam Conference in 1945 stated (II B, Economic Principle 12): "At the earliest practicable date, the German economy shall be decentralized for the purpose of eliminating the present excessive concentration of economic power as exemplified in particular by cartels, syndicates, trusts and other monopolistic arrangements". On the deconcentration policy of the Western allies in the direct aftermath of World War II, see *W. Möschel*, Entflechtungen im Recht der Wettbewerbsbeschränkungen (1979), 4 ff.; *L. Murach-Brand*, Antitrust auf deutsch (2004), 42 ff.

[41] For details, see *Murach-Brand* (n. 40), 164 ff.

implement their ideas in the law. A Draft Competition Act[42] was elaborated by a group of experts, including *Böhm*, under the leadership of *Paul Josten,* who had close ties to the Freiburg School.[43] This so-called Josten Draft was presented to the German administration in 1949.[44] As it was, however, in part too interventionist, it did not play a major role in the following negotiations surrounding the first German competition act, the draft of which was essentially worked out by the officials of the German Federal Ministry of Economics and the three Western powers, under the leadership of the US.[45]

When the first modern competition act, the Act Against Restraints of Competition (*Gesetz gegen Wettbewerbsbeschränkungen*, GWB), was passed in 1957 after a very intense debate, it was neither a mere copy of the Sherman Act nor did it reflect the interventionist thinking of some members of the Freiburg School. Rather, the combined efforts of the US coupled with the insights generated by the Freiburg School and other liberal thinkers made it possible to swing the pendulum towards a system that protects free und unfettered competition, but the fierce resistance of the industry meant that these prohibitions were to an extent watered down in the legislative process. For the first time in Germany, however, the law prohibited cartels as a general rule and allowed them only in exceptional cases. In addition, it established a regime to control anticompetitive conduct of dominant firms.

The German GWB was thus a compromise and far from perfect. Two enormous gaps soon became apparent. First, the prohibition of cartels was too narrowly drafted, as only contracts could be regarded as cartel agreements. This led the *Bundesgerichtshof* (Federal Supreme Court) in 1970 to rule that concerted practices on price fixing which did not involve contractual agreement could not be sanctioned under the GWB.[46] This decision was harshly criticised[47] and corrected by the legislature when the German GWB was aligned in

[42] Entwurf zu einem Gesetz zur Sicherung des Leistungswettbewerbs und zu einem Gesetz über das Monopolamt mit Stellungnahme des Sachverständigen-Ausschuss zu einigen grundsätzlichen Fragen der deutschen Monopolgesetzgebung und Minderheitsgutachten, gedruckt im Auftrag des Bundesministers für Wirtschaft (ohne Jahresangabe).

[43] The economist Paul Josten had served in the Ministry of Economic Affairs during the Third Reich and had close contacts with the Freiburg School. After World War II, he became a high-ranking administrator in the German economic administration established in the British and American Sector of Germany, see *Murach-Brand* (n. 40), 107 with n. 130.

[44] On the Josten Draft, see *E. Günther,* Die geistigen Grundlagen des sogenannten Josten-Entwurfs, in: H. Sauermann/E.-J. Mestmäcker (eds.), Wirtschaftsordnung und Staatsverfassung, Festschrift für Franz Böhm zum 80. Geburtstag (1975), 183–204, 187 ff.; *Murach-Brand* (n. 40), 107 ff.; *Nörr* (n. 7), 163 ff.

[45] For details, see *Murach-Brand* (n. 40), 175 ff., 227.

[46] BGH, judgment of 17 December 1970, Gewerblicher Rechtsschutz und Urheberrecht 1971, 276, 279 f. – Teerfarben.

[47] See *W. Möschel,* 70 Jahre deutsche Kartellpolitik: Von RGZ 38, 155 "Sächsisches Holzstoffkartell" zu BGHZ 55, 104 "Teerfarben" (1972), 24 ff.; *K. Schmidt,*

1998 with the European prohibition of anti-competitive agreements (today Art. 101 Treaty on the Functioning of the European Union, TFEU). Second, there was no mechanism to prevent concentrations. This gap was closed 1973 with the introduction of a merger control regime in 1973. As part of this, the Monopolies Commission was established, which is an independent body comprised of mainly lawyers and economists which monitors merger activity in Germany and advises and informs the legislature and the public on competition policy.

III. The interpretation and application of modern competition law: the European economic approach

Around the same time that the German competition order was being established, the European competition rules were being negotiated. The first antitrust rules were laid down in the 1952 Treaty establishing the European Coal and Steel Community. As they reflected the peculiarities of the coal and steel industry, they were not regarded as a blueprint in the negotiations leading to the 1957 Treaty establishing the European Economic Community, which, *inter alia*, set out the prohibition of anticompetitive agreements and of abusive practices of dominant undertakings.[48] Today these rules are enshrined in Art. 101 and 102 TFEU.

After the German and European rules for the protection of competition became effective, *inter alia*, by establishing proper competition authorities and enforcement rules, the interplay between law and economics also assumed a more practical component. The staff of the enforcement authorities, namely the *Bundeskartellamt* and the European Commission, came to consist of lawyers and economists, with both working closely together when judging industry conduct and sanctioning anticompetitive practices. In addition, courts were more often confronted with economic expert opinions. As consequence, the integration of economic theory into competition law became a very practical topic.

A. Post-Chicago economics and beyond

While prior to World War II a large variety of rather heterogeneous economic approaches to competition law existed, over the course of time the leading approaches taught in the US and Europe have become narrower. The prevailing

Wirtschaftsrecht: Nagelprobe des Zivilrechts – Das Kartellrecht als Beispiel, Archiv für die civilistische Praxis 206 (2006), 169–204, 181, with further references.

[48] On the negotiations leading to the European competition rules, see *W. Wurmnest*, Marktmacht und Verdrängungsmissbrauch (2nd edn., 2012), 66 ff.

doctrines for competition policy have to a greater and greater extent been based on neoclassical microeconomic price theory concepts within the area of industrial organisation. As a starting point, these concepts base the analysis of competition problems at the theoretical level strongly on pricing decisions and decide allocation problems based on the efficiency yardstick. Put simply, price theory became very influential in the US with the rise of the so-called Chicago School of economic thought in the 1970s, which analysed competition problems based on rational market actors and a strong belief in the corrective force of markets. What this meant was that this Chicago School advocated for very limited intervention in the market, an approach which can be contrasted with the Harvard School.[49]

Today, the current lines of thought for competition law and policy are typically grouped under the heading "Post-Chicago-Economics" within the research area of modern industrial organisation.[50] These doctrines are based on much more refined sets of analytical tools than those available to the Chicago School in the 1970s. Such Post-Chicago developments include, amongst other things, game-theory insights on the strategic interactions of market participants. As data is more readily available, econometric studies of real-world examples have also gained increasing importance and are today firmly established in modern economic thinking. At least at the theoretical level, Post-Chicago economics are embraced by a broad majority of competition economists.

That mainstream economic doctrine has become narrower does not however mean that there is a broad consensus on competition policy matters. These doctrines are often very abstract, and thus disputes arise on their application to individual cases. In addition, some findings of modern industrial economics are challenged in part by the findings generated by experimental and behavioural economics, to name two important strands of novel research. Experimental economics is testing general assumptions about market behaviour based on experimental studies conducted in the field or in a laboratory with test subjects.[51] Behavioural economics, a field which was strongly advanced by the psychologists *Daniel Kahneman* and *Amos Tversky*,[52] focuses to a large extent on the issue of bounded rationality by integrating insights from psychology and neuroscience into the economic analysis, thereby adapting the results inferred

---

[49] On the views of the competing schools regarding single firm conduct, see *H. Hovenkamp*, The Harvard and Chicago Schools and the Dominant Firm, University of Iowa Legal Studies Research Paper No. 07-19 (2010), available at https://ssrn.com/abstract=1014153 or http://dx.doi.org/10.2139/ssrn.1014153 (last accessed 15 August 2022).

[50] *C. Ewald*, Grundzüge der Wettbewerbsökonomie, in: G. Wiedemann (ed.), Handbuch des Kartellrechts (4th edn., 2020) § 7 para. 8.

[51] On this approach, see *A.E. Roth*, Introduction to Experimental Economics, in: J.H. Kagel/A.E. Roth (eds.), Handbook of Experimental Economics (2020), 3–109.

[52] See *M. Englerth/E.V. Towfigh*, Verhaltensökonomik, in: E.V. Towfigh/N. Petersen (eds.), Ökonomische Methoden im Recht (2nd edn., 2017), § 8 para. 481.

from the *homo oeconomicus* concept.[53] And even *Friedrich von Hayek*'s definition of competition as an "open discovery procedure" ("*Wettbewerb als Entdeckungsverfahren*")[54] and his plea to keep markets open in order to allow for innovation has not been forgotten. Thus, still today, economists may produce different answers to the same questions.[55]

B. The "more economic approach" by the EU Commission

Professional standards have to be updated regularly. This is generally true and applies equally to the economic insights which are used to resolve legal issues. Since the end of the 1990s, the EU Commission has therefore prepared, advocated and finally applied a "more economic approach" to competition law. This shift, in part driven by US influence,[56] precipitated a heated debate on the reach and usefulness of such an approach, especially in Germany.[57] The intensive debate on the more economic approach should, however, not be seen as a fight between those lawyers in favour of the integration of economic thought into the law and those who oppose economic thinking. There is a broad consensus in the antitrust community today that economic insights are indispensable for the analysis of competition law issues.[58] The debate therefore centres around the question how legal and economic criteria can be optimally assembled to form a coherent regime. In this respect, a reasonable compromise between economic theory and the necessities of the law must be found, as it is impossible to create rules against anticompetitive practices whose application comprehen-

---

[53] On this approach, see *C. Jolls/C. Sunstein/R.H. Thaler,* Behavioral Approach to Law and Economics, Stanford Law Review 50 (1998), 1471–1550; *R.B. Korobkin/T.S. Ulen*, Law and Behavioral Science: Removing the Rationality Assumption from Law and Economics, California Law Review 88 (2000), 1053–1144.

[54] *F.A. von Hayek*, Der Wettbewerb als Entdeckungsverfahren (1968).

[55] See, generally, *H. Fleischer*, Informationsasymmetrie im Vertragsrecht: Eine rechtsvergleichende und interdisziplinäre Abhandlung zu Reichweite und Grenzen vertragsschlußbezogener Aufklärungspflichten (2001), 10.

[56] For details, see *B. Wardhaugh*, Competition, Effects and Predictability: Rule of Law and the Economic Approach to Competition (2020), 92 ff.

[57] See the contributions to *D. Schmidtchen/M. Albert/S. Voigt* (eds.), The More Economic Approach to European Competition Law (2007).

[58] See *P. Behrens*, Comment: Controlling dominance or protecting competition: from individual abuses to responsibility for competition, in: H. Ullrich (ed.), The Evolution of European Competition Law: Whose Regulation, Which Competition? (2006), 224–232, 225 f.; *F. Schuhmacher*, Die stärker ökonomisch orientierte Anwendung der Wettbewerbsregeln, in: S. Griller (ed.), Die europäische Wirtschaftsverfassung de lege lata et ferenda (2007), 193–219, 215; *D. Zimmer*, Der rechtliche Rahmen für die Implementierung moderner ökonomischer Ansätze, Wirtschaft und Wettbewerb 2007, 1198–1209, 1206; *W.-H. Roth*, The "More Economic Approach" and the Rule of Law, in: Schmidtchen et al. (n. 57), 37–57, 54 ff.; *R. Podszun/S. Kreifels*, Digital Platforms and Competition Law, Journal of European Consumer and Market Law 2016, 33–39, 34 ff.

sively reflects economic findings in each individual case, serves legal certainty and can be enforced at reasonable cost.[59]

The term "more economic approach" is slightly misleading as it is not necessarily about "more" economics but also concerns the integration of modern economic theories of harm into the interpretation and application of the law.[60]

A first characteristic of this new approach is a stronger emphasis on consumer welfare as the primary goal of competition law. This change counters the often alleged critique that European competition law prohibits pro-competitive practices in order to protect competitors instead of competition.[61]

Second, the European Commission stresses the need to analyse the actual or at least the likely effects of the conduct in question on the market and consumers to a greater extent than was done before ("effects based approach"). Critics have often alleged that under EU law, a "formalistic" approach prevailed,[62] especially with regard to the block regulation exemptions[63] and the field of exclusionary conduct.[64] Merely looking at the form of conduct has the danger that pro-competitive conduct can be banned although it benefits consumers and competition.

Third, the EU Commission seeks to analyse efficiency considerations in more detail and avoid far-reaching presumptions of illegality. On a more theoretical level, modern insights of competition economics should be integrated into the framework, and on a more practical level the advantages for consumers and competition must be taken into account when judging particular conduct ("efficiency defence").

At an institutional level, the European Commission established the position of chief competition economist within the Directorate-General for Competition; this individual – together with his or her team – is charged with providing sound economic advice for general policy initiatives as well as with regard to

---

[59] *Wurmnest* (n. 48), 230.

[60] *D. Zimmer*, Law and Economics im Recht der Wettbewerbsbeschränkungen, in: Studienvereinigung Kartellrecht e.V. (ed.), Kartellrecht in Theorie und Praxis: Festschrift für Cornelis Canenbley zum 70. Geburtstag (2012), 525–535, 533.

[61] On this critique, see *R. O'Donoghue/J. Padilla*, The Law and Economics of Article 102 TFEU (3rd edn., 2020), 89.

[62] See *R.J. Van den Bergh/P.D. Camesasca*, European Competition Law and Economics: A Comparative Perspective (2nd edn., 2006), 1: "For a long time, European competition law was permeated by legal formalism."

[63] See *E. Bueren*, Der "New economic approach" der Kommission für horizontale und vertikale Wettbewerbsbeschränkungen, Wettbewerb in Recht und Praxis 2004, 567–575, 567.

[64] See *Competition Law Forum Article 82 Review Group*, The Reform of Article 82: Recommendations on Key Policy, European Competition Journal 1 (2005), 179–183, 180 ff.; *E. Rousseva*, Rethinking Exclusionary Abuses in EU Competition Law (2010), 200.

case enforcement.[65] At the national level, equivalent positions have been created, for example in the *Bundeskartellamt*.

The "more economic approach" was first applied to restrictive practices under Art. 101 TFEU, with the adoption of block exemption regulations and corresponding guidelines which took greater notice of the potential effects of agreements.[66] With the adoption of the Merger Regulation 139/2004, this approach was also applied to merger control.[67] The new regime introduced the SIEC-test in lieu of the market dominance test without, however, abandoning the latter criterion completely.[68] Furthermore, the analysis is based on forecasting effects of the merger based on empirical models, and an efficiency defence was created, according to which a merger can be cleared despite a dominant position on the market if the companies can show that their merger generates efficiencies which outweigh the adverse effects of the merger on competition.[69] The modernisation process was complemented by adapted guidelines.[70] Finally, the "more economic approach" was expanded to the application of Art. 102 TFEU. As abusive practices of dominant firms are one of the most disputed areas of competition law, it was no surprise that opinions differed significantly on the question of the extent to which the prerequisites for sanctioning such practices should be adapted. After a very intense debate, also occurring within the European Commission, guidance on the Commission's enforcement priorities in applying Art. 102 TFEU to abusive exclusionary conduct by dominant undertakings was adopted.[71]

---

[65] On the tasks of the chief competition economist, see *L.-H. Röller*, Economic Analysis and Competition Policy Enforcement in Europe, in: P.A.G. van Bergeijk/E. Kloosterhuis (eds.), Modelling European Mergers: Theory, Competition Policy and Case Studies (2005), 13–26, 16 f.

[66] For details, see *Wardhaugh* (n. 56), 95 ff.

[67] Council Regulation (EC) No 139/2004 of 20 January 2004 on the control of concentrations between undertakings (the EC Merger Regulation), Official Journal of the European Union 2004 L 24/1.

[68] *D. Zimmer*, Significant Impediment to Effective Competition: Das neue Untersagungskriterium der EU-Fusionskontrollverordnung, Zeitschrift für Wettbewerbsrecht 2 (2004), 250–267, 250 ff.; *A. Christiansen*, Der "More Economic Approach" in der EU-Fusionskontrolle (2010), 84 ff.

[69] See Recital 29 Merger Regulation.

[70] Guidelines on the assessment of horizontal mergers under the Council Regulation on the control of concentrations between undertakings, Official Journal of the European Union 2004 C 31/5; on these guidelines, see *Christiansen* (n. 68), 83 ff.

[71] Communication from the Commission, Guidance on the Commission's enforcement priorities in applying Article 82 of the EC Treaty to abusive exclusionary conduct by dominant undertakings, Official Journal of the European Union 2009 C 45/7.

C. Economic insights and the rule of law

What makes life for lawyers very difficult is the fact that mainstream economics constantly evolves and even insights propagated by leading voices in the field may change over a span of time that, from a legal perspective, is relatively short. In addition, competing theories may offer different solutions. The reception of economic knowledge must therefore be understood as a continuous process, and caution should be exercised before broad changes are carried out. Usually, novel economic arguments are first examined by scholars and the competition authorities. Later, these insights may be incorporated into the existing legal framework by the courts, exercising the necessary caution.[72] Once a certain economic concept has found its way into the law, the peculiarities of the rule of law apply ("*Eigengesetzlichkeiten des juristischen Entscheidungsprozesses*"[73]). The interpretation and application of legal rules is based on a degree of stability, as certainty and predictability are key components of the rule of law.[74] As a result, when a decision has been delivered by the highest court, competition authorities and lower courts will apply this precedent (or the rule contained therein) to comparable settings. If it becomes apparent that the economic theory on which a certain legal decision was based might be flawed in light of new insights, the antitrust authorities can correct their sanctioning practice relatively quickly. By contrast, it will take much longer for the courts to depart from an established line of case law. In such a scenario there is however, at least in the long run, no other path than to overrule an established precedent. Otherwise, the law would degenerate into a storage medium for outdated economic theory.[75] Nevertheless, this process of adaptation will always be slower than the development of economic knowledge (and certainly too slow from the perspective of economists).[76]

A further problem is the question of which economic theory enforcers and courts should be relying on. In this context it needs to be underscored that economics is not a "hard" science. Rather all theories are based on assumptions which can produce different outcomes. In addition, some approaches have been developed for general application whereas others can only offer insights in very specific settings. Against this background, lawyers need to pragmatically evaluate the economic arguments in light of the given market circumstances and

---

[72] *L.A. Sullivan/W.S. Grimes*, The Law of Antitrust. An Integrated Handbook (2nd edn., 2006), 21.

[73] This expression is attributed to Max Weber, see *H. Fleischer*, Behinderungsmißbrauch durch Produktinnovation: Eine ökonomische und juristische Analyse zum deutschen, europäischen und amerikanischen Kartellrecht (1997), 104.

[74] *Wardhaugh* (n. 56), 40.

[75] *Wurmnest* (n. 48), 234 f.

[76] *Wurmnest* (n. 48), 235.

the facts of the case at hand.[77] Which pieces of economic thought are integrated into the law is thus a genuine legal question.[78]

Competition law cannot focus exclusively on the economic perspective of the individual case but must also keep institutional aspects in mind. Authorities and courts must remain functional. It must be possible to enforce antitrust law within a reasonable time span, and those subject to the law must be able to predict, at least to a certain extent, when their conduct will infringe the law. Thus, legal rules must be framed in a way that courts and administrative bodies can apply them. This not only requires that economic standards of proof are not overly complex, but also that rules are shaped in a way to provide some ex ante guidance on appropriate commercial conduct.[79]

Having said this, it is also necessary to note that the more simply a legal rule is structured, the more its accuracy will decrease, and this can lead to the wrong economic results. Therefore, it is critical to factor in the risks and potential costs to the competitive process that arise from such enforcement errors. Such errors may include over-enforcement by prohibiting pro-competitive conduct (type I error) or under-enforcement by leaving anti-competitive conduct unsanctioned (type II error). The more detrimental a practice is to competition, the more serious the competitive consequences of an economically wrong decision.[80] An approach which incorporates this thinking helps in structuring legal rules even though measuring the precise cost for competition occurring from such errors is not possible.[81]

D. Predatory pricing as an example

I. Two influential cases from the US Supreme Court

Striking the right balance between economic insights and legal needs has been particularly vigorously debated with regard to predatory pricing, i.e. below-cost pricing strategies by firms aimed at driving out or disciplining competitors.[82] This debate was strongly influenced by developments in the US. To

[77] *H. Fleischer/K.U. Schmolke/D. Zimmer*, Verhaltensökonomik als Forschungsinstrument für das Wirtschaftsrecht, in: H. Fleischer/D. Zimmer (eds.), Beitrag der Verhaltensökonomie (Behavioral Economics) zum Handels- und Wirtschaftsrecht (2011), 9–62, 45.

[78] See, generally, *H.-D. Assmann*, Die Transformationsprobleme des Privatrechts und die Ökonomische Analyse des Rechts, in: idem et al. (eds.), Ökonomische Analyse des Rechts (1993), 17–61, 60; *Fleischer/Schmolke/Zimmer* (n. 77), 45.

[79] *Wardhaugh* (n. 56), 217.

[80] *E.-J. Mestmäcker*, Der verwaltete Wettbewerb: Eine vergleichende Untersuchung über den Schutz von Freiheit und Lauterkeit im Wettbewerbsrecht (1984), 98.

[81] *C. Ewald*, Ökonomie im Kartellrecht: Vom more economic approach zu sachgerechten Standards forensischer Ökonomie, Zeitschrift für Wettbewerbsrecht 9 (2011), 15–47, 19: "rechts- und wettbewerbspolitische Spielräume".

[82] For reasons of space, this chapter does not deal in detail with exclusionary conduct of dominant firms by means of above-cost pricing.

better understand its origins, it is important to consider two leading cases of the US Supreme Court that spurred the economic debate on predatory prices and also had a strong impact on the incorporation of economic insights into legal thinking.

In 1911, the US Supreme Court condemned the Standard Oil Trust for an unlawful predatory pricing strategy. The dominant trust had established ways to quite accurately estimate the production and transport costs of its competitors, and this enabled it to offer its products in all sales regions at prices just below those of its competitors. In some cases these prices were below Standard's own cost of supply. The Supreme Court regarded this pricing policy as anti-competitive and an unlawful market monopolisation.[83]

As undercutting a competitor's prices is, however, the essence of competition, condemning low prices as unlawful has the potential to hamper price competition. An example of such an economically unsound judgment can be found in the US Supreme Court's decision in *Utah Pie Co. v. Continental Baking Co.* of 1967. The case concerned a local price war between a regional supplier of frozen pies and its much larger competitors that operated across the entire US market. The local supplier, which sold its products exclusively in Utah and neighbouring states, held around two-thirds of the relevant market, whereas the three national competitors each had a very small share of the market in Utah. When the three competitors undercut the prices of the local supplier in Utah in an attempt to challenge this dominance, the latter sued them for damages and was successful. Since the national producers deliberately undercut prices and acted with the intention of enlarging their position at the expense of the local supplier, the Supreme Court found the pricing strategy to be unlawful price discrimination.[84] The absurdity of this finding is obvious. By relying on predatory intent inferred from internal statements of the defendants, the Supreme Court protected a medium-sized supplier against competition without explaining why the price cuts were harming competition as a whole and not only the challenged competitor.[85]

2. *Competing economic doctrines*

Unsound judgments like *Utah Pie* have fuelled calls for a stronger economic justification for the classification of low prices as predatory. Some proponents of the Chicago School even questioned whether predatory pricing should be banned at all. As far back as 1958, *John S. McGee* published an influential article in which he argued that the *Standard Oil Trust* case was wrongly

---

[83] *Standard Oil Co. of New Jersey v. United States*, 221 US 1 (1911).

[84] *Utah Pie Co. v. Continental Baking Co.*, 386 US 685, 696 ff. (1967).

[85] See the critique voiced by *W.S. Bowman*, Restraint of Trade by the Supreme Court: The Utah Pie Case, The Yale Law Journal 77 (1967), 70–85.

decided.[86] He argued that pricing below cost will not hamper competition but merely harm the firm resorting to such a strategy. Not only will such a step result in the loss of a considerable amount of money during the low price campaign, it also has literally no chance to recoup these losses after having pushed competitors out of the market as new entries will prevent supra-competitive prices. Such a pricing policy is therefore “foolish”.[87] This conclusion was seconded by *Roland H. Koller*, whose study of the cases decided up to 1970 concluded that predatory pricing was essentially a myth as it was hardly ever successful.[88] Against this background, *Robert Bork* offered the following summary in his general critique of the US antitrust law enforcement policy:

> “It seems unwise […] to construct rules about a phenomenon that probably does not exist or which, should it exist in very rare cases, the courts would have grave difficulty distinguishing from competitive price behavior.”[89]

That predatory prices are always irrational was, however, not supported by the empirical evidence.[90] Despite this, *McGee*’s position remained influential in the economic literature for a long time no major economic theory countered the Chicago School model with a rigorous model as to why it would indeed be economically rational for a market participant to engage in predatory pricing.[91] Things changed significantly in the 1980s with the advent of modern industrial economics and game theory models. Building on the work of *David M. Kreps* and *Robert Wilson*[92] as well as that of *Paul Milgrom* and *John Roberts*,[93] game theory could demonstrate that the use of predatory pricing tactics can pay off for market-dominant companies in various scenarios. Losses sustained by below-cost prices cannot be recouped by later supra-competitive prices alone, but the dominant market player may also benefit from a deterrence effect or from

---

[86] *J.S. McGee*, Predatory Price Cutting: The Standard Oil (NJ) Case, Journal of Law and Economics 1 (1958), 137–169.

[87] *McGee* (n. 86), 168: “I am convinced that Standard did not systematically, if ever, use local price cutting in retailing, or anywhere else, to reduce competition. To do so would have been foolish; and, whatever else has been said about them, the old Standard organization was seldom criticized for making less money when it could readily have made more.”

[88] *R.H. Koller*, The Myth of Predatory Pricing: An Empirical Study, Antitrust Law & Economics Review 4/4 (1971), 105–123.

[89] *R.H. Bork*, The Antitrust Paradox: A Policy at War With Itself (1978), 154.

[90] See *A. Edlin*, Predatory Pricing (2012), 22 ff., available at https://works.bepress.com/aaron_edlin/74 (last accessed 15 August 2022). *Edlin* concludes (at 24): “What is learned from this empirical evidence? Even if one takes a narrow view of predatory pricing and considers only below cost pricing as candidates for predation, the view that predation is as rare as dragons is not born of the empirical evidence.”

[91] *Fleischer* (n. 73), 61.

[92] *D.M. Kreps/R. Wilson*, Reputation and Imperfect Information, Journal of Economic Theory 27 (1982), 253–279.

[93] *P. Milgrom/J. Roberts*, Predation, Reputation, and Entry Deterrence, Journal of Economic Theory 27/2 (1982), 280–312. On these studies, see *Fleischer* (n. 73), 62 f.

disciplining competitors. The – thus far very limited – findings of experimental and behavioural economics confirm that predatory pricing indeed may pay off.[94]

But *Utah Pie* also led the proponents of the Harvard School to develop a more sophisticated standard of analysis. In 1975, *Phillip Areeda* and *Donald F. Turner* published an article which formed the basis of a two-prong test to separate unlawful predatory prices from pro-competitive price-cuts, which was later elaborated in more detail.[95] To succeed, *Areeda* and *Turner* argued, the plaintiff must prove that the predatory firm's prices are for a substantial amount of sales below the relevant measure of cost and that there is a market structure from which the predatory firm can reasonably anticipate to recoup its sustained losses through supra-competitive prices after its rivals have been eliminated. As the relevant measure of cost, *Areeda* and *Turner* suggested average variable cost (AVC) measured over a relatively short time span as a proxy for marginal costs. Even though this two-prong test may at first sight look simple and clear, this proves not to be the case. The allocation of costs into the categories of fixed and variable is to a certain extent based on subjective choices and depends on the time span one looks at. Put simply, in the long run all costs are variable.[96] As a result, many other measures of cost have been proposed, such as average avoidable cost, average total cost and long-run average incremental cost – none of which, however, have overcome the application problems.[97] In addition, basing the recoupment test merely on a calculation of sacrificed losses and measurable future gains does not adequately reflect the (newer) findings of Post-Chicago economics, which argue that the economic viability of a predation strategy can also result from disciplining competitors (even on other markets) or from deterring entry by newcomers.[98]

Summing up, today most economists agree that predatory pricing can make economic sense provided that certain market conditions are met. In the following section, the application of these findings by courts in the US and in the EU are analysed.

3. The reception in the United States

(a) In the US, the economic critique ignited by *Utah Pie* led the Supreme Court to adapt a very strict approach towards predatory pricing. In *Brooke Group*, the

---

[94] *Wurmnest* (n. 48), 382 ff.

[95] *P. Areeda/D.F. Turner*, Predatory Pricing and Related Practices Under Section 2 of the Sherman Act, Harvard Law Review 88 (1975), 697–733.

[96] *H. Fleischer*, Gezielte Kampfpreisunterbietung im Recht der Vereinigten Staaten – Der Supreme Court zwischen Chicago School und Post-Chicago Economics, Wirtschaft und Wettbewerb 1995, 796–808, 800 f.; *O'Donoghue/Padilla* (n. 61), 359.

[97] For details see *Wurmnest* (n. 48), 392 ff.

[98] For details see *Wurmnest* (n. 48), 408 ff.

US Supreme Court essentially embraced a price/cost-approach coupled with a very strict recoupment test. These prerequisites apply regardless of whether the action is based on Sec. 2(a) Clayton Act as amended by the Robinson-Patman Act or on the prohibition of market monopolisation as prohibited by Sec. 2 Sherman Act.[99] In *Weyerhaeuser*, a case of predatory buying, this strict test was confirmed in 2007.[100]

(b) With regard to the relevant measure of cost, the Supreme Court did not embrace a certain cost standard, as the parties to the dispute in *Brooke Group* agreed that the relevant measure of cost is AVC.[101] And at the Court of Appeal level the applicable standard is disputed. Many courts rely on standards that are proxies for marginal cost, such as AVC,[102] and regard prices above the average total cost (ATC) as *per se* legal.[103] And though it is disputed at the Court of Appeal level whether prices between AVC and ATC are legal or illegal, even the courts which accept that prices above AVC can in certain instances be unlawful apply very strict standards of proof.[104] All in all, the *Areeda/Turner* price/cost-approach is thus very influential in the US.

(c) Regarding the second prong of the recoupment requirement, it is worth noting that in the earlier *Matsushita* case the Supreme Court had already been very sceptical of successful predation strategies. Referring, *inter alia*, to Chicago School commentators, the court pointed out that "there is a consensus among commentators that predatory pricing schemes are rarely tried, and even more rarely successful."[105] Also in *Brooke Group*, the plaintiff lost because recoupment could not be proven. However, this case concerned a very special setting. The dispute concerned a price war in the cigarette industry following the launch of a generic brand by the plaintiff (Liggett, later renamed Brooke Group), a small cigarette producer with a market share of around 3%. This firm sued its competitor Brown & Williamson, which had a market share of around 10%, for damages arising from unlawful predatory pricing. Given that the market share of the defendant was so low, it was hard so see how a price war could damage competition. The market was, however, characterised by a rather stable oligopolistic structure. Liggett therefore argued that the defendant engaged in the low-price policy to obtain a market share that would give it the price leadership in the oligopoly. Once it had secured that position, the price of no-name cigarettes was to be gradually increased in order to make the cheap brands

---

[99] *Brooke Group Ltd. v. Brown & Williamson Tobacco Corp.*, 509 US 209, 222 f.

[100] *Weyerhaeuser Co. v. Ross-Simmons Hardwood Lumber Co.*, 127 SCt 1069 ff. (2007).

[101] *Brooke Group Ltd. v. Brown & Williamson Tobacco Corp.*, 509 US 209, 222 with n. 1 (1993).

[102] See *Arthur S. Langenderfer, Inc. v. S.E. Johnson Co.*, 729 F2d 1050, 1058 (6th Cir. 1984); *International Travel Arrangers v. NWA, Inc.*, 991 F2d 1389, 1399 (8th Cir. 1993).

[103] *International Travel Arrangers v. NWA, Inc.*, 991 F2d 1389, 1396 (8th Cir. 1993).

[104] For details, see *Wurmnest* (n. 48), 424 f.

[105] *Matsushita Elec. Indus. Co. v. Zenith Radio*, 475 US 574, 589 (1986).

unattractive to consumers and to keep the high profit margins for branded cigarettes. Given the oligopolistic structure in the cigarette industry, the defendant could rely on the behaviour of the other competitors, so that losses from the price war could be recouped through profits in the brand segment. Even though the Supreme Court did not rule out that a recoupment through oligopolistic behaviour was feasible, it underscored the various difficulties of concerted price increases.[106] The majority of the Supreme Court justices therefore found that the evidence presented by the plaintiff was not sufficient to demonstrate the likelihood of such a form of recoupment so that the lower court was right to dismiss the action "as a matter of law" without involving the jury.[107]

(d) US courts deciding on predatory pricing after *Brooke Group* have also relied regularly on the recoupment requirement as a tool to dismiss actions as a matter of law.[108] To understand the procedural implication of this decision, it is worth noting that in the US private enforcement of antitrust law is very strong. The prospect of treble damages coupled with other incentives make claims attractive.[109] Sometimes cases come before the courts that have limited chances of success. Under US procedural law the jury decides on the merits of the claim and – especially – the amount of damages sustained. Before the trial starts the defendant can, however, petition to the court to dismiss the action without proceeding before the jury. Such a motion is granted if the evidence shows there is no genuine dispute as to any material facts such that a fact-finder would not be able to enter a judgment against the party making the motion to dismiss.[110] Deciding a case "as a matter of law" is thus a procedural tool by which judges can strike out apparently unfounded cases. The importance of *Brooke Group* lies in the fact that the hurdle for relying on this instrument was set rather low.

Even though the recoupment test is a barrier that is very difficult to overcome for plaintiffs, courts are nevertheless slowly retreating from the irrationality postulate voiced by the Chicago School. The 10th Circuit has recognised that modern economic thinking has concluded that predatory pricing strategies are much more likely to occur than argued by Chicago economists, so that a slightly more relaxed interpretation of the recoupment test seems in order:

---

[106] *Brooke Group Ltd. v. Brown & Williamson Tobacco Corp.*, 509 US 209, 240 ff. (1993).

[107] The three dissenting judges argued that there was considerable evidence of the existence of an unlawful predation strategy such that the action could not be dismissed "as a matter of law" but should have been decided by the jury, see *Brooke Group Ltd. v. Brown & Williamson Tobacco Corp.*, 509 US 209, 254 ff. (1993).

[108] For details, see *Wurmnest* (n. 48), 436 ff.

[109] On the US system of private enforcement, see *C.A. Jones*, Private Enforcement of Antitrust Law in the EU, UK and USA (1999), 80 f.

[110] See Rule 56 Federal Rules of Civil Procedure.

"Recent scholarship has challenged the notion that predatory pricing schemes are implausible and irrational. [...] Post-Chicago economists have theorized that price predation is not only plausible, but profitable, especially in a multi-market context where predation can occur in one market and recoupment can occur rapidly in other markets. [...] Although this court approaches the matter with caution, we do not do so with the incredulity that once prevailed."[111]

(e) Summing up, the reception of economic insights by the courts in the US has led to a test that focuses very much on type I errors. To avoid over-enforcement by prohibiting pro-competitive price cuts, courts have embraced a very narrow test. This caution can be explained in part by the influence of Chicago School thinking, but it seems to me that the particularities of the private enforcement system have played a much stronger role. In addition, novel economic thinking makes its way rather slowly into the court rooms, and as a consequence the chances for harmed plaintiffs to obtain relief from the courts remain very low.

4. The reception in Europe

The discussion in the US also influenced the reception of economic ideas into the law in Germany and Europe. Put simply, the Chicago School did not receive much acclaim in Europe. Thus, the argument that predatory pricing may not harm competition was not strongly voiced on this side of the Atlantic. In addition, as the European Commission only started to sanction predatory pricing abuses by dominant firms in the 1980s, the experiences gained in the US could be considered when shaping the application of the European competition rules. The US approach was not followed. Rather, the Commission and the European courts took a more critical stand on (selective) price cuts by dominant firms. The major differences between the European approach and the US approach can be summarised as follows:

(a) A first difference relates to the reliance on price/cost standards. Even though the *Areeda/Turner* rule was discussed in Europe, the European Court of Justice (ECJ) did not apply it with the same rigour as many of the courts in the US. The ECJ held in *AKZO* that prices of a dominant firm below AVC are to be regarded as predatory. The Court held that a

"dominant undertaking has no interest in applying such prices except that of eliminating competitors so as to enable it subsequently to raise its prices by taking advantage of its monopolistic position, since each sale generates a loss, namely the total amount of the fixed costs (that is to say, those which remain constant regardless of the quantities produced) and, at least, part of the variable costs relating to the unit produced."[112]

This measure of cost is, however, not regarded as the sole benchmark in testing for abusive conduct. Prices within the range of AVC and ATC can also be

[111] *United States v. AMR Corp.*, 335 F3d 1109, 1112 und 1114 f. (10th Cir. 2003).

[112] ECJ, judgment of 3 July 1991, Case C-62/86, ECR 1991 I-3359 para. 71 – AKZO/Commission.

unlawful if a plan for eliminating competitors can be proven. Such prices, explained the Court, "can drive from the market undertakings which are perhaps as efficient as the dominant undertaking but which, because of their smaller financial resources, are incapable of withstanding the competition waged against them."[113]

Integrating "predatory intent", i.e. the plan to eliminate a competitor, into the analysis bears the danger of coming to false conclusions as reached in *Utah Pie*. This risk is heightened if the *AKZO* judgment is read in a way that creates a presumption that a proven plan can be effectively implemented to the detriment of competition without looking further at the specific features of the market.[114] This threat has, however, not materialised because the Commission in its recent decision practice has relied on very strong evidence and not only on isolated statements of the management.[115] If the predatory pricing strategy cannot be proven directly with internal documents, the anti-competitive intentions can also be shown by looking at the specific factors of the pricing policy to show that the low-price strategy makes no commercial sense for the dominant form or is profitable only if it achieves an anticompetitive goal.[116] In this context the effect of the pricing strategy on the market needs to be taken into account to ensure that the low prices actually do harm competition and not only competitors.

It is worth noting that enforcement practice adapted the relevant measure of cost to reflect the unique aspects of the industries in question. The idea behind the adaptation is that dominant firms must be stopped from driving out competitors that are, in principle, as efficient as the predatory firm.[117] Accordingly, the *Tetra Pak* judgment, in which the ECJ held that prices below AVC must always be regarded as unlawful,[118] is too strict[119] and is no longer to be regarded as good law. The Tribunal of First Instance correctly softened this rule to a rebuttable presumption by holding that "prices below [AVC] give grounds for

---

[113] ECJ, judgment of 3 July 1991, Case C-62/86, ECR 1991 I-3359 para. 72 – AKZO/Commission.

[114] Cf. ECJ, judgment of 3 July 1991, Case C-62/86, ECR 1991 I-3359 para. 72 – AKZO/Commission.

[115] See, e.g., European Commission, decision of 16 July 2003, COMP/38.233, paras. 110 ff. – Wanadoo Interactive.

[116] TFI, judgment of 6 October 1994, Case T-83/91, ECR 1994, II-755 para. 151 – Tetra Pak/Commission; TFI, judgment of 30 January 2007, Case T-340/03, ECR 2007, II-107 para. 197 – France Télécom/Commission.

[117] ECJ, judgment of 27 March 2012, Case C-209/10, ECLI:EU:C:2012:172 para. 38 – Post Danmark/Konkurrencerådet.

[118] ECJ, judgment of 14 November 1996, Case C-333/94 P, ECR 1996, I-5951 para. 41 – Tetra Pak/Commission.

[119] *O'Donoghue/Padilla* (n. 61), 368.

assuming that a pricing practice is eliminatory".[120] The ECJ as well has subsequently hinted that dominant firms may have reasons to price below some measures of cost.[121] In its guidance notice on Art. 102 TFEU, the Commission therefore states that it will usually take the average avoidable cost as a starting point, and it reasons further that only pricing below long run average incremental cost is capable of foreclosing efficient competitors from the market.[122] The applied cost standards thus reflect novel economic insights quite well.

(b) The second important difference in comparison to US law regards the recoupment criterion. The European Court of Justice held in *Tetra Pak* that "in the circumstances of the present case" it is not necessary "to require […] proof that Tetra Pak had a realistic chance of recouping its losses."[123] This is a remarkable statement because the sanctioned dominant firm relied on *Brooke Group* to argue that its prices were lawful[124] – ultimately to no avail. In *France Telecom*, the ECJ confirmed that under EU law no recoupment test is necessary to condemn price cuts as abusive.[125] That does not, however, preclude the Commission from assessing "the possibility of recoupment of losses" when considering the economic rationality of the below-cost pricing.[126] In its guidance notice on Art. 102 TFEU, the Commission also does not advocate a strict recoupment test but instead seeks to prove likely foreclosure effects with structural considerations such as high entry barriers.[127] In addition, the enforcement authority underscores the necessity of taking into account the findings of Post-Chicago economics. For example, the notice refers to the possibility of dominant firms using low prices to influence the expectations of potential entrants or to deter entry by acquiring the reputation of being a predator.[128]

(c) A third difference between US law and the European practice is that under EU law "above-cost" pricing is not *per se* legal, even though such prices

---

[120] TFI, judgment of 30 January 2007, Case T-340/03, ECR 2007, II-107 para. 130 – France Télécom/Commission.

[121] ECJ, judgment of 2 April 2009, Case C-202/07 P, ECR 2009, I-2369, para. 111 – France Télécom/Commission; ECJ, judgment of 27 March 2012, Case C-209/10, ECLI:EU:C:2012:172 paras. 40 f. – Post Danmark/Konkurrencerådet.

[122] Communication from the Commission (n. 71), paras. 64, 67.

[123] ECJ, judgment of 14 November 1996, Case C-333/94 P, ECR 1996 I-5951 para. 44 – Tetra Pak/Commission.

[124] The applicant relied on *Brooke Group* before the TFI, but the Tribunal held that "it is not necessary to demonstrate specifically that the undertaking in question had a reasonable prospect of recouping losses so incurred", see TFI, judgment of 6 October 1994, Case T-83/91, ECR 1994 II-755 paras. 143, 150 – Tetra Pak/Commission.

[125] ECJ, judgment of 2 April 2009, Case C-202/07 P, ECR 2009, I-2369, para. 110 – France Télécom/Commission.

[126] ECJ, judgment of 2 April 2009, Case C-202/07 P, ECR 2009, I-2369, para. 111 – France Télécom/Commission.

[127] Communication from the Commission (n. 71), para. 70.

[128] Communication from the Commission (n. 71), para. 68.

have only been prohibited in very specific circumstances.[129] For example, in *Compagnie maritime belge*, a liner conference that was exempted under a block exemption regulation selectively cut prices for transport services for those ships matching the schedule of a newcomer that competed with the conference. The European Court of Justice held that the shipping cartel intended a dual benefit from this strategy: first, to eliminate "the principal, and possibly the only, means of competition open to the competing undertaking" and, second, to "continue to require its users to pay higher prices for the services which are not threatened by that competition".[130] Without generally ruling on the right of the liner conference to meet competition by cutting prices, the Court underscored that

> "the conduct at issue here is that of a conference having a share of over 90% of the market in question and only one competitor. The appellants have, moreover, never seriously disputed, and indeed admitted at the hearing, that the purpose of the conduct complained of was to eliminate [the newcomer] from the market."[131]

Summing up, the reception of economic thinking in Europe has paid much more attention to type II errors. This development has been influenced by various factors. One factor is certainly that the Chicago School never gained much ground in Europe, and therefore the irrationality argument had hardly any impact in Europe. Another factor might be that the law of predatory pricing was shaped much later in Europe, at a time when on the one hand the irrationality argument was already on the decline and on the other hand it was apparent that *Utah Pie* was wrongly decided. In addition, home grown problems have shaped the course of legal development by the courts. Whereas in Europe only dominant firms can be sanctioned for predatory pricing, under US law, the Robinson-Patman Act can apply to non-dominant firms. Coupled with a strong private enforcement system, it seems that safeguards against type I errors are less important under EU law as compared to US law.

IV. Lessons to be learned from the modern interplay between law and economics

A. Lesson no. 1: Competition law must be based on sound legal concepts

There can be no doubt that the early cooperation between law and economics was a disaster for competition and consumers. The *Historische Schule* was

[129] For details, see *O'Donoghue/Padilla* (n. 61), 404 ff.

[130] ECJ, judgment of 16 March 2000, Joined Cases C-395/96 P and C-396/96 P, ECR 2000, I-1365, para. 117 – Compagnie maritime belge transports/Commission.

[131] ECJ, judgment of 16 March 2000, Joined Cases C-395/96 P and C-396/96 P, ECR 2000, I-1365, para. 119 – Compagnie maritime belge transports/Commission.

beholden to the idea that the economy should be governed by private actors, as had been the case with guilds and other institutions, without adequately considering the devastating effect of such structures on consumers and firms not participating in the arrangement. Over the years, the negative side effects of such economic structures became clearly visible. Unfortunately, even in the Weimar Republic the economic belief in a private ordering of the market remained strong. Although the impact of the *Historische Schule* faded, new economic justifications came up to defend the cartel movement. It would, however, be wrong to blame Germany's failure to develop a modern competition law before World War II on economists alone. The legal profession, too, played its part in the drama. First, lawyers and courts too readily absorbed economic thoughts in favour of a private ordering of the market instead of developing a system to constrain economic power based on the rule of law. As the legal historian *Knut Wolfgang Nörr* has put it:

> "We can see that the legal profession sought and found justifications for cartel conduct in neighbouring sciences. Cartels, lawyers were taught, were children of the times, witnesses of modern development, and the dawn of a new economic phase. But is this sufficient to approve cartels from a legal point of view? Were they also from a legal perspective children of their time, did they reflect modern developments in the legal system?"[132]

Unfortunately, these questions were not at the forefront of the legal debate even though the regulation of economic power is a fitting task for the legal profession. Thus, the law can take up insights from other disciplines but only as far legal principles allow. In this respect, legal scholars and courts do not deserve much credit for their actions up to the end of the Weimar Republic. The debate focused too greatly on the rights of cartels to rely on freedom of contract and the so-called internal perspective of the contract, i.e. the relationship between the cartel and its members. Only where the stipulations restricted a contractual party excessively would the contract be declared void. That unlawful restrictions of competition by agreement also have an effect on the market was a legal issue that was discovered rather late; one can even say: too late.[133] Even though the *Reichsgericht* hinted in the Saxon wood pulp cartel case of 1897 that not all cartel agreements are enforceable and named as examples cartels aiming at a "real monopoly" and a "usurious exploitation" of consumers,[134]

---

[132] *Nörr* (n. 7), 71: "Wir sehen also, dass die Juristen bei den Nachbarwissenschaften Rechtfertigungen für die Kartelle suchten und fanden. Kartelle, so ließen sie sich gern belehren, seien Kinder der Zeit, Zeugen der modernen Entwicklung, und mit ihnen bräche der Morgen einer neuen Wirtschaftsepoche an. Waren die Kartelle aber mit dieser Begründung rechtlich legitimiert? Waren sie Kinder ihrer Zeit auch unter dem Gesichtspunkt des Rechts, spiegelten sie die modernen Entwicklungen in der Rechtsordnung wider?"

[133] *Schmidt* (n. 47), 181: "Die Außenwirkung wettbewerbsbeschränkender Verträge: ein zu spät erkanntes Rechtsproblem".

[134] RG, judgment of 4 Feburary 1897, RGZ 38, 155, 158 – Sächsisches Holzstoffkartell: "Verträge der in Rede stehenden Art können somit vom Standpunkte des durch die

these exceptions never played a role in later decisions.[135] For too long, courts neglected the external effects of contracts concluded to the detriment of competition as it was difficult to integrate these negative effects into the traditional instruments of private law.[136] Tort law was turned into a sword against certain anti-competitive practices only quite late and thus did not provide comprehensive protection against such conduct. It was consequently scholars like *Böhm* whose writings broadened this narrow perspective by also focusing on the effects of anticompetitive agreements on third parties.

Thus, the key lesson from the beginnings of the interplay between law and economics is that lawyers must develop their own concepts to safeguard legal values in competition regulation.

B. Lesson no. 2: Respect the rule of law

The second lesson to be learned from the evolution of the competition law and economics movement is that the rule of law must be respected when integrating economic insights into competition rules. This is the essence of the debate on the "more economic approach". There is no doubt that economic findings have developed significantly over the last decades. Thus, today the task of the competition lawyer is to refine the prohibitions in a manner that reflects economic thinking but that does so in a way respecting the rule of law. The two central questions are which economic findings should be integrated and how should we structure the tests for the detection of anticompetitive conduct. The integration of economic insights into competition law is an ongoing task, and the outcome also depends on the structure of the law. Different structures of the law (as, for example, encountered in different jurisdictions) may mean that the reception of comparable economic in-sights will nevertheless translate into different rules and different approaches for the assessment of anti-competitive conduct. This was demonstrated above for predatory pricing.

Economists are quick to criticise the decisions of authorities and courts, saying that determinations do not sufficiently reflect economic insights. What these observers often overlook is the necessity to reduce economic complexity to a level that can be handled by litigants and courts. Such simplification is critical in keeping the application of the law manageable and ensuring that competition law can also be enforced through actions by private parties. Some economists might regard this necessity as regrettable. Nonetheless, it is the

---

Gewerbefreiheit geschützten allgemeinen Interesses aus nur dann beanstandet werden, wenn sich im einzelnen Falle aus besonderen Umständen Bedenken ergeben, namentlich wenn es ersichtlich auf die Herbeiführung eines thatsächlichen Monopols und die wucherische Ausbeutung der Konsumentenabgesehen ist, oder diese Folgen doch durch die getroffenen Vereinbarungen und Einrichtungen thatsächlich herbeigeführt werden."

[135] *Möschel* (n. 47), 32.

[136] *Schmidt* (n. 47), 181.

price to be paid for the legislature having placed the protection of competition in the hands of the law and entrusted the courts with the task of deciding on the existence of a restriction of competition.[137] Respect for the rule of law demands that rules are shaped in a way that provides some ex ante guidance on appropriate commercial conduct.[138] In the discussion on the more economic approach, the "form vs. effect" dichotomy often did not grasp the necessities of legal regulation. There can also be no doubt that market effects and efficiency gains must be taken into account when judging the lawfulness of a business practice. Requiring excessive economic proof will, however, turn competition law into a blunt sword in the fight against anti-competitive conduct and may undermine the rule of law.[139]

C. Lesson no. 3: Economists on the bench are not the solution

This overview has demonstrated that lawyers and courts sometimes struggle to understand and assess economic insights. Often such insights are presented as expert opinions to support a case or practice. Against this background the question arises whether economists should be appointed to the bench of competition courts.

In this regard it is worth noting that the integration of competition economics into competition law is a rather smooth process in the area of public enforcement. Economists and lawyers ideally work hand-in-hand in competition authorities, and thus economic insights can be competently scrutinised. As legal recourse against decisions of competition authorities is centralised before certain courts, these courts also have access to the necessary knowledge to deal with economic insights.

The proper evaluation and reception of economic thinking is more burdensome when it comes to private enforcement as the (local) jurisdiction of the ordinary courts is less concentrated. Even though economic expert opinions, for example on the amount of damages caused by anti-competitive conduct, have become increasingly frequent in private enforcement actions, it would not in my view make sense to appoint economists – who are not qualified to serve as proper judges – to every competition court. Experience tells us that the assessment of economic evidence is only a small fraction of the judge's role in proceedings, and most decisions concern other issues, often related to civil procedure. The latter issues cannot be decided by an economist who is not also trained as a lawyer. Even though an economist on the bench would help in dealing with expert opinions, this person would be of no help for most decisions to be taken by courts in the course of the proceeding. This would have the effect of increasing the workload for the other judges and counsels against

[137] *Wurmnest* (n. 48), 247.
[138] *Wardhaugh* (n. 56), 217.
[139] *Wurmnest* (n. 48), 256.

the appointment of economists to courts on a large scale.[140] I think further consolidations of jurisdiction and the training of antitrust judges in economic matters are better ways to ensure a sound reception of economic insights. These steps will help the courts to build up the necessary expertise to deal with such economic evidence.[141]

[140] For details, see *Wurmnest* (n. 48), 238 ff.
[141] *Wurmnest* (n. 48), 241 f.

The Interplay of Law and Economics from the Perspective of Polish Competition Law

Tomasz Długosz

I. A short history of Polish competition law

Wolfgang Wurmnest has shown in his work that the path to reach a modern competition protection system in Germany was long and that the ordoliberal doctrines that were implemented after World War II played an important role in the process of achieving this system. The path of development of Polish competition law was similar, and the teachings of German ordoliberals played a similar significant role, although Poland has long been regarded as a socialist country in which the competition of economic entities was not important.

Poland regained its independence in 1918. Previously, the territory of Poland was under the occupation of three states: Germany, Russia, and Austria-Hungary. After the creation of the Polish state, the legislation of the former partitioning powers remained in force, which in various ways referred to competition protection issues. As regards the former German partition, the 1909 Act against Unfair Competition (*Gesetz gegen den unlauteren Wettbewerb*) was still in force. As regards the former Austrian partition, there were rules which regarded business agreements leading to price increases invalid if they were detrimental to purchasers. By contrast, there were no competition rules in the former Russian partition.[1] After regaining its independence, the Polish state dealt relatively quickly with the regulation of competition relations. The first Polish source of cartel law was the ban on selling at excessive prices contained in the Law on Combating War Liches of 2 July 1920.[2] In 1926, an act was

[1] *D. Miąsik*, Rozwój polskiego prawa konkurencji i prawa antymonopolowego, in: M. Kępiński (ed.), Prawo konkurencji System Prawa Prywatnego, vol. 15 (2014), 20–26.

[2] Ustawa z 2.7.1920 r. o zwalczaniu lichwy wojennej (Dziennik Ustaw 1920, Nr. 67, poz. 449, with further amendments).

adopted to combat unfair competition.[3] However, the first comprehensive Polish antitrust act was the Cartel Act of 28 March 1933.[4] Just before the outbreak of World War II, it was replaced by the Cartel Agreements Act of 13 July 1939.[5] Previous to World War II, business agreements which were intended to control or regulate the production, sale, prices, and conditions for the exchange of goods and which had the potential of having anti-competitive effects (cartels) were in general not negatively assessed. Instead, they were treated as a normal market phenomenon, which should nevertheless be overseen by the state. The German approach was very similar, exactly as *Wurmnest* has shown. The legal framework established by the 1933 and the 1939 Acts was designed to establish a public-law supervision of cartel relations and even to use cartels as a state policy measure. Both Acts did not prohibit cartels but imposed an obligation that cartel agreements, resolutions, and provisions had to be drawn up in writing and that they had to be registered by the Minister for Industry and Commerce. It was a public registry, and its entries were published. Furthermore, the Acts authorized the Minister of Industry and Commerce to intervene against a cartel if he came to the conclusion that it threatened the public good. It was initially laid down in the Act of 1933 that the Minister could, in the name of the public good, initiate a proceeding before the Cartel Court to, among other measures, terminate the entire contract or to annul specific contractual provisions. A few years after the 1933 Act had come into force, the position of the Minister was strengthened. He was given the power to rule on matters of cartels himself with the Cartel Court reviewing appeals against his decisions. The Cartel Court ruled in panels, and it is interesting to note that these panels were intended to include lay judges who had an expertise in economic relations. This may be considered an early manifestation of an interdisciplinary approach to law. Lay judges were chosen with the participation of self-governing trade organizations. This model was maintained by the 1939 Act, yet it also included some new elements. It introduced the obligation to specify in the registration notification the economic objectives which the cartel agreement pursued as well as the means of how to achieve these objectives. At the same time, every such objective had to be in line with the interests of the national economy. When assessing the agreement, the Minister for Industry and Commerce based his ruling on the objectives and measures so specified, and he could refuse to register the agreement or he could decide to terminate it in whole or in part. Overall, it is believed that cartels were thereby used as a tool to achieve the

[3] Ustawa z dnia 2 sierpnia 1926 r. o zwalczaniu nieuczciwej konkurencji (Consolidated text Dziennik Ustaw z 1930 r., Nr. 56, poz. 467, with further amendments).

[4] Ustawa z 28.3.1933 r. o kartelach (Dziennik Ustaw 1933, Nr. 31, poz. 270 with further amendments).

[5] Ustawa z dnia 13 lipca 1939 r. o porozumieniach kartelowych (Dziennik Ustaw 1939, Nr. 63, poz. 418).

government's economic policy,[6] and the entire pre-war period is characterized by the progressive tightening of powers against cartels – moving from tolerating cartels or even supporting their activities to fully subordinating cartels to state policy.[7]

After the Second World War, Poland had an economy that was centrally controlled by the state. There was no need to protect competition and no place for antitrust legislation. When towards the end of the 1980s an attempt was made to get the desolate economy back on track, the Act against Monopolistic Practices in the National Economy of 28 January 1987 was passed.[8] The Act fundamentally changed the approach to cartels.[9] It prohibited monopolistic practices of economic entities because such practices were understood to negatively affect social interests as well as the interests of other economic entities and those of consumers. According to the Act, both the behaviour of an individual enterprise as well as the collective behaviour of multiple enterprises could constitute monopolistic practices. Moreover, so-called business combinations were subject to ex ante scrutiny by the Ministry of Finance, which was the competition authority. Its decisions were reviewed by the Supreme Administrative Court. In a volume on interdisciplinary approaches to law, it is again interesting to note that the 1987 Act also created an advisory body, the Antitrust Council, consisting of representatives of the state administration and diverse societal organizations as well as representatives from academia.

In 1989, Poland witnessed a systemic shift affecting Poland's political, economic, and social system. As a result, the 1987 Act was replaced by the Act against Monopolistic Practices and Consumer Protection of 24 February 1990.[10] The text of the Act was similar to the current regulations. In comparison with the old legislation, the changes were fundamental. The previous law was nonetheless designed to capture inefficient activities of state-owned enterprises and achieving price stability. The 1990 Act put in place a modern model for protecting competition in the public interest.[11] The new law was created in an ordoliberal vein. The *Balcerowicz* Plan included an aggressive antitrust policy

[6] *A. Moszyńska*, Instytucjonalne ramy ochrony konkurencji w Polsce – historia i współczesność, Ekonomia i Prawo 12 (2013), 245–259, 253.

[7] *Moszyńska* (n. 6), 247 f.

[8] Ustawa z dnia 28 stycznia 1987 r. o przeciwdziałaniu praktykom monopolistycznym w gospodarce narodowej (Dziennik Ustaw 1987, Nr. 3, poz. 18, with further amendments).

[9] On the importance of this Act, see *A. Piszcz*, Sankcje w polskim prawie antymonopolowym (2013), 114.

[10] Ustawa z dnia 24 lutego 1990 r. o przeciwdziałaniu praktykom (Dziennik Ustaw 1990 r., Nr. 14, poz. 88).

[11] *C. Banasiński* (ed.), Polskie prawo antymonopolowe (2018), 22.

and was inspired by the social market economy model, which draws on the doctrine of ordoliberalism.[12]

The 1990 Act included an open catalogue of monopolistic practices. Furthermore, it introduced a relative ban on monopolistic practices, providing also for exemptions from the general prohibition of such practices. The Act contained prohibitions directed at undertakings in a dominant market position but also in a monopoly market position. There was also an obligation to notify the competition authority of the intention to merge economic operators, thereby allowing ex ante oversight in respect of concentration. The competition authority was titled the Antitrust Authority, a special central authority of the state administration that was subject to the Council of Ministers. Appeals against its decisions were examined by competition courts that were part of the common court system of the Polish judiciary. The overall aim of the 1990 Act was both to protect competition and to ensure its development, and it was envisaged that the competition authority had the power to influence the structure of the economy. The Act has been amended several times, and over time consumer protection has also become its objective.

On 15 December 2000, the Competition and Consumer Protection Act was enacted.[13] Instead of the notion of "monopolistic practices", it introduced the idea of "practices restricting competition". Overall, it is, in terms of content, closer to the current regulation than the 1990 Act was. The prohibition on restrictive agreements and on the abuse of a dominant position has been maintained, but the prohibition on the abuse of a dominant position has lost – in normative terms – its relative character. Furthermore, the special powers of the competition authority with regard to undertakings in monopoly positions have been abandoned. In connection with Poland's preparation for membership in the European Union – and later in connection with its membership – many changes have been made to the 2000 Act. Among other things, the 2002 amendment extended the scope of the Act to practices infringing collective consumer interests.

Eventually, the 2000 Act was replaced by the current Act on the Protection of Competition and Consumers of 16 February 2007.[14] It is not known why it was decided to introduce a new Act and not to reform the existing law. The 2007 Act simply replicated the 2000 Act in terms of structure and content. The relative prohibition of restrictive agreements, the absolute prohibition of the abuse of a dominant position on the market, and the ex ante review in respect of concentrations have been maintained. The inclusion of competition and

[12] As early as 24 August 1989, Prime Minister Tadeusz Mazowiecki spoke of a "social market economy" as the desired economic and social system of the state. See *T. Włudyka*, Dwa dwudziestolecia gospodarki rynkowej w Polsce (2008), 245 f.

[13] Ustawa z 15.12.2000 r. o ochronie konkurencji i konsumentów (Consolidated text Dziennik Ustaw 2005 r., Nr. 244, poz. 2080, with further amendments).

[14] Ustawa z dnia 16 lutego 2007 r. o ochronie konkurencji i konsumentów.

consumer protection in one piece of legislation is also retained. Consequently, the objective of the present Act is to develop and protect competition and to protect the interests of consumers in the public interest. The Polish competition authority is currently the President of the Competition and Consumer Protection Office, which is a central government administration body supervised by the Prime Minister. At the same time, it is a competition authority of a European Union Member State within the meaning of Art. 35(1) of Regulation (EU) No 1/2003.[15] It takes administrative decisions, which can be brought before the Competition and Consumer Protection Court. This Court belongs to the common court system and, in fact, is a division of the Warsaw Regional Court. In court proceedings, the President of the Office for Competition and Consumer Protection has the status of a party. The proceedings before the Competition and Consumer Protection Court are not restricted to checking the legality of the operations of the President of the Office for Competition and Consumer Protection as a public administration body. This would be the approach taken by administrative courts. The purpose of the proceedings is, instead, to fully reconsider the case previously settled by the President of the Office for Competition and Consumer Protection. As Poland is a member of the European Union, EU competition law is, in addition to the national competition protection regime, in force in Poland, too. As we know, the rules of EU competition law are applied by the competition authorities of the Member States of the European Union, one of which is the President of the Competition and Consumer Protection Office in Poland. Consequently, it is natural that Poland's competition law and its application is strongly influenced by EU competition law. EU competition law is a separate system, but its ideas, models, and approaches are significantly affecting national competition laws. Often, decisions of EU courts in the field of competition protection are invoked by Polish courts even in strictly national cases where EU competition law does not apply.[16] I can agree with *Wurmnest* that under the conditions of EU integration, the interplay between law and economics gains in importance, and this is because the application of EU competition law is characterized by a distinctive functional approach. Legislative amendments are also made to national law to conform to EU law. For example, the provision which had given the President of the Office for Competition and Consumer Protection the power to decide that the prohibition of agreements restricting competition was not applicable in a particular case was repealed because it did not comply with Art. 5 of Regulation (EU) No. 1/2003.

---

[15] Council Regulation (EC) No. 1/2003 of 16 December 2002 on the implementation of the rules on competition laid down in Articles 81 and 82 of the Treaty, Official Journal of the European Union 2021 L 1/1.

[16] See, e.g., Polish Supreme Court, judgment of 5 December 2019, I NSK 1/19 (published in Orzecznictwo Sądów Polskich of 2021, No. 12, 79).

Currently, two fundamental trends in understanding competition and the legal conditions for the protection of competition have been identified in Polish legal scholarship and antitrust case law. At times, both trends interfere with each other, but at times they also merge together in the case law. The first trend is the freedom oriented approach (also called the subjective or structural approach), which refers to the findings of the Harvard School and German ordoliberalism. This trend looks at competition as a state of independent undertakings and therefore focuses on preserving the freedom of each market participant. The second trend is called the efficiency oriented trend. It refers to the findings of the Chicago School and focuses on the protection of competition as an effective mechanism for the functioning of the market that ensures the efficiency of the economy as a whole. *Wurmnest* explains that the efficiency oriented trend is essentially reflected in EU competition policy, as the Commission has applied a "more economic approach" since the end of the 1990s. *Maciej Bernatt*, *Agata Jurkowska-Gomułka* and *Tadeusz Skoczny* – three leading Polish competition law scholars – argue that the freedom oriented trend was initially dominant under the 1990 Act, but over time – starting in academic writing and later on in the case law – the efficiency oriented trend has gained in importance. According to their view, the latter trend has even become dominant – at least at the declaratory level – in the policies of the President of the Office for Competition and Consumer Protection as well as in the case law, especially in that of the Polish Supreme Court. The said authors summarize the development as follows: "Today, no one questions that competition is based on an efficiency mechanism and that this mechanism is *differentiam specificam* of market competition."[17]

II. The request for a "more economic approach" in competition law

I agree with *Wurmnest* that certainty and predictability are key components of the rule of law, and from this perspective it is difficult to incorporate economic insights into the law. Of course, the rule of law must be respected when integrating economic insights into competition rules. However, I would like to draw attention to additional issues that relate to the debate on the "more economic approach" in competition. In my opinion, the proper reception of economic thinking in competition cases raises three fundamental issues. The first relates to the extent to which non-competition objectives can be pursued by competition law. In fact, it is a political issue, and lawyers do not have much to say on it. Competition law objectives may vary, and legal systems differ in

[17] *M. Bernatt/A. Jurkowska-Gomułka/T. Skoczny*, Podstawy i zakres publicznoprawnej ochrony konkurencji, in: Kępiński (n. 1), 728–730.

that regard.[18] The question arises whether the pursuit of these other objectives does not distort the basic premise that it is necessary to ensure rivalry between independent entrepreneurs on markets. It can be said that the further state intervention in the economy goes, the more objectives competition law pursues and the more difficult it is to reconcile these objectives in legislation and in the application of this legislation. The second issue relates to the extent of discretionary power in the application of competition law and how the courts control that discretion. These are important legal issues that relate to the protection of values such as legal certainty, legal stability, specificity of law, clarity of regulation, legal consistency, citizens' legal security, and certainty of business operations. Finally, the third issue is the extent to which the argumentative discourse, which concerns legislative decisions and decisions on the application of competition law, can be based on the findings of economics, given that economics is not a "hard science".[19]

The problems mentioned above are challenging and cannot be fully addressed in the present comment. It may however be concluded, considering the preceding chapter, that currently the Polish competition law, influenced by EU law, considers the arguments of efficiency and consumer welfare to be at the core of competition protection. It can also be said that competition protection regulation and, in certain infrastructure sectors, the reinforcement of competition require that a relatively wide discretion be left to the competent authority. This is linked to the fact that the principle of proportionality must play a major role in the judicial review of regulatory decisions. The principle of proportionality has to be used to balance the public interest in the protection or development of competition against the interests of individual market players.[20] It can also be noted that the scope of antitrust analyses carried out in specific cases may be subject to differing assessments. It is also a discretionary matter of the authorities applying competition law. In this way, various economic theories are implemented that – as *Wurmnest* clearly recognizes – may lead to different outcomes. In this regard, the judgment of the Polish Supreme Court of 20 March 2018 is of interest.[21] In its judgment, the Court expressed its views on the antitrust analysis used for the assessment of excessive prices, and it commented on the position of the Court of Appeal in Warsaw, which had considered foreign literature relating to the application of competition law. The Court of Appeal in Warsaw addressed the issue of how difficult it is to overcome barriers to entry into the relevant market and made a very detailed

---

[18] See *D. Miąsik*, Controlled Chaos with Consumer Welfare as the Winner – a Study of the Goals of Polish Antitrust Law, Yearbook of Antitrust and Regulatory Studies 1/1 (2008), 33–57, 36 (with further references).

[19] See the general criticism of *P.M. Romer*, Mathiness in the Theory of Economic Growth, American Economic Review 105 (2015), 89–93.

[20] See Polish Supreme Court, judgment of 2 April 2009, III SK 28/08.

[21] Polish Supreme Court, judgment of 20 March 2018, III SK 5/17, LEX no. 2510667.

analysis. The Supreme Court found that such a far-reaching analysis was not necessary and that not every case of abuse of a dominant position entailed "a need for complex antitrust analyses, including the verification of counterfactual scenarios, as accepted by the Court of First Instance in this case".

In view of the specificity of law, it can only be said that according to the case law of the Polish Constitutional Court, it follows from the principle of democratic rule of law (see Art. 2 of the Polish Constitution of 1997) that any legal regulation which gives state authorities the power to enter the sphere of civil rights and freedoms must meet the requirement of sufficient specificity of law. It is understood that it is necessary to determine precisely the extent of the restriction of civil rights and freedoms, and it is also necessary to define how an entity that is restricted in its rights and freedoms can defend itself against an unjustified violation of its rights. It is stressed that, under the conditions of a democratic rule of law, any form of interference by a state authority in individual rights must be combined with the possibility of reviewing the legitimacy of that authority.[22] However, the language of legal rules on competition law is often (in the terminology of *Herbert L.A. Hart*) to a high degree "open textured", and this often makes it difficult to enforce legislation in a particular case, and therefore there are matters that need to be left to the courts and the administrative authorities to deal with in the light of the circumstances of the case.[23]

Dawid Miąsik and *Anna Laszczyk* have carried out studies on the application of the "more economic approach" by Polish competition authorities. *Miąsik* reviewed antitrust cases in 2008 and found that the Polish authorities did not have a coherent approach to the goals of Polish competition law. However, he concluded that Polish competition law is consumer oriented and generally follows the rule that "what is good for consumers, is good for competition".[24] *Laszczyk* reached the conclusion that economic considerations were present in Polish competition policy even before Poland's EU accession, but that they became more institutionalized in Polish law after 2004 and after the development of the "more economic approach" in EU competition law (the last observation confirms the observation of *Wurmnest*). She also found that the economic considerations on which competition law is based became more sophisticated, although, at the same time, she agreed with *Jurkowska-Gomulka* that the President of the Competition and Consumer Protection Office mainly repeated the considerations of the European Commission and the CJEU.[25] She also added that the President of the Competition and Consumer Protection

---

[22] See Polish Constitutional Court, judgement of 19 June 1992, U 6/92.

[23] *H.L.A. Hart*, Pojęcie prawa (translated by *J. Woleński*, 2020), 221.

[24] *Miąsik* (n. 18), 55 f.

[25] *A. Laszczyk*, Forgotten Issues When Talking about the More Economic Approach to Competition Law in Poland, Yearbook of Antitrust and Regulatory Studies 7/9 (2014), 161–184, 182 f.

Office primarily relied on the tools of neoclassical economics whereas behavioural economics was not explicitly applied.[26]

III. Similar regulatory challenges in infrastructure sectors

The above-mentioned problems in applying competition law are also present in the infrastructure sectors, and here they are even more acute. In these sectors, many undertakings are highly important for the economy as a whole, and these sectors are highly important for the functioning of the state and society. Examples are the telecommunications sector and the energy sector. Regulatory developments in these sectors have led to the emergence of specific regulatory authorities. These specific regulatory authorities face problems in the application and enforcement of law similar to those faced by competition authorities but in more challenging circumstances. They must have an excellent understanding of the functioning of the specific sector and must take into account various overarching policy considerations, such as energy security, market competition, protection of personal data, and the need for innovation. And just like competition authorities, they must balance their objectives with the need for economic efficiency. Moreover, they often have to take action in advance (ex ante regulation), and they, therefore, operate in a context of uncertainty as to the further development of the market situation and the effects of their regulatory decisions. The broad discretion of sectoral regulators is considered to be one of the key features of sectoral regulation, with a distinction being made between discretionary power in assessing whether the market situation, in general, justifies government intervention and discretionary power in assessing which regulatory measures to apply.[27] It may be noted that sectoral laws contain many different measures both to ensure this regulatory discretion and to restrict and oversee it – based on substantive, procedural, and constitutional administrative law.[28] For example, the cooperation of the sectoral authorities and the President of the Office for Competition and Consumer Protection grants the former access to the latter's expertise in competition issues, and this ensures that the sectoral regulators are in a position to exercise their discretion. Furthermore, the independence of the sectoral regulatory authorities is guaranteed in order to ensure that their discretionary power is not "taken over" by other authorities looking to achieve other objectives or interests. Nevertheless, sectoral law may inspire antitrust law. This was the case with Directive (EU)

---

[26] *Laszczyk* (n. 25), 182.

[27] *W. Hoff*, Prawny model regulacji sektorowej (2008), 79.

[28] See further *Hoff* (n. 27), 77 ff.

2019/1 on EU competition law,[29] which provides guarantees of independence for national competition authorities. Thus, if *Wurmnest* says that we should learn lessons as regards the incorporation of economics in law, it is worth taking a look at the law of infrastructural sectors.

Sectoral regulators have highly specialized knowledge and operate in an area of wide discretion. Consequently, it is difficult to organize an effective judicial review of regulatory decisions. The question of criteria and limits on the review of decisions based on discretion is dealt with in different ways in Polish literature and jurisprudence.[30] In this context, it should be noted that in Poland, the decisions of the sectoral authorities as well as the competition authorities are scrutinized by the Competition and Consumer Protection Court. The scope of the review of this court is full, which means that it is not limited – as has been mentioned above – to assessing the legality of the administrative authority's decision; rather, it is a full re-examination of the case by the court. The Competition and Consumer Protection Court is a part of the common court system, but it is a highly specialized court. It is questionable whether the same is true for the court of the second instance, which is the Court of Appeal in Warsaw that hears appeals against judgments of the Competition and Consumer Protection Court. The Court of Appeal is not specifically designed to deal with competition and regulatory matters. By contrast, in the Polish Supreme Court, the recently established Extraordinary Audit and Public Affairs Chamber has jurisdiction in respect of competition and consumer protection matters, energy regulation, telecommunications and postal regulations, rail transport, and regulation of the water and wastewater market.[31]

The Competition and Consumer Protection Court is specifically designed to handle competition and sector-specific regulatory matters. From this point of view, a centralization of judicial decisions has taken place in Poland. Although *Wurmnest* considers it helpful to integrate economics into competition law, we are still dealing with the problem of unclear criteria for the judicial review of decisions made by the sectoral regulatory or competition authorities. One of the judges of the Competition and Consumer Protection Court recently highlighted the practical problems of reviewing regulatory decisions of sectoral regulatory authorities – and these problems presumably exist also with respect

---

[29] Directive (EU) 2019/1 of the European Parliament and of the Council of 11 December 2018 to empower the competition authorities of the Member States to be more effective enforcers and to ensure the proper functioning of the internal market, Official Journal of the European Union 2019 L 11/3.

[30] See further *M. Jaśkowska*, Dopuszczalny zakres kontroli sądowej decyzji uznaniowych, in: R. Hauser et al. (eds.), System Prawa Administracyjnego, vol. 1 (2010), 290 f.

[31] This Chamber was introduced by the new act on the Supreme Court, i.e. ustawę z dnia 8 grudnia 2017 r. o Sądzie Najwyższym (Dziennik Ustaw 2018 r., poz. 5).

to the decisions of the competition authorities.[32] She noted that regulatory authorities in practice tend to make factual findings based on documents and their own analyses, and they occasionally use the opinion of external specialists. Moreover, she indicated that these authorities issue their decisions without gathering evidence, and they also resort to their own "life experience". All of this creates difficulties in the substantive review of decisions made by the sectoral authorities.[33] In conclusion, she proposed a further specialization of the courts and a solution that ensures the participation in the judicial process of non-lawyers who are experts in the regulated sectors.[34] I personally disagree with such a step and share the view of *Wurmnest* that lawyers must develop their own concepts to safeguard legal values and that there are limits to the economization of law.

---

[32] *E. Stefańska*, Pozycja prawna przedsiębiorców telekomunikacyjnych o znaczącej pozycji rynkowej (2019), 277.

[33] *Stefańska* (n. 32), 277 f.

[34] *Stefańska* (n. 32), 338.

Law and the Study of the Commons: The In Personam and In Rem Rights Paradigms*

Grzegorz Blicharz

I. Introduction

"Two co-owners of a farm agree to hold it under hire in alternate years for a fixed price".[1] This sentence introduces a sequence of cases related to the hiring of a farm by multiple users that is analyzed by *Africanus*, a Roman jurist of the second century (D. 19.2.35.1), and it depicts in a compressed form two legal paradigms: property and obligation as well as the resulting rights *in rem* and *in personam*. *Africanus*' analysis reveals the inclination of people to cooperate rather than act independently, to shape mutually beneficial relationships founded on trust, and to appeal to power only as a last resort. Further, it highlights that some resources retain their productivity only as a unit, and users of such resources are more inclined to cooperate and modify their use rather than to abandon or change the resource itself. The two co-owners retain rights *in rem* with regards to their shares of the resource. Instead of following the typical fate of anti-commons (underinvestment of commonly-held property), which is usually overcome only by the dissolution of co-ownership, they decide to reshape the use of the farm by entering into a lease contract: *locatio conductio*. They want individual use and common management. They decide to attain this result not by using their power to divide the resource, which may be impractical, nor by one side taking over the entire farm, which would impair the economic interest of the other. Instead, the co-owners apply a more flexible,

* The paper has been made possible thanks to the National Science Centre (Poland) PhD holder Grant – Sonata 14 no. 2018/31/D/HS5/01951.

[1] English translations of Roman legal sources follow the translation of Justinian's Digest as edited by Alan Watson.

though less stable arrangement by establishing rights *in personam*. The ancient Romans did not stop at this point but went further yet in applying *in personam* rights to land use. *Africanus* recalls a second – real-life – case of "two men, both owning their own farms, who agree that each take the farm of the other on hire with the crops to be counted as the rent" (D. 19.2.35.1), thus without creating common property.[2] *Gaius*, a jurist of the same *saeculum*, presents yet another common example of a *colonus partiarius* (a métayer[3]) who "bears both profit and loss in common with the farm's owner, much like the law in partnership" (D. 19.2.25.6). *Ulpian*, a Roman jurist of the second and third centuries, recalls the case analyzed by another jurist, *Pomponius* (first century), who allows that "the owner of an estate", who gave usufruct of his land to another can hire his own land from the usufructuary (D. 7.4.29 *pr*.). The flexibility of sharing possession of goods by using *in personam* rights to land without interfering with *in rem* rights seems to be neglected, however, in the study of the commons.

It is common to enrich legal debate with the principles of good governance or with data regarding the nature of goods or of services. Much less frequently, however, do we see questions regarding the influence in the opposite direction: whether, in interdisciplinary research, it is economics that could gain from the application of legal constructs, even assuming the presence of nongermane tangential matters. I see such an opportunity in the interdisciplinary research on law and economics developed within the *Vincent* and *Elinor Ostrom* school of thought, usually called "The Ostrom Workshop".[4] First, their research was based on a methodology that rejects the categorical assumption of a rational actor aiming at profit maximization and loss minimization and instead takes into account the broader circumstances of each individual case, moving away from formulating ready-made solutions that apply to all. Second, law and the study of the commons both operate on a similar terrain, i.e. that of the sharing and using of goods by multiple users that requires collective action towards a variety of goods and physical contexts which due to their nature are called "commons", but which are not limited to common property. When we look at the institutional analysis of collective action taken by multiple users, an aspect arises which any lawyer will immediately recognize as proximate and rele-

---

[2] *R. Fiori*, La definizione della "Locatio conductio". Giurisprudenza romana e tradizione romanistica (1999), 234 n. 169.

[3] One who cultivates land for a share of its yield, usually receiving stock, tools, and seed from the landlord.

[4] *V. Ostrom*, Property, Proprietorship and Politics: Law and the Structure of Strategic Opportunities in the California Water Industry, Resources for the Future 47 (1964), 98–111; *V. Ostrom/E. Ostrom*, Public Goods and Public Choices, in: E.S. Savas (ed.), Alternatives for Delivering Public Services: Toward Improved Performance (1977), 7–49; *V. Ostrom/E. Ostrom*, A Theory for Institutional Analysis of Common Pool Problems, in: G. Hardin/J. Baden (eds.), Managing the Commons (1977), 157–172.

vant – the associated bundle of property rights. The study of the commons developed by *Vincent* and *Elinor Ostrom* is centred around collective action taken by users of a particular type of goods ("the commons") which are common pool resources, i.e. goods that are available to many users and that are described by low excludability but high subtractability (like groundwater in the West Basin in California).[5] Their study challenges creed of both the tragedy of the commons (overuse of a shared resource) and the tragedy of the anti-commons (underuse of a shared resource). The concept of indivisibility of a resource also influences the analysis of the commons. Some resources may be fairly divisible although they have clear legal (jurisdictional) boundaries like groundwater. Other resources may be technically divisible but because of human design and underlying economic or cultural reasons are treated as commons.[6] The *Ostroms*, however, sought to frame collective action in various physical contexts, including, but not limited to, commons. Private law is focused on the ideas of property rights and of contractual sharing of diverse types of goods or services. The study of the commons treats contracts as, at best, merely *one* of the *de jure* sources of property rights to the resource, but a close study shows that arrangements *in personam* as seen operating in Roman law have, by contrast, much in common with *de facto* rights which originate among resource-users finding themselves at the bottom of collective action.

Unlike in common law, where land lease is a property right (a right *in rem*), in Roman law it was conceived as a contract (a right *in personam*). Although in the study of the commons all discussion regarding collective action is focused on trust, the framework of property rights to the commons – possibly influenced by common law – is modelled on rights *in rem* and does not refer to relations *in personam*. It seems highly probable that the typology of property rights to the resource which is applied in the analysis of collective action would benefit from taking into account the distinction known to legal scholarship between rights *in rem* and rights *in personam*, a distinction which arises in both civil law and common law precisely in the case of a lease relationship. It is not a matter of merely expanding the bundles of property rights, a course which has been proposed in the studies on commons.[7] Nor is it, of course, an attempt to return to the ambiguity that the authors of those studies were rightly concerned with avoiding, i.e. with the imposition of legal qualifications on the bundles of property rights concerned. It is, rather, about deepening the typolo-

---

[5] *V. Ostrom/E. Ostrom*, Legal and Political Conditions of Water Resource Development, Land Economics 48 (1972), 1–12.

[6] *R.J. Oakerson*, Analyzing the Commons: A Framework, in: D.W. Bromley et al. (eds.), Making the Commons Work: Theory, Practice, and Policy (1992), 41–59, 45–46.

[7] *C. Doss/R. Meinzen-Dick*, Land tenure security for women: A conceptual framework, Land Use Policy 99 (2020), 105080, 2 f.; *T. Sikor/J. He/G. Lestrelin*, Property Rights Regimes and Natural Resources: A Conceptual Analysis Revisited, World Development 93 (2017), 337–349.

gy by adding a new dimension – the matter of whether either *de jure* or *de facto* rights to the resource are *in rem* or *in personam*, where the *in personam* dimension can be directly related to the idea of trust and collective action originating among multiple users. The distinction between rights *in rem* and rights *in personam* is unique to legal scholarship and is one of the most enduring and widespread legacies of Roman law, a legacy which evolved differently in civil and common law traditions, resulting in the different concepts of property rights and contracts (obligations).

In a first step, this work discusses the bundle of property rights in the study of the commons. Then, the legal division between rights *in rem* and rights *in personam* is presented. In a final step, cases of lease are analyzed as lease represents a legal relationship which is particularly relevant to the commons and anti-commons and as cases of lease are often overlooked, being located on the borderline between rights *in rem* and rights *in personam*. Since the concepts of property rights and contracts differ in civil law and common law, we analyze lease using Roman law cases and the Roman law framework.

II. Bundles of property rights: Where law meets the commons

One should be wary of superficial similarities. They are most often deceptive, and especially so in interdisciplinary analyses. For the most part, interdisciplinary studies of law are based on identifying an object of analysis (phenomenon, concept) common to law and an extra-legal discipline and applying the findings of the extra-legal discipline to the study of law, perhaps because these extra-legal disciplines always seem more scientific and stable than law, the application of which "always depends on" interpretation. Sometimes, however, there is entanglement that signals that there is, nevertheless, a sphere characteristic only of law. The application of external theory to law usually gives rise to new problems that have to be resolved using that theory. The study of law and economics involves the application of economic principles to the interpretation of the law, to law-making and to the construction of legal theory.[8] In principle, economic analysis of law has become a permanent feature of legal thought, but it has not been without its unwanted side effects. Take, for example, the doctrine of efficient breach. Breaching a contract on the condition of the payment of damages in situations in which the breaching party had been offered a better contract for the same service by a third party was regarded by *Richard Posner* as economically "efficient" (according to both the *Kalder-Hicks* and *Pareto*

---

[8] *T.J. Zywicki*, The Rise and Fall of Efficiency in the Common Law: A Supply-Side Analysis, Northwestern University Law Review 97 (2003), 1551–1633.

principles) if the breaching party's gain from breach exceeds both parties' losses:[9]

"[T]he promisor is allowed to breach at will so long as he leaves the promisee as well off after breach as he would have been had the promise been performed, while any additional gain is retained by the contract breaker."[10]

However, it turns out that not all is well with this solution: the one who gains most is the party *breaking* the contract, and this runs counter to the very basis of private law and the freedom of contract based on the premise of keeping a promise, which increases stability and trust. In response to this problem, *Posner* made a correction to introduce the concept of "opportunistic breach", a step which, however, undermines the economic sense of breaching a contract in the first place, since the breaching party must give back the profit he made by breaking the contract.[11] Moreover, *Posner* does not explain why he introduced this correction: Is it because breaking the contract undermines the institution of contracts in general or because such action is morally reprehensible?[12] From the point of view of neither legal principles nor intuitive social expectations is breaching a contract normal behaviour. It seems, therefore, that legal efficiency is different from economic efficiency, since in contract law efficiency should be adjusted in accord with autonomy theories.[13] In the case under consideration, however, one of the doctrines of contract itself may come to the rescue, according to which the purpose of every contract is to agree on damages and not on performance[14] – which makes contract itself little different from tort – and then the classic form of efficient breach could be maintained. The doctrine of efficient breach has, however, given rise to serious criticism in American legal scholarship, though it has also opened up a debate on the relationship between contracts and morality, as well as on how economic efficiency itself is understood in law, and it has also had an impact on shaping the idea of contract, i.e. whether it should promote social welfare or the benefit of the parties.[15] Common law solutions are very often intuitive and commonsensical, their being developed from a succession of individual cases over a broad span of time. They often considered effective solutions despite not always being economically efficient or logically explained, with decisions sometimes resting

[9] *R. Posner,* Economic Analysis of Law (3rd edn., 1986), 107; *R.E. Scott/J.S. Kraus*, Contract Law and Theory (2014), 104.

[10] *D. Friedmann*, The Efficient Breach Fallacy, The Journal of Legal Studies 18 (1989), 1–24, 2.

[11] *Posner* (n. 9), 105 f.

[12] *Friedmann* (n. 10), 2.

[13] *N.B. Oman*, The Failure of Economic Interpretations of the Law of Contact Damages, Washington & Lee Law Review 64 (2007), 829–875, 860 and 875.

[14] *G. Klass*, To Perform or Pay Damages, Virginia Law Review 98 (2012), 143–158, 152.

[15] *M.L. Stearns/T.J. Zywicki/T.J. Miceli*, Law and Economics: Private and Public (2018), 177.

merely on judges' intuitions and underlying path dependence.[16] Efficiency depends not only on maximizing the profit of the parties to the contracts, but also on what is efficient from the point of view of the institutional structure – legislative and judicial – the so-called "supply side", which can influence the introduction of economically efficient or inefficient solutions.[17] It is not always possible to explain these solutions on the basis of economic theory, and such attempts sometimes lead to prima facie counterintuitive constructions. This approach to efficiency, however, is very close to institutional economics and the study of the commons, which deviate from the profit maximization paradigm and the promotion of wholesale solutions. Law and the study of the commons operate on similar terrain, which in the commons research is centred around collective action and which in private law is focused on the idea of contract; in both fields the crux of the matter is to "deter those who are tempted to break rules and thereby assure quasi-voluntary compliers that others also comply",[18] this according to the rule: "I will if you will".[19] Legal rules usually operate on the general level, but rules governing the commons, although carved out for a specific group on a case-by-case basis, also apply indiscriminately, in fact universally, among the members of the group. What unites both fields is the common phenomenon of collective action, which happens even in a group of two members only, and the social dilemma of sharing goods and services.

The goal of *Vincent* and *Elinor Ostrom*'s study on the governing of the commons was to determine "how human beings in interdependent social situations find ways to solve problems, coordinate their behaviour, and establish and sustain mutually beneficial relationships"[20] – which is close to what a lawyer should do and what courts and legislators are concerned with. At the inception of their study, they focused on the search for

> "understanding the conditions under which boundedly rational individuals may coordinate their behavior to achieve collective action for the provision of public goods and services, the mitigation and resolution of shared problems, or both through the creation, maintenance, and reform of institutional arrangements".[21]

---

[16] See *Posner* (n. 9), 24 f.; *Y. Chang/H.E. Smith*, An Economic Analysis of Civil versus Common Law Property, Notre Dame Law Review 88 (2012), 1–56, 9.

[17] Cf. *Zywicki* (n. 8), 1632 f.

[18] *E. Ostrom*, Governing the Commons. The evolution of institutions for collective action (1990), 95.

[19] See *M. Goetzmann*, The Building Blocks of Social Trust: The Role of Customary Mechanisms and Property Relations for the Emergence of Social Trust in the Context of the Commons, Philosophy of the Social Sciences 51/4 (2021), 347–370, 348.

[20] *W. Blomquist*, Linking the Origins and Extensions of Commons Theory, in: S. Foster/C. Swiney (eds.), The Cambridge Handbook of Commons Research Innovations (2021), 17–25, 18. Cf. *V. Ostrom*, Public Choice Theory: A New Approach to Institutional Economics, American Journal of Agricultural Economics 58 (1975), 844–850, 848; *Ostrom* (n. 18), 183 f.

[21] *Blomquist* (n. 20), 18.

The research for such institutional analysis of collective action was associated with a particular type of goods – the commons – that is characterized by low excludability but high subtractability, such that collective action is necessary for the survival of a given community of users due to the exhaustibility of the resource. The research has subsequently led to a grid of factors that influence collective action in commons management and that allow each users' community to be analyzed individually. It was developed first by *Elinor Ostrom* and *Larry L. Kiser*,[22] and then followed by the highly successful framework of *Ron Oakerson*, who distinguished four factors that should be taken into account when analyzing the commons: (1) the physical attributes of the resource and technology used; (2) the decision-making arrangements that affect relationships between users; (3) patterns of interactions between decision makers; and (4) outcomes or consequences.[23] What *Elinor Ostrom* had developed started to evolve into the "elements of institutional analysis". Among the factors that influence the way collective action is shaped, she included: attributes of the community of users; attributes of the physical resource; boundary rules and users' rights; and levels of action.[24] Boundary rules explain who may be considered a user of the resource: who is in and who is out, and how these positions are come by.[25] At this point – where the study of the commons dives into the concept of "use" and "user" and rules pertaining to uses and users, of principles of inclusion and exclusion – it overlaps with the realm of law. With relation to the study of boundary rules, *Elinor Ostrom* and *Edela Schlager* proposed different bundles of property rights to resources associated with different types of users and uses, rules which may originate either from the legal order (*de jure* rights) or among resource users (*de facto* rights).[26] As property rights in relation to the commons, the authors enumerated the right of access and withdrawal, the right of management, the right of exclusion, and the right of alienation. Bundles of property rights are intended to be conceptual schemes for organizing property rights systems that distinguish between different bundles of rights: whatever legal structure (*de jure* or *de facto* rights) is adopted, it can be described using bundles of rights. The term "rights" is understood following *Vincent Ostrom*'s analysis of *John R. Commons*'s framework as inspired by *Wesley N. Hohfeld*, which is composed of "authorized transactions" and "authoritative transactions". The former allocate authority to act, the latter allocate authority to enforce and determine authority relationships. Rights are understood as

[22] *L.L. Kiser/E. Ostrom*, The three Worlds of Action: A Metatheoretical Synthesis of Institutional Approaches, in: E. Ostrom (eds.), Strategies of Political Inquiry (1982), 179–222.

[23] *Oakerson* (n. 6), 41–49, 41, 43.

[24] *E. Ostrom*, Formulating the Elements of Institutional Analysis, a conference paper, in: Studies in Institutional Analysis and Development (1985), 1–20; *Blomquist* (n. 20), 24.

[25] *Blomquist* (n. 20), 24.

[26] *E. Ostrom/E. Schlager*, Property-Rights Regimes and Natural Resources: A Conceptual Analysis, Land Economics 68/3 (1992), 245–255.

"particular actions that are authorized", and "rules" "refer to the prescriptions that create authorizations".[27] Along with the proposed typology of rights, a new nomenclature of users is also introduced – "authorized user" (rights of access and withdrawal), "claimant" (rights of access, withdrawal and management), "proprietor" (rights of access, withdrawal and management, and exclusion), "owner" (rights of access, withdrawal and management, exclusion, and alienation) – which to some extent corresponds to the legal qualifications of the property rights holders. *E. Ostrom* and *Schlager* introduced their own framework of property rights to illuminate the erroneous identification of common-pool resources with common-property resources. Commons or common-pool resources may be encountered in a variety of property structures: private ownership, private co-ownership, collective or state ownership – what matters are the rules in use, not the legal categories.[28] According to *E. Ostrom* and *Schlager*,

> "unchallenged *de facto* rights are as much a factor affecting action as are *de jure* rights. Only if *de facto* rights are challenged do the differences between the two classes of rights become apparent".[29]

In principle it is irrelevant to the determination of rights in the bundle whether those rights are *de facto* or *de jure*, because that will only be decided when they are challenged in court. Such duality of rights existed even within Roman law, where new solutions more suited to socio-economic needs were introduced by the praetor, bypassing the legislative path, and provided, as long as they were not challenged by the *de jure* rights holder, effective protection for the rights granted *de facto*: alongside the quiritary owner was the *bona fide* holder (*possessor ad usucapionem*); alongside the civil law heir was the *bona fide* holder of the inheritance (*bonorum possessor*) – the grant of possession guaranteed by a less powerful title offered by the praetor allowed the promotion of factual solutions as opposed to *de jure* arrangements.

Nevertheless, it must not be overlooked that, according to the way things work in practice, rule-making and rule-following are affected by the initial attitude or consciousness of the users – in particular, whether we perceive our rights as strong or not and, hence, whether we will defend ourselves in the future if there is a judicial challenge to them. We know from legal scholarship that the power of an entitlement – *in rem* or *in personam* – affects the user in terms of his or her commitment to expenditures made on the good he or she enjoys, and the more a given entitlement is protected *de jure*, the more it favors future investment and even provides an intergenerational perspective if it is of a heritable nature. To make the power of an entitlement depend only on the

---

[27] Cf. *V. Ostrom*, John R. Common's Foundation for Policy Analysis, Journal of Economic Issues 10 (1976), 839–857, 842–846.

[28] *Ostrom/Schlager* (n. 26), 250.

[29] *Ostrom/Schlager* (n. 26), 254 n. 13.

question of the interference or otherwise of the legislature – which can change everything, as happens, for instance, in the case of the granting or revoking of a license – is too simple a view. It overlooks situations where the state cannot easily exclude users, e.g. where the rights in the bundle are strong and are *in rem* (such as rights jointly owned as private property), and thus where it becomes necessary to trigger extraordinary measures (such as expropriation), especially where there is a judicial route to protect those rights. However, such considerations as to whether and to what extent given rights can be effectively defended in court would already belong to rules at the constitutional level and not to the boundary rules. They also naturally affect the awareness of users – i.e., whether the rights granted to them by law have a real path to protection in court or are just a sham. How users behave can be influenced by their awareness of the nature of the rights at the boundary rules level, i.e. whether they are temporary or long-term, whether they guarantee protection or are fragile. My proposal, then, is that each of the rights proposed by *E. Ostrom* and *Schlager* – of access; of withdrawal; of management; of exclusion; of alienation – can be described as both *in rem* and *in personam*. This would be a reflexive relationship, consistent with the authors' intention, who assumed that every right to a thing regardless of the legal classification adopted can be described by the rights in the bundle.

III. In personam and in rem rights paradigms

The situation of using someone else's property involves obligations incumbent upon us and thus is situated on the border not only between the spheres of I–you, but also between the spheres of rights in relation to things and rights in relation to persons: mine–yours. People operating on such a border are at the heart of the study of the commons. The key to a better understanding of this new dimension may lie not only in applying *in rem* and *in personam* distinctions to the bundle of property rights as proposed by *E. Ostrom* and *Schlager*, but also in answering the question of what function may be played in these communities by a lease relationship – which for its part is a combination of powers and trust – in the sphere of property rights and obligations, i.e. a sphere of rights both *in rem* and *in personam*. This approach will make possible a determination of the stability of rights as regards both their institutional stability and perceived stability.

The idea of a bundle of property rights confirms that legal scholarship and the study of the commons have in fact already overlapped. Although with regard to property rights, the decision was made to eliminate legal connotations that distort the picture created by researchers of the commons, both areas are in practice combined by researchers, and they have influenced each other for a long time. This proposition immediately steers the legal mind towards concepts of ownership and bundles of property rights present already in Roman law and European legal traditions of both civil and common law.[30] At the border, however, we see revealed the distortions produced by the *prima facie* well-ordered constructions of legal dogmatics. In the case of the concept of property, its weaknesses are exposed by the legal relationship of lease, which sits on the boundary between property rights and contracts, becoming a propertized contract.[31]

The distinction between rights *in rem* and *in personam* is unique to legal scholarship and is one of the most enduring and widespread legacies of Roman law. The distinction between *in rem* and *in personam* procedural claims (*actiones*) that was conveyed in *Justinian*'s compilation and that is present in the pronouncements of ancient jurists has enduringly entered the civil law and common law traditions. Even today many fresh theories and interpretative ideas continue to sprout up around this distinction. One particularly illuminating example of a legal relationship between users of land is the lease of land: in civil law the lease is considered a contract (an obligation), while in common law it is considered a right *in rem* (a mix of obligation and property). In Roman law, a lease (i.e. *locatio conductio*) was considered a classic example of a contract even though it evolved over time and allowed the creation of new types of *in rem* lease (especially when the lease was long-term).[32]

Lease is located at the intersection of property and contract, and it is where the property rights model reveals its limits, where functionality disappears and where one can detect differences between civil law and common law, between property and obligation, between rights *in rem* and rights *in personam*.[33] It is also where you can observe commons and anti-commons (relating to the problems of both the maximization ideal which leads to one owner model and the partition of shared resources as a way out of tragedy and destruction of the resource); the issue of internal governing (conditions necessary for successful governance); and defining and assigning different bundles of rights (nature of users' rights to resource). The question is whether economics may take advantage of legal scholarship. The *in rem* and *in personam* distinction runs right across civil law and common law – it is unquestionable, regardless of bundle or dominion theory or of a bottom-up or top-down approach to property. We must remember that civil law did not take everything from Roman law (discovering a parallel in Roman law may mean fewer costs to change the law of

---

[30] *G. Blicharz*, Commons – dobra wspólnie użytkowane. Prawnoporównawcze aspekty korzystania z zasobów wodnych (2017), 83–89.

[31] *Y. Chang/H.E. Smith*, An Economic Analysis of Civil versus Common Law Property, Notre Dame Law Review 88 (2012), 1–55, 9.

[32] *Fiori* (n. 2), 261 f.; *P.J. du Plessis*, Letting and Hiring in Roman Legal Thought: 27 BCE–284 CE (2012), 1, 7–9; *G. Mancinetti*, L'emersione dei doveri "accessori" nella locatio conductio (2017), 1–2.

[33] *Chang/Smith* (n. 31), 9.

things); sometimes Roman law presents parallels to the feudal-based common law of property (featuring different kinds of property) which implicate the Janus-face of Roman law.

In Roman law, the division between *in rem* and *in personam* claims was intended to describe two different litigation strategies: whether the litigation would be with regard to the property or against a particular person; and whether the dispute was to defend a thing or to defend the defendant's own person.[34] If it concerned a thing claimed as one's own, then the claimant did not need to name the defendant – who at the beginning of the litigation was unknown. If someone other than the claimant had an interest in keeping the thing concerned, then he would self-disclose so as not to lose the thing to the claimant. If the litigation concerned something owed to the claimant by another person – i.e., a performance from another person on behalf of the claimant – then the action had to be directed precisely against that particular person.[35] Naturally, today we cannot simply resort to Roman distinctions, and it is clear also that with regard to *in rem* claims, the Romans took into account passive legitimacy and, therefore, who could actually be adjudicated in a suit – the possessor of the thing, the *detentor* of the thing, or the fictitious possessor. This last case essentially meant that the claim from *in rem* became *in personam*,[36] which perfectly captures the flexibility of the Roman conceptual grid.

This distinction naturally had broader implications within the legal process: consumption of claims referred only to *in personam* claims, and consequently with regards to *in rem* actions there could be no plea of *bis de eadem re agi non potest*; *in rem* actions were normally not attached to persons but to things – they were in pursuit of the thing not the person. As *Paulus* explains: "for property cannot be mine more than once, but it can be due several times" (D. 44.2.14.2). In the case in which an *in rem* action was granted to a particular person, it could then be a matter of a usufruct, which encompassed most of the bundle of rights associated with the use of the *res* and which meant that the case was *in rem* – i.e. that it was pursued by a particular person who could defend his right (that is, litigate the case) against anyone. If an action was only against a particular person, then it would concern a lease (*in personam* claim) – and that is where the idea of using tenancy as an example comes from.

The same idea of distinguishing *in rem* and *in personam actiones* on the basis of the range of their application – general or particular – was extrapolated to *pacta in rem* and *pacta in personam*. Agreements in the form of a pact did

[34] *C.A. Cannata*, Profilo istituzionale del processo privato romano, vol. 1 (1980), 30 f.

[35] *R.A. Epstein*, One Step at a Time in Roman Law: How Roman Pleading Rules Shape the Substantive Structure of Private Law, in: G. Dari-Mattiacci/D.P. Kehoe (eds.), Roman Law and Economics: Exchange, Ownership, and Disputes, vol. 2 (2020), 301–326, 312 f.; *P. Bonfante*, Corso di diritto romano, vol. 3 (1933), 6.

[36] *F. Longchamps de Bérier*, Law of Succession. Roman Legal Framework and Comparative Law Perspective (2011), 30.

not give rise to an *actio*, unlike agreements called *conventio* or *contractus*. *Pacta* only granted defenses (*exceptiones*) when being sued, and only step by step did they become enforceable in praetorian law. *Ulpian* explains that pacts are "*in rem* whenever I agree generally that I will not sue", and they are "*in personam* whenever I agree that I will not sue a particular person, that is, that I will not sue Lucius Titius" (D. 2.14.7.8). *Paulus* further develops this idea, pointing out that pacts *in rem* are transmittable to the heirs of the parties to the agreement, whereas pacts *in personam* after the death of a particular person will not benefit the heirs (D. 2.14.21.1).

Ancient Romans never used the formula of *ius in rem* and *ius in personam*, focusing on the more important notion of *actio*, and only partially referring to *pactum*. This abstraction was developed only during the time of the glossators and the commentators, and it is known until today as a division between rights *in rem* and rights *in personam*. We have to redefine *in personam* and *in rem* rights as a framework for asset sharing. It is a very convenient distinction which was translated by *Johannes Apel* (1486–1536) into property and obligations (rights *in rem* and rights *ad rem*[37]) and which ended as the distinction in the law of property and law of obligations – real and personal rights.[38] In any case, we already know that this distinction, although useful, is somewhat ineffectual and unable to deal with the entire territory of the asset-sharing phenomenon understood as the sharing of services and goods. This evaluation is confirmed by recent research on real obligations,[39] which stand exactly on the border between *in rem* and *in personam*: It is argued that nineteenth-century property law was the natural enemy of contract law, and that nowadays "[too many] interferences between property and contract risk to trigger a return to a feudal structure of society"[40] – i.e. a mix of proprietary burdens and personal burdens related to real estate risk a connection between the personal obligation to do something and a submission of persons in relation to land.

If one pushes the argument further, one can claim that the same happened when real obligations were created in relation to other persons, which justified the phenomenon of slavery. In a somewhat similar manner, it is represented in the *in rem* right of children to their parents and *vice versa*, which grants a general claim towards anyone when a family member is endangered.[41] A feudal structure of society was derived, however, only by misunderstanding, or by misusing, Roman law sources. Some claim, especially with regard to common

[37] *J. Apel*, Methodica dialectices ratio ad jurisprudentiam adcommodata (Nuremberg 1535), cap. 7 *in fine*.

[38] *H.J. Berman*, Law and Revolution, II: The Impact of the Protestant Reformations on the Western Legal Tradition (2009), 169 f.

[39] *S. Demeyere*, Real Obligations at the Edge of Contract and Property (2020).

[40] *Demeyere* (n. 39), v.

[41] Cf. *J. Austin*, Lectures on Jurisprudence, Or, The Philosophy of Positive Law (edited by R. Campbell, 1875), 177.

law, that the division into property and obligations maintains the same error; they claim that a common personal right or a right *in personam* is a property right[42] and that obligations are simply one side of one type of property right. This understanding challenges *John Austin*'s (1790–1859) adaptation of Roman law and his defence of the classic understanding of *in rem* and *in personam* rights and the distinction between property and non-property rights.[43] Indeed, according to this view, *Henry de Bracton* had already gotten it right in the twelfth century when he translated *in personam* and *in rem* claims into personal and real property. He deviated, however, from Roman law sources when he limited *in rem* claims to only immovables. *Bracton* argued that when vindicating movables, the defendant could have paid compensation instead of returning the thing.[44] In fact, in Roman law *in personam* and *in rem* claims were differentiated regardless of the final outcome, i.e. the compensatory effect was up to the defendant also in *in rem* claims (*condemnatio pecuniaria*), which changed only with introduction of new imperial procedure (*extra cognitionem*).

On the other side is *Gregory S. Alexander*, who speaks about the moral foundation of property, that property rights are inherently relational and that, because of this, owners necessarily owe obligations to others.[45] The social-obligation theory builds on the claim that the basic purpose of property is to enable the individual to achieve human flourishing. The theory further builds on *Amartya Sen*'s famous insight that flourishing is a matter of what a person is able to do rather than what he has.[46]

Indeed, in the quest for a better understanding of the playing field and the frameworks that are available, we need to realize that in Roman law *in rem* and *in personam* rights were not about our now-traditional division into property and obligation but about the different nature of the claims and as a consequence the different nature of the obligations, i.e. one which a concrete person, an individual, has towards the right holder, or one which everyone and anyone has towards the right holder. Pragmatic transitions in Roman law from *in rem* to *in personam* claims only confirm this. In the case of leases the Romans allowed an equally pragmatic transition from *in personam* claims to *in rem* claims. Thus, in the postclassical and *Justinian* periods, the lease of public land gave rise to limited rights and protection *in rem* to the use of *emphyteusis* and the use of buildings on another's land (*superficies*), which earlier had been regarded as an example of a *locatio conductio* contract.

---

[42] *J. Tarrant*, Obligations as Property, University of New South Wales Law Journal 34 (2011), 677–695, 677 f.

[43] *Austin*, (n. 41), 173–178, 473.

[44] *H. de Bracton*, De Legibus Et Consuetudinibus Angliae: Libri Quinque in Varios Tractatus Distincti, vol. 2 (edited by T. Twiss, 1879), f. 102b.

[45] *G.S. Alexander*, Ownership and Obligations: The Human Flourishing Theory of Property, Hong Kong Law Journal 43 (2013), 451–462, 452.

[46] *A. Sen*, Commodities and Capabilities (1999), 2 f.

One can argue, then, that both *in rem* and *in personam* rights are interpersonal bonds, so both create an obligation, and property is in fact an obligation, but an obligation that has become more complex. In sum, the difference boils down to the very basic observation and experience of what is mine and what is yours: *in personam* rights are always connected with obtaining what is yours, and that is why they are oriented towards a particular person, while *in rem* rights refer to what is (entirely or partially) mine and are oriented generally against anyone. The idea of property with a relational character can be even traced to *Apel*, who defined law as a relationship – "ius vero nihil aliud quam relatio" ("but the right is nothing else than a relationship") and who explained that "nam et obligatio est ius, actio est ius, et dominium, et ususfructus" ("for an obligation is a right, an action is a right, and ownership and usufruct"), so evidently also *dominium* and *obligatio* are relationships.[47]

A change in the approach to understanding property rights was particularly noticeable in the first years of the twentieth century. Unknown outside Polish-speaking circles, *Stanisław Wróblewski* postulated, even before the Italian lawyers, that the right to property should be defined as a social, personal relation between persons, i.e. between the owner and the rest of society. In this understanding, the right is based on the key relation of exclusion – i.e. that the rest of society has a negative obligation, an obligation not to interfere with the right of the owner – and so *Wróblewski* analogously invented a negative side to possession.[48] Defining property through a negative prism was meant to show that the right to property is not in fact a right to a thing, but rather the relationship of the owner to the other participants in the life of a society. This was naturally connected with creating a network of rights and duties on both sides of the relationship, although *Wróblewski* did not stop describing rights *in rem* as absolute rights, using the phrase that they are rights to things. Previous approaches to property oscillated between the positive theory of property, which pointed to the specific rights that the owner had over the thing, and the negative theory, which postulated a wide scope of property, pointing only to the limitations resulting from the law. Nevertheless, *Austin* already claimed that *in rem* rights avail against persons generally, which meant that there is always a negative duty on others to forbear or abstain.[49] In the 1920s, *Hohfeld* constructed his theory of the division of *in rem* and *in personam* rights around the same model – with *in rem* rights conceived as an interpersonal relationship rather than as something in relation to things.[50] As he argued, more radically than *Wróblewski*, it would be absurd to construct a relation with a thing; a relation –

[47] *Apel* (n. 37), cap. 1, *Quartum definiendi genus*.

[48] *S. Wróblewski*, Zarys wykładu prawa rzymskiego. Prawo rzeczowe (1919), 1 f.; *idem*, Posiadanie na tle prawa rzymskiego (1899), 121 f.

[49] *Austin* (n. 43), 177.

[50] *W.N. Hohfeld*, Fundamental Legal Conceptions as Applied in Judicial Reasoning, Yale Law Journal 26 (1917), 710–770, 721–723.

a legal relationship – can only exist between persons. *Hohfeld*'s theory seems close to that proposed by *E. Ostrom* and *Schlager* in that he views rights *in rem* and *in personam* as being contracted on the basis of the same bundle of rights: in the case of rights *in rem*, the personal relation is to all other participants in society; in the case of rights *in personam*, on the other hand, it is to specific individual persons. The similarity comes without surprise since *Vincent* and *Elinor Ostrom* used *Hohfeld*'s analysis of power and authoritative relationships in their treatment of decision-making.[51] This theory has been criticized as both insufficiently grounded and based on an overly literal understanding of the right "to things." The theory of rights *in rem* as interpersonal – not vis-à-vis a thing – can, however, be understood less radically if we translate *in rem* and *in personam* not as rights vis-à-vis a person or vis-à-vis a thing but as a right *in* a person or *in* a thing, meaning that the other person or thing is a token, a carrier of our rights. With regards to the other, without naming him or her personally it would be impossible to discern rights and duties; however, with regards to things, they always belong to someone, and thus rights and duties are discernible without the necessity of specifying the identity of the right holder.[52] *Hohfeld*'s analysis comes close to *E. Ostrom*'s and *Schlager*'s idea of describing various legal constructs using non-legally binding bundles of rights. *Hohfeld*, however, sees differences that *E. Ostrom* and *Schlager* do not, i.e. that the bundle of rights is of greater intensity in the *in rem* case than in the *in personam* case. *Hohfeld*'s critics considered the bundle of rights theory to be a threat against the protection of private property as it was intended to be in opposition to an absolute conception of property and deprived property of its core meaning, treating it as a mere collection of sticks which are equally important. However, pointing to the contrary, it was noted first of all that the bundle of rights does not have to have that meaning, because it can in fact broaden the cases which can be regarded as expropriation: since all sticks can be treated as equally important, appropriating even one small stick can be treated as undue interference with ownership title. Secondly, the recognition of property rights in the category of separate bundles has been present in legal thought since Roman times and was used particularly in the *ius commune*. It was on this understanding of the right to property that the positive definition of the right to property was based. Roman law did not develop a definition of property rights; nevertheless, Roman jurists spoke of certain rights – bundles of rights to things. What is intriguing is that these bundles referred to rights considered to be *in rem*, what we would today call incidents of ownership. However, it is in the context of the earliest of these bundles (*ususfructus*) that the Romans proposed

[51] *Ostrom/Ostrom* (n. 5), 3–5.

[52] *C.M. Newman*, Hohfeld and the Theory of In Rem Rights: An Attempted Mediation, in: S. Balganesh et al. (eds.), Wesley Hohfeld a Century Later. Edited Work, Select Personal Papers, and Original Commentaries (2022), 273–292.

a broad understanding of *utitur* that includes both *in rem* and *in personam* relationships. The invention of *ususfructus* is considered the turning point which allowed to separate from the original bundle of powers of the owner what may be called "ordinary enjoyment" of the object and to vest it in a person other than its *dominus*,[53] from which other property rights to things later evolved. For a long time usufruct was not considered an example of servitude, being very close to ownership: deprived only of heritable character and the right to consume (*abusus*) and alienate the thing. On the other hand, a special place is occupied by the contract of lease *locatio conductio*, especially the leasing of public land (*vectigal*), from which the property right of *emphyteusis* partially evolved, which in the Middle Ages would underlie the concept of feudal property – the property of use and supremacy. This in turn would become the basis for the concept of common law property based on various fragmentary estates, rather than property understood as *dominium*, which leads to the description of common law property based on a bundle of rights.

In any event, Roman law enjoyed an open and flexible framework which was especially triggered by Roman contract *locatio conductio* – letting and hiring – which crossed even the division between different claims, thereby revolutionizing the rights system with *emphyteusis* and *superficies* and leading to medieval real obligations. Unfortunately, this ended up with the medieval misunderstanding of these matters and the creation of the feudal system – and nowadays the bewildering system of property and obligation paradigm that prevails.

IV. A contract between the co-owners of a farm: At the grassroots of collective action

The bundle of rights proposed by *E. Ostrom* and *Schlager* is not enough to capture the overall framework of rights that allow the use of resources. There is yet another dimension that should be highlighted. It is possible to look at each of the rights in the bundle and divide them into *in rem* rights and *in personam* rights. By virtue of this division, the understanding of the framework of the bundle of rights is deepened – it is possible to look at specific users and classify them not only according to the rights that were assigned to them from the bundle but also according to what kind of rights have been assigned to them – *in rem* or *in personam*.

Lease can be described according to the rights in the bundle: it allows the holder to access, withdraw, manage, exclude and alienate (e.g. sublease). The question is whether lease creates an *in rem* or an *in personam* version of rights

[53] *L. Capogrossi Colognesi*, Ownership and Power in Roman Law, in: P.J. du Plessis et al. (eds.), The Oxford Handbook of Roman Law and Society (2016), 524–536, 528.

from the bundle. In this we find the difference between common law and civil law. And note that it is the Roman law perspective that allows us to understand this difference. In Roman law lease did not create an *in rem* action to the leased object. It allowed only *in personam* actions between the parties.[54] This was changed only in the case of *emphyteusis* and *superficies*, which became *in rem* legal relationships. In the case of lease (*locatio conductio*), protection of possession through *interdict* remained with the *in rem actio* holder. A "limping" possessory protection could have been assigned to a lessee only if he gained possession of the thing against the will of the lessor. If the lessee was then expelled from possession by a third party, he could employ an *interdict* to recover it. In Roman law, everything is based on the structure composed by the range of exclusion: the right of possession, the imminency of compensation, reciprocity (monetary or in kind) for the use.

In the property-obligation paradigm, it is all about security and risk – about powers and trust. *In rem* claims associated with property are driven by security and powers whereas *in personam* claims associated with obligations are driven by risk and trust. The only power that we have, however, is a symbolic power – the power of the legal order, of enforcement by law. Property offers us the prospect of securing power over the thing, but even this power can end up as mere compensation, as in the case of eminent domain (public takings) or the loss sustained by creditors when the debtor's property disappears. Thus it is still the case that protection offered by rights *in rem* is based on a fictitious power as well. The only true, physical power that plays a role in this scheme is connected with the concept of possession, and this does indeed play a huge role in the present-day mix of obligation and property. In the management of the commons, everything is about trust.

The *de facto* rights created by such communities are necessarily based on consent, which can create a strong obligation to obey the rules, and thus at the heart of the community's success is a duty-obligation rather than a strong substantive right *in rem*. The micro-legal order that communities create often meets all the criteria of a legal order with the difference that in its radical version it is created entirely from below and provides sanctioning and monitoring without the involvement of an agent of the state. From this point of view, looking at property rights from an *in personam* perspective much better reflects the way collective action actually works than does the distribution of property rights.

In common law, property is based on diverse interests (bundles of rights), which owe their distinction to the feudal structure. Anglo-Saxon lease and continental tenancy are on the periphery of the doctrinal construction of property. In civil law, on the other hand, property – following the example of Roman law – is treated as the fullest right to a thing called *dominium*, from which rights

[54] *Berman* (n. 38), 170.

of a smaller scope may be separated. Anglo-Saxon lease belongs to property rights while continental lease, as in Roman law, belongs to contracts. In both systems of law, however, the lease relationship is subject to changes: Anglo-Saxon lease, under the influence of the case law, acquires increasingly more features of a contract, especially with regards to residential lease, while farm lease seems to retain the character of property. Continental lease, especially the residential type, gains protection against third parties and becomes a contract in name. Regardless of the categorization of these systems, we find that lessees enjoy in both the protection of possession, which differs from lessees in Roman law, who were protected only as contractors and not as possessors. The distinction between property rights and contracts is derived, on the one hand, from the Roman distinction of actions *in rem* and actions *in personam*, and on the other from the distinction of a legal relationship called obligation, which "consists not in making some thing or servitude ours, but in giving, doing, or rendering what I am obliged to do" (*Paulus* D. 44.7.3 *pr*.). The distinction between relations concerning what other people owe us (i.e. obligations) and relations concerning what is ours was closely connected with procedural means: obligations were protected by *in personam* actions, while the protection of what is ours was ensured by *in rem* actions. For this reason, European legal scholarship, breaking down the Roman category of actions, distinguishes *in rem* and *in personam* rights, which, however clear and fundamental, in the case of lease is nevertheless a distortion of the issue as a whole. This is not surprising, since even in Roman law a controversy arose concerning the case of a long-term and hereditary lease, the so-called perpetual public lease (*emphyteusis*) or *superficies*, which was eventually distinguished from both property and lease, being recognized as in itself a new type of *in rem* right.

Let us look at five cases in an attempt to grasp the correlation between rights *in rem* and rights *in personam*. All cases come from the 19th Book of *Justinian*'s Digest, which covers leases and sales as well as undefined flexible contracts. I have selected cases which involve both kinds of rights (i.e. *in rem* and *in personam*) and a plurality of users, and which deal with land – to be precise, with farms.[55]

The first case: "Two co-owners of a farm agreed to hold it under hire in alternate years for a fixed price." (*Africanus* D. 19.2.35.1).

As owners they both have the full set of rights from the bundle, and all of these are *in rem* rights with regard to their shares. Their rights of ownership can be quite strong, potentially excluding third parties from interfering with it. However, they may still be unable to act collectively, thus inviting the tragedy of the commons. Instead of abolishing co-ownership, they decided to enter into a lease contract by virtue of which they gain new rights (all of them from the

[55] *Fiori* (n. 2), 234 n. 169.

bundle) towards the shares of the other; however, these rights differ from the rights that originate from the ownership title. According to Roman law they are *in personam*, not *in rem*.

The situation between equal users was regulated by contract. New users were not added to a farm, however. Rather, what was added was new *uses* and the decision how to share each of them. Together with the lease might be added, for example, a new right of exclusion towards the share of the other co-owner, an exclusion *in personam* – by contract. In this case, each of them has both an absolute and a relative right of exclusion. While the absolute right allows effective exclusion of the other co-owner from their own shares, the relative right of exclusion is granted towards the share of the other co-owner. In fact it gives a right of only compensatory effect, in the event of breach of contract, and only towards the other co-owner, and not to a physical exclusion and return of possession such as is allowed by a right *in rem*.

The second case: "[W]hen your year was about to end, you deliberately destroyed the crops for the next year. I may sue you through two actions, one on lease and one on hire; in the action on lease, my own share will be given judicial consideration; in the action on hire, your share. He [Julian] then remarks: 'In an action for dividing common property, will you not be held responsible to me for the loss as far as my share is concerned?' His remark is apt, but I think the opinion of Servius is also correct, namely that when I preserve my property by one of these actions, the other action with him is obviously extinguished." (*Africanus* D. 19.2.35.1).

This contract is peculiar in that it does not imply a simple lease, but an economic interdependence of one lease on the other: The destruction of the crops prevents the use of the land in the following year – so when crops are destroyed, it violates both the lease by which the land was cultivated (action on lease – *actio locati*) and the lease of a share of land for the next year (action on hire – *actio conducti*).

Is a co-owner free to destroy half of the crops, i.e. his own share? Although an *in rem* right allows a co-owner to defend his use against others (and against another co-owner) and although an *in rem* right even allows the destruction of his own thing, the other co-owner would be protected by an *in rem* claim with regards to his share of the farm by an *actio communi dividundo*. However, the *in personam* right created on the basis of a lease contract makes co-owners liable also for mismanagement of their own share of the resource. They cannot deliberately destroy the crops as in doing so they would breach the contract. So, we see that the *in personam* right governs the relationship between users, but that it also affects the use itself. Such arrangements between co-owners were used in Roman law more often than one can imagine, although sometimes without setting price for rent, allowing only to harvest the fruits in alternate years (e.g. *Ulpianus* D. 10.3.23); this would not constitute a *locatio conductio* contract, but rather an unnamed contract (protected by an *actio praescriptis verbis*). The alternate organization of property cultivation facilitated relationships and community continuity.[56] The two co-owners decided to agree on usage in the face of possible conflicts in harvesting the fruits. The fact that they paid rent for the use of the entire farm, and thus deprived themselves of part of the profits, does not invalidate the rationality of this solution, since the possibility of cultivating the entire acreage on their own could have increased the productivity of the land, while the rent still was at a fixed rate.

A similar case (the third case) would be when "two men, both owning their own farms, agree that each take the farm of the other on hire with the crops to be counted as rent" (*Africanus* D. 19.2.35.1).

Here we have two *in rem* right holders who create *in personam* rights for each other. So, with regard to the exchanged farms, we can look at them as pure *in personam* users. However, the essence is productivity, and consequently the price depends on the crop, so it is an example of *locatio conductio* in which, for the use of land, one owes rent in the form of crops. They contract to create commons, and this contract is based on reciprocity. Since the example is similar to the first two cases, it should be understood that the two owners decide to cultivate two pieces of land in alternate years as a unity: one owned by each of them, and the other rented from a neighbour. There are only two differences from the previous cases: They are separate owners, and rent is due in a share of the crops.[57] Both have separate ownership; nevertheless, they still want single though common management: The two lands will be managed together, but by different people in subsequent years. They decide to reach this result not by the way of changing ownership status, but by using the more flexible, though less stable, *in personam* arrangement. From that point of view, *in personam* rights seem to be weaker than *in rem* rights, and their fragility depends on their particular range of exclusion and on the imminency of compensation and the right of possession.

The fourth case: "You gave me permission to sow on your farm and to remove the [resulting] crop. I sowed, but now you do not allow me to remove the crop. Aristo says that there is no action at civil law, and that it can be doubted whether one in factum should be granted. But there will be one for fraud." (*Pomponius* D. 19.5.16.1).

In this case, we have no lease, no *in rem* right, just a mere permission, apparently a generous act incurring no obligation and with no benefit to the owner. However, there arises the question as to whether such informal permission creates a sufficient bond to cover the man who actually sowed the crop. It shows the limits of the contract system. Here, permission was a means to include a new user. However, the way in which it is done is crucial, since it might

[56] *A. Murillo Villar*, Acerca de la locatio-conductio de una cosa común efectuada por uno solo de los condóminos, in: J. García Sánchez (ed.), Fundamentos romanísticos del derecho contemporáneo (2021), 629–647, 637.

[57] *Fiori* (n. 2), 232.

possibly give rights neither *in rem* nor *in personam* – a pure *de facto* arrangement which does not create obligation. That is why Roman jurists discuss the option of granting an *actio in factum*, considering it an indefinite contract. However, *Aristo* and *Pomponius* cannot in this situation allow any typical contract action nor any *actio in factum*, their treating it instead – as *Bruce W. Frier* suggested – as a conditional gift (permission to sow and harvest is not correlated to the owner's benefit).[58] *Aristo* allows resort to a subsidiary action for fraud (*actio de dolo*) in order to protect against abuse of the law and to deprive the owner of the land of the benefits (crops).[59] One should remember that even gratuitous permission to cultivate the ground gives way a crucial benefit to the owner: the land is kept fertile without his own effort.

By contrast, common law does accept that sometimes our right in the property of others is only *in personam*, i.e. when such a relation is not based on lease but is only a "licence", e.g. when I agree that you may live in my apartment with me as my lodger.

The fifth case: "I am speaking about a tenant farmer who hires for a fixed sum of money; on the other hand, a métayer bears both profit and loss in common with the farm's owner, much like the law in partnership" (*Gaius* D. 19.2.25.6).

A *colonus partiarius* (a métayer) shares profit and loss with the *in rem* right holder. In the case of lease, an *in rem* right holder always has a benefit (monetary or in kind); an *in personam* right holder bears both the profit and the loss of the yield. Roman law and civil law allowed a modification of this only in the case of extraordinary circumstances that caused the loss of the crop (*remissio mercedis*) and obviously not in all cases which involved sharecropping arrangements.[60] Usually, when there is a fixed sum of money agreed as rent, the risk is on the side of the *in personam* user, which demonstrate yet another important element in such cases. In the case of an *in rem* and *in personam* mix, the *in personam* users assume more risk, i.e. (1) of instability, the temporality of using another's land and (2) of loss if the reciprocity is based on monetary exchange and not on crops counted as rent. As regards the latter risk, such a contract is more similar to a partnership, which reveals yet two more elements of what we understand as commons: first of all, a stable group of users, and, secondly, the sharing of profit and loss.

The evolution of law changed the attitude towards a lease, which is, indeed, one of the most important contracts in land management. In civil law, possession is granted; in common law, an *in rem* right is always granted, which is merged also with the protection of possession. What is the import of this? Contractual users gained more protection, which may influence existing *in rem* users, and their situation is more stable.

[58] *B.W. Frier*, A Casebook on the Roman Law of Contracts (2021), 400 f.

[59] *Frier* (n. 58), 401.

[60] *Fiori* (n. 2), 235.

An awareness of the differences between common law and civil law approaches towards *in rem* and *in personam* rights allows another dimension to be added to the bundle of rights, and it allows the economic effectiveness of both kinds of rights to be explored in more depth.

In English and American common law, every use of a resource is covered by *in rem* rights, even use not preceded by any agreement, like bailment in the case of personal property. By contrast, in European civil law, the difference between *in personam* and *in rem* users is still in place; it is usual, however, that *in personam* users are protected in their possession (although they are not granted strong *in rem* rights). In this we see the difference between possession (a mere fact, but one protected by law) and property rights (title, entitlement, *in rem*). *In rem* rights allow the exclusion of anyone. *In personam* rights allow the exclusion of the contractual party, but only if the *in personam* right is connected with the protection of possession. On the one side is Roman law. There, *in personam* users have no possession nor any protection of their ownership. They may use the resource and they may be included among users, but their protection rests on users who hold *in rem* rights – such *in personam* users may request the *in rem* user who granted them the *in personam* right to protect them, and then we see that their protection originates in the authority of the *in rem* user. So in Roman law, *in rem* rights serve to effectively exclude at the system boundary. If the *in rem* user does not provide protection, then *in personam* users may only sue for damages due to breach of contract. Moreover, *in personam* rights may even be granted by someone who has no *in rem* rights, since it is always possible to sue for damages. *In personam* rights can thus serve as a principle of inclusion and exclusion as *in rem* rights do, but by defining particular persons and not abstract categories of persons or criteria of qualification. Thus, it may highlight the importance of *in personam* rights to explain how collective action operates. On the other side is common law, which always grants an *in rem* right in using another's resource. And *in personam* rights serve to regulate the use of the resource by the *in rem* user. In common law, if such use was granted by the owner in the contract, the user is protected even against the owner if he or she acts according to the contract. In civil law, the *in personam* user is protected as a possessor, not as a holder of *in rem* rights. Civil law, surprisingly, assimilates to the common law approach by ordering that such an *in personam* user be protected not only as a possessor, but also by an analogous application of the owner's protection.

In Roman law, however, the understanding of the possession of property was carefully developed, becoming even a non-physical concept, one which literature refers to as the spiritualization of possession – *corpus* and *animus* – in which it is possible to retain possession not only through the physical access to a resource (*corpus*) but through our will (*animus*); consequently not every physical possessor was actually granted possessory protection.[61] Today, both in civil law and in common law every physical (*corpus*) and spiritual (*animus*) access to a good is connected to a possessory protection.

To the end of clarifying this matter in Roman law, it is worth tracing the co-occurrence of *locatio conductio* in relations between owners and, thus, in the case of joint tenancy (where, as a rule, the contractual relationship is replaced by the settlements of the parties and the possibility of abolishing joint ownership). For this reason, the use of *locatio conductio* by the ancient Romans in such cases is even more interesting. Such an inquiry may capture the differences between the use interest in the case of *in rem* and *in personam* rights. But it was from the *locatio conductio* and the public lease that a new *in rem* right evolved – the perpetual lease and subsequently the *emphyteusis*, which in the fifth century was distinguished from both property and the *locatio conductio* as being protected by an *in rem* action, hereditary, transferable and subject to possessory protection. Thus, in this case, first the praetor gave public tenancy *in rem* qualities, and then the emperor adopted into Roman law the Greek *emphyteusis*, which supplanted the earlier public tenancy.

From *locatio conductio* there was distilled not only new types of contracts but also new rights *in rem*. *Locatio conductio* coexisted in relationships based on rights *in rem*.[62] The proposed analysis of rights *in rem* and rights *in personam* is derived from the study of the Roman contract of *locatio conductio*, at the heart of which lies a common legal and economic use interest in the use of other people's property and services. The Romans expressed this interest most broadly in the context of *ususfructus*: "for he who rents and he who sells also uses. But even if the usufructuary transfers the usufruct on request or makes a gift, I believe that he continues to make use of it and therefore retains the usufruct […]" (*Ulpian* D. 7.1.12.2). On the other hand, as *Ulpian* reports in the same fragment: "Julian writes that I retain the usufruct not only if I myself make the lease, but also if someone else does it in the course of my business"; "if someone leases the usufruct from me to a third party, I retain the usufruct." And *Pomponius* adds "[b]ut when the owner has leased this right in his own name, it must be said that it is lost, for the direct lessee no longer exercises it in my name" (*Ulpian* D. 7.4.29 *pr.*). The attraction in playing with the idea of using *in personam* arrangements regardless of *in rem* claims proves further that the distinction between *in personam* and *in rem* claims could have originated already with *Julian*, who adopted the distinction before *Gaius*. Firstly, *Julian* distinguished between two kinds of testamentary bequests: *legatum per damnationem* (covered by an *in personam* claim) and *vindicationem* (protected by

[61] *W. Dajczak/T. Giaro/F. Longchamps de Bérier*, Prawo rzymskie. U podstaw prawa prywatnego (2018), 395.

[62] *A.R. Gonçalves Moniz*, A locatio-conductio e a utilização do domínio público pelos particulares, in: García Sánchez (n. 56), 158–162.

an *in rem* claim); and, secondly, in the context of *res iudicata*, Julian invoked the non-consumability of an *in rem* claim.[63]

Usufruct originated in Roman law as the right closest to ownership – being incident of ownership – and according to some it is an example of the earliest right closest to ownership, one protected with an *in rem* claim and one that is personal in nature and therefore not transferable either *inter vivos* or *mortis causa*. The use interest found in usufruct is connected in the examples given with the *locatio conductio* contract, which is the most typical Roman contract for the use of another person's property for a fee. We note that use interest is also the subject of economic research, particularly within the framework of the *Vincent* and *Elinor Ostrom* school of thought.

Table 1: *In personam* and *in rem* division of rights to a resource

Inclusion and exclusion	Use (access, withdrawal, management, alienation)
in rem	*in rem*
in rem	*in personam*
in personam	*in personam*
in personam	*in rem*

The analysis of Roman law cases as well as of civil and common law developments creates the possibility of four different combinations in terms of how *in rem* and *in personam* rights could be incorporated into the framework of inclusion/exclusion of users, on the one hand, and use (governance) of a resource (e.g. the commons) on the other hand. This is depicted in Table 1, above, with each of the four rows representing a different type of legal institution. Both, the inclusion/exclusion of users and the use of a resource can be the subject of either *in rem* or *in personam* rights and obligations: both *in rem* (line 1); inclusion/exclusion *in rem* and use *in personam* (line 2); both *in personam* (line 3); use *in rem* and inclusion/exclusion *in personam* (line 4).[64] A farm co-owned by two individuals creates the first type of legal institution. If both enter into a contract that creates new obligations of the *in personam* sort, they thus transform their situation into the second type. If two neighboring owners contract to hire their farms in alternate years, the third type is established. If an owner hires his own farm from a usufructuary, he regains inclusion on the basis of an *in personam* claim, but his use is protected by an *in rem* claim. In all cases of a contractual creation of *in rem* rights, inclusion is effectuated by *in personam* claims, which gives rise to *in rem* use and exclusion. In Roman law, *emphy-*

[63] *F.M. Silla*, Sulla distinzione gaiana tra "actio in rem" ed "actio in personam", in: L. Garofalo (ed.), "Actio in rem" e "actio in personam". In ricordo di Mario Talamanca, vol. 1 (2011), 3–52, 43–45.

[64] I am indebted to R.J. Oakerson for his discussion of the applicability of *in rem* and *in personam* rights to the analysis of the commons, which emerged during our discussion of this article.

teusis or *superficies* was created within *locatio conductio*: by way of contract, use was established that was protected with *in rem* claims. In modern civil law, although an *in personam* relationship within a lease contract does not create pure *in rem* rights, it gives possessory protection which elevates the position of the user above the Roman law user within the *locatio conductio* contract.

V. Conclusion

Roman lawyers understood that in the case of a plurality of *in rem* right holders, as in co-ownership or co-usufruct, it was quite normal for people to disagree over the way to use the resource together, and very often disagreements ended up with the dissolution of co-ownership or co-usufruct. This is exactly what scholars analyzing the commons observe to not always be the adopted solution to such a problem: dissolution of co-ownership and co-usufruct may be technically impossible and may even lead to immediate tragedy. These scholars also know that legal divisions may not work in practice and that such arrangements are modified *de facto*. However, in several ancient Roman real-life cases, co-owners decided to remain in co-ownership and shape their relation on the basis of a lease contract – *locatio conductio*. They decided to implement sharing on the level of possession of goods – and not on the level of property rights – and to boost the productiveness of land by contracting for alternate use of land in alternate years, replacing fruits with rent or taking fruits as rent. They preferred *in personam* arrangements rather than those *in rem*. A very common form was *colonia partiaria* (sharecropping), which was based on the model of partnership where both profits and losses were shared by owner and tenant. Unlike usufruct, lease was a long-term reciprocal obligation, which helped to create a community of users. Moreover, *in rem* rights can indeed be divided among a number of right holders, but their relations collide and they have to find a way out of this quandary or by some means come to terms with each other. And one of the ways of doing this is through making an agreement, i.e. a contract, and thus binding themselves reciprocally – bound, that is, *in personam*.

Alternate uses as regards time (years, months, days, hours) or place (pasture, fishery, forest zones) show how a reshaped use of commonly-held property can be devised without dissolving a community of users. In the bigger picture, we may observe a legal distinction between *in rem* rights and *in personam* rights – between property and obligations – which highly resembles the community of users and their arrangements. Even today it is usually assumed that joint-tenancy or tenancy in common is anti-commons, and in the majority of cases such arrangements will indeed end with dissolution of the commonly-held land – and it is less likely that a continued shared use will be reshaped by contractual arrangement.[65] Roman law cases give support for both solutions and provide real life examples – not invented cases – that ideally and happily confirm the ability or eagerness of users to continue with a shared use of the resource – real life examples in which the mode of use is adjusted on the basis of contract. These cases confirm that collective action is in fact based on *in personam* relationships, relationships predicated on trust and mutual obligation, where everyone gives something of themselves – something that is theirs *de facto*. Having refrained from withdrawing, individuals participant to collective action rather engage in monitoring and taking care to maintain the state of the shared resource. The *in personam* and *in rem* distinction can also apply to *de facto* rights, which can be assessed as to their strength and as to whether such rights can be upheld against any user or only against specific users – situations which will often involve the issue of the sharing of one's entitlement, i.e. sharing use with others. The type of entitlement involved affects the perceived tenure stability.[66] And in the study of commons, all discussion regarding collective action is based on trust, and thus bundles of property rights should be modelled also on *in personam* relations rather than on *in rem* rights only.

---

[65] *Y. Chang*, Tenancy In "Anticommons"?, A Theoretical and Empirical Analysis of Co-Ownership, Journal of Legal Analysis 4 (2012), 515–553, 517.

[66] *E. Sjaastad/W.D. Bromley*, The Prejudices of Property Rights: On Individualism, Specificity, and Security in Property Regimes, Development Policy Review 18 (2000), 365–389, 371–373.

Reflections on D. 19.2.35.1 from a (Roman) Law and Economics Perspective

Constantin Willems

I. Introduction: Roman law and economics

Roman law and economics have become *en vogue* in recent years.[1] Various scholars not only from the United States, where the law and economics movement had its origin, but also from countries all across Europe have ventured to apply a law and economics perspective when it comes to analysing Roman law, thereby taking "another view at the Cathedral".[2] Of course, there is no singular law and economics approach. The same is true when it comes to having a look at Roman law: Various scholars focus on different aspects, be it efficiency of the law,[3] the arrangement of legal institutions and organisations,[4] or elements of behavioural economics.[5]

---

[1] To mention just some recent edited volumes, see *K. Verboven/P. Erdkamp* (eds.), Law and Economic Performance in the Roman World (2022); *G. Dari-Mattiacci/D.P. Kehoe* (eds.), Roman Law and Economics, 2 vols. (2020); *D. Mantovani/E. Lo Cascio* (eds.), Diritto romano e economia: due modi di pensare e organizzare il mondo (nei primi tre secoli dell'Impero) (2018).

[2] On this metaphor, see the famous paper by *G. Calabresi/A.D. Melamed*, Property Rules, Liability Rules, and Inalienability: One View of the Cathedral, Harvard Law Review 85 (1972), 1089–1128, 1090 n. 2: "this article is meant to be only one of Monet's paintings of the Cathedral at Rouen. To understand the Cathedral, one must see all of them".

[3] See e.g. *J.J. del Granado*, The Genius of Roman Law from a Law and Economics Perspective, San Diego International Law Journal 13 (2011), 301–350.

[4] See e.g. *B.W. Frier/D.P. Kehoe*, Law and Economic Institutions, in: W. Scheidel et al. (eds.), The Cambridge economic history of the Greco-Roman world (2007), 113–143.

[5] See e.g. *G. Dari-Mattiacci/A. Plisecka*, Luxury in ancient Rome: an economic analysis of the scope, timing and enforcement of sumptuary laws, Legal Roots 1 (2012) 189–216.

II. Blicharz's approach

Accordingly, *Grzegorz Blicharz*'s paper on "Law and the Study of the Commons: The *In Personam* and *In Rem* Rights Paradigms", which discusses Roman law from a law and economics perspective, fits well into current academic paradigms. Of course, Roman law needs to be studied using the tools scholars of Roman law habitually employ, but additional insights can be gained by taking recourse to the toolkit of law and economics.[6]

Going one step further, *Blicharz* focusses on the question of whether in some cases "it is economics that could gain from the application of legal constructs".[7] In essence, he has a look at "commons", but he does not restrict this to considering only common property, i.e. the perspective of rights *in rem*, instead also examining other forms of common usage of certain goods, thereby incorporating the perspective of rights *in personam*. This is indeed a valuable undertaking. Studies on the law,[8] and some studies on law and economics,[9] usually differentiate between contract and property rights, thereby losing sight of the interdependencies between both legal institutions, while at the same time genuine economic studies often[10] tend to ignore this legal differentiation. According to *Blicharz*, it is "probable that the typology of property rights to the resource which is applied in the analysis of collective action would benefit from taking into account the distinction".[11]

---

[6] For other examples, see e.g. *C. Willems*, Justinian als Ökonom. Entscheidungsgründe und Entscheidungsmuster in den quinquaginta decisiones (2017), reviewed by *D.P. Kehoe*, Zeitschrift der Savigny-Stiftung für Rechtsgeschichte – Romanistische Abteilung 136 (2019), 500–506; *C. Willems*, Roman Law and Economics – Ökonomische Analysetools als Erweiterung des "klassischen" romanistischen Methodenspektrums, Studia et Documenta Historiae Iuris 83 (2017), 521–537.

[7] *Blicharz*, p. 284, above.

[8] For instance, *M. Kaser/R. Knütel/S. Lohsse*, Römisches Privatrecht (22th edn., 2021), has different chapters on property law ("Sachenrecht") and the law of obligations ("Obligationenrecht").

[9] For instance, the volume by *H.B. Schäfer/C. Ott*, Lehrbuch der ökonomischen Analyse des Zivilrechts (6th edn., 2020), offers different parts on contract ("Ökonomische Analyse des Vertragsrechts") and property rights ("Property Rights (absolute Rechte)".

[10] An exception is *E. Korn*, (Neue) Institutionenökonomik und ihre Anwendung auf die Alte Welt, in: K. Droß-Krüpe et al. (eds.), Antike Wirtschaft und ihre kulturelle Prägung – The Cultural Shaping of the Ancient Economy (2016), 1–10, 5, pointing out the role of contracts in the distribution of rights of usage as a second category besides property rights.

[11] *Blicharz*, p. 285, above.

III. Some additional considerations on D. 19.2.35.1

In order "to grasp the correlation between rights *in rem* and rights *in personam*",[12] *Blicharz* analyses a selection of five "cases" taken from *Justinian*'s Digest involving a plurality of interested parties and a combination of rights *in rem* and rights *in personam* alike in the context of a farm. The following remarks shall be limited to his first two "cases", both taken from the initial case of D. 19.2.35.1, an excerpt from the *quaestiones* of the Roman jurist *Africanus* (second century CE[13]), preserved in the Roman emperor *Justinian*'s Digest. Offering some additional considerations, this commentary wants to show that a thorough analysis of Romanist doctrine on this case could pave the way to further insights on the relevance of the usage of rights *in rem* and *in personam*. These additions are not intended to criticize *Blicharz*, but rather to show how fruitful indeed *Blicharz*'s very promising approach and the recourse to the insights of this aspect of Roman law and economics could prove to be.

A. The basic constellation

In *Blicharz*'s "first case", a farm (*fundus communis*) is co-owned by two persons who have concluded an agreement stipulating that one of them is to cultivate the whole farm for one year in return for a fixed price (*certo pretio*), while the next year they will change roles. *Karlheinz Misera* stresses that such a special case of "barter of use" ("Gebrauchs- und Nutzungstausch")[14] is not just a theoretical option discussed by legal scholars in the ivory tower, but is a real-life problem[15] also mentioned in the literary sources of that time.[16] It is with good cause that *Blicharz* stresses that, while the joint ownership (a right *in rem*) is upheld in this situation, a contractual solution (a right *in personam*) has been added which mitigates problems of joint administration and cultivation of the farm. In trying to outline such problems, two scholia on Bas. 20.1.34.1, schol.

[12] *Blicharz*, p. 300, above.

[13] See *H.H. Seiler*, Africanus (Sextus Caecilius), in: M. Stolleis (ed.): Juristen. Ein biographisches Lexikon. Von der Antike bis zum 20. Jahrhundert (2nd edn., 2001), 19 f.

[14] *R. Fiori*, La definizione della locatio conductio: Giurisprudenza romana e tradizione romanistica (1999), 229, calls this "scambio di godimento".

[15] *K. Misera*, Der Nutzungstausch bei Nachbarn und Miteigentümern, Zeitschrift der Savigny-Stiftung für Rechtsgeschichte – Romanistische Abteilung 94 (1977), 267–292, 268: "Bei der Frage des Gebrauchs- und Nutzungstausches geht es nicht um einen theoretischen Schulfall, der um seines juristischen Reizes willen untersucht wird, sondern um ein praktisches Problem, das insbesondere bei landwirtschaftlichen Kleinbetrieben auftaucht".

[16] *T. Mayer-Maly*, Locatio conductio: Eine Untersuchung zum klassischen römischen Recht (1956), 131 and *Misera* (n. 15), 268 n. 4 refer to Apul. apol. 17: "an ipse mutuarios operas cum vicinis tuis cambies, neque scio neque laboro" ("Neither do I know nor care to know whether you exchange hired workers with your neighbours").

Κοινὸν ἀγρὸν[17] and schol. Ἵνα δὲ,[18] float the idea of repeated disputes (φιλονεικίας, φιλονεικίας [...] πολλάς) that might have arisen between co-owners, though the specific details of these disputes are not given.[19] In modern economic literature, it is commonplace that a situation of several persons using a common resource is seen as leading to conflicts of interest.[20]

It has been an object of a dispute among scholars of Roman law whether *certo pretio* should mean that a certain sum of money is paid to the co-owner not using the plot of land in the year at hand,[21] or whether the *pretium* does not consist of money, but rather the right to use the whole land in the next year on the other co-owner's own account.[22] If the first alternative is correct, the co-owner taking on the role of *locator*, or landlord, in the year at hand has a certain income guaranteed (the fixed rent agreed upon) at a clear and straightforward risk (namely, his co-owner not being able to pay), whereas the other co-owner taking on the role of *conductor*, or tenant, can make use of the potential of the farm according to his own agenda and thereby has the chance to obtain a higher gain,[23] at the same time having to carry the risk that his plans do not work out. If, however, the second alternative is correct, only the second branch of the argument just made pertains. In any event, such an arrangement between both co-owners, taking recourse to alternate administration and cultivation, had an impact on the income and proceeds of a farm and led to "un sistema que facilitaba las relaciones y la continuidad de la *communio*".[24]

B. The problem and the jurists' answers to it

This being said, it is of interest to have a look at the rest of the fragment: What *Blicharz* calls his "second case" is in fact the continuation of the "first case", the issue that proved to provoke legal problems in the arrangement mentioned above. In the case reported by *Africanus*, the co-owner acting as the tenant in the year at hand, called *Tu* ("you"), deliberately (*consulto*) "corrupted" (*cor-*

---

[17] *G.E. Heimbach/C.G.E. Heimbach*, Basilicorum Libri LX, vol. 2 (1840), 357 f.

[18] *Heimbach/Heimbach* (n. 17), 358.

[19] See also *Misera* (n. 15), 277 n. 52.

[20] See *Korn* (n. 10), 4.

[21] See e.g. *J.A.C. Thomas*, D. 19,2,35,1, Bullettino dell'istituto di Diritto Romano Vittorio Scialoja 74 (1971), 83–88, 84; *Fiori* (n. 14), 232; *A. Murillo Villar*, Acerca de la locatio-conductio de una cosa común efectuada por uno solo de los condòminos, in: J. García Sánchez/A. Díaz-Bautista Cremades (eds.), Fundamentos romanísticos del derecho contemporáneo, vol. 5 (2021), 629–648, 637.

[22] See *Misera* (n. 15), 281 f.

[23] This point is also stressed by *R. Zimmermann*, The Law of Obligations: Roman Foundations of the Civilian Tradition (1990), 355.

[24] *Murillo Villar* (n. 21), 637.

rupisti), or better destroyed,[25] what was to bear fruit in the following year (*fructum insequentis anni*), and what would consequently have been the basis of the profit of the other co-owner, called *Ego* ("I"). In another fragment, D. 10.3.23, originating from the writings of the jurist *Ulpian* (second to third century CE[26]), we find an example of such corruption: *Tu*, in his year of use, allowed his sheep to graze on the common land, thereby destroying what was growing there and what *Ego* otherwise could have later harvested.[27] If this were the background of the case at hand in D. 19.2.35.1, the conflict between both co-owners could also be related to preferences concerning the way the land is economically used, whether as a pasture to raise sheep or as a field to grow crops.

In D. 19.2.35.1, we are confronted with several legal possibilities for how to indemnify *Ego*. The first solution presented by *Africanus*, probably coined by the jurist *Servius Sulpicius Rufus* (second to first century BCE[28]),[29] argues that *Ego*, in order to be fully indemnified, must[30] sue *Tu* with two actions, based on his rights *in personam*: He must first raise the *actio locati*, the remedy of the tenant against the landlord, pleading the loss accruing to *Tu*'s share of property rented out to *Ego* in the next year when *Ego* will be tenant. Additionally, he must raise the *actio conducti*, the remedy of the landlord against the tenant, pleading the loss accruing to his own share of property in the year at hand when *Ego* is the landlord.[31] *Blicharz* is right to conclude that, by destroying the crops, not only this year's lease contract has been breached (by the tenant, who therefore has to respond to the *actio locati*), but also next year's lease contract (by the then landlord, who has to respond to the *actio conducti*). Secondly, *Africanus* reports that another jurist, *Julian* (early second century CE – *Africanus*' teacher[32]), advocated another solution, based on *Ego*'s rights *in rem*: *Ego* could sue *Tu* with the *actio communi dividundo*, the remedy for dividing common property, based on the damage done to his share in the land. In fact, this is the

[25] On this meaning of corrumpere, also concerning this case, see *B. Spagnolo*, Quasi and (Cor)ruptio, in: idem/J. Sampson (eds.), Principle and pragmatism in Roman law (2020), 171–194, 178 with n. 62.

[26] *R. Knütel*, Ulpianus (Domitius), in: Stolleis (n. 13), 640 f.

[27] Ulp. 32 ed. D. 10.3.23: "[…] eadem quaestio est et si socius, qui convenerat, ut alternis annis frueretur, pecus immisit et effecit, ut futuri anni fructus, quos socium percipere oportuit, corrumperentur […]"; see also *Mayer-Maly* (n. 16), 134 and *Misera* (n. 15), 277.

[28] *O. Behrends*, Servius Sulpicius Rufus, in: Stolleis (n. 13), 577 f.

[29] See *E. Levy*, Die Konkurrenz der Aktionen und Personen, vol. 2 (1922), 143; *Mayer-Maly* (n. 16), 132; *Thomas* (n. 21), 84; *Misera* (n. 15), 277 n. 56; *Fiori* (n. 14), 231.

[30] Consequently, *O. Behrends/R. Knütel/B. Kupisch/H.H. Seiler*, Corpus Iuris Civilis: Text und Übersetzung, vol. 3 (1999), 580, correctly translate *agam* as "muß vorgehen", whereas *B. Frier*, trans. of D. 19.2.35.1, in: A. Watson (ed.), The Digest of Justinian, vol. 2 (1985), 110, translates this as "may sue".

[31] See *Misera* (n. 15), 282 f. For the additions to the case that are necessary to understand what is meant, see *Behrends/Knütel/Kupisch/Seiler* (n. 30), 580.

[32] *H.H. Seiler*, Iulianus (Salvius), in: Stolleis (n. 13), 327 f.; *Seiler* (n. 13), 19.

solution also given by the jurist *Ulpian* in the parallel case, D. 10.3.23.[33] It has been observed that the raising of this *actio* would have put an end to the co-ownership.[34] *Africanus* himself[35] seems to propose a third opinion, namely that both sets of action are in principle applicable, but only alternatively: If *Tu* has obtained a verdict[36] on the *actiones locati* and *conducti*, he cannot raise the *actio communi dividundo* anymore, with the inverse also being true; accordingly, there shall be no overcompensation or even double compensation.[37] Being confronted only with *Africanus*' version and not with the original statements issued by *Servius* and *Julian*, one can only speculate whether the solution via rights *in personam* might be the older solution (second to first century BCE), while the solution using rights *in rem* came afterwards (second century CE),[38] or whether *Servius* already thought both approaches pertinent but deliberately decided to focus his remarks on the situation concerning the rights *in personam*.[39]

As to *Blicharz*'s point concerning the differentiation between rights *in rem* and rights *in personam*, one might add that the legal solutions put forward by *Servius* and *Julian* also differ in that the solution proposed by *Servius*, granting the *actiones locati* and *conducti* and being based on the contractual relationship between both parties, ties in with the legal position *in personam*, while the solution taken by *Julian*, considering the *actio communi dividundo*, ties in with the legal position *in rem*, the joint ownership in the plot of land. This appears to indeed be an "important factor",[40] also from an economic perspective, given that the solution based on rights *in personam* allows for a continuation of the economic partnership between *Ego* and *Tu* once the dispute at hand is resolved and the damage is amended,[41] while the solution based on rights *in rem* would

---

[33] See *Mayer-Maly* (n. 16), 133 f.; arguing to the contrary and building heavily on the assumption of interpolations in the text, *Thomas* (n. 21), 87 f.; *Fiori* (n. 14), 236–238.

[34] *Levy* (n. 29), 144; *Mayer-Maly* (n. 16), 133; *Thomas* (n. 21), 85.

[35] See *Mayer-Maly* (n. 16), 133; *Thomas* (n. 21), 84.

[36] See *Levy* (n. 29), 144–146; conversely, *Fiori* (n. 14), 232, seems to deem the assertion ("ricorso") sufficient for the other remedy to be precluded.

[37] *D. Liebs*, Die Klagenkonkurrenz im römischen Recht: Zur Geschichte der Scheidung von Schadensersatz und Privatstrafe (1972), 246 with n. 35, stressing that the remedy based on contract and the *actio communi dividundo* could coincide only in part; likewise, ibid., 208, arguing that Africanus' opinion could open the path for a supplemental claim concerning the remaining difference ("Nachforderung von Differenzbeträgen").

[38] See *Mayer-Maly* (n. 16), 135.

[39] See *Thomas* (n. 21), 84 f.; *Misera* (n. 15), 278 with n. 60.

[40] *Thomas* (n. 21), 85.

[41] See *R. Backhaus*, Rechtsromanistik in Heidelberg von 1918 bis zum Ende des 20. Jahrhunderts, in: C. Baldus et al. (eds.), Geschichtliche Rechtswissenschaft: 100 Jahre Heidelberger Institut (1918–2018) (2018), 57–97, 94 with n. 228, stressing that the contractual claims awarded by Servius leave the basic relation between both socii intact, albeit by using a "legal device" ("Kunstgriff").

lead to a termination of the joint ownership; by contrast, the third solution, put forward by *Africanus*, would leave it up to the aggrieved party whether he would like to continue the joint enterprise (by opting for an enforcement of his rights *in personam*) or whether he preferred to terminate the latter (by choosing to enforce his right *in rem*). The discussion at hand in D. 19.2.35.1 should consequently not be reduced to a dispute among jurists on some formal points of the law, for instance, which form of action is pertinent, whether the counter-performance in a contract of lease and hire could also be in kind, or what the relationship between the two legal remedies is. Rather, we are informed as to the extent which Roman jurists put a set of remedies at the disposal of an economic subject, allowing him to use the scalpel and maintain the common basis of economic coexistence with his fellow economic subject, or alternatively to pull out the sword and cut all ties by splitting up the joint ownership. This is economically convincing, as "[n]o legal set of rules can indicate when these property divisions should take place; that choice depends on economic factors of which the transactors have the best knowledge".[42] Both options are rendered possible by certain basic concepts of Roman law that are unique to either the specific rights *in personam* or the given right *in rem*. The Roman jurist *Africanus* has suggested a flexible response to the described institutional setting, thereby allowing the parties to make some adjustments and continue to profit from their shared use of the commons, or, as necessary, preventing a further tragedy of the commons.

IV. Conclusion

Blicharz's paper touches upon Roman law as viewed from a law and economics perspective. What makes his approach special is that, unlike other studies on Roman law and economics, *Blicharz* not only strives to improve his insights as a Roman lawyer and legal historian by taking recourse to the findings of another discipline, but, beyond that, he tries to show how scholars of economics could profit from a deeper knowledge of structures and patterns of (Roman) law. The additional considerations in section III of this commentary are in no way intended to criticize *Blicharz*'s approach, but are rather to show how insightful and advantageous *Blicharz*'s methods could prove to be when examining this aspect of Roman law and economics. As Roman law – the law of Roman Antiquity – is a common object of study across borders, there is no particular "Polish" approach and there is no genuine "German" approach to Roman law. What the sequence of *Blicharz*'s paper and this commentary have, however, hopefully unveiled is that a continued cooperation of Roman lawyers

[42] See *R.A. Epstein*, The Economic Structure of Roman Property Law, in: P. du Plessis et al. (eds.), The Oxford Handbook of Roman Law and Society (2016), 513–523, 517.

across borders could even further advance our knowledge of Roman law, which is important not only in understanding the history and genesis of the different national laws but also in learning lessons for future legal developments.

Part 6

Law and Psychology

The Role of Emotions in Law: The Impact of Empathy on the Interpretation of Non-Pecuniary Harm*

Marta Soniewicka and *Julia Wesołowska*

I. Introduction

Traditional jurisprudence has been dominated by a positivist approach aimed at the development of a conceptual framework in which law is defined as a rational, objective, neutral, certain and scientific discipline as claimed by *Jeremy Bentham* and *John Austin*.[1] On the grounds of the legal positivist approach, legal subjects/actors are seen as rational and as being endowed with a cognitive capacity based on reason (the capacity to understand and justify legal rules) and with volitional capacity (the capacity for acting according to legal rules).[2] In contrast to legal positivism, legal scholars such as *Leon Petrażycki* have advocated a concept of law which refers to emotions.[3] *Petrażycki* distinguished between legal and moral emotions, arguing that they both have a passive-active

* The writing of this chapter was funded by the National Science Centre of Poland, according to Decision no. 2017/27/B/HS5/01053.

[1] *R. Grossi*, Understanding Law and Emotions, Emotion Review 7 (2015), 55–60; *K. Lee*, The Positivist Science of Law (1989).

[2] *H. Hart*, The Concept of Law (1994); *idem*, Punishment and Responsibility (2008).

[3] *L. Petrażycki*, Teoria prawa i państwa w związku z teorią moralności, vol. 1 (1959), vol. 2 (1960); *idem*, Wstęp do nauki polityki prawa (1969); *idem*, O nauce, prawie i moralności. Pisma wybrane (1985); *idem*, O pobudkach postępowania i o istocie moralności i prawa (2002); *E. Fittipaldi,* Everyday legal ontology. A psychological and linguistic investigation within the frame of Leon Petrazycki's theory of law (2012); *B. Brożek*, Morality, Law and Emotions, in: J. Debiec et al. (eds.), The Emotional Brain Revisited (2014), 5–34.

character, motivate our behavior, and produce our judgments and normative claims. The positivist paradigm of objective and rational law has also been challenged by legal realism, which defines legal norms as social or mental facts,[4] and by critical jurisprudence (critical legal studies),[5] which claims that law is political and is related to a socially created identity of legal actors. According to all these critical views, law should address real individuals and not abstract categories or entities; it should take into account existing social and political settings as well as actual (not ideal) human behavior and capacities.

Currently, we are being confronted by a new trend in scholarship, including legal philosophy, known as "the affective turn". This trend has resulted in the development of law and emotions scholarship,[6] interdisciplinary research drawing on the humanities, social sciences, and life science, which has challenged the traditional positivist view. Law and emotions scholarship has made significant contributions to our understanding of both law and emotions, and we would like to explore its results in this paper. Its contributions include descriptive analysis, critical-reforming postulates, and normative claims. Law and emotions scholarship sheds light on the emotions that pervade legal reasoning and the legal system. The biological (neural) aspects of emotions, the physiological mechanisms of their manifestation and functioning, and their biological evolution are the subject of scientific research carried out in evolutionary psychology, neurobiology, and affective science. Yet the understanding of the nature and social functions of emotions – what they are and what kind of role they play in our self-understanding, how we experience them, how they are shaped by our culture, education, and social interactions, how they are expressed – is the subject of studies carried out in the humanities and social science. What is more, since emotions have a narrative structure, their cultural aspect cannot be well understood without reference to different sorts of art, literature, poetry, and music.[7] As *Eric Posner* accurately points out, legal methodology is not well-adjusted to work on emotions.[8] The field of law and emotions attempts to fill this gap.

Law and emotions scholarship provides a better understanding of legal reasoning and may improve both jurisprudence as well as lawmaking. One of the issues concerning judicial decision-making is whether judges make their decisions based on careful deliberation or based on intuition (or, rather, on both combined) and how contemporary cognitive and psychological research may

---

[4] *O.W. Holmes Jr.*, The Path of the Law (2009); *A. Ross*, TU-TU, Harvard Law Review 70 (1957), 812–825.

[5] *R.M. Unger*, The Critical Legal Studies Movement (2015).

[6] *S. Bandes*, The Passions of Law (2001); *J. Wesołowska*, Prawo i emocje. Synteza ruchu, Forum Prawnicze 2 (2021), 84–105.

[7] *P. Goldie*, The Mess Inside: Narrative, Emotion, and the Mind (2012).

[8] *E.A. Posner*, Law and the Emotions, Georgetown Law Journal 89 (2001), 1977–2012, 1977 f.

help us understand and improve this process. Some scholars have already addressed these issues, working on the impact of emotions on legal actors, such as judges,[9] juries,[10] lawyers,[11] and on witnesses and victims.[12] It is worth stressing that a group of legal scholars has recently started to expand the scope of research on emotions and their role in different branches of law. Legal scholars have analyzed the role of emotions in various legal dimensions, such as in criminal law,[13] family law (especially domestic violence),[14] contract law (especially the negotiation process),[15] international relations, and world politics.[16] They have also analyzed the impact of emotions on mediation, risk assessment, consumer choices, and market behavior with reference to behavioral economics and law.[17] What is more, there are scholars who are probing some specific

---

[9] *S. Bergman Blix/A. Wettergren*, Professional Emotions in Court. A Sociological Perspective (2018); *N.R. Feigenson*, Sympathy and legal judgement: A psychological analysis, Tennessee Law Review 65 (1997), 1–78; *L. Little*, Adjudication and emotion, Florida Coastal Law Journal 3 (2002), 205–218; *M.C. Nussbaum*, Emotion in the language of judging, St. John's Law Review 70 (1996), 23–30.

[10] *K.S. Douglas/D.R. Lyon/J.R. Ogloff*, The impact of graphic photographic evidence on mock jurors' decisions in a murder trial: Probative or prejudicial?, Law and Human Behaviour 21 (1997), 489–509; *B.S. Myers/J. Lynn/J. Arbuthnot*, Victim impact testimony and juror judgements: The effects of harm information and witness demeanour, Journal of Applied Social Psychology 32 (2002), 2393–2412.

[11] *S. Bandes*, Repression and denial in criminal lawyering, Buffalo Criminal Law Review 9 (2006), 339–390.

[12] *S. Bandes*, Empathy, narrative and victim impact statements, University of Chicago Law Review 63 (1996), 361–412.

[13] *D. Kahan/M.C. Nussbaum*, Two conceptions of emotion in criminal law, Columbia Law Review 96 (1996), 269–374.

[14] *C. Huntington*, Repairing family law, Duke Law Journal 57 (2008), 1244–1319; *M. Becker*, The passions of battered women: Cognitive links between passion empathy and power, William & Mary Journal of Women and the Law 8 (2002), 1–72; *N. Seuffert*, Domestic violence, discourses of romantic love, and complex personhood in the law, Melbourne University Law Review 23 (1999), 211–240.

[15] *H. Keren*, Considering affective consideration, Golden Gate University Law Review 40 (2010), 165–234.

[16] *R. Bleiker/E. Hutchison*, Fear no more: Emotions and world politics, Review of International Studies 34 (2008), 115–135.

[17] *E.A. Posner*, A Theory of Contract Law under Conditions of Radical Judicial Error, Northwestern University Law Review 94 (1999), 749–774; *idem* (n. 8); *R.H. Thaler/C.R. Sunstein*, Nudge: Improving Decisions About Health, Wealth, and Happiness (2009); *Ch. Jolls/C.R. Sunstein/R. Thaler*, A behavioral approach to law and economics, Stanford Law Review 50 (1998), 1471–1550; *C.R. Sunstein*, Why Nudge?: The Politics of Libertarian Paternalism (2015); *idem*, The Ethics of Influence: Government in the Age of Behavioral Science (2016); *idem* (ed.), Behavioral Law & Economics (2000); *R. Korobkin/T. Ulen*, Law and behavioral science: removing rationality assumption from law and economics, California Law Review 88 (2000), 1051–1144; *G. Mitchell*, Taking Behavioralism

emotions in terms of their relationship to law; these include disgust,[18] shame,[19] anger,[20] fear,[21] empathy,[22] mercy,[23] hope,[24] and love.[25]

The interaction between emotions and law is dynamic, i.e., on one hand, some emotions are necessary for the creation of an effective, responsive and legitimate law,[26] and on the other, legal institutions may not only regulate or affect emotions but also encourage the emergence of socially valuable emotions and produce specific emotions.[27] Much of the research on law and emotions has been narrowed to a limited scope of criminal law and to judicial review. Interest has mostly focused on "negative" emotions, such as anger, disgust, shame, guilt, indignation, vengeance, and outrage. The main problems

---

Too Seriously? The Unwarranted Pessimism of the New Behavioral Analysis of Law, William & Mary Law Review 5 (2002), 1907–2021.

[18] *D.M. Kahan*, The progressive appropriation of disgust, in: S. Bandes (ed.), The passions of law (1999), 63–79; *M.C. Nussbaum*, "Secret sewers of vice": Disgust, bodies and the law, in: ibid., 19–62.

[19] *T.M. Massaro*, Shame culture and American criminal law, Michigan Law Review 89 (1991), 1880–1944; *M.C. Nussbaum*, Hiding from Humanity: Disgust, Shame, and the Law (2015).

[20] *M.C. Nussbaum*, Anger and Forgiveness: Resentment, Generosity, Justice (2016).

[21] *S. Bandes*, Fear factor: The role of media in covering and shaping the death penalty, Ohio State Journal of Criminal Law 1 (2004), 585–598; *M.C. Nussbaum*, The Monarchy of Fear. A Philosopher Looks at Our Political Crisis (2018).

[22] *L.N. Henderson*, Legality and empathy, Michigan Law Review 85 (1987), 1574–1654; *T.M. Massaro*, Empathy, legal storytelling, and the rule of law: New words old wounds, Michigan Law Review 87 (1989), 2099–2127; *M.L. Hoffman*, Empathy, Justice, and the Law, in: A. Coplan/P. Goldie (eds.), Empathy. Philosophical and Psychological Perspectives (2011), 230–254; *T. Colby*, In Defense of Judicial Empathy, Minnesota Law Review 96 (2012), 1944–2015; *S. Bandes*, Empathy, Narrative and Victim Impact Statements, University of Chicago Law Review 63 (1996), 361–412.

[23] *J.G. Murphy/J. Hampton*, Forgiveness and mercy (1998); *M.C. Nussbaum*, Equity and mercy, Philosophy and Public Affairs 22 (1993), 83–125.

[24] *K. Abrams/H. Keren*, Law in the cultivation of hope, California Law Review 95 (2007), 319–382.

[25] *P. Goodrich*, Law in the courts of love: Literature and other minor jurisprudences (1996); *idem*, The laws of love: Literature, history and the governance of kissing, New York University Review of Law & Social Change 24 (1998), 183–234; *idem*, Erotic melancholia: Law literature, and love, Law & Literature 14 (2002), 103–129; *idem*, The laws of love: A brief historical and practical manual (2006); *H. Petersen*, Informal law and/of love in the European community, in: idem (ed.), Home knitted law norms and values in gendered rule making (1998), 114–155; *Seuffert* (n. 14).

[26] See *P. Selznick*, The Moral Commonwealth: Social Theory and the Promise of Community (1992); *idem*, The Communitarian Persuasion (2002); *idem*, A Humanist Science: Values and Ideals in Social Inquiry (2008); *P. Nonet/P. Selznick*, Law and Society in Transition: Toward Responsive Law (2000).

[27] *R. West*, Law's emotions, Richmond Journal of Law and the Public Interest 19 (2016), 339–362.

which have been addressed include: how legal instruments can be used to control socially unacceptable expressions of emotions; how emotions could and should be embodied in criminal law and penal systems; how law can be used for channeling and rationalizing retribution in criminal law; and how legal actors may be influenced by emotions. However, there is also ongoing research on the role of "positive" emotions in law – especially in legal judging – with an eye to emotions such as compassion and mercy. In this research, special attention has been paid to empathy. Our paper intends to contribute to the existing debate on the understanding and role of empathy in law. We pose questions with regard to how empathy should be defined and whether it is useful in the legal context (Section III). Furthermore, we focus on the role of empathy in interpreting and defining the concept of non-pecuniary harm (Sections IV to V). To address these issues properly, we first need to briefly introduce theories of emotions which could be useful in the legal context (Section II).

II. Theories of emotions applied to law

Since ancient times, emotions – which appear in the literature under many different labels, such as passions, affects, appetites, desires, drives, sentiments, feelings, upheavals, and impulses – have been a subject of interest in philosophy. The English term "emotion" comes from French, and from the middle of the nineteenth century forward it began to find use as an umbrella term covering the meaning of all, or almost all, these words.[28]

There are two main traditions of thinking about emotions in philosophy: (1) dualism, which makes a sharp distinction between reason and emotions, considering them as opposite to each other; (2) holism, which combines reason and emotions within a psycho-physical unity of a person, considering both spheres as complementing each other.[29] The former stems from *Plato*, while the latter can be traced back to *Aristotle*.[30] Both, however, have been further developed and refined by their successors.

---

[28] *A. Scarantino/R. de Sousa*, Emotion, in: E.N. Zalta (ed.), The Stanford Encyclopedia of Philosophy (Summer 2021 edn.), https://plato.stanford.edu/archives/sum2021/entries/emotion/ (last accessed 11 June 2022).

[29] *J. Jaśtal*, Natura cnoty. Problematyka emocji w neoarystotelesowskiej etyce cnót (2009), 34–38, 390 f.

[30] In Plato, we can find both ideas: the idea of a distinction and/or opposition between reason and emotion, as well as the idea of their cooperation. Yet the philosophical tradition which further developed Plato's ideas – including the movement of Neoplatonism and authors such as Saint Augustine and Descartes – followed the former way of picturing reason and emotion and radicalized the view.

The Aristotelian holistic approach had been long neglected while dualism has dominated mainstream philosophy.[31] The dualism of mind (reason) and body (emotions) is usually associated with the Cartesian view of the body as a machine and intellect as being added to, but still being distinct from, the machine.[32] This very influential way of thinking reduces emotions to bodily functions which cause certain mental states and affect agency. This mechanistic view is at odds with the ancient and scholastic tradition of thinking, which conceived emotions as a part of our spiritual life (as parts of the soul – *psyche*). Taking the idea of a "machine body" one step further brings about a conception of "man the machine", where both body and intellect are understood as mechanisms.[33] The dualism of reason and emotion produced two competing approaches to morality: rationalism and sentimentalism. The former perceives reason as a "control center", while the latter sees reason rather as a "spokesperson", using the metaphors adopted by *Steven Pinker*.[34] The rationalistic approach to morality, defended by such influential philosophers as *René Descartes* and *Immanuel Kant*, assumes that moral truths are grasped by reason and that moral judgments result from deliberation. Emotions are identified within this framework as irrational drives, often unconscious sensations, automatic reactions, blind passions. They can support moral judgments, yet they can also corrupt reasoning and lead us astray – thus emotions should be governed by reason and used as drives for action. In response to the rationalistic approach, British empiricists such as *David Hume* and *Adam Smith* advocated the priority of emotions in moral life. They argued that emotions play a fundamental role in our moral lives and enable moral valuing, thus reason should be governed by emotions. This approach, called sentimentalism, has been further developed by evolutionary psychologists such as *Jonathan Haidt* and *Daniel Kahneman*, who have claimed that moral judgments are the result of the *ex post* rationalization of our automatic, emotional reactions which occur prior to any reflection and reasoning.[35]

The traditional continental positivist approach to law was deeply influenced by rationalism. Thus, within the positivist paradigm of law, emotions have a rather negative meaning and are identified with such characteristics as irrationality, unpredictability, subjectivity, chaos, and unbalanced states. Reason, on the other hand, has a positive meaning, and is identified with such characteris-

---

[31] *Jaśtal* (n. 29).

[32] *C. Schmitt*, Lewiatan w teorii państwa Thomasa Hobbesa (2008), 51; *A. Damasio*, Descartes' Error: Emotion, Reason, and the Human Brain (2005).

[33] *J.O. de La Mettrie*, Człowiek-maszyna (1984). The contemporary materialist doctrine utilizes a metaphor of a machine even further – referring to a particular machine such as a computer.

[34] *S. Pinker*, Tabula rasa. Spory o naturę ludzką (2005).

[35] *J. Haidt*, The Emotional Dog and Its Rational Tail: A Social Intuitionist Approach to Moral Judgment, Psychological Review 108 (2001), 814–834.

tics as rationality, predictability, objectivity, order, stability, neutrality, and impartiality.[36] Emotions are seen in a mechanistic way as factors corrupting reason and leading to erroneous decisions. They are defined as biological impulses which we are subject to and are difficult to control. According to this account, it is claimed that emotions should be described and studied by the life sciences (biology, neuroscience) and not by social science and the humanities. Thus, emotions are largely overlooked by legal scholars working in the traditional continental positivist paradigm and are treated as unwanted irrational factors of human behavior which should be either prevented or limited in the public and legal spheres. Legal realism, on the other hand, has referred to the moral sentimentalism of *Hume* and *Smith*, emphasizing the role of emotions in decision-making process. Additionally, the behavioral law and economics movement, which is rooted in both legal realism and law and economics, has followed this path, concentrating on cognitive errors, heuristics, and biases all of which are closely connected with our emotional structure.

The dualism of reason and emotion has been challenged strongly in the field of neuroscience, cognitive science, modern psychology,[37] and philosophy (in particular by the phenomenological, neo-Aristotelian, and neo-Stoic traditions).[38] Since the "affective turn" of the 1980s and 90s, emotions have attracted considerable attention in cognitive science, humanities, and social science, including jurisprudence. Yet there is no agreement between either philosophers or psychologists as to how we should understand emotions.[39] There are ongoing disputes about essential components which constitute emotions, about what qualify as emotions,[40] about how to distinguish between emotions and other states such as moods, attitudes, or appetites, and about the main functions and origins of emotions. Depending on which components are considered as essential, one may distinguish three main ways of conceptualizing emotions: (1) emotions as experiences (feelings); (2) emotions as evaluations; (3) emotions as motivation.[41] Each of these approaches considers different components of emotions as essential. And each of them has been challenged with respect to different issues. Despite many unsolved and perhaps unsolvable disputes among both affective scientists and philosophers, there is a broad consensus among contemporary thinkers that emotions can no longer be considered as being opposed to reason. On the contrary, most thinkers agree that emotion and

[36] See *A. Peczenik*, On Law and Reason (1989).

[37] *A. Damasio*, The Feeling of What Happens: Body and Emotion in the Making of Consciousness (2000); *idem* (n. 32).

[38] *R. Solomon*, What Is An Emotion?: Classic and Contemporary Readings (2003).

[39] *Scarantino/de Sousa* (n. 28).

[40] Most thinkers agree on the obvious candidates, such as fear, joy, anger, and disgust, but there are many less obvious and more complex borderline cases, such as boredom, pride, awe, love, hope, resentment, respect and honor.

[41] *Scarantino/de Sousa* (n. 28).

rationality are complementary[42] or continuous.[43] The rationality of emotions can be understood as: (1) cognitive, i.e., their ability to represent the world as it is; and (2) strategic, i.e., their ability to lead to action that promotes an agent's interests.[44] Both aspects are important and constitute something that we usually recognize as the intelligence of emotions. Among most contemporary thinkers, there is a general agreement about the intentionality of emotions, about the variety of their manifestations, about their biological and cultural nature, and that they determine salience, involve cognitive aspects, and play a motivational role. Yet each of these aspects constitutes a separate subject of studies and generates heated debate concerning its meaning. Let us shortly summarize the most significant aspects of emotions that we will refer to in our further considerations.

Emotions are intentional, i.e., they have an object (e.g., fear of a lion, anger about an insult) or have representational qualities, i.e., represent the world as it is (e.g., fear represents danger arising from a given situation).[45] Emotions involve appraisal of the significance of a given trigger situation – in a most basic form they appear as attraction or aversion. Most emotions have an evaluative-cognitive component, i.e., they refer to personal beliefs related to decisions concerning human well-being and provide insights concerning the world and other people.[46] Emotions also play an important role in motivation and decision-making, they are sometimes considered as commitment devices which help us to make a decision which is not driven by self-interest alone.[47] Emotions can do both – they can distract us and lead easily to errors and biases, but they can also fine-tune our thinking and provide us with the necessary insights to make a good decision, or they could be the basis of an intuition or a hunch.[48] Emotions have also physiological, phenomenological, expressive, behavioral,

---

[42] *Damasio* (n. 32); *R. de Sousa*, The Rationality of Emotion (1987); *A. Etzioni*, Normative-Affective Factors: Toward a New Decision-Making Model, Journal of Economic Psychology 9 (1988), 125–150.

[43] *J.M. Barbalet*, Emotion social theory and social structure: A macrosociological approach (1998); *L.F. Barrett*, How emotions are made: The secret life of the brain (2017).

[44] *Scarantino/de Sousa* (n. 28).

[45] Objectless emotions are treated as moods (e.g., irritation, depression).

[46] Some authors claim that an evaluative-cognitive component, i.e., judgment or belief, is a necessary and sufficient element of emotions: *M.C. Nussbaum*, Upheavals of Thought. The Intelligence of Emotions (2003), 44. Yet this neo-Stoic view is highly disputed (see n. 98, below). We assume a less absolutist view, one holding that most emotions involve beliefs and perceptions but that they are not identical with them.

[47] *Ł. Kurek*, Moral Emotions as Evaluations and their Role in Decision Making, in: *J. Stelmach/W. Załuski* (eds.), Studies in the Philosophy of Law: Game Theory and the Law (2011), 197–212.

[48] See *T. Pietrzykowski*, Intuicja prawnicza. W stronę zewnętrznej integracji teorii prawa (2012).

and mental components. Emotions have both a biological[49] and a cultural nature.[50] Emotions manifest themselves in a variety of ways, and their expressions as well as their intensity and duration may differ depending on their personal structure and cultural context. The rules on feeling emotions, as well as the rules on the expression of emotions (social standards of emotional expressions) are culturally structured and socially produced to guarantee the social management of emotions.[51] Emotions cannot only be socially produced but also instrumentally used and commercialized.[52] Emotions are interpersonal; they are learned in interactions with the others and constitute a "feeling mind". They cannot be reduced to subjective, inner experience since they have a significant social dimension.[53] Emotions are embodied yet culturally shaped. As *Steven M. Parish* claims, emotions are "embodied culture".[54] Referring to the legal context, one could add that while emotions are embedded in the law some emotions constitute "embodied laws". Therefore, on the one hand, we can use the law as a lens in order to enhance our understanding of emotions, in particular their public and social aspects. But on the other hand, studies on emotions can contribute to a better understanding of the law and its functioning.

Building on the ongoing studies on emotions, law and emotions scholarship incorporates emotions into law by recognizing both their cognitive-evaluative, and motivational aspects.[55] This is a very promising approach to law and may help in redefining the relationship between law and morality, providing new insights on human cognition, agency, and decision-making,[56] as well as elucidating legal concepts such as culpability, agency, responsibility, accountability and harm.

In our further considerations we will follow the neo-Aristotelian holistic tradition, as well as the phenomenological approach, focusing especially on cognitive-evaluative and motivational aspects of emotions as applied to the concepts of empathy, liability, and non-pecuniary harm. In particular, we will analyze the concept and role of empathy in interpreting non-pecuniary harm and its impact on ascribing liability (Section V). In order to realize these aims, we

---

[49] *P. Ekman/R.J. Davidson*, The Nature of Emotion: Fundamental Questions (1994).

[50] *C. Lutz/L. Abu-Lughod*, Introduction, Emotion, Discourse, and the Politics of Everyday Life, in: idem (eds.), Language and the Politics of Emotion (1990), 1–23.

[51] *A.R. Hochschild*, The Managed Heart: Commercialization of Human Feeling (1983).

[52] *Hochschild* (n. 51); *idem*, The Outsourced Self: Intimate Life in Market Times (2012).

[53] *Barbalet* (n. 43); *C. Calhoun/R. Solomon*, What is an emotion? Classical readings in philosophical psychology (1984); *D. Evans*, Emotions. The Science of Sentiment (2001); *P. French/H.K. Wettstein* (eds.), The Philosophy of Emotions (1998); *K. Oatley/J.M. Jenkins*, Understanding Emotions (1996).

[54] *S.M. Parish*, Moral Knowing in a Hindu Sacred City. An Exploration of Mind, Emotion, and Self (1994).

[55] *H. Petersen*, The language of emotions in the language of law, in: *idem* (ed.), Love and law in Europe (1998), 12–26.

[56] *M. Peterson*, An Introduction to Decision Theory (2009).

will first introduce the concept of empathy (Section III) and then the concepts of liability and non-pecuniary harm (Section IV).

III. The understanding of empathy and its role in law

The contemporary revival of the sentimentalist approach to morality has also focused special attention on the concept of empathy in many fields, such as cognitive science (theory of mind) and neuroethics,[57] ethology,[58] evolutionary psychology,[59] psychology (especially developmental and social psychology,[60] clinical psychology,[61] and studies on mental disorders such as autism and psychopathy),[62] political and legal philosophy (especially the ethics of care, feminist scholarship, law and literature scholarship, critical legal studies),[63] political science,[64] and aesthetics.[65] Affective scientists usually follow the path of reasoning introduced by *Hume* and *Smith*.

Lord Shaftesbury, *Herbert Spencer,* and representatives of the Scottish Enlightenment, such as *Francis Hutcheson*, *Hume*, and *Smith*, analyzed the phenomena of sympathy, which is frequently considered to be the equivalent of empathy by contemporary authors, and claimed that sympathy provides the

[57] *A.I. Goldman*, Simulating Minds: The Philosophy, Psychology, and Neuroscience of Mindreading (2006); *idem*, Two Routes to Empathy: Insights from Cognitive Neuroscience, in: Coplan/Goldie (n. 22), 31–44; *M. Iacoboni*, Mirroring People: The New Science of How We Connect with Others (2008); *J. Decety/A.N. Meltzoff,* Empathy, Imitation, and the Social Brain, in: Coplan/Goldie (n. 22), 58–81.

[58] *M. Iacoboni*, Within Each Other: Neural Mechanisms for Empathy in the Primate Brain, in: Coplan/Goldie (n. 22), 45–57; *F.B. de Waal*, The Age of Empathy: Nature's Lessons for a Kinder Society (2009).

[59] *R. Plutchik*, Evolutionary Bases of Empathy, in: N. Eisenberg/J. Strayer (eds.), Empathy and its Development (1987), 38–46; *F.B. de Waal*, Putting the Altruism Back into Altruism: The Evolution of Empathy, Annual Review of Psychology 59 (2008), 279–300.

[60] *M.L. Hoffman*, Empathy and Moral Development: Implications for Caring and Justice (2000); *C.D. Batson*, The Altruism Question: Toward a Social-Psychological Answer (1991).

[61] *H. Kohut*, Introspection, Empathy, and the Semicircle of Mental Health, International Journal of Psycho-Analysis 63 (1982), 395–407.

[62] *S. Baron-Cohen*, Autism: the Empathizing-Systemizing (ES) Theory, Annals of the New York Academy of Sciences 1156 (2009), 68–80; *R.J.R. Blair/K.S. Blair*, Empathy, Morality, and Social Convention: Evidence from the Study of Psychopathy and Other Psychiatric Disorders, in: J. Decety/W. Ickes (eds.), The Social Neuroscience of Empathy (2009), 139–152.

[63] See *Henderson* (n. 22), 1578; *Massaro* (n. 22), 2099.

[64] *G. Lakoff,* Moral Politics: How Liberals and Conservatives Think (2002).

[65] *M. Smith*, Empathy, Expansionism, and the Extended Mind, in: Coplan/Goldie (n. 22), 99–117; *D. McIver Lopes*, An Empathic Eye, in: Coplan/Goldie (n. 22), 118–133.

foundation for morality.[66] In other words, sentimentalism can be considered as the ethics of sympathy (empathy). The term "sympathy" is vague and is used with different meanings which cover a variety of psychological phenomena, such as the transmission of emotions from one person to another, grasping the content of other people's minds by analogy and perspective-taking, communication, and the formation of moral and aesthetical responses. *Hume* mainly used the term in its affective meaning – a capacity for feeling what other people feel – as an involuntary, automatic, natural process. *Smith* developed this idea further by adding to it an imaginative perspective-taking which involves the idea of an observer – making it a voluntary, controlled cognitive process. The proponents of sympathy ethics emphasize both the cognitive and motivational role of sympathy. They claim that ethical evaluations, as well as a proper moral response, are founded on sympathy, i.e., experiencing other people's feelings makes us aware of them, helps us to understand them, and motivates a proper response to them. The ethics of sympathy assumes an egoistic human nature, and sympathy is a necessary and evolutionarily developed mechanism allowing self-interested human beings to perform altruistic, i.e., moral acts. Sympathy enables an extension of our circle of interest to other people, especially those close to us with whom we have direct interactions. In fact, this idea does not promote altruism but is rather an extended egoism in which, by the transmission of emotions, your pain becomes my pain and I therefore care about its mitigation.

The sentimentalist conception of the ethics of sympathy was highly criticized by philosophers such as *Edmund Husserl*, *Edith Stein*, and *Max Scheler*, who represented the philosophical movement called phenomenology. They provided an insightful analysis of the phenomena of both sympathy and empathy. In order to understand their objections to the ethics of sympathy, it is worth following the distinction provided by *Stein* and *Scheler* between (1) empathy (*Einfühlung*); (2) emotional contagion (sharing feelings with another person); and (3) sympathy (*Mitgefühl*).[67]

Phenomenology is aimed at the explanation and justification of knowledge. Thus, philosophers in this tradition were particularly interested in the issue of intersubjectivity – the knowledge of other people's minds. *Stein* addressed this issue in her philosophical work.[68] She rejected the three main theories of experiencing other people's minds asserted by, among others, *Theodor Lipps* in the field of aesthetics, British empiricists, and contemporary psychologists: (1) imitation; (2) reasoning by analogy; (3) association. Imitation theory assumes

---

[66] *D. Hume*, A Treatise of Human Nature (edn. by D.F. Norton/M.J. Norton, 2000); *A. Smith*, The Theory of Moral Sentiments (edn. by K. Haakonssen, 2002). Cf. *M. Scheler*, The Nature of Sympathy (1986), xlv; *A. Coplan/P. Goldie*, Introduction, in: *idem* (n. 22), ix–xi.

[67] *Scheler* (n. 66), 8–12.

[68] *E. Stein*, O zagadnieniu wczucia (2014).

that we must share the feelings of another person to understand them, e.g., when we see somebody who is suffering pain, we share this feeling with her, and we also suffer pain. Yet this assumption is wrong since in the state of "emotional infection" we concentrate on our own feelings, not the other person's feelings, and the assumption thus has no epistemological value. We do not need to feel sad ourselves to understand that someone is sad. In contrast to imitation, empathy is an active and intentional process.

Reasoning by analogy, on the other hand, assumes "putting oneself in someone else's shoes" and understanding her experience by analogy to our own – "I know what you feel since I also had a similar experience". This approach does not provide direct knowledge about somebody's mental state, and it limits our knowledge solely to mental states which we have already experienced. This is certainly false since we do not need to experience fighting in a war to understand fear of dying in combat, bravery, cowardice, etc. Empathy may extend our understanding of others and contribute to the understanding of ourselves by opening us up to new experience.[69] Reasoning by analogy may enhance our understanding of other people's experience when our empathy fails or is limited by different factors. In contrast to reasoning by analogy, empathy is an emotional rather than intellectual experience, it provides direct knowledge based on a content given indirectly. It is a spontaneous act which does not require reflection; it precedes conceptual knowledge, providing its content.

Association assumes that our knowledge of another's emotional experience is based on the expression of emotions. For instance, when we see someone's sad face, we associate it with the feeling of sadness. *Stein* emphasizes the distinction between knowledge derived from observation ("I know you are sad because I see you crying"), statement ("I know about your sadness because you told me"), and empathy ("I know you are sad because I grasped your sadness directly").[70] Through empathy we grasp other people's mental states directly and there is no need for reasoning, association, or representation. By means of empathy, someone's sadness is given to us together with its expressions (crying is not a result of sadness but an external part of the experience of sadness) and not as a result of reasoning based on its expressions.

---

[69] *Stein* (n. 68), 229–231. Stein points out that our psycho-physical structure sets limits for empathy by defining what is intelligible for us and what is not. Therefore, in some cases we can have an empty representation of someone's mental state without deep insight; for instance, an atheist can understand a religious person but is unable to fully grasp her mental states. The same could be the case with villains who have committed atrocities – most people would have empathetic obstacles in grasping their mental states: see *A. Morton*, Empathy for the Devil, in: Coplan/Goldie (n. 22), 318–330; *Henderson* (n. 22), 1584 f. Another issue is with other species – we have no direct access to their mental states, which is a significant obstacle for empathy: cf. *T. Nagel*, What is it like to be a bat?, in: *idem*, Mortal Questions (2012), 165–180.

[70] *Stein* (n. 68), 134–173.

While *Stein* was analyzing empathy, *Scheler* provided an in-depth analysis of sympathy.[71] Empathy (*Einfühlung*) is a special cognitive skill which plays a significant role in epistemology, yet it is neither sufficient nor necessary for morality. Grasping other people's experience provides knowledge, but it does not involve an evaluation of the experience. It is a morally neutral skill.[72] We can grasp someone's grief and feel happy about it (*Schadenfreude*). We can even imagine a highly empathetic sadist who perfectly grasps the suffering of the victim and therefore enjoys inflicting pain on her.[73] Yet transmitting emotions from one person to another or reproducing her emotions in our own minds does not have a moral value either. Emotional contagion results in experiencing our own emotional states which are the central subject of our focus. Firstly, this preoccupation with our own feelings distorts the perception of the other and her experience. Secondly, the focus on ourselves may significantly limit our proper moral response to the given situation. For instance, instead of helping the suffering person, we will try to avoid any contact with suffering which could be transmitted to us. Thirdly, understanding that harming somebody is wrong does not require that we feel this person's suffering. In other words, emotional contagion is neither a prerequisite for moral judgment nor a moral motivation.[74] Quite the contrary, it may distort our judgment and mislead our action. True sympathy (fellow-feeling), as *Scheler* claims, does not involve feeling someone's suffering but rather involves feeling sad *for* that person who is suffering.[75]

Sympathy in *Scheler*'s meaning is: (1) intentional, (2) cognitive-evaluative, (3) other-centered, and (4) involves differentiation of the self from the other. With sympathy, I do not grasp your sadness, but I am sad for you because you suffer. In other words, empathy is not required for sympathy, thus we may also feel sympathy for those whom we do not understand (such as villains) or even with entirely unintelligible beings, such as animals.[76] To be sad for someone who is suffering or to be happy for someone who is in joy, I need to evaluate her experience as good or bad and I need to see the person who experiences it as significant to me. Sympathy is cognitive in the prelogical sense; since it does not require reflection or reasoning, it is an act of including the other in the circle of my own concern, a recognition of the real and separate existence of

---

[71] *Scheler* (n. 66).

[72] See the distinction between virtues, skills, and capacities provided by *H.D. Battaley*, Is Empathy a Virtue, in: Coplan/Goldie (n. 22), 277–301.

[73] *B. Williams*, Ethics and the Limits of Philosophy (1985), 91.

[74] *J.J. Prinz*, Is Empathy Necessary for Morality?, in: Coplan/Goldie (n. 22), 211–229.

[75] Sympathy (Mitgefühl) in this sense includes both rejoicing with the other (Mitfreude) and feeling sorry for someone who is suffering (Mitleid), *Scheler* (n. 66), 97.

[76] See n. 69, above; *Nussbaum* (n. 46), 330.

the other[77] and its significance. Sympathy, in *Scheler*'s meaning, is tightly related to love – we feel sympathy with everybody we love, yet we can also feel sympathy with someone we do not love. Sympathy, in *Scheler*'s understanding, can be best expressed by the term "compassion".[78] One may pose the question of whether compassion is a good candidate for the foundation of morality. In contrast to emotional contagion, its relation to morality is clear.[79] Compassion can be understood as a moral virtue (a disposition to respond with an adequate feeling and thought to the other person's experience). Yet it is not a free-standing virtue but rather one rooted in our moral character and dependent on our system of values and beliefs. Thus, compassion is not sufficient for moral judgments, yet without compassion they would be like a ghostly simulacrum.[80]

One of the challenges in studies on empathy which must be faced by the philosopher is the ambiguity of the term and the variety of its meanings as utilized by various thinkers. Most contemporary studies address three main components of empathy: (1) the affective element (feeling the emotion of another person – sharing affections); (2) the cognitive element (understanding the situation of another person); (3) the motivational element (an action brought about by empathic distress). Definitions of empathy may include only the first or second element, or they may combine both of them or even all three elements – keeping in mind that theorists may understand the elements differently. What is more, many studies distinguish between (1) lower-level empathy (also called mirroring, basic empathy, affective empathy) and (2) higher-level empathy (also called mindreading, perspective-shifting, re-enactive empathy, reconstructive empathy).[81]

---

[77] We can have empathy with the fictional protagonists in books or movies, yet we cannot have full sympathy with them since we know that they do not in actuality exist, *Scheler* (n. 66), 160.

[78] *M. Soniewicka*, Granice sprawiedliwości, sprawiedliwość ponad granicami (2010), 94–100; *Nussbaum* (n. 46), 297–454.

[79] The most famous philosophers to have advocated building morality on compassion, however differently understood, include Rousseau, Schopenhauer, and Smith. Yet there were many opponents of compassion in moral philosophy, such as the Roman Stoics, Spinoza, Kant, and Nietzsche. They claimed that compassion is either irrational (noncognitive) or false (due to partiality, superiority, etc.). Most of these objections addressed a different meaning of compassion than given above. See the discussion of these objections in *Nussbaum* (n. 46), 356–364.

[80] *Nussbaum* (n. 46), 390.

[81] Lower-level empathy means picking up on another's person thoughts and emotions, while higher-level empathy means adopting another person's perspective and understanding other people's thoughts, feelings, and motivations (i.e., reasons for thoughts, feelings, and behavior). Both lower- and higher-level empathy are usually explained by the simulation theory which replaced the "theory theory" based on a folk psychology. The "theory theory" is a view in the philosophy of the mind which assumes that our commonsense understanding of people's behavior rests on a speculative theory (a "folk psychology") which deploys mental state concepts (e.g., perception, belief, desire). In other words, "theory theory" assumes

As mentioned above, contemporary studies mainly follow the Humean tradition criticized by phenomenology. In our considerations, we will build upon the major insights from the phenomenological studies and adopt the following typology, which seems to cover all the most important issues discussed above: (1) cognitive empathy (*Einfühlung* – mindreading and/or perspective-taking)[82] – understanding other people's minds); (2) affective empathy (transmission and/or replication of other person's emotions); (3) compassion (empathic concern).[83] Pondering the role of empathy and compassion in law, we will pose the question of whether any of these is a suitable tool to guide legal deliberation.[84] In our further considerations we will defend the following three assertions. Firstly, we claim that cognitive empathy is neither sufficient nor necessary for legal judgments and fair decisions, yet it may help in legal decision-making. Secondly, we claim that affective empathy is not only unnecessary for legal decisions but may also distort reasoning and contribute to injustice. Thirdly, we claim that compassion should complement justice to guarantee fairness. Let us briefly discuss these claims before we turn to verifying these theses in the analysis of such concepts as liability and non-pecuniary harm.

Cognitive empathy is a very useful tool which can contribute to the better understanding of others. Law regards persons and their interactions, and therefore understanding the human mind is certainly important in both the legislation process as well as in the application of law. Yet cognitive empathy understood as direct knowledge of other people's mind or perspective-taking is not necessary in the legal context since it can be replaced by indirect knowledge

---

that to understand mental states which explain people's behavior, we have to refer to theoretical concepts, and predicting someone's behavior rests on theoretical argumentation, which involves "what if" reasoning or "by analogy" reasoning and also generalizations; cf. *L. Röska-Hardy*, Theory Theory (Simulation Theory, Theory of Mind), in: M.D. Binder et al. (eds.), Encyclopedia of Neuroscience (2009), 4064–4067, 4064. Simulationism, on the other hand, assumes that we simulate the minds of others to understand and predict people's behavior: *Coplan/Goldie* (n. 66), xxxiii.

[82] Perspective-taking can either be self-oriented (I imagine myself being "in someone's shoes" and come to the conclusion: "I know what you feel") or other-oriented (I imagine another person in her situation, thus I am moving beyond myself), as Coplan points out: *A. Coplan*, Understanding Empathy: Its features and Effects, in: Coplan/Goldie (n. 22), 9–15. Other-oriented perspective taking is very similar to Stein's Einfühlung. Both are defined as understanding the other "from inside", an intersubjective engagement which requires going beyond oneself. This is the meaning of empathy which we also utilize in this chapter. We also follow Stein's claim that self-oriented perspective-taking can be helpful when empathy fails. Coplan calls self-oriented perspective-taking quasi-empathy, while other-oriented perspective-taking is considered as mature empathy: ibid., 5, 9–15.

[83] The term "empathic concern" comes from the famous empirical studies on the relation between empathy and altruistic behavior which were conducted by *C.D. Batson*, Empathic Concern and Altruism in Humans (2009). Empathic concern seems to be closely related to Scheler's sympathy, which we call compassion.

[84] Cf. *Nussbaum* (n. 46), 297.

based on reasoning by analogy or *as if* reasoning. In fact, most of the legal terms and definitions refer to folk psychology concepts and do not require cognitive empathy. Certainly, in the process of the application of law, cognitive empathy may play an important role in legal judgments – e.g., in the courtroom, when judges or jurors face witnesses, victims, and defendants.[85] Yet we must remember that cognitive empathy is value-neutral, and therefore fair judgment would require something more than knowledge of other people's minds – it would require its adequate evaluation. So-called mindreading can be used for both morally right and wrong purposes and/or for both legal and illegal goals, such as manipulation and cheating. Therefore, cognitive empathy is a useful tool, but it must be shaped and constrained by legal principles. It has also its limitations which we will discuss further below in Section V.

As argued above, we do not have to share feelings with other people to understand them, nor do we need to in order to respond to their problems in an adequate way. Affective empathy is not only unnecessary in the legal context, but it can be also particularly dangerous, as many authors have claimed.[86] Affective empathy reflects our judgments, beliefs, preferences, and biases. In particular, critics emphasize the following features of affective empathy as potentially leading to injustice: (1) partiality (preferential treatment of known persons, e.g., "identifiable victim effect"); (2) selectivity (neglecting facts and paying special attention to emotionally highlighted issues, such as a victim's dramatic confessions or graphic images); (3) its being subject to proximity (bias towards "the near and dear"); (4) its being subject to the salience effect (here-and-now bias and neglect of consequences); (5) in-group bias (preferential treatment of those who belong to the same ethnic, political, social, cultural, etc. group); (6) cuteness bias (positive emotional reactions to infants, puppies, nice-looking faces etc.); (7) paralyzing effect (strong emotional arousal caused by emotional contagion may paralyze action and block reasoning).[87] Due to these features, affective empathy is at odds with impartiality and is very prone to manipulation, and it may lead to unfair decisions. Since affective empathy may distort legal judgments, legal procedures are constructed in a way which aims at guaranteeing the impartiality of adjunction[88] and minimizing the risk of emotional manipulation.

Compassion (empathic concern) reflects our interdependence and vulnerability[89] and recognizes human dignity (inner worth and autonomy).[90] Building

---

[85] *Colby* (n. 22).

[86] See *P. Bloom*, Against Empathy. The Case for Rational Compassion (2016).

[87] *Bloom* (n. 86); *Hoffman* (n. 22), 250; *Prinz* (n. 74), 226 f.

[88] Art. 86 § 2 Ustawy z 27.07.2001 r. Prawo o ustroju sądów powszechnych, Dz.U. z 2020 r. poz. 2072, English translation to be found under https://www.venice.coe.int/webforms/documents/default.aspx?pdffile=CDL-REF(2017)046-e (last accessed 12 September 2022).

[89] *Nussbaum* (n. 46), 300 f.

[90] Cf. *J. Deigh*, Empathy and Universalizability, Ethics 105 (1995), 743–763.

on these assumptions, compassion promotes evaluative engagement with the other and the recognition of the significance of the other and her experience, and it can therefore play an important role in law.[91] Firstly, it can be important in the application of law. It can be considered as the judicial virtue of paying attention to all the sides at a trial.[92] Judicial impartiality does not mean indifference, and we should expect virtuous judges to be engaged with the participants of the legal procedure. What is more, compassion may help to identify unfairness in the application of legal rules in a given case and contribute to a correction of rule-driven results by resort to equity.[93] It can similarly be considered as a virtue of other legal actors, such as jurors, lawyers, or prosecutors. Secondly, it can be important in the process of legislation – incorporating compassion into legal institutions which protect and respect human dignity. It may also encourage adequate legal changes. Thirdly, it can have an important motivational role in fostering respect for the law. Compassion builds strong attachments and provides meaning to our ends. Therefore, it may also motivate people to follow the rules beyond or contrary to self-interest, for the sake of the other or the common good. Yet compassion is not sufficient for guaranteeing fairness since it depends on the underlying system of values. It is also prone to partiality and should therefore be a subject of moral education. Moreover, it should not replace justice based on principles, but rather complement it.

IV. Emotions, liability, and non-pecuniary harm

A. Emotions and liability

Emotions and liability interact, although this relationship is not always obvious. There seem to be two ways in which this interaction may appear: the influence of our emotion on legal liability, and, conversely, liability for emotions that we provoked in someone else.

Firstly, emotions may modify the legal responsibility for a crime. The widely known term "crime of passion" refers in common usage to cases when anger overpowers someone's self-control and logical thinking to the point where they cannot be held responsible for their actions.[94] Such a perception of

---

[91] *Nussbaum* (n. 46) 401–454; *M. Del Mar*, Imagining by feeling: a case for compassion in legal reasoning, International Journal of Law in Context 13 (2017), 143–157.

[92] *M. Soniewicka*, Integralność sędziego z perspektywy etyki cnót, Krytyka Prawa 13 (2021), 81–98, 86.

[93] As guided by another virtue referred to as prudence (Greek: phronesis), *Soniewicka* (n. 92). See also *idem* (n. 78), 89–100; *M.C. Nussbaum*, Equity and Mercy, in: *idem*, Sex and Social Justice (1999), 154–183.

[94] See e.g. *P. Mullen*, The crime of passion and the changing cultural construction of jealousy, Criminal Behaviour and Mental Health 3 (1993), 1–11. In Polish law the so called

emotion subscribes to the mechanistic view on affect, which according to *Martha C. Nussbaum* and *Dan Kahan* holds that "emotions are forces more or less devoid of thought or perception – that they are impulses or surges that lead the person to action without embodying beliefs, or any way of seeing the world that can be assessed as correct or incorrect, appropriate or inappropriate."[95]

However, does the law actually assume that emotions are wild, uncontrollable impulses that excuse crimes? This perception has been increasingly questioned by researchers working in the law and emotions movement. As an example of such studies, it is worth referring to *Kahan* and *Nussbaum*, who advocate replacing the traditional mechanistic conception of emotions in law with an evaluative conception of emotions which is much more sophisticated, coherent, adapted to the legal context, and accords with current discoveries in cognitive science and psychology.[96] The evaluative conception assumes that emotions: (1) embody beliefs, ways of seeing, and of evaluating or appraising an object as valuable or significant; (2) involve reference to personal well-being.[97] While the mechanistic approach emphasizes the passive role of agents (emotions befall them and impact their volition), an evaluative approach assumes an active role of agents whose beliefs, values, and choices shape their emotional lives (emotions can be educated). Thus, within the evaluative approach to emotion, we can argue that we should be held responsible for who we are and how we emotionally respond to different situations. The evaluative approach to emotion does not focus solely on the intensity of emotions, but foremost on their quality; thus we can ponder in legal discourse whether a particular emotional reaction was *adequate* or not.[98] As the authors argue, emotions embody judgments about what kind of goods are valued – including how and by whom – and thus we should assess emotions against the background of the community *mores* and social norms which usually specify their intensity, duration, and ways of expression.[99] A standard of a good person or citizen

"murder in the heat of passion" is regulated in Art. 148 § 4 of the Penal Code: "Whoever kills a person under the influence of strong agitation justified by the circumstances, shall be subject to the penalty of deprivation of liberty for a term of one to ten years."

[95] *Kahan/Nussbaum* (n. 13), 277 f.

[96] *Kahan/Nussbaum* (n. 13), 277 f., analyze the application of the evaluative conception of emotion to criminal law. Yet Nussbaum's other works, in which she promotes an evaluative conception of emotions rooted in neo-Stoic and Aristotelian tradition, go far beyond criminal law.

[97] *Kahan/Nussbaum* (n. 13), 286–291. According to Kahan and Nussbaum, beliefs constitute emotions, and emotions are identical with value-laden cognitive attitude, thus constituting the so-called identity thesis. This gives rise to many objections, see *Scarantino/de Sousa* (n. 28); *J. Deigh*, Nussbaum's Defense of the Stoic Theory of Emotions, Quinnipiac Law Review 19 (2000), 293–308. In our paper we do not follow the neo-Stoic tradition and do not apply the identity thesis, see n. 46, above.

[98] *Kahan/Nussbaum* (n. 13), 325.

[99] *Kahan/Nussbaum* (n. 13), 308.

provides reasons and criteria for judging our emotions, as claimed by the neo-Aristotelian tradition: "A good person not only values the right things but values them in the right amount in relation to other goods".[100] Thus, we can be held responsible for the emotions we experience in a given context.[101] Of course, there are many factors which matter in shaping our character, and therefore all such judgments have to take into account the limited control that individuals have over shaping their emotions.

Emotions, therefore, may mitigate punishment or even excuse one's actions, but they need to be contextually sound, adequate, and appropriately expressed according to moral or social norms – in other words, one has to be reasonably angry or understandably scared for the law to approve these emotions as modifiers of responsibility. Thus, the law should acknowledge the evaluative and cognitive components of emotions in order to adequately address these issues. The mechanistic conception of emotions is inadequate and misleading.

However, the interaction between emotions and liability is not limited to criminal law. In civil law one's own mental state is to some extent legally protected, and, therefore, one can – under special circumstances – be held liable for causing someone else's emotions. Just as *Nussbaum* and *Kahan* considered which factors determine the responsibility for one's own emotions, it must be investigated in what way law conceives of our responsibility for other people's emotions. Accordingly, we must ask which conception of emotions is best fitted to the law in terms of holding people liable for other people's emotions, and we must similarly examine the role that empathy plays in these considerations. In the following part of our paper we will focus on private law liability for other people's feelings, sometimes commonly referred to as "liability for emotional distress" or "emotional harm". As we have mentioned in Section I, a sizable part of law and emotions scholarship has focused on criminal law and the impact of emotions in that sphere. As civil law scholarship falls short of examining the impact of emotions, it seems worthwhile to analyze the role of emotions and empathy with reference to liability for emotional harm. It remains a paradox that while in many jurisdictions emotional distress is one of the rare places in law where feelings, suffering, or other affective states are explicitly mentioned, few law and emotions' scholars have focused on this problem.

At first glance, it may seem counterintuitive that one can be held responsible for how another person feels. *Lisa Feldmann Barrett* asks a rhetorical question – should you be able to sue someone for breaking your heart?[102] Why should law ever protect emotions in this way and under which conditions? Perhaps an attempt to answer this question should begin by retracing the historical roots of the idea. In some European countries (Austria, Ireland, Germany,

[100] *Kahan/Nussbaum* (n. 13), 315.

[101] *Kahan/Nussbaum* (n. 13), 339.

[102] *Barrett* (n. 43), 220.

Poland), there appeared from the eighteenth to twentieth centuries laws which made "offense to religious sentiments" a punishable crime.[103] Their formulation differed from the previous laws of blasphemy. It must be noted that blasphemy was theoretically an offense against God, and it was criminalized out of fear that God would strike the community of the blasphemer.[104] However, beginning with the Enlightenment, western jurisdictions included the protection of people's feelings to some degree, and the new laws were supposed to prevent the public outrage that people may feel when their religion is questioned or mocked – preventing as well the social unrest that might consequently be triggered.[105] Later, it became even clearer that, even though offending religious feelings was a public act, it constituted an injury to the emotions of individual believers – not causing them primarily anger, but rather sadness, indignity, and emotional pain.[106]

It was relatively recently that feelings unrelated to God and religion became an object of interest – and eventual protection – of the law. Emotional distress claims were first raised in the nineteenth century in the United States, as a byproduct of the fright resulting from traffic incidents or insensitive pranks.[107] In the common law systems of today there exist tort provisions or precedents that explicitly define harm to emotions as an object of liability, such as, but not limited to, the intentional infliction of emotional distress.[108] While these regulations and their judicial functioning have been a subject of heated debate in Anglo-American legal scholarship, in this paper we want to focus on the less explored continental version of liability for emotional distress, in some jurisdictions known as non-material or non-pecuniary harm.[109]

The assimilation of the concept of emotion to this construction gives rise to problematic questions; for example, if one is to restore all the loss caused by her unlawful action, how is this possible in respect of emotions? On the other hand, is there a sufficient ground to exclude emotions from the conception of

---

[103] *G. Taylor*, Austria's law against defamation of religion: A case study, Journal of Law and Religion 30 (2015), 80–106. In Polish law Art. 196 of the Penal Code states: "Whoever insults the religious feelings of others by publicly insulting an object of religious honor or a place intended for the public performance of religious rites, shall be subject to a fine, restriction of liberty or imprisonment for up to 2 years."

[104] *Taylor* (n. 103), 80–106.

[105] See e.g. *P. Goldman*, Religious convictions: the law of blasphemy in Ireland, Adelaide Law Review 32 (2011), 265–285; *Taylor* (n. 103), 80–106.

[106] See e.g. *L. Greenfeld,* Transcending the nation's worth, Daedalus 122(3) (1993), 47–62.

[107] *J.G. Curenton,* The Twilight Zone of Danger: Negligent Infliction of Emotional Distress as an Actionable Tort, Cumberland Law Review 15 (1984), 519–541.

[108] *D. Givelber*, The Right to Minimum Social Decency and the Limits of Evenhandedness: Intentional Infliction of Emotional Distress by Outrageous Conduct, Columbia Law Review 82 (1982), 45–75.

[109] *J. Lahe/I. Kull*, Compensation of non-pecuniary damage to persons close to the deceased or to the aggrieved person, International Comparative Jurisprudence 2 (2016), 1–7.

restitution, as they could – potentially – come into the range of legally protected interests? The doctrinal problems of liability also resurface in the context of emotions. For example, stating the extent of responsibility may be problematic due to the interactive nature of emotions and their immeasurability.[110] How do feelings alter meanings of agency and ownership? Moreover, should the existing rules of liability (fault, risk-based, and strict liability) apply to emotion in a similar manner or somehow be modified? All these questions – pertinent to the emotion-related common law torts – will be considered here in reference to what can be called a continental counterpart: non-pecuniary damages.

B. The concept of emotional harm

What we understand by emotional harm in this chapter is an amalgam of philosophical and legal takes on the concept, but it will be exemplified using an example from a continental legal system – the Polish one. *Joel Feinberg* famously defined harming as follows: "A harms B in the strict and narrow sense employed by the harm principle when (i) A sets back B's interests, and (2) A does this in such a manner as to violate B's rights (i.e. wrong him)".[111] In *Feinberg*'s opinion, the interests to be protected include primarily so-called "welfare" interests such as "the absence of absorbing pain and suffering or grotesque disfigurement, minimal intellectual acuity, emotional stability, the absence of groundless anxieties and resentments, the capacity to engage normally in social intercourse and to enjoy and maintain friendships".[112] Accordingly, his definition of harm would extend to emotional harm. The law was not so generous, however, and mental distress was long thought to be subservient to physical damage. This was evident in nineteenth-century American cases where liability for emotional fright could be ascribed only where the endangering object (be it a vehicle or a fist) was in immediate physical proximity to one's body.[113] Over time, purely non-physical injuries inflicted with words alone began to be recognized, such as tasteless pranks, tactless ways of informing someone of a loved one's death,[114] intentional infliction of distress, defama-

---

[110] *R. Elphick/J. Dugard*, Jus Cogens and Compensation, in: D. Tladi (ed.), Peremptory Norms of General International Law (Jus Cogens) (2021), 413–440.

[111] *J. Feinberg*, Harm to others (1984), 65.

[112] *Feinberg* (n. 111), 37.

[113] *J.J. Kircher*, The Four Faces of Tort Law: Liability for Emotional Harm, Marquette Law Review 90 (2007), 789–920, 815.

[114] *W.H. Theis,* Intentional Infliction of Emotional Distress: A Need for Limits on Liability, DePaul Law Review 27 (1977), 275–292, 278.

tion (the revilement of someone's character having roots in Roman *iniuria* suits)[115], and offending one's religious or patriotic sentiments.[116]

The question posed above relates to the problem of the "interpretation of emotions", which can be exemplified by the treatment of non-material (emotional) harm in Polish law.[117] In the Polish legal system, it is well-established that some constitutionally guaranteed basic rights have executable counterparts in private obligations in the form of personal goods (dobra osobiste). An early and very prominent conception of personal goods was emotional in nature. This idea, stated by *Stefan Grzybowski* in the 1960s, defined personal goods as "individual values of the world of feelings, of the mental state of a person".[118] Polish scholarship has labeled this definition a "psychological" or "subjective" concept of personal goods,[119] and it had a tremendous impact on the judiciary throughout the second half of the twentieth century. Despite critiques and attempts to revert to an "objective" conception in the last decades (protecting legal interests by virtue of social agreements about their importance), the subjective definition still resounds in court cases.[120]

The Polish judiciary, as evident from court cases, considers emotional harm as distress brought about by an unlawful attack on what a person holds dear, besides their property, as well as pain or loss of dignity.[121] The family is an example of what is protected, due both to its emotional weight and social agreement about its value and importance. Many cases concern the loss of a loved one: a considerable amount of attention is consequently paid to the special relationship existing between two people prior to a death and the resulting emptiness in the grieving person's life (cases based on Art. 446 § 4 of the Civil Code). Harm to personal goods (Art. 448) is more vague, but it often also involves damage to what people hold dear, like their reputation, their beloved belongings, and their religious beliefs and family heritage. These kinds of

[115] *T. Wallinga,* Review of E. Descheemaeker/H. Scott (eds.), Iniuria and the Common Law, Roman Legal Tradition 10 (2014), 46–50.

[116] Court of Appeal Gdańsk, judgment of 5 July 2018, I ACa 981/17, LEX no. 2694630.

[117] *J. Wesołowska*, Legal (un)translatability of emotion: an empirical study of non-pecuniary harm in Polish courts (doctoral dissertation, Jagiellonian University, Faculty of Law and Administration, expected 2023).

[118] *S. Grzybowski*, Ochrona dóbr, in: idem (ed.), System Prawa Cywilnego, vol. 1 (1985), 297.

[119] *J. Regan (Balcarczyk),* Komentarz do art. 23 k.c., in: M. Załucki (ed.), Kodeks cywilny. Komentarz (2019), Legalis no. 1116028.

[120] See e.g. District Court Gdańsk, judgment of 27 July 2018 r., IV Ca 359/18, LEX no. 2549873.

[121] Dignity as "the right of personage". *M. Soniewicka/J. Holocher*, Human Dignity in Poland, in: P. Becchi/K. Mathis (eds.), Handbook of Human Dignity in Europe (2017), 1–23, 11: "In Polish jurisprudence one distinguishes between two aspects of the dignity of the person: dignity as an inherent and inviolable value; and dignity as 'the right of personage' which includes values of the mental life of every human being, as well as those values that determine the subjective position of an individual in a society."

injuries often, but not always, have to do with dignity: a defamed person has not only lost something valuable (reputation) but also suffered shame, ostracism, and humiliation. A prisoner who feels that her dignity was undermined by oppressive conditions can also bring a lawsuit based on this regulation, asserting a right not to be dehumanized and demeaned. Health is another important personal good, as is sexual integrity, but they are framed in separate regulations – Art. 445 § 1 and Art. 445 § 2, respectively. Perhaps dealing with them separately from other personal goods served to emphasize their importance. However, health and sexual integrity are also related to value and dignity – most people feel that it is important for their health not to be worsened and to not feel crippled, maimed or to lose agency. A component of this kind of harm is pain, which is perceived by the law to be both a physiological state and an unpleasant emotion.[122] This is interesting, as unpleasant emotions alone do not trigger liability in Polish law; they must, rather, be connected to something important, like a value or an interest, which confirms that the cognitive-evaluative component of emotions is crucial and should be acknowledged in legal scholarship.

The way non-material harm is framed in Polish law constitutes an interesting problem for liability in the context of emotions. The Civil Code describes it succinctly, not providing the definition of harm but denoting it as "experienced", which points to the emotional aspect. Similarly, the courts "may order suitable compensation" for the harm suffered. Such a formulation leaves a lot to be determined in the discretion of judges, ranging from the definition of harm itself (coined by courts as: suffering, negative experiences, and distress) to how rules governing liability should be applied. In the following section, we will use this example to show how emotions affect the application of civil law. As we have mentioned in Section II, not only do emotions affect the law, but law has also a reciprocal impact on the functioning of social norms with respect to emotions and their manifestations.

C. Emotional aspects of harm and their consequences for liability

In Polish civil law, one can be held accountable for emotional harm based on all forms of liability: fault, sometimes including negligence (Art. 448); equity principles (Art. 417^2); or fault and strict liability combined (Art. 445 and Art. 446 § 4). Although these forms of responsibility also feature in the regime of awarding damages for material harm, applying them to emotional harm is not a matter of simple analogy. To the contrary, determining legal liability for harm to feelings raises legal, philosophical, and practical issues which need to be integrated into theory of liability. Firstly, there is the matter of how law should understand emotions in order to determine non-pecuniary harm. As we

[122] From the perspective of the theories of emotions, pain would not be considered as an emotion, although it could be a physiological part of emotions such as grief, anger, and fear.

have mentioned in Section II, three ways of conceptualizing emotions should be distinguished: the evaluative or cognitive conception, the affective or experiential conception, and the motivational conception. For harm, the evaluative meaning of emotions seems to be essential as the validity of claims is dependent on the harmed person's relationship to the interest that is impinged – be it one's own reputation, a beloved person, or a sentimental souvenir. As *Nussbaum* insightfully notes, her grief over the death of her mother contains essentially the judgment that her mother was important to her and that a meaningful part of her life has now been lost.[123] Courts agree that grief at the loss of a loved one is not only a result of the striking image of their lifeless body but also a result of the thought of having to live without them. However, in the eyes of the law, while the evaluative sense of emotional experience may provide it with enough information to decide that harm has been done, it is not enough. There is also a matter of assessing the true scope and impact of the harm, which then determines the amount of the compensation. For that, the law must approach emotions not only as evaluations but also as real, lived experiences. The individual specificity of each harm is assessed through reconstructing the affective experience that is also embodied. This is significant in relation to the dual nature of emotions which we addressed in Section II – their simultaneous biological and cultural character. The law on harm recognizes both these aspects. Emotions are embodied and traumatic events which deeply affect the overall health of a person. Often, in cases of non-pecuniary harm, the loss of health and the necessity of treatment is employed as a measure of the intensity of emotions. On the other hand, emotions that are subject to the scrutiny of law are expected to follow cultural norms and the unwritten rules on how a given society experiences honor, pain, loss, and happiness. What it means to thrive is contextual, and if harm is a thwarting of the possibility of thriving, then we need cultural norms that are able to recognize this.

Emotional harm is traditionally thought of in law as less tangible, trustworthy or "serious" than physical ailments or material losses. *Barrett* refers to the assumption that physical harm is worse than emotional harm as being "baked into the law at its deepest levels, driving verdicts of guilt and innocence and gauging punishments on a massive scale".[124] The influence of this assumption on the process of assigning civil liability should, therefore, be expected. In fact, the courts attempt to "objectify" harm to emotions, making it more amenable to legal scrutiny. The first aspect of that process is refusing to attribute liability to states that do not pass the "threshold" of emotional harm. Some Polish courts have stated that certain feelings, although unpleasant and arising from a harmful event, are not sufficient to warrant liability for emotional harm. For instance, in one of these judgments we can read: the "negative feelings reported

[123] *Nussbaum* (n. 46), 37.

[124] *Barrett* (n. 43), 220.

by one person after the death of a loved one did not suffice to declare harm to her personal rights".[125] In a different judgment, although the court noted that "departure of a family member always causes sadness and gloom", it also stated that "it is not identical with emotional harm, sanctioned by law".[126] Therefore, it seems that liability for emotional harm does not extend to psychological pain that is commonly perceived as a normal part of life in society; individuals have to demonstrate a degree of suffering that passes a certain mark in order to have their grievance recognized.

When the plaintiff's injured feelings are recognized as sufficient to constitute harm, the law strives to hold defendants liable only for the part of trauma that their action caused. But that can be difficult, as emotions arise in complex ways and bring about psychological and physiological changes that are often difficult to measure and predict. In view of this complexity and unpredictability, liability for emotional harm complicates the matter even further. How much of the trauma was provoked by a defendant's actions, and what part of it depended on the individual psychological make-up of the harmed individual? As the borders of liability shift between the injured party and the offender, courts scramble to isolate the responsibility exclusively to factors on the offender's side.

Firstly, it needs to be underlined that law only ascribes liability for the "normal effects" of one's action. This legal term takes on a different meaning in the case of emotional harm – as there is a need to set the limits for liability – defining the normal or appropriate response to traumatizing events. In many court cases the view surfaced that the law on emotional harm was not designed to cater to "persons with a weaker psyche" who experience trauma deeper and that it was appropriate to brush off the harm of people who "bottle up" emotions.[127] This is, in a way, a contradiction of the eggshell skull doctrine, according to which the unexpected frailty of the injured person does not excuse one from liability.[128] Polish courts thus convey the idea that one is only liable for what "a reasonable person" may feel.[129] This not only encompasses the initial reaction but also more distant emotional impact. In some cases, there seems to be almost a limit on the suffering, in which "normal" and "prolonged" grief are distinguished. The latter is sometimes seen by courts as a failure by plaintiffs to "cope with" or "work through" their emotion, shifting a part of the

---

[125] Regional Court Ciechanow, judgment of 20 February 2017, I C 861/16.

[126] District Court Słupsk, judgment of 10 April 2017, I C 316/16.

[127] See e.g., Regional Court Słupsk, judgment of 12 April 2017, IV Ca 161/17; Regional Court Olsztyn, judgment of 11 June 2019, I C 135/19, LEX no. 2691720.

[128] *S.J. McQuade*, The eggshell skull rule and related problems in recovery for mental harm in the law of torts, Campbell Law Review 24 (2001), 1–45.

[129] *J. Jastrzębski*, Kilka uwag o naprawieniu szkody niemajątkowej, Palestra 50/3–4 (2005), 32–50, 43.

liability for harm back to them.[130] This approach can be best explained by the cognitive-evaluative conception of emotions, described above, according to which emotions are educable and one is responsible for her character.

Attempting to decontextualize harm means trying to isolate other factors – besides unusual frailty – that can contribute to emotional harm. Some courts have noted that trauma may appear and even feel amplified in people with dramatic, outgoing personalities – but that is no reason to ascribe to them greater harm.[131] Others stress the necessity of separating harm caused by the offender from harm brought about by different traumatic events in the plaintiff's life, such as losing other family members, undergoing serious illnesses, or experience professional troubles.[132] Such factors are not considered as the part of the liability of the defendant but as "co-existing conditions". Similarly, if a mental illness or disorder is an effect of the trauma suffered as emotional harm, the court engages clinical experts to exclude any "organic" causes of the illness – the defendant cannot be made fully liable for a disease that was "dormant" in the injured person and merely triggered by the harmful event.[133]

In trying to isolate and pinpoint the exact degree of liability for emotional harm, Polish courts operationalize trauma and scrutinize biological or psychosocial factors that could have amplified and prolonged it. This signifies the treatment of emotional harm in a medical, professional way, which is evidenced by the ample use of expert witnesses, mainly psychiatrists and psychologists. Such dissection of an individual's mental suffering may appear to be a cold and clinical trivialization, aimed at dispassionate monetary compensation. However, another tendency may be observed which is almost opposite in nature: determining liability for emotional harm turns out to be closely correlated with the moral dimension of responsibility. In many cases, the feelings of condemnation or compassion may also be detected in how the court has described the harm and assigned blame. There are good reasons to think that cases dealing with material goods rarely evoke the same level of moral sentiment.

The fact that the moral dimension of liability is especially underlined with regards to emotional harm shows that the outcome of a case largely depends on the state of mind of the defendant. Those who have inflicted emotional harm on others for especially contemptible reasons are deemed more liable, and although the damages awarded are meant as compensation, sometimes they are

---

[130] Court of Appeal Szczecin, judgment of 27 March 2019, I ACa 533/18, LEX no. 2668028; Court of Appeal Szczecin, judgment of 27 April 2017, I ACa 1000/16, LEX no. 2335156.

[131] Court of Appeal Szczecin, judgment of 27 March 2019, I ACa 533/18, LEX no. 2668028.

[132] Regional Court Białystok, judgment of 31 January 2017, I C 986/16, LEX no. 2667680.

[133] Court of Appeal Gdańsk, judgment of 22 January 2019, V ACa 554/18, LEX no. 2692586.

awarded punitively.[134] This can be seen, for example, when courts award especially high damages to tabloids who tarnish the public reputations of individuals "because they can afford it".[135] Such damages are not only meant to satisfy the plaintiff's expectations but also to punish, in a quasi-penal way, the inflictor of harm, and even function as a warning to the general society.[136] The possibility of negligently inflicting emotional harm demands that the law introduce a standard of care not only with regards to others' physical and material safety but also in terms of the handling of emotions, e.g. treating patients with basic respect and compassion.[137]

As moral consideration enters the deliberation on emotional harm, it may serve not only to increase the liability of the defendant, but sometimes, surprisingly, to decrease it. Feelings of justice and propriety and social norms dictate that inflicting emotional harm on someone is sometimes, if not exactly justifiable, at least understandable. This was curiously illustrated in a case of a spurned woman who harassed the new partner of her husband via text messages. The harassed woman brought a case for emotional harm. The court condemned the behavior of the defendant but at the same time acknowledged that her motives were somehow understandable, as she perceived her years-long relationship and life having crumbled because of the plaintiff, who flaunted her new relationship.[138] The emotional state of offenders (like anger or despair) may in an interesting turn diminish their liability for inflicting emotional harm on others. Two explanations are possible: either the law assumes the irrationality of emotions or, alternatively, in certain circumstances some emotional reactions are deemed understandable and thus constitute a mitigating factor. The latter explanation, as *Nussbaum* argues, is more appropriate since it does not concentrate on the intensity of emotions only, focusing instead on their cognitive element, i.e., their appropriateness or inappropriateness for a given situation.[139] The meaning of legality and morality as standards for responsibility also converges, as emotional harm can be brought about by actions incompatible with social norms (*zasady współżycia społecznego*).

Emotions influence the shape of legal liability on many levels. Emotions as the good endangered by harm spread to the other aspects of the legal process. They influence legal concepts such as "facts", "immediate causes", and "normal effects"; they shape the ways in which the courts perceive credibility; and

---

[134] Regional Court Warsaw, judgment of 6 February 2017, III C 544/15, LEX no. 2632265.

[135] District Court Warsaw, judgment of 9 January 2017, III C 1454/15, LEX no. 2244428.

[136] Court of Appeals Gdańsk, judgment of 22 January 2019 r., V ACa 554/18, LEX no. 2692586.

[137] Court of Appeals Gdańsk, judgment of 22 January 2019 r., V ACa 554/18, LEX no. 2692586.

[138] District Court Warsaw, judgment of 6 February 2017, III C 544/15, LEX no. 2632265.

[139] *Kahan/Nussbaum* (n. 13), 277 f.

they demand engaging with and integrating many, often conflicting, visions of the human psyche. The presence of emotions as the object of harm therefore significantly alters the process by which legal responsibility is assigned, interpreted, and absolved. The emotional character of cases may evoke strong moral feelings in legal actors, which can influence the process of assigning liability, and these actors try to distance themselves from these feelings by means of increasing professionalization and medicalization. Moreover, declaring someone legally responsible for emotional harm makes that person not only financially but also morally liable for the suffering. As emotions are malleable and harm to them is neither beyond change or remedy nor easily compensated with money, courts strive for new ways of assigning liability, blame, and compensation.

V. The role of empathy in the interpretation of non-pecuniary harm

Thomas E. Kadri, following in *Smith*'s footsteps, writes that "a comprehensive response to harm relies on empathy".[140] But how exactly are harm and empathy related, and is this relationship really so inevitable? What role does the latter play in conceptualizing the former, and what shape should this relationship take in the law? In this section of our paper, we will evaluate the three aforementioned kinds of empathy (affective empathy, cognitive empathy and compassion) in order to show that while cognitive empathy is neither necessary nor sufficient for the law to evaluate emotional harm, affective empathy may cause dangerously impartial judgments on the matter of harm. We will also attempt to show why compassion (empathic concern) should take place in the legal evaluation of harm.

Cognitive empathy is defined as mindreading and/or perspective-taking. Following *Stein*'s analyses of *Einfühlung* in Section III, we understand it as emotional experience which provides a direct knowledge of somebody's state of mind. Grasping people's minds is a special cognitive skill which provides knowledge but does not involve evaluation of the grasped experience. Perspective-taking should not be confused with *Einfühlung*. As *Stein* pointed out, we grasp other people's mental states directly, and there is no need for reasoning, association, or representation. Perspective-taking – "putting oneself in someone's shoes" – can be helpful when mindreading fails. Thus, cognitive empathy

---

[140] *T.E. Kadri*, Networks of empathy, Utah Law Review (2020), 1075–1120, 1078. Kadri understands empathy as perspective-taking combined with affective empathy (sharing affection). According to him, "fellow-feeling," to use Adam Smith's term, rests on imagination since perspective-taking brings about an "imaginary change of situation", thanks to which we can conceive of another person's suffering as a part of our own experience.

should be understood first and foremost as mindreading, while perspective-taking can be described rather as cognitive quasi-empathy.[141] Cognitive empathy is a useful tool, yet it is neither necessary nor sufficient in interpreting harm. Contemporary legislation and case law are mainly based on folk psychology concepts and seem to be well-informed as to what kinds of emotions should be met with recognition and legal protection. But even in the more unclear cases where more proactive judicial action is needed, cognitive empathy is still not the best suited tool since it is value-neutral and thus unable to evaluate suffering as good or bad or as right or wrong, determinations which are essential for the concept of harm. This means that cognitive empathy requires reference to moral and legal principles if it is to be of any use in this context.

What is more, cognitive empathy and cognitive quasi-empathy (perspective-taking) are not always reliable – they can be both erroneous and limited. Studies confirm that people routinely use flawed theory of mind in assessing both their own emotions or those of others, be it due to a lack of knowledge or their own biases.[142] Furthermore, due to a social norm placing stigma on mental health, people do not recognize the impact which traumatic events may have on the overall functioning of an individual.[143] This shortcoming is caused by the fact that our psycho-physical structure sets limits on cognitive empathy by defining what is intelligible for us and what is not, as *Stein* notes.[144] Thus, we may lack meaningful insight into someone's mental state, particularly in cases of people with whom we do not share all the dimensions of experience, such as mentally ill, blind, or deaf people. In such cases, when we are unable to directly grasp someone's mental state, we usually make use of perspective-taking, which requires a special kind of imagination. As a result, instead of grasping people's minds, we think what others feel or should feel in certain situations, and this can be highly erroneous and should not be the basis for the protection of their legal interests. If cognitive quasi-empathy (perspective-taking) is essentially imagining the situation of the plaintiff, then it means that the limits of someone's imagination could become the limits of legal protection. This sort of rigid thinking endangers the protection of subjective rights and causes harm judgments to become overly dependent on the judge and her personal background, rather than on the functioning of the law. For example, if a bereaved parent brings a case against whoever caused them to lose their child, a childless judge – if we were to apply the logic of imagination – may theoretically fail to grasp all the implications of the situation. Similarly, an atheist judge may not only be unable to fully grasp the mental state of a religious

---

[141] See n. 82, above.

[142] *S. Stich/S. Nichols*, Folk psychology: Simulation or tacit theory?, Mind & Language 7 (1992), 35–71.

[143] *M. Slade/E. Longden*, Empirical evidence about recovery and mental health, BMC Psychiatry 15 (2015), 1–14.

[144] On what follows, see n. 69, above.

person but also unable to imagine herself as the victim of offence to religious feelings. These limitations of cognitive empathy and quasi-empathy should not, however, restrict moral and legal judgments: as we argued in Section III, we cannot imagine how animals perceive the world, but we may – and nevertheless should – protect them from suffering and surround them with care.

Though not a primary instrument of justice, imagination should aid law as an auxiliary instrument. Conversely, its absence should not hinder the application of the law. This was aptly shown by Justice *Ruth Bader Ginsburg* during a case where other judges – all male – were prone to ruling that a strip search of a 14-year-old girl in a room full of her peers (which caused them to see her naked body) was not an abuse of her legal rights. *Terry A. Maroney* noted that the justice who dismissed that assertion, comparing it to his experience in a boy's locker room, "was promptly schooled by [Justice *Ginsburg*] who, speaking from her more particular experience with having been a teenage girl, expressed a strong view that of course it was traumatic".[145]

Affective empathy involves, as we established, sharing the emotion of another person by the transmission/replication of another person's emotion. It may seem at first glance to be a better basis for emotional judgments, especially if we assume sentimentalism, according to which moral judgments come after automatic, emotional reactions which are prior to any reflection or reasoning.[146] If this were true, harm should be protected in accordance with the feeling of injustice. Yet this approach would endanger legal reasoning with subjectivity, partiality, and biases, as mentioned in Section III. Clearly, there is a danger that judges may act on their own emotions, out of pity or anger, or there may be a lackluster reaction if the plaintiff did not manage to "infect" the judge with her emotion. A judge will often choose legal consequences while feeling pity for the plaintiff – due to the motivational aspect of emotions, the pity may soon turn into anger toward the defendant. If we follow the logic of affective empathy, it does not matter whether the anger is justified or not, as it was borne out of emotional infection rather than having been filtered through reason. Law has long fought to minimize the impact of affective empathy in both judges and juries – this is evidenced by limits on the use of vivid, emotion-evoking imagery in the courtroom (graphic evidence bias, victim impact statements).[147]

Another problem with affective empathy is that it is prone to creating often unconscious stereotypes on how people should display their emotions. There is a problem with this on several levels. Firstly, there is a danger that the person

---

[145] *T.A. Maroney*, Lay conceptions of emotion in law, in: S.A. Bandes et al. (eds.), Research Handbook on Law and Emotion (2021), 15–27, 18.

[146] *J.M. Paxton/L. Ungar/J.D. Greene*, Reflection and reasoning in moral judgment, Cognitive Science 36 (2012), 163–177.

[147] *S.A. Bandes/J.M. Salerno*, Emotion, proof and prejudice: The cognitive science of gruesome photos and victim impact statements, Arizona State Law Journal 46 (2014), 1004–1056.

may not display their feelings well or that the judge may not grasp them well. As we mentioned in Section II, the dual nature of emotions – both biological and cultural – means that their expression, intensity, and duration may differ greatly depending on personal structure and cultural context. People vary in how they show and feel emotion, and especially in how they cope with traumatic events. Various coping mechanisms may appear inexplicable if seen from outside – fits of hysterical laughter at a funeral being one of them.[148] Basing judgments on displayed emotions is unfair: it is biased towards expressive people and against those who are more closed off or incapable of expressing emotion due to neurodiversity. Secondly, affective empathy means measuring the intensity of suffering by its external displays. The message of a sobbing, hysterical plaintiff should not automatically mean more to the court than a tight-lipped and stoic plaintiff since such behavior is not an accurate measure of feeling. Thirdly, emotional expressions can be faked, especially when they are expected by the law, as for instance remorse.[149] The problem of distinguishing authentic emotions from fake ones is not a simple task, and therefore affective empathy may be an easy way to manipulate and corrupt emotions.

Assessing emotional harm through the perception of people's emotions should also not be the basis for legal decisions because there are instant empathy biases that we associate with genders, age, and social roles. Prominent examples are the expectation of remorse for having committed a crime and a negative subconscious reaction to women showing anger and men showing weakness. According to *Jessica M. Salerno*, unconscious biases resulting from social stereotypes permit men to be angry and to act on anger, whilst a woman showing that emotion evokes negative perceptions as it seems incompatible with her perceived gender role.[150]

Just as with our display of emotions, our ability to read other people's feelings varies, depending not only on personality but on upbringing and even such things as the number of mirror neurons.[151] Therefore it is not only the plaintiff that may fail to communicate emotions; the judge as well may fail to grasp or share them. This is also due to a real possibility of affective fatigue. We have a limited capacity to maintain intensive focus on emotionally draining issues –

---

[148] *Barrett* (n. 43), 42.

[149] *C. Sanger*, The Role and Reality of Emotions in Law, William & Mary Journal of Women and the Law 8 (2001), 107–113, 111.

[150] *J.M. Salerno/L.C. Peter-Hagene*, One angry woman: Anger expression increases influence for men, but decreases influence for women, during group deliberation, Law and Human Behavior 39 (2015), 581–592.

[151] *P. Schober/B. Sabitzer*. Mirror neurons for education, INTED2013 Proceedings (2013), 40–45.

thus people get tired of bad news after some time.[152] The waning attention that is devoted to a tragedy with the passage of time is not due to our callousness but is rather a matter of our limited capacity to worry very strongly for a long time, which consumes great amounts of energy and upsets homeostasis. Judges should manage their emotions wisely and sparingly so they do not become burnt out – emotional currency should not be spent all at once.

In contrast to cognitive and affective empathy, the mechanism by which compassion works is more complicated, as we have argued in Section III. Compassion is an empathetic concern – this does not mean taking the perspective of the person who has been hurt and imagining ourselves in her place (that would be an egoistic concern); it is instead taking the perspective of someone who deeply cares about the pain of others. Compassion for somebody who is in pain does not imply feeling her suffering or grasping her state of suffering, but acknowledging her suffering and therefore feeling sorry *for* that person. However, this concern is not purely affective and intuitive; rather, it is mediated with consciously embraced values. As we have mentioned in Section III, empathetic concern recognizes human dignity, inner worth, and autonomy. Therefore, it is not only needed but is even essential in deciding about non-pecuniary harm, which often stems from the legal recognition of subjectivity and the dignity of human person and the interests that are crucial to her thriving, like love, health, and enjoyment of life. Using compassion, judges act in accordance with the spirit of the law, not just its rules.

Compassion starts with a demarcation of the separate individuality of the judge, yet at the same time it is a recognition of shared humanity. Judicial impartiality does not mean disregard or indifference. In surrounding the vital interests of plaintiffs with empathetic concern, the judge does not have to become infected by the plaintiff's emotions, nor is she limited by whether she grasps and/or imagines the person feelings. Compassion begins with the recognition of shared humanity – a recognition that is written into the law at the level of basic freedoms. But the feeling of kinship is not allowed to go so far that our concern would become extended egoism. Rather, it immediately engages faculties of reason and morality because, as we have mentioned, compassion is a sort of perspective through which people can recognize the "good and ill of others and its full meaning"; its logic is inevitably tied into the nature of harm.[153] Most common philosophical ways of defining harm involve assessing how the life of the harmed person has worsened in comparison to what it was or what it could have been; in other words, calculating the absolute bill of damages in the microcosm of the individual's life. Compassion allows judges to

---

[152] *K.N. Kinnick/D.M. Krugman/G.T. Cameron*, Compassion fatigue: Communication and burnout toward social problems, Journalism & Mass Communication Quarterly 73 (1996), 687–707.

[153] *Nussbaum* (n. 46), 401.

understand why certain states of affairs are bad and unfair for a human being, and it lets them express the sentiment that the law, a guardian of values, should do something about it.

Moreover, it is empathetic concern that may prevent judicial impartiality from turning into indifference. While many guidelines see judges as dispassionate actors, scholars working in the field of law and emotions question this assumption, arguing that emotions are not to be avoided and should instead be shaped into moral virtues. Judges should be taught to be impartial, but not dismissive towards subjective or lived individuality. *John Noonan* claimed that a just and equitable jurisprudence can only be founded based on respect for individuality and personality.[154] It is compassion that creates room for that, simultaneously safeguarding against bias and partiality. A judge using empathetic concern will approach emotional harm carefully but seriously, acknowledging innate human interdependence and vulnerability. She will refer to values and try to assess individual situations using shared moral intuition as to human happiness and suffering. Such a judge will use emotional language in judging (as *Nussbaum* would recommend),[155] doing so not to express emotions or biases, but to recognize the individual reality of each harm and the dignity of each person that experiences it.

Finally, since cognitive empathy is not a prerequisite for compassion, we can feel compassion also with those beings whom we do not understand, such as the mentally ill, villains, and even entirely unintelligible beings, such as animals. All those beings require our moral concern, care, and legal protection.

VI. Conclusions

In this paper, we have emphasized the limitations of the use of cognitive and quasi cognitive empathy, and argued against the use of affective empathy and for the use of compassion (empathetic concern) in the law. Our basis for investigation was the civil institution of non-pecuniary harm, in which injuries to emotions and feelings are essentially important. We have shown that cognitive empathy is a limited and insufficient source of information about harm and that using affective empathy may trigger unfair and biased legal outcomes. We have identified compassion (empathetic concern) as a not only useful but desired factor in the adjudication of harm, as its mechanism essentially mirrors the legal conception of harm and allows us to recognize emotions as protected interests while grounding this protection in shared values. It might be even argued that the recognition of non-pecuniary harm is the law's way of showing

[154] *M.H. Hoeflich/J.G. Deutsch*, Judicial Legitimacy and the Disinterested Judge, Hofstra Law Review 6 (1977), 749–754.

[155] *Nussbaum* (n. 9).

compassion (empathetic concern), something visible at the level of the law's application but nevertheless also written into the law as such.

As for the significance of our investigation against the backdrop of law and emotions scholarship, we hope to have both further explicated the conception of emotions in the context of civil law and shown what empathy may mean in the context of applying legal institutions such as non-pecuniary harm. We share the assumption that the evaluative component of emotions plays an extremely important role in the law. Emotions protected by non-pecuniary harm must be intentional and are often judgments of value, e.g., the value of a deceased person in the eyes of the bereaved. However, the legal treatment of non-pecuniary harm cannot do without paying attention to the affective, emotive aspects of feelings that reveal themselves in embodied experience. The motivational aspect of emotions in conceptualizing non-pecuniary harm is also quite remarkable. Non-pecuniary harm requires the evaluation of the change that has occurred in the plaintiff's life, and it requires paying attention to the interests that are important to that person, even if the judge herself cannot easily imagine them or has not seen the plaintiff's suffering with her own eyes. Yet evaluation is not the end – empathetic concern also provides a sense of how to act and what should be done in this situation. Therefore, empathetic concern also involves the motivational as well as the informational aspects of emotion, which are indispensable to judgments about non-pecuniary harms. Applied as such, emotion aids in the mobilization of other people's rights – rather than imagining herself in this place or simply feeling bad for this person, the judge's compassion prompts her to protect the subjectivity of this person.

Emotions in German Law

Phillip Hellwege

I. Introduction

Marta Soniewicka and *Julia Wesołowska* argue for a greater relevance of emotions in law, claiming that law and emotions scholarship will increase our understanding of legal reasoning and that it will improve legislation and jurisprudence. They base their arguments primarily on US but also on Polish scholarship on law and emotions. First, they discuss the role of emotions from the perspective of legal theory, reminding their readers that legal positivism is based on the "paradigm of [an] objective and rational law"[1] leaving, prima facie, no room for emotions. Legal positivism was challenged first by legal realism, then by critical legal studies, and most recently by law and emotions scholarship. These schools of thought not only take into account that legal actors are also driven by their emotions but in addition claim that the "law should address real individuals",[2] including their emotions. Thereby, they open the door to interdisciplinary studies, including law and emotions scholarship.

Soniewicka and *Wesołowska* observe that the discourse on the role of emotions in law has to distinguish three sets of questions. First, there are the questions regarding the psychological mechanisms of emotions, their manifestations, their functioning, and their biological evolution. These questions are foremost the domain of evolutionary psychology, neurobiology, and affective science. Secondly, there are the questions as to the social functions of emotions and their cultural aspects. These questions are addressed in the humanities and the social sciences. Thirdly, there is the question of how jurisprudence, legislation, and legal scholarship may benefit from these extra-legal insights.

It follows that we have different levels of interdisciplinarity: When analysing the social functions of emotions, the humanities and the social sciences may take the findings of evolutionary psychology, neurobiology, and affective science into consideration. Lawyers, too, may directly draw on the findings of these latter disciplines. However, lawyers may also base their reflections on the findings of the humanities and the social sciences, which themselves may have taken into account the results of evolutionary psychology, neurobiology, and affective science. Law and emotions scholarship, thus, does not simply link two disciplines together. Rather, the scholarship on law and emotions appears to be a single knot in a complex net woven from different disciplines – a picture that will be qualified further below.[3]

With respect to the third set of questions – that is, the "legal knot" in the net of disciplines – *Soniewicka* and *Wesołowska* refer to the well-known research on judicial decision-making and, more generally, to "the impact of emotions on legal actors, such as judges, juries, lawyers, and on witnesses and victims",[4] but they also refer to the growing research on "the role of emotions in […] criminal law, family law […], contract law […], [and] international relations".[5] They argue that "the interaction between emotions and law" is multidimensional, as "some emotions are necessary for [the] creation of an effective, responsive and legitimate law", and on a different level "legal institutions may

[1] *Soniewicka/Wesołowska*, p. 320, above.

[2] *Soniewicka/Wesołowska*, p. 320, above.

[3] See p. 359, below. See also *Susan A. Bandes*, Introduction, in: eadem (ed.), The Passion of Law (1999), 1–15, 8.

[4] *Soniewicka/Wesołowska*, p. 321, above.

[5] *Soniewicka/Wesołowska*, p. 321, above.

not only regulate or affect emotions but also encourage the emergence of socially valuable emotions and produce specific emotions".[6]

The concept of emotion used by law and emotions scholars is, as *Soniewicka* and *Wesołowska* point out, wide and, one may add, contested.[7] It may include "disgust, shame, anger, fear, empathy, mercy, hope, and love" as well as "passions, affects, appetites, desires, drives, sentiments, feelings, upheavals, and impulses",[8] and these concepts are again vague and open to different meanings. *Soniewicka* and *Wesołowska* introduce their readers to two fundamentally different concepts of emotions in philosophy: dualism and holism. Whereas traditional mainstream dualism looks upon emotions as something negative, equating them with irrationality, modern holism overcomes the antagonism of reason and emotion. Thereafter *Soniewicka* and *Wesołowska* turn to empathy, again discussing its different concepts, its possible components, its relation to (or difference from) emotion, and its role in law, for example, in judicial decision making.

In the last part of their paper, *Soniewicka* and *Wesołowska* analyse in detail the impact and importance of emotions in the field of non-pecuniary harm in both criminal law and the law of delict. In the last part of this comment, I will, as well, discuss this aspect from the perspective of German law.[9]

II. An irrelevance of law and emotions scholarship in Germany?

A. A search in the catalogue of the Bavarian Library Network

Whereas the scholarship on law and emotions is thriving in the US and gaining ground in other countries, such as Poland, the same is, at first glance, not true for Germany. A title search in the catalogue of the Bavarian Library Network (*Bibliotheksverbund Bayern*)[10] using a combination of the words *Recht* (law) along with *Emotion*, *Emotionen*, *Gefühl*, or *Gefühle* (emotion, emotions, feeling, feelings) produces only three relevant hits.[11] The first two hits are edited volumes published in 2016 and 2018. They have been edited not by legal scholars but by philosophers. Of the 15 authors contributing to the first volume, only

[6] *Soniewicka/Wesołowska*, p. 322, above.

[7] A narrower approach is, for instance, taken by *H. Landweer/D. Koppelberg*, Der verkannte Zusammenhang von Recht und Emotion, in: eadem/idem (eds.), Recht und Emotion I. Verkannte Zusammenhänge (2016), 13–47, 24–26. See also *Bandes* (n. 3), 10.

[8] *Soniewicka/Wesołowska*, p. 323, above.

[9] See pp. 378 f., below.

[10] https://www.bib-bvb.de/. The search was carried out on 9 January 2023.

[11] *Landweer/Koppelberg* (n. 7); *H. Landweer/F. Bernhardt* (eds.), Recht und Emotion II. Sphären der Verletzlichkeit (2018); *H.P. Bull*, Gefühle der Menschen in der „Informationsgesellschaft" – Wie reagiert das Recht? (2011).

one is a German-speaking lawyer, and of the 14 authors participating in the second volume, two co-authors of a single contribution are lawyers. The third hit – a booklet of 36 pages that appeared in 2011 – is the published version of a lecture held by a lawyer on how the law should respond to emotions in our modern information society. There is a further volume published in 2023 on *Rechtsgefühle*.[12] Of the eight participating authors, three are legal scholars at a German university. A keyword search applying the same words brings four further relevant hits published between 1978 and 2017.[13] Two hits are doctoral dissertations on emotional advertising in competition law that were published, respectively, in 1978 and 1983. Another hit is a dissertation in legal sociology on the concept of *Stimmungsdemokratie* (emotion-driven democracy) as coined by the Danish-German sociologist *Theodor Geiger* (1891–1952). It was published in 2012. The final hit is an edited volume on *Gerechtigkeitsgefühle* (senses of justice) and the affective and emotional legitimatization of norms, published in 2017. It has been edited by two anthropologists, one of whom also holds a law degree. Among the seven further authors, there are only two additional lawyers. Finally, a title search and a keyword search using other word combinations, such as *Hass* (hate) and *Recht*, *Angst* (fear) and *Recht*, or *Empathie* (empathy) and *Recht*, produce two further relevant hits.[14] The first is a conference volume on empathy and law edited in 2012 by two lawyers. In total, the volume has 13 contributors, of whom seven hold a law degree. The second hit was published in 2012 by a criminal lawyer and was titled "Angst als juristische Kategorie" ("Fear as a Legal Category").

B. Distinguishing three different kinds of discourse on emotions in law

For the purpose of the present volume, we cannot stop with the simple observation that there seems to be at least a nucleus if not burgeoning body of law and emotions scholarship in German-speaking literature: The present volume wishes to add a comparative perspective to the existing debates on interdisciplinarity and law.[15] More specifically, the present volume wishes to explore how the diverse doctrinal contexts of different national legal systems affect

---

[12] *Thorsten Keiser/Greta Olson/Franz Reimer* (eds.), Feelings about Law/Justice: The Relevance of Affect to the Development of Law in Pluralistic Legal Cultures. Rechtsgefühle: Die Relevanz des Affektiven für die Rechtsentwicklung in pluralen Rechtskulturen (2023).

[13] *M. Bernet*, Die wettbewerbsrechtliche Beurteilung der gefühlsbetonten Werbung (1978); *A. Mylaeus*, Die "gefühlsbetonte Werbung" als Erscheinungsform der "unsachlichen Werbung" und ihre Beurteilung nach § 1 UWG (1983); *B.W. Czok*, Theodor Geigers Stimmungsdemokratie. Eine rechtssoziologische Untersuchung des Legitimationsdefizits im 21. Jahrhundert. (2012); *J. Bens/O. Zenker* (eds.), Gerechtigkeitsgefühle. Zur affektiven und emotionalen Legitimität von Normen (2017).

[14] *M.C. Gruber/S. Häußler*, Normen der Empathie (2012); *J. Dallmeyer*, Angst als juristische Kategorie (2012).

[15] *Hellwege/Soniewicka*, p. 13, above.

interdisciplinary discourse in law, and it wishes to do so by comparing interdisciplinary discourse in Polish and German law. Research findings on emotions in evolutionary psychology, neurobiology, and affective science should be the same regardless of where – the US, Poland, or Germany – the research has been conducted. The findings of these disciplines will presumably claim to have universal validity. A non-lawyer may be led to believe that, consequently, such findings have, or at least should have, the same impact on the law regardless of the specific legal system. Yet we have to distinguish between three different kinds of legal discourse. The distinctions drawn here reflect German legal commentary and differs from those made in English-speaking law and emotions scholarship.[16]

1. Emotions and the study of the foundations of law

First, there is research in those legal sub-disciplines which German legal scholarship refers to as *Grundlagenfächer*: research on the foundations (*Grundlagen*) of law. Legal *Grundlagenfächer* are, for example, legal history, legal philosophy, legal theory, legal methodology, legal sociology, legal anthropology, comparative law, and law and economics. Research on the foundations of law transcends a single legal order because arguments are not developed from within a single legal system.[17] Rather, this kind of research adopts a perspective whereby law is viewed from the outside. Thus, where scholarship on law and emotions engages in research on the foundations of law, it will transcend a single legal order. It follows that the findings of such research will be valid for more than one legal system and that references to a specific legal system will usually be of an exemplary nature only. Nevertheless, the findings of such research will not be able to claim universal validity. Rather, such research may reflect the specifics of different legal systems and legal cultures. Research "on the impact of emotions on legal actors, such as judges, juries, lawyers, and on witnesses and victims",[18] to which *Soniewicka* and *Wesołowska* refer, is an example of such research. It transcends a single legal order, but its findings still cannot claim universal validity. Juries do not exist in every legal system, and where they exist, their roles may differ. Furthermore, the training of judges in different legal systems, their social background, or the divergent procedural

---

[16] On these distinctions, see *T.A. Maroney*, Law and Emotion: A Proposed Taxonomy of an Emerging Field, Law and Human Behaviour 30 (2006), 119–142, 125–133; *R. Grossi*, Understanding Law and Emotion, Emotion Review 7 (2015), 55–60, 57.

[17] On the concept of legal Grundlagenfächer as distinguished from the doctrinal study of law, see, e.g., *O. Muthorst*, Grundlagen der Rechtswissenschaft. Methode – Begriff – System (2nd edn., 2019), § 2 para. 24; *J. Krüper*, Für wen dieses Buch geschrieben ist, wie und warum, in: idem (ed.), Grundlagen des Rechts (4th edn., 2021), 17–21, 19.

[18] *Soniewicka/Wesołowska*, p. 321, above.

laws may, but do not have to, impact how judges are influenced by their emotions in the judicial decision-making process.

2. Emotions and the doctrinal study of law

Secondly, there is what German legal scholarship calls *Dogmatik*, that is, the doctrinal study of law.[19] It engages in the analysis of a given national legal system as it is in force, i.e. positive law. The doctrinal study of law does not transcend the national legal system, it does not adopt a perspective whereby law is viewed from the out-side, instead, it argues from within the legal system. In the process of understanding and explaining a legal norm, the doctrinal study of law starts with its wording (*wörtliche Auslegung*), then analyses its *ratio* (*teleologische Auslegung*), places it in its systematic legal context (*systematische Auslegung*), and takes into account its historical genesis (*historische Auslegung*): Each legal norm of a given legal system is explained and applied, using the tools of legal methodology.[20] It is the interplay of such doctrinal study of law and extra-legal research on emotions that is of particular interest for the present volume. A judge is, according to the rule of law, bound to a specific national law, but not to the findings of extra-legal research on emotions.[21] However, she may be confronted with the findings of such extra-legal research and may feel that she should take these findings into account when solving the specific case in front of her. Then she has to link these extra-legal findings on emotions to the specific national law, to which she is bound, in a way that is "state of the art" from the perspective of legal methodology. Or to put it differently: A judge is bound to a specific legal system; she may not ignore the law to which she is bound in order to give effect to the findings of law and emotions scholarship; yet she may consider such findings if state-of-the-art legal methodology allows her to incorporate such findings in her legal arguments. The interplay of the doctrinal study of law and extra-legal research on emotions is of particular interest for the present volume because the present volume wishes to add a comparative perspective to our understanding of law and interdiscip-

---

[19] On the concept of Dogmatik, *B. Rüthers/C. Fischer/A. Birk*, Rechtstheorie mit Juristischer Methodenlehre (12th edn., 2022), paras. 309–330; *A. Kaufmann*, Rechtsphilosophie, Rechtstheorie, Rechtsdogmatik, in: W. Hassemer et al. (eds.), Einführung in die Rechtsphilosophie und Rechtstheorie der Gegenwart (9th edn., 2016), 1–22, 1.

[20] Examples of standard textbooks on legal methodology in the German language include *E.A. Kramer*, Juristische Methodenlehre (6th edn., 2019) and *R. Wank*, Juristische Methodenlehre. Eine Anleitung für Wissenschaft und Praxis (2019).

[21] On what follows, *A. Beckers*, Empathie im Wettbewerbsrecht: Gesellschaftliche Rationalitätskonflikte statt Emotionen des Verbrauchers, in: Gruber/Häußler (n. 14), 93–114, 95. See, with different foci, also *S.A. Bandes*, Empathetic Judging and the Rule of Law, Cardozo Law Review de novo (2009), 133–148; *eadem*, Compassion and the rule of law, International Journal of Law in Context 13 (2017), 184–196; *L.N. Henderson*, Legality and Empathy, Michigan Law Review 85 (1987), 1574–1653.

linarity: it wishes to analyse how the specificities of a national legal system affect our approaches to interdisciplinary discourse in law.

3. Emotions and discourse on the reform of law

When the findings of extra-legal research on emotions and positive law contradict each other – when, in other words, a judge does not find a way to link the extra-legal findings on emotions to the specific law to which she is bound – then the question needs to be asked whether the law is in need of reform in the light of these extra-legal findings. This third kind of legal discourse is again of interest for the present volume that wishes to compare the interplay between law and extra-legal research in Poland and Germany.

4. Adding a further variable

Evolutionary psychology, neurobiology, and affective science may claim that their findings have universal validity. However, *Soniewicka* and *Wesołowska* remind us that the scholarship on emotions also addresses questions as to their social functions and cultural aspects. These questions are addressed in the humanities and social sciences. Their findings do not necessarily have universal validity. The findings of research on the cultural aspects of emotions may, for example, depend on the specific cultural context that is analysed. It follows that there is a further variable in the three aforementioned types of legal discourse – a variable that a lawyer needs to be aware of: When a lawyer conducts research on the foundations of law, undertakes a doctrinal study of law, or reflects on the reform of law, and when – in so doing – she wants to take into account findings on emotions in the humanities and social sciences, she first has to assess whether these findings are also valid for the specific context in which she works. In summary, we need to qualify the above description of law and emotions scholarship as a knot in a net woven from different disciplines.[22] It rather seems that evolutionary psychology, neurobiology, and affective science are the mountings from which hangs the net woven of various disciplines researching emotions in the humanities, the social sciences, and the legal sciences; however, the legal sciences also have a further mounting: the specific national legal system to which lawyers are bound.

C. Conclusion

Let us revisit the above-mentioned literature: Most of the mentioned titles belong to the so-called *Grundlagenfächer* and involve research on emotions in legal history, legal sociology, or legal anthropology.[23] That explains the in-

---

[22] See p. 354, above.

[23] *Landweer/Koppelberg* (n. 7); *Landweer/Bernhardt* (n. 11); *Bens/Zenker* (n. 13); *Czok* (n. 13); the contributions of *M.-C. Gruber*, *K. Brukamp*, *F. von Harbou*, *S. Häußler*,

volvement of non-lawyers in these volumes. Consequently, these publications do not link together the doctrinal study of law and research on emotions. This observation is not a qualitative statement. These publications are innovative and have the potential of stimulating new research. Nevertheless, for the purpose of the present contribution, they are of little relevance. The two dissertations on emotional advertising published in 1978 and 1983 are doctrinal studies of law.[24] Both authors seem to understand emotional advertising to be a legal concept, even though they do take notice of extra-legal research, especially in economics. It follows that both dissertations are again of little relevance for the present volume. Of the above-mentioned titles, only a few link together the doctrinal study of law and scholarship on law and emotions. In 2012, *Anna Beckers* took on the problem of emotional advertising and embedded her analysis in law and emotions scholarship.[25] And in his monograph on "Angst als juristische Kategorie" ("Fear as a Legal Category") of 2012, *Jens Dallmeyer* engages in an interdisciplinary analysis of law and emotions.[26] He first presents the findings on fear in neuroscience, psychoanalysis, and neuropsychoanalysis and then discusses the relevance of fear in § 20, § 21, § 33, and § 46 of the German Penal Code (*Strafgesetzbuch* – StGB).

In conclusion, scholarship on law and emotions seems to be only a marginal field of research in German legal literature.[27] This observation may be put into historical perspective. *Soniewicka* and *Wesołowska* claim that the "paradigm of [an] objective and rational law",[28] which leaves no room for emotions, was first challenged by legal realism, later by critical legal studies, and finally by law and emotions scholarship. Furthermore, law and emotions scholars claim that "the study of law and emotions has historically been very much a North American phenomenon" and that only recently are there signs of "a growing interest amongst scholars elsewhere".[29] However, *Sandra Schnädelbach* has recently presented a study analysing the German interdisciplinary discourse on emotions in the process of legal decision-making between 1870 and 1933,[30] and in August 2022, at the *43. Rechtshistorikertag* (Forty-Third Conference of

---

K. Mathis/F. Diriwächter, M. Uebelhart, S. Müller, M. Doll, L. Belkin and *V. Hildebrand-Schat*, in: Gruber/Häußler (n. 14); *Keiser/Olson/Reimer* (n. 12).

[24] *Bernet* (n. 13); *Mylaeus* (n. 13).

[25] *Beckers* (n. 21), 93–114.

[26] *Dallmeyer* (n. 14). See also the contribution of *M. Schulte*, Strategien der posttraumatischen Behandlung – Psychoanalytische Randnotizen zur Regulierung der Finanzmärkte, in: Gruber/Häußler (n. 14), 165–190.

[27] *Landweer/Koppelberg* (n. 7), 13.

[28] *Soniewicka/Wesołowska*, p. 320, above.

[29] *H. Conway/J. Stannard*, Contextualising Law and Emotions: Past Narratives and Future Directions, in: eadem/idem (eds.), The Emotional Dynamics of Law and Legal Discourse (2016), 1–8, 5.

[30] *S. Schnädelbach*, Entscheidende Gefühle. Rechtsgefühl und juristische Emotionalität vom Kaiserreich bis in die Weimarer Republik (2020).

Legal Historians) held at the University of Zurich, *Hans-Peter Haferkamp* presented a paper on irrational elements in legal decision-making in nineteenth-century Germany.[31] Is German legal literature perhaps not lagging behind US scholarship on law and emotions? Rather, are German commentators in fact ahead of their US colleagues, having already moved beyond law and emotion scholarship? I will return to this question further below.[32]

III. The relevance of emotions in German law

The provisional conclusion that law and emotions seems to be only a marginal field of research in German academic literature does not mean that emotions are of no relevance in German law or in the German legal scholarship. A search in the German legal database *juris*[33] using the word *Emotion* (emotion) results in 3,856 hits: 1,924 from case law, 148 from legislation, 327 from commentaries and books, 1,426 from journals, and 31 from further sources. A search using the word *Empathie* (empathy) produces 1,865 hits: 888 from case law, 162 from legislation, 144 from commentaries and books, 662 from journals, and 9 from further sources. And a search using the word *Gefühl* (feeling) results in 40,256 hits: 24,465 from case law, 2,697 from legislation, 2,626 from commentaries and books, 10,190 from journals, and 278 from further sources. A search using other emotions will reveal further hits. *Dan M. Kahan*'s and *Martha C. Nussbaum*'s observation on American criminal law, thus, holds equally true for German law: "Emotions are ubiquitous in [...] law, as they are in life."[34] A closer look into the results, however, reveals that not every hit is, at least at first sight, of relevance for the present contribution. § 138(1) of the German Civil Code (*Bürgerliches Gesetzbuch* – BGB), for example, reads:

"Ein Rechtsgeschäft, das gegen die guten Sitten verstößt, ist nichtig."

"A legal transaction which is contrary to good morals [public policy] is void."

The case law and legal literature define *gute Sitten* (good morals, public policy) as the "Anstandsgefühl aller billig und gerecht Denkenden" ("sense of decency of all those who think fairly and equitably").[35] The definition includes the word

---

[31] *H.-P. Haferkamp*, Entspricht das jetzt dem Volksgeist? Geltungsfragen im "Heutigen Römischen Recht", Zeitschrift der Savigny-Stiftung für Rechtsgeschichte – Germanistische Abteilung 140 (2023), 307–332.

[32] See p. 393, below.

[33] https://www.juris.de/jportal/. The search was carried out on 9 January 2023.

[34] *D.M. Kahn/M.C. Nussbaum*, Two Conceptions of Emotion in Criminal Law, Columbia Law Review 96 (1996), 269–374, 270.

[35] Compare *H.P. Haferkamp*, in: M. Schmoeckel et al. (eds.), Historisch-kritischer Kommentar zum BGB, vol. 1 (2003), § 138 para. 1.

Gefühl (sense, feeling, emotion). Yet *gute Sitten* are mostly understood to be a *legal* concept reflecting fundamental values in the constitutional and legal order and furthermore to be a concept referring to the moral order as an extra-legal value system.[36] The definition does not refer to any sort of emotion that could be the research object of interdisciplinary scholarship on emotions. Of the 40,256 hits for the search using the word *Gefühl*, 984 relate to § 138 BGB and are thus mostly irrelevant to law and emotions scholarship. Nevertheless, the sheer number of hits signals that German case law, legislation, and legal scholarship do not ignore emotions. It seems that *Renata Grossi*'s general observation is not true for German law: "While law names emotions it deals with them only obliquely […]."[37] Rather, *Eric A. Posner*'s nuanced observation on US law, echoing the conclusion reached by *Kahan* and *Nussbaum*,[38] holds true also for Germany: "The role of the emotions is much neglected in legal theory. This should be puzzling, because emotions play an important role in many areas of the law."[39]

IV. References to emotions in legal texts

Even though this simple search in the legal database *juris* signals that German case law, legislation, and legal literature do not ignore emotions, we should not too hastily conclude that all hits equally invite for law and emotions scholarship, as the example of § 138(1) BGB has already proven. For the purposes of the present comment, it is helpful to distinguish two possible uses of the word emotion (and related concepts) in legal texts: emotion as a legal concept, on the one hand, and emotion as a "factual" phenomenon on the other hand. If a lawyer uses the word emotion as a legal concept, then there is – from the perspective of the doctrinal study of law – no room for law and emotions scholarship in the sense of an interdisciplinary undertaking. In such case, a lawyer will define the word emotion autonomously. Law and emotions scholarship may of course question that it is correct to use the word emotion as a purely legal concept. It is only when a lawyer uses the word emotion as a "factual" phenomenon which could be a research object of extra-legal disciplines that scholarship on law and emotions becomes conceivable in the sense of an interdisciplinary undertaking. The word "factual" is used in the present context as a shorthand for

---

[36] *J. Neuner*, Allgemeiner Teil des Bürgerlichen Rechts (12th edn., 2020), § 46 para. 12; *R. Bork*, Allgemeiner Teil des Bürgerlichen Gesetzbuchs (4th edn., 2016), para. 1180; *D. Medicus/J. Petersen*, Allgemeiner Teil des BGB (11th edn., 2016), para. 680; *F. Faust*, Bürgerliches Gesetzbuch. Allgemeiner Teil (8th edn., 2023), § 10 para. 1.

[37] *Grossi* (n. 16), 55.

[38] *Kahan/Nussbaum* (n. 34), 270.

[39] *E.A. Posner*, Law and the Emotions, Georgetown Law Journal 89 (2001), 1977–2012, 1977.

all non-legal uses of the word. Furthermore, it is helpful to distinguish between two categories of texts in which these two concepts are used: legal norms on the one hand and other legal texts, including case law and academic legal literature, on the other hand. In a codified system such as German law, case law belongs, in principle, to the second category of texts because it interprets and applies legal norms as they are codified.[40]

A. The reference to emotion as a legal concept

Legal texts may use the word emotion as a legal concept. An example of such use of the word emotion has already been discussed:[41] In the context of § 138(1) BGB, *gute Sitten* are defined as the "Anstandsgefühl aller billig und gerecht Denkenden". In this definition the word *Gefühl* does not refer to a factual phenomenon – real emotions of real people – that could be the research object of law and emotions scholarship. This is a conclusion that may, however, be questioned by law and emotions scholars. I will return to this point later in this comment.[42]

B. The reference in legislation to emotion as a factual phenomenon

Legal norms may refer to emotions as factual phenomena. They may do so in two fundamentally different ways. First, the word emotion may already point to the extra-legal importance of emotions without the need to engage in law and emotions scholarship for understanding or analysing these norms. Rather the fact that these norms refer to emotions is the result of extra-legal scholarship on emotions. A large number of the 148 hits from legislation that were found with the database search using the word *Emotion* refer to the training regulations for certain professions or come from regulations on schools and education. Annex 1 to § 1(1) of the Federal Training and Examinations Regulations for Occupational Therapists (*Ausbildungs- und Prüfungsverordnung für Ergotherapeutinnen und Ergotherapeuten*) issued by the Federal Ministry of Health (*Bundesministerium für Gesundheit*), for example, requires that occupational therapists are also trained on "motivation and emotions" ("Motivationen und Emotionen"). And the Bavarian Guidelines for Family and Sex Education in Bavarian Schools (*Richtlinien für die Familien- und Sexualerziehung in den bayerischen Schulen*) issued by the Bavarian Ministry of Education and Cultural Affairs, the Sciences and the Arts (*Staatsministerium für Bildung und Kultus, Wissenschaft und Kunst*) require that the "possible emotional consequences of rationally communicated factual information have to be

[40] On the controversy regarding how to categorize case law in the German legal order see, e.g., *Neuner* (n. 36), § 4 paras. 9–16.

[41] See, p. 362, above.

[42] See, pp. 375 f., below.

taken into account" ("Mögliche emotionale Auswirkungen rational vermittelter Sachinformationen werden mit bedacht") when engaging in family and sex education. These regulations and guidelines point directly to the extra-legal scholarship on the importance of emotions in the contexts of family and sex education in schools and occupational therapy, and they require schoolteachers as well as those who train occupational therapists to apply state-of-the-art methods. The cited passage from the Bavarian Guidelines for Family and Sex Education in Bavarian Schools allows for another observation. In 2015, *Grossi* wrote:[43]

> "Indeed the history of ideas has been dominated by a seemingly impenetrable distinction between reason and emotion, which not only sharply distinguishes between the two, but values the former over the latter."

When the Bavarian Guidelines require that "possible emotional consequences of rationally communicated factual information have to be taken into account", they indeed sharply distinguish between reason and emotion. However, the Guidelines require that emotions be taken into consideration even where they are irrational, and the Guidelines, thus, do not value reason over (irrational) emotions. However, is the approach adopted by these Guidelines perhaps outdated because modern holism overcomes, as *Soniewicka* and *Wesołowska* argue, the antagonism of reason and emotion as promoted by traditional dualism?[44] I do not think so. The Bavarian Guidelines for Family and Sex Education in Bavarian Schools simply address a possible conflict which is best solved by reference to traditional dualism. If a teacher thinks that he may simply present to his class factual information, he may cause great harm. He has to take into consideration any emotional (even irrational) consequences that factual information may have on children. This conflict is best addressed by identifying the two opposing poles (factual information v. emotional consequences) and not by any sort of holism. Or in other words: Modern trends in philosophy will hinder rather than facilitate the drafting of legal norms in the fashion of the Bavarian Guidelines for Family and Sex Education in Bavarian Schools.

We have just analysed two examples in which legislation uses the word emotion as referring to a factual phenomenon and in which legislation points to the extra-legal importance of emotions without, however, the need to engage in law and emotions scholarship for a further understanding the respective norm. However, legal norms may refer to emotion as a factual phenomenon also in a second fashion. Legislation may use the word emotion as referring to a factual phenomenon, and the application of the respective legal norm benefits from extra-legal findings, as three examples will prove. § 211 StGB on murder reads:

---

[43] *Grossi* (n. 16), 55.

[44] *Soniewicka/Wesołowska*, pp. 323 ff., above.

"(1) Der Mörder wird mit lebenslanger Freiheitsstrafe bestraft.
(2) Mörder ist, wer aus Mordlust, zur Befriedigung des Geschlechtstriebs, aus Habgier oder sonst aus niedrigen Beweggründen, heimtückisch oder grausam oder mit gemeingefährlichen Mitteln oder um eine andere Straftat zu ermöglichen oder zu verdecken, einen Menschen tötet."

"(1) A murderer incurs a penalty of imprisonment for life.
(2) A murderer is someone who kills another person out of a lust to kill, for sexual satisfaction, out of greed or otherwise base motives, insidiously or cruelly or by means constituting a public danger or to facilitate or cover up another offence."

By contrast, § 212(1) StGB on manslaughter reads:

"Wer einen Menschen tötet, ohne Mörder zu sein, wird als Totschläger mit Freiheitsstrafe nicht unter fünf Jahren bestraft."

"Whoever kills a person without being a murderer [according to § 211 StGB] incurs a penalty of imprisonment for a term of at least five years."[45]

The characteristic elements that define murder according to § 211(2) StGB and that distinguish it from manslaughter in the meaning of § 212 StGB are usually divided into three groups, the first of which pulls together those characteristics elements that point to the motivational reprehensibility.[46] Emotions will play an important role for the overall assessment of whether the accused fulfils any of the characteristic elements of the first group. Indeed, lust to kill, sexual satisfaction, and greed may themselves be categorized as emotions. Furthermore, "otherwise base motives" may be fury, anger, jealousy, hate, or revenge.[47] For the purpose of this paper, it is important to note that German law has always followed an evaluative approach and not a mechanistic approach:[48] the murderer's motive has to be base.[49] Finally, it is important to note that German case law and literature have developed numerous competing theories on how to evaluate the motives as being base.[50]

§ 81d(1)(1) of the Code of Criminal Procedure (*Strafprozeßordnung* – StPO) refers to the sense of shame (*Schamgefühl*) of those who are exposed to physical examinations in criminal proceedings:

---

[45] The translation is a modified version of the translation found on https://www.gesetze-im-internet.de/englisch_stgb/ (last visited on 17 February 2023).

[46] *A. Eser/D. Sternberg-Lieben*, in: Schönke/Schröder. Strafgesetzbuch (30th edn., 2019), § 211 paras. 14–20; *M. Heger*, in: Lackner/Kühl/Heger. Strafgesetzbuch (30th edn., 2023), § 211 paras. 4–5c; *H. Schneider*, in: Münchener Kommentar zum Strafgesetzbuch, vol. 4 (4th edn., 2021), § 211 paras. 48–124; *R. Eschelbach*, in: B. von Heintschel-Heinegg (ed.), BeckOK StGB (55th edn., 2022), paras. 15–35; *T. Fischer*, Strafgesetzbuch mit Nebengesetzen (69th edn., 2022), § 211 para. 7.

[47] *Schneider* (n. 46), § 211 para. 73.

[48] See p. 379, below.

[49] See, e.g., BGH, judgment of 11 May 2022, 2 StR 445/21, Neue Zeitschrift für Strafrecht 2022, 541–543.

[50] See e.g. the discussion of *Schneider* (n. 46), § 211 paras. 73–82.

"Kann die körperliche Untersuchung das Schamgefühl verletzen, so wird sie von einer Person gleichen Geschlechts oder von einer Ärztin oder einem Arzt vorgenommen."

"If a physical examination may offend the sense of shame, then it shall be performed by a person of the same sex or by a female or male medical practitioner."[51]

Finally, § 90(1)(1) of the Youth Courts Act (*Jugendgerichtsgesetz* – JGG) refers to the sense of honour (*Ehrgefühl*). The Youth Courts Act implements special provisions of criminal law and criminal procedure for delinquents who are still juveniles, foremost introducing a wider range of responses to an offence, stressing the importance of educational aspects.[52] § 90(1)(1) JGG reads:

"Der Vollzug des Jugendarrestes soll das Ehrgefühl des Jugendlichen wecken und ihm eindringlich zum Bewußtsein bringen, daß er für das von ihm begangene Unrecht einzustehen hat."

"The execution of youth detention should awaken the juvenile's sense of honour and make him fully aware that he must take responsibility for the wrong he has committed."

Youth detention combines both punitive and educational aspects.[53] § 81d StPO and § 90 JGG invite for extra-legal scholarship on the sense of honour (*Ehrgefühl*) and the sense of shame (*Schamgefühl*), and they point to the importance of extra-legal expertise:[54] Those who apply these legal provisions should know how, for example, a juvenile's *Ehrgefühl* is best addressed when implementing a measure of youth detention. Youth detention is, for example, to be immediately executed, as it is known that overly lengthy time gaps between the offence, the sentence, and the execution impair the educational effects of youth detention.[55] Furthermore, the Youth Courts Act explicitly acknowledges the importance of extra-legal expertise. In 2020, § 37 JGG was reformed to reflect the special expertise that a judge working in a youth court should have. § 37(1)(1) and (2) JGG read:

---

[51] The translation is a modified version of the translation found on https://www.gesetze-im-internet.de/englisch_stpo/ (last visited on 17 February 2023).

[52] See, in general, *W. Beulke/S. Swoboda*, Jugendstrafrecht. Eine systematische Darstellung (16th edn., 2020), para. 1; *F. Streng*, Jugendstrafrecht (5th edn., 2020), para. 14.

[53] *H. Diemer/H. Schutz/B.-R. Sonnen*, Jugendgerichtsgesetz mit Jugendstrafvollzugsgesetzen (7th edn., 2015), § 90 paras. 2 f.; *H. Schöch/K. Höffler*, Vollstreckung, Vollzug und Registrierung jugendstrafrechtlicher Entscheidungen, in: B.D. Meier et al. (eds.), Jugendstrafrecht (4th edn., 2019), 298–322, 303. Criticizing the concept of Ehrgefühl as being antiquated, *R. Wulf*, in: B.D. Meier et al. (eds.), Jugendgerichtsgesetz. Handkommentar (2nd edn., 2014), § 90 para. 6; *H. Ostendorf/K. Drenkhahn*, in: H. Ostendorf (ed.), Jugendgerichtsgesetz (11th edn., 2021), § 90 para. 3.

[54] On the importance of training judges in Youth Courts in forensic psychology, see, e.g., *Streng* (n. 52), para. 14.

[55] See *Ostendorf/Drenkhahn* (n. 53), § 90 para. 4a; *Streng* (n. 52), para. 417. See also § 4 of the Verordnung über den Vollzug des Jugendarrestes (Regulation on the Execution of Youth Detention); § 87(4)(1) JGG; *U. Eisenberg*, Jugendgerichtsgesetz (20th edn., 2018), § 87 para. 10a.

"Die Richter bei den Jugendgerichten und die Jugendstaatsanwälte sollen erzieherisch befähigt und in der Jugenderziehung erfahren sein. Sie sollen über Kenntnisse auf den Gebieten der Kriminologie, Pädagogik und Sozialpädagogik sowie der Jugendpsychologie verfügen."

"Judges sitting in the youth courts, and youth public prosecutors handling matters involving juveniles, are to have appropriate education skills and training, as well as experience in the education and upbringing of juveniles. They are to have knowledge in criminology, education, and social education as well as youth psychology."[56]

Finally, according to § 38 JGG, *Jugendgerichtshilfe* (youth courts assistance service) will add further extra-legal expertise in the court room. § 38(2) JGG reads:

"Die Vertreter der Jugendgerichtshilfe bringen die erzieherischen, sozialen und sonstigen im Hinblick auf die Ziele und Aufgaben der Jugendhilfe bedeutsamen Gesichtspunkte im Verfahren vor den Jugendgerichten zur Geltung. Sie unterstützen zu diesem Zweck die beteiligten Behörden durch Erforschung der Persönlichkeit, der Entwicklung und des familiären, sozialen und wirtschaftlichen Hintergrundes des Jugendlichen und äußern sich zu einer möglichen besonderen Schutzbedürftigkeit sowie zu den Maßnahmen, die zu ergreifen sind."

"The representatives of the youth court assistance service shall highlight the supervisory, social and other aspects that are significant with regard to the goals and tasks of youth welfare in proceedings before the youth courts. For this purpose, they shall support the participating authorities by researching into the personality, the development, and the family, social and economic background of the juvenile, and they shall make a statement with regard to any potential particular vulnerability, as well as to the measures that are to be taken."[57]

The extra-legal expertise of judges in youth courts and of the youth courts assistance service will allow judges and members of the service to assess, among other things, the personality and emotional maturity of the accused juvenile.[58]

C. The reference in case law and literature to emotion as a factual phenomenon

Finally, the case law and legal literature may use the word emotion in reference to a factual phenomenon although the legal norm at issue conceptualizes the issue without reference to emotion, as three examples from different areas of law will illustrate. The first example relates again to § 138(1) BGB, according

[56] The translation is a modified version of the translation found on https://www.gesetze-im-internet.de/englisch_jgg/ (last visited on 17 February 2023).

[57] The translation is a modified version of the translation found on https://www.gesetze-im-internet.de/englisch_jgg/ (last visited on 17 February 2023).

[58] In general, with reference to the many reform discussions and the European framework of Directive (EU) 2016/800 of 11 May 2016 on procedural safeguards for children who are suspects or accused persons in criminal proceedings, Official Journal of the European Union 2016 L 132/1, see *J. Schady*, in: Ostendorf (n. 53), § 37 paras. 3–5; *M. Sommerfeld*, in: Ostendorf (n. 53), § 38 paras. 15–25a; *B.D. Meier*, in: idem (n. 53), 286–288; *Streng* (n. 52), paras. 103 f, 106–121.

to which a "legal transaction which is contrary to public policy [good morals] is void".[59] § 138(1) BGB is a so-called general clause (*Generalklausel*) relying on an open-textured concept requiring concretization: good morals (*gute Sitten*). The standard definition of *gute Sitten* – "sense of decency of all those who think fairly and equitably" – is equally in need of concretization. The case law and legal scholarship usually concretizes general clauses such as § 138(1) BGB by developing specific requirements for different groups of cases (*Fallgruppen*).[60] One of these groups of cases involves surety contracts (*Bürgschaftsverträge*) in family relations. Accordingly, a surety contract is void when the following requirements are met:[61]

1. The first family member (e.g., a child) gives a surety for the debts of a second family member (e.g., the child's father) to a third party (e.g., a bank) in order, for example, to secure a loan which the second family member has applied for with the third party.
2. The first family member has no economic reason of her own to give the surety.
3. The first family member is grossly overburdened financially by the surety.
4. The third party knew of the family ties and of the fact that the first family member is grossly overburdened by the surety.

The case law has identified criteria to determine when the first family member gives a surety for economic reasons of her own and is grossly overburdened by the surety. If these four requirements are met, then it is presumed that the third party has exploited the first family member's factual emotional bond to the second family member.[62] In certain situations, the third party may, however, be able to rebut the presumption. In this example, § 138(1) BGB uses a normative concept (public policy, good morals) which is in certain groups of cases concretized by reference to, among other factors, emotions. Nevertheless, for reasons of legal certainty, the first family member who wishes to claim that the legal transaction is void does not need to prove that she was driven by her emotional bond to the second family member. Rather, when the four abovementioned requirements are met, it is presumed that she entered the surety contract because of the emotional bond and that the third party exploited the emotional bond. In all, for the application of these requirements it is not necessary to engage in law and emotions scholarship because the emotional bond is presumed. Nevertheless, I will return to this example further below for a different reason.[63]

---

[59] https://www.gesetze-im-internet.de/englisch_bgb/ (last visited 9 January 2023).

[60] *Neuner* (n. 36), § 46 para. 29.

[61] *C. Armbrüster*, in: Münchener Kommentar zum Bürgerlichen Gesetzbuch, vol. 1 (9th edn., 2021), § 138 paras. 154–160; *Medicus/Petersen* (n. 36), para. 706; *Faust* (n. 36), § 10 para. 5; *Bork* (n. 36), para. 1197.

[62] *Armbrüster* (n. 61), § 138 para. 156; *Faust* (n. 36), § 10 para. 5; *Bork* (n. 36), paras. 1196 f.

[63] See p. 375, below.

The second example in which the case law and legal literature use the word emotion in reference to a factual phenomenon despite the discussed legal norm conceptualizing/framing the issue differently comes from family law. § 1684 BGB concerns a child's contact with its parents. § 1684(4)(1) BGB reads:

"Das Familiengericht kann das Umgangsrecht oder den Vollzug früherer Entscheidungen über das Umgangsrecht einschränken oder ausschließen, soweit dies zum Wohl des Kindes erforderlich ist."

"The family court may restrict or exclude the right of contact or the enforcement of earlier decisions on the right of contact, to the extent that this is in the best interests of the child."[64]

Even though § 1684 BGB refers not to emotions but the "best interests of the child", the emotional ties between the child and its parents, the child's emotional wellbeing, and its fears are, among other aspects, important factors when applying § 1684 BGB.[65] However other than in the context of void surety contracts under § 138(1) BGB, in which emotions are presumed, in the context of § 1684 BGB the child's true emotions are of relevance and need to be assessed for the application of the norm. Let us return to the two fundamentally different concepts of emotions in philosophy: dualism and holism. Traditional mainstream dualism looks upon emotions as something negative, equating them with irrationality. By contrast, modern trends follow the holistic approach. We have already observed that the Bavarian Guidelines for Family and Sex Education in Bavarian Schools rightly follow a dualistic approach.[66] By contrast, § 1684 BGB rightly follows a holistic approach. For the assessment of what is in a child's best interests, all relevant factors – regardless of whether they belong to the sphere of reason or whether they represent (irrational) emotions – have to be taken into account. § 211 StGB rightly follows an evaluative approach:[67] the offender's motives have to be base for the offender to be punished for murder rather than for manslaughter.[68] By contrast, § 1684 BGB does not follow an evaluative approach[69] or, rather, it follows a different evaluative approach: The judge who has to decide what is in the best interests of the child does not evaluate the child's emotions as morally desirable. The child's own best interests are decisive. Finally, § 23b(3)(3) of the Federal Judicature Act

[64] The translation is a modified version of the translation found on https://www.gesetze-im-internet.de/englisch_bgb/ (last visited on 16 January 2023).

[65] See, e.g., the comprehensive discussion by *H. Hennemann*, in: Münchener Kommentar zum Bürgerlichen Gesetzbuch, vol. 10 (8th edn., 2020), § 1684 paras. 70–92; *J. Gernhuber/D. Coester-Waltjen*, Familienrecht (7th edn., 2020), § 58 paras. 32–34, § 67 para. 6; *D. Schwab*, Familienrecht (29th edn., 2021), paras. 967–970, 982 f.

[66] See p. 364, above.

[67] See pp. 379 f., below.

[68] See p. 365, above.

[69] See pp. 379 f., below.

(*Gerichtsverfassungsgesetz* – GVG) again explicitly acknowledges the importance of extra-legal expertise of judges working in family courts:

"Richter in Familiensachen sollen […] über belegbare Grundkenntnisse der Psychologie, insbesondere der Entwicklungspsychologie des Kindes, und der Kommunikation mit Kindern verfügen."

"Family court judges must have […] proven basic knowledge of psychology, particularly in terms of developmental psychology of, and communication with, children."[70]

The third and last example in which the case law and legal commentary use the word emotion as a factual phenomenon, despite the discussed legal norm framing the issue differently comes from criminal law. § 20 StGB reads:

"Ohne Schuld handelt, wer bei Begehung der Tat wegen einer krankhaften seelischen Störung, wegen einer tiefgreifenden Bewußtseinsstörung oder wegen einer Intelligenzminderung oder einer schweren anderen seelischen Störung unfähig ist, das Unrecht der Tat einzusehen oder nach dieser Einsicht zu handeln."

"Whoever, at the time when the offence is committed, is incapable of recognizing the unlawfulness of his actions or of acting in accordance with such appreciation due to a pathological mental disorder, a profound disturbance of consciousness or intellectual disability or any other serious mental disorder is deemed to act without guilt."[71]

Emotional aspects may be an ingredient when assessing whether the requirements of § 20 StGB are met: Anger, fear, shock, and desperation may – but do not necessarily – cause a "profound disturbance of consciousness".[72]

Previously, I have already pointed to the complex interplay between the doctrinal study of law and extra-legal findings on emotions. A legal actor such as a judge is bound to a specific national law, but not to the findings of extra-legal research on emotions. If a legal actor wants to apply such findings, she must find an anchor in the law to do so. § 1684 BGB and § 20 StGB indeed allow the consideration of extra-legal findings on emotions.

D. The absence of references to emotions in legal texts

There is a fourth possibility as well: The concept of emotions is not used in legal texts, but the introduction of law and emotions scholarship to that specific legal question would in fact facilitate sound legal reasoning and improve legislation, jurisprudence, and legal literature.

---

[70] The translation is a modified version of the translation found on https://www.gesetze-im-internet.de/englisch_gvg/ (last visited on 18 February 2023).

[71] The translation is a modified version of the translation found on https://www.gesetze-im-internet.de/englisch_stgb/ (last visited on 17 January 2023).

[72] See, e.g., *H. Schöch*, Schuldfähigkeit, in: E. Hilgendorf et al. (eds.), Handbuch des Strafrechts, vol. 2 (2020), 755–789, paras. 32–39; *Dallmeyer* (n. 14), 123–162.

V. Interdisciplinarity or a division of labour?

Thus far it has become clear that interdisciplinary scholarship on law and emotions is, at first glance, only a marginal field of research in Germany, but that German case law, legislation, and legal scholarship nevertheless do not ignore emotions. The discussed examples raise a further question: Are these examples invitations to engage in interdisciplinary law and emotions scholarship? Or are they rather examples of a division of labour between actors positioned in different disciplines? To assess what, in the context of § 1684 BGB, is in the child's best interests, the court will in many cases obtain an expert opinion.[73] § 163(1) of the Act on Proceedings in Family Matters and in Matters of Non-Contentious Jurisdiction (*Gesetz über das Verfahren in Familiensachen und in den Angelegenheiten der freiwilligen Gerichtsbarkeit* – FamFG) requires the consulted expert to have certain qualifications:[74]

> "In Verfahren nach § 151 Nummer 1 bis 3 ist das Gutachten durch einen geeigneten Sachverständigen zu erstatten, der mindestens über eine psychologische, psychotherapeutische, kinder- und jugendpsychiatrische, psychiatrische, ärztliche, pädagogische oder sozialpädagogische Berufsqualifikation verfügen soll. Verfügt der Sachverständige über eine pädagogische oder sozialpädagogische Berufsqualifikation, ist der Erwerb ausreichender diagnostischer und analytischer Kenntnisse durch eine anerkannte Zusatzqualifikation nachzuweisen."

> "In proceedings according to § 151 numbers 1 to 3, the expert opinion has to be submitted by somebody who has a professional qualification at least in psychology, psychotherapy, child and juvenile psychiatry, psychiatry, medicine, pedagogy, or social pedagogy. If the expert has a professional qualification in pedagogy or social pedagogy, the acquisition of sufficient diagnostical and analytical skills has to be certified by an accredited additional qualification."

§ 151 FamFG includes proceedings in matters concerning parental care, and this in turn includes matters relating to § 1684 BGB.[75] Similarly in the context of § 211 StGB and § 20 StGB, courts will almost always obtain an expert opinion in order to assess whether, in the case of § 20 StGB, the accused really suffered from "a pathological mental disorder, a profound disturbance of consciousness or intellectual disability or any other serious mental disorder" that made him "incapable of recognizing the unlawfulness of his actions or of acting in accordance with such appreciation".[76] As expert opinions are evidence, the principle of the judge's free evaluation of evidence (*Grundsatz der freien rich-*

---

[73] See, e.g., *Hennemann* (n. 65), § 1684 paras. 56 and 114.

[74] See, e.g., *N. Dethloff*, Familienrecht. Ein Studienbuch (33th edn., 2022), para. 211.

[75] *D. Zorn*, in: A. Dutta et al. (eds.), FamFG. Kommentar zum Gesetz über das Verfahren in Familiensachen und in den Angelegenheiten der freiwilligen Gerichtsbarkeit (4th edn., 2022), § 151 para. 5.

[76] *J. Kaspar*, Strafrecht – Allgemeiner Teil (4th edn., 2023), para. 355; *K. Rogall*, in: Systematischer Kommentar zur Strafprozessordnung, vol. 1 (5th edn., 2018), § 73 para. 27.

terlichen Beweiswürdigung) as laid down in § 37(1) FamFG and in § 261 StPO applies. § 261 StPO, for example, reads:

"Über das Ergebnis der Beweisaufnahme entscheidet das Gericht nach seiner freien, aus dem Inbegriff der Verhandlung geschöpften Überzeugung."

"The court shall conclude as to the result of taking evidence at its free persuasion based on the entire trial."

Thus, it is in the power of the court to decide whether to find the expert opinion convincing and whether to draw from the expert's findings the legal/normative conclusion that the accused acted, in the case of § 20 StGB, without guilt.[77] Nevertheless, § 20 StGB – as well as § 211 StGB and § 1684 BGB – are examples of a division of labour and not of true interdisciplinarity.

VI. Emotions and the doctrinal study of law

However, there is room for law and emotions scholarship in German law – not only in the sense of a division of labour, with legal actors taking, where necessary, extra-legal findings on emotions in the form of expert opinions into consideration – but also in the sense of true interdisciplinary scholarship. It is, for example, possible to link the behavioural economics embodied in consumer law with law and emotions discourse.[78] In this last section, I will link law and emotions scholarship to the doctrinal study of German law.

A. Emotions and standards of practices

Interdisciplinary scholarship, including law and emotions scholarship, may help to critically assess standards of practice that have developed concerning the application of legal provisions. Let us return to § 81d(1)(1) StPO.[79] Unlike in the case of § 1684 BGB, § 211 StGB, and § 20 StGB, where a judge will obtain expert opinions in many if not most cases, the same is not true in the case of § 81d(1)(1) StPO. Individuals conducting physical examinations will apply objective standards that should reflect when a sense of shame may typically be offended by an examination. However, those conducting physical examinations will not first assess the examined person's individual sense of shame. It falls on the examined person to articulate her personal sense of shame. A literal interpretation of § 81d(1) StPO supports this understanding:

---

[77] On the many problems, see, e.g., *Schöch* (n. 72), para. 23 f., 35, 37; *C. Roxin/B. Schnünemann*, Strafverfahrensrecht. Ein Studienbuch (30th edn., 2022), § 45 para. 46; *H.H. Kühne*, Strafprozessrecht (9th edn., 2015), paras. 872–874; *C. Pegel*, in: H. Radtke/O. Hohmann (eds.), Strafprozessordnung. Kommentar (2011), § 261 paras. 72–76.

[78] *Posner* (n. 114), 1977–2012.

[79] See p. 366, above.

"Kann die körperliche Untersuchung das Schamgefühl verletzen, so wird sie von einer Person gleichen Geschlechts oder von einer Ärztin oder einem Arzt vorgenommen. Bei berechtigtem Interesse soll dem Wunsch, die Untersuchung einer Person oder einem Arzt bestimmten Geschlechts zu übertragen, entsprochen werden. Auf Verlangen der betroffenen Person soll eine Person des Vertrauens zugelassen werden. Die betroffene Person ist auf die Regelungen der Sätze 2 und 3 hinzuweisen."

"If a physical examination may offend the sense of shame, then it shall be performed by a person of the same sex or by a female or male medical practitioner. Where there is a legitimate interest, the request to have a person or a physician of a particular sex appointed to perform the examination shall be granted. Upon the request of the person concerned, a trusted person is to be admitted. The person concerned is to be instructed as to the provisions of sentences 2 and 3."[80]

Sentence 1 provides for the application of certain objective standards, though it is important to note that these standards have to take the examined age into account and have to distinguish between different communities that may have divergent senses of shame based on, for example, the examined individual's religion or cultural background.[81] Sentence 2 allows the examined person to invoke her personal sense of shame. However, sentence 2 adopts an evaluative approach,[82] as the examined person's request needs to be legitimate in order to be granted. Finally, sentence 4 ensures that the examined person knows of her rights under sentence 2 (and sentence 3). Nevertheless, § 81d(1) StPO leaves room for interdisciplinary scholarship on emotions. The applied objective standards of practice have to withstand a critical review, and research may conduct a critical analysis of these standards of practice.

B. Emotions and public policy

Guten Sitten (good morals, public policy) in the meaning of § 138(1) BGB are defined as the "Anstandsgefühl aller billig und gerecht Denkenden" ("sense of decency of all those who think fairly and equitably). Even though this definition includes the word *Gefühl* (emotion, feeling), it does not refer to a factual phenomenon. It follows that there is no room for interdisciplinary law and emotions scholarship. However, could law and emotions scholarship claim that factual emotions should have relevance for our understanding of § 138(1) BGB? Could law and emotions scholarship increase our understanding of § 138(1) BGB? *Beckers* has indeed argued that there is room for a judge to take empathy

[80] The translation is a modified version of the translation found on https://www.gesetze-im-internet.de/englisch_stpo/ (last visited on 17 February 2023).

[81] *S. Beukelmann*, in: Radtke/Hohmann (n. 77), § 81d paras. 2 f.; *T. Trück*, in: Münchener Kommentar zur Strafprozessordnung, vol. 1 (2nd edn., 2023), § 81d paras. 1, 5–8; *Rogall* (n. 76), § 81d paras. 1 f., 6–9.

[82] See pp. 379 f., below.

into consideration when positive law uses open-textured concepts in general clauses (*Generalklauseln*):[83]

"Grundlage der Rechtsentscheidung ist jedenfalls zunächst, dass Richter an 'Gesetz und Recht' […] gebunden sind. Sie haben sich bei ihrer Entscheidung daher an die kodifizierte Norm zu halten, das Gesetz nach juristischer Methodik auszulegen und ihre Entscheidung durch rechtliche Argumentation zu begründen […]. Hiernach dürfte für eine empathische Rechtsentscheidung kein Raum bleiben. Empathie ist jedoch vor allem dann möglich, wenn Gesetze unbestimmt und abstrakt gefasst sind. Besonders offensichtlich ist dieser weite Auslegungsspielraum bei der Generalklausel, […]."[84]

"The starting point of any legal decision is that judges are bound to the law […]. They have to adhere to the codified law when deciding a case, they have to interpret the law in accordance with legal methodology and they have to base their decision on legal arguments […]. Accordingly, there will be no room for a legal decision based on empathy. Empathy may, however, play a role when the law is formulated in a general and abstract fashion. This wide scope of interpretation is most evident in the case of a general clause, […]."

Beckers develops her argument in favour of a wider consideration of empathy when applying general clauses in the context of competition law, more specifically in the context of assessing whether emotional advertising is prohibited under § 3(2) of the Act against Unfair Competition (*Gesetz gegen den unlauteren Wettbewerb* – UWG), which reads:[85]

"Geschäftliche Handlungen, die sich an Verbraucher richten oder diese erreichen, sind unlauter, wenn sie nicht der unternehmerischen Sorgfalt entsprechen und dazu geeignet sind, das wirtschaftliche Verhalten des Verbrauchers wesentlich zu beeinflussen."

"Commercial practices targeting or reaching consumers are unfair if they are not in compliance with professional diligence and are suited to materially distorting the economic behaviour of consumers."[86]

Beckers then distinguishes different forms of empathy. First, she identifies a tendency whereby judges rely on their personal experiences, on their own empathy, *pars pro toto* for assessing the effects of emotional advertising on consumers, and she convincingly argues against such a way of considering emotions in applying the law.[87] Secondly, she raises the question whether the way forward is "empirische Empathie" (empirical empathy), where courts rely on the opinions of non-legal experts. Again, she is critical because different nonlegal disciplines will reach different conclusions as to the effects of emotional advertising on consumers. The court's decision will depend on which expert

---

[83] On the concept of a general clause, see p. 368, above.

[84] *Beckers* (n. 21), 95.

[85] *Beckers* (n. 21), 96. Beckers refers to an older version of the UWG. For the purpose of the present paper, this is of no relevance, and I cite here to § 3 UWG as it is currently in force.

[86] https://www.gesetze-im-internet.de/englisch_uwg/ (last visited 5 February 2023).

[87] *Beckers* (n. 21), 100 f.

the court has resorted to or which expert the court follows.[88] *Beckers* concludes that it is impossible for the law to identify the factual emotions of consumers.[89] She argues in favour of a third possibility, which she calls "Empathie für die Gesellschaft" ("empathy for society"):[90]

"Wenn der Verbraucher, seine Motive bei der Kaufentscheidung und seine Präferenzen für das Recht nicht erreichbar sind, so ist die Forderung nach empathischer Entscheidung im Wettbewerbsrecht umzudenken. Empathie heißt dann nicht, 'Partei ergreifen' für den schutzbedürftigen Verbraucher, sondern das Verständnis über den sozialen Bereich, in dem er agiert, offenzulegen und an veränderte Verhältnisse anzupassen. Es muss darum gehen, in die rechtliche Entscheidung die divergierenden Interessen und Rationalitäten im Wettbewerb einzubeziehen und diese abzusichern, damit das Individuum in diesem sozialen Bereich frei entscheiden kann."

"When it is impossible for the law to grasp the consumer, his motives for a specific purchase decision and his preferences, then the call for empathic decision in competition law has to be rethought. In such a situation empathy should not mean taking sides in favour of the consumer who is in need of protection. Rather, our understanding of the social sphere in which the consumer acts has to be made transparent and has to be adapted to the changed general framework. It is necessary to consider the divergent interests and rationalities in competition in the process of judicial decision-making so that the individual is able to act freely in this social sphere."

With respect to § 138(1) BGB, I am doubtful, but for a different reason. Understanding social morals as something that may be uncovered by empirical studies is problematic.[91] Doctrinal scholars of law interpret *gute Sitten* to reflect primarily the fundamental values of the constitutional and legal order, and they then analyse how these fundamental values are of importance in the different groups of cases (*Fallgruppen*).[92] This approach has proven to be workable. Of course, from the perspective of the *Grundlagenfächer*,[93] there is room for law and emotions scholarship. It may, for example, reflect on the affective and emotional legitimatization of moral norms as understood by doctrinal scholars of law in the context of § 138(1) BGB.

The appreciation of the importance of emotions may also help to further our understanding of the groups of cases (*Fallgruppen*) which case law and legal literature have developed in order to handle the general clause of § 138(1) BGB. One such group of cases has already been discussed above.[94] It involves surety contracts in family relations. The above-mentioned requirements which

---

[88] Beckers' critique refers to a general problem that exists when courts wish to rely on an expert opinion. See *Kühne* (n. 77), para. 861; *Roxin/Schünemann* (n. 77), § 27 para. 12.

[89] *Beckers* (n. 21), 101–104.

[90] *Beckers* (n. 21), 104.

[91] See, e.g., *Neuner* (n. 36), § 46 para. 9.

[92] See p. 362 and p. 368, above.

[93] See p. 357, above.

[94] See p. 368, above.

have to be met for the surety contract to be void under § 138(1) BGB do not explicitly refer to emotions. However, if these requirements are met, it is presumed that the third party has exploited the first family member's emotional ties to the second family member, and this is the reason for the contract being deemed void. However, comparative law scholars and legal historians have criticized the case law on void surety contracts in family relations. They do not criticize the outcome of these cases, but rather that these cases are discussed as a *Fallgruppe* within § 138(1) BGB. In English and Scots law these cases are discussed as involving an "undue influence", allowing the first family member to rescind the contract.[95] Comparative law scholars and legal historians argue that German law should *de lege ferenda* recategorize this *Fallgruppe* following the examples of English and Scots law.[96]

Indeed: (1) It is incoherent to argue first that *gute Sitten* are a normative concept which is concretized to reflect fundamental values of the constitutional and legal order but then to argue subsequently that in a specific group of cases a contract is void because of the presumed exploitation of emotions. There is no fundamental value of the constitutional and legal order forbidding the exploitation of emotions. (2) Furthermore, the fact that the validity of the contract may be contested for an exploitation of emotions rather aligns this *Fallgruppe* with cases of error, misrepresentation, deceit, and duress. (3) Moreover, the recategorization of this *Fallgruppe* would lead to an improvement with respect to the legal consequences: According to § 138(1) BGB, a contract is *ipso iure* void. However, if the validity of the contract may be contested for an exploitation of emotions, it should fall onto the first family member whose emotions were exploited to decide whether the contract should be avoided. Voidability is, just as in cases of error, misrepresentation, deceit, and duress, the more rational legal consequence in this *Fallgruppe*. (4) Finally, the recategorization of this *Fallgruppe* may allow law and emotions scholarship to openly reassess and fine-tune the requirements that need to be met in order to presume that emotional family ties have been exploited.

By contrast, *Gunther Teubner* focuses not on the exploitation of emotions but on the institutional dimension: The surety contract is void because the third

[95] An analysis of undue influence from the perspective of law and emotions scholarship is offered by *J. Stannard*, The Emotional Dynamics of Undue Influence, in: Conway/Stannard (n. 29), 59–82.

[96] *S. Martens*, Undue influence, in: J. Basedow et al. (eds.), Handwörterbuch des Europäischen Privatrechts, vol. 2 (2009), 1534–1537. See also *R. Zimmermann/J. du Plessis*, The Relevance of Reverence. Undue Influence Civilian Style, Maastricht Journal of European and Comparative Law 10 (2003), 345–379.

party economically instrumentalizes the family as an institution governed by solidarity:[97]

"Wenn Kredite aus erwerbswirtschaftlicher Tätigkeit durch Personalsicherheiten aus der Familiensphäre abgesichert werden, dann ist dies kein Problem der Verletzung individueller Grundrechte durch private Macht. Vielmehr kollidieren unverträgliche Handlungslogiken. [...] Familienbürgschaften sind deshalb unter verfassungsrechtlichen Gesichtspunkten problematisch, weil sie solidarisches Handeln innerhalb der Familie ökonomisch instrumentalisieren. Trotz der kaum noch übersehbaren Literatur zum Thema werden nur wenige Autoren dieser speziellen Konfliktproblematik gerecht. Und wenn sie sie ansprechen, dann zielen sie meist am Kern der Sache vorbei. Formulierungen wie 'Kommerzialisierung von Liebe und Dankbarkeit' weisen zwar in die richtige Richtung, sind aber viel zu vage und unbestimmt. Es gibt Myriaden von strukturellen Kopplungen von wirtschaftlich-instrumentalem und emotional-expressiven Handeln, in denen Gefühle kommerzialisiert werden, ohne dass dies Grundrechtsprobleme aufwürfe."

"When a loan that has been granted in an entrepreneurial context is secured by personal surety coming from the family sphere, then the problem is not that individual basic rights may be infringed by private power. Rather incompatible logics of actions collide. [...] Surety contracts in family relations are problematic from the perspective of the fundamental values of the constitutional order for the reason that family solidarity is economically instrumentalized. Even though there is abundant literature on the problem, only few authors correctly identify the true problem. And when they touch upon the true problem, they nevertheless are not on point. Formulations such as 'the commercialization of love and gratitude' point in the right direction, but they are too vague and uncertain. There are myriads of situations in which economic-instrumental action is coupled with emotional-expressive action, in which emotions are commercialized, without any problems being raised from the perspective of basic constitutional rights."

Read in such way, voidness under § 138(1) BGB would be the correct legal response. *Teubner*'s analysis recalls an important point: The doctrinal study of law rationalizes legal decisions by arguing from within a legal system.[98] However, the doctrinal study of law has different points of reference in the legal system to which a decision may be linked. Those scholars stressing the importance of emotions being exploited will link the case law on void surety contracts to the rescission of contracts and will argue *de lege ferenda* in favour of a recategorization of this *Fallgruppe*. By contrast, *Teubner*'s doctrinal explanation of the case law links the issue to fundamental constitutional values. Consequently, his analysis can do without any reference to emotions. The question of which analysis is to be followed cannot be answered by law and emotions scholars. The question which analysis is to be followed depends on the doctrinal persuasiveness of each analysis.

---

[97] *G. Teubner*, Ein Fall von struktureller Korruption? Die Familienbürgschaft in der Kollision unverträglicher Handlungslogiken (BVerfGE 89, 214 ff.), Kritische Vierteljahresschrift für Gesetzgebung und Rechtswissenschaft 83 (2000), 388–404.

[98] See p. 358, above.

C. Emotions and the judicial review of contracts in terms of fairness

In 2019, *Matthias Wendland* has offered a new theoretical approach to the judicial review of contracts as regards the fairness of a given term.[99] He bases his approach first on the negotiation model that was developed in 1981 by *Roger Fisher* and *William Ury* in the framework of the Harvard Negotiation Project[100] and that has since been further developed by others; secondly, he incorporates the theory of the stages of moral development as formulated by *Lawrence Kohlberg*.[101] *Wendland* thus draws on research that discusses the importance of emotions. I have reservations against *Wendland*'s approach.[102] First, as I have stated previously, he offers no "reasoning that the model – which [he] has derived above all from empirical research on negotiations, from developmental psychology, and from the philosophy of law – is the model on which the German Civil Code is based" ("Begründung, daß das Vertragsmodell, das *Wendland* vor allem aus der empirischen Verhandlungsforschung, aus der Entwicklungspsychologie und aus der Rechtsphilosophie herleitet, auch gerade das Modell ist, das dem BGB zugrunde liegt").[103] In other words, he has not been able to link the research on negotiations to German positive law on the review of contracts for fairness.[104] Secondly, it should follow from *Wendland*'s approach that such a judicial policing of contracts for fairness is legitimate whenever a contract has not been negotiated in accordance with the negotiation model as first developed by *Fisher* and *Ury*. However, *Wendland* himself does not draw this conclusion, instead simply trying to justify the fairness review as practised by German courts, limiting it to a fairness review of standard contract terms.

D. Emotions, liability, and non-pecuniary harm

In the last part of their paper, *Soniewicka* and *Wesołowska* discuss the interaction between emotions and liability. They distinguish different questions.

---

[99] *M. Wendland*, Vertragsfreiheit und Vertragsgerechtigkeit. Subjektive und objektive Gestaltungskräfte im Privatrecht am Beispiel der Inhaltskontrolle Allgemeiner Geschäftsbedingungen im unternehmerischen Geschäftsverkehr (2019), especially 234–277.

[100] *R. Fisher/W. Ury*, Getting to Yes. Negotiating Agreement without Giving in (1981). *Soniewicka/Wesołowska*, p. 321, above, also refer to research on the role of emotions in negotiations when claiming that law and emotions scholarship has started to expand to contract law. They cite *H. Keren*, Considering the affective consideration, Golden Gate University Law Review 40 (2010), 165–234.

[101] *L. Kohlberg*, The Philosophy of Moral Development. Moral Stages and the Idea of Justice (1981).

[102] *P. Hellwege*, Archiv für die civilistische Praxis 221 (2021), 279–285.

[103] *Hellwege* (n. 102), 283.

[104] See p. 358, above.

1. Emotions excluding or modifying personal guilt in criminal law

"Firstly, emotions may modify the legal responsibility for a crime. The widely known term 'crime of passion' refers in common usage to cases when anger overpowers someone's self-control and logical thinking to the point where they cannot be held responsible for their actions."[105]

Soniewicka and *Wesołowska* question, however, whether "the law [does] actually assume that emotions are wild, uncontrollable impulses that excuse crimes", they point out that this "perception has been increasingly questioned by researchers working in the law and emotions movement", and they claim that the approach developed by law and emotions scholars "is much more sophisticated, coherent, adequate for the legal context, and accords with current discoveries in cognitive science and psychology".[106] They draw on a distinction that is rooted in law and emotions scholarship:

"Emotions, therefore, may mitigate punishment or even excuse one's actions, but they need to be contextually sound, adequate, and appropriately expressed according to moral or social norms – in other words, one has to be reasonably angry, or understandably scared, for the law to approve these emotions as modifiers of responsibility. Thus, the law should acknowledge the evaluative and cognitive components of emotions in order to adequately address these issues. The mechanistic conception of emotions is inadequate and misleading."[107]

German law follows neither a purely mechanistic conception of emotions nor a purely evaluative approach. § 20 StGB reads:

"Ohne Schuld handelt, wer bei Begehung der Tat wegen einer krankhaften seelischen Störung, wegen einer tiefgreifenden Bewußtseinsstörung oder wegen einer Intelligenzminderung oder einer schweren anderen seelischen Störung unfähig ist, das Unrecht der Tat einzusehen oder nach dieser Einsicht zu handeln."

"Whoever, at the time when the offence is committed, is incapable of recognizing the unlawfulness of his actions or of acting in accordance with such appreciation due to a pathological mental disorder, a profound disturbance of consciousness or intellectual disability or any other serious mental disorder is deemed to act without guilt."[108]

Furthermore, the punishment may be mitigated according to § 21 StGB for the same reasons as mentioned in § 20 StGB:

"Ist die Fähigkeit des Täters, das Unrecht der Tat einzusehen oder nach dieser Einsicht zu handeln, aus einem der in § 20 bezeichneten Gründe bei Begehung der Tat erheblich vermindert, so kann die Strafe nach § 49 Abs. 1 gemildert werden."

---

[105] *Soniewicka/Wesołowska*, p. 335, above.

[106] *Soniewicka/Wesołowska*, p. 336, above.

[107] *Soniewicka/Wesołowska*, p. 337, above. See, e.g., *Kahan/Nussbaum* (n. 34), 275–301.

[108] The translation is a modified version of the translation found on https://www.gesetze-im-internet.de/englisch_stgb/ (last visited on 17 January 2023).

"If the offender's capacity to appreciate the unlawfulness of the act or to act in accordance with any such appreciation is substantially diminished at the time of the commission of the offence due to one of the reasons indicated in § 20, the punishment may be mitigated pursuant to § 49(1)."[109]

German law does not follow a mechanistic conception according to which an offender acting under emotions is without guilt or according to which emotions diminish the punishment automatically. § 20 and § 21 StGB do not even mention emotions. Emotions may, however, be relevant for assessing whether the offender suffered from "a profound disturbance of consciousness". This disturbance is only of relevance if the offender was, due to such disturbance, "incapable of recognizing the unlawfulness of his actions or of acting in accordance with such appreciation" or if this capability was "substantially diminished". As pointed out above, in assessing whether these requirements are met, a court will obtain an expert opinion,[110] thereby guaranteeing that the court's findings are in accordance with current psychological and psychiatric research. Literature points out that, when examining the accused, German courts and experts will regularly follow the WHO's International Classification of Diseases or the Diagnostic and Statistical Manual of Mental Disorders edited by the American Psychiatric Association.[111] Finally, § 20 and § 21 StGB simply leave no room for an evaluative component assessing whether the offender's emotions were "contextually sound, adequate and appropriately expressed [...] according to moral or social norms",[112] and there is rightly no room for such evaluative assessment. § 20 and § 21 StGB concern the offender's personal guilt, which may be diminished or excluded due to the aforementioned disorders, disturbances, or disability. Disorders, disturbances, and disabilities simply cannot be judged against moral or social norms. Finally, § 20 and § 21 StGB do not follow modern holism.[113] It seems best to understand those emotions that may establish a disturbance in the meaning of § 20 and § 21 StGB as something distinct from reason and, thus, to follow traditional dualism. The offender's personal guilt may also be excluded according to § 35(1)(1) StGB:

"Wer in einer gegenwärtigen, nicht anders abwendbaren Gefahr für Leben, Leib oder Freiheit eine rechtswidrige Tat begeht, um die Gefahr von sich, einem Angehörigen oder einer anderen ihm nahestehenden Person abzuwenden, handelt ohne Schuld."

---

[109] The translation is a modified version of the translation found on https://www.gesetze-im-internet.de/englisch_stgb/ (last visited on 28 January 2023).

[110] See p. 371, above.

[111] *Schöch* (n. 72), para. 23, who in 2020 referred to the now outdated editions of the respective classification and manual.

[112] *Soniewicka/Wesołowska*, p. 337, above.

[113] See p. 355, above.

"Whoever, when faced with a present danger to life, body or freedom of movement which cannot otherwise be averted, commits an unlawful act to avert the danger from himself, a relative or another close person acts without guilt."[114]

§ 35(1)(1) StGB is limited to relatives and other close persons because only then does the law presumes that the offender acted under emotional/motivational pressure in order to save his relative or other close person and only then does the law acknowledges this pressure to be of relevance. In order to decide who counts as "another close person", an evaluative assessment is made.[115] If the other person counts as being close, then it is again presumed that the offender acted under emotional pressure. Thus, in the context of § 35(1)(1) StGB, a kind of mechanistic conception is combined with an evaluative approach. However, the foundations of § 35(1)(1) StGB are contested:[116] Some argue that the individual emotional/motivational pressure cannot explain § 35(1)(1) StGB as the law does not exclude guilt in other, equivalent situations of emotional pressure. For the present contribution, it is important to note that this academic controversy is not linked to law and emotions scholarship, and such scholarship is not of any help in resolving the controversy. It is uncontested that the law should take note that people may act under emotional pressure when they try to avert a present danger threatening people to whom they feel close. The problem faced in § 35 StGB is how to best phrase this idea. The drafters of § 35(1) StGB apparently wanted to limit this notion to certain situations: They require the danger to be objectively present, with the consequence that an emotional pressure based on a merely assumed situation of danger will not do. Furthermore, even though § 35(1)(1) StGB is based on emotional pressure, the drafters do not require the judge to assess the offender's motivational pressure as long as he acted with the intention to avert the danger faced by a relative or another close person. However, the concept of presumed emotions seems to be at odds with the concept of personal guilt. § 35 StGB, thus, raises primarily doctrinal problems.

Finally, emotions may be a relevant factor in fixing the measure of punishment. § 46(1) and (2) StGB read:

"(1) Die Schuld des Täters ist Grundlage für die Zumessung der Strafe. Die Wirkungen, die von der Strafe für das künftige Leben des Täters in der Gesellschaft zu erwarten sind, sind zu berücksichtigen.

---

[114] The translation is a modified version of the translation found on https://www.gesetze-im-internet.de/englisch_stgb/ (last visited on 28 January 2023).

[115] See, e.g., *F. Zieschang*, Entschuldigungs- und Strafausschließungsgründe, in: Hilgendorf (n. 72), 791–848, para. 49.

[116] Compare, for instance, the discussions by *Heger* (n. 46), § 35 para. 1; *C. Momsen/L.I. Savić*, in: von Heintschel-Heinegg (n. 46), § 35 paras. 2–7; *W. Perron*, in: Schönke/Schröder (n. 46), § 35 para. 2; *B. Müssig*, in: Münchener Kommentar zum Strafgesetzbuch, vol. 1 (4th edn., 2020), § 35 paras. 36 f.

(2) Bei der Zumessung wägt das Gericht die Umstände, die für und gegen den Täter sprechen, gegeneinander ab. Dabei kommen namentlich in Betracht:
die Beweggründe und die Ziele des Täters, besonders auch rassistische, fremdenfeindliche, antisemitische, geschlechtsspezifische, gegen die sexuelle Orientierung gerichtete oder sonstige menschenverachtende,
die Gesinnung, die aus der Tat spricht, und der bei der Tat aufgewendete Wille,
das Maß der Pflichtwidrigkeit,
die Art der Ausführung und die verschuldeten Auswirkungen der Tat,
das Vorleben des Täters, seine persönlichen und wirtschaftlichen Verhältnisse sowie
sein Verhalten nach der Tat, besonders sein Bemühen, den Schaden wiedergutzumachen, sowie das Bemühen des Täters, einen Ausgleich mit dem Verletzten zu erreichen."

"(1) The offender's guilt provides the basis on which the penalty is fixed. The effects which the penalty can be expected to have on the offender's future life in society are to be taken into account.
(2) When fixing the penalty the court weighs the circumstances which speak in favour of and those which speak against the offender. The following, in particular, may be taken into consideration:
– the offender's motives and objectives, in particular including racist, xenophobic, antisemitic, gender-related, motives against the sexual orientation or other motives evidencing contempt for humanity,
– the attitude reflected in the offence and the degree of force of will involved in its commission,
– the degree of the breach of the offender's duties,
– the modus operandi and the consequences caused by the offence to the extent that the offender is to blame for them,
– the offender's prior history, personal and financial circumstances, and
– the offender's conduct in the period following the offence, in particular efforts to make restitution for the harm caused as well as efforts at reconciliation with the victim."[117]

Each offence of the German Penal Code (StGB) defines a range of sentences – the range of sentences for manslaughter is, for example, imprisonment between five and fifteen years: § 212 and § 38 StGB. The court will fix a specific sentence, and § 46 StGB guides the court how to do so. According to § 46 StGB, the offender's emotions may, again, be of relevance.[118] § 46 StGB seems to be based on modern holism, not on traditional dualism: The court has to identify all relevant factors and weigh them against each other.[119] At the same time § 46 StGB follows not a mechanistic but rather an evaluative approach: A court will only be able to weigh the different factors, including the different emotions involved, against each other if it evaluates them. Finally, the judgment of the court has to openly state how it reached the specific sentence.[120]

---

[117] The translation is a modified version of the translation found on https://www.gesetze-im-internet.de/englisch_stgb/ (last visited on 30 November 2023).

[118] *J. Kinzig*, in: Schönke/Schröder (n. 46), § 46 paras. 13, 16; *Dallmeyer* (n. 14), 163–185.

[119] *Kinzig* (n. 118), § 46 paras. 6 f., 58.

[120] *Kinzig* (n. 118), § 46 para. 65.

2. Liability for emotional distress in private law

Soniewicka's and *Wesołowska*'s focus is on delictual liability in private law for emotional harm. The starting points of Polish and German law seem to be similar: *Soniewicka* and *Wesołowska* observe that in Polish law "unpleasant emotions alone do not trigger liability".[121] Unlike French or Austrian law, German law does not know a general clause (*Generalklausel*) of delictual liability; instead, it has different bases for claims, the most important of which are § 823(1), § 823(2), and § 826 BGB.[122] § 823(1) BGB reads:

> "Wer vorsätzlich oder fahrlässig das Leben, den Körper, die Gesundheit, die Freiheit, das Eigentum oder ein sonstiges Recht eines anderen widerrechtlich verletzt, ist dem anderen zum Ersatz des daraus entstehenden Schadens verpflichtet."

> "A person who, intentionally or negligently, unlawfully injures the life, body, health, freedom, property or another right of another person is liable to make compensation to the other party for the damage arising from this."[123]

By contrast, the Austrian general clause of liability in damages as codified in § 1295(1) of the General Civil Code (*Allgemeines Bürgerliches Gesetzbuch* – ABGB) reads:

> "Jedermann ist berechtigt, von dem Beschädiger den Ersatz des Schadens, welchen dieser ihm aus Verschulden zugefügt hat, zu fordern; [...]."

> "Every person is entitled to claim compensation from the damaging person for the damage which the latter has caused to him through fault; [...]."

Prima facie, the damaged party may claim compensation for any damage whatsoever under § 1295(1) ABGB. By contrast, § 823(1) BGB is more restrictive: The damaging party must have injured one of the enumerated protected interests (life, body, health, etc.) and the so damaged party may then claim compensation for the damage caused by the infringement of such right.[124] Emotions are not specifically mentioned as a protected interest. Furthermore, emotions as such are not regarded to be "another right of another person" within the meaning of § 823(1) BGB. Nevertheless, the legal rights protected by § 823(1) BGB may have an emotional spin to them: An injury of the body may, for example, be accompanied by the feeling of being emotionally hurt. The emotional side to an infringement of an interest protected under § 823(1) BGB is most obvious in the general right to privacy counting as "another right of another person".[125] Furthermore, even though marriage is not regarded to be "another right of another person", so that a person does not have a claim in

---

[121] *Soniewicka/Wesołowska*, pp. 340 f., above.

[122] *D. Looschelders*, Schuldrecht. Besonderer Teil (17th edn., 2022), § 58 para. 7.

[123] https://www.gesetze-im-internet.de/englisch_bgb/ (last visited on 30 January 2023).

[124] *Looschelders* (n. 122), § 58 para. 5, § 59 para. 2.

[125] *Looschelders* (n. 122), § 61 para. 2.

damages against a person who is having an affair with her spouse, it is generally accepted that the "räumlich-gegenständlicher Bereich der Ehe" ("spatial aspect of marriage") is protected by § 823(1) BGB, such that the betrayed spouse may apply for an injunction preventing that the extramarital affair is carried out in the matrimonial home.[126] In this case, the protected right is defined objectively (the spatial aspect of marriage), but what we truly mean is that the spouse does not have to experience the feeling that she has been betrayed in her own home.

Finally, the case law on damages for shock is of relevance in the present context. People may suffer emotionally distress upon witnessing, or hearing of, an accident. Has the emotionally distressed person himself a claim in damages against the person who unlawfully caused the accident intentionally or negligently? The case law starts with the premise that it is a general risk of life to experience situations that may cause emotions of sadness. Damages for shock are nevertheless allowed under restrictive requirements, and these requirements in essence react to two problems.[127] First, the claimant who suffers the shock must himself suffer an injury to a legal interest protected by § 823(1) BGB. It is not enough that the claimant feels sad. The shock must be of such a nature that it amounts to an injury of health as protected under § 823(1) BGB. Secondly, there is the problem that the shock is only an indirect consequence of the accident, i.e., that the shock is mediated through the shocked person's psyche. Consequently, the case law requires that the shock must be a comprehensible reaction to witnessing an accident. If a person witnesses an accident in which a close person is severely injured or killed or if a person receives the information that a close person is so injured or killed in an accident, shock is a comprehensible reaction. In other words: German law follows in the present context an evaluative approach as promoted by *Soniewicka* and *Wesołowska*.[128]
§ 823(2)(1) BGB continues:

"Die gleiche Verpflichtung trifft denjenigen, welcher gegen ein den Schutz eines anderen bezweckendes Gesetz verstößt."

"A person who commits a breach of a statute that is intended to protect another person has the same obligation [as under § 823(1) BGB]."[129]

In the present context, § 185 StGB on insults and § 238 StGB on stalking are of relevance, as there will often be an emotional aspect to insults and stalking.[130] Furthermore, § 825 BGB introduces a specific liability in damages for

---

[126] *Looschelders* (n. 122), § 60 para. 22.

[127] *Looschelders* (n. 122), § 60 para. 7.

[128] See p. 379, above.

[129] The translation is a modified version of the translation found on https://www.gesetze-im-internet.de/englisch_bgb/ (last visited on 30 January 2023).

[130] With respect to § 238 StGB see *J. Gericke*, in: Münchener Kommentar (n. 46), § 238 para. 1.

inducing other people to sexual acts – an offence that has again strong emotional consequences even though the protected interest is defined as sexual self-determination.[131] Finally, the German legislature has recently reformed § 844 BGB:

"(1) Im Falle der Tötung hat der Ersatzpflichtige die Kosten der Beerdigung demjenigen zu ersetzen, welchem die Verpflichtung obliegt, diese Kosten zu tragen.
(2) Stand der Getötete zur Zeit der Verletzung zu einem Dritten in einem Verhältnis, vermöge dessen er diesem gegenüber kraft Gesetzes unterhaltspflichtig war oder unterhaltspflichtig werden konnte, und ist dem Dritten infolge der Tötung das Recht auf den Unterhalt entzogen, so hat der Ersatzpflichtige dem Dritten durch Entrichtung einer Geldrente insoweit Schadensersatz zu leisten, als der Getötete während der mutmaßlichen Dauer seines Lebens zur Gewährung des Unterhalts verpflichtet gewesen sein würde; […].
(3) Der Ersatzpflichtige hat dem Hinterbliebenen, der zur Zeit der Verletzung zu dem Getöteten in einem besonderen persönlichen Näheverhältnis stand, für das dem Hinterbliebenen zugefügte seelische Leid eine angemessene Entschädigung in Geld zu leisten. Ein besonderes persönliches Näheverhältnis wird vermutet, wenn der Hinterbliebene der Ehegatte, der Lebenspartner, ein Elternteil oder ein Kind des Getöteten war."

"(1) In cases where death is caused, the person liable in damages must reimburse the costs of a funeral to the person under a duty to bear these costs.
(2) If the person killed, at the time of the injury, stood in a relationship to a third party on the basis of which he was obliged or might become obliged by operation of law to provide maintenance for that person and if the third party has as a result of the death been deprived of his right to maintenance, then the person liable in damages must provide the third party damages by payment of an annuity to the extent that the person killed would have been obliged to provide maintenance for the presumed duration of his life; […].
(3) The person so liable has to pay to a surviving person, who at the time of the injury was in a special personal relationship with the person killed, an adequate compensation in money for the emotional distress caused to the surviving person. A special personal relationship will be presumed if the surviving person was the spouse, life partner, parent, or child of the person killed."[132]

Again, § 844(3) BGB explicitly follows an evaluative approach as promoted by *Soniewicka* and *Wesołowska*. By contrast, in the context of damages for nervous shock, such an evaluative approach has been developed by the case law.

In summary, the German law of delict does not in most cases directly protect emotions. German (case) law rather defines objective legal interests and factual situations that may involve emotions. Thus, emotions are in most cases protected indirectly only. It is only § 844(3) BGB that directly refers to "seelisches Leid" ("emotional distress"). It seems that German law adopts a piecemeal approach that can best be explained as being the result of historical development and not as the result of coherent analysis.

---

[131] *Looschelders* (n. 122), § 66 para. 12.

[132] The translation of § 844(1) and (2) BGB is a modified version of the translation found on https://www.gesetze-im-internet.de/englisch_bgb/ (last visited on 30 January 2023).

It is against this backdrop that law and emotions scholarship may help in critically assessing the German law of delict. Consider the question of whether marriage is "another right of another person" in the meaning of § 823(1) BGB.[133] Marriage as such is not such right, with the consequence that a person does not have a claim in damages against another person who is having an affair with her spouse. Marital problems do involve strong emotions, yet an evaluative assessment may tell us that the law of delict does not provide the correct answers to such emotional problems. On the other hand, an evaluative approach as promoted by *Soniewicka* and *Wesołowska* may equally tell us that one's own home should be an emotionally safe space, so that the betrayed spouse may rightly apply for an injunction so as to prevent that the extramarital affair is carried out in the matrimonial home. To analyse these questions from the perspective of the involved emotions would open the door to interdisciplinary scholarship. At the same time, to openly acknowledge that the law of delict protects one's own home as an emotionally safe space seems to be more rational than to protect such emotions in the guise of an objectively framed interest, i.e. the "räumlich-gegenständlicher Bereich der Ehe" ("spatial aspect of the marriage"). Finally, to openly acknowledge that the law of delict protects one's own home as an emotionally safe space would allow a further development of the law: Why may the betrayed spouse only apply for an injunction which prevents that the extramarital affair is carried out in the matrimonial home? Why does the betrayed spouse not have a claim in damages for emotional distress when the affair has already been carried out in the matrimonial home?[134] This question leads to the next subsection.

3. Assessing damages in cases of emotional distress

In the preceding section, the relevance of emotions for the different causes of actions in delict has been discussed. However, emotional distress suffered by the victim may also be of importance in assessing damages which the wrongdoer has to pay to the victim. German law takes a restrictive approach to the recoverability of non-pecuniary damage. § 253 BGB reads:

"(1) Wegen eines Schadens, der nicht Vermögensschaden ist, kann Entschädigung in Geld nur in den durch das Gesetz bestimmten Fällen gefordert werden.
(2) Ist wegen einer Verletzung des Körpers, der Gesundheit, der Freiheit oder der sexuellen Selbstbestimmung Schadensersatz zu leisten, kann auch wegen des Schadens, der nicht Vermögensschaden ist, eine billige Entschädigung in Geld gefordert werden."

"(1) Compensation in money may be demanded for a non-pecuniary damage only in the cases stipulated by law.

[133] See p. 384, above.

[134] See also *J. Hager*, in: J. von Staudingers Kommentar zum Bürgerlichen Gesetzbuch (new edn., 2017), § 823 para. B180.

(2) If damages have to be rendered for an injury to body, health, freedom or sexual self-determination, reasonable compensation in money may also be demanded for non-pecuniary damage."

Beyond the situations of § 253(2) BGB, non-pecuniary damage may be compensated in the case of § 844(3) BGB[135] and in the case of infringement of the general right to privacy under § 823(1) BGB.[136] Law and emotions scholarship may again open the door to a critical evaluation of this restrictive approach. Extra-legal research on the importance of the matrimonial home as an emotionally safe space may, for example, suggest that a betrayed spouse should have a claim in damages for emotional distress when an affair has already been carried out in the matrimonial home and that the betrayed spouse's rights should not be limited to applying for an injunction. Furthermore, extra-legal research may find that in our modern society pets are of a greater important emotional value to, for example, elderly people who live alone than are their closest relatives who may live far away or who may not even exist. Why should such a person not be able to claim compensation for the emotional distress caused to her by the loss of her pet in addition to the pecuniary damage that is already recoverable under § 823(1) BGB. As the law stands, damages for emotional distress are in such a situation not granted.[137] The evaluative approach as proposed by *Soniewicka* and *Wesołowska* may again help to go beyond the situations defined in § 253(2) and § 844(3) BGB without opening the floodgates to the compensation of non-pecuniary damage for any manner of emotional distress. Legal commentators have already identified the present state of German law as being unsatisfactory and inconsistent, and authors have proposed an evaluative approach that is similar to that promoted by *Soniewicka* and *Wesołowska* without, however, subscribing to law and emotions scholarship.[138]

VII. Conclusion

I am not a law and emotions scholar. Nevertheless, I happily took on the opportunity to comment on *Soniewicka*'s and *Wesołowska*'s contribution from the perspective of German law. My plan was to comment on their contribution from the perspective of the doctrinal study of German law. However, as I am approaching law and emotions scholarship for the first time and as scholarship on law and emotions is seemingly only a marginal field of research in German

[135] *Looschelders* (n. 122), § 71 para. 12.

[136] *Looschelders* (n. 122), § 61 paras 3 f., 13.

[137] *Looschelders* (n. 122), § 60 para. 7.

[138] *G. Wagner*, in: Münchener Kommentar zum Bürgerlichen Gesetzbuch, vol. 1 (8th edn., 2020), § 823 paras. 218 f.

legal scholarship, I feel that it is necessary to put my comments into greater context. My tentative conclusions are as follows.

A. *Soniewicka* and *Wesołowska* refer to *Posner* stating that "legal methodology is not well adjusted to work on emotions".[139] And *Grossi* writes: "While positivism […] bars emotion from law, critical jurisprudence […] makes room for it."[140] Yet, the fact that positivists claim that the law is "purely rational"[141] does not mean that positivism bars emotions from law and that positive law has to ignore that the world is largely irrational/emotional. If positive law ignored the fact that the world is irrational/emotional for the simple reason that positive law is "purely rational", there would be no such thing as criminal law. However, emotions in law are, as some have argued, not limited to criminal law: "In the conventional story, emotion has a certain, narrowly defined place in law. It is assigned to the criminal courts. It is confined to those – like witnesses, the accused, the public – without legal training."[142] The debate would greatly benefit from distinguishing the following layers (B–E, below).

B. Lawgivers must act rationally when drafting positive law. However, that does not imply that they must blind themselves to the fact that people are led by emotions, and the numerous examples taken from German law which I have discussed above prove that German legislators take emotions into account. Furthermore, German legislators acknowledge that emotions may have different relevance in real life and in law. (1) Emotions may need to be protected. In addition to the examples discussed above, § 383 of the Civil Procedure Act (*Zivilprozeßordnung* – ZPO) and § 52 StPO come to mind. They privilege – among other people – close relatives and spouses in court proceedings in criminal and private law matters by allowing them to refuse to testify as witnesses, and they thereby protect these individuals from a situation of emotional conflict. Nevertheless, for the application of these norms it is irrelevant whether the witness feels such a situation of conflict. It is enough that the requirements of § 383 ZPO and § 52 StPO are objectively met.[143] (2) Emotions may affect legal responsibility. (3) Emotions may allow a party to escape a contract. (4) Beyond the examples discussed above, emotions may corrupt legal decision-making. § 20 of the Administrative Proceedings Act (*Verwaltungsverfahrensgesetz* – VwVfG), for example, excludes a person from acting for a public authority in administrative proceedings if that person is a relative or a

---

[139] *Soniewicka/Wesołowska*, p. 320, above, referring to *Posner* (n. 114), 1977 f.

[140] *Grossi* (n. 16), 56. In a similar vein, e.g., *H. Petersen*, The Language of Emotions in the Language of Law, in: eadem (ed.), Love and Law in Europe (1998), 12–26, 12.

[141] *Grossi* (n. 16), 56.

[142] *Bandes* (n. 3), 2.

[143] *Roxin/Schünemann* (n. 77), § 26 para. 14; *Kühne* (n. 77), para. 812.1; *H. Kreicker*, in: Münchener Kommentar (n. 81), § 52 para. 1; *J. Damrau/A. Weinland*, in: Münchener Kommentar zur Zivilprozessordnung, vol. 2 (6th edn., 2020), 383 para. 1.

spouse to a party in the proceedings, thereby guaranteeing the impartiality of administrative proceedings.[144]

C. The same is true for those who apply the law, such as judges: They must act rationally. Furthermore, they are bound to the law. However, that does not imply that they must close their eyes to the fact that people are led by emotions. To the contrary, positive law does allow them to consider emotions. To assess when judges may take emotions into consideration or when they are allowed to act with empathy, we have again to distinguish different layers: (1) In Germany, a first instance judge working in the field of private law will often try to convince the parties to enter into a settlement. Such settlement is for the parties often the emotionally sounder solution.[145] To reach such settlement, it may be helpful for the judge to be empathic towards both parties' situations, and in this context German literature refers to the Harvard Negotiation Project.[146] (2) Even if a judge is not successful in reaching a settlement, she will try to understand the parties' situation and act with empathy. After all, a judgment will fulfil its function of appeasing the parties only if the parties accept the judgment, and this requires that the judge understands both parties' positions. Above, we have seen two areas of practice where legislators even expressly require judges to act with empathy and require judges to have extra-legal expertise in psychology: judges sitting in youth courts and family court judges. Furthermore, the former are assisted by the youth courts assistance service, and special training is also required for public prosecutors handling criminal matters involving juvenile offenders. (3) In order to apply the law, a judge must first establish the relevant facts. The legal norm which the judge wishes to apply will guide her in this process. It tells her which facts are relevant for the case. When the judge hears witnesses, she may have to be empathic towards them in order to understand the witness and in order to assess the evidential value of the testimony.[147] (4) However, even when it comes to questions of law, a judge may take emotions into consideration when positive law directly or indirectly refers to emotions. All of this is unproblematic from the perspective of positivism.

D. Nevertheless, in positivism there are limits to a judge being empathic and taking emotions into consideration: (1) She must remain impartial, and (2) she cannot act *contra legem*. (3) Furthermore, she may only take evidence that is

---

[144] *U. Ramsauer*, in: Kopp/Ramsauer. Verwaltungsverfahrensgesetz. Kommentar (23th edn., 2022), § 20 para. 1.

[145] *H.J. Musielack/W. Voit*, Grundkurs ZPO (16th edn., 2022), para. 518.

[146] *T. Husemann*, Der moderierte Vertrag (2021), 115. On the Harvard Negotiation Project see p. 378, above.

[147] *Pegel* (n. 77), § 261 para. 55–59; *R. Bender/A. Nack*, Tatsachenfeststellung vor Gericht, vol. 2 (1995), passim; *C. Balzer/B. Walther*, Beweisaufnahme und Beweiswürdigung im Zivilprozeß (4th edn., 2018), paras. 152–171. Expert opinion may be necessary to assess the credibility of the witness, see *Rogall* (n. 76), § 73 para. 26; *Kühne* (n. 77), para. 851–855.

relevant for resolving the case. She cannot investigate the parties' situation and emotions any further. After all, a judge is a judge and not a therapist.

E. Where it is impossible to take emotions into consideration even though they should be of relevance, a positivist may engage in discourse on reforming the law. Finally, legal scholars may always consider emotions in research on the foundations of law. Summarizing points B–E, *Franz von Liszt*'s (1851–1919) statement made in 1892 with respect to criminal law still holds true today:[148]

> "Wer aber das Verbrechen bekämpfen will, muß das Verbrechen kennen, er muß es studieren nicht als begriffliche Abstraktion, sondern als Erscheinung, als Ereignis des gesellschaftlichen sowohl, wie des individuellen Lebens."

> "He who wants to fight crime has to understand crime; he must study it, not as conceptual abstraction, but as a phenomenon, as incident of societal as well as individual life."

And societal and individual life includes emotions. One may reformulate this idea on a more abstract level: He who wants to regulate life has to understand life; he must study it, not as conceptual abstraction, but as a phenomenon, both from the perspective of society and the individual, including emotions.

F. However, even if German law and legal scholarship already take emotions into account and even if they already address real individuals, does law and emotions scholarship have nevertheless something to offer? The answer very much depends on the agenda of law and emotions scholars. *Heather Conway* and *John Stannard* have recently argued – referring to earlier writings by *Terry A. Maroney* – that "there is still some way to go before law and emotion becomes established as a discipline in its own right […]. A number of issues can be identified, the first of which is the somewhat disjointed nature of the work in this field, with different groups approaching the topic from different angles instead of taking a more holistic approach."[149] If German law leaves, as I have argued, so much room for emotions, should German legal scholars follow the path mapped out by *Conway* and *Stannard*? For a number of reasons, I remain critical of the idea (G–L, below).

G. In German law, some norms are based on dualism, whereas others are phrased to reflect holism. Some legal provisions reflect a mechanistic conception of emotions, whereas others are based on an evaluative approach, and again others implement both. Some norms explicitly name emotions, others only indirectly refer to them, again others are phrased objectively but subcutaneously address emotions; and some legal texts explicitly refer to emotions but use the word as a normative concept. Often it is sufficient to take the findings

---

[148] *F. von Liszt*, Die Zukunft des Strafrechts. Vortrag, gehalten in der Budapester juristischen Gesellschaft, den 4. April 1892, in: idem, Strafrechtliche Aufsätze und Vorträge, vol. 2 (1905), 1–24, 3.

[149] *Conway/Stannard* (n. 29), 4 f.

of other disciplines into consideration (a division of labour), but in other cases true interdisciplinary work is necessary. In some cases, emotions are presumed; in other cases they have to be proven. Finally, in some cases legal actors will apply objective standards which take emotions into account in a typified fashion, and it falls on the individual to point to her individual emotions, as is the case in § 81d StPO. It seems that lawgivers, legal actors, and legal commentators each time adopt the approach that is most suitable for the problem to be resolved or analysed and that is most suitable to the role emotions play in the specific legal context. Law and emotions as a discipline in its own right adopting a holistic approach may wish to overcome such fragmented approach. To adopt a one-size-fits-all solution would, however, be overly simplistic. Nevertheless, law and emotions scholarship may critically analyse the different approaches in order to assess whether German law follows a piecemeal approach and in order to develop a rational matrix regarding when to implement which approach.

H. Furthermore, law and emotions scholarship may overemphasize the relevance of emotions. *Kahan* and *Nussbaum* correctly observe that "[e]motions are ubiquitous [...] in life",[150] yet they are not always important for legal analysis. Often emotions are simply part of a greater bundle of criteria that positive law requires to be taken into consideration when resolving a case, as the examples of § 1684(4) BGB and § 46(2) StGB have proven. To limit the analyses of what is in a child's best interests in the case of § 1684(4) BGB to the child's emotions would simply be flawed.

I. In other cases, law and emotions scholarship may bring the wrong spin to legal analyses. Law and emotion scholars discuss emotions modifying the legal responsibility for crimes. In German law, § 20 and § 21 StGB do not even mention emotions. Yet emotions may be relevant for assessing whether the offender suffered from "a profound disturbance of consciousness". Such disturbance is only of relevance if the offender is due to it "incapable of recognizing the unlawfulness of his actions or of acting in accordance with such appreciation" or if this capability is "substantially diminished". Thus, emotions may be one ingredient in a complex normative analysis. And *Heinz Schöch* reminds his readers that a judge may not simply implement an expert opinion based on the WHO's International Classification of Diseases or the American Psychiatric Association's Diagnostic and Statistical Manual of Mental Disorders:[151]

> "Ob der sachverständige ICD-10-Befund unter ein Eingangsmerkmal des § 20 StGB subsumiert werden kann, ist eine juristische Frage, die letztlich allein das Gericht entscheidet."

---

[150] *Kahan/Nussbaum* (n. 34), 270.

[151] *Schöch* (n. 72), para. 23, who in 2020 referred to the now outdated editions of the respective classification and manual.

"Whether the findings of the expert based on the WHO's International Classification of Diseases fulfils the requirements of § 20 StGB, is a purely normative question, which in the end the court has to answer autonomously."

J. Furthermore, law and emotions scholars discuss questions that, to a German lawyer, simply have nothing to do with emotions. *Kahan* and *Nussbaum*, for example, want to analyse the excuse of self-defence in criminal law in terms of emotions.[152] In German criminal law, such an approach would be untenable.[153]

K. *Conway* and *Stannard* criticize "the somewhat disjointed nature of the work"[154] in law and emotions scholarship. However, it seems that discourse on emotions in law has to be disjointed. Each legal problem raises different questions requiring the help of different extra-legal disciplines to understand the problem. A holistic approach seems impossible.

L. Finally, *Beckers* reminds us of the limits of interdisciplinary research on emotions in law:[155]

"[D]ie Vorstellung, dass die gesellschaftliche Kommunikation in der Lage ist, individuelles Handeln, die Bedürfnisse und Emotionen des Individuums in Gänze zu verstehen, [stößt] zwingend an eine Grenze [...]. Diese Einsicht hat insbesondere für das Empathieverständnis tiefgreifende Konsequenzen. Um einer Empathie des Rechts überhaupt wieder auf die Füße zu helfen, bedarf es der drastischen Einsicht, dass die juristische Personenbeschreibung – der verantwortliche Täter, der verständige Kaufmann oder eben der durchschnittliche Verbraucher – keinesfalls eine Abbildung der Wirklichkeit, sondern ihrerseits wiederum eine rechtliche Konstruktion ist. Sie wird vom Recht nur benutzt, um eine spezifische Operation, die normative Entscheidung, durchzuführen [...]. [...] Der Durchschnittsverbraucher, auf den sich das Recht festlegt, ist nicht der Mensch selbst, sondern eine wandelbare Rolle, die der Mensch innerhalb einer sozialen Institution spielen kann [...] und die ihm das Recht zuweist."

"[T]he ability for societal communication to entirely comprehend individual action, individual needs, and individual emotions is limited [...]. This insight deeply impacts the understanding of empathy. In order to promote empathy in law one has to adopt the drastic insight that references to persons in law – the responsible offender, the reasonable merchant, or the ordinary consumer – are not images of reality. Rather, they are legal constructions which the law makes use of in order to put a specific operation into action: the normative decision [...]. [...] The ordinary consumer to which the law refers is not a person in a true sense. The ordinary consumer is a changing role which a person may take within a social institution [...] and which the law assigns to the person."

M. Against this background, let us revisit *Conway*'s and *Stannard*'s claim that "the study of law and emotions has historically been very much a North

[152] *Kahan/Nussbaum* (n. 34), 327–333.
[153] See only *V. Erb*, in: Münchener Kommentar (n. 116), § 32 paras. 1–260.
[154] *Conway/Stannard* (n. 29), 4 f.
[155] *Beckers* (n. 21), 103 f.

American phenomenon".[156] Above, I have already referred to *Schnädelbach*'s recent study on the German interdisciplinary discourse on emotions in the process of legal decision making between 1870 and 1933,[157] and I have posed the question whether German legal scholarship perhaps does not lag behind US scholarship on law and emotions, and is perhaps ahead of it in terms of having already moved beyond law and emotion scholarship in the vein as it is promoted by US scholars.[158] There are further examples where German law has in the past stressed the importance of emotions in law. *Soniewicka* and *Wesołowska* correctly observe that in "some European countries (Austria, Ireland, Germany, Poland), there appeared from the eighteenth to the twentieth centuries laws which made 'offense to religious sentiments' a punishable offense".[159] Today, § 166(1) StGB reads:

"Wer öffentlich oder durch Verbreiten eines Inhalts […] den Inhalt des religiösen […] Bekenntnisses anderer in einer Weise beschimpft, die geeignet ist, den öffentlichen Frieden zu stören, wird mit Freiheitsstrafe bis zu drei Jahren oder mit Geldstrafe bestraft."

"Whoever publicly or by disseminating content […] reviles the religion […] of others in a manner that may cause a disturbance of the public peace incurs a penalty of imprisonment for a term not exceeding three years or a fine."[160]

§ 166(1) StGB does not any longer protect religious sentiments, instead preserving public peace.[161] And *Beckers*'s claim that interdisciplinary research on emotions in law is of limited explanatory power reminds us that also in other legal contexts German law has moved away from an approach that directly acknowledges the importance of subjective aspects, including emotions, and has moved towards an approach that tries to frame the respective points of reference in a normative fashion. In all, a historical analysis may reveal that the law has extensively discussed emotions in different legal contexts already in the past but has for good reasons decided that emotions should be irrelevant in the specific context at issue. Even if emotions are in life ubiquitous, they should be of relevance in law only where they strengthen the explanatory persuasiveness of legal arguments. Thus, German law, German case law, and German legal scholarship have adopted a nuanced approach to emotions. Especially

---

156 *Conway/Stannard* (n. 29), 5.

157 *Schnädelbach* (n. 30).

158 See p. 361, above.

159 *Soniewicka/Wesołowska*, p. 337, above. On the history of the respective provisions in Germany, see, e.g., *U. Frevert*, Vom Schutz religiöser Gefühle: Rechtspraxis und -theorie in der Moderne, in: Landweer/Koppelberg (n. 7), 321–347.

160 The translation is a modified version of the translation found on https://www.gesetze-im-internet.de/englisch_stgb/ (last visited on 28 January 2023).

161 See, e.g., the critical discussion by *T. Hörnle*, in: Münchener Kommentar zum Strafgesetzbuch, vol. 3 (4th edn., 2021), § 166 para. 2, referring to literature that calls for the total abrogation of criminal offences in the fashion of § 166 StGB.

German criminal lawyers have a very sophisticated approach to the relevance of emotions in law, taking note of the many problems emotions raise in law and taking note of extra-legal research on emotions. However, the treatment of emotions does not follow a holistic approach as promoted by law and emotions scholars. German law follows a contextual approach, according to which the relevance of emotions is discussed in specific legal contexts. I quote *Dallmeyer*'s general conclusion to precisely reflect this finding:

> "Es drängt sich nach alledem die Schlussfolgerung auf, dass man die Frage, ob Angst eine juristische Kategorie ist, letztlich auf sich beruhen lassen sollte. Wichtig ist allein ein zutreffendes Verständnis des angstspezifischen Gehalts der Strafrechtsdogmatik, dessen Voraussetzung ein zutreffendes Verständnis der Angst als psychisches Phänomen ist."

> "The conclusion to be drawn from the present study is obvious: One may leave unanswered the question whether fear is a legal category. What is important is to understand where fear is relevant in the doctrinal study of criminal law and that where it is relevant a correct understanding of fear as a psychological phenomenon is essential."

N. Even though I am, thus, sceptical towards law and emotions scholarship "as a discipline in its own right" and "with taking a more holistic approach",[162] I do acknowledge that interdisciplinary reflections on emotions in law are important (see already G, above) in order to test the way how the law deals with emotions. If one, for example, analyses how the German law of delict approaches the problem of emotional distress, it becomes clear that it adopts a piecemeal approach that is in need of reform. In the law of delict, the evaluative approach promoted by *Soniewicka* and *Wesołowska* seems to be the way forward. In order to openly implement such an evaluative approach, it is necessary to take note of the findings on emotions in extra-legal disciplines.

O. The present volume wishes to explore how the diverse doctrinal contexts of different national legal systems affect interdisciplinary discourse in law, and it wishes to do so by comparing interdisciplinary discourse in Polish and German law. The findings of research on emotions in evolutionary psychology, neurobiology, and affective science will claim for themselves universal validity. German criminal lawyers, for example, refer to the WHO's International Classification of Diseases or the Diagnostic and Statistical Manual of Mental Disorders edited by the American Psychiatric Association when applying § 20 and § 21 StGB.[163] And a non-lawyer may be led to believe that, consequently, such findings should have the same impact on the law regardless of the specific legal system. The social functions of emotions and their cultural aspects are the object of study in the humanities and the social sciences, and even though the findings of these disciplines may not claim to enjoy universal validity, the social functions of emotions and their cultural aspects are most probably converging in the Western World, so that a non-lawyer may again be led to believe

[162] *Conway/Stannard* (n. 29), 4 f.

[163] See p. 380, above.

that the findings of the social sciences and the humanities on emotions should have the same impact on the law regardless of the specific legal system. However, the examples discussed in the present comment prove how positive law affects discourse on law and emotions. With respect to the application of the WHO's International Classification of Diseases or the Diagnostic and Statistical Manual of Mental Disorders edited by the American Psychiatric Association, *Schöch* stresses that the judge, at the end of the day, has to answer a normative question when applying these classifications and manuals.[164] Furthermore, my reading of *Soniewicka* and *Wesołowska* leads me to believe that Polish and German law are similar in their approaches to the liability for non-pecuniary harm in the law of delict. By way of final comparison, it is instructive to consider the article published in 1997 by *David F. Partlett*, in which he analyses the different approaches to the recoverability of damages for nervous shock.[165] He comes to the conclusion that US law has developed an approach that must be puzzling to law and emotions scholars, and he plausibly explained the US approach by pointing to the specific doctrinal framework of US law.

---

[164] See pp. 391 f., above.

[165] *D.F. Partlett*, Tort Liability and the American Way: Reflections on Liability for Emotional Distress, American Journal of Comparative Law 45 (1997), 171–193.

The Personalist Objection against the Volitional Component of the Insanity Defense*

Wojciech Załuski

I. Introduction

Legal scholarship distinguishes between two types of legal defenses: justification and excuse.[1] The distinction is of special importance in criminal law, but it applies equally to the law of tort. The present paper will focus on the criminal law side. Justification includes, for example, self-defense or necessity, and it implies that an agent cannot be held responsible for his *prima facie* wrongful act because, due to some special circumstances, this act is justified and therefore cannot ultimately be regarded as wrongful. Excuse implies that – even though the agent is considered to have acted wrongfully in the sense that he committed an objective wrong – the agent himself, due to some fact relating typically to his state of mind, cannot be regarded as having acted culpably and for that reason cannot be held responsible for the act.

The insanity defense belongs to the group of legal excuses. It appears in two variants: the cognitive and the cognitive-volitional variant. The former assumes that a perpetrator of an offense is excused if, and only if, he could not understand the nature and/or the normative quality of his act,[2] whereas the latter recognizes, apart from cognitive failures, also volitional failures as a ground

* In this paper I develop an argument presented already in Chapter 3 of my book *W. Załuski*, The Insanity Defense: A Philosophical Analysis (2021). In some parts of the present contribution I draw on materials from this book or rework them.

[1] See, e.g., *L. Alexander/K.K. Ferzan*, Crime and Culpability. A Theory of Criminal Law (2009), 86–160.

[2] In most jurisdictions this refers to the legal quality of the act, but in some jurisdictions it refers also to the moral quality of the act.

for the release from legal responsibility, namely that the agent could not control/direct his actions.

When studying the history of the insanity defense, it becomes immediately apparent that it has always included the cognitive component, and at times also the volitional one.[3] Yet at no time has it been confined solely to this volitional component. This historical observation already suggests that this component of the insanity defense is more controversial than the cognitive one.

Against this background, the present paper will critically analyze the volitional component of the insanity defense. However, I will not present the whole gamut of objections raised against it. Rather, I shall confine myself to presenting and developing one objection which literature rarely expounds on in a systematic way; it is the objection that I will call the "anthropological", or more precisely, the "personalist" objection.[4] However, prior to developing this objection, a short overview of the history of legal regulations concerning the insanity defense is in order, highlighting especially the different ways that common law systems and continental legal systems approach its volitional component.

II. A short history of the insanity defense

Today, the volitional component of the insanity defense is only of marginal importance in the US legal system, but this was not always the case as it was contained in the Model Penal Code drafted by the American Law Institute in 1962. The rule (also called the "substantial capacity test") provided by the Model Code in section 4.01 was a kind of combination of the cognitive and volitional (or affective) criteria; it reads as follows:

"(1) A person is not responsible for criminal conduct if at the time of such conduct as a result of mental disease or defect he lacks substantial capacity either to appreciate the criminality (wrongfulness) of his conduct or to conform his conduct to the requirements of law.

(2) As used in this Article, the terms 'mental disease or defect' do not include an abnormality manifested only by repeated criminal or otherwise antisocial conduct."

By 1980 the Model Penal Code rule was adopted by approximately half of the states of the US and by its federal government. Yet the subsequent evolution of the insanity defense in the US legal system proceeded in the direction of eliminating the volitional component.

---

[3] See, e.g., *D. Robinson*, Wild Beasts and Idle Humours. The Insanity Defense from Antiquity to the Present (1996).

[4] It is "anthropological" (or "philosophically-anthropological"), since it appeals to a general view of human nature, and this view is the personalist one.

This process was accelerated by the attempt on *Ronald Reagan*'s life by the schizophrenic *John W. Hinckley, Jr.* in 1982: *Hinckley, Jr.* successfully claimed insanity in reliance on this rule, a fact which caused considerable public outcry. Finally, in 1984 Congress adopted the Insanity Defense Reform Act, which substantially narrowed down the scope of application of the insanity defense. This federal test of criminal responsibility, which resembles the famous *M'Naghten* rule,[5] provides that a person is not responsible if

> "at the time of the commission of the acts constituting the offense, the defendant, as a result of a severe mental disease or defect, was unable to appreciate the nature and quality or the wrongfulness of his acts. Mental disease or defect does not otherwise constitute a defense".

The restrictive character of this rule derives not only from the fact that it eliminates the volitional component, but also from two other details: (1) It requires the mental disease or defect to be "severe". (2) It provides that the defendant was *unable* to appreciate the nature and quality or the wrongfulness of his acts. Thereby, it does not seem to be sufficient that the ability to appreciate was impaired only, even if it was impaired to a substantial degree. Rather, the rule seems to require the ability to have been totally absent. Moreover, the rule has shifted the burden of proof, laying it upon the accused. Prior to the reform, after the defendant presented a *prima facie* case of insanity, the prosecution had to prove that the defendant was sane beyond a reasonable doubt. After the reform, the defense has become an affirmative defense: the defendant must prove by clear and convincing evidence that he was insane at the time of committing the crime.

In general, it can be said that in common law systems, especially in the US legal system and to a lesser degree in the English system, the insanity defense has been narrowed down to the cognitive component: The volitional component is either explicitly rejected or treated with skepticism and reluctantly invoked.[6]

This approach to the insanity defense is essentially different from the one adopted in continental European legal systems, which tend to recognize the volitional component as an equally legitimate part of the insanity defense alongside the cognitive one. The continental European approach can be exemplified by reference to the Polish regulation of the insanity defense. In the

---

[5] This rule was formulated by the House of Lords in 1843 in the aftermath of the trial of Daniel M'Naghten, who killed Edward Drummond, the private secretary to British Prime Minister Robert Peel, leader of the Tory Party, mistaking him for Peel himself. He was declared not guilty by reason of insanity. But the verdict caused an outcry, which led to the attempt to make more precise the rules governing the insanity defense. The result was the formulation of the M'Naghten rule, which became the law of England and was subsequently adopted in several American states. See *Robinson* (n. 3), 163–169.

[6] See, e.g., *P.E. Erickson/S.K. Erickson*, Crime, Punishment, and Mental Illness (2008), 99–110.

Polish Penal Code, the "two-component" variant of the insanity defense is explicitly introduced by Art. 31:

"§ 1. Whoever, at the time of the commission of a prohibited act, was incapable of recognizing its significance or controlling his conduct because of a mental disease, mental deficiency or other mental disturbance, shall not be held responsible for committing an offence.

§ 2. If at the time of the commission of an offence the ability to recognize the significance of the act or to control one's conduct was diminished to a significant extent, the court may apply an extraordinary mitigation of the penalty.

§ 3. The provisions of § 1 and 2 shall not be applied when the perpetrator has brought himself to a state of insobriety or intoxication, causing the exclusion or reduction of accountability which he has or could have foreseen."[7]

Similar solutions have been adopted, for example, in France and Germany. Article 122-1 of the French *Code pénal* provides:

"N'est pas pénalement responsable la personne qui était atteinte, au moment des faits, d'un trouble psychique ou neuropsychique ayant aboli son discernement ou le contrôle de ses actes."

"A person who, at the time of the commission of the offence, was suffering from a psychological or neuropsychological disorder which destroyed his comprehension or his capacity to control his actions, is not criminally responsible".[8]

And § 20 of the German *Strafgesetzbuch* formulates the conditions of a "Schuldunfähigkeit wegen seelischer Störungen" ("inculpability due to mental disorders") as follows:

"Ohne Schuld handelt, wer bei Begehung der Tat wegen einer krankhaften seelischen Störung, wegen einer tiefgreifenden Bewußtseinsstörung oder wegen einer Intelligenzminderung oder einer schweren anderen seelischen Störung unfähig ist, das Unrecht der Tat einzusehen oder nach dieser Einsicht zu handeln."

"Whoever, at the time of the commission of the offence, is incapable of appreciating the unlawfulness of their actions or of acting in accordance with any such appreciation due to a pathological mental disorder, a profound disturbance of consciousness, mental deficiency or any other serious mental abnormality is deemed to act without guilt."[9]

In the remainder of this paper I shall present the already mentioned personalist objection to the volitional component. I find it to be of substantial philosophical weight and importance, although it is surprisingly seldom invoked in the relevant literature (or, if it is invoked, it is not developed at any great length).

---

[7] Available at www.legislationonline.org (last accessed 22 April 2022). Some modifications to the (anonymous) translation have been introduced by the author.

[8] English translation by the author.

[9] English trans. by M. Bohlander/U. Reusch: www.gesetze-im-internet.de/englisch_stgb/index.html (last accessed 22 April 2022).

I discount here other – in my view less important – objections that I have systematically analyzed elsewhere.[10]

III. The anthropological objection to the volitional component of the insanity defense

A. An outline of the personalist view of human nature

The most general and, in my opinion, most fundamental argument against the volitional component is provided by the personalist view of human beings and the specific concept of will implied by it: The will is the fundamental power of a human being, which constitutes personhood. As such, the personalist view implies a strong presumption in favor of the effectiveness of the power of will among offenders. Of course, this argument against the volitional component will convince only those who endorse the personalist view of human nature and its central reliance on free will. It is impossible, within this limited space, to develop a systematic argumentation in favor of this view, but it is at least possible to present it at some length.[11]

The personalist view of human nature implies that human beings are endowed with a number of unique capacities which justify calling them "persons" (a person being *nomen dignitatis*, thus justifying the claim about human beings' dignity): (1) Human beings are not "closed" in their concrete perceptions (which can be called "first-level representations of the world"). Owing to their capacity to use abstract notions, they create abstract representations of the world (which can be called "second-level representations of the world"). This capacity creates, as one may call it, an "ontological crevasse" between themselves and the world, and thereby leaves them fundamentally "detached from" the world. Accordingly, a human being can direct his attention beyond his

---

[10] *W. Załuski*, The Insanity Defense: A Philosophical Analysis (2021), 112–122. Three such regularly discussed objections may be described as the "epistemic", the "non-existence", and the "slippery slope" objections. The "epistemic" objection says that it is impossible to state with certainty whether the perpetrator chose not to resist the impulse or whether he could not resist it. The "non-existence" objection asserts that irresistible impulses do not exist (with the exception of some biological necessities which cannot be postponed indefinitely, like the impulse to sleep, urinate, or sit after standing for a long time – the things people will finally do even with a gun to their head) or occur very rarely. Finally, the "slippery slope" objection implies that, by admitting the volitional component, "[w]e enable other types of offenders to offer 'excuses' for behavior to escape the criminal justice process […]. [T]he numerous novel insanity and diminished-capacity defenses, such as battered women's syndrome, gave credence to the fear that the behavioral sciences were excusing behaviors never before conceived as products of a mentally ill mind," *Erickson/Erickson*, (n. 6), 17.

[11] For a more detailed presentation of the personalist view, see, e.g., *K. Wojtyła*, Osoba i czyn (2000, 1969), or *E. Mounier,* Manifeste au service du personnalisme (1936).

immediate (concrete) perceptions: either towards the "inside" – the depth of his self – or towards what lies "outside" his immediate perceptions. It is this capacity that *Ernst Cassirer* was referring to when saying that a human being is an *animal symbolicum*.[12] (2) The capacity to create second level-representations of the world is strictly connected with or even constitutive of self-consciousness, i.e., the capacity to direct one's attention at one's own acts of consciousness. (3) Self-consciousness, in turn, underlies typically and specifically human – reflective – rationality, which consists in the capacity to consciously search for, deliberate over, and attach weight to various reasons for action or judgment. (4) Human beings' perhaps most unique faculty is that of free will. According to the most common definition, an agent can be said to have free will if, and only if, when choosing a given action *a* at a given moment *m*, he is not causally determined to choose action *a*, i.e., that he has the ability to choose (without positing any change in the "state of the world" preceding the moment of choice *m*) also a different action (*not-a*) at the moment *m*.

Interestingly, while most scholars agree that human beings possess the first three features – (1) the capacity to create abstract representations of the world, (2) self-consciousness, and (3) reflective rationality – many deny the existence of the fourth: free will. But this seems to entail an inconsistency because the first three features imply each other and also imply the fourth one. Thus, for instance, if we assume that human beings are capable of making rational judgments (i.e., judgments "produced" by the capacity for reflective rationality), then we must agree that they are endowed with free will. As *Thomas Aquinas* put it in the "Summa Theologiae":

"Et pro tanto necesse est quod homo sit liberi arbitrii, ex hoc ipso quod rationalis est."

"And forasmuch as man is rational is it necessary that man have a free will"[13]

Human rationality cannot, therefore, be separated from the power of will and its freedom. I shall not present all arguments that can be invoked for this claim. I shall present just one of them, which rests on the uncontroversial assumption that an essential feature of a reflectively rational agent is self-consciousness. In fact, this feature is built into the above definition of rationality: One can hardly imagine that the very process of weighing reasons, comparing them – especially when these reasons are, as is often the case, inconclusive (i.e., when they have such character which excludes subjecting them to formal methods such as the rules of mathematics, logic, or probability) – and grasping and being guided by them could proceed without the active participation of self-

[12] *E. Cassirer*, An Essay on Man. An Introduction to a Philosophy of Human Culture (1972).

[13] *Thomas Aquinas*, Summa Theologiae I, q. 83, art. 1: www.corpusthomisticum.org/ (transl. Fathers of the English Dominican Province: www.documentacatholicaomnia.eu/03d/1225-1274,_Thomas_Aquinas,_Summa_Theologiae_%5b1%5d,_EN.pdf).

consciousness. And self-consciousness can hardly be separated from the free will: The final decisions of what weight to assign to various reasons for action – of what action to take – belong to the prerogative of the will. This last point can be developed along the lines indicated by *John Searle*, who wrote about the subjective experience of three "gaps": (1) between reasons for an action and a decision to take this action, (2) between a decision what to do and performing the action, and (3) between starting an action and carrying it through to a conclusion. In *Searle*'s view, these three gaps "are all parts of a continuous causal gap of conscious voluntary action" – they are the experiences "of thoughts and actions where we do not sense the decisions and actions as causally fixed by the antecedent conditions".[14] Thus, determinism arguably has insurmountable difficulties in accounting for the very existence of self-consciousness and of the related fact of typically human – reflective – rationality.

If we agree that human beings are endowed with free will, the next step in our presentation of the personalist view of human nature must be an attempt at the explication of the very concept of will, highlighting its capacity for freedom. Accordingly, the will is the power responsible for making a choice/decision which leads to action and, therefore, constitutes the power of initiating an action. It is the will which makes an agent's action his own and which justifies holding him responsible for it. The existence of will has often been denied, but those who have affirmed it have always insisted that will is a *spiritual* and *rational* mental power, a part belonging to a person's spiritual sphere.[15] Furthermore, it must be stressed that the will is a power (*potentia*) and not a disposition (*habitus*). This point is important because it puts the emphasis on the active, sovereign character of the will. This is precisely the way in which the will was characterized by, for instance, *Thomas Aquinas*.[16] He stressed that this power enables a human person to distance himself from the pressure of his sensual sphere – somatic (instinctive) and emotional (psychic) impulses. He defined it as an *appetitus intellectivus*, which he distinguished from *appetitus sensitivus*, *concupiscibilis*, or *irascibilis*. Thus, will is a rational power, constitutive of human agency and justifying responsibility attributions since it is owing to the will that our actions are *ours* – that we are their masters – and hence they can be attributed to us. Furthermore, will is – precisely by virtue of being will – *free* will.[17] This means that free will and will are one and the same power,

[14] *J. Searle*, Consciousness and the Problem of Free Will, in: R. Baumeister et al. (eds.), Free Will and Consciousness. How Might They Work? (2010), 121–134, 123.

[15] One can hardly provide an example of a philosopher who would affirm the free will hypothesis (and thereby treat will as a *sui generis* power) and who would, at the same time, endorse a materialistic view of the human mind.

[16] See *Thomas Aquinas*, Summa Theologiae I (n. 13), q. 83, art. 2.

[17] As *H. Arendt*, Willing, in: eadem, The Life of the Mind (1978), 14, aptly noted, "a will that is not free is a contradiction in terms – unless one understands the faculty of volition as a mere auxiliary executive organ for whatever either desire or reasons has proposed".

though the aspect of will's freedom becomes prominent in the act of choosing, and in this case it is more properly called "free will".[18] One should also note that the Thomist philosophers, who believed in the existence of will, always emphasized its strong connection to reason (which should be clear if we remember that they treated will as *appetitus intellectivus*). It is apt here to once again quote the relevant fragment from *Summa Theologiae*:

"Et pro tanto necesse est quod homo sit liberi arbitrii, ex hoc ipso quod rationalis est."

"And forasmuch as man is rational is it necessary that man have a free will"[19]

And will and reason are connected not just in a trivial sense – *nihil volitum nisi praecognitum* – but in a substantial sense, such that rational deliberation is part of the very act of will (though this deliberation need not be conscious). Nonetheless, in classical philosophy the two powers – intellect and will – though both belonging to the spiritual sphere of human beings, were distinguished for the simple reason that the specific acts are different (cognition and action, respectively).

An important implication of this account of will is a *volitional theory of action*.[20] On this theory, human action cannot be fully described in terms of desires and beliefs as its causal factors. They play their important role of providing motives and directing action, but they do not lead to action *directly* or *on their own*: The direct cause of action is an act of will. In other words, the action is, obviously, preceded by other mental states (desires, beliefs, etc.), but these states are not themselves sufficient to bring about an action. If human action could be fully explained in terms of desires and beliefs, then the concept of person (and agency) would be a fiction. It would be just a shorthand (and misleading) way of describing the fact that a certain psycho-physical entity (human being) is no more than a vehicle for a stream of events (beliefs and desires) which deterministically cause him to act in a given way. On this account, the aspects of personhood and agency would be lost. The personalist view admits, of course, that mental states (desires and beliefs) are real (and not epiphenomenal) and thereby have a causal power, but it implies that this causal power is not decisive and deterministic, since an additional – special – executive operation of the mind, attributable to the mind's part – an act of will – is necessary to generate an action.

From what has been said so far, the impression may arise that will, as part of the personalist view of human beings, is an omnipotent faculty (i.e., one which can always easily overcome temptations). But this is not the case: such thinkers as, e.g., *Thomas Aquinas*, *Jacques Maritain*, or *Karol Wojtyła*, who developed this picture with great subtlety and gave to it its classical shape, fully

---

[18] *Thomas Aquinas*, Summa Theologiae I (n. 13), q. 83, art. 4.

[19] See the reference in n. 13, above.

[20] See, e.g., *E.J. Lowe*, An Introduction to the Philosophy of Mind (2001), 246–251.

recognized the phenomenon of weakness of will. Nonetheless, it should be mentioned that there have been many thinkers who claimed that will is strongly independent from reason, that it can be capricious and irrational, and that man may find particular satisfaction in expressing his *independent* will against the commands of reason, no matter what consequences it may lead to. This stance was taken, for instance, by the narrator of *Fyodor Dostoyevsky*'s "Notes from the Underground". A less radical form of this view was endorsed by medieval "voluntarists" such as *Duns Scotus* or *William of Ockham*.[21] They ascribed to will a stronger power to oppose reason than did, for example, *Thomas Aquinas*. *Duns Scotus* asserted that freedom is a fundamental feature of the will, in contrast to *Thomas Aquinas*, who asserted that freedom is the result of the cooperation of the will and reason. Furthermore, *Duns Scotus* also emphasized – much more strongly than *Thomas Aquinas* – will's capacity to resist strong desires. *Hannah Arendt* summarized *Duns Scotus*'s view on this point in the following manner: The will "consists in freely affirming or negating or hating whatever confronts it. It is this freedom of the will mentally to *take a position* that sets man apart from the rest of creation"; consequently, *Duns Scotus*, unlike *St. Paul*, believed that "there is an I-can inherent in I-will".[22] On this account, the will to do x implies therefore the power to do x. As a result, will should easily overcome various desires and temptations. This conception of the sovereign power of the will took an even more extreme form in *William of Ockham*'s philosophy. It therefore constituted an even more distinct departure from the classical – Thomist – conception. *Ockham* maintained that will can reject happiness (*eudaimonia*) as its goal, can hate God, may at the same time desire contrary objects, and even is free to choose evil for the sake of evil (thus, even if the agent knows that it is neither really nor apparently good); in these respects it resembles the will of the protagonist of "Notes from the Underground".

Since the agent who exhibits the capacities sketched out above can be called "a person", this view of a human being can aptly be called "personalist". Thus, it bears stressing that it is an essential feature of the personalist view that it defines a human being in terms of self-consciousness, reflective reason, and (free) will – his spiritual powers – rather than in terms of desires or instincts – his affective and instinctual side. These characteristics are well captured by two Latin phrases (the first coming from *Boethius*'s treatise *Contra Eutychen et Nestorium*, the second from Roman jurists). The first one says that "persona est naturae rationabilis individua substantia" ("a person is an individual substance having a rational nature").[23] Thus, it is precisely by virtue of his nature,

[21] For an in-depth discussion of their views, see, e.g. *E. Gilson*, La Philosophie au Moyen Âge (1944).

[22] *Arendt* (n. 17), 142 (emphasis in original).

[23] Author's translation.

which includes a rational appetite which is will, that a person can generate free actions – that he can himself decide his own actions (this is the precise content of self-determination and, in consequence, of freedom of will). The second phrase states that "persona est sui iuris et alteri incommunicabilis" ("a person is a being of his own and does not have his being in common with any other").[24] Thus, the essential feature of a person is belonging to oneself and being a highly individualized master of oneself who is thus incapable of renouncing oneself (*incommunicabilis*). A person exists *per se* and has "dominium sui actus".[25] A person's action therefore does not simply flow from his nature: "personae non solum aguntur, sicut alia, sed per se agunt" ("persons are not only acted upon, like other entities, but also of themselves").[26] It bears stressing that the non-classical view of will – i.e., as being independent from reason, capricious, undisciplined, recalcitrant, and almost omnipotent – is not part of the personalist view of man. The latter assumes – as should be stressed – that will is *appetitus rationalis*: Even if it does not follow reason's commandments automatically (because it is autonomous and not fully subordinate to reason), it manifests a *tendency* to comply with them. It is easy to notice that the view underlining will's strength and the primacy of will over intellect leads to an even greater skepticism towards the volitional component of the insanity defense than does the view of *Thomas Aquinas*'s – I shall return to this important point in the further part of this paper.

In summary, being a person is a special way of existence – one characteristic of human being – in which actions do not *simply* flow from one's "nature" (a set of predispositions, beliefs, preferences, etc.) but are "filtered" through one's spiritual sphere, a part of which is free will. Thus, there is in every human being an "inner difference" – between himself and his qualitative constitution.[27]

B. Implications

As already mentioned, the personalist view of human nature implies a strong presumption in favor of the effectiveness of the power of will among offenders. It entails that only in exceptional circumstances can the functioning of this power be questioned. By contrast, no such presumption is generated by the naturalistic view of human beings, which, necessarily, must dispense with the metaphysical concept of free will and give priority, in the explanation of their actions, to those factors which belong to, or are strongly influenced by, their affective/instinctual side. Within this view, human beings are perceived as being moved by only those inner factors which can be analyzed by methods of the natural sciences. If the concept of will appears in this view, it takes a trun-

[24] Author's translation.
[25] See *Thomas Aquinas*, Summa Theologiae I (n. 13), q. 30, art. 4.
[26] *Thomas Aquinas*, Summa Theologiae I (n. 13), q. 29, art. 2.
[27] See *R. Spaemann*, Osoby. O różnicy między czymś a kimś (2002), 20.

cated form of the "capacity for self-control" or the "capacity for self-regulation", which is just a pale reflection of the will understood as a spiritual power, as *appetitus rationalis*, strictly connected with the capacity for metaphysical freedom (for generating new causal chains). This naturalistic – and thereby reductionist and deterministic – view strips the phenomenon of crime or evil of *mysterium iniquitatis*, which is its essential part. This *mysterium* is rooted in the fact that crime and evil's final source is human freedom. As *Victor Frankl* memorably and forcefully put it:

> "A crime in the final analysis remains inexplicable insomuch as it cannot be fully traced back to biological, psychological, and/or sociological factors. Totally explaining one's crime would be tantamount to explaining away his or her guilt and to seeing him or her not a free and responsible human being but a machine to be repaired. Even criminals themselves abhor this treatment and prefer to be responsible for their deeds."[28]

This unpalatable consequence is avoided if one assumes, as *Frankl* does, a non-naturalistic view of the human being, i.e., the view according to which human beings are spiritual beings, whose inner selves are beyond the reach of the natural sciences. In those selves there resides the source of their freedom: "[E]verything can be taken from a man but one thing: the last of the human freedoms: to choose one's attitude in any given set of circumstances, to choose one's own way".[29]

However, it should be stressed that the personalist objection against the volitional prong of the insanity defense does not substantiate the claim that irresistible impulses (and thereby the offender's incapacity to conform his behavior to legal rules) *never* occur. It does not imply that the volitional component should be abolished, but it does imply that the volitional defense should be interpreted very restrictively, that it should be allowed only with regard to absolutely uncontroversial cases, because irresistible impulses can occur, if at all, only among those who are afflicted with severe mental illnesses, e.g., among schizophrenics. This restrictiveness can hardly be achieved at the legislative level by adopting a "restrictive" formulation of the volitional component (since it is difficult to say how such a formulation should look), but it can be achieved at the judiciary level, in the process of accepting or rejecting the "volitional" insanity defense in concrete cases.[30] In this context it is important to recall the difference between the personalist view of human nature from the view – inspired by the voluntarist philosophies of *Duns Scotus* and *William of Ockham* – which can be called "radically libertarian". In contrast to the former, the latter assumes that free will is never "suspended" among the agents, and, consequently, it is as effective among the mentally ill as among the mentally sound.

---

[28] *V. Frankl*, Man's Search for Meaning (transl. I. Lasch, 2008), 149.

[29] *Frankl* (n. 28), 75.

[30] These conclusions are supported (but not radicalized) by non-anthropological objections that I could not analyze here in any detail.

It is precisely this conception which was, often implicitly, assumed by many of those who advocated abolition not only of the volitional component, but of the insanity defense as a whole, as advocated in some "conservative" US states such as Idaho.

In Idaho, the insanity defense was abolished in 1982 for the first time in the history of the US.[31] The consideration of insanity was thus eliminated from criminal trials. The Idaho legislation provides that trials are to be restricted to solely ascertaining *actus reus* and *mens rea*, and the only possible verdicts are guilty or not guilty. If the defendant is declared guilty but there is reason to believe that his mental state is a relevant factor for the determination of his sentence, then a psychiatric examination is to be conducted in order to ascertain the extent of his mental illness, the prognosis for rehabilitation, the availability of treatment, and the level of required care (since the defendant is guilty, all forms of care should, strictly speaking, be viewed as a punishment). The motivation for the enactment of this law was, of course, complex:

> "Persons in positions of authority in regard to mental health law reform in Idaho had formed a virtual consensus supporting abolition. That consensus was firmly based on a belief that the insanity plea had been blatantly misused and had failed to provide either satisfactory treatment for offenders or adequate community protection against them. Combined with this conviction was the popular view, strongly held by residents of this isolated, highly religious state, that all human beings ought to take personal responsibility for their behavior, that they should not be able to avoid punitive consequences of criminal acts by reliance on either a real or a faked plea of insanity."[32]

It is obvious that the general view leading to the abolition of the insanity defense implies the (above-described) non-Thomist conception of will as being an almost omnipotent faculty. It should be recalled that the personalist conception assumes a less rigid account of free will. It stresses the uniqueness of human beings, which stems from the fact that, unlike other beings, they have a "spiritual side", but it does not deny the fact that their unique faculties (e.g., free will) may sometimes fail to function properly. Thus, while the radically libertarian conception implies that the volitional component should be abolished, the personalist one implies that the volitional defense should be interpreted very restrictively.

IV. Concluding thoughts

If it were not only true that the volitional defect appeared exclusively among the severely mentally ill, but – also – that it was always accompanied (and

[31] Idaho Code §18-207 (Supp. 1983).

[32] *G. Geis/R.F. Meier*, Abolition of the Insanity Plea in Idaho: A Case Study, The Annals of the American Academy of Political and Social Science 477 (1985), 72–83, 73.

caused) by some cognitive defect, then it might be reasonable to entirely dispense with the volitional component. But it is hard to unequivocally answer the question of whether the volitional defect/failure can ever appear without the cognitive one. The connection between cognition and volition was also emphasized by *Anthony Kenny*:

> "Precisely because the intellect and the will are not separate compartments, it is rash to conclude that a set of criteria like the M'Naghten rules, which are framed in cognitive terms, automatically fail to capture the volitional dimension. The will is the capacity to behave in pursuit of long-term goals and in the light of the comparative attractiveness of alternative courses of action: because of this, an investigation of an agent's ability to understand what he is doing and its relevance to long-term goals, and of his judgments of comparative value, is not something distinct from, and irrelevant to, an inquiry into the effectiveness of his will."[33]

This thesis – that an agent cannot control his actions only if he exhibits cognitive defects – seems to hold also for the personalist view of human nature, which assumes that the relationships between the intellect and the will are very close. At any rate, it seems that there are few, if any, cases in which an impulse is irresistible, yet cognitive capacities are fully retained (an example of this type of case, undoubtedly controversial, may be bipolar disorder);[34] the general rule, confirmed by empirical research, seems to be that the main factor regarded by judges as resulting in the loss of volitional control is psychotic delusions, which is a cognitive failure. But since the matter is not entirely clear, it seems reasonable to retain the volitional component, but to interpret it, as mentioned, very restrictively (only with regard to offenders having serious mental illnesses). In order to make this postulate of restrictiveness more precise, one can say that the personalist conception provides a first strong presumption in favor of volitional capacity, while the second one would be a lack of cognitive impairments. Consequently, the evidentiary threshold for admitting the insanity defense based on the volitional component should be set very high. This conclusion is strengthened by the remark that will is not only a psychological fact but also a task – a challenge. Each human being should seek to make their will the root of his actions. This kind of task would obviously be undermined by an overly liberal understanding of the volitional component, as it justifies or excuses a human being's volitional failures and weakens his motivation to

---

[33] *A. Kenny*, Freewill and Responsibility (2012), 44. Please note that Kenny writes about "M'Naghten rules", while I use the term "M'Naghten rule"; this is just a matter of style: since the M'Naghten rule can be decomposed into two rules (one concerning the nature, the other the normative quality of the act), both names are justifiable.

[34] See the following quotation: "Those in favor of preserving a volitional test maintain that debilitating but readily treatable psychiatric disorders, such as bipolar disorder, result in loss of volitional control, while cognitive knowledge and appreciation of wrongfulness/criminality remain intact": *A. Donohue/V. Arya/L. Fitch/D. Hammen*, Legal Insanity: Assessment of the Inability to Refrain, Psychiatry 5/3 (2008), 58–66, 60.

develop his will. Thus, there is also another aspect of the naturalistic view of human beings, the aspect which gives rise to a "pragmatic" argument against the volitional component, particularly that the negation of man's freedom becomes a self-fulfilling prophecy:

> "There is a danger inherent in the teaching of man's 'nothingbutness', the theory that man is nothing but the result of biological, psychological and sociological conditions, or the product of heredity and environment. Such a view makes a neurotic believe what he is prone to believe anyway, viz. that he is the pawn and victim of outer influences or inner circumstances. This neurotic fatalism is fostered and strengthened by a psychotherapy which denies that man is free."[35]

But it bears repeating that the skepticism justified by the personalist view of human being towards the volitional component is not radical. It would be radical if one assumed such a conception of the will that – unlike, for example, *Thomas Aquinas*'s conception – would emphasize the will's sovereign character (its independence from reason).

[35] *Frankl* (n. 28), 132.

Free Will for (almost) Everyone? Problems of a Restrictive Normative Approach to the Insanity Defense

Johannes Kaspar

I. Introduction

The contribution of *Wojciech Załuski* deals with a complex and controversial topic that relates to fundamental aspects of criminal law, both from a theoretical and a practical perspective – the "insanity defense". Whether you call it a "defense" (like in the US) or an "excuse" or "exculpation" (like Poland and Germany) – either way, each legal order has to come up with an answer to the question of how to define and assess a potential absence of criminal responsibility due to mental disorder and to what extent an interdisciplinary approach should be followed in this context. Therefore, the topic is well chosen with respect not only to comparative law but also to this volume's overarching theme of interdisciplinary approaches to law.

In German criminal law, there is a specific provision concerning the absence of "culpability" (*Schuldfähigkeit*) due to pathological mental disorders or comparable mental states.[1] § 20 of the German Criminal Code (*Strafgesetzbuch* – StGB) reads as follows:

> "Ohne Schuld handelt, wer bei Begehung der Tat wegen einer krankhaften seelischen Störung, wegen einer tiefgreifenden Bewußtseinsstörung oder wegen einer Intelligenzminderung oder einer schweren anderen seelischen Störung unfähig ist, das Unrecht der Tat einzusehen oder nach dieser Einsicht zu handeln."

> "Whoever, at the time of the commission of the offence, is incapable of appreciating the unlawfulness of their actions or of acting in accordance with any such appreciation due to a

[1] *R.E. Rauxloh*, Insanity in German Criminal Law, in: R. Mackay/W. Brookbanks (eds.), The Insanity Defence: International and Comparative Aspects (2022), 247–273. For a German-Anglo-American comparative summary, see *M.D. Dubber/T. Hörnle*, Criminal Law. A Comparative Approach (2014), 500 ff.

pathological mental disorder, a profound disturbance of consciousness or intellectual disability or any other serious mental disorder is deemed to act without guilt."[2]

In these cases, punishment is not possible and one may only impose measures of rehabilitation or incapacitation (*Maßregeln der Besserung und Sicherung*), which are called the "second track" of criminal sanctions (*Zweispurigkeit*).[3]

The wording of § 20 StGB clearly shows that an absence of culpability can be alternatively based on two grounds in connection with one of the four deficient mental states specified above: either the offender is not capable of appreciating the unlawfulness of the act in question (*fehlende Einsichtsfähigkeit*) – which is often referred to as the cognitive component of the insanity defense; or the offender is not capable of acting in accordance with his (existing) appreciation of committing a wrongful act, or, to put it in more simple terms, he is not able to control himself (*fehlende Steuerungsfähigkeit*) – which is called the control component or (as termed by *Załuski*) the volitional component.

In his contribution, *Załuski* questions the latter on the basis of in-depth deliberations of a predominantly philosophical nature, also taking into account historical aspects. In his introductory remarks, he stresses that from a historical point of view, the volitional component has not always been acknowledged as being part of the culpability test and is by far more controversial than the cognitive component.[4]

As *Załuski* rightly points out, this different acceptance of both components also shows in recent developments in the US, where the insanity defense was restricted in the aftermath of the famous *Hinckley* case.[5] *John W. Hinckley, Jr.*, who had tried to assassinate former US president *Ronald Reagan* while he was in office in 1981, was acquitted based on the insanity defense and confined in a psychiatric hospital. Even though he ended up spending 35 years in this type of detention (i.e. much longer than he would have probably ever potentially spent in prison),[6] the acquittal of *Hinckley* had produced public outrage and

---

[2] https://www.gesetze-im-internet.de/englisch_stgb/ (last accessed 28 November 2023).

[3] For an overview of possible sanctions resulting from full, diminished or missing culpability, see *J. Kaspar/S. Stübner*, A German Perspective, in: M. van der Wolf (ed.), Safeguarding the Quality of Forensic Assessment in Sentencing. A Review Across Western Nations (2022), 146–174, 147.

[4] *Załuski*, p. 398, above. See e.g. the criticism against the control element raised by *S.J. Morse*, Moore on the Mind, in: K. Kessler Ferzan/S.J. Moore (eds.), Legal, Moral and Metaphysical Truths (2016), 233–250, 243 ff.; see also *idem*, Against Control Tests for Criminal Responsibility, in: P.H. Robinson et al. (eds.), Criminal Law Conversations (2009), 449–459.

[5] *Załuski*, p. 398 f., above. See *S.J. Morse*, Before and After Hinckley: Legal Insanity in the United States, in: Mackay/Brookbanks (n. 1), 199–222.

[6] This is an important aspect that is sometimes neglected in the discussion: With regard to potential preventive measures, exculpation is not always an advantage for the defendant. For the example of Canada, see *Dubber/Hörnle* (n. 1), 511. For an extreme case in Germany, where the detention of the mentally ill offender in a psychiatric hospital lasted much longer

ultimately led to various legal reforms restricting or even abolishing the insanity defense. Until then, federal as well as state provisions relating to the insanity defense had frequently contained both components. One of the reasons was that § 4.01(1) of the quite influential Model Penal Code published by the American Law Institute in 1962 included a test featuring both a cognitive and a volitional component, of which only one had to be fulfilled for acquittal.[7] Following the *Hinckley* verdict, in order to restrict the insanity defense, especially the volitional component (if not the complete insanity defense as such) was abolished in many states.[8] In a recent decision, the Supreme Court has confirmed the constitutionality of this development (including the total abolition of an insanity defense): The Court ruled that an affirmative defense of legal insanity was not constitutionally required in the US and that it would be sufficient if the defendant could introduce evidence of mental abnormality to negate *mens rea*.[9] Four states have followed this approach and fully abolished the defense.[10] One has to acknowledge, however, that even severe mental disorder rarely negates *mens rea*, so most of such offenders will be convicted.[11]

The situation in continental European systems is different, as *Załuski* points out:[12] Most countries, like Poland and Germany, acknowledge both components. With this in mind, it is interesting to note that *Załuski*'s criticism is to a certain extent in line with the development in the US, even though he suggests applying the volitional component with caution rather than completely abolishing it. In Germany, the scope of § 20 StGB, including the volitional component, has not been the object of such controversy. Unlike in the US, both components are seen as independent and of equal value.[13]

Recent reforms have dealt only with changes in the (formerly rather outdated and stigmatizing) wording. Previously used terms like "*Schwachsinn*" (idiocy) and "*seelische Abartigkeit*" (psychological abnormality) were replaced by more neutral ones.[14] There was, probably for two reasons, no serious

---

than a prison sentence could possibly have been for the same offence (intentional destruction of valuable paintings), see *J. Kaspar*, Aussetzung und Erledigung der Unterbringung in einem psychiatrischen Krankenhaus nach §§ 67b und d StGB, Forensische Psychiatrie, Psychologie, Kriminologie 1 (2007), 217–225, 225.

[7] *Morse* (n. 5), 200; *Dubber/Hörnle* (n. 1), 509.

[8] See *Morse* (n. 5), 201 f.; *Hörnle/Dubber* (n. 1), 515 f.

[9] See *Kahler* v. *Kansas*, 140 SCt 1021 (2020). In *Clark* v. *Arizona*, 548 US 735 (2006), the Supreme Court had generally stated that the insanity rule was "open to state choice". See also *Morse* (n. 5), 204 ff.

[10] In a fifth state (Nevada), a similar reform was held unconstitutional by the State Supreme Court, see *Morse* (n. 5), 202.

[11] *Morse* (n. 5), 202.

[12] *Załuski*, p. 399, above.

[13] *Hörnle/Dubber* (n. 1), 517.

[14] For the background of the recent reform, see *A. Schiemann*, Weg mit dem Schwachsinn – zur längst überfälligen Ersetzung der Begriffe "Schwachsinn" und "Abartigkeit" in

debate about restricting or abolishing § 20 StGB: First, there is a strong belief that mentally ill offenders should not be punished as they cannot be held accountable for what they did. This so-called "guilt principle" (*Schuldprinzip*)[15] is based on the guarantee of human dignity in Art. 1(1) of the German Constitution (*Grundgesetz* – GG), i.e. on the most fundamental legal provision in German law. Second, in most of these cases, as a consequence of the previously mentioned two-track system German of criminal sanctions, a preventive measure of rehabilitation and incapacitation (see §§ 61 ff. StGB) is imposed by criminal courts, especially detention in a psychiatric hospital (§ 63 StGB). Even though these offenders go unpunished in a formal sense, their assumed dangerousness is dealt with by the criminal courts (which might be a relevant difference compared to the *Hinckley* case). As long as public safety is taken care of in this way, so it seems, there remains no further "need for punishment".

In addition to these two primary explanations, it can be further observed that some recent (and critical) publications on culpability under § 20 StGB did not specifically focus on the volitional element, with the works by *Anja Schiemann* and *Gunnar Spilgies* being two examples. In her comprehensive and thorough analysis, *Schiemann* criticizes the vagueness of the criteria found in § 20 StGB in general with respect to legal certainty (Art. 103(2) GG).[16] She also disapproves of their unclear (normative or rather empirical) nature and the difficult division of labor between courts and forensic experts in this field. In the end, however, *Schiemann* does not suggest removing the volitional component from § 20 StGB, favoring instead its rephrasing and a clarification of how it is addressed procedurally, just as is the case regarding the cognitive component.

In his discussion of culpability, *Spilgies* criticizes the indeterministic concept of guilt as well as "agnostic" positions dominating the German discussion.[17] He claims (in this regard similar to *Schiemann*) that the assessment of culpability is unclear and possibly arbitrary – but again, his criticism is directed at both components simultaneously. *Spilgies* argues in favour of a reformed (deterministic) concept of guilt, without suggesting the restriction or abolishment of the volitional component in particular.

---

§ 20 StGB und der verpassten Chance einer umfassenden Reform der Schuldfähigkeitsfeststellung, Kriminalpolitische Zeitschrift (2019), 338–346.

[15] See *T. Hörnle*, Guilt and Choice in Criminal Law Theory – A critical Assessment, Bergen Journal of Criminal Law and Criminal Justice 4 (2016), 1–24.

[16] *A. Schiemann*, Unbestimmte Schuldfeststellungen. Verstoß der §§ 20, 21 StGB gegen den Bestimmtheitsgrundsatz nach Art. 103 II GG (2012).

[17] *G. Spilgies*, Über Schuld und Strafe auf deterministischer Grundlage. Mit einem abolitionistischen Epilog (2021).

II. Wojciech Załuski's main arguments

In his contribution, *Załuski* argues that from a "personalist" or "anthropological" point of view,[18] the volitional component is doubtful and should be applied cautiously, i.e. restricted to clear cases of severe mental illnesses like schizophrenia.[19] Even though the term "anthropological" could point at something like a natural science approach, this is not what *Załuski* has in mind:[20] Biological or medical-psychiatric aspects do not play a central role in his argumentation. Instead, on the basis of philosophical considerations going back to *Thomas Aquinas*, a certain (normative) concept of "personhood" is developed. It relates to human beings' capacity for abstract representation, their self-consciousness, their ability to make rational decisions and (as a consequence of rationality, which is defined as the "capacity to consciously search [...] for reasons for action") to exercise free will.[21] Summarizing this view at the end of his contribution,[22] *Załuski* speaks of the "uniqueness of human beings" and their "spiritual side", distinguishing them from other living creatures.

The classic controversy of determinism *versus* indeterminism in the context of criminal responsibility, including the question of whether new results of "neuroscience" and brain research support a deterministic view,[23] is not directly addressed. But it becomes very clear that *Załuski*'s position is an indeterministic one, as the existence of free will (i.e. "the power of initiating an action"[24]) is assumed. He emphasizes the "active, sovereign character of will", which would make actions "ours" – and, as a consequence, obviously also allows that we are held responsible for crimes we have committed; *Załuski* explicitly speaks of (legitimate) "responsibility attributions" based on his concept of personhood.[25] According to the author, an important argument supporting this view is the subjective experience of three "gaps" described by *John Searle*, i.e. the fact that human beings do sense a distinction between having reasons to act and actually deciding to act accordingly, and, in the next two steps,

---

[18] *Załuski*, p. 398 and p. 401, above.

[19] *Załuski*, p. 407, above.

[20] See *Załuski*, p. 398 n. 3, above.

[21] *Załuski*, p. 402, above.

[22] *Załuski*, pp. 408 f., above.

[23] On this (complex) debate, see the recent summary by *V. Schrader*, Über Schuld und Durchschnittsmenschen – auch ein Beitrag zum Verbandsstrafrecht (2021), 27 ff.; see also *T. Hillenkamp*, Strafrecht ohne Willensfreiheit? Eine Antwort auf die Hirnforschung, JuristenZeitung 2005, 313–320 and *idem*, Hirnforschung, Willensfreiheit und Strafrecht – Versuch einer Zwischenbilanz, Zeitschrift für die gesamte Strafrechtswissenschaft 127 (2015), 10–96.

[24] *Załuski*, p. 403, above.

[25] *Załuski*, p. 403, above.

between having decided to act and actually starting the action and, then, in carrying the action through to a conclusion.[26]

Załuski's argument is based on a "volitional theory of action", with the direct cause of action being the will (and not "inner factors" like beliefs or human desires). Otherwise, he contends, the concept of "person" would be fiction;[27] *Załuski* explicitly rejects a "naturalistic view" of human beings where people are seen as being moved only by the above-mentioned "inner factors" that can be analyzed by "methods of the natural sciences".[28] From his point of view, free will is necessary to generate an "action". Even though the existence of "weakness of will" is acknowledged,[29] as is the possibility of free will's "sovereignty" to decide against rational expectations, *Załuski* argues that there is a general "tendency" of human beings to "comply with reason".[30]

As a consequence, a "presumption" of the effectiveness of free will among offenders is formulated – meaning that an offender is generally held criminally responsible for his actions and the volitional component of the insanity defense can become relevant only under "exceptional circumstances", i.e. in "absolutely uncontroversial cases" of severe mental illnesses such as schizophrenia.[31]

In his concluding remarks, *Załuski* discusses whether the volitional component could be totally abolished, as – one might argue – a relevant lack of control due to a severe mental illness necessarily also leads to a relevant cognitive defect.[32] Even though, according to *Załuski*, this is true in most cases (including cases of psychotic delusions), he argues that there might be constellations (like bipolar disorders) where there is indeed a relevant lack of control despite cognitive capacities still being intact. This uncertainty leads him to the conclusion that the volitional component should be retained but at the same time used in a very restricted manner by the courts: They should, as a start, work with a "strong presumption" in favor of full volitional capacity.[33] He adds the argument that free will is not only a "psychological fact" but also a "task" or a "challenge": "Each human being should seek to make their will the root of his actions"[34] – which could be classified as a criminal policy argument that is quite close to the slippery slope argument that he briefly mentioned earlier in his paper.[35] A final "pragmatic" argument in favor of a restrictive use of the

[26] *Załuski*, p. 403, above.
[27] *Załuski*, p. 404, above.
[28] *Załuski*, pp. 406 f., above.
[29] *Załuski*, p. 405, above.
[30] *Załuski*, p. 406, above.
[31] *Załuski*, p. 407, above.
[32] *Załuski*, pp. 408 f., above.
[33] *Załuski*, p. 409, above.
[34] *Załuski*, p. 409, above.
[35] *Załuski*, p. 400 n. 10, above.

volitional component is that a harmful self-fulfilling prophecy should be avoided, where offenders with mental problems are given the general impression that they are mere objects of certain circumstances and not responsible in any event for what they do, possibly contributing to future offences.

III. Comparative comment

Załuski's contribution contains philosophical reflections on the concept of personhood which are used as an argument in a legal context, regarding the question of criminal responsibility and the scope of the insanity defense. Therefore, the two disciplines directly referred to are law and philosophy. It is not, however, an interdisciplinary approach where "extra-legal" findings in a strict sense are applied to legal questions; in our context, there is no clear-cut division between both disciplines, as concepts like "personhood", "action" and (even more so) "responsibility" are strongly related to the legal sphere and to classical topics of legal philosophy, where both disciplines converge.

It is important to note that the topic of criminal responsibility has an even broader interdisciplinary dimension, which is implicitly also mentioned by *Załuski* – it is the fundamental question of how empirical facts are related to (normative) legal terms and categories. In our context this becomes relevant within substantive as well as procedural law. On the one hand, substantive law is touched upon when it comes to the question whether statutory prerequisites regarding an absence of culpability (or regarding legally relevant "insanity" for that matter) contain empirical facts, normative value judgments or both – for Germany, at least, the latter is the case, with a certain preponderance of normativity. On the other hand, the question of how and by whom these elements are to be assessed in court is, obviously, a question of procedural law. In Germany, there is a complex interplay between forensic (especially psychiatric) experts and the courts.[36] Whereas the final decision on culpability is up to the courts alone (as it is perceived to be a normative value judgement),[37] in practice the forensic expert's diagnosis seems to exert considerable influence.[38]

Załuski's point of view is predominantly a normative one, even though in a way he also argues with factual aspects of "human nature", e.g. with the subjective perception of free will[39] or with free will as a presumed "psychological

---

[36] See *Kaspar/Stübner* (n. 3), 154 ff.

[37] *Hörnle/Dubber* (n. 1), 512.

[38] There is not much empirical research regarding this question in Germany; for homicide cases, see *T. Verrel*, Schuldfähigkeitsbegutachtung und Strafzumessung bei Tötungsdelikten. Eine empirische Untersuchung zur Bedeutung des psychowissenschaftlichen Sachverständigen im Strafverfahren (1995).

[39] *Załuski*, p. 403, above.

fact".[40] But at the same time he dismisses what he calls a "naturalistic" view of human beings being dominated by desires and beliefs as measured by "methods of the natural sciences".[41] It is free will that constitutes "persons" in a normative sense, and therefore, according to *Załuski*, criminal responsibility based on free will and sufficient control should be presumed and only in exceptional cases rejected.

From a comparative perspective, it is noteworthy that this normative, legal-philosophical "personalist" argument appears in the German discussion on culpability and criminal responsibility in a similar way, but it is usually used only to support an indeterministic concept of culpability as such and to defend this concept against its deterministic opponents – and not to criticize or restrict the widely acknowledged volitional component.

One famous example for this different use of the personalist argument is an early verdict issued by the German Federal Court of Justice (*Bundesgerichtshof*) of 1952. The court had to deal with the question of mistake of law (§ 17 StGB), which can – although rather exceptionally – exclude criminal responsibility. The court used this opportunity to make a general statement about the concept of "guilt" and culpability. A famous and frequently cited part of the verdict reads as follows:

"Strafe setzt Schuld voraus. Schuld ist Vorwerfbarkeit. Mit dem Unwerturteil der Schuld wird dem Täter vorgeworfen, daß er sich nicht rechtmäßig verhalten, daß er sich für das Unrecht entschieden hat, obwohl er sich rechtmäßig verhalten, sich für das Recht hätte entscheiden können. Der innere Grund des Schuldvorwurfes liegt darin, daß der Mensch auf freie, verantwortliche, sittliche Selbstbestimmung angelegt und deshalb befähigt ist, sich für das Recht und gegen das Unrecht zu entscheiden, sein Verhalten nach den Normen des rechtlichen Sollens einzurichten und das rechtlich Verbotene zu vermeiden, sobald er die sittliche Reife erlangt hat und solange die Anlage zur freien sittlichen Selbstbestimmung nicht durch die in § 51 StGB genannten krankhaften Vorgänge vorübergehend gelähmt oder auf Dauer zerstört ist."

"Guilt is a prerequisite for punishment. Guilt is blameworthiness. With the judgment of guilt, the perpetrator is accused of not having behaved lawfully, that he has decided in favor of wrongdoing, although he could have behaved lawfully and could have decided in favor of the law. The inner reason for blaming the offender lies in the fact that man is destined for free, responsible, moral self-determination and is therefore capable of deciding in favor of the law and against wrongdoing, of adjusting his behavior to the norms of the legal "ought" and of avoiding illegal behavior as soon as he has reached moral maturity and as long as his disposition for free, moral self-determination is not temporarily paralyzed or permanently destroyed due to one of the pathological disorders mentioned in § 51 StGB."[42]

---

[40] *Załuski*, p. 409, above.

[41] *Załuski*, p. 406, above.

[42] BGHSt 2, 194, 200. § 51 StGB was the former regulation on an absence of culpability due to mental disorders, which is now located in § 20 StGB. The translation is a modified version of that prepared by *Rauxloh* (n. 1), 247.

A similar understanding of human beings and their criminal responsibility also shows in a more recent verdict of the German Constitutional Court (*Bundesverfassungsgericht*), the so-called Lisbon Decision of 2009, where the importance of the principle of guilt (*Schuldprinzip*) and the underlying presumptions were expressed in the following manner:

"Das Strafrecht beruht auf dem Schuldgrundsatz. Dieser setzt die Eigenverantwortung des Menschen voraus, der sein Handeln selbst bestimmt und sich kraft seiner Willensfreiheit zwischen Recht und Unrecht entscheiden kann. Dem Schutz der Menschenwürde liegt die Vorstellung vom Menschen als einem geistig-sittlichen Wesen zugrunde, das darauf angelegt ist, in Freiheit sich selbst zu bestimmen und sich zu entfalten (vgl. BVerfGE 45, 187 227). Auf dem Gebiet der Strafrechtspflege bestimmt Art. 1 Abs. 1 GG die Auffassung vom Wesen der Strafe und das Verhältnis von Schuld und Sühne (vgl. BverfGE 95, 96, 140). Der Grundsatz, daß jede Strafe Schuld voraussetzt, hat seine Grundlage damit in der Menschenwürdegarantie des Art. 1 Abs. 1 GG (vgl. BverfGE 57, 250, 275; 80, 367, 378; 90, 145, 173)."

"Criminal law is based on the principle of guilt. This principle presupposes a human being's own responsibility; it presupposes human beings who themselves determine their actions and can decide in favor of right or wrong by virtue of their freedom of will. The protection of human dignity is based on the idea of Man as a spiritual and moral being which has the capabilities of defining himself, and of developing, in freedom (see BverfGE 45, 187, 227). In the area of the administration of criminal law, Article 1.1 of the Basic Law determines the idea of the nature of punishment and the relationship between guilt and atonement (BverfGE 95, 96, 140). The principle that any sanction presupposes guilt thus has its foundation in the guarantee of human dignity under Article 1.1 of the Basic Law (see BverfGE 57, 250, 275; 80, 367, 378; 90, 145, 173)."[43]

It becomes apparent that both courts seem to share with *Załuski* similar convictions concerning the nature of human beings and free will; interestingly enough, even the aspect of "spirituality" is mentioned both by *Załuski* and the German Constitutional Court in our context. Consequently, we are left to – pointedly – ask why German discourse does not more frequently adopt the personalist argument in the (restrictive) way it is used by *Załuski* – one rare example is a question which was posed (though not answered) by *Tatjana Hörnle* and *Markus D. Dubber* in their comparative discussion of insanity in Germany and the US. They ask whether "respect for the autonomy of accused persons" might "preclude rather than support the recognition of a broad insanity defense (and perhaps any insanity defense), and most particularly of an insanity defense that turns on a finding that the accused lacked the requisite capacity for autonomy".[44]

(1) A (legal) reason for this difference might be the previously mentioned guilt principle (*Schuldprinzip*) and its constitutional basis, the protection of human dignity (Art. 1(1) GG). The principle is considered to be a very important

---

[43] BVerfGE 123, 267, 413. The translation is a modified version of that prepared by *Hörnle* (n. 15), 1.

[44] *Hörnle/Dubber* (n. 1), 517.

barrier against an excessive use of criminal punishment (being the state's *ultima ratio* and a grave intrusion into liberty rights).[45] It strictly forbids punishing a person who is deemed not to be criminally responsible due to a relevant (severe) mental disorder or a comparable deficient mental state like acute intoxication. Of course, the question as to which persons actually fall under this description is open to debate and cannot be answered just by taking into account quite abstract principles of constitutional law. But still, it would be a peculiar result to derive from human dignity and the embodied notion of human beings (in German: the *Menschenbild*) both the protection of mentally ill offenders against punishment as well as a restrictive use of the respective protective regulations (in our case: § 20 StGB). One probably has to distinguish between two dimensions here: It is one thing to argue with human dignity and the nature of human beings when it comes to defending free will and criminal responsibility in general, like the highest German courts do – but it is a different situation if the same argument is used in concrete cases to insist that a certain person should be punished because the insanity defense has to be used in a restrictive manner and therefore does not apply. Even if we accept the premise that persons in general share certain abilities making them criminally responsible, this premise itself (and the underlying concept of "personhood") does not answer the question of how many persons lack the prescribed abilities and therefore have to be protected from criminal punishment due to the guilt principle and human dignity. A need for differentiation concerning the use of the personalist argument in different contexts is also expressed (though in a more general way) by *Hörnle* in her contribution on "Guilt and Choice in Criminal Law Theory":

> "It is one thing to consider the unique features of a human being in a philosophical discourse or within constitutional theory, but it is quite another to do so in a criminal verdict."[46]

(2) A legal-theoretical reason could be that in the German discussion many scholars would hesitate to draw far-reaching (restrictive) conclusions from a predominantly normative concept in a context that, according to the leading opinion, also contains factual elements – which is why the structure of § 20 StGB is often described as containing two steps or stages, with both normative and factual elements that cannot be entirely separated but instead interact with each other.[47] That leads us (again) to the difficult question of the relationship between normative value judgements and empirical facts, a question that is also relevant in *Załuski*'s analysis. When he mentions a "subjective experience" of free will[48] or, following *Viktor Frankl*, a "preference" of offenders to be

---

[45] See *J. Kaspar*, Grundrechtsschutz und Verhältnismäßigkeit im Präventionsstrafrecht (2014).

[46] *Hörnle* (n. 15), 4.

[47] *Kaspar/Stübner* (n. 3), 154 f.; *Hörnle/Dubber* (n. 1), 512.

[48] *Załuski*, p. 403, above.

responsible for their deeds,[49] he refers to factual circumstances that could be measured and confirmed by means of empirical research. But it is clear that these facts alone are proof neither of the actual existence of free will nor that it is justified to generally treat people as criminally responsible. First, because it is problematic to immediately draw normative conclusions from empirical facts (a false conclusion which is called a "natural fallacy"). And second, because the subjective experiences and expectations mentioned by *Załuski* are probably also shared by many mentally ill persons who in the end are considered not to be criminally responsible – which indicates that subjective experience alone is not a good distinguishing factor here.

Apart from these factual elements of his position, *Załuski* criticizes a "naturalistic view" of human beings. According to him, the latter are "spiritual beings, whose inner selves are beyond the reach of the natural sciences".[50] But if this means that, in the end, natural sciences and their (e.g. biological or psychiatric) findings and results cannot meaningfully contribute to the question of criminal responsibility, then a number of questions arise: Why bother with forensic experts and their diagnoses at all? Why is, according to *Załuski*, a diagnosis of a "severe mental illness" like schizophrenia supposed to be relevant, leading to one of the "exceptional cases" he identifies where the volitional component and as a consequence culpability are indeed missing? How (if not by the help of natural science) do we know that schizophrenia is one of these clear and uncontroversial cases? What other mental disorders – and according to what findings – should be included in this category? Why do we make exceptions at all for that matter? Couldn't we attribute responsibility to all human beings just because they are human beings? And finally: how do we deal with the fact that legislators both in Poland and Germany obviously assumed that there was indeed a group of people not criminally responsible due to a relevant lack of control – and that the statutory terms are factual rather than normative ones? The wording of the relevant regulations in both countries relates to people who are incapable of controlling their conduct – which is the description of a factual circumstance, no matter if this circumstance contradicts our general view on human beings and their free will and no matter if it disappoints social or legal expectations.

Załuski's argument goes in a different direction. For perfectly understandable reasons, he speaks of the "task" of human beings to act according to their free will,[51] and he warns that a too generous exoneration of mentally ill offenders might lead to unfavorable consequences.[52] But is that supposed to mean that we should also punish people who actually could not control themselves

[49] *Załuski*, p. 407, above.

[50] *Załuski*, p. 407, above.

[51] *Załuski*, p. 409, above.

[52] *Załuski*, p. 410, above.

because they failed to fulfill the above-mentioned task or because we are afraid of the consequences for society as a whole if we refrain from punishment? Wouldn't it be a "normative fallacy"[53] to ignore an existing lack of control because it does not align with a certain philosophical (idealistic) image of how persons "should be"? And wouldn't this restrictive normative approach also affect the use of the cognitive element, as one could easily argue that it is at the same time a "task" of everyone to apprehend the wrongfulness of one's actions?

(3) Finally, a simple (practical) reason might be that there does not seem to be a need for (further) restricting the application of § 20 (absence of culpability) or § 21 StGB (diminished culpability) in Germany because courts use both regulations quite cautiously anyway.[54] The legislative framework in § 20 and § 21 StGB as such is understood as a presumption that adults are generally responsible for their crimes and only exceptionally exculpated[55] – this understanding resembles the restrictive approach by *Załuski*, but it relates both to the volitional component and the cognitive one at the same time.

In 2021 (the last year with available data), 815,199 persons were dealt with by German criminal courts.[56] Of these defendants, only 1,147 (0.14 %) were fully exculpated due to a mental disorder according to § 20 StGB. Unfortunately, these data do not show if culpability was denied with regard to the cognitive or the control element. But it is a fair assumption that (unlike in the US[57]) the control element plays a significant role in German judicial practice as cases of acute intoxication are acknowledged as a potential case where culpability is absent.[58]

Even diminished culpability according to § 21 StGB, which does not exclude criminal responsibility but solely allows for a facultative mitigation of punishment, was found rather sparingly: only 15,120 persons (1.85 % of all defendants in court) were considered to have fulfilled the prerequisites of § 21 StGB. This explains why the fear of a "slippery slope" or of an overly generous exoneration of many offenders, which had played a considerable role in the German discussion before the introduction of today's culpability regulations in

---

[53] *T.D. Campbell*, The Normative Fallacy, The Philosophical Quarterly 20 (1970), 368–377.

[54] *J. Kaspar*, in: H. Satzger et al. (eds.), Strafgesetzbuch (5th edn., 2021), § 20 paras. 7 ff.

[55] *Schrader* (n. 23), 20 ff.

[56] See *Statistisches Bundesamt*, Rechtspflege. Strafverfolgung (2021), 370, available online: https://www.destatis.de/DE/Themen/Staat/Justiz-Rechtspflege/Publikationen/_publikationen-innen-strafverfolgung.html (last accessed 1 March 2023).

[57] For a comparative discussion, see *Dubber/Hörnle* (n. 1), 506 and 511.

[58] On this complex topic (including the legal construction of an actio libera in causa in cases of negligent or even intentional intoxication), see *S. Gless/N. Jain/ A. Loughnan*, Imputation of Responsibility and Intoxicated Offending, in: K. Ambos et al. (eds.), Core Concepts in Criminal Law and Criminal Justice, vol. 2 (2022), 95–131.

1975, is no longer part of the current debate. Furthermore, as mentioned above, acquittals due to the insanity defense rarely become scandals, as in many cases other stationary measures of rehabilitation and incapacitation are imposed, such as detention in a psychiatric hospital (§ 63 StGB) or detention in an addiction treatment facility (§ 64 StGB). In 2021, for example, of 1,147 persons who were acquitted due to an absence of culpability under § 20 StGB, only 125 (10.85 %) were not sanctioned at all, whereas 922 (80.38 %) were detained in a psychiatric hospital and 100 (8.72 %) in an addiction treatment facility.[59] Against this background one can understand why a further restriction of the application of § 20 StGB is not on the agenda in Germany.

[59] See *Statistisches Bundesamt* (n. 56), 370.

Rationalization in Legal Theory

Łukasz Kurek

I. Introduction

Rationalization is the human cognitive capacity to explain and predict the behaviour of other persons in terms of reasons for action. This cognitive capacity is the subject of interdisciplinary investigation that aims to describe the cognitive mechanism which underpins rationalization. This cognitive mechanism gathers, processes and applies the information in a specific way that enables the attribution of reasons. At the present moment, the investigation on the cognitive mechanism in question suggests that it consists of two components: theory of mind and mental simulation. Theory of mind comprises common-sense information about the mind whereas mental simulation consists in using one's own decision-making mechanisms to attribute reasons to another person. The present chapter discusses how the investigation into the cognitive mechanism underlying rationalization is relevant for legal theory.

More specifically, the chapter argues that theorizing about law involves a rationalization of the behaviour of agents guided by law. Going further, when legal theorists engage in the cognitive activity which eventually leads them to reach the explanatory targets of their discipline, they use theory of mind and they mentally simulate the hypothetical and real-world persons in various legal settings to attribute to them reasons for action. The chapter describes how theorizing about law is underpinned by a theory of mind and how mental simulation sheds new light on the method of legal theory which is conceptual analysis of law.

II. Two modes of behaviour explanation: causal explanation and rationalizing explanation

Philosophers tend to differentiate between two modes of explanation: causal explanation and rationalizing explanation.[1] Causal explanations target unintentional behaviour. Unintentional behaviour is passive in the sense that things only happen to entities that behave unintentionally. Some entities, such as planets, clouds and rocks, always behave unintentionally. On the other hand, some entities behave unintentionally only from time to time. These entities are intentional agents, and the foremost kind of intentional agents are human beings. Intentional agents behave unintentionally when their behaviour is not goal-directed. If a football player is shoved by his opponent and crashes into another player, his crashing into another player is unintentional behaviour. It only happened to him that he crashed into someone else, and his unintentional behaviour can be explained by citing its cause which is that he was shoved.

In addition to the fact that things happen to human beings, there are also things that human beings *do*. When human beings do things, they engage in intentional behaviour which is behaviour guided by a goal. This behaviour requires a rationalizing explanation referring to the inner states of an intentional agent – to his reasons for action. In particular, rationalization refers to the intentional agent's desires, i.e. to the fact that the agent strives towards something, and to his beliefs, i.e. to the fact that he is aware of how to achieve what he wants. Rationalizing explanations are required to explain intentional behaviour because intentional behaviour is influenced by what happens inside intentional agents – by the fact that they consider their reasons and their behaviour to be guided by these considerations. If a person is lightly pushed and uses this situation to crash into someone else on purpose, her crashing into someone else is intentional behaviour. Imagine a football player who is lightly pushed by an opponent, but he wants to make this push look like a shove so that the opponent is penalized. To achieve what he wants, the football player lunges himself towards another player in his path and crashes into him. The football player wanted that his crashing into the player in his path looked like it only happened to him, that it was caused by the push of his opponent. But it would be wrong to explain his behaviour in this way. His crashing into another player was something that he did because there was a reason why he did it – he wanted his opponent to be penalized.

An important feature of reasons for action is that reasons render the behaviour rational in the sense that they rationally support behaviour. Minimally, all rationalizations render the target behaviour instrumentally rational. Instrumental rationality assumes that the person whose behaviour is the target of rational-

---

[1] *L. Wittgenstein*, Philosophical Investigations (1986), 161–163; *D. Dennett*, From Bacteria to Bach and Back (2018), 44 f.; *Ch. List*, Why Free Will is Real (2019), 58–64.

ization is capable of (1) gathering information about her environment (her reasons correspond to her environment), (2) processing this information in a particular manner (her reasons are internally consistent) and (3) guiding her behaviour in accordance with this information processing (her reasons guide her behaviour). The cheating football player mentioned in the above paragraph is instrumentally rational in this way. First, his reasons appropriately correspond to his environment, as he correctly believes that he can use the fact that his opponent lightly pushed him to his advantage. Second, his reasons are internally consistent in the sense that his desire that his opponent be penalized is consistent with his desire to make his opponent's push look like a shove. Third, his reasons guide his behaviour in the sense that his beliefs and desires influence what he does.

In the above paragraph, rationalization was used to describe what happens when an intentional behaviour is carried out. But apart from this descriptive dimension of rationalization, it also has a normative dimension: It may be used to normatively assess behaviour. That is, rationalization may be used to assess whether a particular behaviour is instrumentally rational, i.e. whether the reasons which guided it corresponded to the environment, whether these reasons were internally consistent or whether they guided behaviour. In this context, instrumental rationality provides information about how the agent – under certain idealized conditions such as correspondence between reasons and the environment, internal consistency of reasons and the behaviour's conformity to reasons – ought to behave. Thus, the behaviour of the cheating football player may be evaluated as correct, given that his overriding desire is that his opponent be penalized.

The normative standards used to rationalize behaviour may be more demanding than instrumental rationality even though all these more demanding standards require a minimal assumption that intentional behaviour is carried out by agents capable of being instrumentally rational. These more demanding standards assume that certain goals go beyond consistency or the factual correctness which agents ought to strive for when they consider their reasons for action. As a result, these more demanding standards allow the rationalizer to go beyond the reasons which guide behaviour and assess these reasons. Rationalizations that adopt these more demanding standards aim to describe what happens when an intentional action is carried out and to explain how – under certain idealized conditions – agents ought to behave, although in cases of these rationalizations their normative dimension is more prominent. One such rationalization targets behaviour guided by moral reasons. Another such rationalization – which will be discussed in more detail below – targets behaviour guided by law.

The fact that rationalization has the above-mentioned normative dimension distinguishes this mode of behaviour explanation from its causal counterpart. The causal explanation may be used to describe the process leading to behaviour which is its explanatory target, but causes do not rationally support behaviour. For example, in the case of the football player who was shoved by his opponent and crashed into another player, the shoving describes the process leading to the crash, but it does not render the crash rational.

III. The cognitive mechanism underpinning rationalization

The above considerations, according to which unintentional behaviours *ought to* be explained causally and intentional behaviours *ought to* be explained by rationalizations, correspond to how people explain and predict intentional and unintentional behaviour. That is, when people explain behaviour in ordinary situations, the default mode of explaining unintentional behaviour is to look for its causes, and the default mode of explaining intentional behaviour is to look at its reasons.[2] The interdisciplinary research on rationalization – which involves the cooperation of philosophers, social and cognitive psychologists as well as neuroscientists – aims to determine how the mechanism which underpins rationalization works. To describe the explanatory strategy adopted here, it is useful to distinguish between three notions: cognitive capacity, cognitive mechanism and cognitive tasks.[3]

A cognitive capacity is characterized by the goal which it aims to achieve. The goal of the cognitive capacity to rationalize is to explain and predict intentional behaviour. A different cognitive capacity is categorization. The goal of categorization is to classify objects into different kinds. A cognitive mechanism is a specific way of how information is gathered, processed, and applied to bring about the goal of a particular cognitive competence. A cognitive mechanism describes the logical structure of the procedure required to achieve the goal of a particular cognitive competence. In the case of rationalization, the logical structure of the procedure required to explain and predict behaviour consists in attributing to others the already mentioned reasons for actions, such as beliefs and desires. A lot more can be said about the mechanism which underpins rationalization, and we will come back to this issue in a moment. In the case of categorization, one of the proposed mechanisms which underpin it consists in building, storing, updating and applying prototypes.[4] That is, people classify objects into different kinds of objects based on how similar these

---

[2] *B. Malle*, How the mind explains behavior. Folk explanations, meaning, social interaction (2004), 92–112.

[3] *E. Machery*, Doing without concepts (2009), 121–125.

[4] *E. Rosch/C.B. Mervis*, Family resemblance: Studies in the internal structure of categories, Cognitive Psychology 7 (1975), 573–605; *J.A. Hampton*, Concepts as prototypes, in: B.H. Ross (ed.), The psychology of learning and motivation: advances in research and theory (2006), 79–113.

objects are to the object considered to best represent each kind, i.e. to prototypes. Objects very similar to prototypes will be classified as belonging more to a particular kind than objects that are only a little similar to prototypes. Finally, a cognitive task is a concrete situation that requires using a particular cognitive competence. Explaining the behaviour of a football player who crashed into another player by appealing to the fact that he *wanted* to crash into another player is a cognitive task that requires rationalization. For example, categorization is required to solve the cognitive task consisting in attributing to the animal pictured on the poster for the film *Jaws* the property of being a shark.

Above it was mentioned that research on rationalization aims to determine the workings of the mechanism which underpins rationalization. An important and fairly recent development on this issue concerns the realization that the logical structure of the procedure required to attribute to others reasons for action is much more complex than had been typically assumed. To be more specific, in the first stage of the research on the mechanism underpinning rationalization the dominant view was that people have a partially tacit, commonsense theory of mind which is stored in a linguistic format. That is, people believe that there are certain regularities in how reasons drive behaviour, and when they rationalize they engage in a partially covert dialogue with themselves which results in reason attribution.[5]

In the second stage of the research under discussion, a novel mechanism underpinning rationalization was proposed. According to this view, to attribute reasons, people simulate the target behaviour using their decision-making mechanisms. The advantages of the simulation mechanism over the theory mechanism are threefold. First, the former is simpler. Simplicity is always an advantage when different views on the same issue are compared. More importantly, however, in this particular context simplicity helps the simulation theory to avoid the so-called frame problem – a difficulty that often troubles investigations of mechanisms underpinning human cognitive competences. The frame problem is the challenge of describing the logical procedure required to achieve the goal of a particular cognitive competence without taking into account a large amount of obvious information which is typically associated with achieving this goal.[6] In many cases, people intuitively know what information is relevant when they make quick decisions, but it is difficult to describe the logical procedure followed in assessing this relevance. If the proposed logical procedure is too simple, it can lead to simple mistakes which

[5] *W. Sellars*, Empiricism and the philosophy of mind, in: H. Feigl/M. Scriven (eds.), The foundations of science and the concepts of psychology and psychoanalysis: Minnesota studies in the philosophy of science (1956), 253–329, 317.

[6] *M. Shanahan*, The frame problem, in: E. Zalta (ed.), The Stanford Encyclopedia of Philosophy (Spring 2016 edn.), https://plato.stanford.edu/archives/spr2016/entries/frame-problem/ (last accessed on 5 May 2022).

people rarely make in the real world, making the procedure psychologically unrealistic. For example, people are quite adept at attributing to others the most basic emotions such as anger or surprise. At least part of the logical procedure involved in this attribution consists in taking into account the facial expression of the attribution's target – anger and happiness are associated with characteristic facial expressions. However, the logical procedure used to attribute emotions is more complex than just taking into account the relevant facial expression. This is illustrated by the fact that most of us realize that when someone else is telling a story involving an angry or a surprised person and the storyteller makes an angry or a surprised face to make the story more appealing this does not entail that the storyteller is really angry or surprised. On the other hand, if the logical procedure proposed to underpin a cognitive competence is too complex, the amount of information required by this competence is too large to exercise it quickly which also makes the logical procedure psychologically unrealistic. According to the proponents of the simulation mechanism, rationalization does not require a theory of human behaviour that indicates the relevant information to attribute reasons. Instead, rationalizers take a shortcut and reason what they would have done in the situation of the person whose behaviour is the explanatory or predictive target. Second, the simulation mechanism is in line with at least part of the phenomenology of rationalization.[7] In many cases, reasons are attributed almost instantly. In these cases, there is certainly no overt inner dialogue that results in reason attribution, and it is implausible to hypothesize that in these cases reasons are attributed as a result of engaging in a covert inner dialogue. There is simply no time for this covert dialogue to take place. Third, there have been discoveries in psychology and neuroscience which support the view that people use their decision-making mechanisms to attribute reasons to others.[8]

In the third stage, which is also the present stage of the discussed research, it was recognized that the mechanism which underpins rationalization needs to include the elements of both theory and simulation.[9] This is mainly because, on the one hand, simulation alone is not a mechanism that is sufficiently information-rich to handle rationalization. Even simple cognitive tasks which involve rationalization seem to require a mechanism that is information-rich to a greater extent than pure simulation. One such cognitive task, known as a "false-belief task", consists in answering the following question: Where will the person look for the object which she left in place A and which was then moved to

---

[7] *S. Gallagher*, In defense of phenomenological approaches to social cognition: Interacting with the critics, Review of Philosophy and Psychology 3/2 (2012), 187–212.

[8] *A. Goldman*, Simulating minds (2006), 113–146.

[9] *T. Stone/M. Davies*, The Mental Simulation Debate: A Progress Report, in: P. Carruthers/P. Smith (eds.), Theories of Theories of Mind (1996), 119–137, 136.

place B without her seeing that the object was relocated?[10] The correct answer is that the person will look for the object in place A – even though this is not the place where the object is located. To arrive at the correct solution of this cognitive task, one needs to acknowledge the implications of the fact that the person whose behaviour is predicted in the false-belief task did not see that the object was relocated. It follows from this fact that this person is unaware that the object is in place B. Going further, it follows from these two facts – (1) that this person did not see that the object was relocated and (2) that this person is unaware that the object is in place B – that she will look for the object in place A.

However, if the logical structure of the procedure which underpins rationalization conformed to what is proposed by the proponents of the simulation mechanism, then it would be unclear how we arrive at the correct solution to the false-belief task. To predict where the person will look for the object, one cannot simply use one's own decision-making mechanism. Using one's own decision-making mechanism would lead to the incorrect conclusion that the person will look for the object in place B because the decision-making mechanism of the person who is predicting is updated with the information that the object was moved to place B. If I know that the object was moved to place B and someone asks me where to look for this object – this is what using one's own decision-making mechanisms amounts to, i.e. it amounts to solving this cognitive task on one's own – the correct answer is that this object ought to be looked for in place B. To correctly solve this cognitive task the person who is predicting needs to perceive the important differences between herself and the person whose behaviour is the predictive target. The difference in question is that the latter person did not see that the object was relocated and because of this she is unaware that the object is in place B. Simulation typically requires that the person who simulates acknowledges the difference between herself and the person whose behaviour is rationalized – these differences include, for example, differences in what one believes – because if it is not the case that both persons are identical in all the relevant aspects, then simulation would always lead to incorrect solutions to cognitive tasks which require rationalization. However, people often correctly and even effortlessly solve cognitive tasks which involve rationalization. What is more, to determine which differences between oneself and the person whose behaviour is the target of rationalization are relevant and what follows from these differences, one needs to have some kind of a theory of mind. For example, solving the false-belief task entails knowing two things about the mind. First, a person who did not see that an

[10] *H. Wimmer/J. Perner*, Beliefs about Beliefs: Representation and Constraining Function of Wrong Beliefs in Young Children's Understanding of Deception, Cognition 13 (1983), 103–128.

object was relocated ought to be unaware that this object was relocated. Second, a person ought to look for an object in the place where she last saw it.

To sum up the above discussion on the cognitive mechanism underpinning rationalization, its logical structure comprises both the common-sense theory of mind and mental simulation. The theory of mind allows the rationalizer to acknowledge the differences between himself and the person who is the target of rationalization. Mental simulation, on the other hand, provides the necessary shortcut in gathering, processing and using the information needed to attribute reasons. Because of this dual nature of rationalization, one can expect characteristic divergencies between what rationalization tells us about behaviour and the behaviour's actual features. In particular, one can expect that solving cognitive tasks which involve rationalization will result in an egocentric bias in the case where the rationalizer mistakenly assumes that the person who is the target of rationalization is like him in all the relevant aspects, failing to acknowledge the discrepancy between his reasons and the reasons of his explanatory or predictive target.

To illustrate that this expectation is correct, consider the psychological research on the malleability of eyewitnesses' beliefs about events that they have seen.[11] In one experiment related to this phenomenon, subjects have seen a film of a car accident. Some subjects were asked about the speed of the car involved in the accident. Other subjects were asked about this as well, but their question also mentioned that the car involved in the accident passed a white barn. After a week all participants in the experiment were asked whether they saw a barn in the film of the car accident. Even though there was no barn on the film, 17% of the subjects who were asked the question which mentioned the barn reported having seen the barn and only 3% of the other subjects reported this. Experiments on the malleability of beliefs about events that people have witnessed have illustrated that even the mentioning of objects or events which people did not witness significantly increases the likelihood that people will believe that they have seen these objects or events. This leads to the conclusion that eyewitness testimony is much less reliable evidence in legal proceedings than it was previously assumed. For the present discussion, this experimental research is significant because its results are surprising. The extent to which eyewitness memory can be modified as a result of a post factum intervention was not taken into account in legal proceedings before it was empirically demonstrated, because this phenomenon is unavailable for someone who merely rationalizes the eyewitness's behaviour. That is, when participants in the legal proceedings mentally simulate what they would believe about events that the witness has seen and then attribute the beliefs produced in this way to the witness, they fail to notice the phenomenon in question because their common-sense theory of

[11] *E. Loftus*, Planting misinformation in the human mind: A 30-year investigation of the malleability of memory, Learning & Memory 12 (2005), 361–366.

mind does not include information that this is how the mind works. It may be hypothesized that the theory of mind used when people attribute beliefs about events to the witnesses of these events includes the following information: Witnesses' recollections of events ought not to be significantly malleable as a result of a casual, post factum mentioning of a non-existent object or event. Let us describe as "blind spots" those features of behaviour that are difficult, if not impossible, to determine on the grounds of rationalization alone. In general, blind spots are quite a common feature of behaviour, including law-guided behaviour.[12]

IV. The nature of law and the concept of law

This section will describe how theorizing about law involves a rationalization of the behaviour of agents whose behaviour is guided by law. This requires some stage setting. First, it will be discussed how answering the question "What is law?" – a question whose answer is perhaps most associated with what legal theory is about – is related to the so-called conceptual investigations of law.[13] Second, it will be argued that conceptual investigations of law involve the rationalization of law-guided behaviour.

Describing legal theory as aiming to answer the question "What is law?" indicates that legal theory aims to determine the universal features of law, i.e. features which all particular instances of law share, at least to some extent. Answering this question does not consist in determining the features of particular legal orders, particular branches of law or particular legal rules. This general scope of legal-theoretic inquiries can be illustrated by pointing to what is the most discussed topic in this discipline: Whether what counts as law depends on moral considerations. This issue is not associated with any particular law but with law wherever and whenever it exists. Still, solving this issue may be of consequence to particular laws. For example, there have existed rules – regarded as valid law by the communities where these rules were in force – widely recognized to be at odds with moral considerations. If it is indeed the

[12] Apart from the one blind spot of law-guided behaviour already identified, i.e. the malleability of eyewitness's beliefs about events that they have seen, another much-discussed blind spot is the influence of heuristics on legal decision-making. Heuristics are simple, practical rules which people follow when they make decisions in legal settings. The problematic feature of heuristics is that in certain situations they lead to erroneous decisions: *J. Rachlinski/J. Jeffrey/A.J. Wistrich*, Judging the Judiciary by the Numbers: Empirical Research on Judges, Annual Review of Law and Social Science 13 (2017), 203–229; *B. Brożek*, The legal mind. A new introduction to legal epistemology (2020), 23–29.

[13] *J. Stelmach/B. Brożek*, Methods of legal reasoning (2006), 216; *S. Shapiro*, Legality (2011), 3; *H.L.A. Hart*, The concept of law (3rd edn., 2012), 1; *B. Tamanaha*, A realistic theory of law (2017), 37.

case that what counts as law depends on moral considerations, then, in reality, these rules did not count as law. These rules merely appeared to be laws.

Determining the universal features of a thing boils down to explaining this thing's nature. Thus, the question "What is law?" is interchangeable with the question "What is the nature of law?". Because explaining the nature of things is a philosophical undertaking, legal theorists engaged in looking for the answer to the question "What is law?" are best conceived as philosophizing about law. One of the most important developments in contemporary legal theory consists in the insight that answering the questions "What is law?" and "What is the nature of law?" is somehow related to answering the question "What is the concept of law?".[14] Some legal theorists think that all three questions are interchangeable.[15] Let us describe this view as an "interchangeability claim". The interchangeability claim is at least unobvious. This is because this claim rests on the counterintuitive assumption that the concept of law and the phenomenon to which this concept corresponds are the same thing. This assumption, however, appears to be based on a categorical mistake: Concepts are entities of a different kind than the phenomena to which these concepts correspond. Concepts determine how we understand phenomena and our understandings of phenomena are something different from the phenomena themselves.

Admittedly, some legal theorists disagree with the interchangeability claim. However, even these legal theorists typically adopt the following, weaker claim: Answering the conceptual question about law goes some way towards answering what law is and explaining the nature of law. Let us describe this view as a "hermeneutical claim". It appears that the hermeneutical claim is attributed, *inter alia*, to *Joseph Raz*, who writes:

> "Is it not our aim to study the nature of law, rather than our culture and concept of law? Yes and no. We aim to improve our understanding of the nature of law. The law is a type of social institution, the type that is picked up – designated – by the concept of law. Hence in improving our understanding of the nature of law we assume an understanding of the concept of law, and improve it."[16]

Notice that the hermeneutical claim is unobvious for the same reason that the strong claim is: The weaker claim appears to be based on a categorical mistake as well. One may wonder why it is the case that investigating our understanding of law goes some way towards explaining what law is. The concept of law determines how we understand law, and our understanding of law is something different from the phenomenon of law itself. To illustrate this, notice that it follows from the hermeneutical claim that, in the case of law, everyone cannot be mistaken about what law is. On this view, there is a necessary connection

---

[14] *Hart* (n. 13), 110.

[15] *J.L. Coleman/O. Simchen*, Law, Legal Theory 9/1 (2003), 1–41, 5 f.

[16] *J. Raz*, Authority and interpretation (2009), 31.

between the concept of law and what law is. This is because if we agree with the hermeneutical claim that answering the conceptual question about law goes some way towards answering what law is, we also need to agree that how law is understood law contains information about what it is. Although in many cases it is true that how we understand phenomena ought to be distinguished from the phenomena themselves because there is no significant relationship between our concepts of these phenomena and the phenomena themselves, this observation does not hold – or at least it does not hold completely – for law. In the case of law, the distinction between how we understand it and the phenomenon itself blurs. However, before it will be explained why the hermeneutical claim is correct, we need to take a closer look at what concepts are. This will shed some light on why the hermeneutical claim appears to be mistaken.

Although concepts are a rather controversial issue within philosophy, philosophers agree that concepts are the basic elements of thoughts.[17] Philosophers also agree that concepts mediate between mind and world in the sense that concepts are tools for thinking about phenomena.[18] For example, the concept of a dog is a tool for thinking about dogs. In philosophy, thoughts about dogs are something different from the concept of a dog. The difference is that having a concept of a dog means that one can think about dogs.[19] Thoughts about dogs contain a great variety of information about dogs but only some of this information is required to be able to think about dogs. For example, the information that there are therapy dogs is not the kind of information one needs to know to be able to think about dogs. One may not be aware that there are therapy dogs and still be able to think about dogs. Thus, that there are therapy dogs is not information that is stored within the concept of a dog. On the other hand, that dogs eat and breathe or that they are unable to fly is information stored within the concept of a dog. If an agent is unaware that dogs eat and breathe or that they are unable to fly, she is unable to think about dogs. Not taking into account the disputed issue of what exactly concepts are – for example, whether concepts are abstract, timeless entities or abstractions from the use of words, or whether they are mental entities located inside our heads – the talk about concepts entails that there are three kinds of entities: (1) phenomena, (2) thoughts about phenomena and (3) concepts which mediate between (1) and (2).

Now, let us go back to the question "What is the concept of law?". Taking into account the above considerations, the concept of law is an entity that mediates between law and thoughts about law. The last piece of the puzzle is the phenomenon to which the word "law" in the previous sentence corresponds.

---

[17] *J. Prinz*, Concepts, in: D.M. Borchert (ed.), Encyclopedia of philosophy (2006), 414.

[18] E. Margolis/S. Laurence, Concepts, in: E. Zalta (ed.), The Stanford Encyclopedia of Philosophy (2021 edn.), https://plato.stanford.edu/archives/spr2021/entries/concepts/ (last accessed on 5 May 2022).

[19] *E. Machery*, Doing without concepts (2009), 32.

The phenomenon in question is social: It comprises all instances of law-guided behaviour.[20] Law-guided behaviour is behaviour in the case of which the reasons which guide are legal reasons which include, but are not limited to, legal provisions, judicial decisions and generally accepted rules of legal interpretation. Thus, the concept of law mediates between law-guided behaviour and thoughts about law-guided behaviour. Now we can see in more detail why the hermeneutical claim appears to be based on a categorical mistake. Namely, this claim appears to preclude the mediating role of the concept of law: The claim in question conflates the mediator (which is the concept of law) with one of the things between which this concept mediates (which is law-guided behaviour).

The objection that the hermeneutical claim appears to be based on a categorical mistake will be convincing if there is a clear-cut distinction between law-guided behaviour and the concept of law. A "clear-cut distinction" in this context means that the concept of law does not influence what law-guided behaviour is. For the categorical mistake argument to work, the relationship between law-guided behaviour and the concept of law-following needs to be one-way only: from law-guided behaviour to the concept of law-following. That is, it is the law-guided behaviour that needs to influence our understanding of this social phenomenon and not the other way around. In other words, law-guided behaviour needs to be mind-independent if we want the argument of categorical mistake to work against the hermeneutical claim. On the other hand, if law-guided behaviour is mind-dependent, then the argument in question loses its force. If law-guided behaviour is mind-dependent, then its explanation needs to appeal to its concept.

To a large extent, there seems to be a clear-cut distinction between world and mind in the case of the natural – as opposed to the social – world. For example, water is a part of the natural world. The relationship between water and the concept of water is one-way only: from water to the concept of water. It is the physical, observable features of water that influence how we understand water. The concept of water, on the other hand, does not influence what water is. For example, how we understand water does not make it the case that water is a transparent substance with the chemical structure of H_2O. It is physical, observable features of water that make it the case that we understand water as having these qualities.

However, in the case of the social world, the situation is different. How we understand the social world is of immense significance in its explanation. Theft, for example, is a part of the social world. Theft consists in an *intentional* taking of something that belongs to someone else. Thus, in the explanation of what theft is, there is an appeal to how the agent who commits it needs to understand his behaviour. To determine whether a person stole an umbrella or

[20] *Hart* (n. 13), v; *R. Dworkin*, Law's empire (1986), 90; *J. Raz*, Two views of the nature of the theory of law: a partial comparison, in: idem (n. 16), 47–90, 47.

took someone else's umbrella by mistake, we need to know which reasons she considered before taking the umbrella. In particular, we need to know whether she knew that the umbrella she took was someone else's. Thus, to determine whether a particular behaviour counts as theft of an umbrella, one needs to solve a cognitive task that involves rationalization and determine how the person who took the umbrella understood her behaviour.

Law-guided behaviour is mind-dependent as well. It is mind-dependent in the simple sense that to determine whether a particular behaviour counts as an instance of law-guided behaviour, one needs to determine the reasons which guide this behaviour. Otherwise, an instance of law-guided behaviour may be indistinguishable from instances of other kinds of behaviour. If a pedestrian waits for the green light to cross the road, his behaviour may count as an instance of law-guided behaviour (if the reason why he waits is that he follows the legal rule according to which you ought not to cross the road if the light is red) or it may count as an instance of behaviour guided by prudential reasons (if he waits because he considers it dangerous to cross the road when the light is red). Thus, to determine whether a particular behaviour counts as law-guided, one needs to solve a cognitive task that involves rationalization and determine how the person who undertakes this behaviour understands it.

More importantly, however, law-guided behaviour is mind-dependent in the sense that there are some features which at least most instances of law-guided behaviour share, and these features may be identified by investigation of the concept of law. Some of these features are quite rudimentary, such as the fact that law-guided behaviour involves following rules which are valid, public, possible to obey, coherent and prospective. Conceptual investigations of law involve predicting what fictional or real-world persons would think or do in various legal settings and explaining the law-guided behaviour of real-world persons. In short, conceptual investigations of law involve rationalizing law-guided behaviour. Thus, a simple thought experiment involving a fictional person obliged to follow a retrospective rule reveals that law-guided behaviour cannot comprise behaviours guided by retrospective rules – at least not for the most part. More specifically, a retrospective rule changes the conditions under which decisions in a legal setting ought to be made, and this change pertains to decisions that are already in the past and cannot be changed. As such, retrospective rules demand that what the law requires in the case of past behaviours and past behaviours cannot be changed.

Most probably, there are only few supporters of retrospective legal rules. This makes the claim that law-guided behaviour comprises behaviour guided by prospective rules a truism. However, other controversial features of law-guided behaviour have been put forward which were more popular. One such feature was proposed by the proponents of the predictive theory of law.[21] According to this theory, legal rules are predictions of what the courts will do. However, on this view, legal rules are not merely tools that aid in predicting what the courts will do in the sense that legal rules exist even if, in some cases, they fail to predict courts' decisions. According to the predictive theory, legal rules *are to be identified* with these predictions, i.e. with descriptive statements about the future courts' decisions. For example, the contractual obligation of the buyer to pay a particular amount of money to the seller *is* the prediction that the court will order the buyer to pay the price to the seller. If the buyer predicts that the court will not order him to pay because he thinks that he will be able to deceive the court into thinking that he already paid, then the buyer does not have the contractual obligation to pay. The problem with the predictive theory of law is that it is mistaken at the conceptual level. This can be demonstrated if one adopts the perspective of the judge who needs to decide whether the buyer ought to pay to the seller. If the judge needs to decide this, then, on the view under discussion, he needs to hypothesize what his decision will be in this particular case.[22] The problem is that to hypothesize about his future decision he needs to consider the legal rules which are relevant in the case at hand, and he cannot consider these rules because, according to the predictive theory, these rules are predictions of his future behaviour. At least at face value, the predictive theory entails that the descriptive statement about the judge's future decision in this particular case is the law in this particular case.[23] To demonstrate that this cannot be a feature of law-guided behaviour, it is not necessary to look at how judges actually decide cases. To demonstrate this, it is sufficient to rationalize the behaviour of a fictional judge who wants to decide a particular case and hypothesize how he will arrive at this decision.

V. The limits of conceptual analysis of law: the issue of sanction

Above, it was mentioned that legal theory aims to determine the universal features of law understood as a kind of a social phenomenon, i.e. as law-guided behaviour. What is more, because law-guided behaviour is mind-dependent,

---

[21] *O.W. Holmes*, The path of the law, Harvard Law Review 10 (1898), 457–478; *B. Leiter*, Legal realism, in: D. Patterson (ed.), A companion to philosophy of law and legal theory (1996), 249–266, 250.

[22] *Hart* (n. 13), 136.

[23] Because, at least on face value, the predictive theory of law entails the unwanted and, frankly speaking, absurd consequence that judges are unable to engage in law-guided behaviour, a more charitable reading of this theory was proposed which says that proponents of the predictive theory of law claimed that when judges decide cases, their behaviour is guided by both legal and non-legal reasons: *B. Leiter*, Naturalizing jurisprudence: Essays on American legal realism and naturalism in legal philosophy (2007), 24–26.

the method of legal theory is a conceptual analysis of law. There are some uncontroversial features of law-guided behaviour – such as the fact that it involves following rules which are valid, public, possible to obey, coherent and prospective – embraced by the concept of law. The drawback of these features is that they are rather truistic. There are also some controversial claims about law-guided behaviour – such as the claim that legal rules are predictions of what the courts will do – which are relatively easy to undermine with the aid of conceptual investigations into the nature of law. There is, however, a third and more interesting category of claims about law-guided behaviour. These are claims of a conceptual nature that are, interestingly, at odds with the actual features of law-guided behaviour. We will discuss one such claim according to which sanction is not a necessary feature of law-guided behaviour.

In contemporary legal theory, the discussion about the relationship between sanction and law-guided behaviour began with *Herbert Hart*'s critique of the command theory of law. According to this theory, particularly as it was developed by *John Austin*, law-guided behaviour consists in following commands of the sovereign backed by threats of sanction. An important condition here is that, in this view, a sovereign is an individual or a group of individuals wielding the actual power to govern society. The sovereign's orders are habitually obeyed by the majority of the population, and the sovereign does not habitually obey anyone else. Opposing this view of law-guided behaviour, *Hart* asks us to imagine a robbery in which the robber points a gun at his victim and says: "Hand over the money or I will shoot". The victim hands over the money. The victim's behaviour can be rationalized as following the command of the sovereign backed by a threat of sanction. First, the victim follows a command because handing over the money is nonoptional. Second, there is also a clear threat of punishment. Third, the robber has the actual power to govern the behaviour of the victim. The final premise in *Hart*'s argument is that legal rules impose obligations. Now, if we agree that the victim is following the command of the sovereign backed by a threat of sanction and that legal rules impose obligations, then it cannot be a feature of law-guided behaviour that it consists in following commands of the sovereign backed by a threat of sanction. This is because there is no obligation for the victim to guide her behaviour in accordance with the robber's command. Thus, if it were a feature of law-guided behaviour that it is simply "a gunman situation writ large", this would mean that legal rules do not impose obligations – yet we have already agreed that legal rules impose obligations.

For the purposes of the present discussion, it is worthwhile to observe that the "gunman situation" is yet another exercise in rationalizing law-guided behaviour. This argument works against the command theory of law because it is easy to observe for the rationalizer of the victim's behaviour that fulfilling an obligation will not be among the reasons for action which the victim considers before handing over the money to the robber. Many legal theorists and philosophers agree with *Hart* that any theory of law which puts forward sanction as a necessary feature of law-guided behaviour distorts the nature of this social phenomenon. Some of them defend the view that a sanction-free legal system is not only a conceptual but even an empirical possibility.[24] Others, however, are at least uneasy with claims about sanctions being merely an optional feature of law-guided behaviour.[25] One of the reasons for this uneasiness is that sanctions are always a central feature of law-guided behaviour. Some go even further and argue that sanctions are a conceptual necessity in the case of law-guided behaviour.[26]

One can attempt to outline an explanation of this diversity of opinions on the relationship between sanction and law-guided behaviour by an appeal to the fact that theorizing about this relationship involves a rationalization of law-guided behaviour. More specifically, solving both the conceptual and the empirical issues of whether sanctions are a necessary or merely an optional feature of law-guided behaviour requires solving cognitive tasks that require rationalization. Going further, in theorizing about this issue, one's own theory of mind mechanism is used, as well as the mechanism of mental simulation, which makes it possible to hypothesize whether fictional or real-world persons require sanctions to guide their behaviour in accordance with what the law requires. The diversity of opinions on the relationship between sanction and law-guided behaviour may be accounted for by an appeal to the theory of mind mechanism or to the simulation mechanism.

First, the theory of mind mechanism is responsible for the fact that a particular legal theorist finds certain claims about how the mind works – and, in consequence, how legal reasons guide behaviour – more convincing than others. One can observe that a theory of mind is used in the case of inquiries into the relationship between sanction and law-guided behaviour when legal theorists engage in a sort of inner dialogues with themselves and an outer dialogue with their peers. This results, first, in the attribution of reasons to fictional and real-world persons – and even to entities such as angels – and, second, in hypothesizing how these agents would solve decision problems in various legal settings. However, divergencies between the theories of mind – i.e. divergencies in the beliefs about regularities in how reasons guide behaviour – of different legal theorists may result in their different views on the conceptual possibility of sanction-free and law-guided behaviour. As regards the empirical possibility of there being sanction-free and law-guided behaviour, there may be a blind

[24] For a defence of the claim that a sanction-free legal system is conceptually possible, see e.g. *J. Raz*, Practical reason and norms (1994), 159 f.; for a defence of the claim that a sanction-free legal system is empirically possible, see e.g. *G.D. Caruso*, Rejecting Retributivism. Free Will, Punishment and Criminal Justice (2021), 184–228.

[25] *F. Schauer*, Was Austin right after all? On the role of sanctions in a theory of law, Ratio Juris 23/1 (2010), 1–21.

[26] *K.E. Himma*, Coercion and the nature of law (2020), 4.

spot involved. That is, it may be difficult, if not impossible, to solve the cognitive task of accurately predicting how real-world persons would behave in a legal setting completely devoid of sanctions.

Second, the simulation mechanism may be responsible for an egocentric bias in the case of rationalizations of law-guided behaviour in sanction-free legal settings. More specifically, when legal theorists solve these cognitive tasks they may mistakenly assume that the persons who are the targets of their rationalizations are like them in all relevant aspects and fail to acknowledge the discrepancy between their reasons and the reasons of the targets of their rationalizations. That this not a mere possibility is indicated by the fact that, as it was already mentioned, actual law-guided behaviour is always associated with coercion, and the coercive component of law is an important part of how many, if not most, persons who engage in law-guided behaviour understand law. Moreover, egocentric bias caused by mental simulation may be responsible for the fact that some legal theorists deny the possibility of sanction-free law. In particular, this bias may make them sceptical towards the possibility of persons – sufficiently different from the persons that these legal theorists can imagine – who would engage in law-guided behaviour even in sanction free legal settings.

VI. Conclusion

In the case of any theoretical inquiry, one can differentiate between the context of discovery and the context of justification. The context of discovery pertains to how ideas come to the mind of the theorist, and the context of justification pertains to the fact whether ideas put forward by a theorist are appropriately justified. It is often the case that inquiries into the former issue are regarded as having at most a minor role in the assessment of a theory. What matters in this assessment is whether a theory is appropriately justified. Furthermore, inquiries into the former issue may be regarded as undermining the objectivity of the investigated theory. Although in many cases the context of discovery is indeed of minor importance in the assessment of a theory, how ideas come to the mind of a theorist is significant in cases of social phenomena because their nature depends on our ideas about them. In the context of social phenomena, it is important to notice that some of our ideas about them might be produced not by our concepts of these phenomena or by these phenomena themselves, but by the cognitive mechanisms which operate, at least to some extent, independently of our beliefs and concepts. In the case of theorizing about law, the mechanisms in question are the theory of mind and mental simulation, which produce powerful intuitions about law-guided behaviour whenever we engage in its rationalization. It is also important to acknowledge that these intuitions may be easily mistaken with features of reality.

Being (Un-)Reasonable: Rationalization and Rationality in Law and Legal Theory

Svenja Behrendt

I. Introduction

When I approached the essay "Rationalization in Legal Theory", I expected it to be mostly about issues of coherence and sense-making with respect to enacting and applying the law – maybe as an interdisciplinary study of law and logic mixed with insights from psychology. Instead, the author focuses mostly on rationalization as a potential for explaining and understanding the behaviour of fellow human beings. He distinguishes *causally* from *rationally* effected events, addresses human decision-making and rationality, and applies rationalization to what he describes as concepts of law. *Łukasz Kurek*'s essay is situated at the interdisciplinary crossroads between philosophy (especially the philosophy of mind), cognitive and social psychology, neuroscience and law. These crossroads and the issues explored in the essay have long since been under discussion in legal philosophy and legal theory. However, *Kurek* frames and connects them in a somewhat unusual way.

In this (commenting) paper, I address some of the phenomena that *Kurek*'s essay focuses on and offer a different perspective, mostly on what role human behaviour plays within the law. I begin by addressing the meaning of rationalization and the two different modes of explanation (causal and rational). I elaborate on the connection between human reasoning and law and on *Kurek*'s notion of connecting intentional with rationalizable behaviour and of contrasting it with only causally explainable events. The essay also touches upon highly selective issues of rationality in law and legal theory – these topics and their conceptual entanglement are, however, simply too big to fully cover them in a short commenting paper.

II. The meaning of the term "rationalization"

The term rationalization is often used to describe a (self-)deceptive process: Whenever somebody convinces him- or herself that there were good reasons for harmful behaviour, this is considered to be rationalizing behaviour. The American Psychological Association states that rationalization is

> "an ego defense in which apparently logical reasons are given to justify unacceptable behavior that is motivated by unconscious instinctual impulses. In psychoanalytic theory, such behavior is considered to be a defense mechanism. […] Rationalizations are used to defend against feelings of guilt, maintain self-respect, and protect oneself from criticism."[1]

People act for certain reasons, but they try to convince themselves and/or others that they were acting for *other* reasons – reasons which make the behaviour look good because it would have been guided by goals that the agent considers to be good or that he perceives to be valued as good by others. Insofar, rationalization is mostly addressed as a *post hoc* phenomenon. According to *Fiery Cushman,* "[r]ationalization takes an action that has already been performed and then concocts the beliefs or desires that would have made it rational. It is, therefore, exactly the opposite of rational action".[2] Rationalization would thus have to be separated from the question of whether an action was *actually* rational.[3] If we look at it like this, rationalization is simply a means to cope with epistemic limitations with respect to factual rationality. First and foremost, rationalization produces plausible narratives; it is strongly connected with the concept of *coherence* and *consistence*. To make sense of complex, ambiguous and contradictory information, coherent stories are developed. Information in support of the narrative is accepted while contradicting information is rejected.[4] Rationalization is about creating sound narratives – whether they align with the truth is a completely different question.

---

[1] See https://dictionary.apa.org/rationalization (last accessed on 23 February 2023).

[2] *F. Cushman*, Rationalization is rational, Behavioral and Brain Sciences 43 (2020), 1–59, 1.

[3] Rationalization is a phenomenon that is connected to a variety of cognitive biases and dissonances. For an overview and sources, see *Cushman* (n. 2), 2.

[4] In relation to juror decision-making, see e.g. *J. Nadler/P. Mueller*, Social Psychology and the Law, in: F. Parisi (ed.), The Oxford Handbook of Law and Economics, vol. 1 (2017), 124–160, 126, with further references. *J.M. Balkin*, Understanding Legal Understanding: The Legal Subject and the Problem of Legal Coherence, Yale Law Journal 103 (1993), 105–

Insofar as the actual reasoning for one's behaviour is crucial, (post hoc) rationalization poses problems. In order to establish criminal wrongdoing on the conceptual basis of *personal misconduct*,[5] we would need to be able to determine what actually motivated someone and to separate antecedent reasoning from any post hoc rationalization. Since criminal proceedings are *post hoc* by nature, asking people about their prior mental events (e.g. past decisions, witnessed events) generally involves rationalization. *Introspection* – i.e., exploring one's prior mental events – pressures the agent to rationalize his own behaviour.[6] This cannot be avoided because it is simply how the brain works. What can be influenced is how we deal with the information people give us about their prior mental events: We would have to try to avoid cognitive biases and dissonances (e.g. the anchor effect) that could be caused by receiving an account of past events that might have been highly influenced by rationalization.

In his essay, *Kurek* mostly addresses rationalization as a sense-making process of the *onlooker*. He uses the term rationalization in a very specific and somewhat different way than defined above: he defines rationalization as "the human cognitive capacity to explain and predict the behaviour of other persons in terms of reasons for action". Insofar, rationalization is a social phenomenon: It is about processing information about others, making sense of their past behaviour and predicting their future conduct. He attempts to perceive it as an endeavour to gain insight into the *true* reasoning of an agent – otherwise it could not be an attempt to forecast future behaviour. In this respect, it does not suffice to attribute any sound reason which can explain an agent's behaviour. To predict an agent's future behaviour by analysing his past behaviour would require the analysis to be correct – past behaviour would have had to be based on exactly those reasons. Predicting future behaviour by logically inferring it from reasons attributed for past behaviour seems highly fallible. In addition, people can behave inconsistently: An agent's behaviour on one occasion might be soundly explainable by certain reasons but those reasons might not provide a sound explanation for the agent's behaviour in another setting (even if the parameters are the same).[7] However, people *do* anticipate behaviour of other

176, 114 ff., distinguishes three types of coherence: The first pertains to factual beliefs, the second refers to normative systems like the law and the third to making sense of the world around us.

[5] Since modern criminal law is based on culpability, this idea is core to most modern concepts of criminal law.

[6] *E. Schwitzgebel*, Introspection, in: E.N. Zalta (ed.), The Stanford Encyclopedia of Philosophy (2019 edn.), https://plato.stanford.edu/archives/win2019/entries/introspection/ (last accessed 12 February 2023).

[7] *J. Bernacer/I. Martinez-Valbuena/M. Martinez/N. Pujol/E. Luis/D. Ramirez-Castillo/M.A. Pastor*, Neural correlates of effort-based behavioral inconsistency, Cortex 113 (2019), 96–110.

human beings, and the anticipation of other people's behaviour influences one's own behaviour.[8] It is only because people anticipate behaviour that they can be confused, maybe even irritated, if the other person behaves differently.[9] It seems plausible that forecasting future behaviour is done by a simulation mechanism that takes into account the informational basis of the targeted agent (whose future behaviour is in question). It seems to be a coping mechanism for dealing with uncertainty and epistemic limitations: We do not know how the other agent will behave because we do not yet have the knowledge of all the causal factors at play in human decision-making processes, nor do we know what, for example, the agent's biochemical and neurological determinants will look like at the respective time nor do we know all the data that is going to be processed by the individual in order to make the concrete decision. So, we derive our prognosis from knowledge of human behaviour and of their needs in general as well as from knowledge about the concrete agent (including his preferences). Some of this knowledge may be acquired by rationalizing people's behaviour: People usually eat something when they are hungry (or when they find themselves in a situation in which the social convention dictates to share food) and drive to a shopping mall if they need something that can be bought there (or if they work there). As an observer, we can attribute reasons for every behavioural decision, and we therefore engage in rationalization. It also seems to be accurate that rationalization leads to good predictions of future behaviour in some simple cases. It is hardly an unwarranted assumption that a person will consume food again once he gets hungry and that he will shop at the mall again at some point if he needs something. To predict a *concrete* behaviour of an agent at a *certain* point of time would be much more difficult: When exactly will he be driving to the mall? Which food will he choose? The aptitude of rationalization as a tool to predict future behaviour depends on whether the target agent's reasons for behaving in a certain way mirror the "normal" or common reasons for the behaviour and the accuracy of the observer's knowledge about the agent's circumstances. Rationalization enables an agent to come up with behavioural expectations despite a multi-faceted lack of knowledge but, to conclude, there are certain limits.

III. Autonomy, culpability and normatively relevant behaviour

Kurek constructs his essay on the premise that events can be explained either by *causal explanation* or by *rationalization* and that those modes of explanation are categorically and qualitatively different from one another. He describes it as a dichotomy; there is no overlap. Furthermore, *Kurek* connects *rationality*

---

[8] *N. Luhmann,* Die Wissenschaft der Gesellschaft (1992), 33.

[9] *Luhmann* (n. 8), 40.

with *intentionality*. Due to the aforementioned distinction, intentionality can only be perceived as part of events that are explainable by rationalization.

On some level, rationality and intentionality are connected: An event is intended if the agent wanted it to happen, i.e., if he strives to achieve it. It is certainly true that rationalizing – and not causal – explanation is required here: Rationality comes into play when the acting agent's behaviour is *observed* by a different agent and when the observer interprets this behaviour to be goal-driven, i.e., intentional. However, this does not mean that setting the goal and deciding to follow that goal by performing a certain action cannot be understood by causal explanations. We do not have the necessary knowledge yet, but if we knew exactly and in full detail how the brain works and could determine all the criteria that drive the *concrete* decision-making process of the individual in question, then it would be explainable causally – *if* there is truly nothing metaphysical about human decision-making.

A. (In-)Determinism and normatively relevant behaviour

Kurek's two categories of *causal* and *rational* modes of explanation touch on the old controversy between determinist and indeterminist world views in a somewhat complex way. Nowadays, the determinist world view is widely accepted, but with one remaining battlefield: the debate about the existence of free will and the related question of whether human decision-making processes fall within the scope of the determinism paradigm.[10]

Human behaviour can be understood as being generally autonomous by nature only if human behaviour is the result of an autonomous decision. According to the indeterminist paradigm, human agents are understood as beings capable of causing events *without being caused*. The human being is setting his or her goals freely and independently, and his or her action can be measured against those goals by referring to rationality.[11] Whenever a behaviour *cannot* be understood as being guided by an autonomous decision, the agent does not behave in a normatively relevant fashion; his behaviour cannot be understood as infringing upon or complying with legal obligations. The event is attributed to the "causal" world.[12] In that sense, the football player who is pushed by his opponent and crashes into someone else (*Kurek*'s example) does not perform a

---

[10] Cf. e.g. *G. Caruso*, Rejecting Retributivism: Free Will, Punishment, and Criminal Justice (2021), 14 f.; *D. Dennett*/*G. Caruso*, Just Deserts: Debating Free Will (2021), passim, and *R. Kane*, Rethinking Free Will: New Perspectives on an Ancient Problem, in: idem (ed.), The Oxford Handbook on Free Will (2nd edn., 2011), 381–401; *B. Bröckers*, Strafrechtliche Verantwortung ohne Willensfreiheit (2015), 98.

[11] See *Kane* (n. 10), 384 f.

[12] Günther Jakobs attributes these normatively non-relevant events to nature, cf. *G. Jakobs*, System der strafrechtlichen Zurechnung (2012), 59 f.

normatively relevant behaviour. He is not culpable for the event; it is not the result of *his* decision.

The legal concepts of autonomy, responsibility and guilt seem to require the existence of free will. From the face of it, this seems to suggest that only the indeterminist paradigm could support rationalization as an explanatory mode. However, according to *compatibilist* stances,[13] this is not the case: It is possible to conceive responsibility and guilt even if one understands human decisions as events that are (fully) explainable by causal dynamics.[14] This has consequences for *Kurek*'s dichotomy of distinguishing two modes of explanations (rationalization and causal explanation). Rationalization would not be qualifiable as a mode of explanation genuinely different than causality – everything would be explainable by causal parameters. This does not mean that rationalization would lose its relevance as a problem-solving method. Just because there would be a causal explanation for any event does not mean that an event cannot also be analysed by asking for the *reasons* that drove the agent to undertake the action and cause the event. The individual's reasoning can – if he or she

[13] Whether moral and legal accountability is compatible with determinism is debated, see e.g. *Dennett/Caruso* (n. 10), passim. Proponents of compatibilist stances argue that moral accountability is compatible with determinism; proponents of incompatibilist stances argue the opposite, see e.g. *Bröckers* (n. 10), 23, 98 f. This descriptive meaning of an (in-)compatibilist stance needs to be distinguished from the descriptive meaning of an (in-)compatibilist stance in the discussion on whether free will is compatible with determinism, see e.g. *Caruso* (n. 10), 13 f. The categorization of an account as (in-)compatibilist refers to how it answers the question of compatibility of one thing/concept with another. To avoid confusion, it is important to pay attention to what the account refers to when discussing compatibility. The question of whether free will is compatible with determinism is *different* than the one of whether determinism is compatible with moral/legal accountability. If you take a compatibilist stance in one discussion it does not necessarily follow that you need to take a compatibilist stance in the other.

[14] See *Kane* (n. 10), 381; *G. Caruso/D. Pereboom*, Moral Responsibility Reconsidered (2022); *T. Hörnle*, Kriminalstrafe ohne Schuldvorwurf: Ein Plädoyer für Änderungen in der strafrechtlichen Verbrechenslehre (2013), 51 ff.; *B. Bröckers* (n. 10); *R.D. Herzberg*, Willensunfreiheit und Schuldvorwurf (2010), 265 ff.; *idem*, Das Anderskönnen in der strafrechtlichen Schuldlehre, in: J.C. Bublitz et al. (eds.), Recht – Philosophie – Literatur: Festschrift für Reinhard Merkel zum 70. Geburtstag (2020), 371–393, 387 ff.; *S. Behrendt*, Entzauberung des Rechts auf informationelle Selbstbestimmung: Eine Untersuchung zu den Grundlagen der Grundrechte (2023), ch. 19 B. Mostly, the discussion revolves around the practice and/or the legitimacy of ascribing responsibility and accountability, cf. *Bröckers* (n. 10), 259 ff.; *Hörnle*, op.cit., 51 ff. Additionally, there is a discussion on whether believing in (causal) determinism is compatible with rational deliberation, see e.g., *G. Caruso*, On the Compatibility of Rational Deliberation and Determinism: Why Deterministic Manipulation is not a Counterexample, The Philosophical Quarterly 71 (2021), 524–543, 524. Deliberation-incompatibilists argue against the compatibility of a person believing in determinism and being rational and engaging in deliberation. Deliberation-compatibilists argue in favour of it.

acted upon it – call for a response.[15] Because we cannot determine the necessity of a response by referring to the actual reasoning of another agent (due to epistemic limitations), we need to refer to rationalization.

B. Legal accountability and normatively relevant decision

Insofar as *Kurek*'s approach aims at differentiating between events for which an agent can be held *accountable* and events for which he could not be, the concept seems to leave a gap.

Legal accountability can be established even if the cognitive processes of the acting agent lack rationality from the perspective of the observer. The observer's judgment about the acting agent's behaviour in terms of *rationality* can be separated from the question of whether the agent's behaviour was actually based on a *normatively relevant decision.* A normatively relevant decision requires that the concrete cognitive processes have taken sufficient data into account to arrive at a rational decision and be sufficiently complex.[16] It does not necessarily meet the observer's understanding of a rational decision – if that were the case, there could be no criminal liability for an "irrational attempt". Whether *Kurek*'s approach roughly matches the existing differentiation is not clear. His approach *could* entail that those cases commonly classified as irrational attempts would be qualifiable as rational attempts by way of thorough mental simulation. The common classification refers to the judgement of an "objective third party" in terms of the rationality of the attempt but, according to *Kurek*, mental simulation requires putting yourself in the shoes of the acting agent and acknowledging the difference between yourself and the person whose behaviour is rationalized. Whether *Kurek*'s approach leaves room for irrational attempts depends on how far he would take the idea of mental simulation.

Normatively relevant behaviour is not limited to *intentional* – and thus rationalizable – behaviour: Not every act of human behaviour is perceivable as goal-oriented and non-intentional behaviour may still be normatively relevant. An agent might cause an event by being negligent even though he did not arrive at a sufficiently reasonable decision about creating the risk as long as he could and should have. Negligent behaviour can thus be normatively relevant if it is based on cognitive processes with which the agent *could* have arrived at a

---

[15] Cf. *R.A. Duff*, Guiding Commitments and Criminal Liability for Attempts, Criminal Law and Philosophy 3 (2012), 411–427, 417 f.; *idem*, Responsibility and Reciprocity, Ethical Theory and Moral Practice 21 (2018), 775–787, 776 ff.

[16] *H. Frister*, Die Struktur des "voluntativen Schuldelements" – zugleich eine Analyse des Verhältnisses von Schuld und positiver Generalprävention (1993), 120; *Behrendt* (n. 14), ch. 19 B.; *eadem*, Die beiden Säulen der Rechtssubjektivität: Autonomie und Anerkennung eines grundrechtstheoretischen Rechtsverhältnisses als Fundamente für die Entstehung von Rechtssubjektivität, Rechtstheorie 52 (2021), 45–68, 51, 54 ff.

normatively relevant decision but did not due to his/her negligence. The behaviour in question does not have to be specifically goal-driven to be normatively relevant negligent behaviour in this sense. However, negligence can also be a *by-product* of intentional behaviour: When you want event x to occur and intend to achieve it by performing a certain task, you might be unaware that this will also lead to event y. The occurrence of this event would not be explainable by rationalization; the agent would *not* have made a sufficiently reasonable decision about creating the risk – if such a decision had occurred, he would have wilfully created the risk. Insofar as negligence occurs as a by-product of intentional behaviour, it might fall within *Kurek*'s definition of rational – and therefore normatively relevant – behaviour. However, not all cases of negligence can be understood in this manner.

As a consequence, the observer does not necessarily have to perceive the behaviour of the other agent as rational to consider the behaviour as normatively relevant. He only needs to perceive that person as being *capable* of making rational decisions.[17] Whether the behaviour can normatively trigger a response (e.g. punishment) depends on whether it was truly based on a normatively relevant decision (or could have been but was not due to negligent behaviour).[18] It is important to differentiate between the *attribution of rationality* and the *ontological substrate* which is required for a normatively relevant decision.[19] The fact that the observer calls the rationality of the attempt into question does not necessarily mean that there is no normatively relevant behaviour. The existence of normatively relevant behaviour does not depend on whether or not the observer thinks that the behaviour is explainable by rationalization.

Human beings have limited insight into the real world. They perceive the world not as it is; it is always a hermeneutic endeavour.[20] People are limited by the constraints of their physical senses, their cognitive capacities, the limitations of biological data processing and so forth. This means that a normatively relevant decision cannot require that the cognitive results have led to an objectively correct result – even if it would only need to be "objectively correct" in relation to the goals set by the individual. To be clear: I am not stating that it

---

[17] Cf. *M. Pawlik*, Normbestätigung und Identitätsbalance: Über die Legitimation staatlichen Strafens (2017), 10 f.; *T. Scanlon*, Moral Dimensions: Permissibility, Meaning, Blame (2008), 139 f.

[18] *Frister* (n. 16), 126 ff.; *idem*, Überlegungen zu einem agnostischen Begriff der Schuldfähigkeit, in: G. Freund et al. (eds.), Grundlagen und Dogmatik des gesamten Strafrechtssystems: Festschrift für Wolfgang Frisch zum 70. Geburtstag (2013), 533–554, 546 ff.; *idem*, Strafrecht Allgemeiner Teil (9th edn., 2020), ch. 18 paras. 12–14.

[19] *Behrendt* (n. 14), ch. 19 B.

[20] Hermeneutics is the study of interpretation in general; it is not only about understanding texts, see e.g. *T. George*, Hermeneutics, in: E.N. Zalta (ed.), The Stanford Encyclopedia of Philosophy (2021 edn.), https://plato.stanford.edu/archives/win2021/entries/hermeneutics/ (last accessed 12 February 2023).

is always impossible to get it right when it comes to perceiving the world. Determining whether there are three apples on the table in front of oneself is a task most adults would master effortlessly. Being brought up in an environment in which apples are available everywhere and are commonly described with that term, the agent has simply learned all he needed to learn to make sense of the world insofar as he can reliably perceive an object that is described as an apple and distinguish it from other objects. However, normatively relevant decisions are not only about perceiving the world, they are about concretizing interests and about understanding and accepting or creating risks or chances. The decision to pick one of the apples up and eat it seems to be perceivable as a normatively relevant decision without any difficulties. However, whether and to what extent there are normatively relevant decisions requires more substance than that: It would be about understanding what eating that apple would mean regarding one's own interests and the interests of others. Usually, eating an apple does not cause any problems in that respect either, but what if the person eating the apple is a diabetic and eating that apple would cause him/her bodily harm? What if someone else would need that apple to stay alive? If we conceptualize normatively relevant decisions in this manner, the question would be whether the agent (1) has processed data that is deemed to be sufficient to decide about the risk/the chance in a normatively relevant fashion and (2) whether the cognitive processes were sufficiently complex.[21] This would be an unavoidably interdisciplinary issue: Drawing the line between sufficiently and non-sufficiently complex cognitive processes would be a *normative* issue, but the law does not provide the necessary insight into the *ontology* of cognitive processes.

If the behaviour of the acting agent is based on a decision that meets these criteria, it will qualify as a normatively relevant behaviour. At first glance, neuroscientific research casts doubt on the thesis that behaviour can actually be *based* on a decision: If the decision is made *after* the action has already been performed, the behaviour cannot be based on the decision. Consequently, it would not qualify as normatively relevant behaviour. The famous experiments

[21] If the circumstances of eating an apple are unproblematic, we do not have a problem with perceiving that decision as normatively relevant – we might even find it hard to argue why we should describe it like this in light of the banality of the decision. The conceptual necessity only becomes visible if we back away from only trying to solve problematic cases and try to see the big picture instead.

by *Benjamin Libet*[22] seem to suggest this.[23] However, the experiments have only shown that the *awareness* of making the decision took place after the initiation of the act – and even that is called into question because these findings relied on the recording of the participant and the measured readiness potential could be connected to other cognitive processes.[24] Furthermore, awareness cannot be a necessary element if negligent behaviour can qualify as normatively relevant. Even if awareness only took place after an action was initiated, it does not necessarily mean that there could not be any normatively relevant behaviour which is based on a wilful decision to create the risk or chance: The action might not be fully determined by the initiation but might occur only in the absence of a neural stopping sequence. If we set aside the question of whether the action was initiated by a decision that was (partially) consciously deliberated on in that particular decisive moment, we might want to consider that the factors involved in initiating that action were previously "formed" by cognitive processes. For example: Choosing and applying for a university program is behaviour which is obviously preceded by a significant amount of reflection.

C. (Ir-)rational attempts and the need to respond

The term "rationalization" does not seem to be a good fit for the differentiation of rational and irrational attempts. The *acting agent* will usually qualify his behaviour as rational and thus assume to undertake a rational attempt to achieve the goal – otherwise he would not have opted for said action. The *observer* can qualify action x as being a *rational* or an *irrational* means to achieve the goal (event y). If one adopted mental simulation to determine whether a rational attempt took place, it would depend on the depth and success of the endeavour to simulate the agent's mindset. In order to differentiate between rational and irrational attempts, one would have to determine what should not be considered within this process of mental simulation (otherwise every intentional behaviour would have to qualify as rational). The observer would have to engage in mental simulation (which might be somewhat superficial due to epistemic limitations) and then measure it against an abstract threshold used for labelling decision-making processes as rational.

---

[22] In reference to these experiments, see *B.W. Libet*, Do We Have Free Will?, Journal of Consciousness Studies 6 (1999), 47–57, 47 ff. For recent developments in neuroscientific research on the subject, see e.g. *I. Fried/P. Haggard/B.J. He/A. Schurger*, Volition and Action in the Human Brain: Processes, Pathologies, and Reasons, Journal of Neuroscience 37 (2017), 10842–10847; *K. Fifel*, Readiness Potential and Neuronal Determinism: New Insights on Libet Experiment, Journal of Neuroscience 38 (2018), 784–786.

[23] The experiments have been discussed thoroughly (and vigorously) mostly with regard to their implications on free will, but they also impact the related question of whether behaviour can be the result of a decision.

[24] See e.g. *Fifel* (n. 22), 784.

Whether the means are deemed (a) rational or (b) irrational by the observer can make a difference with regard to criminal law. This question touches upon the discussion about *factual* and *legal* impossibility and the controversy between *subjectivist* and *objectivist* accounts of (criminal) wrongdoing,[25] which – in turn – touch upon the challenging problem of the unavoidable subjective perception of the ontological world. A verdict of irrationality does not dismiss criminal liability, but – to simplify a very complicated discourse – the less rational the attempt, the better are the chances of criminal liability being called into question.[26] Whether criminal liability is actually called into question depends on the stance the observer takes on these conceptual matters.[27]

Additionally, we could also discuss the rationality of the reaction towards an agent's behaviour. Whether the acting agent is held criminally liable and how the state formally reacts can be subject to an analysis of rationality. Here, it is not the perpetrator's behaviour that is under scrutiny – it is about the rationality of the reaction. This relates to the academic disagreement as to whether *retributivism* or *consequentialism* is the proper justification for punishment.[28] Retributivism argues that punishment is justified simply because of the criminal wrongdoing; punishment would be in no need of further justification.[29] In contrast to this stance, consequentialism argues that punishment is justifiable only because such a response is required by a *further* reason, e.g. deterrence, norm stability (and/or trust in the validity of the behavioural norm), public safety. Consequently, the response to an agent's behaviour can also be

[25] For an overview, see e.g. *R.A. Duff*, Subjectivism, Objectivism and Criminal Attempts, in: A.P. Simester/A.T.H. Smith (eds.), Harm and Culpability (1996), 18–44; *S. Mathis*, Criminal Attempts and the Subjectivism/Objectivism Debate, Ratio Juris 17 (2004), 328–345, 330–333, and – with a slightly different perspective on the discourse – *S. Behrendt*, Attempting the Impossible: Impossibility in Criminal Law Theory and the Constructivist Discourse-Theoretical Concept of Law, Zeitschrift für Internationale Strafrechtswissenschaft 2023, 20–32, passim.

[26] Cf. *J. Hasnas*, Once More unto the Breach: The Inherent Liberalism of the Criminal Law and Liability for Attempting the Impossible, Hastings Law Review 54 (2002), 1–77, 74; *Mathis* (n. 25), 340 ff.; *A. Ashworth*, Attempts, in: J. Deigh/D. Dolinko (eds.), The Oxford Handbook of Philosophy of Criminal Law (2011), 125–144, 136 f.; *G.P. Fletcher*, Rethinking Criminal Law (1978), 160 f.

[27] In my opinion, it would be more prudent to link the issue of rationality to the question of whether it is necessary to formally respond to the behaviour (by a declaration of guilt and possibly by imposing punishment) – it is not a matter of criminal liability because a breach of a behavioural norm is conceivable. If the agent has attempted to commit a crime by use of *reasonable* means, there is cause to respond to it.

[28] For an overview, see e.g. *D. Dolinko*, Retributivism, Consequentialism, and the Intrinsic Goodness of Punishment, Law and Philosophy 16 (1997), 507–528; *G.P. Fletcher*, Punishment and Responsibility, in: D. Patterson (ed.), A Companion to Philosophy of Law and Legal Theory (2nd edn., 2010), 504–512, 506; *M.N. Berman*, Two Kinds of Retributivism, in: R.A. Duff/S. Green (eds.), Philosophical Foundations of Criminal Law (2011), 433–458.

[29] *Caruso* (n. 10), 11 f.

analysed with respect to its rationality in this regard. Furthermore, these question about the rationality of the response also touch upon the discussion about the relevance of moral luck (or more precisely outcome luck)[30] for criminal wrongdoing and blameworthiness: These issues matter with respect to the question of whether there was any criminal wrong-doing in the first place and if so, to what extent. According to some, the outcome is more than just an event that triggers the investigation of possible wrongful behaviour influence – it influences blameworthiness.

IV. Rationalization within the legal system

(Post hoc) rationalization is not privy to accountability in the realm of criminal law. The phenomenon is linked to *decisions* and is, therefore, observable everywhere. Decisions within the legal system – i.e., verdicts and judgments, legislative decisions – are not exempt since they are also human decisions. However, some decisions are made only after a long process of deliberation: Thoughts are outlined in writing, discussed in fora, and so forth. *Antecedent* rationalization is strong in those cases.[31] Making the final decision can be up to one person or a collective (e.g. parliament, panels, court senates/chambers). Collective decision-making processes work differently than those of an individual.[32] This needs to be taken into account when the rationality of a decision is in question.

Once a decision – be it an individual or a collective decision – is communicated in society, it gains its own footing. Others attribute a claim to correctness to the decision insofar as they understand the decision to be based on reason. From then on, the decider's task is to explain the decision, rationalize it, argue why it was reasonable to decide in this manner and not in another. In those

---

[30] Cf. *J.P. Manalich*, The structure of criminal attempts: An analytic approach, Revus 34 (2018), paras. 50 ff., https://journals.openedition.org/revus/4118 (last accessed 12 February 2023).

[31] Whether antecedent rationalization is conceptually possible depends on one's understanding of the term. If it were restricted to post hoc processes, it might be more prudent to describe it as strong reasoning.

[32] *W. Hoffmann-Riem*, Die Klugheit der Entscheidung ruht in ihrer Herstellung – selbst bei der Anwendung von Recht, in: A. Scherzberg et al. (eds.), Kluges Entscheiden: Disziplinäre Grundlagen und interdisziplinäre Verknüpfungen (2006), 3–23, 20. Cf. the literature on collective intentionality, collective decision-making and human rationality from a sociological stance (e.g. "discursive dilemma", "doctrinal paradox"): e.g. *L.A. Kornhauser/L.G. Sager*, Unpacking the Court, Yale Law Journal 96 (1986), 82–117; *P. Pettit*, Deliberative Democracy and the Discursive Dilemma, Philosophical Issues 11 (2001), 268–299; *C. List/P. Pettit*, Group Agency: The Possibility, Design, and Status of Corporate Agents (2011), 42 ff.

situations, additional information might come to light or the agent might understand the relevant issues more thoroughly than before. Maybe the new information/perspective would cause the agent to decide differently. How the agent deals with this dilemma (either argue for the old decision even though one does no longer believe it to be right or correct the decision even though it has already been made and communicated to others) seems to have something to do with whether the decision already had some real impact and to depend on personality traits of the agent himself (e.g. does he avoid correcting himself because he fears it would make him look weak or unreliable?). *Post-hoc rationalization* on the part of the decider in these scenarios seems to be highly influenced by socio-psychological factors.

When it comes to decisions within the legal system – a judgment, enacting a law, issuing an administrative act – an agent is bound by his own (communicated) decisions much more profoundly than by informal decisions in the social sphere. If a friend changes his mind about being free for dinner, we might be disappointed, and if it was an important event, we might expect him to have and provide a valid reason. That is, we might hold him accountable. There might even be some form of "social sanction", but the agent is generally free to change his mind. This is different if it is about a decision attributable to the state. Once made, the decision is generally out of the state's hand. After having delivered the verdict, the judge is generally bound by his decision. A post hoc written reasoning needs to support the verdict otherwise the decision may be overturned simply on the basis that the decision is unsupported by adequate reasoning. Therefore, the pressure to rationalize one's prior decision is higher than in common, non-intimate social relationships.

A. Rationality, the law and the legal system

Law as a social construct serves as a means to organize society (inter alia by setting/stabilizing behavioural expectations and thus enabling people to anticipate the behaviour of other people). According to *Jürgen Habermas*, the function of law is to relieve the individual of having to engage in communicative action in order to reach consensus because the matter is already settled by the law.[33] However, there is much more uncertainty and ambiguity to law than most of us like to believe. Disagreement and the necessity for discourse is not removed simply because there are norm texts (statutes and regulations).[34] Norm texts leave substantial room for interpretation. There is not "one right answer"

---

[33] *J. Habermas*, Faktizität und Geltung (2016), 110. See also *A. Engländer*, Grundrechte als Kompensation diskursethischer Defizite? Kritische Anmerkungen zu Jürgen Habermas' Diskurstheorie des Rechts, Archiv für Rechts- und Sozialphilosophie 81 (1995), 482–495, 484; *idem*, Diskurs als Rechtsquelle (2002), 18.

[34] Discourse theory acknowledges this fact because it acknowledges that the requirements of an ideal discourse can never be met in reality.

to the question of what the law dictates.[35] In addition, norm texts need to be seen as part of the "bigger picture": Preconceptions and other (especially higher ranking) texts impact the interpretation. Insofar as rationalization takes place in these contexts, it would seem to be about developing a plausible narrative for a certain text (norm text, decision and so forth). However, conflicting decisions can be reasoned for with equal claim to professional standards.[36] Insofar as rationalization has a (self-)deceptive element, rationalization would only take place when a decision was made for some reasons and the rationalizer explains it with *different* reasons and/or sounder reasoning.

This ambiguity and openness of law[37] does not conflict with the assumption that the law provides considerable guidance. If it did not, we would see far more chaos, conflict and legal disputes.[38] The search for consensus, the establishment of relatively stable and counterfactual behavioural expectations by means of law,[39] and the search for rationality in law and the application of law have always been core issues of legal theory. This essay does not, however, leave enough room to even sketch the discourse on this issue and the connected topics (objectivity, legitimacy etc.).

Another problem is the grander setting of decisions, and legislative decisions are no exemption. A decision might have effects that do not have anything to do with the rationality of the decision with regard to the subject matter and the axioms the decider believes to be true. If a problem is perceived from only an isolated, siloed perspective, the rational solution might cause problems elsewhere. If a member of parliament votes against the party line, for example,

---

[35] The "one-right-answer"-thesis is ascribed, inter alia, to Ronald Dworkin. Most scholars refute it, see *T. Herbst*, Die These der einzig richtigen Entscheidung: Überlegungen zu ihrer Überzeugungskraft insbesondere in den Theorien von Ronald Dworkin und Jürgen Habermas, Juristenzeitung 2012, 891–900; *C. Bäcker*, Die diskurstheoretische Notwendigkeit der Flexibilität im Recht, in: idem/S. Baufeld (eds.), Objektivität und Flexibilität im Recht (2005), 96–110, 97.

[36] See e.g. *C. Becker*, Was Bleibt? Recht und Postmoderne: Ein rechtstheoretischer Essay (2014), 74, 111.

[37] *Hoffmann-Riem* (n. 32), 4, 14; *Bäcker* (n. 35), passim.

[38] To elaborate on the basis of the constructivist discourse-theoretical concept of law: In light of the uncertainty about normative contents, the interpreter is challenged with the task of generating an understanding of what the law dictates with reference to the concrete circumstances by engaging with the norm texts and communicative acts he perceives to be relevant. Creating a concrete "ought" pressures the interpreter to be reasonable, especially if it is the lawfulness of his behaviour that is in question. If another interpreter is not convinced, reasons differently and comes to a different assessment of the law, he will judge the acting agent's behaviour according to his own perception of what the law dictates. On the basis of the constructivist discourse-theoretical view, the rationality of legal interpretation is therefore enriched with a socio-psychological element.

[39] See e.g. *N. Luhmann*, Ausdifferenzierung des Rechts: Beiträge zur Rechtssoziologie und Rechtstheorie (1999), 17; *idem*, Rechtssoziologie (1983), 342.

this might lead to a loss of influence within the party and thus weaken one's ability to support other valuable causes within the party later on. If these socio-legal and political issues are so grave that a siloed, materially rational decision would cause more harm than good, then it might be rational to decide differently.[40] The rationality of a decision therefore depends on the goal the decision is measured against.

Additionally, a politician's stance on *one* matter can be influenced by *another*, giving room for political trade-offs. The German constitution has built-in provisions to avoid this (Art. 38 (1)(2) *Grundgesetz* – GG), but some decisions are subject to party discipline. Additionally, no one can have expert knowledge on all of the subject matters that he/she has to vote on. Consequently, the party line has a big influence on some of the voting behaviour even when there is no party discipline.[41] Additionally, informal social arrangements could still take place. Whether they do take place, and to what extent, would be a matter of empirical research. Arrangements according to which a member of parliament would be obliged to vote a certain way are illegal (but would be difficult to detect). However, though policy compromises might not suit our ideals, they are to some extent necessary and well-accepted practice. Coalitions would not be possible otherwise.

Insofar as the public explanation of legislative decisions does not account for political and strategic issues (to the extent they have played a role) or the complexity of parliamentary and political processes, such explanation reduces complexity and argues a siloed material reasoning. Deploying the understanding that rationalization is a practice by which an event is explained by a plausible narrative which is expected to be more acceptable to others than the real reasoning, public explanations of legislative decisions are not exempt from rationalization.

B. Rationality, law and reality

The core function of the law is to shape society by guiding the behaviour of state and non-state actors. The law should tell them what to do and what not to do in order to achieve some sort of goal.[42] This implies a connection between law and reality because one can only meet an objective if the means – i.e., the norms or, to be more precise, the norm texts – are apt. Under the assumption that the state is fully accountable to its members, every state action needs to serve a goal. Therefore, every state action would need to be rational. What that entails depends on the subject matter and the time-sensitivity of a decision, but,

---

[40] *Hoffmann-Riem* (n. 32), 19.

[41] *M. Morlok/C. Hientzsch*, Das Parlament als Zentralorgan der Demokratie – Eine Zusammenschau der einschlägigen parlamentsschützenden Normen, Juristische Schulung 2011, 1–9, 4.

[42] See e.g. *A. Steinbach*, Rationale Gesetzgebung (2017), 10, 132 ff.

generally speaking, this means that the circumstances which determine the reality and the effectiveness of potential measures would need to be investigated before a decision is made.[43] Such an approach to legislation is often called naïve due to political realities.[44] There is some truth to this characterization. Mainly, there are two issues that impact the connection between legislative decisions and reality: (1) Parliament cannot investigate all relevant circumstances or it would never get anything done. Moreover, the necessary knowledge base is limited not only by what can possibly be investigated within a certain period of time but also by the availability of resources (some epistemic obstacles may be impossible to overcome with the methods and resources available in the present). If the state approached every task in an ideal fashion, he would most likely require more resources than are available. If this is true, then we should perceive legislation and government as a form of managing limited resources; political debates can sometimes also be framed as differences of opinion regarding prioritization. (2) Furthermore, parliamentary voting decisions are often influenced by factors that have little to do with the subject matter at hand (party line and political recognizability; the desire to be reelected, to gain power or to stay in power). While those issues point to the problems of an idealised understanding of legislation and a siloed focus on the concrete decision – they are separable from the necessity of basing a decision on sufficient knowledge about the reality.

C. Rationality, rationalization and accountability

Whether the rationality of a decision can be reviewed depends on whether the objective was communicated truthfully.[45] A decision can be rational even if no other agent can determine the rationality. However, if no review is possible, the acting agent exempts himself from accountability. Under the assumption that the state is fully accountable to its members, giving reasons would therefore be a requirement of legitimate state action. Making rational decisions does not require the communication of reasons, but accountability does – and communicating one's reasons typically implies rationalization.

[43] See e.g. *A. Gromitsaris*, Rationalität und Recht, Rechtstheorie 50 (2019), 307–328, 323 f.; *A. Steinbach*, Gesetzgebung und Empirie, Der Staat 54 (2015), 267–289; *idem* (n. 42), 132 ff. For a critical perspective, see e.g. *P. Dann*, Verfassungsgerichtliche Kontrolle gesetzgeberischer Rationalität, Der Staat 49 (2010), 630–646, 640 f.

[44] Cf. e.g. *Dann* (n. 43), 641.

[45] The differences between the production and the portrayal of a decision have been worked out most prominently by *N. Luhmann*, Legitimation durch Verfahren (1969).

V. Summary

Rationalization and rationality in law and legal theory is a scintillating and conceptually demanding topic. *Kurek* has made some intriguing and thought-provoking points. I hope to have hinted to additional and associated matters and to have insinuated their complexity. In the end, we seem to be only at the beginning of true interdisciplinary work on the topic.

Part 7

Law and Aesthetics

Aesthetic but Artefactual? – In Search of the Lost Object of Protection in Copyright Law*

Ewa Laskowska-Litak

In 1969, *Michel Foucault* published his famous and widely discussed essay titled "What Is an Author?", in which he questioned the definition of a work of art and its relationship to its author.[1] His answers sparked controversy and considerable debate in the social sciences.[2] Contrary to common aesthetic theories at that time searching for original and aesthetic properties in a work's structure, *Foucault* claimed that it is the author who identifies the work and who communicates it to the public, and therefore it is the author who shall remain the sole point of reference for a work of art.[3] A few years later, *Roland Barthes* answered the same question in his illustrious but ominously titled essay "The Death of the Author". He desanctified the figure of the author by assigning a greater role to the recipient and to the communication between authors and the public rather than to the artefact and its author.[4] This discussion occurred several decades ago, and even though it has since been superseded by new concepts from postmodernism and *Derrida*'s theory of deconstruction,[5] it has

---

* The research for this paper was funded by the National Science Centre of Poland (2016/23/D/HS5/01792). The author would like to express her gratitude to Lionel Bently, Cambridge University, and Ryszard Markiewicz, Jagiellonian University, for their support and the many relevant discussions. Any errors, inaccuracies, or omissions are the author's own.

[1] *M. Foucault*, What is an Author?, in: J.V. Harari (ed.), Textual Strategies. Perspectives in Post-Structuralist Criticism (1979), 141–160.

[2] *M. Lloyd/A. Thacker* (eds.) The Impact of Michel Foucault on the Social Sciences and Humanities (1996); *L. Downing*, The Cambridge Introduction to Michel Foucault (2008).

[3] *L. Bently*, Copyright and the Death of the Author in Literature and Law, Modern Law Review 57 (1994), 973–986; *Downing* (n. 2), 38–52.

[4] *R. Barthes*, The Death of the Author, in: *idem*, Image – Music – Text (trans. S. Heath, 2003), 142–148.

[5] *B. Stocker*, Derrida on Deconstruction (2006).

greatly influenced the humanities and social sciences. By contrast, the passionate debate in the social sciences questions has impacted the discourse on copyright law on only a relatively small scale.[6] Similarly, although cognitive science has over the past 30 years witnessed significant advances and there has been fundamental technological progress, the definition of a work in copyright law has not changed since the first international provisions emerged during the nineteenth century.[7] Against this background, the current paper aims to explore the relationship of copyright law and modern conceptions of aesthetics with particular reference to the impact that technology carries for the subject matter of copyright. The first part of the paper summarizes what impact modern technology has had on copyright law, and it explores the questions raised by modern technology as well as the challenges that the every-day use of technology poses for the current legal framework of intellectual property law. The second part provides a critical assessment of selected contemporary aesthetic theories (in particular perceptualism and the institutional theory of art) regarding the notion of a work and analyses them against the background of the current problems of copyright law. The final part discusses the possibility of re-evaluating a phenomenological approach to the notion of a work in the direction set up by modern aesthetic concepts and new technologies, pointing out the necessity of bringing a more interdisciplinary approach to the contemporary theories of copyright law.

I. Copyright law and technological progress

The very first copyright act dates back to the eighteenth century: the Statute of Anne (passed in 1710 by the Parliament of Great Britain), which, for the first time, allowed for the granting of a temporary monopoly right to a person who undertook an investment effort to publish a manuscript and introduce it to the

---

[6] *M.A. Lemley*, Romantic Authorship and the Rhetoric of Property, Texas Law Review 75 (1997), 873–906; *M. Woodmansee*, The Genius and the Copyright: Economic and Legal Conditions of the Emergence of the "Author", Eighteenth-Century Studies 17/4 (1984), 425–448; *idem*, On the Author Effect: Recovering Collectivity, Cardozo Arts and Entertainment Law Journal 10 (1992), 279–292; *P. Jaszi*, Toward a Theory of Copyright: The Metamorphoses of Authorship, Duke Law Journal 40 (1991), 455–502; *J.C. Ginsburg*, The Concept of Authorship in Comparative Copyright Law, DePaul Law Review 52 (2003), 1063–1092; *L. Bently*, R. v The Author: From Death Penalty to Community Service, Columbia Journal of Law and the Arts 32 (2019), 2–109; *M. van Eechoud* (ed.), The Work of Authorship (2014); *L. Zemer*, Three Arguments on Locke, Authorship, Communication and Solitude, WIPO Journal 7 (2015), 40–50.

[7] *Woodmansee*, Genius and Copyright (n. 6), 445–447; *Jaszi* (n. 6), 500.

market.[8] It coincided with the first court disputes between different publishers of the same books (also known as the "battle of booksellers"). The points at issue were guaranties on investment returns for, and profits resulting from, publishing works amid growing competition and the emergence of easier and cheaper print techniques. For the first time parties discussed paradigms of copyright law: What constitutes a work? How shall it be addressed in the normative framework? And what is its function regarding different publication models?[9] However, not only did the dissemination of print techniques cause a revolution in copyright law, but whenever technological progress occurred, copyright law witnessed similar challenges and disputes:[10] With the advent of pianola (piano rolls), the early US jurisprudence had to address the problem of what constitutes a musical work and its legal protection.[11] The introduction of computer programmes to the private market forced a quick (yet incomplete) introduction of their protection within the copyright regime – not without question marks and emerging criticism.[12] A similar situation took place as regards databases and *sui generis* rights in favour of the producer of a database.[13] The

[8] *Woodmansee*, Genius and Copyright (n. 6), 425, 434; *M. Rose*, Authors and Owners. The Invention of Copyright (1993), 31; *idem*, The Author as Proprietor: Donaldson v. Becket and the Genealogy of Modern Authorship, Representations 23 (1988), 51–85, 56; *Bently* (n. 6), 16.

[9] *L. Bently/B. Sherman*, The Making of Modern Intellectual Property Law (2003), 15; *U. Andersch*, Die Diskussion über den Büchernachdruck in Deutschland um 1700 bis 1815 (2018), 70 f., 73–76.

[10] *Bently/Sherman* (n. 9), 159–191.

[11] See the famous pianola case, *White-Smith Music Publishing Co. v. Apollo Co.*, 209 US 1 (1908); *J. Butt*, What is a "musical work"? Reflections on the origins of the "work concept" in western art music, in: A. Rahmatian (ed.), Concepts of music and copyright: How music perceives itself and how copyright perceives music (2015), 1–20, *G. Mania*, Muzyka w prawie autorskim (2020), 67 f.; *E. Laskowska-Litak/G. Mania*, Copyright as a service – A perspective on the axiological nature of the copyright system, in: S. Frankel (ed.), Is Intellectual Property Pluralism Functional? (2019), 267–287, 268–270.

[12] See e.g. *J.H. Reichman*, Legal Hybrids Between the Patent and Copyright Paradigms, Columbia Law Review 94 (1994), 2432–2558, 2488–2453; *P.S. Menell*, Tailoring Legal Protection for Computer Software, Stanford Law Review 39 (1987), 1329–1372, 1359–1361; *D.S. Karjala*, Copyright, Computer Software, and the New Protectionism, Jurimetrics Journal 28 (1987), 33–96; see also *G. Schricker*, Farewell to the "Level of Creativity" (Schöpfungshöhe) in German Copyright Law?, International Review of Intellectual Property and Competition Law 26 (1995), 41–48.

[13] Directive 96/9/EC of the European Parliament and of the Council of 11 March 1996 on the Legal Protection of Databases, 1996 OJ L77/20. See also *C. Garrigues*, Databases: A Subject-Matter for Copyright or for a Neighbouring Rights Regime?, European Intellectual Property Review 19 (1997), 3–5; *C. Geiger/G. Frosio/O. Bulayenko*, Text and Data Mining in the Proposed Copyright Reform: Making the EU Ready for an Age of Big Data? Legal Analysis and Policy Recommendations, International Review of Intellectual Property and Competition Law 49 (2018), 814–844.

growing popularity of internet piracy (with the invention of peer-to-peer services and their introduction to the private market) implied a broader interest in technological protection measures (particularly digital rights management systems) and autonomous protection of these innovations within copyright law.[14] And most recently, an equally controversial problem regarding the growing relevance of aggregation services in respect of press information has finally forced an introduction of a separate neighbouring right in favour of press publishers,[15] despite the concerns raised during the legislative process within the EU.[16] The same tendency can be seen in examples of the current CJEU's jurisprudence, which has evolved into a more casuistic (and technology-centred) line of judgments, in particular if we consider the detailed decisions on linking infringement cases.[17]

The above-described close relationship between technology and business models constitutes a fundamental justification for the international character of copyright regulation – national provisions are not able to address problems that have a global character as such problems do not recognise any territorial limitations.[18] The international character of copyright law is thus reflected in the shape of the normative framework that has been commonly applied in the vast majority of countries, irrespective of different national legal traditions or legislative policies. Legislation and the respective case law usually recognise the "work" as the copyright's subject matter, followed by the construction of authorship, the scope of exclusive rights (here, some national differences are found), the choice of a limitation or exception system (a closed system is

[14] See *P. Goldstein*, Copyrights Highway (2003), 170 (quoting C. Clark, the Legal Advisor to the International Publishers Copyright Council, in 1995).

[15] *L. Bently/M. Kretschmer/T. Dudenbostel/M. C. Calatrava Moreno/A. Radauer*, Strengthening the Position of Press Publishers and Authors and Performers in the Copyright Directive (2017).

[16] *Bently/Kretschmer/Dudenbostel/Calatrava Moreno/Radauer* (n. 15), 17–23.

[17] See discussion in the literature by, e.g., *N. Cordell/B. Potts*, Communication to the Public or Accessory Liability? Is the CJEU Using Communication to the Public to Harmonise Accessory Liability across the EU?, European Intellectual Property Law Review 40 (2018), 289–294; *J. Nordemann*, Recent CJEU Case Law on Communication to the Public and Its Application in Germany: A New EU Concept of Liability, Journal of Intellectual Property Law & Practice 13 (2018), 744–756; *E. Rosati*, Why the CJEU Cheese Copyright Case Is Anything but Cheesy, Journal of Intellectual Property Law & Practice 12 (2017), 813 f.

[18] The international tendency to create and maintain a relatively harmonised legal framework for intellectual property law should not raise any concerns. As of today, copyright law is the subject of more than 200 international agreements (not counting bilateral agreements), these including 26 agreements that are administered by the WIPO, the international organisation created as part of WTO for the sole purpose of governing intellectual property goods, 15 EU directives, 2 regulations, and several additional instruments governing the EU system of copyright law.

usually recognised in continental Europe; an open system of fair dealing/fair use clauses is found in common law countries), and infringement constructions (secondary, primary, or accessory liability and a system of remedies and enforcement mechanisms).

It is the notion of a work that remains the common denominator and, thus, the cornerstone of every copyright's normative framework. In essence, one is able to reduce the notion of a work to two key elements: the "fixation" requirement (a copyright subsists only with respect to fixated forms of expression[19]) and the originality requirement (which, under EU law, is also known as the requirement of the "author's own intellectual creation"[20]). The rationale of the first requirement is the assumption of the objectivity for legal relationships and trade circulation. Only such expressions might constitute a copyright's subject matter which can be an object of human perception. In the advent of rapid technological development and the growing availability of luxury or cuisine products, a question was raised whether a copyright's subject matter may subsist in cases of perception based on the sense of smell or taste. From the CJEU's decision on the *Levola Hengelo* case, it follows that aural or olfactory identification might introduce too much subjectivity.[21] Thus, currently the first requirement still excludes such works from copyright's regime. The justification for the second requirement – the creativity premise (also known as originality requirement in common law countries) – refers to a copyright's main function: to grant temporary exclusive rights solely to those authors whose intellectual efforts can be distinguished as compared with commonly available and known intellectual goods. The originality requirement aims (but in practice usually fails) to exclude from protection works that are banal, typical, or present

[19] For instance, according to the Polish Copyright Act, only a fixated form of expression constitutes a work of authorship.

[20] This requirement has been confirmed by a relatively constant line of judgments starting with the Infopaq decision: ECJ, judgment of 16 July 2009, Case C-5/08 – Infopaq International A/S v. Danske Dagblades Forening; later affirmed by, e.g., ECJ, judgment of 1 December 2011, Case C-145/10 – Eva-Maria Painer v. Standard Verlags GmbH; ECJ, judgment of 22 December 2010, Case C-393/09 Bezpečnostní softwarová asociace – Svaz softwarové ochrany v. Ministerstvo kultury; see also *E. Rosati*, Originality in EU Copyright: Full Harmonisation through Case Law (2013); *S. van Gompel/E. Lavik*, Quality, Merit, Aesthetics and Purpose: An Inquiry into EU Copyright Law's Eschewal of Other Criteria than Originality, RIDA – Revue Internationale Du Droit d'Auteur 236 (2013), 100–295; *E. Laskowska-Litak*, Between Scylla and Charybdis: A Comparative Look at Copyright's Protected Subject Matter and the (CJ)EU Harmonization, Journal of Intellectual Property Law & Practice 14 (2019), 761–770.

[21] ECJ, judgment of 13 November 2018, Case C-310/17 – Levola Hengelo BV v. Smilde Foods BV; *S. van Gompel*, Smaak, auteursrecht en objectafbakening: over perceptie en bepaalbaarheid, Tijdschrift voor auteurs-, media & informatierecht 43 (2019), 9–16; *C. Sganga*, The notion of work in EU copyright law after Levola Hengelo: one answer given, three question marks ahead, European Intellectual Property Review 41 (2019), 415–424.

obvious solutions. Considered together, both requirements exclude mere ideas from protection. Furthermore, they do not allow a monopolisation over vague concepts. From the point of view of the law's recipients, it would be as unjustified a solution as allowing subjective judgements based solely on the personal feelings or taste of judges.[22]

Even though it seems to be justified to reduce the notion of a work to these two key elements, it also raises concerns when one considers contemporary technologies, their impact on everyday life, and their potential further development. The first concern relates to the relatively excessive emphasis on a necessary reification (or objectification) of a copyright's subject matter, excluding every immaterial good that might not fit the aforementioned definition of an artefact.[23] Consequently, "works" like a smell of a perfume[24] or the taste of a cheese[25] are not considered as being protected under copyright law, even if their commercial, aesthetic, or cultural value is commonly recognised and appreciated. On the one hand, this guarantees a certain objectivity in identifying a copyright's subject matter. On the other hand, it also excludes some valuable assets resulting from modern technologies: the interactivity of a computer game,[26] the functionality of computer code,[27] or the responsiveness of a website.[28] If compared with a general classification of a computer program as a literary work, one may conclude that copyright law might not fit the digital age

---

[22] *B. Brożek*, The Legal Mind: A New Introduction to Legal Epistemology (2019), 11–37; *L. Tvrdíková*, Do Not Ignore the Elephant … Exploring the Role of Intuition and Experience in Judicial Decision-Making, in: T. Smejkalová et al. (eds.) Argumentation 2021. International Conference on Alternative Methods of Argumentation in Law (2021), 32–50, 39–41.

[23] *J. Pila*, The subject matter of intellectual property: inventions, works, signs and designs (2017), 8–11.

[24] See, however, the opposite approach by the Dutch Hoge Raad, decision of 16 June 2006, C04/327HR, Lancome Parfums et Beaute et Cie SNC v. Kecofa BV, International Review of Intellectual Property and Competition Law 37 (2006), 997. See also *C.C. von Scholten Illum*, On Copyright Protection of Smell, Taste and Texture, European Intellectual Property Review 34 (2012), 704–710.

[25] See the Levola Hengelo case (n. 21). See also *T. Su Li Cheng*, Copyright Protection of Haute Cuisine: A Recipe for Disaster?, European Intellectual Property Review 30 (2008), 93–101, 99.

[26] *J. Griffiths*, Infopaq, BSA and the "Europeanisation" of United Kingdom, Media & Arts Law Review 16 (2015), 59–72; *I. Stamatoudi*, Copyright and Multimedia Products. A Comparative Analysis (2001), 3–5, 18–20; *N. Hitsevich*, The Accessibility of a Website as a Basis of Jurisdiction in the Case of IPR Infringement over the Internet, Journal of Intellectual Property Law & Practice 11 (2016), 846–855, 854.

[27] *P. Samuelson*, Functionality and Expression in Computer Programs: Refining the Tests for Software Copyright Infringement, Berkeley Technology Law Journal 31 (2016), 1215–1300.

[28] *Hitsevich* (n. 26), 854.

and will not be able to respond to all future technological developments (e.g. works generated by artificial intelligence).

Even though such limitations of present copyright law may be acceptable as they reflect current legislation policies, this issue nevertheless relates to the second concern which I would like to raise – an ever lower threshold with respect to the originality requirement. The problem with the judicial tendency to lower the threshold of originality and grant exclusive rights in cases of questionable works (simple, banal solutions; *kleine Münze*) is already known and has been the subject of wide criticism.[29] In the advent of an increasing tendency to expand monopoly rights, it is surprising that copyright scholars rarely discuss alternatives to the contemporary interpretations of the originality requirement.[30] Moreover, regarding the broadly understood reification of a copyright's subject matter, the lack of uniformly developed interpretations of the notion of originality, individuality, or one's "own intellectual creation"[31] gradually leads to the replacement of vague notions like "individuality" or "originality" with even more vague or arbitrary criteria as to whether the work in question has an appropriate "structure", whether it is constructed in a "specific" ("original" or "individual") way, or whether it is reflected in a form already recognised in the literature or within professional circles.

For instance, in the Polish case, where the work in question was a breadbox, it was confirmed that "the concrete product has to be substantially distinguishable from the other products of this kind and that it furthermore has to be in such way different from other products that, at the same time, it is to be considered as the result of a creative process", yet in the written rulings of the courts of the different instances, there is no indication of what methodology was used in choosing the comparative material for such a test.[32]

The Polish Supreme Court's decision of 1969 provides us with another example concerning the originality of a research paper: the Court required "development of a substantive formula, a creative transfer of data from files to the manuscript including map legends that are attached to the work, and a creative editing of the entire paper".[33] Two objections may be raised against this decision. Firstly, according to the court, for a copyright to subsist in the case of a research paper, the work in question must contain certain elements recognised

---

[29] *J. Nordell*, The Notion of Originality – Redundant or not?, Scandinavian Studies in Law 42 (2002), 97–111; *van Gompel/Lavik* (n. 20), 16; *A. Ohly*, The Case for Partial Cumulation in Germany, in: E. Derclaye (ed.), The Copyright/Design Interface: Past, Present and Future (2018), 128–170, 154 f.

[30] However, there are exceptions; these will be mentioned in subsequent paragraphs.

[31] ECJ, judgment of 16 July 2009, Case C-5/08 – Infopaq International A/S v. Danske Dagblades Forening.

[32] Polish Appellate Court Warsaw, judgment of 1 February 1995, I ACz 1208/94 (author's translation).

[33] Polish Supreme Court, judgment of 9 May 1969, I CR 77/69 (author's translation).

by the court (attachments, descriptions, data edits, etc.), but the court leaves unanswered the question of why these elements (and no other) were decisive for the research paper's constituting a subject matter of a copyright. And secondly, even if we agree on the fact that it is not the mentioned elements of a work that are constitutive for the subject matter of copyright, but its creativity or originality, it was not fully explained how or according to what standard the "editing of the whole paper" was "creative".

In another judgment of the Polish Appellate Court, disputed pictures were described as "attractive [and] interesting, especially among such companies dealing with extreme sports, [so that these pictures] may be considered as the subject matter of copyright". The photos showed a person during a skateboard competition while jumping against the background of a building and observing residents.[34] There are, however, no indications of how the attractiveness of the pictures was measured, nor did the court provide criteria for the "interesting character" and identification of the copyright's subject matter, which here would be solely based on the court's evaluative description relating to the content depicted in the photo (jumping person, background, and the people involved). It is also worth mentioning that the description referring to the skateboard competition contextualises the photo even though from the photo itself it might not be possible to recognise this specific context. The question thus remains whether the context or the background of a work must be a part of a judicial (therefore normative) description of a copyright's subject matter.

Another example reflects a disputed (yet several times confirmed) line of judgments of Polish courts regarding "a specification of the essential terms of the contract" (also known as a "specification for goods and services procurement"). In several decisions, Polish courts have argued in favour of the status of a copyright's subject matter because of the uniqueness of the use of specific clauses or phrases applied in the disputed specifications.[35] This line of judgments expands copyright law beyond being a concept (a concept of a compilation of contractual provisions) and reduces the requirement of originality to a statistical analysis of how often or how possible it is for an author to apply a specific combination of clauses.

Finally, it is worth mentioning the decision by the appellate court in Warsaw regarding an advertisement designed for a real estate developer's media campaign. According to the court, the advertisement had an original character because it was "an artistic composition […], organised around the building's outline, which – in the shape of a gable roof with the defendant's logo integrated and two vertical walls having a maroon stripe at the bottom – is a permanent

[34] Polish Appellate Court, judgment of 8 November 2012, I ACa 602/12 (author's translation).

[35] Polish Appellate Court, judgment of 23 October 2015, I ACa 121/15. Similarly, Polish Supreme Court, judgment of 3 February 2017, II CSK 400/16.

compositional element of all the plaintiff's advertisements".[36] The quoted description of the copyright's subject matter includes both an aesthetic evaluation of the work in question ("artistic composition"), and it focuses on the structure of the disputed objects (a detailed description of the roof, the walls, and the defendant's logo).

In summary, both the terminology used to describe the notion of a work and the interpretation of a copyright's subject matter as applied in the quoted court's decision reflect an increasing tendency to reify the abstract intangible good (copyright's subject matter) and to identify it as a reflection of descriptive tangible properties. The objectification of a copyright's subject matter alone might not justify too much criticism. However, when trying to verify the originality threshold by analysing the disputed artefact itself (considering its internal properties such as its structure, features, and characteristics), this might end with a gradual ossification of the notion of a work.[37] Finally, the following question remains: How should we address future problems regarding the notion of a work if already today there are multiple difficulties in determining what the subject of copyright law can be?

II. The abandonment of the structuralist approach in aesthetics

In copyright theory, there have been several attempts to use aesthetic concepts to justify and construct a model for the protection of the copyright's subject matter. For example, *Alois Troller*, *Eugen Ulmer*, and *Joseph Kohler* explicitly referred to *Nicolai Hartmann*'s theory,[38] and Polish scholar *Andrzej Kopff* implemented *Roman Ingarden*'s phenomenological theory of a layered structure of a work of art in the Polish copyright law.[39] Inspired by *Hartmann*'s approach to the notion of a work of art, *Troller* argued for a structured interpretation of a copyright's subject matter, which consists of two layers: an external layer (*Vordergrund*) and an internal layer (*Hintergrund*). Only by combining these two layers – reflecting a constant character (*Daseinkonstanz*), which is provided by the external layer, and the beauty of a work (*ästhetischer Reiz*), which is provided by the internal layer[40] – it is possible to identify a whole work.[41] A similar approach has been implemented in jurisprudence, as the above-mentioned examples from the Polish courts prove. It could be summarised as a

[36] Polish Appellate Court, judgment of 29 June 2007, I ACa 546/07.

[37] *Laskowska-Litak* (n. 20), 769.

[38] *J. Kohler*, Urheberrecht an Schriftwerken und Verlagsrecht (1906); *E. Ulmer*, Urheber- und Verlagsrecht (3rd edn., 1980); *A. Troller*, Immaterialgüterrecht, 2 vol. (1985).

[39] *A. Kopff*, Dzieło sztuk plastycznych i jego twórca w świetle przepisów prawa autorskiego, (1961).

[40] *Troller*, vol. 1 (n. 38), 446.

[41] See also *Kopff* (n. 39), 433 f.

strategy for recognising specific internal properties of a work that should justify their qualification as a copyright's subject matter (e.g. external/internal layers).

However, the structuralist approach to the notion of a work of art has been the subject of criticism in aesthetics. The postmodernist shift towards Derridean deconstructionism and the influence of *Wittgenstein*'s analytical philosophy have broadened the discussion in aesthetic theory so as to include many new trends and concepts relating to, *inter alia*, the definition or qualification of a work of art.[42] By referring to these trends in aesthetic theory, *Richard Shusterman* formulated in aesthetics philosophy three general propositions indicating the necessity of abandoning a phenomenological approach as a way to define a work of art: a radical indeterminacy of notions; a logical multiplicity of aesthetic discourse; and a historical character of art and aesthetic evaluation.[43] The first proposition challenges the deductive model of argumentation in aesthetics – a method that is based on observing an artefact itself in order to define it. Contrary to the phenomenological approach, contemporary aesthetic concepts do not consist of analysis of the artefact (also known as dissection of an artefact)[44] but instead focus on different methods to identify and describe it. In his second proposition, *Shusterman* underlines the existence of a multiplicity of aesthetic predicates and contexts that they are applied to:[45] for an appropriate decoding of the notion of a concrete work, it is necessary to take into consideration its context and to reflect on its whole cultural complexity and meaning.[46] The third point rightly stresses that every historical era creates its own cultural characteristics, influencing the rules, traditions, and the character of the art created at a specific point in time. Consequently, the identification of a work of art implies recognising the moment of its creation by taking into account the cultural and historic foundations of that era.[47]

---

[42] *A. Carr/P. Hancock*, Art and Aesthetics at Work: An Overview, Journal of Critical Postmodern Organization Science 2/1 (2002), 1–7; *B. Gaut/D. McIver Lopes* (eds.), The Routledge Companion to Aesthetics (2013); *A. Savile*, A History of Modern Aesthetics, British Journal of Aesthetics 55 (2014), 406–409.

[43] *R. Shusterman*, Wittgenstein and Aesthetic Argument, in: R. Haller (ed.), Aesthetics – Proceeding of the 8th International Wittgenstein Symposium (1984), 44–46.

[44] Such an approach was rejected due to the limitations of descriptive language and based on an assumption that any aesthetic notion should remain vague and flexible: *Shusterman* (n. 43), 44 f.

[45] *L. Sosnowski*, Sztuka. Historia. Teoria. Światy Arthura C. Danto (2007), 190.

[46] *L. Wittgenstein*, Lectures and Conversations on Aesthetics, Psychology and Religious Belief (1970), 2 f. It is worth mentioning that such a statement is in accordance with the information theory developed by *L. Floridi*, The philosophy of information (2013).

[47] *Wittgenstein* (n. 46), 23. Critically *W. Eltron*, Aesthetics and Language (1954), 13–35; affirmative *W.E. Kennick*, Does Traditional Aesthetics Rest on a Mistake?, Mind 67/267 (1958), 317–334, 319; *M. Sułkowska*, Postwittgensteinowska estetyka analityczna, in: A. Noras/D. Kubok (eds.), Między kantyzmem a neokantyzmem (2012), 112–129.

This approach has been adopted in the broadly discussed concept of aesthetic perceptualism. Its most prominent representative was *Monroe C. Beardsley*, who defined a work of art as an arrangement of conditions intended to be capable of affording an aesthetic experience.[48] According to *Beardsley*, the assessment of an artefact is determined only by its external factors. The author's intention to provide an aesthetic character is the basic point of reference for the assessment of the nature of a work of art and may manifest itself in the use of particular tools or means of artistic expression, for example, in the title of the work or in the application of appropriate artistic conventions. Hence, it is not about the subjective intention but rather its manifestations that can be verified by an external recipient[49] (and not the internal structure of an artefact). However, the concept of including the artist's intention into an identification of a work of art is limited: the intention to create a work does not extend to the intention of providing a specific meaning and does not imply that the work will eventually be interpreted according to that meaning initially intended by the artist.[50] To put it simply, the author's intention does not have to be successful. Additionally, artistic conventions and the manner in which a work of art is created are of great relevance in identifying a work of art.[51] Reference to them or the use of typical forms of expression is a visible manifestation of the intention to create a work of art. On the other hand, artistic conventions do change and they are not imposed top down by the artworld;[52] they are always exposed to current trends and undergo certain changes – exactly like technology or artistic practices.

Beardsley's approach was severely criticised, mainly because of its inconsistency in defining the aesthetic experience.[53] Although *Beardsley* attempted to address the criticism and presented various (even phenomenological) approaches on how to determine the aesthetic experience of the recipient, these were not satisfactory solutions[54] – partially due to the lack of scientific proof (in particular through cognitive or neuro-aesthetic studies), partially due to the

---

[48] *M. Beardsley*, Redefining Art, in: M. Wreen/D.M. Callen (eds.), The Aesthetic Point of View (1982), 298–315; *idem*, In Defense of Aesthetic Value, Proceedings and Addresses of the American Philosophical Association 52/6 (1979), 723–749; *S. Davies*, Definitions of Art (1991), 52 f.; *idem*, Aesthetic judgements, artworks and functional beauty, Philosophical Quarterly 56 (2006), 224–241.

[49] On the distinction between internal and external evidence, *M. Beardsley*, An Aesthetic Definition of Art, in: H. Curtler (ed.) What Is Art? (1983), 15–29, 20; *W.K. Wimsatt/M. Beardsley*, The Intentional Fallacy, The Sewanee Review 54 (1946), 468–488.

[50] *Beardsley*, Aesthetic Definition of Art (n. 49), 18 f., 21, 25 f.

[51] *Davies*, Definitions of Art (n. 48), 203 f.

[52] The term "the artworld" was initially introduced by A. Danto and later used by G. Dickie, though not without disagreement arising from the several proposals the second author presented, see *Davies*, Definitions of Art (n. 48), 81.

[53] *Davies*, Definitions of Art (n. 48), 66–69.

[54] *A. Danto*, Transfiguration of the Commonplace (1981).

fact that "the aesthetic experience" constitutes a rather vague notion. One of the most important accusations raised against perceptualism is the disregard of the fact that an aesthetic experience might be significantly affected by the recipients' awareness that they are dealing with a work of art, which in itself contradicts the objectivity of the discussed criterion.[55]

Interestingly, perceptualism has been discussed in copyright doctrine.[56] For example, having analysed the possibility of the implementation of such an approach into copyright law,[57] *Robert Kirk Walker* and *Ben Depoorter* identified copyright case law that reflects a perceptualistic approach to a work (e.g., *Burrow-Giles Lithographic Company v. Sarony*[58]). In their opinion, the courts have already recognised the author's intention as a relevant indication of the fixation requirement.[59] In *Mazer v. Stein*,[60] one of the reasons for rejecting copyright status for handcrafted statuettes was that the plaintiff had the intention to use the disputed objects as objects of utility desk lamps) rather than as works protected under copyright law.[61] By adopting such a position, one may as well argue that in the *Painer* case – where the copyright status of portrait photographs was at issue[62] – the CJEU implemented a perceptualistic perspective by referring to the manifestations of the author's intentional actions in the disputed photograph's features:[63]

"In the preparation phase, the photographer can choose the background, the subject's pose and the lighting. When taking a portrait photograph, he can choose the framing, the angle of view and the atmosphere created. Finally, when selecting the snapshot, the photographer may choose from a variety of developing techniques the one he wishes to adopt or, where appropriate, use computer software. By making those various choices, the author of a portrait photograph can stamp the work created with his 'personal touch'."

The British decision in *Ravenscroft v. Herbert and New English Library Ltd.*[64] may also be interpreted as following the perceptualistic approach. The case involved two literary works – the former being a fictional novel and the latter

[55] *Danto* (n. 54), 13.

[56] In particular *R.K. Walker/B. Depoorter*, Unavoidable Aesthetic Judgments in Copyright Law: A Community of Practice Standard, Northwestern University Law Review 109 (2015), 343–381.

[57] *Walker/Depoorter* (n. 56), 355.

[58] 111 US 53 (1884). See also *A.C. Yen*, Copyright Opinions and Aesthetic Theory, Southern California Law Review 71 (1998), 247–302.

[59] See e.g. *Brandir International, Inc. v. Cascade Pacific Lumber Co.*, 834 F2d 1142 (1987); *C.H. Farley*, Judging Art, Tulane Law Review 79 (2005), 805–858, 846 f.; *Yen* (n. 58), 281.

[60] 347 US 201 (1954), 204 f.

[61] See the analysis by *Yen* (n. 58), 282.

[62] ECJ, judgment of 1 December 2011, Case C-145/10 – Eva-Maria Painer v. Standard Verlags GmbH and Others.

[63] ECJ, judgment of 1 December 2011, Case C-145/10, paras. 91 f.

[64] [1980] RPC 193.

being a nonfictional work from which the former drew historical motifs. The court held that the novelty (originality) of a work should be reflected in the elements created with purposes of catching the interest of recipients and of providing them with a pleasure of experiencing such a work – contrary to the documentary purpose of nonfictional novels, which aim at passing knowledge to recipients.[65] Consequently, because one of the disputed books was fiction and the latter was historical nonfiction, both of the works were considered two autonomous copyright subject matters.[66]

Beardsley's perceptualism is often contrasted with the institutional theory of art, which was introduced and developed by *George Dickie*. In his concept, the status of a work of art rests on two pillars: It is determined by whether it is (1) an artefact and (2) at the same time a candidate for appreciation by some person or persons who are acting on behalf of the artworld.[67] Thus, the creation of a work does not suffice on its own to grant it an artistic status – it is the recipient's reaction that is also of great relevance; and not that of average recipients, but of experts, of members of the artworld.[68] According to *Dickie*, there are, thus, two points of reference for identifying a work of art: its artifactuality and its institutionality.[69]

The first pillar, regarding the object's artifactuality, directly refers to philosophical works by *Marcia Eaton* and *Richard Scalfani*. According to *Eaton*, for an object to be qualified as an artefact, some handcrafted intentional action is required.[70] *Scalfani*, on the other hand, argued that an object might be considered an artefact solely if it was used with the intention to become an artefact or if the process of creating the object was at least initiated with such intention.[71] In the case that some handcraft needs to take place, merely the commencement of such an action with the intention of creating an artefact is sufficient to transform an object into an artefact. Both of the proposals were then combined by *Dickie*. The artifactuality requirement adopts a broad under-

[65] See also *J. Pila*, Copyright and its categories of original works, Oxford Journal of Legal Studies 30 (2010), 229–254, 247.

[66] Similarly *Michael Baigent and Richard Leigh v. The Random House Group Ltd.* [2006] EWHC 719.

[67] *G. Dickie*, The Art Circle: A Theory of Art (1984); *S. Davies*, Philosophical Perspectives on Art (2007), 44; *idem*, Definitions of Art (n. 48), 83; *A.C. Danto*, The Artworld, The Journal of Philosophy 61 (1964), 571–584.

[68] *Dickie* (n. 67), 80–82.

[69] *Davies*, Definitions of Art (n. 48), 120 f.

[70] *M.M. Eaton*, Art, Artifacts, and Intentions, The American Philosophical Quarterly 6 (1969), 165–169, although on the basis of the examples mentioned in the paper, one may doubt if the key element is a change in physical form or instead the change in the recipient's response to a work (e.g. application of a driftwood modified by a nature as a warning sign without changing its appearance).

[71] *R. Scalfani*, The Logical Primitiveness of the Concept of a Work of Art, The British Journal of Aesthetics 15 (1975), 14–28.

standing of the notion of an artefact: as a result of modifications, as a human work (*Eaton*'s proposal), or as an object that presents a meaning for the participants of a certain culture (*Scalfani*'s proposal). The first option does not require a work of art to present any differences from a fixation; the latter does not require any physical changes to the object itself; it is just the social (semantic) meaning that is of great relevance.[72] A variation of the artifactuality concept was presented by *Gary Iseminger*. In his approach, artifactuality is understood as a property of an object that succeeds from some of the object's other properties or that has been intentionally created by the author.[73] Thus, it is necessary that the object's property reflects a certain activity and that a property has been created which itself has an aesthetic character, thus resulting in the creation of an artefact.[74] If a creation process does not result in a final modification of an object and the development (creation) of aesthetic properties that the object in question did not previously contain, it will not be considered an artefact.

Institutionalism's second pillar is that it is based on the expert's decision. *Dickie* concluded that when taking two objects under consideration that are visually undistinguishable – where, however, one is considered a work of art and the other is not (as in the examples of conceptual art by *Marcel Duchamp*)[75] – the difference is the entanglement in the net of cultural or aesthetic relations that makes the first object an artefact, but not the second.[76] The net of such relations cannot be visually perceptible by a recipient, but it is intellectually recognised by conscious recipients. Consequentially, a work of art does not exist outside this context.[77] In *Dickie*'s theory, a work of art places itself within the (broadly understood) artworld, and it shall be the artworld that legitimises the status of a work of art. Therefore, the reference point for the identification of a work of art is the enriched cultural framework of an artefact that makes it possible to distinguish between the different objects.[78]

The institutional approach has been broadly criticised in the literature, making it one of the most discussed concepts of poststructuralist aesthetics. In particular, despite its simplicity, an obvious weakness consists in relying on the opinion of experts – including the presumed objectivity of an opinion voiced

---

[72] *Davies*, Definitions of Art (n. 48), 124–126; *Dickie* (n. 67), 43 f.

[73] *G. Iseminger*, The Work of Art as Artifact, The British Journal of Aesthetics 13 (1973), 3–16.

[74] *Iseminger* (n. 73), 4 f., 9, 11; *Davies*, Definitions of Art (n. 48), 129.

[75] *Danto* (n. 54), 68 f.

[76] *G. Dickie*, The New Institutional Theory of Art, in: idem et al. (ed.), Aesthetics. A Critical Anthology (1989), 196–205, 200.

[77] *Dickie* (n. 76), 201; *W. Stróżewski/P. Taranczewski*, Wykłady lubelskie o estetyce (2016), 141.

[78] *Dickie* (n. 76), 201; *Sosnowski* (n. 45), 202.

with the awareness that the experts are experiencing the work of art[79] or questions regarding the exclusiveness of the artworld[80] – and in the legitimacy of the artworld itself.[81] Despite these reservations, the concept of an institutional approach towards a work of art has drawn attention to an important aspect that could be taken into account when considering the concept of a copyright's subject matter: the audience's reaction towards a work. While identifying the object of protection it which might reflect the real social and economic value of the work, and the author's intention.

In essence, *Dickie*'s concept is based on a search for criteria justifying the work's status as art in terms of its social recognition – the internal properties of a work are fully neglected, tilting the decisive gravity towards the artworld or a group of experts. The result was a broad pluralistic definition of a descriptive-qualifying character that excluded any normative aspect being required for a work to have the status of art (there is no bad or good art) and that had no evaluative character.[82]

Having studied *Dickie*'s works, *Laura Biron* and *Elena Cooper* mentioned that the institutional theory of art might be understood as a compromise between the romantic authorship concept[83] and the modernistic approach to the copyright's subject matter based solely on the internal properties of a work and leaving aside the author's figure.[84]

For the purpose of the present paper on the object of protection in copyright law, the aforementioned attempts to define the notion of an artefact – *Dickie*'s first pillar – are of interest: *Eaton* and *Scalfani* required an intentional act in the creation or use of an object, and according to *Iseminger* an object becomes an artefact only if a new property occurs that is the result of an intentional creative process and that has an aesthetic character. These attempts may be taken into consideration when interpreting the first key element for defining a work in modern copyright law, that is the fixation requirement,[85] and when developing a solution to the problem of derivative works in copyright law. After all, the artifactuality of an object requires an intentional activity, but it requires at the same time a certain objectification, which is verifiable in judicial proceedings. Despite the reservations formulated against this criterion, the inclusion of institutional reaction seems to be an interesting way forward in

---

[79] *Wimsatt/Beardsley* (n. 49), 470–472.

[80] *P. Brand*, Feminist Art Epistemologies: Understanding Feminist Art, Hypatia 21 (2006), 166–189.

[81] *B. Dziemidok*, Główne kontrowersje estetyki współczesnej (2012), 134–135; *Sosnowski* (n. 45), 202 f.; *Davies*, Definitions of Art (n. 48), 87.

[82] *Dziemidok*, (n. 81), 139; *Yen* (n. 58), 259; *Sosnowski* (n. 45), 202.

[83] *Rose*, Authors and Owners (n. 8), 31 f.

[84] *L. Biron/R. Cooper*, Authorship, aesthetics and the artworld: Reforming copyright's joint authorship doctrine, Law and Philosophy 35 (2016), 55–85, 57.

[85] See the text corresponding to n. 19, above.

copyright law. Even if it opens up the possibility of an institutional subjectivity and even if it may be criticised in terms of discrimination, as in some countries there are no institutionalised forms of artistic activities or environments, on the potential subject matter of a copyright could be a reasonable criterion. And even though institutional reaction implies several further questions (with regard to the evaluation criteria, methods, the reification of a copyright's subject matter, expert group selection, etc.), such an approach might nevertheless function as a subsidiary method.

And indeed, at least in some court decisions, the ease of the institutional approach has already been noticed, as, for example, in the British case *Hensher v. Restawile*,[86] which raised the question as to the qualification of furniture as "works of artistic craftsmanship". The House of Lords held that mass-produced furniture cannot be considered the subject matter of a copyright because for such a status, a work must be created by a recognised artist or person who is trained to be such an artist.[87] A similar approach was adopted in the case of *Shelley Films Ltd. v. Rex Features Ltd.*,[88] which required that the author have the appropriate qualifications, experience, and recognition, as well as in the New Zealand case *Bonz Group (Pty) Ltd. v. Cooke*.[89] All three decisions indirectly refer to institutionalism: if the author is a recognised or trained artist, then it justifies the finding that a work created by this author is protected under copyright law.[90] In the US literature regarding the question of the substantial similarity between two disputed works, *Alfred C. Yen* also noted several decisions referring to the reaction of the public as a point of reference in resolving infringement cases.[91] An example is the well-known case *Bleistein v. Donaldson Lithographing Co.*, which used the recipients' reactions as a final

[86] [1976] AC 64. Similarly *P. Masiyakurima*, Copyright in works of artistic craftsmanship: An analysis, Oxford Journal of Legal Studies 36 (2016), 505–534, 515 f.

[87] [1976] AC 64, 94: "It follows, again, that whether the subject matter is or is not a work of artistic craftsmanship is a matter of evidence; and the most cogent evidence is likely to be from those who are either themselves acknowledged artist-craftsmen or concerned with the training of artist-craftsmen […]." See also *A. Barron*, Copyright Law and the Claims of Art, Intellectual Property Quarterly 4 (2002), 368–401, 373.

[88] [1994] EMLR 134.

[89] [1994] 3 NZLR 216. For an interesting analysis on popular music and its legal status in copyright law, see *L. Bently*, Authorship of Popular Music in UK Copyright Law, Information Communication and Society 12 (2009), 179–204.

[90] One has to take into consideration that within the UK system, "a work of artistic craftsmanship" refers directly to "the artistic character" of such a work, although it excludes making any aesthetic evaluation, see *L. Bently/B. Sherman/D. Gangjee/P. Johnson*, Intellectual property law (2018), 80–82; *Masiyakurima* (n. 86), 515.

[91] *Yen* (n. 58), 284–297, 271. In addition to the cases cited below, see also the decision concerning the TV show "The Greatest American Hero": *Warner Brothers, Inc. v. American Broadcasting Companies*, 720 F2d 231 (1983).

criterion to qualify an artefact as a the subject matter of a copyright.[92] According to the court, it is the publicity that influences the commercial success of a work; thus, it is necessary to take this publicity into consideration while identifying the protected intellectual goods. The reason for such an approach is the economic justification for copyright law, i.e. to protect those artefacts that have some commercial value: "these pictures had their worth and their success".[93] A similar test was applied in *Kieselstein-Cord v. Accessories by Pearl, Inc.*,[94] which considered the copyright status of two visually similar belt fasteners. The court relied on the commercial success of one of the disputed "works" and the fact that the Metropolitan Museum of Art accepted a design project as a part of a planned exhibition.[95] As noted by *Yen*, this clearly confirms a reference to *Dickie*'s institutional theory of art; however, in both decisions, we may also find some inspirations from formalism and perceptualism as well.[96]

III. Should we merge copyright law and aesthetics?

Both perceptualism and institutionalism have common denominators: They stress the intentional character of activities undertaken to create a work; they underline the necessity to take into consideration the broader context in which a work stands in order to recognise it as a work of art; and they acknowledge that an analysis limited to using the internal properties of an artefact to identify a work as art falls short. Nevertheless, I do not wish to propose that either concept should be directly implemented into copyright law. After all, not every work of art should be qualified as a subject matter of copyright, and not every copyright's subject matter should be considered a work of art. Some mechanisms, however, are worth paying attention to in the context of resolving contemporary problems of copyright law. In the following paragraphs, I wish to discuss two such problems and one possibility.

The first problem is the identification of a copyright's subject matter. The phenomenological approach applies an analysis of the internal properties of an artefact including the structure of a work and the properties of a form of expression, without, however, considering the broader context of a work and without paying attention to the author's intention or the recipients' reactions. Contemporary trends in aesthetics have abandoned this strategy, and in my opinion, there are several arguments in favour of such an approach also in copyright law. First, a structuralist approach based on an internal analysis of a

[92] *Bleistein v. Donaldson Lithographing Co.*, 188 US 239 (1903).
[93] *Yen* (n. 58), 270 f., 274.
[94] 632 F2d 989, 990 (2d Cir. 1980).
[95] *Kieselstein-Cord v. Accessories by Pearl, Inc.*, 632 F2d 989 (1980), 990 f.
[96] *Yen* (n. 58), 278, 283.

work is not able to take technological and societal progress into consideration when identifying a copyright's subject matter. Even if one assumes the possibility of defining or at least providing a noncategorical enumeration of the properties of the individual components of the work, the evolution of technology and art has led to abandoning the paradigm of this approach: artifactuality. Having analysed modern works and new technologies, *Andrew Christie* noted that with the advent of multimedia works, the subject matter of copyright evolved from something symbolic to something sensual: It is not any longer symbols that constitute a work, but rather what hitherto has been represented by symbols:

> "Towards the middle of the continuum are copyright works embodying not symbolic representations of sounds or images, but the sounds or images themselves".[97]

Furthermore, today the recipients' reactions towards a work have to be taken into consideration. The thus-far passive recipient has become an actively participating actor, who – through available tools and programmes – shapes,[98] communicates with[99] or even co-creates[100] content. Consequently, it is not the content itself (syntax), the meaning of a work (sense), or its interpretation (semantics) that acquires a growing social and economic significance; it is instead the way of co-receiving works together in a massive (online) way and participating in their creation, existence, and development. A similar position was taken by *Niva Elkin-Koren* in her 1996 publication, in which she noted that the subject matter of a copyright had stopped being received in a linear and static manner.[101] Instead, modern exploitation models allow for access to the content in a non-linear way, as chosen by users, which shifts the decision regarding the interpretation of a work (and, thus, its value) from the author to recipients:

> "Non-linearity transfers meaning-making power from authors to readers. If a user is able to enter the text at any point, she may disregard what the author considered to be the meaning of the text, and may use the fragmented material as she wishes."[102]

---

[97] *A. Christie*, Reconceptualising copyright in the digital era, European Intellectual Property Review 17 (1995), 522–530, 523. Christie wrote his paper in 1995, but the vast majority of his statements are relevant even in 2023.

[98] Consider user-generated content in social media: *N. Elkin-Koren*, Cyberlaw and Social Change: A Democratic Approach to Copyright Law in Cyberspace, Cardozo Arts and Entertainment Law Journal 14 (1996), 215–281, 239 (pointing out the fluidity of works and their exploitation in cyberspace and noting that digitalisation has expanded the broad scope of possibilities to exploit information).

[99] Consider communication via mobile apps, social media, and computer software.

[100] Consider online games, e.g. overwhelmingly multiplayer online role-playing games.

[101] *Elkin-Koren* (n. 98), 239 f. See also *Goldstein* (n. 14), 197–234; *O. Bracha*, Who Killed Politics – Past and Present Perspectives on the Political Sphere of Intellectual Property, Journal of Law, Philosophy and Culture 4 (2009), 125–154.

[102] *Elkin-Koren* (n. 98), 240.

It is the user who decides which parts, components, or phrases and in what order or sequence they are going to be exploited. If we further add the fluid shape of the content presented in social media, one might argue that both content, structure, and the "form of expression" of such "work" might vary depending on the user's preferences and his historic decisions (that are observed by algorithms). Even blocking software applied by the user (computer programs that block algorithmic surveillance in social media) and national personal data protection instruments will influence the work and its content. In summary, limiting the analysis of a work and its structure to syntactical and semantical meaning has become insufficient and unsatisfactory against the backdrop of technological (algorithmic and business) changes. Furthermore, the phenomenological approach does not take into account society's shift away from a business model based on the possession and purchase of products towards an entertainment model based on the subscription of services and social media. Finally, it excludes the essential role which the recipient has in shaping the presentation and exploitation of intellectual goods as well as their meaning in, and relation with, cultural contexts.

The second problem is the paradoxical subjectivity of a structuralist approach towards the notion of a work. Contrary to its appearances, some of the criteria for identifying a copyright's subject matter constitute pejorative or evaluative descriptions of a work – its artistic purpose, the individual manifestations of the author's personality, creative edits, unique compilations, etc. But why should some of the internal properties of a work have more meaning or value compared with the content of a work? How can two works that are visually different but contain similar content be distinguished from each other? In other words: why should a formal expression of a work matter more for normative protection than a semantic meaning of the content of a work or its role in shaping culture or science? An intentional approach that analyses the author's intention and an institutional approach that analyses the recipients' reactions to a work, of course, also do not avoid subjectivity, but the combination of them might provide additional value when it comes to counterbalancing the risks. Moreover, contemporary aesthetic trends – as confirmed by culture studies,[103] information theories,[104] and cognitive studies[105] – suggest that in iden-

---

[103] *J.E. Cohen*, Creativity and Culture in Copyright Theory, U.C. Davis Law Review 40 (2007), 1151–1205, 1179, 1185.

[104] *Floridi* (n. 46), 205, 208.

[105] E.g. *J. George/J. Zhou*, Understanding when bad moods foster creativity and good ones don't: The role of context and clarity of feelings, Journal of Applied Psychology 87 (2002), 687–697; *G. Oldham/A. Cummings*, Employee creativity: Personal and contextual factors at work, Academy of Management Journal 39 (1996), 607–634; *I. Reszka Pinheiro/R. Moraes Cruz*, Mapping Creativity: Creativity Measurements Network Analysis, Creativity Research Journal 26 (2014), 263–275; *M. Donald*, Art and Cognitive Evolution, in: M. Turner (ed.), The Artful Mind: Cognitive Science and the Riddle of Human Creativity

tifying and evaluating an artefact, one should take into consideration the broader context of a work, rather than focusing solely on its forms of expression. Such an approach may be helpful in relation to copyright's originality requirement.

In 2007, *Julie Cohen* published a paper in which she accurately identified the current copyright problem as a dichotomous choice between relative and merit-based opinions in intellectual property law. In her view, this approach is based on a false assumption of courts trying to avoid making any aesthetic evaluation of a copyright's subject matter.[106] In general, her criticism is reasonable as subjective opinions on a work exist and as judgments may be based solely on the evaluation of the audience and of the actual work's recipients rather than that of the courts. However, as *Cohen* and other scholars aptly noted, such a perspective solves the copyright problem only superficially:[107] It is based on a paradigm of a romantic notion in which the author is isolated from culture, society, and other authors.[108] Moreover, it supports a concept of the creative process as a linear, teleological progress, and it legitimises frameworks for economic domination.[109] As *Elkin-Koren* mentioned, it also excludes the participation of society in the creative process.[110] This scepticism is shared by *Cohen*, who points out that for many years, copyright theory has avoided confrontation with the postmodernist criticism of authorship and originality, disregarding the fact that the romantic authorship concept, which was a dominant foundation for the modernistic vision of the creative process and the structuralist approach to the notion of a work, no longer fits contemporary technological challenges. Furthermore, the modern copyright discourse has repeatedly emphasised the need to broaden the discussion regarding the delineation

(2011), 3–20 (pointing out the necessity to consider the context of a work of art in order to evaluate and identify it as an artefact); see also *J. Hughes*, Cognitive and Aesthetic Functionality in Trademark Law, Cardozo Law Review 36 (2015), 1227–1285 (noting the role of cognitive and psychological functionality in trademark law).

[106] *Cohen* (n. 103) refers to the US decision on *Bleistein v. Donaldson Lithographing Co.*, 188 US 239 (1903).

[107] *Cohen* (n. 103), 1163 f.; *P. Jaszi*, On the Author Effect: Contemporary Copyright and Collective Creativity, in: M. Woodmansee/P. Jaszi (eds.), The Construction of Authorship: Textual Approaches in Law and Literature (1994), 29–56; *idem* (n. 6), 455; *D. Lange*, Recognizing the Public Domain, Law and Contemporary Problems 44 (1981), 147–178; *Woodmansee*, Genius and Copyright (n. 6), 425; *M. Chon*, Postmodern "Progress": Reconsidering the Copyright and Patent Power, DePaul Law Review 43 (1993), 97–146. See also *R.H. Rotstein*, Beyond Metaphor: Copyright Infringement and the Fiction of the Work, Chicago-Kent Law Review 68 (1993), 725–804; *J. Boyle*, Shamans, Software and Spleens: Law and the Construction of the Information Society (1996); *R.J. Coombe*, The Cultural Life of Intellectual Properties: Authorship, Appropriation and Law (1998), 58 f.

[108] *Boyle* (n. 107), 54, 55 f., 59; *Coombe* (n. 107), 45.

[109] *Boyle* (n. 107), 60, 79 f., 84–96; *Coombe* (n. 107), 54 f.

[110] *Elkin-Koren* (n. 98), 271–274.

of the concepts of creativity, authorship, and a copyright's subject matter; the evaluation of the public domain; fair use; and the production models of cultural goods.[111] As *Cohen* noted, the rejection of culture and the rejection of work's production, aesthetic qualities and social values when identifying a copyright's subject matter wrongly assumes that the functions of supporting culture and science will be fulfilled independently by the conscious choices of consumers who actively participate in the democratic dialogue.[112] As it turns out, years after publishing *Cohen*'s paper, such an approach was found to be idealistic – not every choice made by a consumer is a result of an autonomous and reasonable decision process without any trace of visual or subthreshold manipulation.[113] General disregard for the social sciences and cultural theories seems additionally unjustified because neither of these fields are novel concepts – they have been part of the scientific discourse for years,[114] even if they have not been sufficiently visible in legal scholarship. According to *Cohen*, an interdisciplinary, postmodernist approach requires a deeper and more careful analysis of the social, cultural, and legal mechanisms for evaluating, rewarding, and the creative process – and this might provide additional value for copyright law.[115] From the perspective of what is presented above, my opinion is – particularly in terms of the subject matter of copyright, fair use, or models for the production of cultural goods – that it would be a mistake to avoid referring to what exactly is an intellectual good. Such an approach ignores an essential evolution of the other social sciences, leading towards an isolationism of legal opinions and, eventually, to the ossification of academic discourse.

Thirdly – and this brings me to the future prospects – intentionalism and perceptualism may cause a gradual transformation from an artefactual, strictly reified understanding of what ought to be protected under copyright law into a new concept, one that is more flexible and fitted to the digital environment. As a result, this might lead to a re-evaluation process for works such as computer programmes (and their functionalities, nowadays outside the copyright system) as well as websites and video games (with the interactivity and user-generated content involved). This conclusion has been confirmed also by a comparison of the modern and future problems of copyright law: the problem of delineating

---

[111] *Lange* (n. 107), 147; *J. Litman*, The Public Domain, Emory Law Journal 39 (1990), 965–1023; *M.J. Madison*, A Pattern-Oriented Approach to Fair Use, William & Mary Law Review 45 (2004), 1525–1690.

[112] *Cohen* (n. 103), 1165.

[113] See, e.g., the Cambridge Analytica scandal.

[114] *Cohen* (n. 103), 1165 f. See also *S. Scafidi*, Who Owns Culture? Appropriation and Authenticity in American Law (2005) (exploring relationships between cultural products and communal identities); *K. Aoki*, Adrift in the Intertext: Authorship and Audience "Recoding" Rights, Chicago-Kent Law Review 68 (1993), 805–839 (considering the political implications of postmodernist critique).

[115] *Cohen* (n. 103), 1168 f.

inspiration and authorship, which is particularly evident in cases of *de minimis* works; AI-generated works, where there is no human involvement in the creation process; big data, which involves "massive amounts" of data worth "massive amounts" of money; social media, with a disputable status of user-generated content; as well as additional problems related to the interactivity of multimedia works.[116] An open question remains, however, regarding whether such properties like interactivity and form dynamics (fluidity, flexibility) or even the content's volatility in relation to the individual user's preferences should be included within the normative (and more or less constant) structure of what is subject to copyright.[117] In my opinion, it is at least worth discussing whether there is a social, cultural, or even economic necessity to include such technological developments (and their future changes) within the normative framework before we all agree – consistent with the *Barthes* quote offered at the beginning of this paper – on the "death of a notion of a work".

IV. Final call for an interdisciplinary approach

While technological development has been the driving force and the main motivation behind copyright regulation, the corresponding development of various business models has also become its *nemesis*: It has ultimately led to many ambiguities and contemporary problems of copyright law. The attempts so far to identify and to describe the subject of copyright have failed to fulfil the hopes placed in them: On the one hand, they assume a certain objectification of the legal assessment, and, on the other hand, the enigmatic nature of copyright's structure leads to decisions criticised in the literature. Interestingly, however, in the advent of an increasing tendency to expand monopoly rights, it is surprising that copyright scholars rarely discuss alternatives to the contemporary interpretations of the notion of a work. It seems to me that it is impossible to extricate ourselves from this impasse without an interdisciplinary and holistic approach. This, in turn, may refer to the achievements of aesthetics, with interesting prospects discussed already as institutional and perceptual concepts. Although both of the concepts alone might not be the solution appropriate for copyright law, a combination of them seems more plausible. Such a combination would implement the reasonable postulates of institutionalists and

[116] *Stamatoudi* (n. 26), 3–16.

[117] *P.B. Hugenholtz*, Auteursrecht op Informatie (2005), 60 (arguing in favour of a semantic form as the reference point for the identification of a copyright's subject matter and proposing to replace the duality between idea and form of expression with the semiotic threefold of sign, reference, and referent. See also *N. van Dijk*, Grounds of the Immaterial: A Conflict-Based Approach to Intellectual Rights (2017), 43–45.

perceptualists while at the same time it would reduce the danger of subjective judgments.

The final conclusion to be drawn from this paper should not be reduced solely to a plea for a corresponding re-evaluation of copyright law. The main reason for conducting interdisciplinary research on the subject matter of copyright has long been identified – and it reflects a tradition embraced by my predecessors; it is to recognise, to study, and to be inspired by aesthetic concepts, so that the final construction of copyright law might not disintegrate as a result of artistic practices, economic values, or society's needs. Contrary to the idealistic assumption of the romantic author, who creates his or hers work in a complete void, copyright is not entirely separate from aesthetics, technology, or society. Therefore, it seems most justified to refer to other social sciences and create such a combination of solutions that will begin to fulfil its basic function: it will become the authors' right.

A Context-Based Assessment of Copyrightability: In Search of the Justification

Daria Kim

In her chapter, *Ewa Laskowska-Litak* identifies a number of shortcomings of the existing approach to defining a "work" in copyright law, particularly concerning the originality requirement and its judicial application in Polish case law. In her view, the following "contemporary problems" of copyright law lead to dissatisfaction with the current approach: the "reification" ("objectification") of the notion of a work, the diminishing threshold of originality, vagueness and arbitrariness in the judicial assessment of copyrightability, and the exclusion of certain subject matter which renders copyright law unfit for the digital age. In view of such deficiencies, she notes that "it is surprising that copyright scholars rarely discuss alternatives to the contemporary interpretations of the originality requirement".[1] Such alternatives, she argues, might be inspired and informed by the debate in the field of aesthetics. More specifically, she points to an approach to the copyrightability assessment that would take into account the context of an artefact (hereinafter, a "context-based approach").

Overall, *Laskowska-Litak*'s analysis can be viewed as interdisciplinary in the sense that it makes an excursion into the domain of aesthetics[2] in search of the relevant concepts and theories that might or could inform the definition of a work for the purposes of copyright law. A universal step-by-step methodology for conducting interdisciplinary research can hardly exist, even if the disciplines and research questions of interest are identified. What can provide

[1] *Laskowska-Litak*, p. 469, above.

[2] While Laskowska-Litak generally refers to aesthetics, more specific subfields involved in her inquiry can be defined as the ontology of art and analytical aesthetics.

some guidance are the basic principles regarding the relevance of the chosen disciplines to the purpose of an inquiry and their aptitude to fulfil that purpose in a meaningful and reliable way. Accordingly, this comment reflects on the arguments made in favour of a context-based approach to the definition of a work in copyright law, the prospect of its implementation, its potential to resolve what are posited as "contemporary problems" of copyright law, and the relevance of the selected aesthetic theories for the normative analysis of what qualities and standards should define a work in copyright law.

I. The overall line of argumentation

The starting point of *Laskowska-Litak*'s analysis is the observation that the notion of a work in copyright law is "reduced" to two "elements" – fixation and originality – which raises two concerns: "the relatively excessive emphasis on a necessary reification (or objectification) of a copyright's subject matter" and "an ever lower threshold with respect to the originality requirement".[3] Next, she reviews several decisions by Polish courts where the copyrightability assessment has focused on the constitutive elements and expressive attributes of the objects at issue and where the judicial reasoning has deployed "vague" language.

In search of a more apt approach, *Laskowska-Litak* reviews the discussion in the field of aesthetics on what constitutes a work of art, where she observes an overall tendency to abandon structuralist and phenomenological approaches in favour of intentionalism, perceptualism and institutionalism. Further, she associates the tendency to "objectify" the copyright's subject matter with structuralist and phenomenological approaches to the definition and appreciation of artwork in aesthetics and contrasts them with perceptualism and institutionalism. She sees the main advantage of the latter two approaches in their aspiration to take into account the "broader context of a work".[4] While *Laskowska-Litak* is cautious about arguing for the direct implementation of either institutionalism or perceptualism in copyright law, she suggests that a "context-based" approach, at least, holds the promise of remedying the "contemporary problems" of copyright law – namely, the problem of identifying a work and the subjectivity of the assessment – and making copyright law "more flexible and fitted to the digital environment".[5]

In sum, the main motivation for *Laskowska-Litak*'s inquiry into aesthetics is a dissatisfaction with the originality requirement and how it has been applied in (Polish) case law. In what follows, let us take a closer look at the identified

[3] *Laskowska-Litak*, p. 469, above.

[4] *Laskowska-Litak*, p. 479, above.

[5] *Laskowska-Litak*, p. 483, above.

shortcomings of copyright law and consider the relevance and potential of the selected aesthetic theories to resolve them.

II. The "reification" of the notion of a work in copyright law

By the "reification" or "objectification of a copyright's subject matter", *Laskowska-Litak* refers to a tendency in the judicial assessment of copyrightability to focus on "the disputed artefact itself (considering its internal properties such as its structure, features, and characteristics)"[6] when analysing whether the originality threshold is reached. She further compares such tendency to an approach to the identification of a work in aesthetics that stems from structuralism and phenomenology,[7] both attending to "the internal properties of an artefact including the structure of a work and the properties of a form of expression".[8] Overall, *Laskowska-Litak* argues that what she identifies as a "structuralist" approach to the copyrightability assessment should be abandoned, for structuralism has been criticised[9] and already superseded in aesthetics by other theories.

While the analogy suggested by *Laskowska-Litak* is thought-provoking, we might need to distinguish between the structuralist approach as a method of identifying and interpreting a work of art in aesthetics, on the one hand, and the reference to the structural patterns and properties of an artefact in judicial reasoning, on the other hand. The latter might evidence not the adherence to a structuralist approach in aesthetics but the commitment to the idea-expression dichotomy in copyright law.[10] That judges often refer to the constitutive elements of the subject matter of copyright disputes is, in a way, inevitable: the structure of an artefact, its stylistic features, its form, its shape, its lines and the colour palette are all expressive elements whose consideration keeps the focus

---

[6] *Laskowska-Litak*, p. 471, above.

[7] In her analysis, Laskowska-Litak does not draw a clear distinction between phenomenological and structuralist approaches in aesthetics, and at times she refers to them interchangeably. For instance, she observes that "the structuralist approach to the notion of a work of art has been the subject of criticism in aesthetics" and, next, summarises Richard Shusterman's arguments "indicating the necessity of abandoning a phenomenological approach": *Laskowska-Litak*, p. 472, above. However, even though phenomenological and structuralist approaches share certain common perspectives on the experience and interpretation of art, they have distinct analytical focuses: a phenomenological approach can be viewed as focusing on the subjectivity in aesthetics, while structuralism attempts to reveal the underlying patterns and structures that may fashion how we experience and understand art.

[8] *Laskowska-Litak*, p. 479, above.

[9] In her words, "an analysis limited to using the internal properties of an artefact to identify a work as art falls short": *Laskowska-Litak*, p. 479, above.

[10] The idea-expression dichotomy has been a contested notion in copyright scholarship, and this note would not be a proper place to revisit this fundamental issue.

of the legal analysis on the expression of an idea. In other words, the attention to the structural and constitutive elements of an artefact performs a distinct function in the copyrightability assessment. In this view, the parallel argument – since structuralism has been "abandoned" in aesthetics, it should be abandoned in copyright law – might not be warranted. To justify such parallelism, it would be pertinent to consider how the abandonment of the approach that focuses on "the properties of a form of expression" would square with the copyright law principle that protection extends to expression and not ideas, and to what extent expressive elements should still remain relevant in the copyrightability assessment.

III. An "ever lower threshold" of originality and "vague" judicial reasoning

The second concern pointed out by *Laskowska-Litak* is "an ever lower threshold"[11] of originality. In the chapter, she reviews five Polish cases spanning the period between 1969 and 2015, and observes that "the lack of uniformly developed interpretations of the notion of originality, individuality, or one's 'own intellectual creation' gradually leads to the replacement of vague notions like 'individuality' or 'originality' with even more vague or arbitrary criteria".[12] In particular, she cites as examples the attributes "attractive" and "interesting" (with regard to a picture), "artistic" (with regard to the composition of a real estate advertisement), and "creative editing" (of a research paper).[13] Regardless of the extent to which the Polish case law reviewed by *Laskowska-Litak* presents a problem in terms of vague or unjustified judicial interpretations in Polish copyright law, the issue of the "low" originality threshold has indeed been widely discussed in critical commentary on copyright law. However, the question is rather whether it indicates a deficiency in the originality requirement as such or a fallacy in its judicial interpretation and application. The latter might not automatically warrant the search for an alternative definitional requirement of a work in copyright law – instead, one might first consider the need for guidance on the originality standard and its application.

Furthermore, it would be worth considering how a context-based approach would remedy the issue of the "low" threshold of originality. If a context-based approach to the definition of the copyrightable subject matter were to be applied as an alternative to the originality criterion, it would face the same question of where to set the threshold for the protectability requirement and ensure its proper application.

---

[11] *Laskowska-Litak*, p. 469, above.

[12] *Laskowska-Litak*, p. 469, above.

[13] Here, I rely on the translation provided by Laskowska-Litak in her chapter.

IV. The unfitness of copyright law in the digital age

Notably, *Laskowska-Litak* sees not the objectification of a copyright's subject matter as such as the problem but its consequence of excluding certain subject matter – "valuable assets" – from being eligible for copyright protection, even though their "commercial, aesthetic, or cultural value [might be] commonly recognised and appreciated".[14] Among such "valuable assets", she mentions the functionality of computer code, the responsiveness of a website and the interactivity of a computer game.[15] Having pointed out the lack of copyright protection for such subject matter, she observes that, "[i]f compared with a general classification of a computer program as a literary work, one may conclude that copyright law might not fit the digital age and will not be able to respond to all future technological developments (e.g. works generated by artificial intelligence)".[16] The chapter does not provide further elaboration on how incorporating the functionality of computer code, the responsiveness of a website, and the interactivity of a computer game into copyright protection can make copyright law "fit" for the digital age. Neither is consideration given to the functionality-based rationale for excluding such subject matter. Questions arise: Why is the ineligibility of functional subject matter for copyright protection viewed as symptomatic of the unfitness of copyright law in the digital age? Furthermore, in what way should a context be factored into the copyrightability assessment to help address the challenges posed by "all future technological developments"?[17]

The answers are by far not straightforward because it cannot be taken for granted that copyright protection benefits technological development automatically, unequivocally and across the board. *Laskowska-Litak*'s call to take into account the context and contextually defined value of an artefact points to the consequentialist theory of IP law, which posits that IP protection should be justified by its beneficial consequences for society, including economic and cultural domains. Yet there is no linear relationship between IP protection, creativity, and technological progress. IP rights are not necessarily conducive to or desirable for promoting innovation and creativity.[18] Thus, the statement of the importance of the context of an artefact is neither self-explanatory nor sufficient to justify the extension of copyrightable subject matter as "context"-

[14] *Laskowska-Litak*, p. 468, above.

[15] *Laskowska-Litak*, p. 468, above.

[16] *Laskowska-Litak*, p. 468, above.

[17] *Laskowska-Litak*, p. 469, above.

[18] See, e.g. *G. Dosi/L. Marengo/C. Pasquali*, How Much Should Society Fuel the Greed of Innovators? On the Relations between Appropriability, Opportunities and Rates of Innovation, Research Policy 35 (2006), 1110–1121; *A. Suominen/M. Deschryvere/R. Narayan*, Uncovering Value through Exploration of Barriers – A Perspective on Intellectual Property Rights in a National Innovation System, Technovation 123 (2023), 102719.

based arguments can be raised both for and against protection by exclusive rights.

Laskowska-Litak argues that, by focusing on the constitutive elements of an artefact, assessments fail to account for its value which is derived from the context. However, it is not the attention to the constitutive elements – the "structuralist" approach – in the assessment of copyrightability that leads to the exclusion of the functional subject matter. After all, such subject matter also has a structure and inherent attributes and, hence, could be qualified as protectable under the "structuralist" approach. Thus, the mere observation that "structuralism" has been superseded by the theories in aesthetics that divert the focus away from the structural elements may not suffice for subsuming functional subject matter under copyright protection. In this regard, the contention that "limiting the analysis of a work and its structure to syntactical and semantical meaning has become insufficient and unsatisfactory against the backdrop of technological (algorithmic and business) changes"[19] requires further clarification and argumentation.

Laskowska-Litak observes that, despite "fundamental technological progress, the definition of a work in copyright law has not changed since the first international provisions emerged during the nineteenth century".[20] It is worth noting, technological developments have raised legal uncertainties, led to new categories of subject matter being eligible for copyright protection and affected the statutory definition and the judicial interpretation of the scope of rights. Yet it appears quite a leap to argue that, because a context-based approach inspired by aesthetics theories of institutionalism and intentionalism would allow technological subject matter to be included in the scope of copyright protection, it would make copyright law more fitted to the digital age.

Historically, technological developments have certainly borne on copyright law-making: among other examples, the categories of protectable subject matter such as computer programs or databases and the right of making available certain subject matter to the public would not have come into being had copyright law ignored contextual changes. However, as the example of the sui generis protection of databases in the EU shows, the policymakers' aspiration to "catch up" with technological developments by establishing a new category of a protected subject matter can lead to what is by now widely acknowledged as a regulatory failure.[21] Thus, it may not be the focus on the expressive elements of a work as such in the copyrightability assessment and its consequence of "a

[19] *Laskowska-Litak*, p. 481, above.

[20] *Laskowska-Litak*, p. 464, above.

[21] Neither the first nor the second evaluation of the Database Directive (Directive 96/9/EC on the legal protection of databases) revealed evidence that the sui generis right significantly improved the competitiveness of the EU in the database sector. Furthermore, the case of copyright protection for software has been controversial, as also acknowledged by *Laskowska-Litak*, p. 465, above.

gradual ossification of the notion of a work"[22] that make copyright law "unfit" for the digital age. The problem arises rather due to a limited understanding of the *socio-economic implications* of IP protection – the functional relationship between protection, creativity, and innovation – that can complicate efforts to make copyright law "fit" for technological realities.

Furthermore, *Laskowska-Litak* observes that digital technologies have been allowing technology users and content recipients to take on an increasingly active role in "shaping", "communicating with", or "co-creating" content. Next, she argues that "it is not the content itself (syntax), the meaning of a work (sense), or its interpretation (semantics) that acquires a growing social and economic significance; it is *instead* the way of co-receiving works together in a massive (online) way and participating in their creation, existence, and development".[23] While it might be difficult to empirically assess and causally attribute which of the mentioned factors accounts more for the "growing social and economic significance" of artefacts, one would assume that an appreciation of the content is the prerequisite for it to be chosen and "massively" disseminated through the digital means. Digital communication technologies may amplify and disseminate the value of certain subject matter rather than solely account for the "growing social and economic significance" of such subject matter. Neither does the fact of shifting from "possession and purchase of products" to subscription-based models[24] of consumption appear on its face to attest to a diminishing of the role of the expressive elements of an artefact in aesthetic experience and appreciation.

V. The issue of subjectivity in applying the originality criterion

One of the issues pointed out by *Laskowska-Litak* is "the paradoxical subjectivity of a structuralist approach towards the notion of a work",[25] as some criteria for identifying a copyright's subject matter – including "the individual manifestations of the author's personality"[26] – might "constitute pejorative or evaluative descriptions" of a work.[27] This observation echoes the debate among legal scholars about whether the criterion of "the author's own intellectual creation" implies an objective or a subjective test.[28] However, it is not the expres-

[22] *Laskowska-Litak*, p. 471, above.
[23] *Laskowska-Litak*, p. 481, above (emphasis added).
[24] *Laskowska-Litak*, p. 480, above.
[25] *Laskowska-Litak*, p. 481, above.
[26] *Laskowska-Litak*, p. 481, above.
[27] *Laskowska-Litak*, p. 481, above.
[28] *S. Mendis*, A Copyright Gambit: On the Need for Exclusive Rights in Digitised Versions of Public Domain Textual Materials in Europe (2019), 137, n. 82–84, and the accompanying text.

sive (including structural) elements of an artefact as such that might constitute a shaky (subjective) basis for the copyrightability assessment – after all, lines, shapes, colours and ornaments do have objective points of reference that are ontologically independent from the perceiver.[29] Rather, it is the assessment of these elements as the author's choices by the perceiver – an individual who might happen to be a judge – that is exposed to subjectivity. At issue is, again, whether it is the originality requirement, its standard of assessment, or the way such standard has been applied in the judicial analysis that calls for a critical review and an alternative conception.

While *Laskowska-Litak* acknowledges that an "intentional approach that analyses the author's intention and an institutional approach that analyses the recipients' reactions to a work, of course, also do not avoid subjectivity",[30] she assumes that "the combination of them might provide additional value when it comes to counterbalancing the risks".[31] In other words, the problem of subjectivity would not be an issue as long as it can be compensated by the benefits of an alternative approach, such as the one inspired by intentionalism and institutionalism. If one agrees to follow such "cost-benefit" approach, one would need to identify potential benefits and weigh them against the "cost" of subjectivity, an exercise notoriously difficult, especially when attempting to make such analysis future-proof.

One such benefit pointed out by *Laskowska-Litak* would be the protectability of the subject matter currently excluded under the approach that "reifies" the notion of a work, which would make copyright law "more flexible and fitted to the digital environment".[32] In particular, a context-based approach "might lead to a re-evaluation process for works such as computer programmes (and their functionalities, nowadays outside the copyright system) as well as websites and video games".[33] Even more so, there might be "a social, cultural, or even economic necessity" for the "properties like interactivity and form dynamics (fluidity, flexibility) or even the content's volatility in relation to the individual user's preferences [to] be included within the normative (and more or less constant) structure of what is subject to copyright".[34] Yet it is not immediately clear why the inclusion of technical and functional subject matter would befit and benefit the digital age. As pointed out above, the functional subject matter has been excluded from copyrightability not without reason. Furthermore, a context-based approach might be prone to the same risk of "vague" and "arbitrary" interpretation and application, as discussed in the next section.

---

[29] Unless the matter is viewed from a radical constructionism perspective.

[30] *Laskowska-Litak*, p. 481, above.

[31] *Laskowska-Litak*, p. 481, above.

[32] *Laskowska-Litak*, p. 483, above.

[33] *Laskowska-Litak*, p. 483, above.

[34] *Laskowska-Litak*, p. 484, above.

VI. Uncertainties about the application of a context-based approach

Context is a "catchall term"[35] that can embrace everything – if one wishes to establish a connection between an artefact and its context, there can hardly be a case where this would not be possible. This may lead to a situation where everything can be protected under copyright, which raises the question of whether the idea of delineating copyrightable subject matter would retain any relevance at all. If so, the relationship between an artefact and its context would need to be specified for the purposes of distinguishing between copyrightable and non-copyrightable subject matter. What would be the relevant considerations and concrete criteria? Which particular aspect of the relationship between an artefact and the context should be material and decisive for the copyrightability assessment? In the case of "technological development" referred to in the chapter, would any connection be sufficient? For instance, should "AI-generated" output be copyrightable for the sole reason that it has been produced by or with the aid of computational techniques? Would the functionality of computer code, the responsiveness of a website, and the interactivity of a computer game[36] be copyrightable due to their mere ability to perform a technical function?

While these questions remain open, it is worth noting that examining the relationship between an artefact and a context would constitute an act of interpretation. The very notion of a contextual interpretation implies the variability of an artefact's meaning – each artefact carries in itself a range of (latent) meanings as numerous and versatile as the individual acts of interpretation. Needless to say, a broad variety of hermeneutic approaches exists in analytical aesthetics, the ontology of art and other sub-fields of aesthetics. Which one(s) should inform and serve the purposes of the copyrightability assessment? An artefact's meaning might be obvious or hidden, intended or non-intended by the creator; the creator's meaning might coincide with or diverge from the one of the perceiver; the meaning construed at the time of an artefact's creation might be different from the one construed in hindsight, etc. Furthermore, a context is not "a fixed given",[37] and its constitutive elements can also be subject

[35] *E.D. Hirsch*, Validity in Interpretation (1979), 86, further noting that context is an "undifferentiated set of relevant factors [...] expanding to the entire physical, psychological, social and historical milieu in which the utterance occurs [...] the tradition and convention that the speaker relies on, his attitude, purposes, kinds of vocabulary, relation to his audience, and we may mean a great many other things besides". Thus, "[c]onventions and traditions [...] not directly given by a milieu [are] not outside the meaning of the utterance but constitutive of it". Ibid. While this observation refers to the role of context in interpreting an utterance, the same can be said about the role of context in interpreting an artefact.

[36] *Laskowska-Litak*, p. 468, above.

[37] *Hirsch* (n. 35), 201.

to multiple interpretations. What would determine the validity of the "correct" contextual reading of an artefact, and what would warrant the objectivity of the assessment?

The multiplicity of and uncertainty about contextual interpretations lead to an "inevitable and consistent paradox":[38] given that the context is known to the interpreter only partially, a judgment/interpreted meaning might be valid in light of some contextual elements but invalid in light of others (unknown or inaccessible to the interpreter). How would the copyrightability assessment cope with such uncertainty and contestability of contextual readings? While the idea of integrating contextual considerations into the copyrightability assessment merits further exploration, further analysis would need to address two pivotal issues: Which artefact-context relationship should be material in the copyrightability assessment, and what would be a reliable way of ascertaining its existence in an individual case.

VII. Concluding thoughts on interdisciplinarity

Whether and how the discipline of aesthetics can help copyright law overcome its normative entanglements cannot be answered in general – rather, the explanatory and justificatory potency of individual theories needs to be examined relative to specific legal/normative issues. *Laskowska-Litak*'s analysis presents a case where "extra-legal insights" are sourced from aesthetics and applied *in* the legal analysis.[39] Even though the notion of a work is a common subject of interest in copyright law and aesthetics, the attempts to theorise what should constitute a work pursue different objectives and have different underlying premises in the disciplines of law and aesthetics. The foregoing discussion highlights several aspects regarding the relevance and aptitude of a context-based approach to remedy the "contemporary problems" in copyright law identified by *Laskowska-Litak*. At the same time, it should be emphasised that it is not the existence of the contextually defined value of an artefact or the importance of recognising such value that has been questioned here. Rather, this comment intended to identify the linkages that might need to be elaborated further in order for a context-based approach to present a more grounded case. Such analysis would be valuable should lawmakers in Poland[40] (or elsewhere) decide to adopt proposals inspired by aesthetics for affording copyright protection.

---

[38] *Hirsch* (n. 35), 201.

[39] On the distinction between interdisciplinary reflections on law and interdisciplinary or extra-legal insights applied in law, see *Hellwege/Soniewicka*, pp. 3 ff., above.

[40] *K. Kościński*, Poland, in: S. von Lewinski (ed.), Copyright Throughout the World (2022), § 28:11 (noting that lawmakers in Poland have so far declined such proposals).

Part 8

Law and Mathematics

Law and Mathematics: Old Problems in the Digital Era

A Plea for Reforming Today's Law School Curricula

Wojciech Dajczak

Concerns for the future of law typically include the question of whether traditional "analogue law" will be able to meet the shifting needs of a digital world. However, the impacts of digitalization on law and legal research cannot be reduced to this one question. They are manifold. For the so-called digital humanities, for example, fundamental quantitative methods of analysis are aimed at identifying the characteristics of research objects, determining their prevalence, and formulating conceivable and clear – if at times simplistic – categorizations,[1] and the digital humanities will certainly also impact legal reasoning. Furthermore, the technological developments that emerged in the late twentieth century have raised questions about the utility of science, in particular computer science, in the modernization of law.

Yet it is by no means novel to ask, on the one hand, whether the law is able to meet the shifting needs of a world shaped by modern sciences and, on the other hand, in what ways modern sciences are capable of modernizing the law, as the case of law and mathematics proves. The earliest signs of an impact that mathematics had on law can be found in the antiquity.[2] Traces of mathematical concepts such as addition, subtraction, fractions, and arithmetic proportionality

[1] See *C. Schöch*, Quantitative Analyse, in: F. Jannidis et al. (eds.), Digital Humanities. Eine Einführung (2017), 279–298, 279.

[2] *D. Stephanitz*, Exakte Wissenschaft und Recht. Ein Einfluß von Naturwissenschaft und Mathematik auf Rechtsdenken und Rechtswissenschaft in zweieinhalb Jahrtausenden (1970), 16–24.

appear already in ancient Roman jurisprudence. These concepts were most likely based on the Euclidean geometry and arithmetic that had been passed down to Rome. They underpinned some innovative jurists' findings concerning, for example, the determination of the shares of an estate; previously, this determination had remained arithmetically undefined, being governed by a literal interpretation of the last will[3] – problematic were cases in which the sum of all shares of the estate (expressed as fractions) was greater or less than one. However, the innovative application of arithmetic in these cases was limited. Decision-making in Roman law followed a flexible method of legal reasoning, and Roman jurists never adopted the formalization of proof essential to mathematics.[4] The belief that mathematical notions had limited utility in relation to social life is explicitly reflected in the constitution of Emperors *Diocletian* and *Maximilian*, adopted in 294 AD and reproduced in C 9.18.2:

"Artem geometriae discere atque exerceri publice intersit. Ars autem mathematica damnabilis interdicta est."

"It is in the public interest to learn and practise the art of geometry. However, the damnable mathematics are forbidden."[5]

The two emperors distinguished between geometry, which they believed useful for the public interest, and forbidden mathematics, which was in Roman legal language often equated with magic.[6] *Justinian*'s Codex preserved the constitution, enabling its spread into European legal culture. Legal dissertations discussing this part of the Codex, entitled "De Maleficis et Mathematicis", have, from the early eighteenth century onward, explained the cultural background of this particular dichotomy and detailed its subsequent descent into irrelevance.[7] This shift towards a positive perception of mathematics in the civil law tradition lines up with the reframing of mathematics as a force for modernizing law that emerged in continental Europe in the second half of the seventeenth century.

It is these developments of the seventeenth and eighteenth centuries which the present contribution wishes to focus on in its first part (see below, I). It will

[3] *W. Dajczak*, Matematica e intuizione. Calcolo delle quote ereditarie da parte dei giuristi romani, in: L. Garofalo/L. Vacca (eds.), Studi in ricordo di Carlo Augusto Cannata (2021), 189–204, 194–200.

[4] *Dajczak*, (n. 3), 203.

[5] Author's translation.

[6] This use of the word "mathematica" occurred in the collections of Roman legal texts from the fourth century onwards, such as in the Pauli Sententiae (PS. 5.21); from the fifth century, in texts such as Mosaicarum et Romanarum legum collatio (Coll. 15); in the title De maleficis et mathematicis et ceteris similibus of the Theodosian Code (C.Th. 9.16), promulgated in 438 AD; and in the same title of the Code of Justinian of 534 AD (C. 9.18).

[7] *J. Bücklin*, De Maleficis et Mathematicis (Ulm 1706), 2.; *J.B. Winckler*, Commentationem ad Titulum Codicis de Mathematicis maleficis et ceteris similibus (Leipzig 1725), 67.

do so by distinguishing three questions that have the potential of enriching the modern discourse on law and digitalization: Did the mathematization of law modernize scientific legal methods? (I.A). What were the limits of applying quantitative methods to legal reasoning? (I.B) What was the connection between the idea of mathematizing law and the mathematical expertise of contemporary lawyers? (I.C). Accordingly, the first question relates to innovations in legal methodology; the second question moves beyond the methodological arena and considers different attempts to apply mathematics to the solution of legal questions; and the third question focuses primarily on eighteenth-century mathematical textbooks written for lawyers. In its second part, the present contribution will then work out the lessons we can learn from the process of the mathematization of law in the early modern era for the present-day problems associated with digitalization and the law (II).

I. Law and mathematics in the early modern era

A. The idea of mathematizing legal methods in the seventeenth and eighteenth centuries: The Zeitgeist meets the law

The promising concept of using mathematics to modernize law had shaped much of the legal *Zeitgeist* since the sixteenth century.[8] The idea took deepest root at German universities, where jurisprudence was focused on the modern application of Roman law in practice, today usually referred to as *usus modernus pandectarum*. The idea was also utilized for modern scientific adaptations of Roman law, including *Vernunftrecht*, an enlightened and secularized version of natural law which was based on pure rationality, but which nevertheless strongly drew on Roman law. The idea then spread throughout seventeenth- and eighteenth-century Europe. The clearest call for a mathematically based improvement of law came from outside the field of legal sciences. *Erhard Weigel* (1625–1699), appointed as professor of mathematics and astronomy at Jena in 1653, outlined in two treatises his belief in the highest utility of mathematics for the purpose of modernizing law.[9] With his book "Synopsis iurisprudentiae mnemoneutica e syntagmatae illustris viri Georgii Adamii Struvii", published in 1669, he intended to improve *Georg Adam Struve*'s tract, which for its part had played an important role in the *usus modernus pandectarum* tradition. The

[8] *Stephanitz* (n. 2), 62–65.

[9] Cf. *E. Weigel*, Idea totius encyclopaediae mathematico-philosophico hoc est analysis Aristotelico-Euclidea (Jena 1671), 2: "Acuratissima interim via & methodo usi sunt Philosophorum antiquissimi, qui pro singulari quo prae caeteris ad eruendas scientias flagrarunt, studio Mathematici dicebantur […]." ("Meanwhile, the most appropriate way and method was used by the ancient philosophers, which shines in various sciences and is called mathematics […]." [author's translation]).

changes that *Weigel* sought to introduce to *Struve*'s work rested on two premises. One was the assumption that objects of juridical debate were just as measurable as natural objects,[10] while the other was the belief that geometric illustrations used in cartography were likewise useful in legal debate.[11] However, the implementation of these two premises in an updated edition of *Struve*'s treatise was ultimately limited to the introduction of certain keywords, simplification of the text's formal structure, and a tabular presentation of the content. *Weigel*'s second attempt to implement his belief in the capacity of mathematics to explain social matters was his 1674 book "Die Arithmetischen Beschreibung der Moral-Weißheit" ("The Arithmetic Description of Moral Wisdom"), in which he used numbers and mathematical principles of his own choosing to illustrate the complexity of social relations as well as some of their distinctive regularities. For example, in the difference between whole numbers and fractions he saw a reflection of the difference between complete and incomplete lives: "people", *Weigel* wrote, were "either without frailty or expressly frail." The capacity to discern "the blind, the mute, but also the stupid, the silly, or even the mad" spoke, in *Weigel*'s view, to the possibility of assigning precise numerical descriptions to specific human conditions.[12] Using mathematics in this way to explain social problems was completely separate from existing law and empirical data.

Even before the publication of these works and shortly after his appointment to the Jena chair, *Weigel* gained, on account of his very approachable lecturing style, a reputation for being an exceptionally good mathematics and astronomy teacher.[13] This reputation attracted to Jena his most famous students: *Samuel von Pufendorf* in 1656 and *Gottfried Wilhelm Leibniz* in 1663. It is conceivable that already the clarity of *Weigel*'s mathematical lectures provided some early impetus for efforts to rationalize legal reasoning and legal methodology, as

[10] *E. Weigel*, Synopsis iurisprudentiae Mnemoneutica e Syntagmate Illustris Viri Dn. Georgii Adami Struvii (Frankfurt/Jena 1669), Praefatio IV: "Necessitudo vero illa qua mathematicus juri excolendo adstringimur ipsum tangit professionis suae tum objectum quantitatis nempe speciem civilem, cuius in mathesi generali non minus ac naturalium quantitatem." ("When dealing with law, we as mathematicians are forced by real necessity to stick to our approach and hence the quantities of legal objects are in fact not to be treated differently from natural quantities, as it is done in mathematics in general." [author's translation]).

[11] *Weigel* (n. 10), Praefatio III: "[V]ix infra tertiam totius operis partem subsistere illi norunt, qui geographiae speciali operam dederunt." ("Hardly a third of the entire work is presented in such a way as in the geography of the entire work." [author's translation]).

[12] *E. Weigel*, Arithmetische Beschreibung der Moral-Weißheit von Personen und Sachen (Jena 1674, reprint 2004), 11: "also sind die Menschen auch entweder ohne Gebrechen/ oder sie sind gebrechlich. Da besonders die Blinden/Tauben/Stummen/ wie auch die Blöden […].“

[13] *J. Dorschner*, Erhard Weigel in seiner Zeit, in: R. E. Schielicke et al. (eds.), Erhard Weigel – 1625 bis 1699. Barocker Erzvater der deutschen Frühaufklärung. Beiträge des Kolloquiums anläßlich seines 300. Todestages am 20. März 1999 in Jena (1999), 11–38, 31.

traces of preliminary attempts to apply mathematical modes of thinking to discussions of social relations can be found in some earlier works penned by *Weigel*'s brilliant students.

In *Leibniz*'s legal dissertation of 1666, this approach took the shape of a formal discussion of the rule "Si vinco vincentem te, vinco te ipsum" ("If I defeat the one who vanquishes you, I vanquish you, too") and the scope of its application in questionable cases. In his search for regularity or order in competing rights of different ranking granted by different legal bodies in a pluralistic legal order, *Leibniz* identified thirteen cases. For each case, competing solutions based on ancient Roman law, on early modern *ius commune*, and on local laws were presented and evaluated.[14] The theoretical overview of these findings was compiled in the "Nova methodus discendae docendaequae jurisprudentiae" of 1668. Like *Weigel*, *Leibniz* recognized the "great utility of tables" for a more accessible presentation of legal information.[15] However, *Leibniz* softened *Weigel*'s idea of the numerical measurability of social concepts. Rather, *Leibniz* argued for adopting a "mathematical style" (*more mathematico*) in comparative discussions of legal issues.[16] In his methodological treatise, however, *Leibniz* ultimately made no references to either arithmetic or geometry.

The relationship between traditional interpretations of the nature of law and the idea of its mathematization is illustrated by the parallels between *Weigel*'s and *Leibniz*'s thinking. *Weigel* linked this relationship to his main mathematical *opus*, the quaternary numeral system, which he preferred over the decimal system.[17] According to him, the quaternary *Rechen-Tafel* ("arithmetic board") consisting of four numbers distributed onto two rows was the basis for all "moral calculations". On the first row, the numbers stood for (1) *deum cole* ("honor God") and (2) *honeste vivere* ("live honourably"). On the second row, the numbers represented (3) *neminem laedere* ("harm no one") and (4) *suum cuique tribuere* ("render to each his own").[18] By contrast, *Leibniz*'s natural law was based on a three-tiered structure. On the first tier, he placed the *ius strictum*, which embodies the axiomatic principle of *neminem laedere*.[19] On the second tier, he placed equity (*aequitas*), focused on the application of legal

---

[14] *G.W. Leibniz*, De casibus perplexis in iure (Leipzig 1666, reprint 2014), 89–154 (XXII–XXXIX).

[15] *G.W. Leibniz*, Nova methodus discendae docendaeque jurisprudentiae (Frankfurt 1668), 40 (pars specialis, § 7).

[16] *Leibniz* (n. 15), 148 (pars specialis, § 79): "Elementa enim ita comparata esse debent more Mathematico, ut ex iis omnes quaestiones possint decidi." ("Individual items should be compared as it is done in mathematics, so that a solution to all questions can be found this way." [author's translation]).

[17] *M. Cantor*, Vorlesungen über Geschichte der Mathematik, vol. 3 (2nd edn., 1901), 39.

[18] *Weigel* (n. 12), 138.

[19] *Leibniz* (n. 15), 142 (pars specialis, § 72).

remedies according to the principle of *suum cuique tribuere*.[20] *Pietas* followed on the third tier, which, *Leibniz* believed, was to embody the use of freedom in accordance with the principle of *honeste vivere*.[21]

The parallels between *Weigel* and *von Pufendorf* had a different character. Like his mentor, *von Pufendorf* drew on quasi-geometric concepts, such as the unity of rights, the diversity of wrongful behaviours,[22] and the variety of powers.[23] *von Pufendorf*'s orientation towards the doctrine of rational natural law (*Vernunftrecht*) brings to mind the idea, present already in *Weigel*'s work, of subjectively introducing arithmetic or geometric rigorism to legal argumentation. The phrase *quod erat demonstrandum*, typically concluding mathematical proofs, symbolically illustrated *von Pufendorf*'s approach to the new legal method, which was limited to the meta-level of the new theory of rational natural law.[24]

The understanding of mathematics as a modernizing factor of law was developed further and popularized by a generation of younger mathematicians, alongside the jurist *Christian Wolff*. His methodological approach is well illustrated by the view that the relationship between astronomy and mathematics is analogous to the relationship between law and axiomatic definitions brought forth by philosophy.[25] However, the idea that there could be any analogy between legal and scientific methods provoked fierce disagreement in the eighteenth century. *Johann Christian Claproth*, in his "Verteidigung der mathematischen Lehrart in der Rechtsgerlehrsamkeit" ("Defence of the Mathematical Research Method in Jurisprudence"), argued against latitude in interpretation and for clear distinctions between the certain and the probable in legal reasoning.[26] He critically noted that it was only inherent in human nature that the difference between one person estimating the probability of an event at thirty per cent and another at twenty per cent could be overcome with "but one louis d'or."[27] Disregarding mathematical innovations of the time, *Claproth*

---

[20] *Leibniz* (n. 15), 143 (pars specialis, § 73).

[21] *Leibniz* (n. 15), 144 (pars specialis, § 74).

[22] *S. von Pufendorf*, Elementorum jurisprudentiae universalis libri II (The Hague 1660), 232–234 (I.18.1).

[23] *von Pufendorf* (n. 22), 69 f. (I.7.3).

[24] Cf. *S. von Pufendorf*, Specimen controversiarum circa ius naturale (Uppsala 1678), 11.

[25] *C. Wolff*, Horae subsecivae Marburgenses quibus philosophia ad publicum privatamque utilitatem aptatur (Veronae 1770), 218: "Ius civile cum philosophia arcto adeo vinculo connectere licet, quo partes Matheseos mixta cum pura, veliti Astronomia cum Geometria"" ("It is possible that civil law and philosophy can be linked in the same way as parts of mixed and pure mathematics are linked, like for example, astronomy and geometry." [author's translation]).

[26] *J.C. Claproth*, Vertheidigung Der mathematischen Lehrart in der Rechtsgelehrsamkeit nach eben derselben Lehrart abgefasset, in: ders., Sammlung juristisch- philolosophisch- und critischer Abhandlungen, vol. 2 (Göttingen 1742), 209–277.

[27] *Claproth* (n. 26), 257.

declared that placing any further expectations on the mathematical method was unrealistic due to the perpetual character of disputes between jurists.[28] Thus, in practice, the mathematization of law would mean only, as *Gottfried Heinrich Elend* put it, to apply a "demonstrative" or formalistic reasoning in positive law which could mitigate doubts in arbitrary definitions[29] but which could not "safeguard against human error."[30]

The conflation of the mathematization of law with the "demonstrative method" improved the external framework for decision-making in law. The demonstrative method inspired and, to some extent, influenced subsequent methodological and systemic innovations in the nineteenth-century Pandectist theory of private law.[31] The immediate application of numerical methods in legal reasoning focused further on the use of mathematics in the determination of the length, weight, or size of measurable objects in legal disputes. For cases like these, the earliest records of which come from antiquity, *Leibniz* used the term "legal geometry" and "legal arithmetic."[32] *Weigel*, considered the Baroque founding father of early German Enlightenment, was completely disconnected from the emerging mathematical discoveries of his era, including statistics and probability theory. Long after graduating from the University of Jena, *Leibniz* grew critical of *Weigel*'s ideas and labelled them parochial mathematics.[33] However, neither *Leibniz* nor any other representatives of the "demonstrative" method in law managed to introduce their mathematical discoveries into the legal debate and reshape it "in the mathematical manner." While the *Zeitgeist* made mathematics the ideal science for progress-seeking lawyers, it ultimately failed to break down the barriers between the methodologies used by mathematicians and lawyers. One crucial step in this direction, however, was made by *Nicolaus Bernoulli* some time later, in the early eighteenth century.

---

[28] *Claproth* (n. 26), 255.

[29] *G.H. Elend*, Mediationes ad quaestionem: Utrum methodus demonstrativa sive mathematica in iurisprudentia civili adhiberi possit? (Kiel 1739), 7: "Vel definitions ita sunt comparatae, ut quaedam contineant et continere debeant quae naturaliter subiecto non insunt, ets i eidem non contrarientur, adeoque nec per solam reflexionem indagari possunt; sed quae adiecta sunt vel ex meo vel alterius arbitrio".

[30] *Elend* (n. 29), 23: "Atque haec, ut iam ante monui, non ideo affero ut nullo modo Virum Celeberrimum incuriae, vel ex errore, quem forsam in demonstratio commisit".

[31] *W. Dajczak*, Der Allgemeine Teil des Privatrechts im Kontext der mathematischen Inspirationen der Rechtswissenschaft ab dem 17. Jh. bis zur Entstehung der pandektistischen Systematik, in: C. Baldus/W. Dajczak (eds.), Der Allgemeine Teil des Privatrechts. Historische Wurzeln – Leistungsfähigkeit im 21. Jahrhundert (2018), 43–68, 54 f.

[32] *Leibniz* (n. 15), 101 (pars specialis, § 49).

[33] *Dorschner* (n. 13), 31.

B. Nicolaus Bernoulli's dissertation: a forgotten mathematical-legal treatise

Much of the theoretical foundation for the theory of probability – one of the greatest mathematical discoveries of the seventeenth century – was laid by the Swiss mathematician *Jacob Bernoulli* (1655–1705). His work was posthumously published by his nephew and student, *Nicolaus Bernoulli* (d. 1726).[34] A portion of this work pertained to the applicability of probability calculus to social matters.[35] Furthermore, *Jacob Bernoulli* inspired his nephew's dissertation on the use of the theory of probability in law, which he successfully defended in 1709 at the University of Basel's Faculty of Law. In the introductory chapter, he defined probability as a degree of certainty.[36] *Nicolaus Bernoulli*'s approach stood in stark opposition to the scepticism of legal discourse toward the possibility of determining the degree of probability. The mathematical measurability of this degree, elegantly defined by *Christaan Huygens* and *Jacob Bernoulli*, formed the foundation upon which *Nicolaus Bernoulli* could build upon. It needs to be clear from the outset that *Nicolaus Bernoulli* worked on a different level of abstraction than did *Weigel*, *Leibniz*, and *von Pufendorf*. The latter wanted to systematize the law and improve legal methodology by reference to mathematics. By contrast, *Nicolaus Bernoulli* wanted to apply the theory of probabilities to guide legal practitioners in the application of law and to improve and explain concrete legal rules.

For example, he used the mathematical method in the search for *equilibrium* in disputable legal cases:[37] *Bernoulli* wanted to calculate the probability of events which were the premises of a legal decision. The key rule for calculations in such cases was: multiply the possible outcomes by the number of cases in which they occur, and then divide the sum of all these outcomes by the total number of cases. The result is the expected degree of probability.[38]

However, a mathematically based critique and proposals for refining the *ius commune* formed the core of his dissertation. He discussed issues such as (1) declarations of death; (2) the enforceability of aleatory contracts; (3) the value of perpetual rights such as annuities; (4) risk compensation in insurance and maritime loan contracts; (5) the credibility of testimony at trial; and (6) the liability of a borrower in the event of a *force majeure* loss of a movable lent under a *commodatum* contract. The uncertainty inherent in these cases pertained, for example, to the length of a person's life, the reliability of testimony,

[34] *J. Bernoulli*, Ars conjectandi. Opus posthumum (Basel 1713), I f.

[35] *Bernoulli* (n. 34), 210–239.

[36] *N. Bernoulli*, De usu artis conjectandi in jure (Basel 1709), 4 f.

[37] *Bernoulli* (n. 36), 6: "[E]xhibet distantiam centri gravitatis h.e. illius puncti, ex quo suspensa pondera sunt in aequilibrio […]." ("It shows the distances of the points such that the weights suspended in them, when connected, remain in equilibrium]." [author's translation]).

[38] *Bernoulli* (n. 36), 5.

or the occurrence of an act of God (*force majeure*). For each example, it is possible to identify the innovative feature of, and the advancement achieved by, applying probability calculus in legal reasoning. However, particular problems of such application also become apparent.

Roman law had, for example, developed a range of different, and arbitrary, time periods that had to be fulfilled before someone missing could be declared dead, such as five, seven, ten, or thirty years. In addition, early modern discourse witnessed at times extreme opinions: Some argued in favour of the presumption of a centenarian lifespan, others favoured free judicial discretion.[39] By contrast, *Nicolaus Bernoulli* assessed the odds of being found dead rather than alive as two to one.[40] He then based his calculations on data compiled by the English statistician *John Graunt* that determined mortality rates for specific age groups. For example, *Nicolaus Bernoulli* calculated that a sixteen-year-old boy could be declared dead after twenty-five years, a seventy-six-year-old man already after six years and eight months.[41] *Nicolaus Bernoulli* also recognized the limitations of using data from England rather than the region where the missing person lived and the misrepresentations this could cause.[42]

Another example concerned the legal enforceability of transactions containing a strong aleatory element, such as the purchase of a prospective haul of fish for a fixed sum of money. Roman jurists accommodated this type of agreement within the framework of a sales contract. It was an *emptio spei*, which was believed to come into existence immediately following an agreement. A particular problem involving such contracts drew the attention of many early modern jurists: The buyer's obligation to pay the agreed price even when the goods did not materialize was contrary to the principle of *laesio enormis*, which held that the mutual performances of the parties to the contract should be equivalent. However, according to the prevalent view, the principle of *laesio enormis* was not applicable in this particular case.[43] By contrast, a few jurists suggested, based on considerations of equity, that the principle of *laesio enormis* should at least apply in those cases in which there was a gross disproportion between the mutual benefits of the contracting parties.[44] *Nicolaus Bernoulli* proposed that the fairness of the price for a prospective haul of fish ought to be assessed on the basis of the probability of catching fish: the number of fish caught across a given number of years at a given location was to be divided by that number of years, and the contract was, according to the principle of *laesio enormis*,

[39] *Bernoulli* (n. 36), 19 f.
[40] *Bernoulli* (n. 36), 21.
[41] *Bernoulli* (n. 36), 21.
[42] *Bernoulli* (n. 36), 16.
[43] Cf. *Bernoulli* (n. 36), 23.
[44] Cf. *von Pufendorf* (n. 22), 177 (I.12.55).

valid if the final price were not higher than double and not lower than half the value of the so calculated probable haul.[45]

In the final chapter of his dissertation, *Nicolaus Bernoulli* offered two further examples of how to apply probability theory to the solution of concrete legal problems. The first concerned the credibility of testimony at trial. *Nicolaus Bernoulli* believed that the probability of a witness speaking the truth or the defendant being guilty could ultimately be calculated.[46] Such calculation was to be based on a list of factors, conceived as answers to a series of true/false questions, each of which would be assessed by a lawyer individually. The amount of circumstantial evidence and the number of true answers formed the numerical indications for the calculations. If, as a result, innocence was twice as likely as guilt, *Nicolaus Bernoulli* took it to say that the innocence of the defendant was beyond doubt.[47] He also noted that the greater the number of factors taken into account, the more precise the calculation was.[48] However, he ultimately failed to include any explanation as to how to choose the relevant factors for the calculation. Neither were there any examples referring to social reality. It rather seems that the use of mathematics in this particular case served to formally legitimize intuition.

The final example concerned the use of mathematics to determine the standard of liability of the borrower (*commodatarius*) in cases of a *force majeure* loss of a movable lent under a *commodatum* contract. The contemporary doctrine of the *usus modernus pandectarum*, which followed the opinion of ancient jurists in that the borrower could not be held liable for a *force majeure* loss of the borrowed object,[49] was ultimately challenged by *von Pufendorf* in his treatise on natural law. He argued for the liability of the borrower in cases where the loss would not have happened if the contract had not been concluded. He based his arguments on principles of equity: in such a case, equity required that compensation be paid by the person who was able to use the movable free of charge thanks to the kindness of the person from whom he received it.[50] *Nicolaus Bernoulli* based his solution again on mathematical reasoning. In his laconic but clear argument, he replaced equity with the proportionality between risks and benefits and, somewhat arbitrarily, held that the likelihood of damage from a *force majeure* event was no greater than one in a hundred. According to

[45] *Bernoulli* (n. 36), 23.

[46] *Bernoulli* (n. 36), 54.

[47] *Bernoulli* (n. 36), 54: "[I]n singulis circumstantiis duplo probabilius sit, ut quis sit innocens, quam nocens, & primo nullum contra reum adesset indicium, innocentia ejus poneretur extra dubium […]." ("When, in a particular set of circumstances, it is twice as likely that someone is innocent as that they are guilty, and nothing has been proven to the contrary, their innocence is unquestionable." [author's translation]).

[48] *Bernoulli* (n. 36), 54 f.

[49] *Ulpian* D. 13.6.5.4; *Gaius* D. 13.6.18 *pr.*; C. 4.23.1; *Bernoulli* (n. 36), 55.

[50] *S. von Pufendorf*, De jure naturae et gentium (Frankfurt 1684), 715 (V.3.6).

Bernoulli, it followed that under a *commodatum* contract the borrower ought to be held liable for the resulting damage.[51]

Nicolaus Bernoulli's analysis of these cases may, even today, be regarded as innovative. It is nevertheless clear that his approach is questionable, and the empirical flaws of the statistical data he applied are rather glaring. Although nominally based on mathematics, his reasoning regarding the credibility of testimony and the borrower's liability in *commodatum* contracts was merely a rebranding of opinions already rooted in intuition and equity. His book, however, still makes an important point about the preconditions for, and limits to, mathematically driven innovation in legal reasoning. His work also illustrates the differences between him and the proponents of the "demonstrative" method in law. Unlike *von Pufendorf* and *Claproth*, he derived his solutions from actual calculations, and he was certain of the result. And indeed, after reading *Nicolaus Bernoulli*'s pioneering work today, my doubts do not concern the calculations themselves but the correctness of the underlying data.

The mathematical approach first outlined in *Nicolaus Bernoulli*'s dissertation was later adopted in economics, especially in the calculation of insurance premiums.[52] However contrary to the predictions of Enlightenment authors, mathematics did not become the basis for shaping social relations.[53] *Nicolaus Bernoulli*'s dissertation did not influence the development of codified private law at all. The influence of the Enlightenment on codifications took a different path. The uninfluential fate suffered by Bernoulli's idea of using mathematical innovation in law has a threefold explanation. First, there is the problem of the availability and credibility of empirical data necessary for the relevant calculations. Secondly, the transposition of mathematical results into legal reasoning was all but clear. While *Nicolaus Bernoulli* argued that the application of probability theory in law could be a remedy against the arbitrariness of jurists, his dissertation includes no explanation as to why a certain degree of probability would be considered to be the truth (*veritatem dicit*).[54] In several cases, he simply replaced arguments rooted in equity with ones based on a certain degree of probability. Finally, there was the problem of lawyers having the sufficient mathematical expertise prerequisite for an innovative and interdisciplinary approach as advocated by *Nicolaus Bernoulli*. In the introduction to his dissertation, he praised the opportunity of having had both a legal and a mathematical education and of having had access to his ingenious uncle's unpublished works, which he believed were fundamental for him.

---

[51] *Bernoulli* (n. 36), 55.

[52] The application of mathematics to social matters was also inspirational for the development of physics in the nineteenth century; cf. *T. Siegfried*, A Beautiful Math: John Nash, Game Theory, and the Modern Quest for a Code of Nature (2006), 128–138.

[53] *M. Condorcet*, Esquisse d'un tableau historique des progrès de l'esprit humain (Paris 1798), 282 f.

[54] *Bernoulli* (n. 36), 54.

In the context of the *Zeitgeist*, this third cause warrants a closer look. Although mathematics was certainly *en vogue* in eighteenth-century legal scholarship, sources show that lawyers at the time had a rather weak grasp of even simple mathematical findings and that efforts had been undertaken to mitigate the situation. Let us see whether these efforts may have sparked interest in innovations such as *Nicolaus Bernoulli*'s and helped in understanding them.

C. Eighteenth-century mathematical textbooks for lawyers and mathematical skills of legal practitioners

The first systematic examination of the application of mathematical knowledge to the *usus modernus pandectarum* was compiled by *Johann Friedrich Polack* in his book entitled "Mathesis forensic", first published in 1734.[55] Subsequent editions of this work, published in 1739, 1756, and 1770, were judged to be "at the very least" the proof of how useful forensic mathematics could actually be.[56] *Polack* rejected the direct application of numerical methods to the interpretation of law because of the "untranslatability" of justice into mathematically-driven proportionality.[57] He had a different view of the impact of mathematics on the modernization of legal reasoning. In his opinion, "mathematics cleans up [a law student's and lawyer's] head and makes it more capable of reasoning and reflection."[58] Moreover, he argued that an expertise in mathematics would be more useful than a purely legal education for about two-thirds of law graduates, as these graduates, in his opinion, had in any event no chances of entering the legal professions.[59] The lack of even rudimentary mathematical knowledge among law students in the "mathematization of law" period would later be confirmed by multiple authors. For example, with his "Beyträge zur mathesi forensi" ("Contributions to Forensic Mathematics"), *Johann Unger* sought to teach independent arithmetical expertise even to those students who "did not display much aptitude for algebra."[60] *Friedrich Meinert* lamented the fact that in most schools, mathematics was considered an inessential subject,[61]

---

[55] On Polack, see *M. Cantor*, Polack, Johann Friedrich, in: Allgemeine Deutsche Biographie, vol. 26 (1888), 381.

[56] *C. Chassot de Florencourt*, Abhandlungen aus der juristischen und politischen Rechenkunst (Altenburg 1781), I.

[57] *J.F. Polack*, Mathesis forensis (Leipzig 1756), 53.

[58] *Polack* (n. 57), 54: "Ein Rechtslehrer hat die Mathematik, außer dem, daß sie ihm überhaupt den Kopf aufräumet und zum Schließen und Nachdenken fähiger machet".

[59] *Polack* (n. 57), 5 f.

[60] *J.F. Unger*, Beyträge zur mathesi forensi, vol. 2 (Göttingen 1744), 4: "Dennoch aber die daraus hergeleitete Lehrsätze und Regeln solcher gestalt vorgetragen zu haben vermeine, daß auch diejenige, welche sich mit der Algebra nicht abgeben, die Rechnung selbst einsehen und prüfen können".

[61] *F. Meinert*, Ueber das Studium der Mathematik für Juristen, Cammeralisten und Oekonomen auf Universitäten (Halle 1788), 14.

and he saw universities as a valid venue for teaching mathematics to law students.[62] Some more far-reaching proposals were formulated as well. In the late eighteenth century, *Karl Chassot de Florencourt* argued that mathematics should enjoy a status similar to that of history or other auxiliary courses featured in the curriculum of German law schools.[63] Designed by *Polack* and embraced by other authors, the purely practical nature of forensic mathematics shaped the arithmetical and geometrical skillset that contemporaries desired in lawyers. However, in the *usus modernus pandectarum*, the mathematical skills required by lawyers were as follows: they had to be able to calculate legitimate shares, to divide estates, to calculate partner profits, to determine the division of goods, and to calculate compound interest (*interusurii*)[64] or hereditary annuities.[65] The reference to probability theory was marginal in this body of literature and lacked any examples of actual use in legal argumentation.[66]

In the course of the eighteenth century, forensic mathematics was gradually replaced by political arithmetic, which, in academic training, was to be used in economic studies.[67] In addition – and parallel to the so-called "demonstrative method" – forensic mathematics lost its prominent position in jurisprudence in the second half of the eighteenth century. The question of the utility of contemporary mathematical discoveries for the decision-making process in law simply remained outside the bounds of efforts to modernize the legal method. Furthermore, it became impossible for contemporary lawyers to learn about the possibilities of mathematical processing of social data, and, consequently, they remained oblivious to the idea of incorporating calculations based on such data into legal argumentation. As a consequence, in continental Europe in the first industrial revolution, the idea of modernizing the law was linked not to mathematics but, as it had been before, to Roman law. In the nineteenth century, the law's paradigm ultimately became history.[68]

II. Law and digitalization

Mark Twain famously observed that "[h]istory does not repeat itself, but it does often rhyme."[69] Hence, it is useful to search for functional similarities, and indeed, parallels exist between the seventeenth- and eighteenth-century belief in

---

[62] *Meinert* (n. 61), IX.

[63] *Chassot de Florencourt* (n. 56), III.

[64] Cf. *Polack* (n. 57), 116–128.

[65] Cf. *Polack* (n. 57), 59–64.

[66] Cf. *Chassot de Florencourt* (n. 56), 39–65.

[67] Cf. *K.H. Rau*, Zasady umiejętności skarbowej, vol. 1 (1865), 17.

[68] Cf. *F.C. von Savigny*, System des heutigen Römischen Rechts, vol. 1 (1840), XIII f.

[69] *James George Eayrs*, Diplomacy and its discontents (1971), 121, attributed the quote to Mark Twain.

the power of mathematics to modernize law and present-day predictions envisioning the changes that IT technologies will bring to the legal field.

The digitalization of legal texts, which makes them readable to both humans and machines, brings, for example, a new path of implementation of search functions in law, which were also developed by mathematicians in the seventeenth century in relation to the sprawling Roman law texts within the framework of the "mathematization of law". Recent developments in the field of quantitative data analysis, such as vector-based models used in the representation of the semantic content of words and Deep Learning,[70] bring with them a range of new possibilities in terms of the processing and application of legal texts.

However, while we should acknowledge the possibilities, we should not ignore the fears these developments raise. After all, the design of information influences our thinking, and computers tend to encourage analytical approaches that eschew systemic perspectives in favour of a focus on keyword and individual cases.[71] The impact of science on law is often associated with the story of *Dr. Faust*, as "[e]fficiency, not verity, is the measure."[72] Discussions regarding the future of law in the era of its digitalization often include references to ideas formulated in science fiction literature, such as the laws of robotics conceived by *Isaac Asimov*.[73]

Today, however, jurisprudence is oriented neither toward mathematics nor toward history. Today's debate on the digitalization or algorithmization of law has witnessed nothing comparable to the conditions by which the idea of mathematizing law gripped the field between the sixteenth and eighteenth centuries. The outline of these experiences presented herein provides a useful lens through which to reflect on this debate. The immediate impetus for the practical application of mathematical skills to law stemmed from the work of the mathematics professor *Weigel* and the clarity of his lectures. The further development and subsequent constraining of the mathematically inspired formalization of legal reasoning, however, was the creation of lawyers, some of whom were also mathematicians. By contrast, present-day advances in the digitalization of law are driven primarily by the progress of computer science. Cutting-edge IT innovations, such as smart contracts, fail to recognize the autonomy of law in the way we might have seen in *Weigel*, in his student *Leibniz*, or even in *Nicolaus Bernoulli*'s dissertation.

These developments pose two risks. On the one hand, scientific experts rarely, if ever, take into account the limitations resulting from the nature of

---

[70] *Schöch* (n. 1), 297.

[71] *B. Großfeld*, Zeichen und Zahlen im Recht (2nd edn., 1995), 20–23.

[72] *D. Faigman*, Legal Alchemy: The Use and Misuse of Science in the Law (1999), IX.

[73] See: European Parliament resolution of 16 February 2017 with recommendations to the Commission on Civil Law Rules on Robotics (2015/2103(INL)), Official Journal of the European Union 2018 C 252/239.

law. On the other hand, jurists are unable to perceive the actual breadth of possibilities offered by science. Lessons from the "mathematization of law" in the seventeenth and eighteenth centuries are, in my opinion, not irrelevant to present-day efforts to mitigate these risks. First, we must not forget that the tendency of the predecessors and adherents of the "demonstrative method" to formalize legal argumentation did not imply a rejection of flexibility in legal practice. The flexible nature of human decisions has since been confirmed by neuroscience and game theory, thus overturning economic determinism.[74] These theories are now considered a key in the mathematical representation of human behaviour, illustrating the versatility of decision-making that results from a variety of probable but non-deterministic strategies in human interaction.[75] In this context, the parallel between *Weigel*'s intuitions about the core elements of a legal *Rechen-Tafel* and *Leibniz*'s definition of the three tiers of natural law is striking. Both scholars drew on the Roman law principles of *honeste vivere*, *alterum non laedere*, and *suum cuique tribuere*.[76] *Leibniz*'s conviction that jurists must go far beyond the content of positive legislation and be able to convincingly solve hard cases remains one of the most important parts of his legacy.[77] It should also be noted that both *Weigel* and *Leibniz* clearly emphasized the universal basis of value, which they considered axiomatic for the Christian faith. This axiom corresponds, at least functionally, to present-day scepticism about whether paraconsistent logic is capable of providing law with the power to resolve conflict in cosmopolitan society.[78]

Moreover, *Nicolaus Bernoulli*'s belief in the applicability of probability theory to decision-making in law was based on a purely illusory use of social data. While his method was directed against the arbitrariness of jurists, in many respects it was little more than a formal legitimization of certain moral intuitions that itself relied on an arbitrary use of data. Questions about the shortcomings of social data and whether it was valid to equate a specific degree of probability with truth remain unanswered to this day. Some aspects of these lingering issues were elucidated by the American historian of mathematics *Jeff Suzuki*. Referring to examples of the application of relevant algorithms in legal practice, he argued that we ignore the findings of mathematics at our peril, as such findings not only are capable of reinforcing paths suggested by tradition or

---

[74] *Siegfried* (n. 52), 122–125.

[75] *Siegfried* (n. 52), 213–223.

[76] These three principles marked the understanding of good faith (bona fides) in contract law by Roman jurists; cf. *W. Dajczak*, Zwrot bona fides w rozstrzygnięciach dotyczących kontraktów u prawników rzymskich okresu klasycznego (1998), 150–152.

[77] *S. Meder*, Der unbekannte Leibniz: Die Entdeckung von Recht und Politik durch Philosophie (2018), 332.

[78] *A. Halpin*, The Applications of Bivalent Logic, and the Misapplication of Multivalent Logic to Law, in: H.P. Glenn/L.D. Smith (eds.), Law and the New Logics (2017), 208–235, 234 f.

common sense but can also show alternative ways.[79] The flaws in the application of numerical methods to law, visible in *Bernoulli*'s work and enduring to this day, speak to the difference between using algorithms in a support capacity in decision-making and uncritically basing legal decisions on the results of calculations. Despite its flaws, *Bernoulli*'s work can still serve as a source of inspiration. Even today, it would be reasonable to critically evaluate the results of mathematical calculations in legal argumentation from an equity perspective. As aptly observed by *David Faigman*, democracy needs science, law, and religion, and for each to be a strong presence capable of checking the excesses of the other two.[80]

Lastly, the experience of the seventeenth and eighteenth centuries clearly points us toward the mathematical skills of lawyers. *Nicolaus Bernoulli*'s dissertation revealed the gap between the spirit of "mathematization of law" and the innovative incorporation of mathematics into efforts to modernize legal reasoning. The body of literature on so-called forensic mathematics published throughout the eighteenth century failed to recognize this gap and made little effort to rectify it. To this day, very little has changed in that respect. When it comes to Poland, I would have to agree with *Faigman*'s early twenty-first-century observation that many students who avoided mathematics and science in school went on to become lawyers.[81] As the third decade of the twenty-first century begins, few lawyers in Europe would find it surprising that out of 175 accredited law schools in the US, only one requires a course in basic statistics.[82] After three centuries, the question remains as to what should be required of lawyers who wish to present probabilistic ideas in the courtroom.[83] The picture presented here and the modern experience of law in continental Europe aligns with the American author's observation that while lawmakers in the eighteenth century had some grasp of the sciences, today they remain wilfully ignorant thereof.[84] In 1734, the author of the first textbook on forensic mathematics wrote that it was worthwhile for law students to also study mathematics, because for two-thirds of them it was mathematics rather than their legal studies that would ensure future employment.[85] The lack of mathematical competence, however, would not prove an obstacle for those who would go on to become lawyers. Neither was it of any concern to legal scholars, as evinced by their lack of response to *Nicolaus Bernoulli* and his work. Today, lawyers

---

[79] *J. Suzuki*, Constitutional calculus: The Math of Justice and the Myth of Common Sense (2015), 3.

[80] *Faigman* (n. 72), 201.

[81] *Faigman* (n. 72), XI.

[82] *Faigman* (n. 72), XII.

[83] *C.G.G. Aitken*, Some thoughts at the interface of law and statistics, Law, Probability and Risk 8 (2009), 73–83, 82.

[84] *Faigman* (n. 72), 122.

[85] *Polack* (n. 57), 5 f.

remain secondary actors in the digitalization and, to some extent, the algorithmization of law. For example, the proposal to incorporate smart contracts into existing legal frameworks revealed that the lawyers' poor grasp of the underlying technology and their inability to apply it in legal reasoning remained the greatest challenge to technology's implementation.[86] Lawyers' obliviousness of these issues, however, may not go as unpunished as it had before. I believe that safeguarding the balance between the traditional autonomy of the law and the present-day technological revolution sweeping the legal field requires that we retool our expectations toward law school applicants and expect from them mathematical skills and abilities similar to those demonstrated by prospective computer science students. These changes ought to be followed up with efforts to update law school curricula to include basic computer sciences classes alongside traditional coursework and soft skills workshops. To paraphrase an opinion first uttered three hundred years back, while changes like these could effectively slash the number of law school applicants by two-thirds, the lawyers we would end up with would be much better suited to combine that which constitutes the essence of law in our tradition with the myriad strands of our modern, digital reality.

In the last part of the paper, I highlighted three issues: The flexible nature of human decision-making; the benefits and limitations of using mathematical findings in a support capacity in decision-making by lawyers; and the link between lawyers' mathematical skills and their ability to understand the opportunities and risks of new technologies in law. These three observations demonstrate that the best interdisciplinary relationship between mathematics and law combines mathematical imagination with legal sensitivity – with the latter understood as the ability to grasp how the law reflects values and what those values might be from a legal perspective. Such legal sensitivity is crucial if we are to preserve the autonomy of private law – a fundamental precept of the civil and common law traditions – even at a time when numerical procedures in law are becoming increasingly important.

---

[86] *J.G. Rohr*, Smart Contracts in Traditional Contract Law, Or: The Law of the Vending Machine, Cleveland State Law Review 67 (2019), 67–88, 88.

Law and Mathematics: A Comment*

Herbert Zech

I. Introduction

The article "Law and Mathematics: Old Problems in the Digital Era" by *Wojciech Dajczak* deals with the connection of jurisprudence and mathematics. It focuses on method and education. First, it shows how legal thinking was influenced by mathematical thinking – especially in the 1600s and 1700s. Second, the influence of digitalization on legal practice is addressed. This is finally used as an argument for requiring more mathematical skills from law school applicants.

II. Influence of mathematics on legal thinking

Mathematical thinking played an important role in the 1600s and 1700s. It not only served as an important part of the development of modern sciences (for example, in the philosophy of nature methods developed by *René Descartes* and *Galileo Galilei*[1]) but also influenced thinkers in the field of rational natural law (*Vernunftrecht*) like *Thomas Hobbes*, *Samuel Pufendorf* or *Gottfried*

* The author wishes to thank Prisca von Hagen, Irma Klünker, Finn Schädlich, Simon Schrör and Pablo Schumacher for their valuable comments on the contribution.

[1] Galilei famously calls mathematics the language of the universe; *G. Galilei*, Il Saggiatore (Rome 1623), obtainable at https://www.liberliber.it/online/autori/autori-g/galileo-galilei/il-saggiatore/: "La filosofia è scritta in questo grandissimo libro che continuamente ci sta aperto innanzi a gli occhi (io dico l'universo), ma non si può intendere se prima non s'impara a intender la lingua, e conoscer i caratteri, ne' quali è scritto. Egli è scritto in lingua matematica, e i caratteri son triangoli, cerchi, ed altre figure geometriche, senza i quali mezi è impossibile a intenderne umanamente parola; senza questi è un aggirarsi vanamente per un oscuro laberinto."

Wilhelm Leibniz. This has been described in detail by *Dieter Stephanitz*.[2] Mathematics as a role model for axiomatization and formalization[3] led to a systematization of the law, paving the way for later codifications. However, attempts to formalize the law have been largely unsuccessful until today.

The influence of mathematics on normative thinking was not limited exclusively to legal scholars but is found also in ethics generally. *Spinoza*'s book on ethics, published posthumously in 1677, is famously titled *Ethica, ordine geometrico demonstrate*, that is: Ethics, shown or proven (demonstrated) in a mathematical way. The quest for demonstrability also influenced the development of modern scientific methods among natural philosophers. Arguably, mathematics was an important driver of rationalist thinking in general. And the discussion of method in many different disciplines, inspired by mathematics, was a key element of the rationalist movement.[4]

Formalization and axiomatization remain pressing problems for legal thinkers. Formalization has long played an important role in logic and law.[5] Whereas logic is fundamental to legal thinking, formalized legal logic never caught on.[6] Currently, formal logic in the legal discipline is arguably even in decline. Machine learning enables useful legal tech but at the price of less formal reasoning (see next part, below). Axiomatization, on the other hand, is still strong. It has been realized that deductive thinking with norms (statements of value) is different from deductive thinking with statements of facts. However, systematics and the hierarchy of legal norms are still key components of legal theory and jurisprudence. It has even been argued that mathematical thinking shows several similarities with legal thinking, among them deductive thinking and the use of syllogisms.[7]

---

[2] *D. Stephanitz*, Exakte Wissenschaft und Recht. Der Einfluß von Naturwissenschaft und Mathematik auf Rechtsdenken und Rechtswissenschaft in zweieinhalb Jahrtausenden. Ein historischer Grundriß (1970), 52 ff.

[3] *K. Radbruch*, Mathematik in den Geisteswissenschaften (1989), 130 f.

[4] The success of the mathematical method is largely owed to *R. Descartes* and his Discours de la méthode pour bien conduire sa raison et chercher la verité dans les sciences first published in Leiden in 1637; see *Stephanitz* (n. 2), 62.

[5] There is a significant number of German textbooks on law and logic, e.g. *U. Klug*, Juristische Logik (4th edn., 1982); *J.C. Joerden*, Logik im Recht (3rd edn., 2018); *F.E. Schnapp*, Logik für Juristen (7th edn., 2016).

[6] See *R. Alexy*, Theorie der juristischen Argumentation (1983), 17 ff. For a current example, see *A. Metzger/S. Schrör*, Zwischen Wissenschaft, Praxis und Politik: Wie Juristen Gesetzgebungsverfahren in Fachzeitschriften begleiten (Between Science, Practice and Politics: How Lawyers Reflect on Legislative Processes in Professional Journals), Zeitschrift für Rechtssoziologie 42 (2022), 243–269, 258 f.

[7] *M. Termini*, Proving the Point: Connections Between Legal and Mathematical Reasoning, Suffolk University Law Review 52 (2019), 5–35, 14.

Dajczak's contribution offers reflections on another interesting instance of mathematical influence on legal thinking: the introduction of thinking in probabilities (probability theory). With his doctoral thesis *Dissertatio Inauguralis Mathematico-Juridica de Usu Artis Conjectandi in Jure*, published in 1709, *Nicolaus (I) Bernoulli* alerted the legal community to the importance of the newly developed probability theory. The experience of probability theory is a good example of how mathematical concepts influence thinking in other disciplines. For instance, probability theory can be used in decision theory, an analytical tool relevant in legal practice.[8] Probability rules are also essential in AI, e.g. in supervised machine learning.[9] Likewise, many concepts developed in mathematics have influenced or sometimes even enabled other disciplines. This certainly holds true for the calculus, developed independently by *Leibniz* and *Isaac Newton*, which enables classical mechanics. However, in law, the enabling power of mathematics or natural sciences is limited. The discovery of special relativity did not influence the legal concept of corporeal things.[10] This is because the law is based on everyday life and, accordingly, must consider only what influences everyday life. A discipline exerting a greater influence on the law is economics, which, in turn, makes great use of mathematics.

The influence of mathematical ideas on legal thinking or reasoning follows a path like the influence of other disciplines (economics, natural sciences etc.): The results from other disciplines can be adopted if they can be translated into ordinary language. The mathematical description of socially relevant (and therefore legally relevant) phenomena has become an immense field, for instance with game theory. Resulting mathematical concepts, however, must be translated into ordinary language to become relevant for lawyers. This is a statement of fact on the one hand, but it also seems to be useful interdisciplinary practice on the other hand. Consequences for legal education will be discussed in the last part of this comment.

III. Legal thinking and legal practice

The second part of *Dajczak*'s contribution touches upon law and digitalization. His discussion focusses on changes that information technology (IT) has been bringing to the legal field. These changes, however, are in legal practice rather than in legal thinking. In the form of legal tech, digital technology as a tool for

[8] See *H.E. Jackson/L. Kaplow/S. Shavell/W.K. Viscusi/D. Cope*, Analytical Methods for Lawyers (3rd edn., 2017), 1 ff. (Decision Analysis).

[9] See *S. Russell/P. Norvig*, Artificial Intelligence: A Modern Approach, Global Edition (4th edn., 2022), 673 f.

[10] *H. Zech*, Information als Schutzgegenstand (2012), 104.

legal practice has been remarkably successful, and its ongoing progress carries the chance of completely transforming parts of the legal market. This success is largely owed to a move away from attempts to formalize the law toward a results-oriented application of machine learning to legal decisions. The inherent lack of transparency means that underlying rationales or questions of justice are eclipsed. Although transparency might eventually be increased by developments in the AI sector (explainable AI), this is still a major problem of legal tech.

Dajczak's contribution draws parallels between the influence of mathematics on legal thinking in the era of natural law and the influence of digitalization on legal thinking today. However, the influences seem to be fundamentally different in their effects. While mathematical thinking has driven legal thinkers towards systematization and increased understandability, digitalization in the form of legal tech seems to be having the opposite effect. This effect is increased with the advent of machine learning and by AI with its intrinsic transparency problems. Moreover, while mathematics has influenced legal thinking, digitalization has so far influenced only legal practice. In the future, however, the use of digital tools in legal practice might also influence legal thinking.[11] Arguably, this influence could be rather detrimental. It could lead to an effects-orientation at the expense of procedural justice, transparency and even material justice.

Hence, legal tech is, as *Dajczak* correctly states, a challenge for legal education. However, the educational challenge is not only about teaching technical or mathematical skills, but is even more about teaching how to deal with the legal methodical challenges posed by legal tech. It calls for "a sharpening of methodical skills, the legal sense of responsibility and the intuitive understanding of the law"[12]. The use of digital technology in the legal profession (and in academia) can be beneficial. But, to ensure this, alertness and legal training are required.

---

[11] As an early example, consider the use of upload filters to ensure fulfilment of duties of care affecting platform providers and the influence of their use on liability law, see *H. Zech*, General and specific monitoring obligations in the Digital Services Act. Observations regarding machine filters from a private lawyer's perspective, 2021, https://verfassungsblog.de/power-dsa-dma-07/.

[12] *S. Hähnchen/P.T. Schrader/F. Weiler/T. Wischmeyer*, Legal Tech. Rechtsanwendung durch Menschen als Auslaufmodell?, JuS 2020, 625–635, 625: "Vielmehr bedarf es auch einer Schärfung der methodischen Fertigkeiten, des juristischen Verantwortungsbewusstseins und des Judizes."

IV. Mathematics influencing society

The influence of mathematics on society goes beyond merely describing it or being used as a tool in legal practice. Mathematics nowadays has become a kind of technology.[13] Whereas mathematics previously was only an activity of the human mind, mathematical methods in the form of algorithms are now routinely carried out by machines (information technology).[14] With the help of information technology, mathematics has become more powerful and influential. Algorithms lie at the heart of any digital control, and digital solutions are found almost everywhere in our life. Mathematics increasingly influences the real world.

Mathematics, therefore, together with information technology, greatly influences society. It may even be regarded as a transformative technology,[15] being "capable of significantly changing practice and reorganising concepts".[16] This influence brings with it not only opportunities but also risks. Ethics in Mathematics,[17] itself an emerging field, can be seen as a reaction to the growing societal influence of mathematics.

Thus, mathematics is useful and influential not only as a legal tool but in all aspects of society. The fact that mathematics increasingly influences everyday life can be seen as a boost for the argument made in *Dajczak*'s article that mathematical knowledge is becoming more important for lawyers and that mathematical education for lawyers must be strengthened. This will be addressed in the next and last part of this comment.

The comparison with technology also strengthens the argument that the law is concerned with practical implications rather than to theoretical knowledge. In technology law this is debated as the problem of technology-neutrality:[18] Legal rules should be invariant under technological changes, i.e., their practical

---

[13] For the definition of technology, see *H. Zech*, Einführung in das Technikrecht (2022), 3 ff. Arguably, the influence of information technology led to a dematerialization of the concept of technology (ibid., 6).

[14] Besides mathematics, computer science (informatics) must be mentioned here. Arguably, computer science is in many aspects based on mathematics.

[15] The term "transformative technology" is mentioned in connection with AI by the *European Commission*, Communication from the Commission to the European Parliament, the European Council, the Council, the European Economic and Social Committee and the Committee of the Regions on Artificial Intelligence for Europe, 25. April 2018, COM(2018) 237 final, para. 1. The term was coined by the *Nuffield Council on Bioethics*, Genome editing: an ethical review (2016), 12, 26, for characterizing genome editing; see *B. Fateh-Moghadam*, Genome Editing als strafrechtliches Grundlagenproblem, medstra – Zeitschrift für Medizinstrafrecht 2017, 146–156, 148.

[16] *Nuffield Council on Bioethics* (n. 15), 12.

[17] *D. Müller/M. Chiodo/J. Franklin*, A Hippocratic Oath for Mathematicians? Mapping the Landscape of Ethics in Mathematics, Science and Engineering Ethics 28:41 (2022).

[18] See *Zech* (n. 13), 33 ff.

effects should remain the same (and in consequence they should remain just). Lawyers judge other fields from a layman's perspective (German: *Parallelwertung in der Laiensphäre*). This is because justice hinges on practical effects for humans.

V. Call for teaching interdisciplinary competence

The growing importance of mathematics for the law triggers the question of how legal education should react. *Dajczak* posits "that safeguarding the balance between the traditional autonomy of the law and the present-day technological revolution sweeping the legal field requires that we retool our expectations toward law school applicants and expect from them mathematical skills and abilities similar to those demonstrated by prospective computer science students."[19]

The question must be asked whether the growing importance of mathematics for the law really means a growing importance of mathematical knowledge for lawyers. Without doubt, mathematical knowledge can be useful for lawyers. However, it seems that not all lawyers should be forced to have mathematical skills. Like with any other discipline, the field of law demands a special legal or juridical expertise which is itself unique and which can only be complemented – and not made whole – by other expertise(s).

The solution may be found in interdisciplinary cooperation. Teaching interdisciplinary cooperation is an extraordinarily important part of legal education. Rather than becoming mathematicians (or scientists or engineers), lawyers should learn how to talk to experts from other disciplines. Rather than turning lawyers into mathematicians, lawyers should be trained to speak with mathematicians (and vice versa). It may also not necessarily be expert knowledge that is required for interdisciplinary research. Rather, the implicit methodological assumptions and practices in different academic communities may pose obstacles in collaborative research. These obstacles could be addressed by encouraging complementary interdisciplinary studies. There are existing experiences as regards the fields of engineering (law and technology), the natural sciences, economics, and the social sciences. Not so much experience exists with informatics and mathematics. This should be seen as a call for more interdisciplinary endeavors.

Nevertheless, teaching mathematics and the law seems to be a good idea as a complementary and voluntary educational offering. The same holds true for other sciences and the law. For law students who can cope with the additional workload, introductory training in other disciplines seems useful. This should, however, not be made mandatory. Introductory courses on economics or

---

[19] *Dajczak*, p. 515, above.

analytical methods for lawyers[20] may be seen as a model. A similar approach could be adopted for mathematics, the natural sciences and technology. Law school curricula should thus leave more room for optional interdisciplinary modules.

---

[20] *Jackson/Kaplow/Shavell/Viscusi/Cope* (n. 8).

List of Contributors

Dr. *Svenja Behrendt*
Department of Public Law, Max Planck Institute for the Study of Crime, Security and Law, Freiburg.

Dr. *Grzegorz Blicharz*
Chair for Roman Law, Faculty of Law and Administration, Jagiellonian University in Kraków.

Prof. Dr. *Wojciech Dajczak*
Chair for Roman Law, Legal Traditions and Cultural Heritage Law, Faculty of Law and Administration, Adam Mickiewicz University of Poznań.

Dr. *Michał Derek*
Chair for Criminal Law, Faculty of Law and Administration, Jagiellonian University in Kraków.

Dr. hab. *Tomasz Długosz*
Chair for Business Regulation and Economic Policy, Faculty of Law and Administration, Jagiellonian University in Kraków.

Prof. Dr. hab. *Monika Florczak-Wątor*
Chair for Constitutional Law, Faculty of Law and Administration, Jagiellonian University in Kraków.

Prof. Dr. *Phillip Hellwege*, M.Jur. (Oxford)
Chair for Private Law, Business Law and Legal History, Faculty of Law, University of Augsburg.

Prof. Dr. *Peter Kasiske*
Professor of Criminal Law, Criminal Procedure and Economic Criminal Law, Faculty of Law, University of Augsburg.

Prof. Dr. *Johannes Kaspar*
Chair for Criminal Law, Criminal Procedure Law, Criminology and the Law of Criminal Sanctions, Faculty of Law, University of Augsburg.

Dr. *Monika Kawczyńska*, LL.M. (Leuven)
Chair for European Law, Faculty of Law and Administration, Jagiellonian University in Kraków.

Dr. *Daria Kim*
Max Planck Institute for Innovation and Competition, Munich.

Dr. Dr. *Łukasz Kurek*
Chair for Philosophy of Law and Legal Ethics, Faculty of Law and Administration, Jagiellonian University in Kraków.

Dr. *Ewa Laskowska-Litak*, LL.M. (Heidelberg)
Chair for Intellectual Property Rights, Faculty of Law and Administration, Jagiellonian University in Kraków.

Prof. Dr. hab. *Franciszek Longchamps de Bérier*
Chair for Roman Law, Faculty of Law and Administration, Jagiellonian University in Kraków.

Prof. Dr. *Thomas Marschler*
Chair for Dogmatics, Faculty of Catholic Theology, University of Augsburg.

Prof. Dr. *Thilo Rensmann*, LL.M. (University of Virginia)
Chair for Public Law, Public International Law and European Law, Faculty of Law, University of Augsburg.

Prof. Dr. *Matthias Rossi*
Chair for Constitutional and Administrative Law, European Law and the Theory of Legislation, University of Augsburg.

Dr. *Aqilah Sandhu*
Chair for Constitutional and Administrative Law, European Law and the Theory of Legislation, University of Augsburg.

Prof. em. Dr. Dr. h.c. *Reiner Schmidt*
Emeritus Professor of Public Law, Economic Administration Law and Environmental Law, University of Augsburg.

Assoc. Prof. Dr. Dr. hab. *Marta Soniewicka*
Chair for Philosophy of Law and Legal Ethics, Faculty of Law and Administration, Jagiellonian University in Kraków.

Prof. Dr. Dr. h.c. Dr. h.c. *Jerzy Stelmach*
Chair for Philosophy of Law and Legal Ethics, Faculty of Law and Administration, Jagiellonian University in Kraków.

Julia Wesołowska
Chair for Philosophy of Law and Legal Ethics, Faculty of Law and Administration, Jagiellonian University in Kraków.

Prof. Dr. *Constantin Willems*
Chair for Private Law and Roman Law, Faculty of Law, University of Marburg

Prof. Dr. *Wolfgang Wurmnest*, LL.M. (Berkeley)
Chair for Private Law and Commercial Law, including Maritime Law, Faculty of Law, University of Hamburg.

Prof. Dr. Dr. hab. *Wojciech Załuski*
Chair for Philosophy of Law and Legal Ethics, Faculty of Law and Administration, Jagiellonian University in Kraków.

Prof. Dr. jur. Dipl.-Biol. *Herbert Zech*
Chair of Civil Law, Technology Law and IT Law at Humboldt University, Berlin, Director at the Weizenbaum Institute for the Networked Society.